ALIVE CHRIST

GRADE 3 · CATECHIST EDITION

The Church

aliveinchrist.osv.com

OurSundayVisitor

For permission to reprint copyrighted materials, grateful acknowledgment is made to the following sources:

English translation of the *Catechism of the Catholic Church for the United States of America* copyright © 1994, United States Catholic Conference, Inc.—Libreria Editrice Vaticana. English translation of the *Catechism of the Catholic Church: Modifications from the Editio Typica* copyright © 1997, United States Catholic Conference, Inc.—Libreria Editrice Vaticana. Used by permission. All rights reserved.

Excerpts from the English translation of *Roman Missal* © 2010, International Commission on English in the Liturgy Corporation (ICEL). All rights reserved. Published with the approval of the Committee on Divine Worship, United States Conference of Catholic Bishops.

Gadium et Spes ("Pastoral Constitution on the Church in the Modern World") © Libreria Editrice Vaticana.

Music selections copyright John Burland, used with permission, and produced in partnership with Ovation Music Services, P.O. Box 402 Earlwood NSW 2206, Australia. Please refer to songs for specific copyright dates and information.

Scripture selections taken from the *New American Bible, revised edition* © 2010, 1991, 1986, 1970 by the Confraternity of Christian Doctrine, Washington, D.C., and are used by license of the copyright owner. All rights reserved. No part of the *New American Bible* may be reproduced in any form without permission in writing from the copyright owner.

Additional acknowledgements appear on CE66.

Alive in Christ Parish Grade 3 Catechist Edition
ISBN: 978–1–61278–027–6
Item Number: CU5115
1 2 3 4 5 6 7 8 015016 17 16 15 14 13
Webcrafters, Inc., Madison, WI, USA; August 2013; Job# 104419

ALIVE IN CHRIST   Table of Contents

Vision and Philosophy

66 I am the way and the truth* and the life… I am the resurrection and the life. 99

John 14:6, 11:25

66 Jesus Christ not only transmits the word of God: he is the Word of God. Catechesis is therefore completely tied to him. Thus what must characterize the message transmitted by catechesis is, above all, its 'christocentricity'. 99[1]

General Directory for Catechesis, 98

Jesus Christ at the Center

Welcome to *Alive in Christ*. Christ is at the center of our faith, our Church, our catechesis. *Alive in Christ* is intentional in its focus on the life, mission, and saving work of Jesus Christ. This lays a foundation for a relationship with Jesus, who continually leads us to his Father's love and calls us through the Spirit to share in the divine life through his Church (see *Catechism of the Catholic Church*, 426).

Mirroring the Divine Pedagogy

The catechetical process of *Alive in Christ* mirrors the divine pedagogy—the gradual and relational way God teaches us so that we can know him and his truth, be guided by the Holy Spirit to respond with faith and love, and accept the gift of new life in Christ.

In this unique and effective pedagogy, each lesson encourages a personal and ongoing relationship with God, beginning with God's invitation through Sacred Scripture and leading children to reflect on his Word, deepen their understanding of our Sacred Tradition, and respond with a lived faith within the home and among friends, within the Church and in the community.

Building Knowledge of, and Reverence for, Sacred Scripture

Sacred Scripture from the *New American Bible Revised Edition* is foundational to every lesson in *Alive in Christ*. Scripture from both the Old Testament and New Testament is presented in a variety of ways that encourage children to listen to the voice of God in his written Word and learn about the people and stories of the Bible. Each lesson offers several distinct encounters with Sacred Scripture, giving children the opportunity to pray with, reflect on, study, and apply God's Word to their lives.

Comprehensive Presentation of Catholic Teaching

Alive in Christ provides an authentic and comprehensive presentation of the essentials of the Catholic faith and has been found by the United States Conference of Catholic Bishops' Subcommittee on the Catechism to be in conformity with the *Catechism of the Catholic Church*.

Following a systematically organized scope and sequence, key themes of Catholic teaching are repeated each year, through a grade-level focus, building on the child's knowledge of the faith at each developmental stage. This presentation of Catholic teaching—coupled with a purposeful emphasis on Catholic practices, images, and models of faith—promotes a common language of faith and builds a vibrant Catholic identity.

Developmentally Responsive and Appropriate

Created by a team of experts in catechesis, theology, and child psychology *Alive in Christ* incorporates the most trusted research on how children learn and communicate. Definitions, activities, questions, and reading passages have been reviewed for developmental appropriateness. Targeted on page interactions help children more effectively learn or reinforce lesson content.

Topics are presented at important developmental "windows"—ages when research in child development tells us that learning about a particular topic would be most effective. Illustrations, Catholic art, and photos emphasize Scripture and visually present the chapter objectives in ways children can understand and relate to.

Complete and Purposeful Approach to Prayer and Worship

Every grade level intentionally incorporates each of the five forms of prayer mentioned in the *Catechism*—blessing and adoration, petition, intercession, thanksgiving and praise (see CCC, 2626-2643). Children learn about and pray these basic prayer forms and are introduced to traditional prayers and devotions of the Church. They are taught how to talk with God in their own words and listen silently as he speaks to them. Each grade level also presents many opportunities to deepen children's understanding of the feasts and seasons of the Church year and how we celebrate the Paschal Mystery through them.

Putting Faith into Practice

Alive in Christ presents and effectively implements the six fundamental tasks of catechesis (see *General Directory for Catechesis*, 84–85). Exercises, features, and questions throughout the text prompt children to relate knowledge of our Catholic faith with their life experience. Every chapter has on page activities for immediate application as well as concrete suggestions for children to live out the faith at school, at their parish, and in their homes, and communities.

Each lesson's Our Catholic Life section provides practical examples of the ways we worship, live, pray, and serve together as Catholics. It introduces children to Catholic figures who stand as models of heroic virtue in everyday life. Every lesson has connections to the Catholic social tradition, and each grade level provides catechesis on the seven major themes of the Church's Social Teaching.

Practical Ways to Involve Families in Their Children's Faith Formation

The "Family + Faith" page and an extensive website give parents the tools they need to know what their children are learning, talk about the faith, and recognize how they can more consciously live the faith in their daily family life.

On each lesson's take home page, parents will find information about children's developmental understanding, discussion prompts, and resources for family prayer. Taking into consideration the aims of the New Evangelization, each page includes an opportunity for adult reflection on their own relationship with Jesus and the Church.

Online resources offer multimedia tools to foster family interaction and reinforce the lesson at home.

A Commitment to Support Both New and Experienced Catechists

Alive in Christ Catechist Editions empower catechists with easy-to-use and effective tools for lesson planning, teaching and reinforcing faith concepts, and growing in their own relationship with Christ and his Church.

The key concepts and chapter objectives are fully explained and conveniently located at the beginning of each lesson along with background to strengthen catechist understanding and nurture personal faith. A clear, concise, wraparound lesson plan leads the catechist page-by-page through the effective three-step process with integrated background on Sacred Scripture and doctrine, teaching tips, and connections to music, liturgy, and Catholic Social Teaching.

Extensive Online Resources for Catechists and Families

Alive in Christ provides catechists and leaders comprehensive program level resources and unit, chapter, and seasonal specific tools and activities. Online support includes lesson planning tools, catechist formation, custom test building and eAssessments, connections to the Sunday readings, and the option to share lesson plans via social media.

This extensive site provides children and families access to web-based assessments, interactive games and reviews, and articles and resources targeted specifically to adults—all to support faith sharing and continued learning in the home.

Age-Appropriate Music that Enhances Learning

With the knowledge that music is a means for forming children in Sacred Scripture, Church teachings, and Catholic Identity, *Alive in Christ* integrates multiple music options into every lesson. A variety of music from OCP (Oregon Catholic Press), John Burland, Dr. Jo Ann Paradise, and other sources is tied to chapter objectives and themes.

Music is suggested at point-of-use in the Catechist Edition, with multiple song suggestions for each chapter. Many prayer pages feature a song to be used within the prayer service. Music can be sampled and downloaded.

Also, we now have an all-new music component, *Songs of Scripture: Deepening Children's Understanding of the Word of God*, which features songs that teach, reinforce, and unfold the meaning of Scripture stories presented in the Student Book.

Alive in Christ Development Team

Greg Erlandson
President and Publisher

Beth McNamara
General Manager

Sabrina Magnuson
Associate Publisher

Dr. Jo Ann Paradise   Dr. Joseph White

Ana Arista   Heidi Busse   David Dziena   Dr. Hosffman Ospino   Denise Utter

Alive in Christ Structural Framework

Alive in Christ follows a systematic Scope and Sequence organized around key themes of Catholic teaching that repeat each year within a grade-level focus, building on the child's knowledge of the faith at each developmental stage.

This organizational structure takes into account research in child development that tells us at which age learning about a particular topic is most effective. These developmental "windows" help us to understand when the spiritual, cognitive, emotional, sociological, moral, and physical abilities of a child are "ripe" for learning. Included in the sequence, then, is a sensitivity to when children are ready to learn. A grade level focus based within the structural framework of the seven essential truths allows for optimal learning.

The seven essential, eternal truths of the faith— Revelation, Trinity, Jesus, The Church, Sacraments, Morality and Kingdom of God—provide the structural framework that organizes the content of the grade. Progressing from first to sixth grade, the child deepens understanding as he or she is presented content that is theologically precise and developmentally appropriate.

As you study the Scope and Sequence, you will see how the objectives across grades move the learner to examine and appropriate a greater knowledge of our Catholic faith and how those objectives help to form a vibrant Catholic Identity.

Grade Level Focus	
1: Jesus Christ	"For through faith you are all children of God in Christ Jesus." **Galatians 3:26**
2: Sacraments of Penance and the Eucharist	"This is my body, which will be given for you; do this in memory of me." **Luke 22:19**
3: The Church	"I am the vine, you are the branches. Whoever remains in me and I in him will bear much fruit…" **John 15:5**
4: The Moral Life	"This is my commandment: love one another as I love you." **John 15:12**
5: The Seven Sacraments	"I am the vine, you are the branches. Whoever remains in me and I in him will bear much fruit…" **John 15:5**
6: The Word of God in the Old Testament	"The water I shall give will become in him a spring of water welling up to eternal life." **John 4:14**

 Go to **aliveinchrist.osv.com** for an overview of the developmental windows for each grade level focus and full program Scope and Sequence.

Program Scope and Sequence

This graphic gives a visual image of the scope and sequence as a fourth grader in your group will experience it. The circles on the outside name the essential truths that are the framework (unit structure) for every grade level. The child is holding key developmental factors or "windows" that lead to the grade level focus (for more on this, see page CE29). No matter what unit you are teaching, some component of the grade level focus is being treated.

Unit 1
Revelation

Unit 2
Trinity

Unit 3
Jesus
Christ

Unit 4
The
Church

Unit 5
Morality

Unit 6
Sacraments

Unit 7
Kingdom
of God

**Snapshot of Developmental Factors
Third Grade— The Church**

- Children this age have entered what some social/developmental theorists call the "chumship stage," when same-age peers become very important and children often have "best friends." For this reason, it is an ideal time to focus on the parish community.

- Third graders are more aware of the larger world, so this is a good time to talk about the larger worldwide Church and how it is organized.

- This is also a great year to build "missionary mindfulness" by talking about the work of the Church in various parts of the world and how our one faith is expressed in diverse ways across cultures.

Alive in Christ **Program Components**

Student Books Grades 1 to 6 Parish Edition

Student Books follow a seven unit structure with a grade level focus on a foundational topic in our Catholic faith. They are the perfect tool to teach children to know, love, and live their Catholic faith through Sacred Scripture, doctrine, prayer, practices of the faith, and seasonal celebrations.

Catechist Editions

The Catechist Editions help to build confident, capable, and successful catechists with comprehensive background and lesson preparation pages, timed wrap around lesson plans, optional activities, and point of use information. They are spiral bound and conveniently sized to match the Student Book.

People of Faith Collection

This beautifully illustrated collection of Saints, Blesseds, and Venerables are connected to specific chapters. Children will learn about models of our Catholic faith while deepening their relationship with God and the Church.

Music Resources

Catechists are provided options for developmentally-appropriate music that enhances learning. *Alive in Christ* integrates music into each step of the lesson. A variety of music from Oregon Catholic Press is tied to chapter objectives and themes.

A unique, all new music component, *Songs of Scripture: Deepening Children's Understanding of God's Word*, features songs by John Burland and Dr. Jo Ann Paradise, that teach, reinforce, and unfold the meaning of Scripture stories presented in the Student Book.

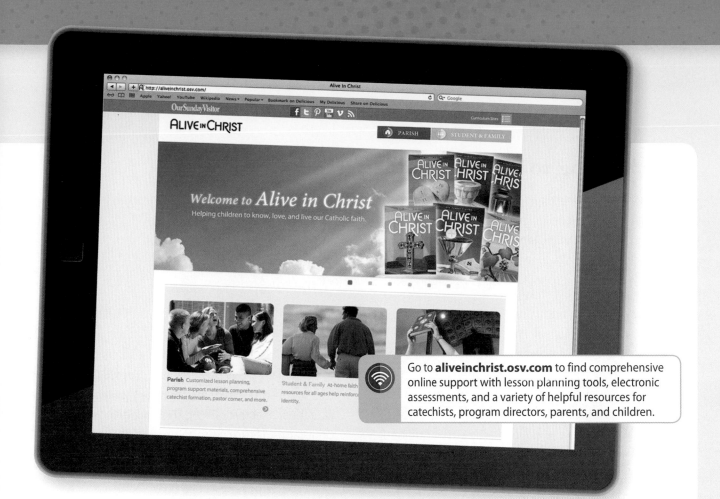

Go to **aliveinchrist.osv.com** to find comprehensive online support with lesson planning tools, electronic assessments, and a variety of helpful resources for catechists, program directors, parents, and children.

Online Resources For the Catechist

- Online lesson planning helps catechists to plan using chapter, seasonal, or Catholic Social Teaching lessons
- Share lesson plans via social media such as Facebook & Twitter
- Unit- and chapter-specific tools, assessments, activities, and multimedia resources
- Build a Custom Test allows catechists to build, print, and distribute tests using a bank of multiple choice, matching, fill in the blank, and long answer questions
- Assign eAssessments to children for completion Online
- Catechetical formation and professional development tools are designed to help catechists hone their skills and grow in the knowledge of God's love
- Sample and download chapter-specific music to enhance catechetical learning or for prayer

Online Resources For the Student & Family

- Interactive Reviews offer children an opportunity for web-based assessment, preparation, and practice
- At-home faith formation resources for all ages help reinforce Catholic identity
- Faith-sharing features and resources geared to parents, children, and families encourage continued learning at home via games, multimedia activities, Lectionary-connected resources, social media interaction, and topical articles
- Sample and download chapter-specific music to enhance catechetical learning or for prayer

Online Resources For the Leader

- Program-level tools and resources provide directors, administrators, and leaders with higher-level materials from correlations to in-service models
- Sample and download chapter-specific music to enhance catechetical learning or for prayer

Responding to Your Vocation

66 Give thanks to the Lord for the gift of your vocation, through which Christ has called you from among other men and women to be instruments of his salvation. Respond with generosity to your vocation and your names will be written in heaven. 99

— Blessed Pope John Paul II, *Guide for Catechists*, 37

These words, taken from a talk by Blessed Pope John Paul II to the catechists of Angola, are both awe inspiring and challenging! You have been called, he said, called by Christ from among other men and women. Have you ever wondered why you responded to the talk of the pastor or DRE that spoke about the need for catechists? Why did the bulletin article that outlined the responsibilities of a catechist stir your heart and prompt you to respond? Who gave your name to the catechetical leader in your parish?

No matter how the invitation came, it was Christ who called you. And by the power of the Holy Spirit, you, like Mary, responded, "Yes!" The vocation to catechesis, like all vocations, first comes from the grace of Baptism,

is strengthened in Confirmation, and sustained by the Eucharist and Penance. "The Church awakens and discerns this divine vocation and confers the mission to catechize….This personal call of Jesus Christ and its relationship to him are the true moving forces of catechetical activity. 'From this loving knowledge of Christ springs the desire to proclaim him, to "evangelize," and to lead others to the "Yes" of faith in Jesus Christ'[2]" (GDC, 231).

You have been called by Christ and been given the mission by his Church to be instruments of his work. Take a moment and ponder that statement. With so many responsibilities and demands on our time, we might sometimes lose sight of this and being a catechist becomes just one of the many things we must do each week. This cannot be so. Every time you gather with your children, you take your place in the long line of those who have for 2,000 years held the sacred duty of bringing others into "communion, in intimacy, with Jesus Christ" (*Catechesi Tradendae*, 5).

Your Role

To support and nurture your children in their baptismal call to a lifetime of growing closer to and more like Jesus, the Church sets out some essential instructions. In order to provide a presentation of the "entire treasure of the Christian message" while adapting it to the "capacity of those being catechized" (GDC, 112), a catechist must do several things.

Teach the comprehensive course of study outlined by the United States Conference of Catholic Bishops' Subcommittee on the *Catechism*. In *Alive in Christ*, you find these doctrines and practices presented in the objectives of the lesson. (See GDC, 112)

Respect the developmental level of your children by understanding how they learn. (See GDC, 112)

Use various methods as they are a "sign of life and richness" that will address multiple learning styles and special needs (GDC, 148).

Model a Catholic life through your own behaviors and practices, for the "charism given to [the catechist] by the Spirit, a solid spirituality and transparent witness of life constitutes the soul of every method" (GDC, 156).

Proclaim with joy and enthusiasm that "God so loved the world he sent his only Son." In the words of Pope Benedict XVI, "Today too, there is a need… to rediscover the joy of believing and the enthusiasm for communicating the faith" (*Porta Fidei*, 7).

As you accept this sacred and challenging vocation be assured that the Holy Spirit will lead and guide you in handing on our Catholic faith to the next generation. Let the love of God pour through so that they see in you the image and heart of our loving God.

The Task of Catechesis

As Jesus Formed His Disciples

There are six fundamental tasks in the ministry of catechesis. These six tasks are named and treated in the *General Directory for Catechesis* (GDC , 85), and later in the *National Directory for Catechesis* (NDC, 20). Each of these tasks corresponds to an aspect of faith in Jesus. The following are the six tasks of catechesis.

General Directory of Catechesis

Promoting Knowledge of the Faith

We cannot live a faith we do not know. For this reason, studying the teachings of Jesus and his Church is an essential task of catechesis. The U.S. Bishops' Subcommittee on the Catechism and the conformity review process direct what is to be contained in this comprehensive presentation of the faith. According to the *National Directory for Catechesis*, this task of catechesis is a response to the individual's desire that God plants in the heart of every person to know. This desire comes naturally when individuals have had opportunities to encounter Christ and his message and have experienced an initial conversion. *Alive in Christ* begins each lesson by giving children an opportunity to meet God in his Word and to wonder about his life and love, followed by a process of helping them to know more about him through Sacred Tradition—the teaching of the Church. In this way, we help children frame questions that drive their desire to know more.

Liturgical Education

This task relates to learning about the ways in which the Church worships and celebrates, including the Seven Sacraments, the Order of Mass, and the liturgical year. According to the *General Directory of Catechesis*, liturgical education includes teaching about the form and the meaning of liturgical celebrations, but also means helping individuals prepare their minds and hearts to enter into these mysteries of our faith. As you use *Alive in Christ*, you will teach your students about the liturgy both through the doctrine presented in the core chapters as well as through seasonal activities and prayerful experiences that echo the words and rhythms of our liturgical celebrations.

Moral Formation

This task of catechesis involves forming the consciences of learners through the moral teachings of Jesus and his Church and fostering understanding of what it means to live these teachings in one's daily life. Morality in the Christian life involves standards and guidelines, but it is more than learning a list of rules. Morality is about discipleship. As you use *Alive in Christ*, you will find opportunities to challenge children to apply what they have learned about the Ten Commandments, Jesus' command to love as he has loved, and the Beatitudes to situations at home and school and in the community.

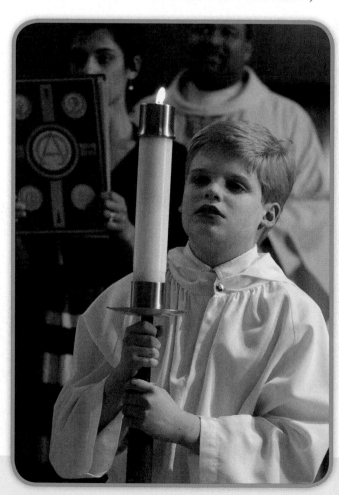

Teaching to Pray

"When catechesis is permeated by a climate of prayer, the assimilation of the entire Christian life reaches its summit" (GDC, 85). The "climate of prayer" in catechesis invites individuals into an ever deeper relationship with God. Teaching to pray is more than merely "teaching prayers"; it involves fostering an understanding of prayer as conversation with God— helping children learn how to talk with God in their own words as well as how to listen to God.

This task of catechesis involves teaching the traditional prayers of the Church and the various forms and expressions of prayer mentioned in the *Catechism of the Catholic Church*. *Alive in Christ* incorporates experiences of all six forms of prayer. You will also have opportunities to help children speak to God in their own words.

Education for Community Life

This task of catechesis relates to developing an understanding of what it means to be a part of the Christian community, including respecting the authority and structure of the Church as well as living out Jesus New Commandment to love one another as he has loved us. "Catechesis prepares the Christian to live in community and to participate actively in the life and mission of the Church" (GDC, 86). Catechesis should prepare us to live and work with one another, both within the Church and in society as a whole. The

bishops write that catechesis "should encourage a spirit of simplicity and humility, a special concern for the poor, particular care for the alienated, a sense of fraternal correction, common prayer, mutual forgiveness, and a fraternal love that embraces all these attitudes." Various chapter features, as well as the "Live Your Faith" sections on Catholic Social Teaching will assist you in this task of catechesis.

Missionary Initiation

While only some may be called to other lands to minister in Christ's name, by Baptism, all are called to live in such a way that we serve as witnesses of the faith to those who are around us. This task of catechesis prepares the learner to share his or her faith with others. *Alive in Christ* helps to form children in the language of the Catholic faith and the behaviors and practices of the faith. Forming them in a vibrant Catholic identity gives them the skills necessary to be strong witnesses of the faith. This is reinforced in the tools we provide the parents in the Family + Faith page, as it equips the parents to talk about faith with their children.

Our bishops state, "all efforts in evangelization and catechesis should incorporate these tasks" (NDC, 20). In this way, we pay attention to several different dimensions of faith, with the ultimate goal of helping children grow into deeper communion with Christ so that they live as disciples in faith, word, and deed.

The Divine Pedagogy

As catechists, we always hold two realities: the "what" and the "how" of catechesis. What do we want our children to know and love about our faith and how do we best communicate the treasure of our faith?

We use the word *pedagogy* to speak about the art, science, or profession of teaching. In other words, pedagogy is the "how" of faith formation. We are called to hand on the truths of our faith by echoing God's own way of teaching us his truths. The *General Directory for Catechesis* tells us that,

66 Catechesis, as communication of divine Revelation, is radically inspired by the pedagogy of God, as displayed in Christ and in the Church… It is the Church's mission to be a visible and actual continuation of the pedagogy of the Father and of the Son. 99

GDC, 143, 141

Each lesson in **Alive in Christ** mirrors the divine pedagogy—the gradual and relational way God teaches us so that we can know him and his truth, be guided by the Holy Spirit to respond with faith and love and accept the gift of new life in Christ. Even as we teach others, God remains active in their hearts, bringing growth to the seeds of faith that are planted there.

Here are five important characteristics of the divine pedagogy that are at the heart of each lesson of **Alive in Christ**.

The pedagogy of God is invitational and person-centered.

God initiates a relationship with each person. He does so by first creating us with a desire to know him and the capacity to respond to him. The ultimate invitation to relationship comes in Jesus. Blessed John Paul II tells us that the purpose of all catechesis is to bring people into intimacy with Jesus.

As God enters into dialogue with us, we are called to follow this example by providing catechesis that it is rooted in interpersonal relationships and involves a process of dialogue, (see GDC, 143). God also meets us where we are and accommodates for our particular needs. Therefore, effective catechesis should be developmentally-appropriate and should make allowances for adapting to special needs.

God's pedagogy is incarnational.

Dei Verbum points out the "inner unity" of deeds and words in God's plan of revelation: "the deeds wrought by God in the history of salvation manifest and confirm the teaching and realities signified by the words, while the words proclaim the deeds and clarify the mystery contained in them" (2). From speaking the universe into existence, to his promise to Noah and his

Jesus the Teacher

covenants with Abraham and Moses, to the Word made flesh in Jesus Christ, it is evident that God's Word becomes action.

An effective pedagogy should make the faith come to life through hands-on activities and applications and multisensory teaching methodologies. It should give learners clear ways to go out and live the Gospel they have received.

The pedagogy of God is familial and communal.

God reveals himself as a communion of persons—Father, Son and Holy Spirit—and creates human beings to be in communion with one another.

Effective catechesis should build community among the children and should involve parents and families as primary catechists, and should connect children to the larger parish community. Connecting the families to the life of the parish, particularly through participation in the Sunday Eucharist, is vital in building up the Body of Christ.

God's pedagogy is structured and comprehensive.

In salvation history, God reveals himself to humanity gradually as people are able to understand. One Revelation builds upon the next, until Revelation reaches its fullness in the Person of Jesus Christ. Effective catechesis also presents key truths of the faith gradually as the learner is able to receive them.

The pedagogy of God is perpetual.

We read in **Isaiah 55:11**, "So shall my word be that goes forth from my mouth; It shall not return to me empty, but shall do what pleases me, achieving the end for which I sent it." God's truths are handed on through the generations in the forms of Sacred Scripture and Sacred Tradition, which is the living memory of the Church. God's covenants do not end, but come to greater fulfillment and realization.

A catechesis based on the divine pedagogy prepares the learner to share the Gospel with others, in word and deed, so that the Good News of salvation is handed on to others and to future generations.

Three Step Catechetical Process

Alive in Christ's catechetical methodology mirrors the divine pedagogy by following a three-step process of **Invite**, **Discover**, and **Live**. This process encourages a personal and ongoing relationship with the Holy Trinity.

1. **The Invite Step** begins the lesson with God's invitation through Sacred Scripture. Children open their minds and hearts to what God is saying to them in Scripture, reflect on it, and transition to the Discover step and chapter objectives.

2. **The Discover Step** helps form Catholic identity through the study of Scripture, knowledge of Church teaching, and an understanding of Catholic practices. It presents the doctrine of the lesson in developmentally appropriate language and images. Charts, on page questions, and gold star activities prompt children to interact directly with the page, and aid in understanding and retention. With large on page activities, children are given the opportunity to process and reinforce what they have learned and apply it to their own lives and the experience of the Church.

3. **The Live Step** helps children relate knowledge of the faith and the ways we worship, live, pray, and serve together as Catholics. Children are given the tools to connect their faith to everyday life and to deepen their relationship with God and the Church through the prayer experiences at the end of each lesson.

If you follow this three-step process, you will in fact mirror the divine pedagogy by offering your children the opportunity to know God and his truth through Sacred Scripture and Sacred Tradition. You will inspire them to be open to the Holy Spirit so that they will respond in faith and love and accept the gift of new life in Christ!

As a catechist, during the **Invite** step you:

- Call the children together to begin in **prayer**.

- Prepare the children to hear the Word of God.

- Guide the children through the **Scripture reflection** process, proclaiming God's Word and inviting quiet thought. (See CE22 for a full description of the Scripture reflection process.)

- After proclamation of the Scripture, allow time (governed by what is developmentally appropriate) for sacred **silence**.

- Invite children **to share** what they have experienced, what they felt God was saying to them or what he wanted them to know in a special way today. Assure them sharing is voluntary.

- Prompt continued thought about God's Word and move to chapter objectives by using the "**What Do You Wonder**" questions.

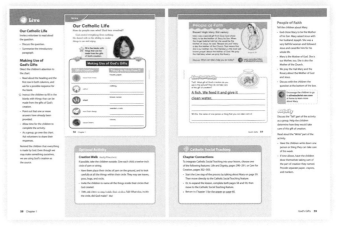

As a catechist, during the **Discover** step you:

- Teach the **objectives** of the lesson which are identified in the Catechist Edition in several places, the overview Lesson Plan in the catechist background section and in the left hand corner of each Discover spread. The Quick Review, highlighted in the bottom right hand corner of the Discover spread, allows you to check that you have fully covered the objectives.

- Follow the **instruction** in the vertical side columns which walks you through the entire lesson. Note that the activities are an integral part of the lesson. They emphasize the essential elements of Church teaching and help the children apply those truths to worship, prayer, and daily life.

- Present the **Catholic Faith Words** which are highlighted in the text and called out in the side boxes. These words build a common language of faith and are explained with precise theological language that is developmentally appropriate.

- Use the **boxes** framed in green at the bottom of the page that provide additional Scripture and doctrinal background, optional activities, quick tips, ways to adapt for special needs, suggestions for including music, and more.

As a catechist, during the **Live** step you:

- Guide the children through a graphic organizer, chart, or reflection activity to **synthesize** what they have learned in the chapter.

- Hold up the Communion of Saints, and introduce the children to a **Saint**, **Blessed**, or **Venerable** whose life exemplifies the content of the lesson. What better way to encourage faith-filled living than through Catholic heroines and heroes?

- Give the children the opportunity through a closing **activity** to relate their knowledge of the faith to their lives and invite them to commit themselves more deeply to what it means to be Catholic with concrete action and future steps.

- Conclude with a **prayer celebration**. Make sure to leave time at the end of the lesson to pray with the children. If the prayer calls for it, you may want to assign parts a week ahead of time.

- Send home the **Family + Faith** page. As the children live their faith primarily in the circle of their families, this page is an excellent resource to connect the children's learning with their home and to form their parents in faith.

Lesson Preparation

Alive in Christ Catechist Editions give you everything you need for lesson planning, teaching and reinforcing faith concepts, and growing in your own relationship with Christ and his Church.

Each chapter has catechist specific content provided in the planning and background pages. These are the five pages that provide Scriptural, doctrinal, and methodological background and formation. You will also find pages that address the different ways children process, understand, and learn lesson content at any given grade level.

Catechist Background easy-to-understand theological background on the chapter content. The Reflect questions help connect faith concepts with the catechist's own life experience.

Key Concept for each lesson is clearly stated at the start of each chapter.

Doctrinal Content correlates to paragraphs from the *Catechism of the Catholic Church*.

Tasks of Catechesis relate lesson components to one of the six Tasks of Catechesis as outlined in the *National Directory for Catechesis*.

Catechist's Prayer offers a moment of reflection for the catechist before planning each lesson.

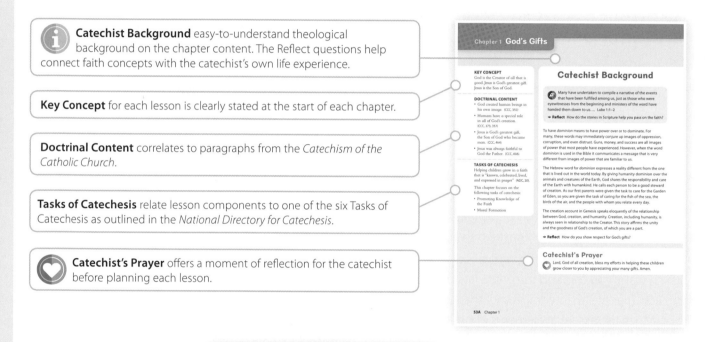

Timed Lesson Plan clearly stated chapter objectives, step-by-step instructions, and a suggested time frame to complete each step of the lesson.

Process Column notes prayer, Scripture, activities, and Catholic Faith Words in each step.

Materials Column materials and online resources needed for the lesson.

Family + Faith / Chapter Review reminders to share chapter content with families and directs catechists to various opportunities for review and assessment.

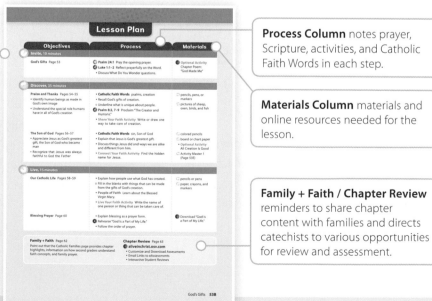

Sharing the Message offers insight on the relationship between the lesson objectives and the child's developmental level of understanding of those topics.

How Grade Level Children Understand provides general background on where children this age typically are with cognitive, social, spiritual, and emotional development.

Online Resources are clearly labeled throughout the Catechist Edition and direct you to downloads, lesson planning tools, interactive reviews, eAssessments, and more.

Chapter Story or poem provides an opportunity to extend the Invite step of the process with additional life experience connections.

NCEA IFG: ACRE Edition correlates the lesson objectives to the domains of *NCEA Information for Growth: Assessment of Children/Youth Religious Education* (2013) and helps catechist measure children's understanding and appropriation of lesson content.

Catholic Social Teaching identifies which principles of Catholic Social Teaching/Live Your Faith pieces connect to this chapter and provide direction for how to integrate them into the Live step of the process. These connections are also noted at point of use in the bottom band of the lesson plan.

Music Options are provided to enhance catechetical learning and in the prayer celebration. These options are also called out at point of use in the wraparound lesson plan.

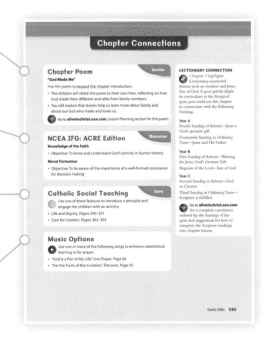

Catholic Bible

✝

NABRE

New American Bible Revised Edition

Sacred Scripture

❝ For in the sacred books, the Father who is in heaven meets His children with great love and speaks with them; and the force and power in the word of God is so great that it stands as the support and energy of the Church…. ❞

Dei Verbum, 21

Sacred Scripture from both the Old Testament and New Testament is at the heart of *Alive in Christ*. The children are invited to understand the importance of Sacred Scripture, as a font of Divine Revelation and the guide for their lives. The Word is always given prominent visual importance to highlight its significance, with a parchment background, an icon and logo. Children are led to know, love, and be formed by God's Word.

Scripture in the Catechetical Process

The children always **pray** with Scripture in the opening prayer of the Invite step and often in the prayer experience in the Live step.

The practice of Scripture **reflection** is an essential element in the Invite step of every lesson and the means by which we enter into the divine pedagogy.

Children are formed by this practice of reflecting on Scripture and being open to the Word of God personally speaking to them. Listening with the ear of the heart and reflecting on Scripture prepares children for practices such as *Lectio Divina*.

Sacred Scripture is **studied** in the Discover step as children learn about God's action throughout salvation history and see how Scripture is a source of Church teaching. Key Scripture accounts are presented in multiple grade levels to encourage biblical literacy, familiarity, and understanding.

Throughout the Discover and Live steps the children **apply** the Word of God to their lived experience and acquire the behaviors and practices of a Catholic life.

Scripture Reflection

Step 1: Begin by using the directions provided on the Invite page of the lesson or you may use the recorded preparation entitled, "Mantra," included in both the *Songs of Scripture* CDs.

Step 2: Help the children enter into sacred space by prominently displaying the Bible, lighting or turning on a candle, and guiding them to become quiet and still.

Step 3: Read the passage in a slow and steady voice, one complete sentence at a time.

Step 4: Ask the question, "What did you hear God say to you today?" This reflection is critical in providing the children an opportunity to encounter God through his Word. It prepares the child to receive and respond in faith to God's personal invitation.

CHAPTER **3**

Invite

God's Commandments

💗 **Let Us Pray**

Leader: Loving Father, you made us to know you and your desire for us.

"I delight to do your will, my God; your law is in my inner being!" Psalm 40:9

All: O God, help us to learn how to listen for your voice so that we will know how to follow you. Amen.

📖 **Scripture**

"When [Moses] looked, although the bush was on fire, it was not being consumed.... When the LORD saw that he had turned aside to look, God called out to him from the bush: Moses! Moses! He answered, 'Here I am.' God said: Do not come near! Remove your sandals from your feet, for the place where you stand is holy ground." Exodus 3:2b, 4–5

What Do You Wonder?

• How does God speak to people today?

• How do the Ten Commandments help you to know God and what

⏱ **Invite**

💗 **Let Us Pray**

Invite children to gather in the prayer space and make the Sign of the Cross. Begin with leader's p... and have a volunteer pray alou... psalm verse from a Bible. Prom... the group's response.

Have the children move out o... prayer space and back to their...

Say: God wanted Moses to lead... People, who were slaves, to freedom. The Word of God we will hear... of Moses' journey of faith.

📖 **Scripture**

Guide the children through... process of Scripture reflection.

• Invite them to close their eyes and open their minds and hearts to what God is saying to them by being silent and still.

• Proclaim the Scripture.

Sacred Tradition

What is necessary for the children to know so that they will develop a vibrant Catholic identity and be able to express their faith with competence, understanding, and love?

The Church guides us, teaching that the catechetical message has "a 'comprehensive hierarchical character'[3] which constitutes a vital synthesis of the faith" (GDC, 114). The truths of the faith are organized in a hierarchy around the mystery of the most Holy Trinity, in a Christ-centered (or *Christocentric*) perspective.

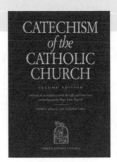

Catechism of the Catholic Church

66 The mutual connections between dogmas, and their coherence, can be found in the whole of the Revelation of the mystery of Christ.[4] 'In Catholic doctrine there exists an order or "hierarchy" of truths, since they vary in their relation to the foundation of the Christian faith.'[5] 99

CCC, 90

In other words, some truths are so basic and foundational to what we believe as Catholics that they must be presented first, and then other related truths can be better understood.

To help us know what is basic and foundational, the USCCB's Subcommittee on the Catechism has identified the truths of the faith deemed essential to the formation of children. *Alive in Christ* has been found to be in conformity with the *Catechism of the Catholic Church*.

In salvation history, God has revealed himself to people in a systematic and gradual way, showing us more of himself as we are capable of understanding. (See GDC, 38 and CCC 54–65.) Our catechesis models this divine pedagogy and includes all of the essential elements of the faith, presenting them in a gradual and systematic way as the learner is ready to hear them.

Alive in Christ organizes the essential truths around seven key themes of Catholic teaching that repeat each year within a grade level focus.

Systematic and Comprehensive

The content of Sacred Scripture and Sacred Tradition are systematically presented in precise theological language in the **lesson objectives** of each lesson. The objectives are found on your Lesson Plan and at point of use where they are presented to the children.

Important **Catholic Faith Words** are highlighted in every chapter with definitions that grow as children's understanding does and their repetition across grades helps to promote the common language of faith.

Each **Unit Opener** summarizes key concepts being presented and references these faith statements to the Catechism of the Catholic Church.

At the back of each Student Book the **Our Catholic Tradition** reference section reinforces the faith basics presented in the lessons. It is referenced in your lesson plan with specific instruction on how to integrate the content into the lesson.

The Theory Behind It

At one point or another in your family life and your ministry as a catechist, you've likely found yourself explaining to a child, "It's not just what you say, it's how you say it." The message is as important as the delivery. You can't separate the *what* from the *how*. Similarly, doctrine and method are not two ends of a spectrum. They are interdependent. In catechesis, you can't have one without the other. And it goes a step further, for it's not just *what* we teach, and how we teach it, but *how* the learner receives it.

"Consequently catechesis starts out with…the integral structure of the Christian message, and proceeds to explain it in a manner adapted to the capacity of those being catechized" (GDC, 112).

When we teach things in a theologically accurate way, and in a manner sensitive to where the children are developmentally, we provide the best chance that they will appropriate the content—process and understand it in a way that has meaning to them and that they can then apply to their own lives.

According to the National Association for the Education of Young Children (NAEYC), *developmental appropriateness* includes multiple components.

1. It is important to know how children develop and learn at particular ages and stages and to create learning environments that are responsive to these general needs.

2. Because every child is unique, knowing the individual children and how they learn best is essential.

3. It is important to know what is culturally appropriate for different ages and stages of development.

The Practice of It

Alive in Christ provides you with carefully selected topics and activities that meet the developmental level of the children you are teaching as well as tips for addressing individual needs. The program includes prayers, Saints, activities, and stories that represent the

Presentation of Text

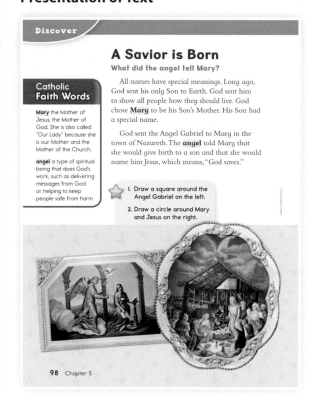

- Information is sequenced and organized in smaller "chunks" to make reading and understanding faster and easier.

- Sentences are shorter in length for younger grades.

- Fonts and type sizes are set with consideration given to the reading level of the child.

- Words are defined consistently at point-of-use and highlighted for easy identification.

- Terms and concepts are introduced, reinforced, and then further defined in advanced ways as they develop across grades.

diversity of cultures found in our Church and introduces these traditions at developmentally-appropriate times.

Alive in Christ takes into account the experience level of today's children with various topics and how they are used to receiving and processing those topics. So, the series is developmentally appropriate not just in what

kids learn at particular ages, but how they learn it.

As a catechist, you can feel confident that you are giving the children the most precise presentation of Church teaching in the most developmentally appropriate way. That's what excellent catechesis is all about.

Use of Visuals

- Fine art, illustrations, and photos advance in detail and sophistication as grades progress.
- Graphic organizers, charts, and call outs are used to present content in easy to track and access formats.
- Captions are used to aid in learning, and the content and purpose of captions advance as the grades do.
- The text-to-art ratio is intentional and customized for each grade level.

Teaching Strategies

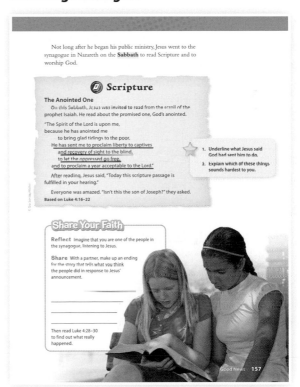

- Questions focus reading, prompt reflection, and reinforce learning.
- On page activities and teaching strategies incorporate dynamic, interactive learning methods.
- Chapter reviews use multiple formats to accommodate different learning styles.
- The Catechist Edition includes a "Teaching This Grade" page that gives details on how children at this age might understand lesson objectives.
- Ideas for customizing content are found in the "Reaching All Learners" boxes in the chapter.

The Use of Images

"" In order to communicate the message entrusted to her by Christ, the Church needs art. ""

—Letter of Pope John Paul II to Artist (1999), 12

While educational research assures us that children make meaning through the interplay of text and images (Carney and Levine, 2002), any adult whose spent time with a young child knows that verbal and visual both tell the story. For hundreds of years the Church has used sacred art and stained glass windows to teach Catholic doctrine and provide a physical presentation of the truths of our faith. Jesus often used images when he preached, giving his disciples a glimpse into his Father's mystery and the Kingdom.

Its use of fine art, stained glass, and Scripture illustrations created specifically for this program is another way that *Alive in Christ* mirrors the divine pedagogy.

Educational research (Carney and Levine, 2002) and our own experience tells us that photos, illustrations, and art closely tied to text

- improve the reader's learning and recall
- direct the child's attention to what's most important on the page
- make the text more understandable and memorable
- help the child connect and apply what's been learned to their lived experience.

In *Alive in Christ* lessons, developmentally appropriate visuals—Scripture illustration, fine art, stained glass, statues, icons, photos, and accompanying captions— meet lesson objectives and build Catholic identity.

You will find historically accurate, child friendly Scripture and Saint illustrations that grow in sophistication and detail as grades advance. This promotes a common visual language of faith and builds a vibrant Catholic identity.

Grade 1   Grade 6
Saints Thérèse of Lisieux and Teresa of Avila

Grade 1   Grade 3
The Sacred Heart of Jesus in statue and fine art

Grade 2   Grade 5
The Parable of the Good Samaritan

The Role of Music

The use of music in *Alive in Christ* is both intentional and purposeful. The music has been chosen to form children in the lesson content and Catholic identity. It is age appropriate and includes children's voices. It has both a formative and an informative purpose.

Long-term Retention

It has been demonstrated that the repeated rehearsal of information has a positive effect on long-term retention. Activities from the arts, such as music integrated into classroom content, can be used as prompts to recall information. Combining music with movement further enhances a child's learning. We "encode" information through both verbal and motor activity. In other words, when we sing and do movement, we are learning in both our bodies and our minds.

Sustain Attention

Music and movement also sustain attention. Translating material into actions (role playing a song) helps learners not only recall a story but can also help them connect that story to a concept they have learned. Besides, moving to music is a universal response, and, with the proper disposition, can enhance prayer.

Emotional and Spiritual Connection

Music can also affect us on an emotional level. Who of us has not been moved by a song to feel something deep within our hearts? Music has helped form us as Catholics throughout the ages and has enabled us to both experience God's presence and respond to him from the depths of our being.

Moral Formation
- Objective: To be aware of the importance of a well-formed conscience for decision making

Catholic Social Teaching Live

 Use one of these features to introduce a principle and engage the children with an activity.
- Life and Dignity, Pages 290–291
- Care for Creation, Pages 302–303

Music Options

 Use one or more of the following songs to enhance catechetical learning or for prayer.
- "God Is a Part of My Life," Live Prayer, Page 60
- "For the Fruits of this Creation," Discover, Page 55

First Sunday of Advent—Waiting for Jesus, God's Greatest Gift
Baptism of the Lord—Son of God

Year C
Second Sunday in Advent—God as Creator
Third Sunday in Ordinary Time—Scripture is fulfilled.

Go to **aliveinchrist.osv.com** for a complete correlation ordered by the Sundays of the year and suggestions for how to integrate the Scripture readings into chapter lessons.

Music options are integrated into every lesson and can be used to celebrate prayer or enhance learning. You will find these options both at point of use in the wraparound and in the Chapter Connections page in the box titled, "Music Options."

Play chapter-specific music to enhance catechetical learning or for prayer. Go to **aliveinchrist.osv.com** to sample and download.

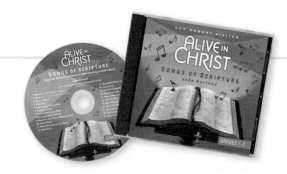

Songs of Scripture Music CDs

To support the commitment to Sacred Scripture, an all new, original resource, *Songs of Scripture Deepening Children's Understanding of God's Word*, by John Burland and Jo Ann Paradise, unfolds one of the Scripture passages in each unit. Activities for these songs are found in bottom-band boxes in the Catechist Edition.

 Go to **aliveinchrist.osv.com** to order the *Songs of Scripture* CDs and for more information.

Reaching All Learners

"Growth in faith is related to human development and passes through stages. Individuals develop as human beings and faithful followers of Christ in different ways according to their own pace...The Church's catechesis—and even more so, the catechist— must take into consideration all the human factors of a particular age level in order to present the gospel message in a vital and compelling way. "

NDC, 48

Benefitting from the work of educators in the past decades, religious educators now have new tools in providing children the fullness of the faith in developmentally appropriate ways.

Not only must we teach the faith related to children's level of human development, we must meet the individual needs of our children. When working with any group of children, it does not take long to realize that they learn in different ways. Many have written about how to best provide strategies to address different learning styles. Dr. Howard Gardner's research on Multiple Intelligences provides particular insight. His theory looks at eight different ways people learn. Applying his theory to your planning will help you reach each child with the Good News of salvation.

Using varying strategies to meet the learning styles of the children is not the only consideration when preparing a lesson. Learning is also affected by learning or emotional disorders and mental or physical challenges. A special feature in your Catechist Edition, called, "Reaching All Learners" will provide you with tips, suggestions and proven ways to include children with different learning styles, and abilities in your lessons.

 Go to **aliveinchrist.osv.com** for additional resources on meeting the challenges of providing for special needs in your faith formation sessions.

Multiple Intelligences	
Verbal/ Linguistic	This learning occurs best through reading, writing, telling stories, and discussing ideas.
Logical/ Mathematical	This learning occurs best through problem solving, analyzing, and applying logic.
Musical	This learning occurs best through singing, listening to music, and remembering melodies.
Bodily/ Kinesthetic	This learning occurs best through physically moving, dancing, acting, and making things.
Visual/Spatial	This learning occurs best through looking at pictures, drawing, and creating.
Interpersonal	This learning occurs best through sharing about one's feelings, talking with others, and collaborating with others on tasks.
Intrapersonal	This learning occurs best through working alone and reflecting.
Naturalist	This learning occurs best through exploring nature and living things.

Teaching Third Graders

It's a blessing to be a catechist to fourth graders. This is an exciting time in the life of a child, when children have a clear sense of cause and effect, making them curious about how and why things work the way they do.

Growth of Social Relationships

The third grade is characterized by a growth in social relationships. Children this age have entered what social/developmental theorist Harry Stack Sullivan called the "chumship stage," when same-age peers become very important and children often have "best friends." As children become more aware of building their own peer community, it is an ideal time to focus on the parish community as well. Make sure children know their parish and how it is organized. If possible, invite leaders from various ministries to share what they do with the class. Make sure the class is aware of ways children their age can serve in the parish, perhaps as an altar server.

Cooperative Learning

The growth in peer relationships at this age gives us an opportunity to use more cooperative learning techniques. Make time for partner and group work. Sometimes catechists are reluctant to do this out of concern that children will be more likely to get off task. However, you can help keep things moving by following a few simple steps: 1) Explain each task thoroughly. You might wish to provide both verbal and written instructions. 2) Assign specific roles to each member of the group. Make sure each child knows the way in which he or she is expected to participate. 3) Provide time limits and transition times for each group activity. Let them know how long they have to complete each step, and give a 5-minute and 1-minute warning.

You can also capitalize on the social nature of third graders by making time for whole-class activities. Group games and group prayer/sharing times can be particularly enjoyable for children this age.

Learning about the Church

Third graders are more aware of the larger world, so this is a good time to talk about the larger worldwide Church and how it is organized. Make sure they know our Pope and also the bishop of your diocese. You might wish to write a class letter to the bishop to talk about what you are learning and thank him for his service. Keep the children up to date on events in the worldwide Church, such as theme years or papal travels. If you have a globe or world map in your room, talk about the Church in various parts of the world, and point out where the Vatican is located. Begin to build that "missionary mindfulness" by talking about the work of the Church in various parts of the world and how our one faith is expressed in diverse ways across cultures.

Living and Learning Together

In the *General Directory for Catechesis* we are told that the "childhood religious awakening which takes place in the family is irreplaceable"[6] (226). The role of the catechetical leader and the catechist in the parish is to help form and support families in this sacred journey.

The Family + Faith page gives families the tools they need to talk about faith and more consciously live the faith in their homes and daily lives. The resources on this page are invaluable in providing adults the practical help they need to grow in faith themselves and to nurture the faith of their children.

Your Child Learned
This section summarizes key Catholic teaching covered in the chapter and introduces families to the Scripture and Person of Faith presented.

Children At This Age
This feature helps families understand the relationship between the content presented and the child's developmental level of understanding. It provides a look at the content through the eyes of the child and equips parents with a perspective that is necessary in order to nurture their child's faith.

Consider This Through the use of targeted questions that encourage reflection, adults are given the opportunity to reflect on their experience and inform that experience with the teaching of the Church.

Let's Talk Adult specific questions or directions help to facilitate discussion with the child about the lesson content.

Let's Pray This provides families with a short prayer that incorporates the key concept of the lesson.

Go to **aliveinchrist.osv.com**. The Family + Faith page sends adults to aliveinchrist.osv.com so that families can reinforce and assess their learning, along with suggestions for family discussions and ways to apply faith to family life.

FAMILY + FAITH
LIVING AND LEARNING TOGETHER

YOUR CHILD LEARNED >>>
This chapter is about God's gift of creation and the special place humans have in it because we are made in the image and likeness of God.

God's Word
Read **Luke 1:1–2** to learn more about those who have worked to tell God's story.

Catholics Believe
• God is the Creator of all that is good.
• Jesus is God's greatest gift. Jesus is the Son of God.
To learn more, go to the *Catechism of the Catholic Church* #256, 319, and 454 at usccb.org.

People of Faith
This week, your child met the Blessed Virgin Mary who we honor as the Mother of God and the Mother of the Church.

CHILDREN AT THIS AGE >>>
How They Understand God's Creation Most second-graders have a strong sense of cause and effect. This makes it natural for them to believe in a Creator when they see the created world. They also have a strong sense that everything has a purpose. For this reason, it is an excellent time for them to learn that everything in the natural world is a gift from God and has a God-given role or meaning.

CONSIDER THIS >>>
When was the last time that God's creation amazed you?

Do you realize creation is one of the many ways God shows himself to you? God... "is living and personal, profoundly close to us in creating and sustaining us. Though he is totally other, hidden, glorious, and wondrous, he communicates himself to us in Jesus Christ, whom we meet in the Church, especially in Scripture and the Sacraments. In these many ways, God speaks to our hearts where we may welcome his loving presence" (*USCCA, p. 51*).

LET'S TALK >>>
• Ask your child to talk about God's gifts. Which is his greatest? (Jesus)
• Talk about ways your family uses God's gifts of creation in your daily routines.

LET'S PRAY >>>
Mary, Mother of God, pray for our family and help us always love your Son, Jesus. Amen.

For a multimedia glossary of Catholic Faith Words, Sunday readings, seasonal and Saint resources, and chapter activities go to **aliveinchrist.osv.com**.

Alive in Christ, Grade 2 Chapter 1 **61**

The **aliveinchrist.osv.com** Student/Family pages extend learning, foster family faith sharing, and provide session plans and tools for home-based catechesis.

Catholic Social Teaching

Blessed Pope John Paul II reminded us that one of the fundamental tasks of the Christian family is to remember that the family is always at the service of God's Kingdom. While the family is to "guard, reveal, and communicate love," it does so knowing that their love is not only to be shared within itself, but meant to be shared with the world (*Familiaris Consortio*, 17). We are called to reach out past our family to build relationships of love and justice in our neighborhoods, communities, and beyond.

Each grade level of **Alive in Christ**, presents the seven principles of Catholic Social Teaching, articulated by the United States Conference of Catholic Bishops. In this **Live Your Faith** component, the scriptural and doctrinal foundations of the principles help the children connect their faith to a life of peace and justice. While peace and justice are taught in many of the core chapters, the seven principles are intentionally treated in Live Your Faith.

You can use these Catholic Social Teaching features in a variety of ways. Every core chapter and seasonal lesson has a Catholic Social Teaching Connection integrated into the lesson plan. A **bottom band box** will provide you with suggestions on how to incorporate the Live Your Faith component with the lesson. Combining these components with the seasonal lessons can help your children connect how Catholics worship with how Catholics live.

Your catechetical leader may choose to schedule these components so that all the children will be focusing on the same principle at the same time. If you schedule your own sessions, you may choose to combine several of the principles and present them at one time.

This presentation of Catholic teaching builds a vibrant Catholic identity and prepares us to evangelize the world through faith and action as we work in service of God's Kingdom.

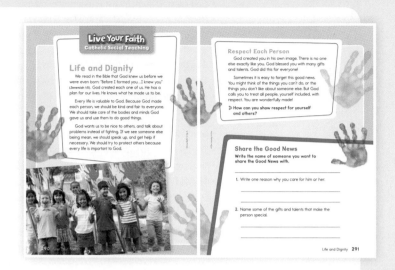

Using This Feature

Lesson Connection

Use this feature to enhance, or in place of, the Live section of the following chapters:

Chapter 1, page 53   **Chapter 5**, page 97

Chapter 3, page 73   **Chapter 12**, page 175

Chapter 4, page 87   **Chapter 20**, page 267

Use this feature after the Discover section, before the Live prayer begins in the following seasonal lessons:

Ordinary Time: All Saints, page 15

Christmas, page 25   **Easter, We Rejoice**, page 43

Scope and Sequence

Unit	Chapter		Lesson Concepts
1 REVELATION	CHAPTER 1	God's Gifts	• God created human beings in his own image. • Humans have a special role in all of God's creation. • Jesus is God's greatest gift, the Son of God who became man. He is always faithful to God the Father.
	CHAPTER 2	God's Promise	• God gives all people the ability to choose. • Original Sin is the first sin committed by Adam and Eve. • Jesus is the Savior because he led people who were lost through sin back to God; Jesus is the Good Shepherd.
	CHAPTER 3	The Word of God	• God tells us about himself through the Bible. • The Bible is God's Word written down by humans, inspired by the Holy Spirit. • Jesus tells stories that help us know and love God the Father. • The Old and New Testaments are the two parts of the Bible, also called Scripture.
2 TRINITY	CHAPTER 4	God the Father	• God the Father is the First Divine Person of the Holy Trinity. • Jesus taught us that God the Father loves and cares for us. • We rely on God the Father, praying to him and trusting he will provide what we need.
	CHAPTER 5	God the Son	• The Angel Gabriel announced to Mary that she would be the Mother of the Son of God, the Savior, Jesus. • The Holy Family of Jesus, Mary, and Joseph lived in Nazareth where Jesus grew up, learning and praying. • Jesus is both the Son of God and a human being. • The Baptism of the adult Jesus by John the Baptist was the beginning of his public teaching.
	CHAPTER 6	God the Holy Spirit	• The Holy Spirit is the Third Divine Person of the Holy Trinity who helps and guides us as Jesus promised. • Jesus is the Son of God who became man, the Second Divine Person of the Holy Trinity. • The Holy Trinity is one God in three Divine Persons. • The Holy Spirit helped the Apostles understand and spread Jesus' teachings and he remains with the Church today.
3 JESUS CHRIST	CHAPTER 7	God's Commandments	• The Ten Commandments are God's laws that teach us to love him and others. • The Great Commandment sums up all of God's laws, telling us to love God above all else and others the way you love yourself. • Jesus told the parable of the Good Samaritan to help us understand that loving God means loving our neighbor. • Jesus gave us a New Commandment to teach us to love as he loves.
	CHAPTER 8	Choose to Do Good	• When we make bad choices that hurt our relationship with God and others, God forgives us if we are truly sorry. • Sin is a free choice to do what we know is wrong. Mistakes and accidents are not sins. • Both venial and mortal sins harm our relationship with God, but in different ways. • Conscience is an ability given to us by God that helps us make choices about right and wrong.
	CHAPTER 9	God's Mercy	• We learn about God's mercy in the story of the Prodigal Son. • The virtues can help us say no to temptation and choose what is good. • Mercy is kindness and concern for those who are suffering; God has mercy on us even though we are sinners. • It's important to ask God and others for forgiveness, and to be forgiving.
4 THE CHURCH	CHAPTER 10	The Sacraments	• The Seven Sacraments are special signs and celebrations that Jesus gave his Church that allow us to share in God's life and work. • Jesus continues to share his life and love with us in the Sacraments. • Baptism, the first Sacrament received, makes a person a child of God and member of the Church, taking away Original Sin and all personal sin. • The Sacraments of Initiation—Baptism, Confirmation, Eucharist—celebrate our membership into the Catholic Church.
	CHAPTER 11	Seek Forgiveness	• An examination of conscience is a prayerful way of thinking about how we have followed the Ten Commandments, Beatitudes, and Church teachings. • Contrition is being sorry for your sins and wanting to live better. • In the Sacrament of Penance and Reconciliation, God's forgiveness for sin is given through the Church. • The Sacrament includes confession, penance, contrition, and absolution.

Sacred Scripture	Catechism of the Catholic Church	Tasks of Catechesis	Catholic Faith Words	People of Faith	Catholic Social Teaching
Handing Down the Stories Luke 1:1–2; The Creator and Humans Psalms 8:2, 7–9	355, 373, 357, 464, 606	Promoting Knowledge of the Faith, Moral Formation	psalms, creation, sin, Son of God	Blessed Virgin Mary	Life and Dignity, Care for Creation
The Sinner Who Repents Luke 15:7; The Garden of Eden Genesis 2:15–17; 3:1–6, 23; The Good Shepherd John 10:11–14	1730–1731, 389, 397, 457, 754	Promoting Knowledge of the Faith, Moral Formation	Original Sin, Savior	St. Cristóbal Magallanes Jara	Call to Community, Human Solidarity
Jesus Among the Crowds Luke 6:17–18; The Great Flood Genesis 6–9; Jesus Teaches Matthew 4:23–25	104, 105, 546, 120	Promoting Knowledge of the Faith, Missionary Initiation	Bible, Old Testament, New Testament	St. Luke	Life and Dignity, Rights and Responsibilities
Trust in the Father Luke 12:29–31; Rely on God Matthew 6:25–32	254, 322, 2779–2781, 2590	Promoting Knowledge of the Faith, Teaching to Pray	Saint, God the Father, prayer, trust	Bl. Julian of Norwich	Life and Dignity, Care for Creation
My Beloved Son Luke 3:21–22; Announcing Jesus' Birth Luke 1:26–38; 2:1–11; The Boy Jesus in the Temple Luke 2:41–52; Baptism of Jesus Matthew 3:13–17	430, 514–515, 723–724, 535	Promoting Knowledge of the Faith, Liturgical Education	Mary, angel, Holy Family	St. Peter	Life and Dignity, Human Solidarity
Risen Jesus Appears to Disciples Luke 24:49; The Promise John 14:15–26; The Spirit Comes Acts 1:4–5, 8; 2:2–3	683–684, 258–259, 253–255, 767–768	Promoting Knowledge of the Faith, Liturgical Education	Holy Spirit, Holy Trinity, disciples, Pentecost, Apostles	St. Arnold Janssen	Call to Community, Rights and Responsibilities
Moses on the Mountain Exodus 24:12; Love the Lord Your God Luke 10.27, The Parable of the Good Samaritan Luke 10:29–37	1962, 2055, 1465, 546, 1970	Promoting Knowledge of the Faith, Moral Formation	Ten Commandments, Great Commandment, parable, New Commandment	St. Elizabeth of Hungary	Rights and Responsibilities, Option for the Poor
Peter Hears the Rooster Mark 14:69–72; Peter Denies Jesus John 18:17–18, 25–27	1441, 1849, 1777–1778, 1854–1855	Promoting Knowledge of the Faith, Moral Formation	free will, mortal sin, venial sin, conscience	St. Thérèse of Lisieux	Rights and Responsibilities, The Dignity of Work
Forgive Seventy-Seven Times Matthew 18:21–22; The Prodigal Son Luke 15:11–32	1439, 270, 2447, 1810, 1459	Moral Formation, Education for Community Life	virtues, temptation, mercy	St. Jane de Chantal	Call to Community, Human Solidarity
Jesus Heals a Blind Man Luke 18:35–43; The Commissioning of the Apostles Matthew 28:19–20	1113, 1116, 1127–1128, 1212, 1213	Promoting Knowledge of the Faith, Liturgical Education	Seven Sacraments, Baptism, grace, Sacraments of Initiation	St. Pius X	Option for the Poor, Care for Creation
Whose Sins You Forgive John 20:21, 23; The Woman Who Was Forgiven Luke 7:36–39, 44–50	1779, 1432, 1422, 1423–1424	Liturgical Education, Moral Formation	examination of conscience, contrition, Sacrament of Penance and Reconciliation, confession, penance, absolution	St. Benedict-Joseph Labre	Call to Community, Human Solidarity

Unit	Chapter		Lesson Concepts
4	CHAPTER 12	The Church Year	• The liturgy is the public prayer of the Church. • The Church Year celebrates the life, Death, Resurrection, and Ascension of Jesus. • The Seasons of the Church year are Advent, Christmas, Ordinary Time, Lent, The Three Days (Triduum), and Easter. • Easter celebrates Christ's Resurrection and is the greatest feast of the Church year.
5 MORALITY	CHAPTER 13	Welcome in the Kingdom	• By the things he said and did, Jesus included those often left out and showed that God welcomes everyone. • The story of Zacchaeus is an example of Jesus welcoming someone who had faith and was willing to repent. • Jesus has a great love for children, and welcomed them along with all others into his Kingdom. • The Kingdom of God is the world of love, peace, and justice that God has in Heaven and wants for us on Earth.
	CHAPTER 14	Share the Good News	• The Gospel message is the Good News of God's Kingdom and his saving love. • In his parable of the Vine and Branches, Jesus teaches us that we need to stay connected to him in order to have life. • The Holy Spirit strengthened the Apostles to share what Jesus had taught them. • Many people in our parish share Jesus' message and work together with God as he builds his Kingdom.
	CHAPTER 15	Ways to Pray	• Jesus taught us to pray the Lord's Prayer, which we also call the Our Father. • There are five basic forms of prayer: blessing, petition, intercession, thanksgiving, and praise. • Prayer is important to deepen our friendship with God, and we can pray in many ways and at different times. • Sacramentals are blessings, objects, and actions that remind you of God and are made sacred through the prayers of the Church.
6 SACRAMENTS	CHAPTER 16	Gather to Worship	• The Eucharist is the Sacrament in which Jesus Christ shares himself and the bread and wine become his Body and Blood. • The Mass is another name for the celebration of the Eucharist. • The assembly is all those gathered for Mass. We take part by praying, singing, and using actions to worship God. • The Introductory Rites gather and unite us, preparing our hearts to hear God's Word.
	CHAPTER 17	Listen to God's Word	• Jesus used stories as a way to help us understand more about God and his Kingdom. • The first main part of the Mass is the Liturgy of the Word during which we hear readings from both the Old and New Testaments. • We listen to the deacon or priest proclaim the Gospel reading and give a homily to help us understand and apply God's Word. • This part of the Mass ends with the Creed and Prayer of the Faithful.
	CHAPTER 18	Remembering Jesus' Sacrifice	• The Mass is a memorial celebration of Jesus' Death, Resurrection, and Ascension. • Jesus' Death on the Cross is a sacrifice and gift that saves all people from the power of sin and everlasting death. • The Liturgy of the Eucharist is the second main part of the Mass in which Jesus Christ gives us the gift of himself, and we receive his Body and Blood in Holy Communion. • In the consecration, through the power of the Holy Spirit and the words and actions of the priest, the gifts of bread and wine become the Body and Blood of Jesus Christ.
7 KINGDOM OF GOD	CHAPTER 19	Supper of the Lamb	• The story of the Loaves and the Fish helps us understand what Jesus gives us in Holy Communion. • Before receiving Communion, we pray together the Lord's Prayer and offer each other a sign of peace. • Through the Eucharist, Jesus' followers are united with him and one another. • Jesus Christ is really and truly present with us in the Eucharist, so we receive Holy Communion with reverence and adore him in the reserved Blessed Sacrament.
	CHAPTER 20	Go Forth!	• In the Concluding Rites of the Mass, we are blessed and sent out to proclaim the Good News and give honor to God by the way we live. • As the Apostles were called to share the Good News, the Church's mission is to share Jesus' message of love and the Kingdom. • All members of the Church share in her mission, and some serve as missionaries who travel far away to spread the Good News.
	CHAPTER 21	A Feast for Everyone	• Heaven is life and happiness forever with God. • The story of the Wedding Feast is compared to God's invitation and our response. • The Eucharist is spiritual food that helps us to live with Jesus forever. • We are called to say "yes" daily to God.

Sacred Scripture	Catechism of the Catholic Church	Tasks of Catechesis	Catholic Faith Words	People of Faith	Catholic Social Teaching
The Holy Family Celebrates Passover Luke 2:41–42	1069–1070, 1171, 1163–1164, 1169	Liturgical Education, Education for Community Life	liturgy, worship, Resurrection	Pope Saint Victor	Life and Dignity, Human Solidarity
Let the Children Come Luke 18:15–17; Zacchaeus the Tax Collector Luke 19:1–10; Blessing of the Children Matthew 19:13–15	542–543, 2412, 526, 559, 2818–2819	Promoting Knowledge of the Faith, Education for Community Life	faith, peace, Kingdom of God	St. Brigid of Kildare	Option for the Poor, The Dignity of Work
Jesus' Disciples Receive a Mission Mark 16:15–16; The Vine and the Branches John 15:4–5	541, 787, 746–747, 941–942	Education for Community Life, Missionary Initiation	Gospel, proclaim, parish	Bl. Mother Teresa of Calcutta	Rights and Responsibilities, The Dignity of Work
The Lord's Prayer Luke 11:1–4; How to Pray Matthew 6:5–9	2759, 2644, 2565, 1668, 1671	Liturgical Education, Teaching to Pray	Lord's Prayer, blessing, petition, intercession, thanksgiving, praise, sacramentals	St. Alphonsus Liguori	Solidarity, Care for Creation
The Road to Emmaus Luke 24:30–32; The Community Gathers Acts 2:42–47	1323–1324, 1382, 1346, 1348–1349	Education for Community Life, Liturgical Education	Eucharist, Mass, assembly	St. Tarcisius	Call to Community, The Dignity of Work
The Parable of the Yeast Luke 13:18–21; The Mustard Seed Matthew 13:31–32	2613, 1154, 131–132, 1349, 1184, 1346	Promoting Knowledge of the Faith, Liturgical Education	Liturgy of the Word, homily, creed, Prayer of the Faithful	St. Paul	Call to Community, Care for Creation
Give God His Due Matthew 6:24; The Rich Young Man Matthew 19:21–22	1330, 616–617, 1408, 1142, 1411	Liturgical Education, Education for Community Life	sacrifice, Last Supper, Liturgy of the Eucharist, consecration	Bl. Imelda Lambertini	Option for the Poor, Human Solidarity
The Bread of Life John 6:30–35; The Feeding of the Five Thousand Luke 9:10–17	1335,1365, 1369–1370, 1374	Liturgical Education, Moral Formation	Holy Communion, Real Presence, reverence, Blessed Sacrament, Tabernacle	V. Pierre Toussaint	Call to Community, Option for the Poor
Paul Proclaims the Kingdom Acts 28:30–31; Peter Preaches Acts 10:42–48	1332, 849, 851–852	Missionary Initiation, Education for Community Life	mission, missionaries	St. Anthony Claret	Life and Dignity, The Dignity of Work
Jesus Knocks Revelation 3:20; The Wedding Feast Matthew 22:2–10 and Luke 14:16–23	326, 1329, 1391, 143	Promoting Knowledge of the Faith, Moral Formation	Heaven	St. Mary Magdalen de Pazzi	Option for the Poor, The Dignity of Work

Unit	Chapter	Lesson Concepts
1 REVELATION	CHAPTER 1 The Creator's Work	• God created human beings in his image and likeness. • Creation is a gift from God that shows his goodness; it is the work of the Holy Trinity. • Humans have the responsibility to care for all of creation, especially each other.
	CHAPTER 2 The Church Gathered	• The Bible is the Word of God written in human words. It is the holy book of the Church. • The Church is the community of all baptized people who believe in God and follow Jesus. • The Church helps us understand God's Word, teaches us about God's love, and gathers us to honor and worship God.
	CHAPTER 3 Families Teach Love	• Families teach us how to care for, respect, and help one another. • We honor Mary as the Mother of God, the greatest of Saints, and our Mother, too. • The Hail Mary begins with the words Elizabeth used to greet Mary. • The Catholic family is the domestic Church where we experience love and learn about God and how we pray and live as Catholics.
2 TRINITY	CHAPTER 4 The Holy Trinity	• A mystery is a truth that is difficult to perceive or understand with our senses, but is known through faith and through signs. • Jesus teaches us about God his Father and the Holy Spirit. • God the Father, God the Son, and God the Holy Spirit are a perfect communion of love. • The Creed is a statement of the Church's beliefs.
	CHAPTER 5 The Church Celebrates	• At the Last Supper Jesus celebrated the Passover with his Apostles. • Liturgy is the public prayer of the Church. It includes the Seven Sacraments and forms of daily prayer. • Catholics are required to attend Mass on Sundays and Holy Days of Obligation. • The Blessed Sacrament is the Holy Eucharist, especially the Body of Christ, which is kept in the Tabernacle.
	CHAPTER 6 Pray Always	• In the Lord's Prayer, Jesus taught his followers to pray to God the Father. • Daily prayer is important. We can pray using traditional prayers and our own words, out loud or silently, and at any time. • The five basic forms of prayer are blessing and adoration, praise, petition, intercession, and thanksgiving.
3 JESUS CHRIST	CHAPTER 7 The Good News	• The Gospel message is the Good News of God's Kingdom and his saving love. • The four Gospel books in the New Testament are about Christ's life, teaching, Death, and Resurrection. • The Kingdom of God is the world of love, peace, and justice that is in Heaven and is still being built on Earth. • In his miracles and parables, Jesus shows us that God's Kingdom is here and yet to come fully.
	CHAPTER 8 The Paschal Mystery	• Jesus offered the greatest sacrifice: he gave his life to save us from sin so that we could have new life with God in Heaven. • The Resurrection is the event of Jesus being raised from Death to new life by God the Father through the power of the Holy Spirit. • The Paschal Mystery is the mystery of Jesus Christ's suffering, Death, Resurrection, and Ascension. • The Church celebrates the Paschal Mystery in each of the Seven Sacraments.
	CHAPTER 9 The Body of Christ	• With the help of the Holy Spirit, members of the Church continue Jesus' work here on Earth. • The Church is the Body of Chirst of which Christ is the head. • All the baptized use their gifts and talents to serve others. • Stewardship is the way we appreciate and use God's gifts, including our time, talent, and treasure and the gift of creation.
4 THE CHURCH	CHAPTER 10 Church Leaders	• The Apostles are the twelve disciples Jesus chose to be his closest followers to share in his work and mission in a special way. • Peter was the leader of the Apostles and first Pope, head of the entire Church. • The bishops are successors of the Apostles. • The Pope, bishops, priests, and deacons lead, guide, and make the Church holy.
	CHAPTER 11 One and Holy	• The Marks of the Church are the four characteristics that identify Christ's Church: one, holy, catholic, and apostolic. • Pentecost is the feast that celebrates the coming of the Holy Spirit fifty days after Easter. • The Holy Spirit continues to unify the Church and make her holy. • The Communion of Saints is everyone who believes in and follows Jesus, people on Earth and in Purgatory and Heaven.

Sacred Scripture	Catechism of the Catholic Church	Tasks of Catechesis	Catholic Faith Words	People of Faith	Catholic Social Teaching
You Formed Me Psalm 139:13–15; The Creation of the World Genesis 1:1–23	355, 293, 292, 2415	Promoting Knowledge of the Faith, Moral Formation	creation, Holy Trinity, image of God	St. Rabanus Maurus	Life and Dignity, Care for Creation
Jesus Prays John 17:20–23; Helping One Another Acts 2:42–47	105–106, 1213, 2030, 942, 1816	Promoting Knowledge of the Faith, Education for Community Life	Bible, Church, Sacred Tradition	St. Francis of Assisi	Call to Community, Human Solidarity
Those Who Hear and Act on the Word of God Luke 8:19–21; Mary Visits Elizabeth Luke 1:39–56	1657, 2207, 963, 435, 2676, 2204	Promoting Knowledge of the Faith, Education for Community Life	Visitation, Mary, domestic Church	Bls. Luigi and Maria	Life and Dignity, Call to Community
This Is How We Know 1 John 4:13–14, 16; The Father and the Spirit John 14:6–7, 16–17	237, 240, 2780, 850, 187	Promoting Knowledge of the Faith, Education for Community Life	mystery, Incarnation, creed, Apostles' Creed	St. John of Matha	Call to Community, Human Solidarity
They Were Hungry Mark 6:34–42; The Last Supper Luke 22:14–20	2097, 1339–1340, 1069–1070, 1389, 1379	Promoting Knowledge of the Faith, Liturgical Education	Seven Sacraments, Last Supper, liturgy, Nicene Creed, Tabernacle, Blessed Sacrament	St. Mary MacKillop	Call to Community, Rights and Responsibilities
Pray Quietly Matthew 6:5–6; The Lord's Prayer Matthew 6:9–13; Praying Well Matthew 6:5–8	2765, 2659, 2644	Teaching to Pray, Liturgical Education	prayer, Lord's Prayer, blessing, adoration, praise, petition, intercession, thanksgiving	St. Gertrude the Great	Life and Dignity, Human Solidarity
The Woman and the Lost Coin Luke 15:8–10; The Rejection at Nazareth Luke 4:16–21; The Mustard Seed Mark 4:30–32	125, 120, 127, 2818–2819, 546	Promoting Knowledge of the Faith, Moral Formation	Gospel, Messiah, Kingdom of God, miracle, parable	St. Isaac Jogues	Life and Dignity, Rights and Responsibilities
No Greater Love John 15:12–13; Mary Meets Jesus John 20:11–18	619, 623, 648, 571, 1113	Promoting Knowledge of the Faith, Liturgical Education	sacrifice, Resurrection, Ascension, Paschal Mystery	St. Mary Magdalene	Life and Dignity, Human Solidarity
Gifts of the Spirit 1 Corinthians 12:4–7; Those Who Helped Matthew 25:31–40	1287–1288, 792, 791, 1937, 2402	Education for Community Life, Liturgical Education	parish, Body of Christ, stewardship	Bl. Joseph Vaz	Call to Community, Option for the Poor
Jesus Sent Out the Twelve Matthew 10:5–10; Peter and Jesus Matthew 16:15–19, 26:69–75, John 21:15–17	551, 552, 861–862, 939	Education for Community Life, Liturgical Education	Pope, bishop, Magisterium, Apostolic Succession	St. Gregory the Great	The Dignity of Work, Care for Creation
Jesus Preached Peace Ephesians 2:19–21; The Coming of the Spirit Acts 2:1–12	811, 731, 2623–2625, 960–962	Education for Community Life, Liturgical Education	Marks of the Church, one, holy, catholic, apostolic, Pentecost, Saint, Communion of Saints	Sts. Perpetua and Felicity	Call to Community, Human Solidarity

Unit	Chapter	Lesson Concepts
4	**CHAPTER 12** Catholic and Apostolic	• Saint Paul was one of the first to take the message of Jesus across many countries, establishing Church communities and writing them letters that became part of the New Testament. • All Church members participate in her mission to announce the Good News of God's Kingdom to people of all nations. • The Church is catholic because she is everywhere and welcomes everyone. • The Church is apostolic because Jesus gave his Apostles the mission of sharing his Good News with people all over the world.
5 MORALITY	**CHAPTER 13** Choose Love	• The Story of Joseph in the Old Testament shows us to forgive and love. • Jesus teaches us to love our enemies. • The Beatitudes are teachings of Jesus that show the way to true happiness and tell how to live in God's Kingdom. • Jesus' New Commandment is for his disciples to love one another as he has loved us.
	CHAPTER 14 Live in the Light	• Vocation is God's plan for our lives, the purpose for which he made us. • Virtues are good spiritual habits that make you stronger and help you do what is right and good. • The Theological Virtues of faith, hope and charity are gifts from God that help us live in relationship with the Holy Trinity. • Virtues grow over time with our practice and openness to God's grace.
	CHAPTER 15 Help With Choices	• Conscience is an ability given to us by God that helps us make choices about right and wrong. • The Precepts of the Church are some of the minimum requirements given by Church leaders for deepening our relationship with God and the Church. • The Holy Spirit and the teachings of the Church help us to make good choices. • In the Sacrament of Penance and Reconciliation, we receive God's forgiveness and the grace to help us change.
6 SACRAMENTS	**CHAPTER 16** Sacraments of Initiation	• People of all ages can be baptized into the Church. • The Sacraments of Initiation celebrate membership into the Catholic Church: Baptism, Confirmation, and Eucharist. • Baptism removes Original Sin, forgives personal sin, and gives new life in Christ. Confirmation seals and completes Baptism. • In the Eucharist, Jesus Christ shares himself with us, giving us the gift of his Body and Blood.
	CHAPTER 17 Sacraments of Healing	• In the Sacraments of Healing, God's forgiveness and healing are given to those suffering physical and spiritual sickness. • In Penance and Reconciliation, we confess our sins to a priest who forgives in the name of Christ and his Church. • In the Anointing of the Sick, the priest prays that God will send his healing love to the person who is being anointed.
	CHAPTER 18 Sacraments at the Service of Communion	• Sacraments at the Service of Communion celebrate people's commitment to serve God and the community and help build up the People of God. • Holy Orders is the Sacrament in which baptized men are ordained as deacons, priests, or bishops to lead and serve the Church. • Matrimony joins a baptized man and a baptized woman in Christian marriage to serve God by loving and serving each other and any children God gives them.
7 KINGDOM OF GOD	**CHAPTER 19** The Church Through Time	• A covenant is a sacred promise or agreement between God and humans. • God established a covenant with Abraham, and from that came the beginning of God's People. • As the Son of God, Jesus fulfills God's promise and his covenant extends to all people. • The first Christians faced difficult times, but they tried to be faithful to him and to the covenant, and the Church grew.
	CHAPTER 20 The Work of the Church	• The Church continues Jesus' work on Earth through her worship, teaching, care for others, and work for peace and justice. • The Church is a sign of God's Kingdom and helps people share in the love of the Holy Trinity. • By our Baptism, we are called to participate in the Church's mission to share the Good News and serve God and others.
	CHAPTER 21 Everlasting Life	• Jesus' Resurrection is proof of his promise of eternal life. • The Particular Judgment is the individual judgment by God at the time of a person's death when God decides where that person will spend eternity according to his or her faith and works. • The Last Judgment is God's final triumph over evil, when Christ will come again and bring the Kingdom of God to its fullness. • The last book of the Bible, Revelation, ends with John's vision of a new creation, God's everlasting Kingdom.

Go to **aliveinchrist.osv.com** for complete program Scope and Sequence.

Sacred Scripture	Catechism of the Catholic Church	Tasks of Catechesis	Catholic Faith Words	People of Faith	Catholic Social Teaching
Do Everything in the Name of Jesus Colossians 3:16–17; Doing God's Work 1 Corinthians 3:5–9	849, 856, 863, 830–831, 869	Education for Community Life, Missionary Initiation	evangelization, mission, missionaries	St. Elizabeth Ann Seton	Option for the Poor, The Dignity of Work
Pray for Those Who Mistreat You Luke 6:27–28, 31; The Story of Joseph Genesis 37–45; Love of Enemies Matthew 5:43–47	312, 1825, 1716, 1970–1971	Promoting Knowledge of the Faith, Moral Formation	Beatitudes, mercy, New Commandment	St. Peter Canisius	Life and Dignity, Option for the Poor
The Light of the World John 8:12; Your Light Must Shine Matthew 5:14–16	1877, 1803, 1813, 1830	Promoting Knowledge of the Faith, Moral Formation	vocation, virtues, Theological Virtues, faith, hope, charity	St. Genevieve	Rights and Responsibilities, Care for Creation
You Know My Thoughts Psalm 139:23–24; Saul and Jesus Acts 9:1–30	1777, 2041, 1783–1785, 1422–1423	Promoting Knowledge of the Faith, Moral Formation	grace, conscience, Precepts of the Church, sin	St. Pio of Pietrelcina	Rights and Responsibilities, The Dignity of Work
A People Chosen by God 1 Peter 2:9–10; Many Are Baptized Acts 2:38–41	1247, 1250, 1212, 1217, 1323	Promoting Knowledge of the Faith, Liturgical Education	Sacred Chrism, Sacraments of Initiation, Real Presence, Eucharist	St. John the Baptist	Life and Dignity, Call to Community
All Were Healed Matthew 14:34–36; Jesus Gives New Life Luke 8:40–42, 49–56	1421, 1424, 1517	Promoting Knowledge of the Faith, Liturgical Education	Sacraments of Healing	St. Marianne Cope	Rights and Responsibilities, The Dignity of Work
Called to Be Free Galatians 5:13–14; Servants of Christ 1 Corinthians 3:21–4:2	1534, 1536, 1601	Liturgical Education, Moral Formation	vows, priest, deacon, Sacraments at the Service of Communion	St. Jean-Baptiste de La Salle	Call to Community, Human Solidarity
They Lived Together Acts 2:42; I Will Be Your God Genesis 17:1–19	56-58, 72, 73, 706, 2471–2472	Promoting Knowledge of the Faith, Liturgical Education	covenant, proclaim, faithful	St. Clement of Rome	Rights and Responsibilities, Human Solidarity
Be Happy 2 Corinthians 13:11; The Commissioning of the Twelve Matthew 10:5–14	759, 763, 2044–2046	Moral Formation, Missionary Initiation	justice, peace	St. Peter Claver	Rights and Responsibilities, The Dignity of Work
Whoever Knows Jesus Has Life 1 John 5:11–12; The New Heaven and the New Earth Revelation 21:1–4; Alpha and Omega Revelation 22:13	655, 1022, 1038–1040, 1044–1045	Promoting Knowledge of the Faith, Moral Formation	Heaven, Hell, Purgatory, Last Judgment	St. Joseph	Life and Dignity, Rights and Responsibilities

Scope and Sequence

Unit		Chapter	Lesson Concepts
1 **REVELATION**	CHAPTER 1	God's Providence	• The first creation account teaches the goodness of all of God's creation. • Providence is God's loving care for all things; his will and plan for creation. • Divine Revelation is the way God tells humans about himself and makes his plan known. • God reveals himself through Sacred Scripture and the Sacred Tradition of the Church.
	CHAPTER 2	God is Faithful	• Death, suffering, ignorance and the inclination to sin all came into the world as a result of Original Sin. • God always remains faithful and promises salvation, desiring humans to be free and faithful to him. • A covenant is a sacred promise or agreement between God and humans. • God called Abraham, and because of his belief and trust in God, God established a covenant with him.
	CHAPTER 3	God's Commandments	• God created people to be free and live as his People, and he called Moses to lead his People from slavery in Egypt. • The Ten Commandments are the summary of laws that God gave Moses on Mount Sinai that tell us what is necessary in order to love God and others. • God gave the Ten Commandments to help us be faithful to him and his covenant.
2 **TRINITY**	CHAPTER 4	In God's Image	• Human dignity comes from being made in God's image and likeness with the ability to love, think, and make choices. • The soul is the spiritual part of a human that lives forever. • Sin is a deliberate thought, word, deed, or omission contrary to the law of God. • Every person is worthy of respect because he or she is created in God's image and made to love.
	CHAPTER 5	Living in Community	• The mission of God the Son and the Holy Spirit is to bring all people into the love of the Holy Trinity. • Morality is living in right relationship with God, yourself, and others. • God created all people for one another and we must all work for the common good. • Our love of our neighbor reflects the love of the Holy Trinity.
	CHAPTER 6	Making Good Choices	• Free will is the God-given freedom and ability to make choices. • God gives us grace, the Ten Commandments, and the Church to help us make good choices and deepen our relationship with him. • We need to know God's laws and form, or strengthen, our conscience so it will help us make good decisions. • Conscience is the God-given ability that helps us judge whether actions are morally good or wrong.
3 **JESUS CHRIST**	CHAPTER 7	The Beatitudes	• The Beatitudes guide us to show mercy and be a blessing to others. • The word beatitude means "blessing" or "happiness." God put the desire for happiness inside each of us. • The Beatitudes are Jesus' teachings about the way to true happiness and living in God's Kingdom now and always. • God wants all of us to have eternal life—to live forever with him and all who die in his friendship.
	CHAPTER 8	Love God and Neighbor	• The Great Commandment is the two-fold command to love God above all and your neighbor as yourself. • The Theological Virtues of faith, hope, and charity are gifts from God that help us to believe in him, trust his plan for us, and love him with all our heart, soul, and mind. • Loving God leads to sharing his love with others, and the Corporal and Spiritual Works of Mercy guide us in the ways to do so.
	CHAPTER 9	Honoring God	• The First Commandment teaches us to worship and honor only God, and not to place things or other people before him. • The Second Commandment calls us to always use the name of God with reverence and respect. • Blasphemy is the sin of showing disrespect for the name of God, Jesus Christ, Mary, or the Saints in words or actions. • We observe the Third Commandment through participation in the Sunday Eucharist, rest, time with family, and works of service.
4 **THE CHURCH**	CHAPTER 10	Called to Serve	• Vocation is God's plan for our lives; the purpose for which he made us. • Priesthood, consecrated religious, committed single life, and married life are four distinct ways people respond to God's call. • All baptized members of the Church are called to serve God and the Church using their gifts.
	CHAPTER 11	Models of Virtue	• A Saint is a person who the Church declares has led a holy life and is enjoying eternal life with God in Heaven. • Mary is the perfect model of holiness, accepting God's will throughout her life and remaining faithful to him. • The Immaculate Conception is the truth that God kept Mary free from sin from the first moment of her life. • Mary is called the Mother of the Church because she holds her Son's followers close to her heart.

Go to **aliveinchrist.osv.com** for complete program Scope and Sequence.

Sacred Scripture	Catechism of the Catholic Church	Tasks of Catechesis	Catholic Faith Words	People of Faith	Catholic Social Teaching
God's Plan Psalm 33:9, 11–12; The Story of Creation Genesis 1:1-31, 2:1–3; The Call of Jeremiah Jeremiah 1:4–8	299, 302–303, 50, 81–82	Promoting Knowledge of the Faith	providence, Sacred Scripture, Divine Revelation, Sacred Tradition	St. Kateri Tekakwitha	Life and Dignity, Care for Creation
The Promise Hebrews 10:16–17, 23; In the Garden Genesis 3; Abram's Call and Journey Genesis 12:1–8; God's Promise 15:1–5, 18; 17:5–9, 15; 21:1–3	402–405, 55, 56–58, 59–60	Promoting Knowledge of the Faith, Moral Formation	Original Sin, salvation, covenant, faithful	St. Bridget of Sweden	Rights and Responsibilities, Human Solidarity
Holy Ground Exodus 3:2b, 4–5; Joseph and His Brothers Genesis 37:1–4, 42:6–8, 44:1–12, 45:4–5; The Exodus from Egypt Exodus 2:1–10, 14:10–31, 15:19–21	2057, 2061, 2062–2063	Promoting Knowledge of the Faith, Moral Formation	Ten Commandments, ark of the covenant	St. Raymond of Peñafort	Call to Community, Rights and Responsibilities
Worthy of the Lord Colossians 1:10, 12–15; In His Image Genesis 1:27	355–357, 366, 1849, 1440, 1700	Promoting Knowledge of the Faith, Moral Formation	human dignity, soul, sin, mortal sin, venial sin	St. Germaine Cousin	Life and Dignity, Care for Creation
Love One Another 1 John 4:9, 11–13, 16b; The Communal Life Acts 2:42–45	258–260, 1950–1951, 1905–1906, 1878	Promoting Knowledge of the Faith, Education for Community Life	Holy Trinity, morality, common good	St. Dominic	Call to Community, Option for the Poor
The Lord's Judgment Isaiah 11:1–4a; The Parable of the Good Samaritan Luke 10.30–35	1704, 1785, 1783–1784, 1777	Promoting Knowledge of the Faith, Moral Formation	free will, grace, conscience	St. Charles Lwanga	Rights and Responsibilities, Option for the Poor
Hear and Observe the Word of God Luke 11:27 28; The Sermon on the Mount Matthew 5:3–10	2444, 1718, 1716, 1720–1721	Moral Formation, Missionary Initiation	mercy, Beatitudes, eternal life, peace	St. Yi Sung-hun	Option for the Poor, Human Solidarity
Live as Jesus Commanded Ephesians 5:1–5; The Greatest Commandment Matthew 22:37–40; The Rich Young Man Matthew 19:16–22	2055, 1814, 1817, 1822, 2447–2448	Moral Formation, Missionary Initiation	Great Commandment, Theological Virtues, faith, hope, charity, Corporal and Spiritual Works of Mercy	St. Katharine Drexel	Life and Dignity, Human Solidarity
Worthy Are You, Lord Revelation 4:11; 7:12; The Golden Calf Exodus 32:1–20	2110, 2142–2143, 2148, 2176–2177	Liturgical Education, Moral Formation	worship, idolatry, blasphemy, Resurrection	St. Mary Ann of Quito	Life and Dignity, Care for Creation
Saul Is Chosen 1 Samuel 10:20–22; The Call of the First Disciples Matthew 4:18–22	1877, 871–873, 912–913	Education for Community Life, Missionary Initiation	vocation, Kingdom of God, vows, laity	Bl. Frédéric Ozanam	Call to Community, The Dignity of Work
Light of the World Matthew 5:14–16; The Canticle of Mary Luke 1:46–50	828, 829, 491, 963	Promoting Knowledge of the Faith, Teaching to Pray	canonization, Saint, beatification, Mary, Immaculate Conception, patron Saint	St. Bernadette Soubirous	Call to Community, Option for the Poor

Unit	Chapter	Lesson Concepts
4	CHAPTER 12 — The Church Teaches	• Jesus chose Peter to be the shepherd of his flock, leader of the Apostles, and head of his Church. • Jesus gave Peter and the Apostles, and their successors the Pope and bishops, the authority to teach and lead in his name. • The Magisterium is the teaching office of the Church, which is all of the bishops in union with the Pope. • The Holy Spirit directs the Magisterium in teaching and guiding the People of God. • The Precepts of the Church are some of the minimum requirements for deepening our relationship with God and Church.
5 MORALITY	CHAPTER 13 — Family Love	• God created humans to live in families and wants family members to respect, love, and protect one another. • The Fourth Commandment teaches children to honor and obey parents, who are to provide for, love, and share faith with them. • The Sixth and Ninth Commandments are about faithful love and commitment between husband and wife, but require all of us to keep promises, be faithful, and act appropriately. • The Cardinal Virtues help us to act wisely, use self-control, give God and others their due, and be disciplined.
	CHAPTER 14 — Respect Life	• Life comes from God. Every human life is sacred from the moment of conception until the time of natural death. • All actions that respect and protect life uphold the Fifth Commandment. • Actions that deliberately harm human life, including that of the unborn, the sick, and elderly, are grave sins. • The Fifth Commandment calls us to respect and take care of our bodies.
	CHAPTER 15 — Live in the Truth	• A martyr is a person who gives up his or her life to witness to the truth of Christ and the faith. • God is the source of all truth. His Word and his law call people to live in the truth. • The Eighth Commandment calls us to be honest in words and actions and forbids lying, gossip, and any acts against the truth.
6 SACRAMENTS	CHAPTER 16 — The Liturgical Year	• The Paschal Mystery is the mystery of Jesus' suffering, Death, Resurrection, and Ascension through which he saved all humans from the power of sin and everlasting death. • The liturgical year is made up of the feasts and seasons of the Church calendar that celebrate the Paschal Mystery of Christ. • The seasons of the Church year are Advent, Christmas, Ordinary Time, Lent, Triduum, and Easter.
	CHAPTER 17 — The Seven Sacraments	• God the Father sent his only Son, Jesus, as a sign of his love for all people. • The Seven Sacraments are effective signs of God's life, instituted by Christ and given to the Church, so that Jesus can continue his saving work in the world. • The visible signs and Divine actions in each celebration give grace and allow us to share in God's work. • The Sacrament of the Eucharist, in which we receive the gift of Jesus Christ's Body and Blood, is at the heart of Catholic life.
	CHAPTER 18 — Healing and Reconciliation	• Conversion involves turning away from sin and responding to God's love and forgiveness. • In the Sacrament of Penance and Reconciliation, we receive God's forgiveness of sins through the Church and are strengthened by grace to make peace and avoid temptation. • The Sacrament of the Anointing of the Sick brings Jesus' healing touch to strengthen, comfort, and forgive the sins of those who are seriously ill or close to death.
7 OF GOD	CHAPTER 19 — A Generous Spirit	• Being detached from our possessions enables us to work for peace and justice in God's Kingdom. • The Seventh and Tenth Commandments teach about the right attitude toward material possessions and require generosity. • Theft, greed, and envy are sins against these Commandments. • God created the world for all creatures and called humans to stewardship.
	CHAPTER 20 — The Church in the World	• The mission of the Church is to proclaim the Gospel and work for the good of all people. • Evangelization is sharing the Good News of Jesus through words and actions in a way that invites people to accept the Gospel. • The Church is made up of people of many cultures and they are all united by their belief in Christ. • Missionaries spread the Gospel message and Jesus' care for all people to countries all around the world.
	CHAPTER 21 — Eternal Life with God	• Heaven is a state of eternal happiness with God. • To spend eternity with God, we must grow in friendship with God. Through the Holy Spirit, God helps us respond to his grace and grow in friendship with him. • At the time of our death, we will be judged by God. This is called the Particular Judgment. • The Last Judgment refers to Jesus' coming in glory at the end of time to judge all the living and the dead and the coming of God's Kingdom in its fullness.

Go to **aliveinchrist.osv.com** for complete program Scope and Sequence.

Sacred Scripture	Catechism of the Catholic Church	Tasks of Catechesis	Catholic Faith Words	People of Faith	Catholic Social Teaching
Building the Body of Christ Ephesians 4:11–13; You Are the Messiah! Mark 8:27–30	881, 85, 890–891, 892, 2041–2043	Moral Formation, Education for Community Life	Magisterium, Precepts of the Church	St. Mary Magdalen Postel	Call to Community, Rights and Responsibilities
Obey Your Parents Colossians 3:20–21; The Boy Jesus and His Family Luke 2:41–52	2203, 2199, 2348–2350, 1804–1805	Moral Formation, Education for Community Life	Cardinal Virtues, temperance, fortitude, modesty, chastity	Bl. Louis Martin and Marie-Azélie Martin	Life and Dignity, Call to Community
You Will Answer for Your Actions Matthew 5:21–22; The Choice Deuteronomy 30:19–20; Love of Enemies Matthew 5:43–45	2258, 2302, 2268–2269, 2288	Moral Formation, Education for the Community Life	sacred, murder	St. Gianna Molla	Life and Dignity, Option for the Poor
Keep Your Promises Matthew 5:33, 37; The Truth Will Set You Free John 8:31–32, 14:6	2473, 2465, 2464, 2487	Moral Formation, Education for the Community Life	martyr, reparation, prudence	St. Joan of Arc	Rights and Responsibilities, Human Solidarity
Trust God Psalm 62:8–9; The Right Time Ecclesiastes 3:1–8	571, 1171, 1168–1169	Promoting Knowledge of the Faith, Liturgical Education	Ascension, Paschal Mystery, liturgical year	St. Juan Diego	Call to Community, Human Solidarity
His Grace Ephesians 1:3, 7–8; The Last Supper Luke 22:17–20	458, 1127, 1128, 1131, 1322, 1324	Promoting Knowledge of the Faith, Liturgical Education	Incarnation, Seven Sacraments, Eucharist	St. Margaret Mary Alacoque	Option for the Poor, Human Solidarity
I Confess Psalm 32:1 3, 5; The Story of Zacchaeus Luke 19:1–10; The Man Born Blind John 9:1–38	1427–1428, 1468–1469, 1532	Liturgical Education, Moral Formation	repent, Penance and Reconciliation, Confession, temptation, sacramental seal, penance, absolution, Anointing of the Sick	V. Matt Talbot	Rights and Responsibilities, Option for the Poor
Give Luke 6:38; The Parable of the Rich Fool Luke 12:16–21; The Poor Widow's Contribution Mark 12:41–44	2545–2546, 2401, 2534, 2408, 2536, 2538, 2402	Promoting Knowledge of the Faith, Moral Formation	envy, greed, humility, justice, stewardship	St. Margaret of Scotland	Call to Community, The Dignity of Work
Be My Witnesses Acts of the Apostles 1:8; The Commissioning of the Disciples Matthew 28:18–20	849, 853–854, 849–851, 781	Education for Community Life, Missionary Initiation	Gospel, mission, evangelization	Bl. Junipero Serra	Option for the Poor, Human Solidarity
Whoever Has the Son Has Life 1 John 5:1–3, 11–12; The Judgment of the Nations Matthew 25:34–40	1024, 1039–1041, 1021–1022, 682, 1038	Promoting Knowledge of the Faith, Education for Community Life	Heaven, Gifts of the Holy Spirit, Particular Judgment, Purgatory, Hell, Last Judgment	St. Martin de Porres	Life and Dignity, Rights and Responsibilities

Endnotes:

1. Cf. CCC 426-429; CT 5-6; DCG (1971) 40.

2. CCC 429.

3. cf. CT, 31; CT 31 which expounds the integrity and organization of the message; cf. DCG (1971) 39 and 43.

4. Cf. Vatican Council I: DS 3016: *nexus mysteriorum*; LG 25.

5. UR 11.

6. CT 68.

Opening Lesson
&
Church Year Feasts
and Seasons

Opening Lesson

The Church Year Feasts and Seasons

KEY CONCEPT

The key concept for each lesson is clearly stated at the start of each chapter.

DOCTRINAL CONTENT

The doctrinal content for each chapter will be found in this section. It will show how the chapter correlates to paragraphs from the *Catechism of the Catholic Church*.

TASKS OF CATECHESIS

The six tasks of catechesis are outlined in the *National Directory for Catechesis*. The relevant tasks of catechesis for a chapter will be found in this section.

Catechist Background

For all of you who were baptized into Christ have clothed yourselves with Christ. There is neither Jew nor Greek, there is neither slave nor free person, there is not male and female; for you are all one in Christ Jesus. **Galatians 3:27–28**

➔ **Reflect** How are we one in Christ Jesus?

The Catechist Background includes a short essay that provides easy-to-understand theological background on the chapter content for both novice and experienced catechists.

The catechetical process of **Alive in Christ** mirrors the divine pedagogy—the gradual and relational way God teaches us so that we can know him in his truth, be guided by the Holy Spirit to respond with faith and love, and accept the gift of new life in Christ. Each lesson encourages this personal and ongoing relationship, beginning with God's invitation through Sacred Scripture. This leads children to reflect on his Word, deepen their understanding of our Sacred Tradition, and respond with a lived faith within the home and in the community.

Alive in Christ incorporates the most trusted research on how children learn and communicate. Topics are presented at important developmental "windows"—ages when research in child development tells us that learning about a particular topic would be most effective. For example, third graders are more aware of the larger world, so this is a good time to talk about the larger worldwide Church and how she is organized. In Chapter 10, they will learn that Peter was the leader of the Apostles and first Pope, head of the entire Church.

➔ **Reflect** What makes the Church the Body of Christ?

Catechist's Prayer

Lord, thank you for calling me to the ministry of catechesis. It is a great privilege and an awesome responsibility to echo your Word to others. Draw me closer to you, so that I may teach by word and example. Amen.

A New Year

 Let Us Pray

Leader: Father, you call us together as your Church. You give us your Son to teach and lead us, and your Spirit to make us one.

"Hallelujah!
 Sing to the LORD a new song,
  his praise in the assembly of the faithful...
For the LORD takes delight in his
  people…"   Psalm 149:1, 4

All: God, thank you for uniting us. Give us life and love as we grow as the Body of Christ on Earth. Amen.

 God's Word

"For all of you who were baptized into Christ have clothed yourselves with Christ. There is neither Jew nor Greek, there is neither slave nor free person, there is not male and female; for you are all one in Christ Jesus." Galatians 3:27-28

What Do You Wonder?

- How are we one in Christ?
- What makes us the Church?

© Our Sunday Visitor

 **Invite**

Ask children how they feel when they are invited somewhere. Point out the *Invite* heading on the page, and explain that every lesson will begin with an invitation.

 Let Us Pray

Introduce the children to the prayer space and invite them into it. Lead them in the Sign of the Cross. Read aloud the leader's prayer and the Psalm verse. Prompt the children's response.

Have the children move from the prayer space back to their seats.

God's Word

Invite the children to close their eyes and concentrate on the message in this passage.

- Proclaim the Scripture.
- Pause for several moments.
- *Ask:* What message did you hear in this passage?
- Invite volunteers to share.

What Do You Wonder?

Point out the picture and ask how the children are unified. Discuss how it feels to belong to a happy group of people.

Invite the children to respond to the questions. Ask what else they might wonder about in their relationship with Jesus or in their belonging to the Church.

(i) **Catechist Background**

Reflecting on Scripture

Each chapter in *Alive in Christ* begins with a focus on Sacred Scripture. On the *Invite* page, the children are called to open their minds and hearts to God's message.

- The Psalm verse and New Testament excerpt set the theme for the chapter. The passage from Galatians is especially appropriate for this opening lesson, as it reflects on membership in the Church.
- For more information on the use of Sacred Scripture throughout the chapters, refer to page CE22.

Objectives

- Chapter objectives relating to this Discover section are clearly stated here
- Begin to understand what will be learned this year, especially about the Church as a faith community

Third Grade

Ask the children to define the word *discover*.

Point out that the Discover pages in this book will help them learn important things about their faith.

Explain that the children will use this book to deepen their understanding of the Church.

- Have the children explore the book by looking at titles in the table of contents.
- Let them preview the illustrations and headings.
- Ask the children to report on what they will learn.

Point out the icons on the page and invite the children to speculate on what they signal. Use the text to expand on their responses.

- As you define the icons, reinforce the importance of Scripture, prayer, and songs in learning about God.
- Call attention to the gold star on the page.
- Point out that this star will be next to directions for an activity.
- Invite the children to circle two items on the page that they will do this year.

Third Grade

What's going to happen this year?

This year is all about learning, loving, and celebrating our Catholic faith!

When you see , you know it's a story or reading from the Bible. You will spend lots of time with God's Word from the Bible. Through Bible stories you will discover more about being a follower of Christ and member of the Church.

When you see 💗, you know it's time to pray. Each time you are together, you have the chance to listen to and talk to God in prayer. You will grow closer as a community as you pray together and get to know Jesus' teachings.

When you see ▶, you will sing songs to praise God and celebrate our faith. During the year you'll explore the Church's feasts and seasons, and meet many Saints, our heroes of the Church.

> ⭐ Circle two things you will do this year.

This gold star begins an activity to help you better understand what's being taught. You may underline, circle, write, match, or draw.

2 Opening Lesson

✓ Quick Tip

Lesson Structure

The chapters in this book will all follow the same three-step process:

- *Invite* begins with prayer that includes Sacred Scripture and calls the children to be open to God's Word.
- *Discover* presents Scripture, Church teachings, and Catholic practices with developmentally appropriate language and art and contains activities to reinforce and apply learning.
- *Live* connects the children's faith knowledge with the ways that Catholics worship, live, pray, and serve in community. It also contains the concluding prayer for the chapter.

For more information on the lesson process, see pages CE18-CE19.

A Community of Faith

This year you will learn a lot about the **Church**, the community of all baptized who believe in God and follow Jesus Christ. Important words like this are **highlighted** in yellow so you don't miss them.

You'll get a deeper understanding of what it means to belong to the Catholic Church. You will explore how the Church is the Body of Christ whose various members work together to share the Good News of Jesus and give thanks through worship and prayer.

Catholic Faith Words

In this box you will again see the **highlighted** words and definitions.

Church the community of all baptized people who believe in God and follow Jesus; the word is often used for the Catholic Church because she traces her origins back to the Apostles

© Our Sunday Visitor

Share Your Faith

When you see these fun green words, you know it's time for an activity!

Think What words would you use to describe the Church?

_____

_____

Share Talk with a partner about your words and what it means to belong to the Church.

3

(i) Catechist Background

Focus on Third Graders

Alive in Christ presents key themes of Catholic teaching in a developmentally appropriate sequence. For more information on how the series framework supports faith development, see pages CE8–CE9.

- The Grade 3 Focus is the Church.
- This year's lessons have been designed to address the children's growing awareness of the larger world, so focusing on the Church as a worldwide organization is appropriate.
- For more information on the abilities and perspectives of the children you are teaching, see pages CE9 and CE29.

A Community of Faith

Elicit from the children that the word *community* refers to a group of people who share something.

- *Ask:* Who belongs to our community of faith?
- Point out that to be good members of the community, they will need to learn about it and how its members work together.

Read aloud the first two paragraphs to explain what they will learn about the Church.

Work with Words

Call attention to the word *Church* in the first paragraph and the Catholic Faith Words definition on the side of the page. Read through the side definition with the children. Tell the children that they will learn many new words this year.

Activity

Point out the Share Your Faith feature.

- Point out that this feature and others like it will help them think about their faith and share it.
- Read aloud the directions.
- Allow time for the children to work independently. Then have them share their ideas with a partner.

Quick Review

This book will teach about the Church and how she follows Jesus. It contains Scripture, prayers, songs, and exercises to help us learn.

Discover

Objectives

- Learn that the Bible is the inspired Word of God written by humans
- Find and recognize the parts of the Bible

God's Word

Explain that we use words to teach important ideas. God also uses words to teach us.

Read aloud the first two paragraphs to show the importance of God's Word.

- Tell the children that the Bible is a collection of books that were written at many different times and by many different people. The books tell the story of God's relationship with his People.

The Old Testament

Read aloud the text to acquaint the children with the Old Testament.

- Emphasize that this part of the Bible tells us about before Jesus was born.

- Point out the text that provides information about the Old Testament. Tell the children that this book will have many lists and illustrations that will help them learn.

God's Word

Where can you read stories about God?

The **Bible** is a holy book. It is God's Word written down by humans. The word Bible means "books." Many different books are included in the Bible. The Bible has two parts, the Old Testament and the New Testament.

The Bible is also called Scripture, which means "writing." We hear readings from Scripture during Mass and the other Sacraments.

The Old Testament

The Old Testament tells the story of the Hebrew people and their covenant with God.

Catholic Faith Words

Bible the Word of God written in human words. The Bible is the Holy Book of the Church.

© Our Sunday Visitor

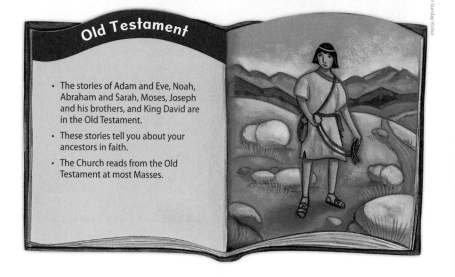

Old Testament

- The stories of Adam and Eve, Noah, Abraham and Sarah, Moses, Joseph and his brothers, and King David are in the Old Testament.
- These stories tell you about your ancestors in faith.
- The Church reads from the Old Testament at most Masses.

 Liturgy Link

Bible Readings

The Old Testament and New Testament are the core of the Liturgy of the Word. However, the priests, deacons, and readers do not read directly from the Bible; they read from the Lectionary and Book of Gospels, which contains passages from the Bible.

- Typically, the first reading on a Sunday is from the Old Testament, followed by a responsorial Psalm. The next is usually from a New Testament Epistle and the last is always from the Gospels.

 Go to **aliveinchrist.osv.com** for Sunday readings, Scripture background, questions of the week, and seasonal resources.

The New Testament

The New Testament tells the story of our faith since Jesus was born. It is about the life and teaching's of Jesus, his followers, and the early Church.

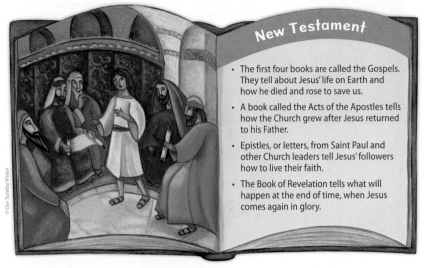

New Testament

- The first four books are called the Gospels. They tell about Jesus' life on Earth and how he died and rose to save us.
- A book called the Acts of the Apostles tells how the Church grew after Jesus returned to his Father.
- Epistles, or letters, from Saint Paul and other Church leaders tell Jesus' followers how to live their faith.
- The Book of Revelation tells what will happen at the end of time, when Jesus comes again in glory.

© Our Sunday Visitor

Connect Your Faith

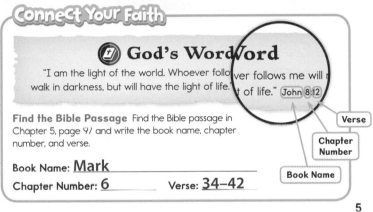

God's Word

"I am the light of the world. Whoever follows me will not walk in darkness, but will have the light of life." John 8:12

Verse

Chapter Number

Book Name

Find the Bible Passage Find the Bible passage in Chapter 5, page 97 and write the book name, chapter number, and verse.

Book Name: **Mark**

Chapter Number: **6**   Verse: **34–42**

5

✓ Quick Tip

Sacred Tradition

Part of the richness of the Catholic faith resides in Sacred Tradition, accrued through two millennia of Church history.

- Every lesson in this book presents truths of the faith.
- At the back of the Student Book, the Our Catholic Tradition reference section expands on the lesson contents. Your lesson plans will contain specific references to this reference section when appropriate.
- You may want to have the children explore this section. For more on Sacred Tradition, see page CE23.

The New Testament

Read aloud the first paragraph. Allow the children to explore the information about the New Testament.

- Explain that the New Testament begins with Jesus' birth and is about Jesus and the early Church.
- Point out that the readings during Mass are from the Old Testament and the New Testament. The Gospel at Mass is always from one of the four Gospels.
- Explain that in Biblical times, the best way to communicate was with letters. The books of Letters were written by Jesus' followers to early Church members and explain what Jesus taught.
- Explain that the Book of Revelation is about the end of time.

Activity

Explain that the Bible is a very big book. To help people find different parts in it, it is divided into books, which are named with words. The books are divided into chapters, and the chapters contain verses. We can find any part of the Bible if we know its book, chapter, and verse.

- Have the children complete the activity. Be prepared to assist them as necessary.

Quick Review

The Bible has two parts. The Old Testament tells about God's People before Jesus was born. The New Testament tells about Jesus and the early Church.

Our Catholic Life

Point out the Live heading on the page.

- Explain that each chapter in this book has a section that will help the children live as good Catholics. Read the text to further explain this.

- Invite volunteers to read aloud the six points in the "Grow as a Follower of Jesus" box.

- Discuss why following each point will make us good Catholics.

- Reinforce that the children will learn about each of these ways to grow during this school year.

People of Faith

Read aloud this paragraph.

- Tell the children that they will learn about Saints and other holy people in this feature.

Allow time for the children to complete the activity.

- Invite volunteers to share their ideas about Jesus and their questions.

Live

Our Catholic Life

What does it mean to be Catholic?

Each chapter in your book has an Our Catholic Life section. It shows in a special way what it means to be Catholic. Words, pictures, and activities help us grow closer to Jesus and the Church.

Grow as a Follower of Jesus

- know more about our faith
- learn about the Sacraments
- live as Jesus taught us
- talk and listen to God in prayer
- take part in Church life
- help others know Jesus through what we say and do

People of Faith

You will also meet People of Faith, holy women and men who loved God very much and did his work on Earth.

Live Your Faith

Spread the Good News! Write one thing about Jesus that you can share with someone you know.

_____

Write one question you have about Jesus or the Church.

_____

© Our Sunday Visitor

Catechist Background

Six Tasks of Catechesis

As a catechist, you are charged with six fundamental tasks as contained in the *National Directory for Catechesis.*

- Each of these tasks corresponds to an aspect of faith in Jesus. They are: Promoting Knowledge of the Faith, Liturgical Education, Moral Formation, Teaching to Pray, Education for Community Life, and Missionary Initiation.

- For more information on these tasks, refer to pages CE14–CE15.

Let Us Pray

Pray Together

Every chapter has a prayer page, with lots of different ways to pray. You may listen to God's Word read from the Bible, pray for the needs of others, call on the Saints to pray for us, and praise God the Father, Son, and Holy Spirit in words and songs.

Gather and begin with the Sign of the Cross.

Leader: Blessed be God.

All: Blessed be God forever.

Leader: Let us pray.

Bow your head as the leader prays.

All: Amen.

Leader: A reading from the holy Gospel according to John.
Read John 15:1–8.
The Gospel of the Lord.

All: Praise to you, Lord Jesus Christ.

 Sing "Alive in Christ"
We are Alive in Christ
We are Alive in Christ
He came to set us free
We are Alive in Christ
We are Alive in Christ
He gave his life for me
We are Alive in Christ
We are Alive in Christ

A New Year **7**

 Let Us Pray

Pray Together

Read the first paragraph aloud to the children.

- Explain that every chapter will end with prayer.

Prepare

Assume the role of leader.

Show the children where their responses are on the page.

 Rehearse "Alive in Christ," downloaded from **aliveinchrist.osv.com**.

Gather

Lead the children into the prayer space.

- Begin with the Sign of the Cross.
- Invite the children to be still and listen to the reading.

Pray

- Follow the order of prayer on the student page.

Conclude by processing around the room with the children singing "Alive in Christ."

 Songs of Scripture

Songs for Deepening Children's Understanding of God's Word

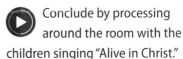

In addition to all of the chapter-specific songs available for download, a program component, *Songs of Scripture: Songs for Deepening Children's Understanding of God's Word* by John Burland and Dr. Jo Ann Paradise helps celebrate faith and support catechesis.

- Two CDs, Grades 1-3 and Grades 4-6, offer songs that teach, reinforce, or unfold the meaning of Scripture stories.
- These and other songs are available through aliveinchrist.osv.com and are searchable by grade and chapter level.

Family+Faith

Distribute the page to the children or parents/adult family members. Point out the chapter highlights, insights on how third graders understand concepts, the opportunity for the adults to reflect on their own experience and faith journey, and the family prayer.

Your Child Learned is a summary of the Catholic teaching that was covered in the chapter and introduces families to the Scripture and the Person of Faith that was presented.

Children At This Age helps parents become aware of how their child comprehends what was taught and suggests ways to help the child gain a deeper understanding of the material.

Consider This invites parents to ponder some of their own experiences and listen as the Church speaks to their personal journey of faith.

Let's Talk offers parents developmentally appropriate questions that lead to discussion of the week's lesson.

Let's Pray provides a short family prayer based on the Person of Faith featured in the lesson.

Online Resources offers multimedia tools to encourage family interaction and reinforce the lesson at home.

FAMILY+FAITH
LIVING AND LEARNING TOGETHER

YOUR CHILD LEARNED >>>

This page is for you, the parent, to encourage you to talk about your faith and see the many ways you already live your faith in daily family life.

In this section, you will find a summary of what your child has learned in the chapter.

God's Word
 In this section, you will find a Scripture citation and a summary of what your child has learned in the chapter.

Catholics Believe
- Bulleted information highlights the main points of doctrine in the Chapter.

Here you will find chapter connections to the *Catechism of the Catholic Church.*

People of Faith
Here you meet the holy person featured in People of Faith.

CHILDREN AT THIS AGE >>>

This feature gives you a sense of how your child, at this particular age, will likely be able to understand what is being taught. It suggests ways you can help your child better understand, live, and love their faith.

How They Understand Your third-grader is beginning to identify him or her self, and others, as members of groups. At this age, they begin to be joiners. They like communal activities such as team sports, hobby clubs, and scouting. Your family and parish community will still be a strong influence for your son or daughter.

For eight or nine year olds, putting someone else's needs ahead of their own is a new concept. They are just learning how to be unselfish. Help them see how Jesus ignored his own comfort to help others.

Find opportunities to affirm your child or other children when they show consideration for others, patience in a difficult situation, and courage in the face of teasing.

CONSIDER THIS >>>

This section includes a question that invites you to reflect on your own experience and consider how the Church speaks to you on your own faith journey.

LET'S TALK >>>

- Here you will find some practical questions that prompt discussion about the lesson's content, faith sharing, and making connections with your family life.

- Ask your child to share one thing they've learned about their book.

LET'S PRAY >>>

 This section encourages family prayer connected to the example of our People of Faith.

Holy men and women, pray for us. Amen.

 For a multimedia glossary of Catholic Faith Words, Sunday readings, seasonal and Saint resources, and chapter activities go to **aliveinchrist.osv.com**.

© Our Sunday Visitor

8 *Alive in Christ,* Grade 3 Opening Lesson

Optional Activity

Explore the Student Book

In addition to what is presented in this opening lesson, there are many other features that help you present the Catholic faith to the children. Ask them to find the following features in their books.

- The Church Year: Children learn about Church feasts and seasons.

- Unit Openers: Preview the doctrinal theme with photos and art that convey the richness of our Catholic Tradition.

- Catholic Social Teaching/Live Your Faith: Introduce the children to important teachings of Jesus and the Church that help us live Jesus' New Commandment to love as he loved.

The Church Year Overview

Check out the activities and resources available for the seasons of the Church Year at the following websites.

Go to **aliveinchrist.osv.com** and click on the Resource Library tab and select a season.

Go to **teachingcatholickids.com** and click on the current month's newsletter.

LESSON OBJECTIVES

- Learn how to honor our ancestors who are now Saints
- Recognize the Communion of Saints, including those in Purgatory

ENVIRONMENT

One or more statues or pictures of Saints

Prayer table

Green cloth

Battery-powered or electric candle

Bible or Lectionary

Holy water and bowl

- Cover the prayer table with the green cloth and arrange the statues, candle, and Bible or Lectionary on top of the table.
- Turn on the candle before beginning the ritual.
- Pour the holy water in a bowl.

MUSIC OPTIONS

Go to **aliveinchrist.osv.com** to sample and download, "I Know That My Redeemer Lives" "Sing a Song to the Saints" "We Gather Around Your Throne" "When the Saints Go Marching In" "Litany of Saints"

CATHOLIC SOCIAL TEACHING

- **Life and Dignity** Pages 290–291
- **Solidarity of the Human Family** Pages 300–301

Catechist Background

> "Amen, amen, I say to you, unless a grain of wheat falls on the ground and dies, it remains just a grain of wheat; but if it dies, it produces much fruit. …Whoever serves me must follow me, and where I am, there also will my servant be. The Father will honor whoever serves me." **John 12:24–26**
>
> ➔ **Reflect** Have you released your personal agenda to God?

All Saints Day is one of the oldest feasts of the Church. According to Pope Urban II, All Saints Day was begun to honor all the Saints known and unknown and to make up for any deficiencies in celebration during the rest of the year. In the early days during the persecutions, Christians celebrated the anniversary of the death of a martyr at the place where the martyr had died. As the number of martyrs increased, the Church declared a special day for all martyrs. As time went on and the persecutions stopped, people began to celebrate the lives of those who had lived in an exemplary Christian manner. Before the process of canonization, many Saints were acclaimed Saints by communities who had known them.

In contemporary times, we are more used to canonized Saints and often look at them as very extraordinary and somewhat distant from us. The feast of All Saints, which celebrates all those who are in Heaven, brings us back to the reality that all Christians are called to holiness and to sharing eternal life with God. It also reminds us that Saints also had moments of doubt and fear. But they continued to say "yes" to God, even in the face of disappointments or challenges. This feast is an invitation to examine our own lives and see how we're doing in the life we promised to live at our Baptism.

➔ **Reflect** How would you describe a Saint for our times?

Catechist's Prayer

> "Make known to me your ways, Lord; teach me your paths. Guide me by your fidelity and teach me, for you are God my savior, for you I wait all the day long." Amen. (Psalm 25:4–5)

All Saints and All Souls

 Let Us Pray

Leader: Dear Jesus, I trust in you. I know you are with me now. You will always be with me. Guide me to stay on your path every day.

"To you, O LORD, I lift up my soul, my God, in you I trust." **Psalm 25:1-2**

All: Amen.

 God's Word

Amen, amen, I say to you, unless a grain of wheat falls to the ground and dies, it remains just a grain of wheat; but if it dies, it produces much fruit.... Whoever serves me must follow me, and where I am, there also will my servant be. The Father will honor whoever serves me. **John 12:24, 26**

What Do You Wonder?

- What makes a grain of wheat grow and bear fruit?
- How many ways can you serve Jesus?

9

© Our Sunday Visitor

Lectionary Connection

John 12:24–26

This Gospel reading is proclaimed on the Fifth Sunday of Lent.

- Jesus foreshadows his suffering and Death as he explains why a "grain of wheat must die."
- He admonishes his followers that they, too, will have to die to themselves in order to inherit the eternal life promised by the Father.

 Invite

 Let Us Pray

Invite the children to gather in the prayer space and make the Sign of the Cross. Pray the leader's part and the Psalm verse. Have the children return to their seats.

Explain that we need to remember that we can always trust God.

Say: In today's reading, Jesus tells his disciples that when we follow him, we may have difficulties but they will change us for good.

God's Word

Guide the children through the process of Scripture reflection.

- Invite them to close their eyes, be still, and open their minds and hearts to what God is saying to them in this passage.
- Proclaim the Scripture.
- Maintain several moments of silence.
- *Ask:* What did you hear God say to you today?
- Invite volunteers to share.

What Do You Wonder?

Say: Saint Paul was reminding the people that no matter what happens, as long as we follow Jesus, God the Father will take care of us.

Invite the children to respond to the questions. Ask what else they might wonder about bearing fruit and serving Jesus.

Remembering the Dead

Say: On All Saints Day, we remember all the people who faithfully followed Jesus. When they died, they found new life in Heaven with God forever.

Have the children silently read the first paragraph.

- Explain your parish's rituals for All Saints and All Souls Day.
- Ask the children to share what they do in their families to remember those who have died.
- If your parish has a book of remembrance of those who have died, explain what it is and when it is used. If possible take the group to see it.

Read aloud the second paragraph.

 Have the children underline how people in Latin America celebrate the Day of the Dead.

Review with the children the information in the side column.

Read aloud the photograph's caption.

- Invite the children to describe what they see and share their impressions of the scene.

Mexico's Día de los Muertos celebrates and honors all the dead with a special focus on ancestors. Families visit the gravesites of their departed loved ones.

The Feast of All Saints

- The feast of All Saints is celebrated on November 1. The day after, November 2, is the feast of All Souls.

- These feasts honor the people who have died and gone before us. Many parishes remember those who have died all month.

Remembering the Dead

The Church has two special days for remembering people who have died. Both of the days are in November. On November 1, we celebrate All Saints Day. We honor everyone who is in Heaven. We honor these people, the Saints, even though we only know the names of some of them. On November 2, we celebrate All Souls Day. We pray for people who have died but who are not in Heaven yet. They are in Purgatory.

In some cultures, All Souls Day is very important. It is an occasion to remember that people on Earth and their relatives in Heaven remain united through prayer. For instance, many Latinos in the United States and in Latin America celebrate El Día de los Muertos (The Day of the Dead). On that day, graves of their relatives are decorated with flowers. They eat special foods. They also make a family altar. Candles and pictures are on the altar. Families gather at the altar and say prayers for their relatives.

➜ **How does your parish remember those who have died?**

© Our Sunday Visitor

10   The Church Year

✓ Quick Tip

Praying for the Dead

Explain to the children that one of the Spiritual Works of Mercy is to pray for the dead.

- Suggest that every day during the month of November they say three Our Fathers and three Hail Marys for the souls in Purgatory.
- Point out that the children can find these prayers on pages 320 and 321 in the Our Catholic Tradition section at the back of the Student Book.

These feasts help us remember that people who have died are very much part of the Church. They are part of the Communion of Saints. You honor the Saints and pray for those in Purgatory.

A Saint is...

Saints are heroes of the Church who loved God very much, led a holy life, and are now with God in Heaven. We know the names of some of the Saints but there are many Saints we do not know. We remember all of them on All Saints Day when we honor all of those who opened their lives to God on Earth and are enjoying life forever with God in Heaven. We can also ask patron Saints to pray for us about specific things. They are connected in a special way to a place, person, or type of work.

© Our Sunday Visitor

Activity

Find a Patron Saint There is a patron Saint for almost anything you can think of, like Saint Cecilia, the patron Saint of music and musicians, or Saint Albert, the patron Saint of scientists and students. Think of some of the things you like to do or the things that are most important in your life. Research the name of the patron Saint for these subjects and write their names here.

_____

_____

_____

_____

_____

11

Invite a volunteer to read aloud the paragraph.

A Saint is...

Ask a volunteer to read aloud the paragraph.

Ask: Do you have a favorite Saint?

- Invite the children to share.
- Write their responses on the board or on chart paper.
- Discuss the details of each image with the children.

 Music Option: Have the children sing "Sing a Song to the Saints" or "We Gather Around Your Throne," downloaded from **aliveinchrist.osv.com**.

Activity

Read aloud the directions.

- Provide research materials, if this is to be completed on site.
- If research is to be completed at home, go over Internet security issues, or recommend/lend hardcopy literature.

ⓘ Catechist Background

The Sign of the Cross

The Sign of the Cross is probably the most used Catholic prayer.

- The Sign of the Cross is used to begin and end most devotions as well as at Mass and for blessings.
- The Sign of the Cross recalls Christ's Cross—the instrument of our salvation—as well as the mystery of the Holy Trinity.
- When talking to the children about praying for those in Purgatory, remind them to begin and end with the Sign of the Cross.

People of Faith

Ask the children what the word *ordinary* means. Possible responses: usual, everyday

- Point out that most days are ordinary days; they are not holidays or birthdays or other special occasions.

- Point out that most Sundays are in Ordinary Time—up to thirty-four Sundays each year are included.

- Tell the children that the liturgical color for Ordinary Time is green and it signifies a time of spiritual growth.

- *Say:* One way we all grow is by learning new things. Here is a list of People of Faith. Try to choose one you have never heard of to look up.

- Have the children tell you which person of faith they want to look up. If possible, try to set it up so no two people are researching the same person of faith.

- Tell the children to look in the chapter that is listed for their Saint, read what they find, and write down some facts to share with the rest of the group.

Saint Francis of Assisi

Saint Elizabeth Ann Seton

Saint Pio

People of Faith		
Chapter	Person	Feast Day
1	Blessed Rabanus Maurus	February 4
2	Saint Francis of Assisi	October 4
3	Blessed Luigi Betrame Quattrocchi and Blessed Maria Corsini	November 25
4	Saint John of Matha	December 17
5	Saint Mary MacKillop	August 8
6	Saint Gertrude the Great	November 16 or 17
7	Saint Isaac Jogues	October 19
8	Saint Mary Magdalene	July 22
9	Saint Elizabeth Ann Seton	May 26
10	Saint Gregory the Great	September 3
11	Saints Perpetua and Felicity	March 7
12	Blessed Joseph Vaz	January 16
13	Saint Peter Canisius	January 23
14	Saint Genevieve	January 3
15	Saint Pio (Padre Pio)	September 23
16	Saint John the Baptist	June 24
17	Saint Damian of Molokai	May 10
18	Saint Jean-Baptiste de la Salle	April 7
19	Saint Clement of Rome	November 23
20	Saint Peter Claver	September 7
21	Saint Joseph	March 19

© Our Sunday Visitor

12 The Church Year

Catholic Social Teaching

Lesson Connections

To integrate Catholic Social Teaching into your lesson, choose one of the following features: Life and Dignity, pages 290–291; or Solidarity of the Human Family, pages 300–301.

- To expand the lesson, complete page 12, then move to the Catholic Social Teaching feature.

- Return to the prayer on page 13.

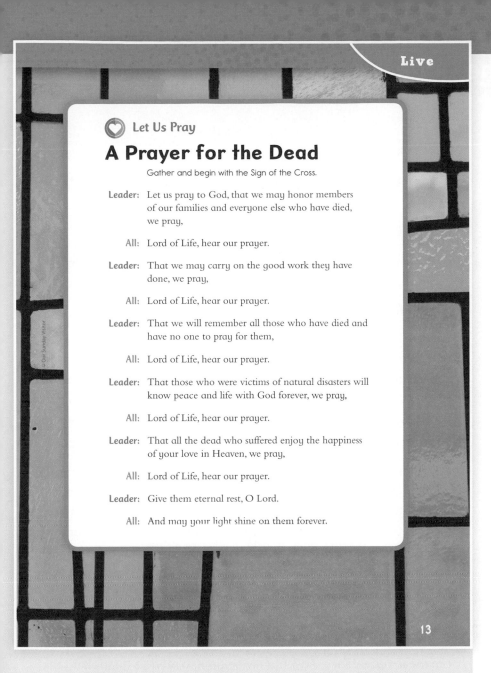

Let Us Pray

A Prayer for the Dead

Gather and begin with the Sign of the Cross.

Leader: Let us pray to God, that we may honor members of our families and everyone else who have died, we pray,

All: Lord of Life, hear our prayer.

Leader: That we may carry on the good work they have done, we pray,

All: Lord of Life, hear our prayer.

Leader: That we will remember all those who have died and have no one to pray for them,

All: Lord of Life, hear our prayer.

Leader: That those who were victims of natural disasters will know peace and life with God forever, we pray,

All: Lord of Life, hear our prayer.

Leader: That all the dead who suffered enjoy the happiness of your love in Heaven, we pray,

All: Lord of Life, hear our prayer.

Leader: Give them eternal rest, O Lord.

All: And may your light shine on them forever.

13

Liturgy Link

Liturgical Colors

The liturgical color for Sundays in Ordinary Time is green. It denotes hope, growth, life, immortality, and fidelity.

- Ordinary Time occurs during the Earth's growing seasons, when green is the prevalent color in nature.
- During Ordinary Time, we, too, grow into the hope of our calling as Christians.

Let Us Pray

A Prayer for the Dead

Set up images of Saints in the prayer space. Prepare the environment with the electric or battery-powered candle and other items.

- You will be the leader.

 Rehearse with the children "I Know That My Redeemer Lives," downloaded from **aliveinchrist.osv.com**.

Invite the children to gather in the prayer space around the images of the Saints.

- Begin by leading the children in the Sign of the Cross using the holy water.
- Follow the order of prayer on the student page.

Conclude by inviting the children to process around the room singing the hymn refrain.

Distribute this page to the children or parents/adult family members.

Advent: **Walk in the Light**

LESSON OBJECTIVES

- See that Jesus, our Savior, is the light that leads us back to God
- Identify Advent as a time to prepare our hearts

ENVIRONMENT

Prayer table
Purple cloth
List of ill parishioners
Advent wreath
Battery-powered candles in colored sleeves
Bible

- Set the prayer table with the purple cloth, the Advent wreath and candles, and the Bible.

 MUSIC OPTIONS
Go to **aliveinchrist.osv.com** to sample and download,
"Jambo, Jesu"
"Candles of Advent"
"Getting Read for Jesus"

 CATHOLIC SOCIAL TEACHING

- **Call to Community**
  Pages 292–293
- **Care for Creation**
  Pages 302–303

Catechist Background

> …the night is advanced, the day is at hand. Let us then throw off the works of darkness [and] put on the armor of light; let us conduct ourselves properly as in the day… **Romans 13:12–13a**

➜ **Reflect** Do you wear the armor of light?

When you are expecting a special guest to visit your home, you probably spend some time making preparations. The house is cleaned, food is prepared, and everyone is expected to show his or her best behavior. If the guest is someone especially beloved, all of these activities become part of a joyful atmosphere of anticipation and welcome.

Advent is a time to prepare for the most special guest that can possibly come to us: Jesus himself. The season reminds us that it is time to put our spiritual house in order, to make careful preparations, and to bring forward the best of ourselves. If we do as much for visitors to our homes, how much more ought we to prepare spiritually for the coming of the Son of God! Like a much-loved guest, Jesus comes not to inspect our housekeeping or grade our hospitality but he comes to be with us because he loves us. The atmosphere of Advent is joyful expectation.

The color of purple in this season reminds the faithful that preparation can mean repentance. Advent may be time to mend a quarrel or seek forgiveness. But above all, the liturgy proclaims that God is faithful to his promises. God will come. The candles of the Advent wreath contribute to a sense of watchful waiting. Advent is a season of hope.

➜ **Reflect** What spiritual preparations will you make this Advent?

Catechist's Prayer

God of Love, help me show my unconditional love to the children in my group as they learn to keep their promises and live in faithfulness. Amen.

Walk in the Light

Let Us Pray

Leader: Lord God of Light,
open my eyes to see you more clearly.
Bring light to my Advent path.

"…let us walk in the light of the LORD!"
Isaiah 2:5b

All: Amen.

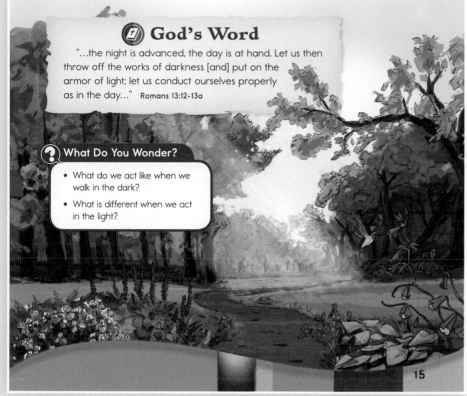

God's Word

"…the night is advanced, the day is at hand. Let us then throw off the works of darkness [and] put on the armor of light; let us conduct ourselves properly as in the day…" **Romans 13:12–13a**

What Do You Wonder?

- What do we act like when we walk in the dark?
- What is different when we act in the light?

15

Lectionary Connection

Romans 13:12–13a

This reading is proclaimed on the First Sunday of Advent, Year A.

- Saint Paul calls Christians in Rome to live differently than they once did, to "put on the armor of light."
- Here, Saint Paul draws a contrast with pagans in Rome, who were known for wild, drunken parties. He calls on the Church of Rome to conduct themselves differently.

Invite

Let Us Pray

Invite the children to gather in the prayer space and make the Sign of the Cross. Have the children proclaim the verse from Isaiah. Then have them return to their seats.

Explain that this prayer helps us see what we need to do to walk in Jesus' light and prepare our hearts for his coming into the world.

Say: In Baptism you were named a child of the light. Listen to what Saint Paul tells the Romans and you about darkness and light.

God's Word

Guide the children through the process of Scripture reflection.

- Invite them to close their eyes, be still, and open their minds and hearts to what God is saying to them in this passage.
- Proclaim the Scripture.
- Maintain several moments of silence.
- *Ask:* What did you hear God say to you today?
- Invite volunteers to share.

What Do You Wonder?

Say: God our Father gave us Jesus so we would not have to walk in darkness. We can always use Jesus' light. Ask the children what else they wonder about how God provides light in the darkness.

Jesus, God's Light

Explain that Advent is a time when we can bring Jesus' light to others.

- Drape the prayer table with the purple cloth, and place the Advent wreath on it.

- Ask the children why Advent wreaths have four candles. one for each Sunday in Advent

- Have the children help you make a list of sick relatives and friends. Add this to the list of ill parishioners.

Summarize the first paragraph.

Read aloud the next two paragraphs.

- Ask the question that follows the text.

- Ask the children why it is hard to walk in darkness. Possible response: You cannot see where you are going.

- Direct the children to underline what the Advent wreath prepares us to do.

- Allow enough time for the children to reread and underline.

Lighting the Advent Wreath

Have the children describe what is happening in the photograph.

- Invite a volunteer to read aloud the bullet points.

Jesus, God's Light

Advent is the first season of the Church year. As you prepare your heart for the coming of Jesus' Kingdom, you pray for his light to help you choose right actions. You ask him to make your heart ready for when he comes again at the end of time.

Long before Jesus was born, God's people waited for a Savior to bring God's light. They "walked in darkness" (Isaiah 9:1). When the time was right, God sent his Son, God's own Light, into the world to be our Savior.

Advent helps you remember that Jesus is the light in your life, too. The Advent wreath reminds you to prepare your heart to welcome Jesus. The Advent wreath has four candles. A candle is lit each week during Advent. A special prayer is prayed to ask that the light of Jesus come into your life.

➔ **What does your family do during Advent?**

 Underline what the Advent wreath prepares you to do.

© Our Sunday Visitor

Lighting the Advent Wreath

- We light purple candles on the first and second Sundays of Advent.

- On the third Sunday, we also light the rose colored candle as a sign of joy and rejoicing: our wait for Christmas is almost over.

- On the fourth Sunday, we add the last purple candle so all are lit.

16

🌐 Catholic Social Teaching

Chapter Connections

To integrate Catholic Social Teaching into your lesson, choose one of the following features: Call to Family, pages 292–293; or Care for Creation, pages 302–303.

- To expand the lesson, complete page 16, then move to the Catholic Social Teaching feature.

- Return to the prayer on page 17.

Let Us Pray

Witness to the Light

Gather and begin with the Sign of the Cross.

Leader: Our help is in the name of the Lord.

All: Who made Heaven and Earth.

Leader: Let us pray.
Bow your heads as the leader prays.

All: Amen.

Listen to God's Word

Reader: A reading from the holy Gospel according to John.
Read John 1:6–9.
The Gospel of the Lord.

All: Praise to you, Lord Jesus Christ.

Leader: Jesus, Light of the World, we ask you to bring your
healing light to those for whom we now pray.

All: Sing "Jambo, Jesu (Hello, Jesus)"
Lord of all life, be with us.
Lord of all life, be with us.
Lord of all life, be with us.
Lord of all life, be near.

Text: Refrain based on African Prayer. "Lord of All Life" Text and music © 1995,
Jack Miffleton. Published by OCP. All rights reserved.

17

Let Us Pray

Witness to the Light

Prepare the prayer table.

- Select a reader.
- You will be the leader.

 Rehearse with the children
"Jambo, Jesu," downloaded
from **aliveinchrist.osv.com**.

Invite the children to gather in the
prayer space around the Advent
wreath and Bible.

- Follow the order of prayer on the
  student page.

Leader's prayer: God our Father, we
are waiting in darkness for the light
of your Son, Jesus. We have faith
that he will come to us and change
our lives. We make this prayer in
Jesus' name.

Conclude by singing with
the children "Jambo, Jesu."

Catechist Background

Cultural Connection: Saint Lucy

Scandinavian customs on the Feast of Saint Lucy (December 13)
remind us of the importance of light.

- On this feast, a daughter in each home wakes up early and dresses
  in white. She wears an evergreen wreath with lit candles, awakens
  her family, and offers them special cakes for breakfast.
- The name *Lucy* means "light." However, for Christians, the most
  important light is the light of Christ.

Distribute this page to the children
or parents/adult family members.

LESSON OBJECTIVES

- See Mary, the Mother of God, as a prominent figure in the Advent season
- Appreciate the love Our Lady of Guadalupe has for everyone, especially the poor

ENVIRONMENT

Crucifix
Marian statue
Prayer table
Battery-powered or electric candle
Bible or Lectionary
White cloth

- Place the prayer table in a central location.
- Cover the table with the white cloth and arrange the statue, candle, and Bible or Lectionary on top of the table.
- Turn on the candle before beginning the ritual.
- Allow plenty of space around the prayer table for the children.
- Consider adding flowers to the prayer table.

 MUSIC OPTIONS
Go to **aliveinchrist.osv.com** to sample and download,
"Mother, Dark and Lovely"
"Immaculate Mary"
"Mary, Our Mother"

 CATHOLIC SOCIAL TEACHING

- **Option for the Poor**
  Pages 296–297
- **The Dignity of Work**
  Pages 298–299

Catechist Background

And Mary said: "My soul proclaims the greatness of the Lord; my spirit rejoices in God my savior. For he has looked upon his handmaid's lowliness; behold, from now on will all ages call me blessed" Luke 1:46–48

➜ **Reflect** How does your soul proclaim God's greatness?

Mary, Mother of Jesus, is lauded above all other Saints. She is honored for many reasons, but above all, as Mother of Christ, she is Mother of God. Mary is also our Mother, for we are all part of Christ's Body, the Church.

In the Gospel according to Luke, the Angel Gabriel calls Mary "full of grace." Mary didn't earn this grace granted to her by God. He made her sinless for a special purpose. She was human, just like we are. Jesus was her Savior just as he is ours and as he was to those who came before him. God gave Mary the special grace that would come through Jesus in advance so she could be a perfect Mother for him.

Through the centuries, Mary has appeared to many holy people. Often, these people were of humble origins—peasants or children—and from different cultures. One such person chosen by Mary to bring her son's message of salvation into the world is Saint Juan Diego, in fifteenth-century Mexico. Through Juan Diego's vision of the Virgin Mary, and his cooperation with her, the Catholic faith and devotion to the Mother of God grew throughout Mexico.

Mary's role as Mother gives her a special place in the lives of all Christians. We can always depend on her motherly care and know that she prays for us and brings our needs before her Son, Jesus.

➜ **Reflect** How do you incorporate the multi-cultural roots of children in your catechetical efforts?

Catechist's Prayer

 God the Holy Spirit, show me the times I should stop what I'm doing and help another. Let me walk in your light for your glory. Amen.

Our Lady of Guadalupe

 Let Us Pray

Leader: Dear Lady of Guadalupe,

Mother of Jesus and our Mother, teach us your ways of gentleness and strength. Guide us to help those experiencing great needs. Hear our prayer.

"Sing a new song to the LORD,
for he has done marvelous deeds." **Psalm 98:1a**

All: Amen.

 **God's Word**

And Mary said: "My soul proclaims the greatness of the Lord; my spirit rejoices in God my savior. For he has looked upon his handmaid's lowliness; behold, from now on will all ages call me blessed. The Mighty One has done great things for me, and holy is his name. His mercy is from age to age to those who respect him."

Based on Luke 1:46-50

? What Do You Wonder?

- How do you reflect God's goodness with your actions?
- What makes other people happy with God's gifts?

19

Lectionary Connection

Luke 1:46–50

This Gospel reading is adapted as the responsorial psalm on the Third Sunday of Advent, Year B, and is one of the optional Gospel readings on the feast of Our Lady of Guadalupe

- This reading, traditionally called the *Magnificat,* has its roots in Hannah's song at the birth of Samuel in 1 Samuel 2:1–10.
- The *Magnificat* is most frequently recited or sung as a canticle during Vespers, the main evening prayer service of the Liturgy of the Hours.

Invite

 Let Us Pray

Invite the children to gather in the prayer space and make the Sign of the Cross. Ask a volunteer to read aloud the leader's prayer and the Psalm verse. Afterwards, have the children return to their seats.

Say: The Psalm part of this prayer is a song of praise and thanks that applies to all of us when we think of the ways that God makes our lives new. Let's listen to Mary's song of praise.

God's Word

Guide the children through the process of Scripture reflection.

- Invite them to close their eyes, be still, and open their minds and hearts to what God is saying to them in this passage.
- Proclaim the Scripture.
- Maintain several moments of silence.
- *Ask:* What did you hear God say to you today?
- Invite volunteers to share.

What Do You Wonder?

Say: You are also God's favored child. God has done wonderful things for all of us, which we should be thankful for.

Invite the children to respond to the questions. Ask what else they might wonder about God's goodness.

The Blessed Mother

Explain that Mary is an important person in the Advent season. She is the one who brought Jesus to us.

Summarize the story of Juan Diego.

- Select four children to role-play the story of Mary's apparition to Juan Diego and his visit to the bishop.

- Have the first child read the story dramatically, while the other three act it out in pantomime.

- Emphasize that Mary was bringing the message that God loves all people especially those who are poor, and he wants them to know his Son.

⭐ Ask the children to underline what Our Lady of Guadalupe wanted Juan Diego to do.

Review with the children the information in the side column on the Feasts of Mary.

- *Ask:* What is the date of the Feast of the Immaculate Conception of Mary? December 8

- *Ask:* What is the date of the Feast of Our Lady of Guadalupe? December 12

Discover

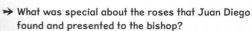

The Blessed Mother

Advent Feasts

- During the four weeks of Advent, the Church celebrates two very special feasts of Mary.

- December 8 is the feast of the Immaculate Conception of Mary. December 12 is the feast of Our Lady of Guadalupe.

Early one morning in December, a Nahuatl Indian named Juan Diego heard the beautiful sound of singing birds. He heard someone call his name, "Juanito," (little Juan). There he saw a beautiful young woman. She told him she was the Virgin Mary. She wanted Juan Diego to tell the bishop of Mexico to build a temple on the hill to honor her.

When Juan Diego gave the bishop Mary's message, the bishop did not believe him and asked him for some proof. Later, Mary appeared to Juan Diego again and told him to go up the hill where he would find roses. It was almost impossible for roses to grow in December. He went up the hill and found beautiful roses, cut them, and put them in his cloak. He returned to the bishop with the flowers. When Juan Diego opened his cloak, roses fell onto the floor and Our Lady of Guadalupe miraculously appeared.

➔ **What was special about the roses that Juan Diego found and presented to the bishop?**

© Our Sunday Visitor

20　The Church Year

🌐 Catholic Social Teaching

Lesson Connection

To integrate Catholic Social Teaching into your lesson, choose one of the following features: Option for the Poor, pages 296–297; or The Dignity of Work, pages 298–299.

- To expand the lesson, complete page 20, then move to the Catholic Social Teaching feature.

- Return to the prayer on page 21.

Our Lady of Guadalupe

This prayer form is called a litany which is a prayer of petition that repeats a line several times.

♥ Let Us Pray

Gather and begin with the Sign of the Cross.

Leader: The Lord be with you.

All: And with your spirit.

Leader: Lord, have mercy on us.

All: Christ, have mercy on us.

Leader: Lord, have mercy on us. Christ hear us.

All: Christ, graciously hear us.

Leader: Our Lady of Guadalupe,

All: Pray for us.

Leader: Mother of those who suffer,

All: Pray for us.

Leader: Patroness of the Americas,

All: Pray for us.

Leader: Mother of all peoples around the world,

All: Pray for us.

Leader: Pray for us, O holy Mother of God.

All: That we may be made worthy of the promises of Christ. Amen.

21

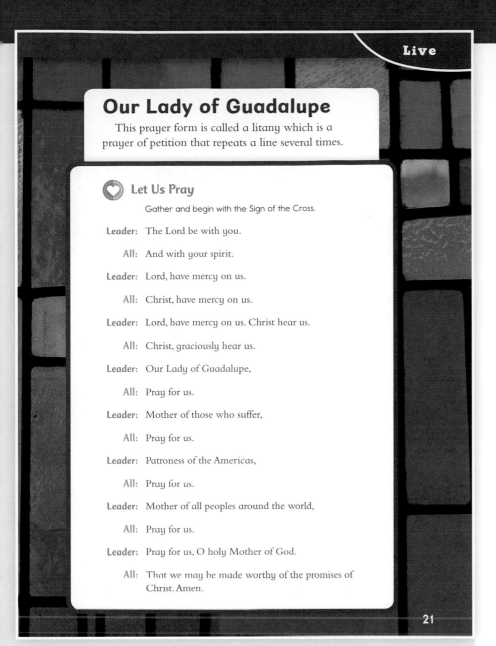

♥ Liturgy Link

Litany

Prayers that consist of short invocations read by the leader and short responses, such as "Pray for us," are called litanies.

- Explain that litanies are often sung in a procession.
- Tell the children that we pray the Litany of the Saints at the Easter Vigil and often at Baptisms throughout the year.
- In Mass, during the Prayer of the Faithful, we use the litany form to pray for the Church, its leaders, and other intentions.

♥ Let Us Pray

Our Lady of Guadalupe

Explain the prayer form.

- You will be the leader.

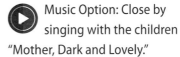 Music Option: Rehearse with the children "Mother, Dark and Lovely," downloaded from **aliveinchrist.osv.com**.

Quiet the children as they arrive in the prayer space.

- Explain that you will lead the litany, and the children will respond to each petition.
- Follow the order of prayer on the student page.

▶ Music Option: Close by singing with the children "Mother, Dark and Lovely."

Or, you might conclude the session, by having the children slowly and reverently process back to their seats.

Distribute this page to the children or parents/adult family members.

Our Lady of Guadalupe **21-22**

LESSON OBJECTIVES

- Describe Christmas as a season to give God thanks and praise
- Recognize that prayer is a way of praising God

ENVIRONMENT

Nativity scene
Prayer table
White or gold cloth
Battery-powered or electric candle

- Place the Nativity scene in an easily accessible area of the room.
- Put the white or gold cloth on the prayer table.

 MUSIC OPTIONS

Go to **aliveinchrist.osv.com** to sample and download, "Hark, the Herald Angels Sing" "Joy to the World"

 CATHOLIC SOCIAL TEACHING

- **Life and Dignity**
  Pages 290–291
- **Care for Creation**
  Pages 302–303

Catechist Background

For a child is born to us, a son is given to us; upon his shoulder dominion rests. They name him Wonder-Counselor, God-Hero, Father-Forever, Prince of Peace. **Isaiah 9:5**

➜ **Reflect** Who is your hero?

The liturgy reveals that Christmas is more than a celebration of Jesus' birth. Certainly the Christmas celebration points out the Infancy Narratives found in the first chapters of the Gospels according to Matthew and Luke. But the liturgy of the season also highlights scenes from Jesus' later childhood in the Feast of the Holy Family, and it illustrates his adulthood in the Feast of the Baptism of the Lord. What these Scripture passages have in common is their emphasis on how Jesus came into our midst. The full mystery of the Incarnation, Jesus as true God and true man, fully human and fully divine, is the essential message of Christmas.

Eight days, called an *octave*, are set aside during the season for the celebration of the great feast of Christmas. The octave of Christmas begins on December 25 and ends on January 1, the Solemnity of Mary, the Mother of God. The duration of the octave reminds us how important it is to take ample time to celebrate the Good News of Christ's coming. Savor the mystery!

➜ **Reflect** How is Christmas a proclamation of Good News for you?

Catechist's Prayer

Father God, thank you for sending your Son to save us from our sins. Thank you for your love and presence in my life. Let my life be a testament of my love and gratitude to you in return. Amen.

Glory to God

 Let Us Pray

Leader: God, our Heavenly Father,
We praise and bless you for the gift of your Son
Jesus. He brings light and peace to our world. We
pray that all people of the world will know peace
in this season.

"Arise! Shine, for your light has come,
the glory of the LORD has dawned upon you."
Isaiah 60:1

All: Amen.

God's Word

For a child is born to us, a son is given to us;
upon his shoulder dominion rests.
They name him Wonder-Counselor, God-Hero,
Father-Forever, Prince of Peace.   *Isaiah 9:5*

© Our Sunday Visitor

What Do You Wonder?

• What does it mean for dominion
to rest on Jesus' shoulders?

• Which title is the best for Jesus?

23

Lectionary Connection

Isaiah 9:5

This reading is proclaimed in the Christmas Mass during the night—
the vigil Mass on Christmas Eve.

• This verse is understood to be a prophecy about Jesus, the Messiah
who would come as a child.

• Isaiah gives some of the titles that would later be given to Christ.

 Let Us Pray

Invite the children to gather in the
prayer space and make the Sign of
the Cross. Pray the leader's prayer,
including the verse from Isaiah.

Have the children move out of the
prayer space and back to their seats.

Say: God's greatest gift to us was to
send his Son to live among us. Jesus
became one of us so we would
know how to give God glory and
to save us from sin. We are invited
now to listen carefully to the words
of Isaiah.

 God's Word

Guide the children through the
process of Scripture reflection.

• Invite them to close their eyes,
be still, and open their minds and
hearts to what God is saying to
them in this passage.

• Proclaim the Scripture.

• Maintain several moments
of silence.

• *Ask:* What did you hear God say
to you today?

• Invite volunteers to share.

What Do You Wonder?

Say: In today's reading, Isaiah is
prophesying that a child, a son, will
be born for us, with all authority,
and he will be called many things as
well as Prince of Peace.

Invite the children to respond to the
questions. Ask what else they might
wonder about titles of Jesus.

Praise Jesus

Tell the children that the reading from Isaiah 9:5 helps us see how awesome the birth of Jesus was. It is so wonderful that we have to keep giving God thanks and praise.

Have a volunteer read aloud the paragraph.

- Ask the children what we celebrate on Christmas. the birth of Jesus

 Direct the children to circle the ways that we worship God during the Christmas season.

Call attention to the photo on the page. Have the children point out and identify the people depicted.

- Reinforce the idea that we re-enact the Nativity scene to praise God for the gift of Jesus.

Read aloud the question.

- Invite the children to respond.
- Write their responses on the board or on chart paper.

Ask the children to accompany you to the part of the classroom where the Nativity scene is displayed.

- Discuss all the elements and why they think each is important.

> ▶ Music Option: Have the children sing "Joy to the World," downloaded from **aliveinchrist.osv.com**.

Discover

Praise Jesus

At Christmas, the Church praises and thanks God for all his gifts, especially for the best gift of all—Jesus! We want to thank God for Jesus and for our many blessings. The Church gives God thanks and honors him in many ways.

The most important prayer of thanks and praise is the Mass. Beginning on Christmas Eve, special Masses are celebrated each day to worship God during the Christmas season. Displaying Nativity scenes is another way to praise God for the gift of Jesus.

Circle the ways that we worship God during the Christmas season.

➡ What is your favorite way to thank and praise God in prayer?

24

ⓘ Catechist Background

Cultural Connection: Oplatki

Polish families and their guests share Oplatki on Christmas Eve.

- These rectangular wafers are similar to Communion hosts and have Nativity scenes embossed on them.
- Each person gets a wafer. The head of the household begins the ritual by offering his or her wafer to family members and guests.
- All join in, exchanging good wishes and words of reconciliation as they share the wafers.

Christmas Day

On Christmas Day the Church gives God thanks and praise for Jesus' birth. The feast of Christmas begins a major season in the Church year. It is so important that the celebration starts in prayer on December 24, at the Christmas Eve Vigil. It continues for a few weeks until the feast of the Baptism of Jesus.

Cardinal Donald Wuerl blesses the altar

God's Great Gift

God gives you a special gift in Jesus. You can give your own gifts to God. Your prayers of thanksgiving are your gifts. You can pray with words, gestures, and actions, during the Mass or at any time.

→ Have you seen other people pray in ways that are different from the way you pray?

Activity

Prayer Journal Keep a prayer journal with your thoughts and feelings about God. Start today using the space below.

_____

_____

_____

_____

_____

_____

Christmas **25**

Christmas Day

Have a volunteer read aloud the paragraph.

- Count with the children how many days the season lasts.
- Have them tell you the beginning and end date and corresponding feast.
- *Ask:* So, is Christmas just one day? No; it lasts from Christmas Eve through the Feast of the Baptism of Jesus, or the Baptism of the Lord.

God's Great Gift

Ask: What are some gifts you can give God? Possible response: prayers of thanksgiving

Read aloud the question.

- Invite the children to share what they have seen.

Activity

Read aloud the directions for the activity.

- Allow time for the children to begin writing on the day of the week that corresponds with the meeting day.

Catholic Social Teaching

Lesson Connections

To integrate Catholic Social Teaching into your lesson, choose one of the following features: Life and Dignity, pages 290–291; or Care for Creation, pages 302–303.

- To expand the lesson, complete pages 24–25, then move to the Catholic Social Teaching feature.
- Return to the prayer on pages 26–27.

Celebrate Jesus

 Let Us Pray

Prepare

Move the Nativity scene to the center of the prayer table, and turn on the candle.

- You will be the leader.

 Rehearse with the children "Hark, the Herald Angels Sing," downloaded from **aliveinchrist.osv.com**.

Invite the children to gather in the prayer space around the Nativity scene and Bible.

- Ask a volunteer to read aloud the opening paragraph explaining the form of prayer.

Pray

Begin by leading the children in the Sign of the Cross.

- Pray the greeting and prompt the response.

Leader's prayer: God, our Father, thank you for the gift of your Son and our brother Jesus. Help us share your gift and spread the Good News of Christmas with joy.

Listen to God's Word

Have the children stand.

- Proclaim the Gospel.
- Have all pray the Lord's Prayer.

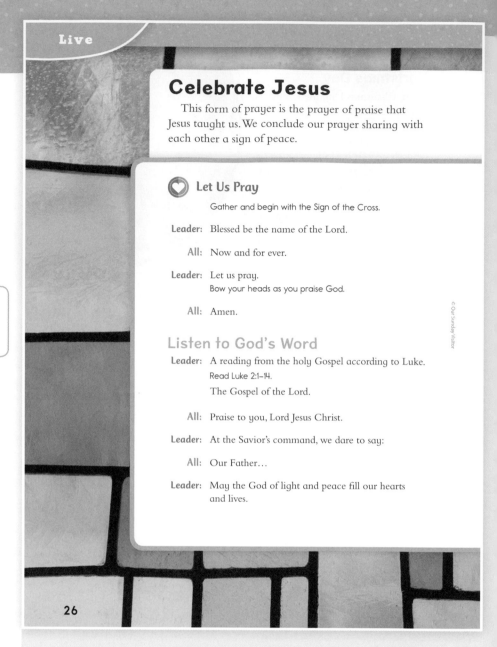

Live

Celebrate Jesus

This form of prayer is the prayer of praise that Jesus taught us. We conclude our prayer sharing with each other a sign of peace.

 Let Us Pray

Gather and begin with the Sign of the Cross.

Leader: Blessed be the name of the Lord.

All: Now and for ever.

Leader: Let us pray.
Bow your heads as you praise God.

All: Amen.

Listen to God's Word

Leader: A reading from the holy Gospel according to Luke.
Read Luke 2:1–14.
The Gospel of the Lord.

All: Praise to you, Lord Jesus Christ.

Leader: At the Savior's command, we dare to say:

All: Our Father…

Leader: May the God of light and peace fill our hearts and lives.

26

Liturgy Link

Christmas

Share information about how the Church celebrates Christmas.

- The Christmas vestments are white and gold, in keeping with the joyful nature of the feast.
- During Christmas, the Church celebrates the mystery of faith that God became fully human—the mystery of the Incarnation.
- The Christmas feast itself is celebrated with three different Masses: Midnight Mass, Mass at Dawn, and Mass during the day.

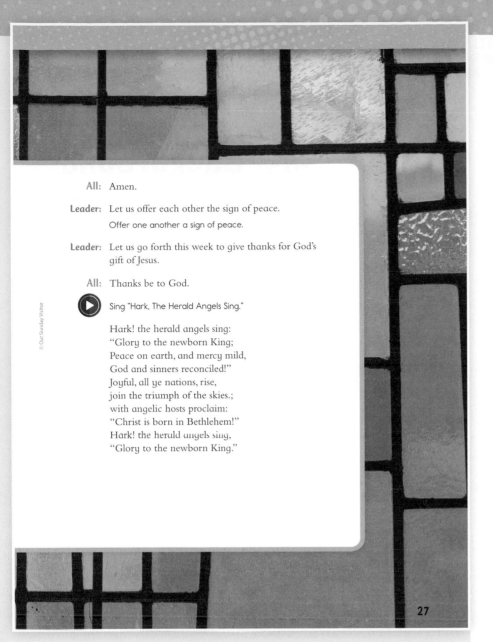

All: Amen.

Leader: Let us offer each other the sign of peace.

Offer one another a sign of peace.

Leader: Let us go forth this week to give thanks for God's gift of Jesus.

All: Thanks be to God.

▶ Sing "Hark, The Herald Angels Sing."

Hark! the herald angels sing:
"Glory to the newborn King;
Peace on earth, and mercy mild,
God and sinners reconciled!"
Joyful, all ye nations, rise,
join the triumph of the skies.;
with angelic hosts proclaim:
"Christ is born in Bethlehem!"
Hark! the herald angels sing,
"Glory to the newborn King."

© Our Sunday Visitor

27

Sign of Peace

Have the children exchange a sign of peace.

- After the lesson, use information from the Catechist Background box to talk with the children about the sign of peace.

▶ Conclude by inviting the children to process around the room singing "Hark, the Herald Angels Sing."

ⓘ Catechist Background

Peace Be with You

The sign of peace is used in the Mass immediately after the Lord's Prayer.

- We share a gesture with those around us, according to local custom: perhaps a handshake, a hug, or a spoken phrase.
- The sign of peace symbolizes that we are at peace with everyone, not just those who are worshipping with us.

Distribute this page to the children or parents/adult family members.

Lent: **Time for Change**

LESSON OBJECTIVES
- Realize that Lent is the season to grow closer to Jesus
- Discuss how good actions bring us closer to Jesus

ENVIRONMENT
Purple cloth
Prayer table
Cross
Bible
Battery-powered candle

- Set the prayer table with the purple cloth, the cross, the candle, and the Bible.

- Arrange the room to provide several areas for quiet prayer.

 MUSIC OPTIONS
Go to **aliveinchrist.osv.com** to sample and download, "Lord, throughout These Holy Days" "With These Ashes" "Ashes"

 CATHOLIC SOCIAL TEACHING
- **Rights and Responsibilities** Pages 294–295
- **Solidarity of the Human Family** Pages 300–301

Catechist Background

> And this is the verdict, that the light came into the world, but people preferred darkness to light, because their works were evil. For everyone who does wicked things hates the light and does not come toward the light, so that his works might not be exposed. But whoever lives the truth comes to the light, so that his works may be clearly seen as done in God. **John 3:19–21**
>
> ➔ **Reflect** Do you know anyone whose works can be clearly seen as "done in God"?

Early in the history of the Church, Lent became a season of preparation for Baptism. The emphasis was on conversion. Lent was also a time of Reconciliation for those who had sinned. The emphasis was on forgiveness. Today both elements are present in the Church's observance. The liturgies of Lent call us to prepare for Baptism or the renewal of baptismal promises. They also proclaim God's forgiveness.

The scriptural image of the desert or the wilderness can provide a key to understanding this season. The Israelites spent forty years in the wilderness before they reached the Promised Land. Jesus also went into the wilderness. Before he began his public ministry, he spent forty days in prayer there. Jesus fasted and resisted temptations from the devil. His struggle with Satan gives the Church a model of faithfulness. For this reason, the Gospel for the First Sunday of Lent each year is the story of Jesus in the desert.

Lent is a time of retreat. Signs of festivity that are normally part of the Sunday liturgy, such as the Gloria and the Alleluia, are set aside. The environment for worship is simple and spare. Lent is a season to rediscover the holy and place it at the center of our lives.

➔ **Reflect** How might you set aside time for God in your own life this Lent?

Catechist's Prayer

 God of Love, let my thoughts remain in love. Help me to forgive others and myself, and let me be forgiven. Amen.

Time for Change

 Let Us Pray

Leader: Lord, God, send your Holy Spirit to guide us in the ways of doing good and avoiding evil. Through Christ, our Lord.

"The LORD is my light and my salvation;
whom should I fear?

The LORD is my life's refuge;
of whom should I be afraid?" **Psalm 27:1**

All: Amen.

God's Word

"And this is the verdict, that the light came into the world, but people preferred darkness to light, because their works were evil. For everyone who does wicked things hates the light and does not come toward the light, so that his works might not be exposed. But whoever lives the truth comes to the light, so that his works may be clearly seen as done in God."

John 3:19–21

? What Do You Wonder?

- Why do we call Jesus the "light"?
- Why do people do evil things?

29

Lectionary Connection

John 3:19–21

This Gospel reading is proclaimed on the Fourth Sunday of Lent, Cycle B.

- In this passage, Jesus explains why he is rejected by some.
- Jesus explains that those who "live in truth" have nothing to hide, and so they should come out into the light so that their works may be seen.

Invite

Let Us Pray

Have the children gather in the prayer space and make the Sign of the Cross. Read aloud the leader's part. Invite the group to pray the Psalm verse aloud with you.

Have the children move out of the prayer space and back to their seats.

Say: We ask God to send the Holy Spirit to help us see how to do good and avoid doing evil—things that are harmful to others, ourselves and our relationship with God. Sometimes this is a challenge, but we remember God is always with us and he sent Jesus to be our guiding light.

God's Word

Guide the children through the process of Scripture reflection.

- Invite them to close their eyes, be still, and open their minds and hearts to what God is saying to them in this passage.
- Proclaim the Scripture.
- Maintain several moments of silence.
- *Ask:* What did you hear God say to you today?
- Invite volunteers to share.

What Do You Wonder?

Say: In today's reading we heard that Jesus brings light into the world.

Invite the children to respond to the questions. Ask what else they might wonder about the light of Jesus and our response to it.

Discover

Growing in Faith

Say: During Lent we take time to think about the actions we need to take to grow in our relationship with God and be bearers of light to those around us.

- Gather the children around the prayer table. Solicit volunteers to help you put the purple cloth, candle, and cross on the table.
- Ask the children what the forty days before Easter are called. Lent

Read aloud the first paragraph.

Lenten Acts

Discuss the custom of giving up special treats during Lent or of taking positive actions toward change.

Ask volunteers to read aloud the two paragraphs.

- Ask the question that follows the text.
- Allow time for silent reflection.
- Remind the children that they do not need to share this information. However, if anyone wants to share, allow them to do so.
- Have the children circle some things they can do to make themselves stronger during Lent.
- Allow the children time to reread and circle the text.
- Check that everyone circled all of the information.

Invite a volunteer to read the facts about Lent in the side column box.

Growing in Faith

To help you grow stronger as a follower of Christ, the Church gives you the forty days of Lent. During Lent you prepare your heart for the joy of Easter by the Lenten practices of fasting, prayer, and almsgiving. These practices help you show sorrow for your sins and the desire to do better.

Lenten Acts

To make yourself stronger, you might decide to give up certain treats or a favorite activity during Lent. You can use any money you save to remember the needs of others.

Your Lenten practice can also include positive actions. You can choose to pray more often, go to Mass more often, or go out of your way to do something good for others.

➔ What will you do this Lent to grow closer to Jesus?

Lent
- The season of Lent begins on Ash Wednesday and lasts for forty days.
- Purple, the color of Lent, reminds us that we need to repent.
- Lent is a season of change for the Church and her members.

Circle some things you can do to make yourself stronger during Lent.

30

© Our Sunday Visitor

(i) Catechist Background

Cultural Connection: Saint Joseph

In Italy, the Feast of Saint Joseph on March 19—which always falls during Lent—is observed with a special feast called Joseph's Table.

- Bonfires begin on March 18, and the next day villagers act out the parts of the Holy Family in a pageant.
- After Mass, an outdoor feast is held. Those who are poor and needy are special guests at the festivities.
- See if your parish celebrates the Feast of Saint Joseph in a special way, and if so, invite the children to attend the celebration with their families.

More Like Jesus

The Cross is the sign of what Jesus was willing to do for all people. God loves us so much that he sent his Son whose death saved us from sin and eternal death.

Making the Sign of the Cross is a reminder of the sacrifice of love that was made for you by Jesus. It is also a reminder that you are his disciple. During Lent you and your faith community strive to become more like Jesus through prayer and helping others.

➤ Who reminds you most of Jesus?

➤ How are you "like Jesus" for others each day?

Activity

Decorate a Lenten Cross Decorate the cross and write Lenten words below that remind you of the extra things you are doing during Lent.

_____

_____

_____

Lent **31**

More Like Jesus

Have a volunteer read aloud both paragraphs.

- Point out that Catholics honor the cross because Jesus won our salvation through his Death on the Cross. The cross signifies all that Jesus did for us and his obedience to the Father.

- Read aloud the questions.

- Pause after each question, and invite the children to respond.

Point out the photograph at the top of the page.

- Invite volunteers to describe what they see.

Have a volunteer read aloud the directions for the activity.

- Ask the children to work in pairs to create a list of Lenten words that have special meaning to them.

- Provide art materials for decorating.

- Allow enough time for the children to decorate their crosses and write in their words.

 Music Option: Have the children sing "With These Ashes," downloaded from **aliveinchrist.osv.com**.

🌐 Catholic Social Teaching

Lesson Connections

To integrate Catholic Social Teaching into your lesson, choose one of the following features: Rights and Responsibilities, pages 294–295; or Solidarity of the Human Family, pages 300–301.

- To expand the lesson, complete pages 30–31, then move to the Catholic Social Teaching feature.

- Return to the prayer on pages 32–33.

Celebrate Lent
 Let Us Pray

Prepare

Turn on the candle.

- You will be the leader.

> ▶ Rehearse with the children "Lord, Throughout These Holy Days," downloaded from **aliveinchrist.osv.com**.

Gather the children in the prayer space with their books.

Pray

Follow the order of prayer on the student page.

Leader's prayer: Dear Father in Heaven, we are trying to grow stronger in your love. We are working to change ourselves to be more like you. Please accept our sacrifices and help us in our efforts. We ask this through Jesus our Savior.

Listen to God's Word

Have the children stand.

- Proclaim the Scripture.
- Invite the children to be seated for silent reflection.

Live

 **Let Us Pray**

Celebrate Lent

Gather and begin with the Sign of the Cross.

Leader: O Lord, open my lips.

All: That my mouth shall proclaim your praise.

Leader: Let us pray.

Bow your head as the leader prays.

All: Amen.

Listen to God's Word

Leader: A reading from the Letter to the Ephesians.
Read Ephesians 5:1–2, 8–10.
The Word of the Lord.

All: Thanks be to God.

32

 Liturgy Link

Postures

This celebration contains two liturgical postures that demonstrate different states of mind in the participants.

- In standing for the Scripture reading, children show that they are respectfully witnessing to the Bible.
- By sitting and casting their eyes downward for the silent prayer, children show that they are reflecting on their lives.

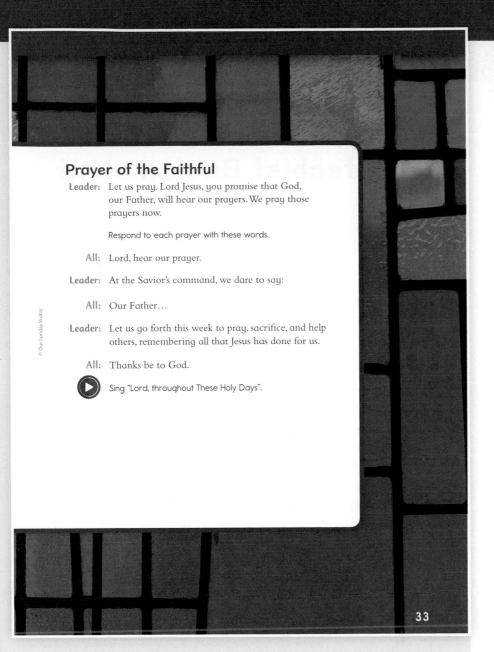

Prayer of the Faithful

Leader: Let us pray. Lord Jesus, you promise that God, our Father, will hear our prayers. We pray those prayers now.

Respond to each prayer with these words.

All: Lord, hear our prayer.

Leader: At the Savior's command, we dare to say:

All: Our Father…

Leader: Let us go forth this week to pray, sacrifice, and help others, remembering all that Jesus has done for us.

All: Thanks be to God.

▶ Sing "Lord, throughout These Holy Days".

33

Prayer of the Faithful

Lead the Prayer of the Faithful. Include the following prayers:

- In thanksgiving for our successes this Lent,
- For the strength to carry our disciplines further as Lent continues,
- For those who need your help most,
- For the grace of a happy Easter.

Lead the children in praying the Lord's Prayer; follow with the concluding rite.

▶ Sing with the children the refrain for "Lord, throughout These Holy Days," as you lead them around the prayer space and back to their seats.

Alternate Music Option: "Ashes"

Optional Activity

Write a Prayer *Verbal/Linguistic*

The children may wish to write prayers to pray before the cross.

- Encourage them to write about their thoughts on Lent and Jesus' sacrifice.
- Have each child compose a short prayer that includes these thoughts.
- Suggest that they create a nice, clean copy of the prayer to put in a special place.
- Encourage the children to pray their prayers every day.

Distribute this page to the children or parents/adult family members.

LESSON OBJECTIVES

- Recognize that Holy Week is a special week for the Church
- Discover what makes up the three days of the Triduum

ENVIRONMENT

Bread
Cross
Holy water
Baptismal candle
White cloth
Prayer table
Bible

- Place the prayer table in the center of the room.
- Set the prayer table with the white cloth, the bread, cross, holy water, baptismal candle, and the Bible.
- Allow space around the table for the children to stand and sit during the celebration.

 MUSIC OPTIONS

Go to **aliveinchrist.osv.com** to sample and download,
"Christ Is Light"
"Jesu, Jesu"
"Were You There?"
"We Remember—The Three Days"

 CATHOLIC SOCIAL TEACHING

- **Call to Community**
  Pages 292–293
- **The Dignity of Work**
  Pages 298–299

Catechist Background

 For as often as you eat this bread and drink the cup, you proclaim the death of the Lord until he comes.
1 Corinthians 11:26

➔ **Reflect** How do you practice rememberance of the Lord's sacrifice in your daily life?

The Easter Triduum begins on the evening of Holy Thursday and continues through Evening Prayer on Easter Sunday. The center and high point of the Triduum is the celebration of the Easter Vigil. It is the oldest liturgy in the Church's calendar. Attendance at the Easter Vigil was mandatory during the first centuries of Christian history. It was the sole celebration of Easter. It also was considered the best time of the year to celebrate Baptism. During the late fifth century, an additional Mass was introduced on Easter Sunday.

Today, the Easter Vigil is the normal time for the Baptism of adults and older children. The renewal of baptismal promises allows us to say "yes" yet again to the new life of grace. The whole celebration invites us to join in praise of the Risen Lord, who died and rose so that we might "live in newness of life" (Romans 6:4).

➔ **Reflect** What are your own high hopes for Easter this year?

Catechist's Prayer

 Jesus, help me be of solemn manner when I should, and joyful manner when I can. Help me to help the children understand the season. Amen.

Holy Week

 Let Us Pray

Leader: Lord, God, we believe you will always love us.
Send your Holy Spirit to help us always love you.
Through Christ, our Lord,

"Forever I will maintain my mercy for him;
my covenant with him stands firm." **Psalm 89:29**

All: Amen.

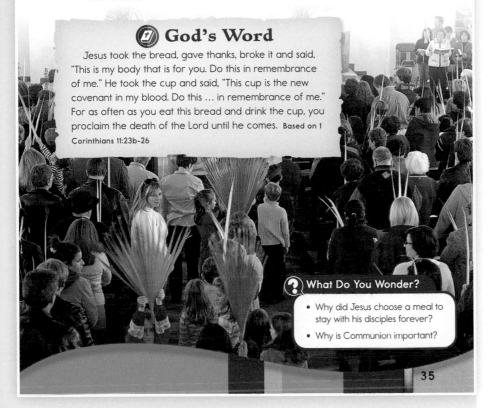

 God's Word

Jesus took the bread, gave thanks, broke it and said, "This is my body that is for you. Do this in remembrance of me." He took the cup and said, "This cup is the new covenant in my blood. Do this … in remembrance of me." For as often as you eat this bread and drink the cup, you proclaim the death of the Lord until he comes. **Based on 1 Corinthians 11:23b-26**

? What Do You Wonder?

- Why did Jesus choose a meal to stay with his disciples forever?
- Why is Communion important?

35

Lectionary Connection

1 Corinthians 11:23b–26

This reading is proclaimed on Holy Thursday.

- Saint Paul is writing to the Church in Corinth, who had not fully understood the teaching regarding the Eucharist and were engaging in liturgical abuses in their worship.

- He reiterates the words of Jesus at the Last Supper, clarifying the teaching that the Eucharist really is the Body and Blood of Jesus Christ.

Invite

Let Us Pray

Invite the children to gather in the prayer space, and make the Sign of the Cross. Read aloud the leader's part and the Psalm verse. Afterwards, have the children return to their seats.

Say: Our prayer today helps us remember that God promised to be with us always. Let's get very quiet and listen to what Saint Paul told the Corinthians about Jesus' promise of presence at the Last Supper.

God's Word

Guide the children through the process of Scripture reflection.

- Invite them to close their eyes, be still, and open their minds and hearts to what God is saying to them in this passage.
- Proclaim the Scripture.
- Maintain several moments of silence.
- *Ask:* What did you hear God say to you today?
- Invite volunteers to share.

What Do You Wonder?

Say: Jesus wanted us to share in the Eucharist so that we could remember him and do what he did.

Invite the children to respond to the questions. Ask what else they might wonder about the importance of Communion.

Discover

Rejoice

Tell the children that during Holy Week, we remember the Lord's Supper and all the events of Jesus' last days.

Read aloud the two paragraphs.

- *Ask:* What did Jesus do on Holy Thursday, Good Friday, and Easter? He gave us the Eucharist, he died on the Cross, and he rose from the dead.

The Three Days

Ask three volunteers to each read aloud one of the paragraphs.

- *Ask:* What special days are included in the celebration of Triduum? Holy Thursday, Good Friday, and Holy Saturday

- Point out to the children that by attending any of the Easter Masses, they are professing their faith. They are standing not only with their parish community but also with Catholics around the world in honoring God and appreciating Jesus' sacrifice.

 Have the children underline what the word *vigil* means.

Read aloud the question.

- Write the children's responses on the board or on chart paper.

> ▶ Music Option: Have the children sing "Jesu, Jesu" or "Were You There," downloaded from **aliveinchrist.osv.com**.

Discover

Rejoice

At the end of Lent, the Church sets aside a very holy week. It begins on Palm Sunday with the procession of palms and reading of the Passion.

The last three days of Holy Week celebrate what Jesus did for all people. The Church calls these three special days the Triduum. The Triduum begins with the Holy Thursday Mass of the Lord's Supper and ends with evening prayer on Easter Sunday.

The Three Days

On Holy Thursday the Church recalls Jesus' Last Supper with his disciples. On Good Friday Jesus' suffering and Death on the Cross is remembered. Holy Saturday is a day of prayerful waiting to celebrate Jesus' Resurrection.

The liturgy on Holy Saturday evening is called the Easter Vigil. The word vigil means "keeping watch by night." At the Easter Vigil the Church community keeps watch with those waiting to be baptized.

To express the joy of Jesus' Resurrection, the deacon or other minister sings the Easter Proclamation.

Underline what the word vigil means.

➔ **What are some other ways people express joy in the Resurrection?**

On Palm Sunday palm branches are sprinkled with holy water and blessed before they are distributed to the assembly.

© Our Sunday Visitor

36

🌐 Catholic Social Teaching

To integrate Catholic Social Teaching into your lesson, choose one of the following features: Call to Community, pages 292–293; or The Dignity of Work, pages 298–299.

- To expand the lesson, complete page 36, then move to the Catholic Social Teaching feature.
- Return to the prayer on page 37.

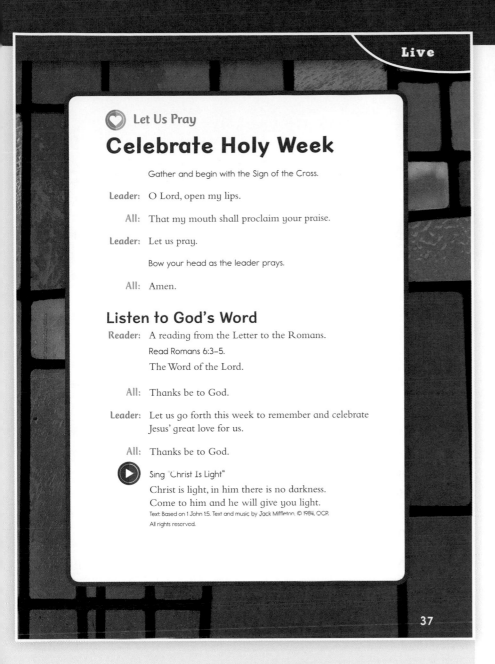

Let Us Pray

Celebrate Holy Week

Gather and begin with the Sign of the Cross.

Leader: O Lord, open my lips.

All: That my mouth shall proclaim your praise.

Leader: Let us pray.

Bow your head as the leader prays.

All: Amen.

Listen to God's Word

Reader: A reading from the Letter to the Romans.
Read Romans 6:3–5.
The Word of the Lord.

All: Thanks be to God.

Leader: Let us go forth this week to remember and celebrate Jesus' great love for us.

All: Thanks be to God.

 Sing "Christ Is Light"
Christ is light, in him there is no darkness.
Come to him and he will give you light.

37

Liturgy Link

Triduum Colors

The liturgical colors used during the Triduum are varied.

- On Holy Thursday, the priest wears white.
- Good Friday is signified with red, the color of blood and martyrdom.
- The joy of Easter is celebrated with white or gold vestments.

Let Us Pray

Celebrate Holy Week

You will be the leader.

Rehearse with the children "Christ Is Light," downloaded from **aliveinchrist.osv.com**.

Invite the children in to gather the prayer space around the Cross.

- Follow the order of prayer on the student page.

Leader's prayer: Lord, we thank you for the three holy days of Triduum. We honor your memory and your gifts to us by recalling the gift of the Eucharist, your Death on the Cross, and your glorious Resurrection. Thank you for these signs of your love for us.

Conclude by processing around the room with the children singing the hymn refrain.

Alternate Music Option: "We Remember—The Three Days"

Distribute this page to the children or parents/adult family members.

Easter: Holy, Holy, Holy

LESSON OBJECTIVES
- Appreciate Easter as a holy day
- Recognize Baptism as a source of holiness

ENVIRONMENT
Prayer table
White cloth
Bowl of holy water
Branch for sprinkling
Candle
Spring flowers

- Put the prayer table at the center of the room.
- Consider decorating the room with Easter flowers and symbols.

MUSIC OPTIONS
Go to **aliveinchrist.osv.com** to sample and download, "This Day Was Made by the Lord," "You Call Us to Live,"

CATHOLIC SOCIAL TEACHING
- **Life and Dignity** Pages 290–291
- **Solidarity of the Human Family** Pages 300–301

Catechist Background

> Your boasting is not appropriate. Do you not know that a little yeast leavens all the dough? Clear out the old yeast, so that you may become a fresh batch of dough, inasmuch as you are unleavened. For our paschal lamb, Christ, has been sacrificed. Therefore let us celebrate the feast, not with the old yeast, the yeast of malice and wickedness, but with the unleavened bread of sincerity and truth. 1 Corinthians 5:6–8
>
> ➜ **Reflect** Have you thrown out the old in preparation for the new?

Easter is the most joyful season of the liturgical year. The signs and symbols of Easter all contribute to the season's atmosphere of joyful celebration. Alleluias are sung, the Gloria returns to the liturgy, and the hymns are full of joy. Churches are decorated with lilies and other spring flowers. The prayers of the liturgy give thanks for the Risen Lord and his life among us.

One of the central motifs of the Easter season is the new life of Baptism. Through Baptism, we come to share in the life of the risen Jesus. Baptisms often take place during the Easter season, and the sprinkling rite is frequently used at the beginning of Sunday Mass in place of the Penitential Act.

The cycle of nature echoes the theme of new life that the Easter season celebrates As winter gives way to spring, however, the Earth comes to life again. During the Easter season, water, light, candles, flowers, song, and silence are used to proclaim a single message: "Jesus is risen!"

➜ **Reflect** What signs of the Resurrection do you see in the world around you?

Catechist's Prayer

Risen Jesus, let my days be filled with expressed love and gratitude for the importance of this season. Let it be first in my thoughts and you first in my life. Amen.

Holy, Holy, Holy

 Let Us Pray

Leader: Lord, God, send your Holy Spirit to guide us to right and loving actions. Through Christ, our Lord,

"Make known to me your ways, LORD; teach me your paths." **Psalm 25:4**

All: Amen.

 God's Word

Do you know that just a little yeast puffs up bread to make it high and big? Get rid of the yeast. Make yourselves like bread without yeast; Christ our Passover has been sacrificed. Let us celebrate the feast not with the old yeast of dishonesty and wickedness but with the new unleavened bread of honesty and goodness. **Based on 1 Corinthians 5:6–8**

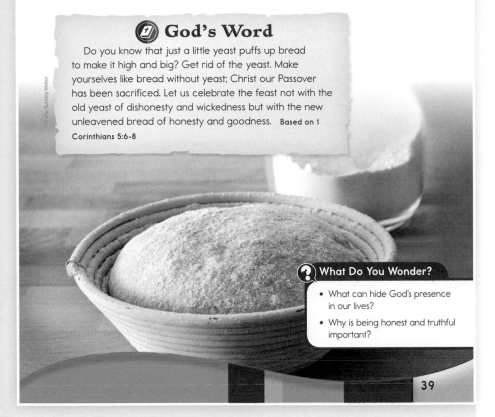

? What Do You Wonder?

- What can hide God's presence in our lives?
- Why is being honest and truthful important?

39

 Lectionary Connection

1 Corinthians 5:6–8

This reading is proclaimed on Easter Sunday.

- Saint Paul calls the Church in Corinth to change their attitudes in light of the sacrifice of Jesus Christ.
- He uses the metaphor of the unleavened bread used in the traditional Jewish Passover meal, calling on Christians to "clear out the old yeast" of sinfulness.

 Let Us Pray

Invite the children to gather in the prayer space and make the Sign of the Cross. Ask a volunteer to pray the leader's prayer and the Psalm verse. Have the children move out of the prayer space and back to their seats.

Say: The Holy Spirit gives us guidance and strength. In today's reading, Saint Paul explains that we will need this help sometimes.

 God's Word

Guide the children through the process of Scripture reflection.

- Invite them to close their eyes, be still, and open their minds and hearts to what God is saying to them in this passage.
- Proclaim the Scripture.
- Maintain several moments of silence.
- *Ask:* What did you hear God say to you today?
- Invite volunteers to share.

What Do You Wonder?

Say: In today's reading, Saint Paul talks about yeast. Sometimes yeast is good because it makes bread rise but yeast is made from bacteria. Saint Paul was suggesting that we don't always need what yeast gives us.

Invite the children to respond to the questions. Ask what else they might wonder about God's presence in our lives.

Discover

The Holiest Day

Say: Easter reminds us that we are all called in Baptism to be holy.

Have a volunteer read aloud the first paragraph.

- *Ask:* Which is the greatest feast of the year? Easter Why is it so important? Possible response: Jesus rose from the dead on Easter.

A Holy People

Ask two volunteers to read aloud the two paragraphs.

- Point out the picture of the priest sprinkling water on the people.
- Tell the children that the Rite of Sprinkling at Mass reminds us of our Baptism.

Read aloud the questions at the end of the text.

- Write the children's responses on the board or on chart paper.
- Instruct the children to underline how Jesus made people holy again.
- Allow the children time to review the text and underline the correct line.

Review with the children the information in the side column.

- *Ask:* How many days do we celebrate the Easter season? fifty days

Discover

The Holiest Day

On Easter day, the holiest day of the Church year, the Church celebrates Jesus being raised from the dead. It celebrates the everlasting life that is yours because of Jesus' Death and Resurrection. Every Sunday we celebrate a "little Easter" because that is the day Jesus rose from the dead.

A Holy People

To be holy means to be like God. God made all people to be like himself. He wants everyone to be holy. <u>By his Death, Jesus made people holy, again.</u> Through the waters of Baptism, Christians share in the life and holiness Jesus won for them.

At Easter Mass the assembly renews the promises made when they were baptized. The priest walks throughout the church and sprinkles everyone with the holy water that was blessed at the Easter Vigil.

➔ **Where is the holy water in your parish church? When do you use it?**

Easter

- During Easter, the whole Church celebrates the Resurrection of the Lord with Alleluias.
- The priest wears white vestments.
- The Church celebrates for fifty days.

Underline how Jesus made people holy again.

© Our Sunday Visitor

40

 Songs of Scripture

Mary Magdalene

Teach the children the song "Mary Magdalene."

- Ask the children to write "He lives!" on a piece of paper.
- Have them roll up the piece of paper, tight at one end and larger at the other, to make a megaphone.
- When the children sing "He lives," have them shout it into their megaphones.

▶ Use *Songs of Scripture*, Grades 1–3 CD, Track 19

Easter celebrates the Resurrection of our Lord Jesus Christ.

Living Water

During the Easter season, the assembly gathered is sprinkled with holy water. This is a reminder of the importance of Baptism. Through Baptism you share in the new life of Jesus who is risen forever.

➜ **Name some people you know who live holy lives.**

Activity

Present an Easter Play Together with your classmates, write a short play about the events of the first Easter morning. Use your own words, and wear simple costumes to act it out. Your class might like to present this as a play for a group of younger children.

Characters: _____

_____

Setting: _____

_____

Costumes and props: _____

_____

Easter **41**

© Our Sunday Visitor

Living Water

Read aloud the paragraph.

- *Ask:* Why is the assembly sprinkled with holy water? to remind us of the importance of Baptism

Have a volunteer read aloud the question.

- Invite the children to share names of people they know.
- Remind the children that everyday people can be holy.

Ask the children to silently reflect on the art at the top of the page.

- After a few moments, ask volunteers to explain what is happening.

Activity

Read aloud the directions for the activity.

- Allow the children to work in groups of three or four to write the play.
- Provide props and Bible-time costumes.
- Allow time for writing and organizing.
- Ask each small group to perform their play before the larger group.

Catholic Social Teaching

Lesson Connections

To integrate Catholic Social Teaching into your lesson, choose one of the following features: Life and Dignity, pages 290–291; or Solidarity of the Human Family, pages 300–301.

- To expand the lesson, complete page 41, then move to the Catholic Social Teaching feature.
- Return to the prayer on pages 42–43.

Celebrate Easter

 Let Us Pray

Prepare

Set up the prayer table and light the Paschal Candle.

- Prepare the environment with the Bible and other items.
- You will be the leader and reader.

> ▶ Rehearse with the children "This Day Was Made by the Lord," downloaded from **aliveinchrist.osv.com**.

Invite the children to gather in the prayer space around the prayer table.

Pray

Begin with Sign of the Cross.

Leader's prayer: All creation gathers to praise God. We rejoice because Jesus, our King and brother, has conquered death. We praise God because we are washed clean. We are not slaves to sin anymore! We pray this through Jesus, our Savior.

Sprinkling Rite

Dip the branch into the holy water and sprinkle the children. Remind them to make the Sign of the Cross and think about being a child of God.

Listen to God's Word

Have the children stand.

- Proclaim the Scripture.

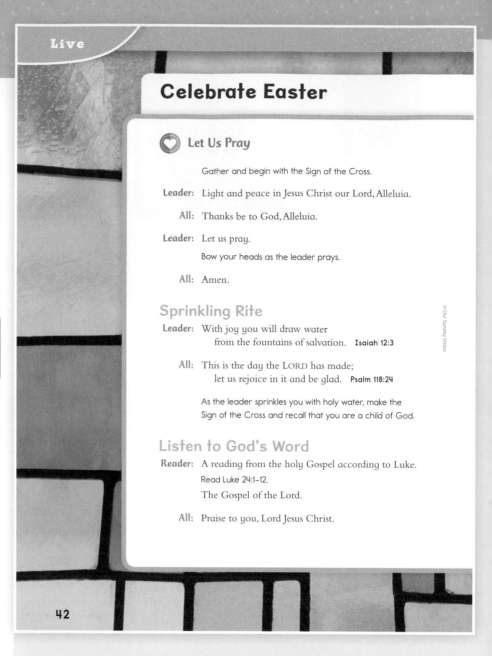

Celebrate Easter

 Let Us Pray

Gather and begin with the Sign of the Cross.

Leader: Light and peace in Jesus Christ our Lord, Alleluia.

All: Thanks be to God, Alleluia.

Leader: Let us pray.
Bow your heads as the leader prays.

All: Amen.

Sprinkling Rite

Leader: With joy you will draw water from the fountains of salvation. *Isaiah 12:3*

All: This is the day the LORD has made; let us rejoice in it and be glad. *Psalm 118:24*

As the leader sprinkles you with holy water, make the Sign of the Cross and recall that you are a child of God.

Listen to God's Word

Reader: A reading from the holy Gospel according to Luke.
Read Luke 24:1–12.
The Gospel of the Lord.

All: Praise to you, Lord Jesus Christ.

© Our Sunday Visitor

42

 Liturgy Link

Paschal Candle

Explain to the group the symbolism and usage of the Paschal Candle.

- The Paschal Candle is decorated with a cross; the year; the Greek letters alpha and omega, symbolic of the eternity of God; and five grains of incense, symbolic of Christ's wounds.
- It is used during the Easter season at all Masses. During the rest of the year it is used at Baptisms and funerals. The Paschal Candle symbolizes Resurrection.

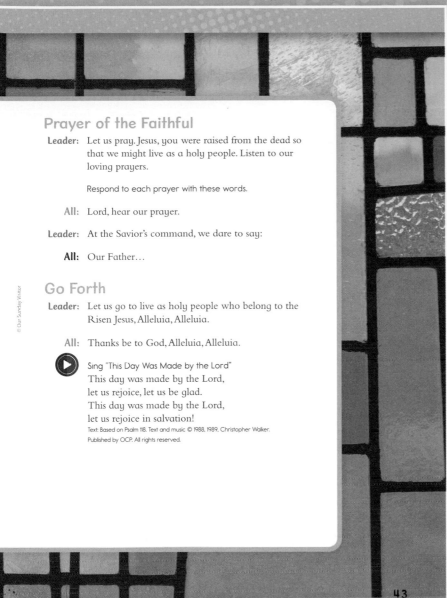

Prayer of the Faithful

Leader: Let us pray. Jesus, you were raised from the dead so that we might live as a holy people. Listen to our loving prayers.

Respond to each prayer with these words.

All: Lord, hear our prayer.

Leader: At the Savior's command, we dare to say:

All: Our Father…

Go Forth

Leader: Let us go to live as holy people who belong to the Risen Jesus, Alleluia, Alleluia.

All: Thanks be to God, Alleluia, Alleluia.

▶ Sing "This Day Was Made by the Lord"
This day was made by the Lord,
let us rejoice, let us be glad.
This day was made by the Lord,
let us rejoice in salvation!

Text: Based on Psalm 118. Text and music © 1988, 1989, Christopher Walker.
Published by OCP. All rights reserved.

43

Prayer of the Faithful

Lead the prayers:

- Help your Church live in holiness and according to your will.
- Help our parish give witness to the Easter miracle.
- Help our families share the joy of Easter.
- Help us share the light of Easter.

Follow this by leading the children in praying the Lord's Prayer.

Go Forth

▶ Conclude the celebration by inviting the children to process around the room singing "This Day Was Made by the Lord."

Distribute this page to the children or parents/adult family members.

Catechist Background

The Sprinkling Rite

The sprinkling rite is a reminder of our Baptism. Although it can take place at other times of the year, it is especially celebrated during the Sundays of Easter.

- Water is a symbol of grace, purity, and eternal life.
- Following the Lent and Holy Week, the holy water that we use in church and in our homes is blessed at the Easter Vigil.

Holy, Holy, Holy **43-44**

Easter: Pentecost

LESSON OBJECTIVES

- Explain that on the Feast of Pentecost, we ask for the coming of the Spirit
- Understand that the Holy Spirit gives us the power to share the Good News

ENVIRONMENT

Red cloth
Prayer table
Electric or battery-powered candle
Bible
Stand for the Bible
Red or yellow flowers

- Place the prayer table in a corner.
- Allow space for the children to move in the prayer area.
- Place a red cloth on the table, along with a candle, Bible (with stand), and red or yellow flowers.

 MUSIC OPTIONS
Go to **aliveinchrist.osv.com** to sample and download,
"Alle, Alle, Alleluia"
"Come to Us, Spirit of Jesus"
"Come to Us, Holy Spirit"

 CATHOLIC SOCIAL TEACHING

- **Call to Community**
  Pages 292–293
- **Option for the Poor**
  Pages 296–297

Catechist Background

"It shall come to pass I will pour out my spirit upon all flesh. Your sons and daughters will prophesy, your old men will dream dreams, your young men will see visions. Even upon your male and female servants, in those days, I will pour out my spirit." Joel 3:1–2

➔ **Reflect** How do you use your gifts?

The Easter season ends with the celebration of Pentecost. The Old Testament background for this feast can be found in the Jewish celebration of Pentecost (also called the Feast of Weeks). Initially, it was a harvest festival during which the first fruits were offered. Later this celebration marked the anniversary of the making of the covenant, fifty days after the Exodus. The Christian celebration is not a harvest of nature, but a harvest of the Holy Spirit's gifts. The new covenant that it celebrates is made with all people.

Once the followers of Jesus had received the Holy Spirit, they became fearless in proclaiming the Gospel. The story of the first Pentecost shows how people from many different places who spoke various languages were brought together to form a community.

Pentecost provides a rich array of vivid stories and images of the newborn Church. But it has also been an occasion for praising the third Divine Person of the Blessed Trinity. The Sequence for Pentecost, a hymn that is sung in the liturgy before the Gospel, is full of such praises. The Holy Spirit is called "comforter," "welcome guest," "sweet refreshment," and "solace."

➔ **Reflect** What gifts of the Holy Spirit do you believe are most needed today?

Catechist's Prayer

 Come Holy Spirit, fill our hearts with the assurance that you are present with us. Let the children in my care recognize you in me. Amen.

Invite

Pentecost

♥ Let Us Pray

Leader: Holy Spirit of the living God, send down your power so we may bring the Good News to others.

"Send forth your spirit, they are created
and you renew the face of the earth."
Psalm 104:30

All: We ask this in the name of the Lord Jesus. Amen.

✝ God's Word

"It shall come to pass
I will pour out my spirit upon all flesh.
Your sons and daughters will prophesy,
your old men will dream dreams,
your young men will see visions.
Even upon your male and female servants,
in those days, I will pour out my spirit." **Joel 3:1–2**

© Our Sunday Visitor

? What Do You Wonder?

- How does the Holy Spirit help you?
- When does God pour out the Holy Spirit on us?

45

✝ Lectionary Connection

Joel 3:1–2

Today's reading is one of the optional readings for the vigil of Pentecost.

- This passage from the book of Joel is considered a prophecy of the coming of the Holy Spirit upon the Church.
- The prophet emphasizes the pouring out of the Holy Spirit on all believers, young and old, male and female, rich and poor.

Invite

♥ Let Us Pray

Invite the children to gather in the prayer space and make the Sign of the Cross. Pray the leader's part and the Psalm verse together as a group. Prompt the group's response. Have the children move out of the prayer space and back to their seats.

Say: The Holy Spirit is powerful. Two of the symbols of the Holy Spirit, fire and wind, have the power to change things in their path. The Holy Spirit has the power to change us if we open our hearts.

✝ God's Word

Guide the children through the process of Scripture reflection.

- Invite them to close their eyes, be still, and open their minds and hearts to what God is saying to them in this passage.
- Proclaim the Scripture.
- Maintain several moments of silence.
- *Ask:* What did you hear God say to you today?
- Invite volunteers to share.

What Do You Wonder?

Say: In today's reading, we hear that when God sends his Holy Spirit, some wonderful things will happen!

Invite the children to respond to the questions. Ask what else they might wonder about how the Holy Spirit helps us.

The Holy Spirit

Say: We celebrate the Feast of Pentecost to remember that God sent his Holy Spirit on the Apostles and he continues to be with us today.

Have volunteers read aloud the paragraphs.

- Remind the children that the Holy Spirit guided the Apostles as they began their work for the Church.

- *Ask:* Why was the Holy Spirit sent to the disciples? Possible response: to help them share the Good News with others

 Ask the children to underline the Good News that Jesus shared.

- Give them time to reread and underline the appropriate text.

Invite a volunteer to read aloud the information about Pentecost in the side column.

- *Ask:* What color does the priest wear for Pentecost? red

Discover

The Holy Spirit

After Jesus returned to his Father, the disciples did not know what to do. Then, as Jesus had promised, the Holy Spirit was sent to them.

The Holy Spirit strengthened the disciples. With his help, they shared the Good News of Jesus with everyone they met.

The Good News that Jesus shared was that everyone is welcome in his Father's Kingdom. Jesus also taught that God's Kingdom is one of peace, justice, and love.

The Holy Spirit gives us the power to share the Good News of God's Kingdom with every person that we meet. On Pentecost, we pray that the Holy Spirit comes to us.

Pentecost

- The Church celebrates Pentecost fifty days after Easter.

- Pentecost celebrates the coming of the Holy Spirit upon Jesus' first disciples.

- The priest wears red vestments on Pentecost.

Underline the Good News that Jesus shared.

46 The Church Year

Songs of Scripture

Holy Spirit

Pentecost is the day we celebrate that the power of the Holy Spirit made the Apostles into one community, the Body of Christ, the Church.

- Pass out construction paper flames and have the children place the flames over their heads each time they hear the words *Holy Spirit* or *you*.

- Have the children sing together "Holy Spirit."

 Use *Songs of Scripture*, Grades 1–3 CD, Track 12

The Power of the Holy Spirit

The Feast of Pentecost celebrates the gift of the Holy Spirit to all of Christ's followers. With the Holy Spirit's guidance and strength, you can follow Christ and work to help build God's Kingdom of justice, love, and peace.

➜ **What are some ways that young people can show others how to follow Christ?**

Activity

Signs of Peace What are some signs of peace and justice in your parish, your school, your country? With a partner make a list of some of these signs. Choose one thing you can do to spread peace and love.

_____

_____

_____

_____

_____

_____

_____

Pentecost **47**

🌐 Catholic Social Teaching

To integrate Catholic Social Teaching into your lesson, choose one of the following features: Call to Community, pages 292–293; or Option for the Poor, pages 296–297.

- To expand the lesson, complete pages 46–47, then move to the Catholic Social Teaching feature.
- Return to the prayer on pages 48–49.

The Power of the Holy Spirit

Talk with the children about how they feel when they receive a gift.

- Ask a volunteer to read aloud the paragraph.
- Emphasize to the children that all of Jesus' followers share in the gift of the Holy Spirit.

Read aloud the question.

- List the children's responses on the board or on chart paper, and encourage them to act upon the ideas presented in the coming weeks.

Activity

Read aloud the directions for the activity.

- Organize the children in pairs.
- Allow time for the children to list their signs of peace and justice.
- Invite volunteers to share their lists.
- Encourage the children to follow through on their ideas for spreading peace and love.

 Music Option: Have the children sing "Come to Us, Spirit of Jesus" or "Come to Us, Holy Spirit," downloaded from **aliveinchrist.osv.com**.

Celebrate the Holy Spirit

 Let Us Pray

Prepare

Set up flowers in the prayer space.

- Prepare the environment with the candle, Bible, and other items.
- You will be the leader.

 Rehearse with the children "Come, Holy Ghost," downloaded from **aliveinchrist.osv.com**.

Invite the children to come to the prayer space.

- Have a child carrying the Bible high above his or her head lead the procession.
- Explain the celebration.

Pray

Begin with the Sign of the Cross

Leader's prayer: God the Father, by strengthening the Apostles on the first Pentecost, the Holy Spirit gave new life to the Church. Give us the same strength to continue your work. We ask this through Jesus, our Lord.

Listen to God's Word

Encourage the children to show respect and reverence for the Bible.

Proclaim the Scripture.

Live

Celebrate the Holy Spirit

Today you will pray a celebration of the Word. You will listen and think about God's Word. You will pray prayers of reverence by kneeling and bowing before the Bible.

 Let Us Pray

Gather and begin with the Sign of the Cross.

Leader: Light and peace in Jesus Christ our Lord, Alleluia.

All: Thanks be to God, Alleluia.

Leader: Let us pray.

Bow your heads as the leader prays.

All: Amen.

Listen to God's Word

Leader: Come, Holy Spirit, fill the hearts of your faithful.

All: And kindle in them the fire of your love.

Kneel as the Bible is carried to the prayer table. When the Bible is placed on its stand, take turns respectfully bowing in front of it.

Leader: A reading from the Acts of the Apostles.
Read Acts 2:1–11.
The Word of the Lord.

All: Thanks be to God.

48

ⓘ Catechist Background

Cultural Connection: European Customs

Some European countries recall the attributes of the Holy Spirit mentioned in today's reading.

- Flower petals are dropped on worshippers in Italy, symbolizing the tongues of fire that appeared at the first Pentecost.
- In France, the sound of the wind is recalled when trumpets are played during services.

Prayer of the Faithful

Leader: Let us pray. God the Holy Spirit, you fill us with your power and strength. Hear the prayers that we bring to you now.

Respond to each prayer with these words.

All: Hear our prayer, O Lord.

Leader: Let us offer praise to the Holy Trinity.

All: Glory be to the Father…

Go Forth

Leader: Let us go forth this week to share God's Word with everyone we meet.

All: Thanks be to God.

Sing "Alle, Alle, Alleluia"
Alle, alle, alleluia,
alle, alle, alleluia.
Alle, alle, alleluia.
Alle, alle, alle, alleluia.
© 1996, Fr. Richard Ho Lung, M.O.P., and Missionaries of the Poor. Published by OCP. All rights reserved.

49

Prayer of the Faithful

Lead the prayers:

- For your Church, that it may continue to follow the inspiration of the Holy Spirit, we pray to the Lord.

- For our parish, that our leaders will find guidance in the Holy Spirit, we pray to the Lord.

- For all of us, that the Holy Spirit will work in our lives to help us serve others, we pray to the Lord.

Lead the children in praying the Glory Be.

Go Forth

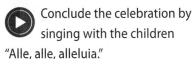 Conclude the celebration by singing with the children "Alle, alle, alleluia."

Distribute this page to the children or parents/adult family members.

♥ **Liturgy Link**

Sights and Sounds

Explain to the children what they will hear and see on Pentecost Sunday.

- On Pentecost, the joyous white of Easter gives way to brilliant red, which symbolizes the wonder and excitement of the Holy Spirit's arrival.

- A sequence is used during the Pentecost liturgy. The sequence is a type of poetic hymn that is read or sung on special feasts before the proclaiming of the Gospel.

Core
Chapters

Revelation

Our Catholic Tradition

- Creation is all things that exist, made by God from nothing. You are part of God's plan. (CCC, 315, 317)

- We can discover God's plan in his Word—Sacred Scripture and Sacred Tradition. (CCC, 289)

- Our families show us God's love and help us know his plan for us. (CCC, 2203)

- Scripture and Tradition also tell us about God's plan for his Church, the People of God. (CCC, 781)

What are some of the ways that God shows himself to us?

© Our Sunday Visitor

Unit 1 Overview

Chapter 1

The children will:

- recall that God created human beings in his image and likeness
- reflect on creation as a gift from God that shows his goodness
- understand that creation is the work of the Holy Trinity
- recognize our responsibility to care for all of creation, especially each other

 Catholic Social Teaching: Live Your Faith

- Life and Dignity, Pages 290–291
- Care for Creation, Pages 302–303

Chapter 2

The children will:

- describe the Bible as the Word of God written in human words, the holy book of the Church
- define the Church as the community of all baptized people who believe in God and follow Jesus
- recognize that the Church helps us understand God's Word, teaches us about God's love, and gathers us to honor and worship God
- realize that we can serve God and the Church by living out the Good News of Jesus

 Catholic Social Teaching: Live Your Faith

- Call to Community, Pages 292–293
- Solidarity or the Human Family, Pages 300–301

Chapter 3

The children will:

- appreciate that families teach us how to care for, respect, and help one another
- recognize the importance of Mary as the Mother of God and our Mother, too
- connect the words Elizabeth used to greet Mary with the Hail Mary
- identify the Catholic family as the domestic Church where we experience love, and learn about God and how we pray and live as Catholics

 Songs of Scripture
"Mary, O Blessed One"

 Catholic Social Teaching: Live Your Faith

- Life and Dignity, Pages 290–291
- Call to Community, Pages 292–293

Preview Unit Theme

Ask: What is the unit theme?

Confirm that the unit focus is on Revelation.

Have volunteers read aloud each of the bullets under Our Catholic Tradition.

Point out that they will learn more about these doctrinal statements as the group reviews this unit.

Ask the children to study the photos on this page. See if they can connect the images to the unit theme and/or the bullet points.

Ask: What are some of the ways that God shows himself to us?

After some discussion, explain that they will be exploring this question in the next three chapters.

KEY CONCEPT

God created everything. All creation shows God's goodness. God created humans in his image and likeness with a unique role in his creation.

DOCTRINAL CONTENT

- God created human beings in his image and likeness. (CCC, 355)
- Creation is a gift from God that shows his goodness. (CCC, 293)
- Creation is the work of the Holy Trinity. (CCC, 292)
- Humans have the responsibility to care for all of creation, especially each other. (CCC, 2415)

TASKS OF CATECHESIS

Helping children grow in a faith that is "known, celebrated, lived, and expressed in prayer" (NDC, 20).

This chapter focuses on the following tasks of catechesis:

- Promoting Knowledge of the Faith
- Moral Formation

Catchist Background

"You formed my inmost being; you knit me in my mother's womb. I praise you, because I am wonderfully made; wonderful are your works! My very self you know. My bones are not hidden from you, When I was being made in secret, fashioned in the depths of the earth." **Psalm 139:13-15**

→ **Reflect** Do you consider yourself wonderfully made?

Only God, in his infinite wisdom, could have conceived and then guided to fulfillment the magnificence of creation. With faith, one has only to hold a newborn baby or stroll on the shore by a rolling ocean wave to know, beyond the shadow of a doubt, that only an almighty God could have created the universe. Part of the mystery of creation is just how perfectly the universe is put together. God's well-ordered plan situates planets and plants, buds and bugs, stars and squirrels so that each functions according to its purpose. All creation gives honor and glory to God, yet only humans are created in his divine image. He has placed humans at the summit of creation.

Their special place in God's creation gives humans a corresponding responsibility to care for the world. People are called to care for all that God has created, including the earth itself and its natural resources. Most important of all, they are called to care for one another.

→ **Reflect** How do you show respect for creation? What has creation taught you about God?

Catechist's Prayer

God Almighty, you have made the world a place of beauty and mystery. Help me be a good steward of all your gifts. Help me always see your glory in the world around me. Amen.

Lesson Plan

Objectives	Process	Materials

Invite, 10 minutes

The Creator's Work Page 53

- **Psalm 148:5** Pray the opening prayer.
- **Psalm 139:13–15** Reflect prayerfully on the Word.
- Discuss What Do You Wonder questions.

- **Optional Activity** Chapter Poem: "A Day at the Beach"

Discover, 35 minutes

The Creation of the World Pages 54–55

- Recall that God created human beings in his image and likeness
- Reflect on creation as a gift from God that shows his goodness

- **Catholic Faith Words** creation
- Give examples of creation and what these examples show about God.
- **Genesis 1:1–23** Proclaim "The Creation of the World."
- **Share Your Faith Activity** Draw or write your favorite part of God's creation.

- ☐ pencils or pens
- ☐ colored pencils or markers
- ☐ drawing paper
- ☐ index cards, one per child
- **Optional Activity** Colorful Creation
- ☐ Activity Master 1: (Page 53E)

The Beauty of Creation Pages 56–57

- Understand that creation is the work of the Holy Trinity
- Recognize our responsibility to care for all of creation, especially each other

- **Catholic Faith Words** Holy Trinity, image of God
- Help the children see that beauty and diversity are important aspects of creation.
- ☆ Underline what you learn from God's creation.
- **Connect Your Faith Activity** Identify likenesses and differences of people in a group.

- ☐ pencils or pens
- ☐ index cards, two per child

Live, 15 minutes

Our Catholic Life Pages 58–59

- Point out that the Earth must be cared for.
- ☆ Place a check mark next to ways to care for and enjoy creation.
- **People of Faith** Learn about Saint Rabanus Maurus.
- **Live Your Faith Activity** Plan an imaginary garden.

- ☐ pencils or pens
- ☐ board or chart paper
- ☐ graph paper

Prayer of Praise Page 60

- Choose a volunteer to read the leader part.
- Follow the order of prayer.
- Sing "And It Was Good."

- Download "And It Was Good."

Family + Faith Page 61

Point out that the Catholic Families page provides chapter highlights, information on how third graders understand faith concepts, and family prayer.

Chapter Review Page 62

- **aliveinchrist.osv.com**
  - Customize and Download Assessments
  - Email Links to eAssessments
  - Interactive Student Reviews

ONLINE RESOURCES

 Go to **aliveinchrist.osv.com**

You will find:

- Interactive lesson planning with web specific content and additional activities
- Step by step lesson instruction from printed Catechist Edition for integrated lesson planning
- Custom-built assessments to download and eAssessment links
- Interactive reviews that provide scores and the option to review answers
- Sunday readings with background and questions of the week

 Go to **osvparish.com**

You will find:
- Ask the Experts Q and A
- General Catechist Helps
- Community Connections and Blogs

Sharing the Message with Third Graders

Creation Third graders enjoy being outside and are often very interested in science and nature. They understand cause and effect and are usually very curious about how things work. This is an excellent age for appreciating God's thoughtful and marvelous design and our responsibility in caring for creation.

Teaching Tip: In case they haven't yet seen it, point out the family page to the parents of the children in your group and discuss ways in which they can use it.

How Third Graders Understand

- Third graders are curious. Help them understand that differences and likenesses are from God.
- Children this age enjoy working in groups. Assign specific tasks to each group member so they will know what to do.
- As children grow and mature, they are learning to be more responsible. Allow them to make mistakes, but help them set realistic goals and limits.

"I am learning to be responsible. Help me to set realistic goals and limits."

Chapter Poem

Invite

"A Day at the Beach"

Use this poem to expand the chapter introduction.

- Tell about something beautiful that you saw earlier in the day.
- Have the children write something that they saw today in creation.
- Encourage the children to share what they wrote with the group.

 Go to **aliveinchrist.osv.com** Lesson Planning section for this poem.

NCEA IFG: ACRE Edition

Discover

Knowledge of the Faith

- Objective: To know and understand basic Catholic teaching about the Incarnate Word Jesus Christ as the way, truth, and life

Moral Formation

- Objective: To be knowledgeable about the teachings of Jesus and the Church as the basis of Christian morality and to understand Catholic Social Teaching

Catholic Social Teaching

Live

 Use one of these features to introduce a principle and engage the children with an activity.

- Life and Dignity, Pages 290–291
- Care for Creation, Pages 302–303

Music Options

 Use one or more of the following songs to enhance catechetical learning or for prayer.

- "And It Was Good," Live Prayer, Page 60
- "God Is Part of My Life," Discover, Page 54
- "The Trinity," Discover, Page 57

LECTIONARY CONNECTION

 Chapter 1 highlights Lectionary-connected themes such as creation, image of God, and Holy Trinity. If your parish aligns its curriculum to the liturgical year, you could use this chapter in connection with the following Sundays.

Year A

Seventeenth Sunday in Ordinary Time—God's Love for All

Twenty-sixth Sunday in Ordinary Time—Personal Responsibility

Year B

Eighth Sunday in Ordinary Time—Jesus as Son of God

Ninth Sunday in Ordinary Time— God as Creator

Year C

Solemnity of the Blessed Virgin Mary, Mother of God—God the Father

Second Sunday of Lent—Creation

Go to **aliveinchrist.osv.com** for a complete correlation ordered by the Sundays of the year and suggestions for how to integrate the Scripture readings into chapter lessons.

Name _____   Date _____

Colorful Creation

What are your favorite parts of creation?

- In the five large stars below, write the name of something you can find in the air or in the heavens. Color the stars yellow.

- In any three spaces where there is land on the Earth, write the names of creatures that live on land. Color the land green.

- In the remaining spaces, write the names of three creatures that live in water. Color the water blue.

If you like a challenge, try thinking of things in each group that begin with the same letter.

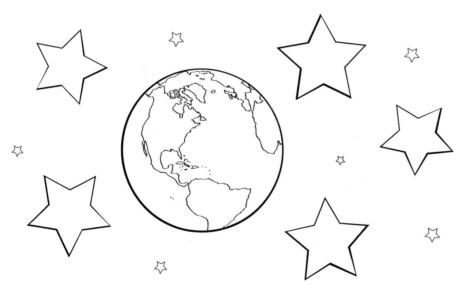

Write a thank-you prayer. Tell God how you will help care for creation.

_____

_____

_____

_____

The Creator's Work

 Let Us Pray

Leader: God, we praise you for your beautiful creation!

"Let them all praise the LORD's name;
for he commanded and they were
created." **Psalm 148:5**

All: We thank you God for the gifts of this world. Help
us to be responsible and respectful to all you have
given us. Amen.

 God's Word

You formed me. You made me in my mother's
womb. I praise you, because I am wonderfully made.
Wonderful is everything you have made. You knew
everything about me; even my bones you could
see. **Based on Psalm 139:13–15**

© Our Sunday Visitor

? What Do Your Wonder?

- If God made all people, why are we
so different?
- Is everything that God made good?

The Creator's Work **53**

Optional Activity

Chapter Poem: "A Day at the Beach" *Verbal/Linguistic*

Use this poem after the opening prayer, before discussing creation.

- Invite eight children to each read aloud one line of the poem.
- Ask the children to identify the feelings about nature that the
poem expresses. excitement, awareness of beauty
- After encouraging them to share beach experiences, transition
back to the lesson instruction.

 Go to **aliveinchrist.osv.com** for Chapter Poem.

 Invite

 Let Us Pray

Invite the children to gather in the
prayer space and make the Sign of
the Cross. Read aloud the leader's
prayer and the Psalm verse. Prompt
the children's response.

Have the children move from the
prayer space back to their seats.

Explain that God made the world
and everything in it. He created
human beings to be able to know
him and live as his friends.

Say: Let's listen to the words of
Psalm 139 to hear what God has to
say to you about how you were
created.

God's Word

Guide the children through the
process of Scripture reflection.

- Invite them to close their eyes, be
still, and open their minds and
hearts to what God is saying to
them in this passage.
- Proclaim the Scripture.
- Maintain several moments
of silence.
- *Ask:* What did you hear God say
to you today?
- Invite volunteers to share.

What Do You Wonder?

Say: You are God's special creation.
There is no one in all of the world
like you. All of creation is a gift
and has a purpose.

Invite the children to respond to the
questions. Ask what else they might
wonder about being God's special
creation.

Objectives

- Recall that God created human beings in his image and likeness
- Reflect on creation as a gift from God that shows his goodness

The Creation of the World

Ask a volunteer to read aloud the paragraph.

God's Word

Challenge the children to envision the changes described in the creation account as they listen to it.

- Proclaim the Scripture reading.

Distribute paper and colored pencils or markers to the children, and encourage them to draw pictures that show their favorite parts of creation.

Emphasize that God created the world and everything in it. The children can learn about God by looking at what he created. Remind them that God made human beings in his image and likeness.

> Music Option: Have the children sing, "God Is Part of My Life," downloaded from **aliveinchrist.osv.com**.

Discover

The Creation of the World

How was everything in creation made?

God is the Creator of all things. Everything he made has a purpose and a plan. Do you remember the story of creation from the Bible?

God's Word

The Creation of the World

On the first day, God made light. He separated the light from the darkness and called them day and night.

On the second day, God separated the sky from the water below.

On the third day, God separated the land from the water. He made plants and trees.

On the fourth day, God made the moon, the sun, and the stars and put them in the sky.

On the fifth day, God made fish and birds.

On the sixth day, God made land animals.

Then God made man and woman in his image and likeness. He blessed them and put them in charge of everything he had created. And God saw that his creation was good.

On the seventh day, God rested. **Based on Genesis 1:1—2:3**

© Our Sunday Visitor

54 Chapter 1

 Scripture Background

Genesis 2:4b–24

The Scripture passage on this page is known as the first account of creation. The second creation account is found in Genesis 2:4b–24.

- The first account tells that God created all things. The second acount emphasizes the creation of humans.
- If time permits, read aloud both accounts.
- Both versions demonstrate for the children the tenderness and generosity of our Creator.

Learning about God

In the Bible, we learn that God alone created the universe and all forms of life. God used his power to create everything that exists. You can learn about God through his **creation**. Only God can create something where nothing existed before.

Because God is good, everything that he creates is good. In the creation story, God is shown to us as the powerful Creator who sees the goodness of all that he has made. God made everything in creation to work together.

Catholic Faith Words

creation everything made by God

Share Your Faith

Think In the green circle below draw or write about your favorite thing in God's creation.

Share Talk about God's creations with your group.

55

Optional Activity

Activity Master 1: Colorful Creation

Distribute copies of the activity found on catechist page 53E.

- Tell the children that they will need to think about creation to finish this activity.
- As an alternative, you may wish to send this activity home with the children.

Learning about God

Ask the children to give examples of creation and what these examples show about God. Possible responses: water—God wants to nourish humans; sunset—God loves beauty.

Ask a volunteer to read aloud the paragraphs.

- If possible, take the children outside for the rest of the lesson.
- *Ask:* What are some signs of God's goodness that you see around you?
- Help the children generate ideas from their personal lives.

Work with Words

Give each child one index card. Have the children write the Catholic Faith Word on one side of the card and its definition on the other side.

- Keep the cards for use in a vocabulary memory game or for chapter or unit review.

Activity

Read aloud the directions for the Share Your Faith activity.

- Provide the children with colored pencils or markers for drawing or writing.
- Ask the children to gather in groups of four to share their work.

Quick Review

God created human beings in his image and likeness. Creation is a gift from God that shows his goodness.

Objectives

- Understand that creation is the work of the Holy Trinity
- Recognize our responsibility to care for all of creation, especially each other

The Beauty of Creation

Direct the children's attention to the question at the top of the page. Tell them we will learn about this as we discuss the next two pages.

Invite three volunteers to each read aloud one of the paragraphs.

- *Ask:* What does God want from all parts of creation? for us to live together in harmony and peace

- ⭐ Have the children underline things we can learn from God's creation.

- Discuss the illustration with the children. Have them describe what they see.

- Ask the question at the bottom of the page. Encourage the children to share with the group.

Work with Words

Have the children locate the highlighted words. Read aloud the definition for *Holy Trinity* from page 57.

- To reinforce the definition and to read more about The Holy Trinity, have the children turn to page 304 of the Our Catholic Tradition section in the back of the Student Book.

The Beauty of Creation

What is the purpose of God's creation?

The **Holy Trinity**—God the Father, God the Son, and God the Holy Spirit—worked as one to create the world. The Holy Trinity continues to care for and support creation. Everything God created is good and can tell you something about the love of the Trinity. You can come to know God through the beauty of creation. You can learn the truth of his goodness.

Everything in God's creation has a purpose. God wants all parts of his creation to live together in harmony and peace.

God's creation includes whales and hummingbirds, lightning and wind, sunshine and rain, and people of every color. These differences make God's world more beautiful and teach us about his greatness.

➔ What are some things you see every day that are part of God's creation?

> Underline the things you can learn from God's creation.

© Our Sunday Visitor

56

Optional Activity

Creation Quilt *Visual/Spatial*

Distribute to each child a six- or eight-inch square of white or light-colored cloth.

- Have each child use fabric markers to draw his or her favorite part of creation on the cloth.
- Sew the pieces together in quilt form.
- Display the creation quilt for everyone to see.
- You could also create something similar with paper and tape.

The Image of God

God created humans in his own image and likeness and asked them to care for all creation. God wants you to live in his friendship and to be happy with him. You have a responsibility to show respect and love for God's creation. You are made in the **image of God**.

There is also sin in the world, and because of this, God's creation sometimes gets out of balance. God relies on humans to help bring back the harmony and peacefulness that he put into his creation.

Responsible to One Another

Your most important responsibility in caring for creation is to the human community. Humans are the most blessed of all God's creatures. God wants you to show respect and love for all people because he created us in his own image. In God's community of love, everyone is your brother or sister. In your unity, you can be a sign of God's goodness and love.

Catholic Faith Words

Holy Trinity the one God in three Divine Persons—God the Father, God the Son, and God the Holy Spirit

image of God the likeness of God that is in all human beings because we are created by him

Connect Your Faith

Show Your Uniqueness Work in groups of four. Next to each fingerprint, write one way that each of you are similar and one way that you are different from one another.

 We are similar because _____

_____.

 We are different because _____

_____.

The Creator's Work **57**

Explore Creation

Children should enjoy learning about all God has created. Emphasize that created beings come in many different sizes and shapes.

- Talk about small creatures, including ants, flies, ladybugs, and gnats.
- Discuss animals and plants that are not native to your city, state, or country and encourage the children to research one.

The Image of God

Ask a volunteer to read aloud the two paragraphs. Ask the children to place their finger on the highlighted words.

- Read aloud the definition for *image of God*.

Responsible to One Another

Read aloud the paragraph.

- Help the children see that beauty and diversity are important aspects of creation. All people deserve respect because we are created in God's image.

▶ Music Option: Have the children sing "The Trinity," downloaded from **aliveinchrist.osv.com**.

Work with Words

Give each child two index cards. Have the children write the vocabulary word on one side of the card and the definition on the other side.

- Encourage the children to use the cards to prepare for chapter and unit reviews.

Activity

- Read aloud the directions.
- Arrange the children to work in groups of four.

Quick Review

- The Holy Trinity worked as one to create the world. We, as a community, are responsible for caring for all of creation, especially each other.

Our Catholic Life

Read aloud the question.

- Point out that the Earth must be cared for, just as people care for the gifts they receive from friends and family members.

Read aloud the paragraph.

- *Ask:* Why is it important to respect the Earth? It gives us food and materials we need to live. It is God's creation and when we care for it, we show we are thankful.

- List all responses on the board or on chart paper.

Enjoy and Care for Creation

Allow volunteers to read aloud the two sections of the chart.

 Instruct the children to place a check mark next to the things they do already, and place an X next to one thing they can try to do this week.

- Ask the children to share some of their answers with the group.

- Help them determine a plan for caring for creation in the future.

Live

Our Catholic Life

How can you show you care for all of God's creation?

God put everything we need here on Earth. The Earth gives us food. It also supplies us with materials for our clothing and our homes. God gave us all of creation to use and enjoy. When we show care for God's creation we are showing respect for other people and for the Earth.

© Our Sunday Visitor

Place a check mark next to the things you do already. Place an X next to one thing you can try to do this week.

Enjoy and Care for Creation

Enjoy Creation

☐ Give the flowers from the Earth as gifts.

☐ Use fruits and vegetables for food.

☐ Play sports on the grass or watch beautiful sunsets.

Care for Creation

☐ Respect other people and care for animals.

☐ Respect the Earth by putting trash in its proper place and recyclable items in recycle bins.

☐ Make a commitment not to waste food or things you use every day.

ⓘ Catechist Background

Creation

This chapter has been all about God's creation. Yet, all around us, we see items made by human hands.

- Remind the children that everything we make comes from things that God created. And many of these things are still further enhanced by God's creation.

- For example, from the outside of a church, the stained-glass windows appear dark. But once you enter the church, God's gift of sunlight illuminates the windows, creating beautiful and colorful images.

People of Faith

Saint Rabanus Maurus, 780–856

February 4

Saint Rabanus Maurus was a German monk and teacher. He lived a very long time ago. He was one of the smartest men of his time. He studied many different things. He opened a special school to help other people learn, too. He wrote many books. One was about the whole universe. Another book helped people figure out the date for Easter. Saint Rabanus wanted us to know God better by learning about the things God created. You can see some of his books in the Vatican library.

Discuss: How can you know God better by learning about the things God created?

 Learn more about Saint Rabanus at **aliveinchrist.osv.com**

Make a Garden One of the best places to use and enjoy God's creation is in a garden. Imagine that you are planting a garden of your own. Write down your plans.

Things I need to start: _____

_____

What I'm going to plant: _____

_____

I'll care for this garden by: _____

_____

How is caring for creation a way to honor God?

_____

_____

The Creator's Work **59**

People of Faith

Tell the children about Saint Rabanus Maurus

- He was a German monk and teacher who cared very much for the poor.
- He loved to study and write comments on books, especially the Bible.
- Have a proficient reader read aloud the paragraph.
- Discuss the question with the children.

 Encourage the children to go to **aliveinchrist.osv.com** at home to learn more about Saint Rabanus Maurus.

Activity

Read aloud the directions for the Live Your Faith activity.

- If possible, supply the children with graph paper so that they can design their written plans.
- Ask for volunteers to share their answers. Encourage the rest of the group to add to their answers if they hear about a tool they forgot or a plant they'd like to add to their imaginary garden.
- Discuss how caring for creation is a way to honor God.

Catholic Social Teaching

Chapter Connections

To integrate Catholic Social Teaching into your lesson, choose one of the following features: Life and Dignity, pages 290–291; or Care for Creation, pages 302–303.

- Start the Live step of the process by talking about Saint Rabanus Maurus on page 59. Then move directly to the Catholic Social Teaching feature.
- Or, to expand the lesson, complete both pages 58 and 59, then move to the Catholic Social Teaching feature.
- Return to Chapter 1 for the prayer on page 60.

The Creator's Work **59**

Let Us Pray

Prayer of Praise

Explain that this prayer is to praise God for his creation.

Prepare

Choose a volunteer to read the leader part. Practice the part with the leader.

> ▶ Rehearse "And It Was Good," downloaded from **aliveinchrist.osv.com**.

Gather

Invite the children to come to the prayer space with their books.

- Lead the children into the prayer space while playing or singing "And It Was Good."

Pray

Follow the order of prayer on the student page.

Leader's concluding prayer (share this prayer with the leader or read it yourself): God our Father, we thank you for your gift of creation. Help us honor your creation and respect all people.

> ▶ Conclude by processing around the room with the children, singing "And It Was Good."

Live

 Let Us Pray

Prayer of Praise

Gather and begin with the Sign of the Cross.

Leader: Loving God, help us appreciate the marvelous gift of this world that you have created.

All: We thank you, God, for the gift of creation.

Leader: You made each of us wonderfully special.

All: We thank you, God, for the gift of creation.

Leader: Dear God, help us love your creation.

All: Amen.

Leader: Let us pray.

Bow your heads as the leader prays.

All: Amen.

 Sing "And It Was Good"
And it was good, good, very, very good,
and it was good, good, very, very good,
and it was good, good, very, very good,
it was very, very, very good.
Text and music: Jack Miffleton. © 1990.
OCP. All rights reserved.

Liturgy Link

Include Visuals

For any prayer celebration, you can reinforce the theme by adding visuals in the prayer space.

- For this prayer, have the children help you gather some symbols of God's creation. You might include flowers, leafy branches, seasonal fruits, or even goldfish in a bowl.

- Have the children look to the visuals and to one another as they thank God for his gift of creation.

> Go to **aliveinchrist.osv.com** for Sunday readings, Scripture background, questions of the week, and seasonal resources.

FAMILY+FAITH
LIVING AND LEARNING TOGETHER

YOUR CHILD LEARNED >>>
This chapter explains how the Holy Trinity — God the Father, God the Son, and God the Holy Spirit—worked as one to create the world.

God's Word
 Read **Psalm 139:13–15** to find out how each one of us is special to God.

Catholics Believe
- God created everything. All creation shows God's goodness.
- God created humans in his image and likeness with a unique role in his creation.

To learn more, go to the *Catechism of the Catholic Church* #339, 358 at **usccb.org**.

People of Faith
This week, your child met Saint Rabanus Maurus, a German monk and prototype scientist. He understood that we know God better when we learn about the things God created.

CHILDREN AT THIS AGE >>>
How They Understand Creation Third-graders enjoy being outside and are often very interested in science and nature. They understand cause and effect and are usually very curious about how things work. This is an excellent age for appreciating God's thoughtful and marvelous design and our responsibility in caring for creation.

CONSIDER THIS >>>
How much does an artist reveal about himself in his work?

Whether it is Michelangelo or your third grader, what a person creates is an extension of him or herself. Human beings are God's creation. "God's image is not a static picture stamped on our souls. God's image is a dynamic source of inner spiritual energy drawing our minds and hearts toward truth and love, and to God himself, the source of all truth and love" (USCCA, p. 67).

LET'S TALK >>>
- Ask your child to name some signs of God's goodness that he or she sees around them.
- Talk about the different ways you can care for God's creation as a family.

LET'S PRAY >>>
 Dear God, Saint Rabanus Maurus said we know you better when we learn about the things you created. We thank you for creating the plants and animals and each one of us. Amen.

 For a multimedia glossary of Catholic Faith Words, Sunday readings, seasonal and Saint resources, and chapter activities go to **aliveinchrist.osv.com**.

Chapter 1 Review

A **Work with Words** Fill in the circle beside the correct answer.

1. To _____ means to make something from nothing.
- ○ pray
- ○ love
- ● create

2. God has given all people _____ to care for creation.
- ● responsibility
- ○ money
- ○ permission

3. The three Divine Persons in one God is called the _____
- ○ Holy Church
- ○ Holy Spirit
- ● Holy Trinity

4. All creation is _____
- ● good
- ○ bad
- ○ old

5. Only _____ are created in the image of God.
- ○ animals
- ○ birds
- ● humans

B **Check Understanding** Write a brief response to each question.

6. What did God create? __everything__

7. Who can make something from nothing?

__God__

8. How can you show that you care for creation?

__take care of it__

9. What causes God's creation to be out of balance?

__Sin__

10. Who can help bring creation back into harmony?

__humans__

 Go to **aliveinchrist.osv.com** for an interactive review.

Family + Faith

Distribute the page to the children or parents/adult family members. Point out the chapter highlights, insights on how third graders understand concepts, the opportunity for the adults to reflect on their own experience and faith journey, and the family prayer.

Chapter Review

Use Catechist Quick Reviews to highlight lesson concepts.

A **Work with Words**
Explain to the children that they will be filling in the circle beside the correct answer.

B **Check Understanding**
Tell the children to write a brief answer to each question.

Go to **aliveinchrist.osv.com** to prepare customized and downloadable assessments, send eAssessments, and assign interactive reviews.

God's Beautiful World   **61–62**

KEY CONCEPT

The Bible is the Word of God written in human words. The Church is the community of all baptized people who believe in God and follow Jesus.

DOCTRINAL CONTENT

- The Bible is the Word of God written in human words. It is the holy book of the Church. (CCC, 105–106)

- The Church is the community of all baptized people who believe in God and follow Jesus. (CCC, 1213)

- The Church helps us understand God's Word, teaches us about God's love, and gathers us to honor and worship God. (CCC, 2030)

- We can serve God and the Church by living out the Good News of Jesus. (CCC, 942, 1816)

TASKS OF CATECHESIS

Helping children grow in a faith that is "known, celebrated, lived, and expressed in prayer" (NDC, 20).

This chapter focuses on the following tasks of catechesis:

- Promoting Knowledge of the Faith

- Education for Community Life

Catechist Background

"I pray not only for them, but also for those who will believe in me through their word, so that they may all be one, as you, Father, are in me and I in you, that they also may be in us, that the world may believe that you sent me." **John 17:20–21**

➜ **Reflect** Do your words reflect your belief?

The word *church* comes from a word meaning "a gathering of people called by God." From the beginning, God has called humans to share in his life. With the passage of time, he has formed a people who know him, believe in him, and follow his plan. Preparation for the Church began when he called the Israelites to be his People. Jesus initiated the Church and established the Reign of God. The Church is called to continue the saving work of Jesus by bringing all people into communion with God.

The word *church* has other meanings as well. It refers to the Eucharistic assembly. In its largest sense, the Church means the universal Church throughout the world.

God did not create humans to live alone. He gives humans families to nurture them and communities in which they can live and work. The Church is a special kind of community. Christians provide one another with strength and hope and help further the Reign of God on Earth. The Church community shares in God's life and plan of salvation.

➜ **Reflect** As part of the Church community, what is your responsibility for carrying on the work of Jesus?

Catechist's Prayer

Loving God, thank you for giving me the Church community to help me in my task of guiding these children. May they grow in this faithful community. Amen.

Lesson Plan

Objectives	Process	Materials

🕐 Invite, 10 minutes

The Church Gathered Page 63

- 💗 **Psalm 84:5** Pray the opening prayer.
- 📖 **John 17:20–23** Reflect prayerfully on the Word.
- Discuss What Do You Wonder questions.

🌐 **Optional Activity**
Chapter Story:
"Here's the Church"

🕐 Discover, 35 minutes

Serving the Community
Pages 64–65

- Describe the Bible as the Word of God written in human words, the holy book of the Church
- Define the Church as the community of all baptized people who believe in God and follow Jesus

- **Catholic Faith Words** Bible
- Explain that it is important for the Church community to work together to solve problems.
- 📖 **Acts 2:42–47** Proclaim: "Helping One Another."
- ⭐ Underline ways Brother André helped.
- **Share Your Faith Activity** Write about having trouble sharing with family or friends.

☐ pencils or pens
☐ board or chart paper
☐ index cards, one per child

- **Optional Activity**
Communities in Action
☐ Activity Master 2 (Page 63E)

God's People Pages 66–67

- Recognize that the Church helps us understand God's Word, teaches us about God's love, and gathers us to honor and worship God
- Realize that we can serve God and the Church by living out the Good News of Jesus

- **Catholic Faith Words** Church, Sacred Tradition
- Discuss how God wants humans to live and work together in communities.
- ⭐ Underline how being part of a community can be of help.
- **Connect Your Faith Activity** Draw how some people honor God and help others.

☐ pencils or pens
☐ crayons, colored pencils, or markers
☐ board or chart paper
☐ index cards, two per child

🕐 Live, 15 minutes

Our Catholic Life Pages 68–69

- Talk about who is called to serve the Church.
- ⭐ Write examples of how to live the Good News.
- Share current parish community projects.
- **People of Faith** Learn about Saint Francis of Assisi.
- **Live Your Faith Activity** List ways young people can do God's work.

☐ pencils or pens

Prayer of Thanksgiving Page 70

- Select six readers.
- ▶ Rehearse "We Come Today."
- Follow the order of prayer.

🌐 Download "We Come Today."

Family + Faith Page 71
Point out that the Catholic Families page provides chapter highlights, information on how third graders understand faith concepts, and family prayer.

Chapter Review Page 72
 aliveinchrist.osv.com
- Customize and Download Assessments
- Email Links to eAssessments
- Interactive Student Reviews

ONLINE RESOURCES

 Go to **aliveinchrist.osv.com**

You will find:

- Interactive lesson planning with web specific content and additional activities
- Step by step lesson instruction from printed Catechist Edition for integrated lesson planning
- Custom-built assessments to download and eAssessment links
- Interactive reviews that provide scores and the option to review answers
- Sunday readings with background and questions of the week

 Go to **osvparish.com**

You will find:

- Ask the Experts Q and A
- General Catechist Helps
- Community Connections and Blogs

Sharing the Message with Third Graders

The Church Community Third grade is an age when the social group often becomes important to children. They want to know that they belong and have friends. This is the perfect age to talk about the Church as our community of faith. It's especially important that they have time to spend with peers at church and are able to form friendships in their parish community.

Teaching Tip: Allow for a few minutes each session for children to talk with one another. This can be accomplished through more open-ended activities in which kids are able to socialize as they work.

How Third Graders Understand

- Third graders like to know the reason for doing things. Tell them why things are done at Mass so they can participate fully.
- Children this age want to be helpful. Assign simple tasks so that they will feel they are a part of the group.
- Young people need to feel and show respect. Give them ways to become successful community builders.

"I enjoy being part of the group. Assign tasks, like reading aloud, that allow me to actively participate."

Chapter Connections

Chapter Story

Invite

"Here's the Church"

Use this story to expand the chapter introduction.

- Take the children to the church and allow them to look around. Remind them to behave in a respectful manner while in the church.
- Open a discussion about who we see in the church and how they are different and alike.
- Write the children's responses on the board or on chart paper under alike and different.

 Go to **aliveinchrist.osv.com** Lesson Planning section for this story.

NCEA IFG: ACRE Edition

Discover

Knowledge of the Faith

- Objective: To know and understand basic Catholic teaching about the Incarnate Word Jesus Christ as the way, truth, and life

Communal Life

- Objectives: To know the origin, mission, structure, and communal nature of the Church; to know the rights and responsibilities of the Christian faithful

Catholic Social Teaching

Live

 Use one of these features to introduce a principle and engage the children with an activity.

- Call to Community, Pages 292–293
- Solidarity of the Human Family, Pages 300–301

Music Options

 Use one or more of the following songs to enhance catechetical learning or for prayer.

- "We Come Today," Live Prayer, Page 70
- "Jesus Is the Word," Discover, Page 64
- "Jesus Is with Us Today," Discover, Page 66

LECTIONARY CONNECTION

 Chapter 2 highlights Lectionary-connected themes such as the Bible, Church, and Sacred Tradition. If your parish aligns its curriculum to the liturgical year, you could use this chapter in connection with the following readings.

Year A

Second Sunday of Easter— Communal Life

Fifteenth Sunday in Ordinary Time—Triumph of God's Word

Year B

Fourth Sunday of Advent—Service

Fifth Sunday of Lent—Word of God

Year C

Ash Wednesday—Word of God

Easter Sunday of the Resurrection of the Lord—Word of God

 Go to **aliveinchrist.osv.com** for a complete correlation ordered by the Sundays of the year and suggestions for how to integrate the Scripture readings into chapter lessons.

Name _____ Date _____

Communities in Action

Below are pictures of communities of people that are cooperating.
Choose your favorite, and write or tell a story about it.

_____

_____

_____

_____

The Church Gathered

 Let Us Pray

Leader: Lord, we want to live in your presence.

"Blessed are those who dwell in your house!
They never cease to praise you." **Psalm 84:5**

All: Make us your house, O God. We are your people gathered in Jesus' name. Open our hearts to the Holy Spirit who makes us one. Amen.

God's Word

"I pray not only for them, but also for those who will believe in me through their word." I pray that everyone who believes in me may be one like I am one with you Father, so that the world will believe you sent me. **Based on John 17:20–23**

? What Do You Wonder?
- How can we be one with people all over the world?
- How can you spread the Good News of Jesus?

63

© Our Sunday Visitor

Optional Activity

Chapter Story: "Here's the Church" *Verbal/Linguistic*

Use this story after the opening prayer, before you tell the children that Jesus called people to follow him.

- Read aloud "Here's the Church." Help the children recall this rhyme and its actions, or teach the actions to the group.
- After discussing why your parish is blessed to have many types of people as members, transition back to the lesson instruction.

 Go to **aliveinchrist.osv.com** for Chapter Story.

Invite

Let Us Pray

Invite the children to gather in the prayer space and make the Sign of the Cross. Read aloud the leader's prayer; have a volunteer proclaim the Psalm verse. Prompt the children's response.

Have the children move from the prayer space back to their seats.

Say: Jesus called people to follow him. The disciples were people who said "Yes" to Jesus. They became a community of believers. Let's listen to some words that Jesus shared with his disciples.

God's Word

Guide the children through the process of Scripture reflection.

- Invite them to close their eyes, be still, and open their minds and hearts to what God is saying to them in this passage.
- Proclaim the Scripture.
- Maintain several moments of silence.
- *Ask:* What did you hear God say to you today?
- Invite volunteers to share.

What Do You Wonder?

Say: Jesus wants us to be one community, one Church. If we say "Yes" to Jesus like his first disciples, we can work together to spread the Good News.

Invite the children to respond to the questions. Ask what else they might wonder about the Church.

Objectives

- Describe the Bible as the Word of God written in human words, the holy book of the Church
- Define the Church as the community of all baptized people who believe in God and follow Jesus

Serving the Community

Ask a volunteer to read aloud the question.

- Write the children's responses on the board or on chart paper.

Read aloud the first paragraph.

- Explain that it is important for the Church community to work together to solve problems.

 Music Option: Have the children sing, "Jesus Is the Word," downloaded from **aliveinchrist.osv.com**.

Saint André Bessette

Choose three volunteers to each read aloud one of the paragraphs.

- *Ask:* Why did they have to build another building for Saint André? for all of the visitors who wanted to talk and pray with him
- Ask the children to underline the ways that Brother André helped his community.
- Give the children time to reread the text and find the correct answer.

 Underline the ways that Brother André helped his community?

Serving the Community

Where do you learn about God?

We live in communities. Life together gives us opportunities to serve one another. Here is a story about a Saint who helped his community.

Saint André Bessette

Saint André belonged to the Order of the Holy Cross. His parents died when he was young, so he did not have much schooling. The job he could do best was answering the door at a Catholic college in Canada.

Many people visited the college looking for help. Brother André helped them get what they needed. Some of the people were sick. He prayed with them and invited them to pray to Saint Joseph. Some of the people he prayed with were cured. Brother André said that God had cured them.

So many people visited Brother André to ask for his prayers that the college had to build a separate building for all of the visitors! After helping at the college, he would go out into Montreal to find more people to help. Brother Andre spread God's love through his life, work, and prayer.

64

ⓘ Catechist Background

Saint André Bessette (1845–1937)

Saint André rose from humble beginnings to be a Saint.

- He was known for his great devotion to Saint Joseph, referring to himself as "Saint Joseph's little dog."
- Saint André was so beloved that more than a million people filed past his coffin.
- Through his efforts, Saint Joseph's Oratory in Montreal was built. Today, the Oratory attracts more than two million visitors each year.

The early Christians gathered in house churches, catacombs, and other hidden spots to pray and break bread in Jesus' name.

God Teaches You

The **Bible** story below tells us how the first followers of Jesus prayed, lived, and worked.

© Our Sunday Visitor

 God's Word

Helping One Another

After the Holy Spirit came, Jesus' followers met often to learn from the Apostles, to break bread together, and to pray. Some members of the group sold what they had and gave the money to help the others. Many early Christians shared their belongings with those who were in need. These followers of Jesus were very happy, and new members joined every day. **Based on Acts 2:42–47**

➔ Why did Jesus' followers share their belongings?

Share Your Faith

Think Write about a time when you've had trouble sharing with a friend or family member.

_____

_____

Share With a partner, talk about how it can sometimes be difficult to share.

Catholic Faith Words

Bible the Word of God written in human words. The Bible is the holy book of the Church.

 Scripture Background

Acts 2:42–47

This passage from the Acts of the Apostles describes the lives of early Christians, but it is similar to today's Church.

- The Church is formed by its celebrations of Eucharist, from which flow the other signs of Christian life: the teachings of the Apostles, communal life, prayers, and generosity.
- Equally important is the spirit of joy shown by being one in mind and heart.

God Teaches You

Read the opening paragraph.

 God's Word

Proclaim the Scripture story.

- *Ask:* So, what did Jesus' followers do?
- Write the children's responses on the board or on chart paper. They met often, learned from the Apostles, broke bread, prayed, gave money to help others, and shared their belongs with those in need.
- Ask the question following the Scripture passage and discuss as a group.

Work with Words

Have the children find the highlighted Catholic Faith Word, *Bible*.

- Ask a volunteer to read aloud the definition.
- Have the children make a vocabulary card that they can use to prepare for chapter and unit reviews.

Read aloud the directions.

- Allow the children time to write.
- Encourage them to pair up and share what they wrote.

Quick Review

The Church, as the community of all baptized people who follow Jesus, believes that the Bible is holy and that it is the Word of God.

Discover

Objectives

- Recognize that the Church helps us understand God's Word, teaches us about God's love, and gathers us to honor and worship God
- Realize that we can serve God and the Church by living out the Good News of Jesus

God's People

Ask: Why is being part of the Church community so important?

- Write the children's responses on the board or on chart paper.
- Tell the children that you will come back to the question after they have covered the text.

Have three volunteers each read aloud one of the paragraphs.

- *Ask:* What is the name for a group of people who come together for a shared purpose? community

 Music Option: Have the children sing, "Jesus Is with Us Today," downloaded from **aliveinchrist.osv.com**.

- Point out that Jesus is with us today in the Church community.

- Ask the children to think again about the question at the top of the page, then have them underline the way that being a part of a community can help them.
- Remind the children that the Church is a special community that God calls us to join.

God's People

Why is being part of the Church community so important?

Underline the way that being part of a community can help you.

The early Christians learned about God from Jesus and from his Apostles. God wants all people to love one another and work together like the early Christians did.

When people come together for a shared purpose, the group they form is called a community. God created you to be part of a community. <u>A community can help you learn things about God that you might never know if you were learning on your own.</u>

You feel God's love and share his life in the Church. The **Church** is the community of all baptized people who believe in God and follow Jesus. The word Church is often used for the Catholic Church because we trace our origins back to the Apostles. Jesus showed all people his Father's love, and he sent the Holy Spirit to guide the Church.

The Church community helps us learn more about God and grow in our faith.

66

(i) Catechist Background

A Spirit of Welcome

In *Welcoming the Strangers Among Us,* the U.S. Conference of Catholic Bishops called Catholic parishes to welcome people of diverse backgrounds with graciousness and concern. Children should be encouraged to do the following.

- Volunteer to assist with greeting people as they enter the church.
- Have an adult with them when they act as greeters.
- Smile and give a special greeting to newcomers to the parish.

Gathered in Jesus' Name

The word *church* comes from two different words. One word means "a community called together." The other word means "belonging to the Lord." These meanings tell you that the Church is different from other communities. Through Baptism, God calls you to be part of this special community gathered in Jesus' name.

As a member of the Catholic Church, you have some very important work to do. Church members gather together to honor and worship God and to help other people. We listen to the teachings of the Church, which came from the Apostles and have been passed down to us by the bishops through **Sacred Tradition**. The Church helps us understand the Bible and the message of Jesus. She teaches us about God and his love.

Catholic Faith Words

Church the community of all baptized people who believe in God and follow Jesus. The word is often used for the Catholic Church because we trace our origins back to the Apostles.

Sacred Tradition God's Word handed down verbally through the Apostles and bishops

Connect Your Faith

God's Work Draw one way some people in your parish honor God and help others.

The Church Gathered **67**

✓ Quick Tip

Start Small

Children may think of the Church's work as being something that they are too young or inexperienced to do. Help them realize that small things done well can serve God and others.

- Point out that children are already doing many of the things listed in the text.
- Reinforce that children who learn with small jobs can handle more responsibility as they grow.

Gathered in Jesus' Name

Ask two volunteers to read aloud the two paragraphs.

Ask: How can someone your age serve the Church?

- Encourage the children to give specific examples.
- Write their answers on the board or on chart paper.
- Encourage them to find ways to practice these things in their parish Church.

Work with Words

Have the children find the highlighted Catholic Faith Words, *Church* and *Sacred Tradition*, on pages 66 and 67.

- Ask two volunteers to each read aloud one of the definitions.
- Give each child two index cards. Have the children make vocabulary cards for each term.
- Keep the cards for use in a vocabulary memory game or to prepare for the unit review.

Activity

Read aloud the directions.

- Provide the children with crayons, colored pencils, or markers.
- Allow the children to share their drawings with the group.

Quick Review

The Church helps us, teaches us, and gathers us. We can serve God and the Church by living out the Good News of Jesus.

Live

Our Catholic Life

Have a volunteer read aloud the question at the top of the student page.

- Ask the group to share their thoughts.

Read aloud the first paragraph.

- Ask the children if they are aware of or involved in any current parish projects. Encourage them to share.

- Ahead of time, gather together information on parish projects that you can share with the group.

- Ask one of the children to read the next paragraph.

- *Say:* Let's explore some ways to do this by reviewing the chart.

Live the Good News

Read aloud the chart heading and allow several volunteers to read the examples.

⭐ Ask the children to write some examples of how they can live the Good News.

- Let the children work in pairs.

- Ask volunteers to share what they wrote.

- To read a little more about the Church, have the children turn to page 305 in the Our Catholic Tradition section in the back of the Student Book. Go over both sections—"The Church" and "Body of Christ."

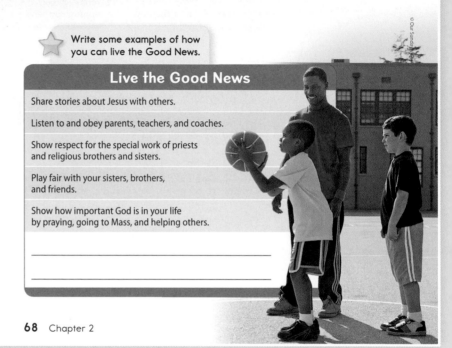

Our Catholic Life

Who is called to serve the Church?

Members of the Church are called together to do God's work on Earth. Each person has a special role in the Church community. You are not too young to help your Church community. Many parishes have projects that people your age can work on. Some projects go on all year. Other projects may be finished in a shorter time.

You can also serve God and the Church by living out the Good News of Jesus. You can do this in many ways.

⭐ Write some examples of how you can live the Good News.

Live the Good News

Share stories about Jesus with others.

Listen to and obey parents, teachers, and coaches.

Show respect for the special work of priests and religious brothers and sisters.

Play fair with your sisters, brothers, and friends.

Show how important God is in your life by praying, going to Mass, and helping others.

_____

_____

68 Chapter 2

Optional Activity

Activity Master 2: Communities in Action

Distribute copies of the activity found on catechist page 63E.

- Tell the children that they will write or tell a story about people who are cooperating.

- As an alternative, you may wish to send this activity home with the children.

People of Faith

Saint Francis of Assisi, 1182–1226

October 4

Saint Francis was the son of a man who sold beautiful cloth. His father wanted Francis to work with him, but Francis wanted to tell people about Jesus. One day while he was praying, Jesus asked him to rebuild the Church. Francis knew that God was calling him to do this special work. Soon other people came to help Francis. He helped people see the beauty of the world. He preached the Good News of Jesus. He helped make the Church more holy. He lived a simple life and was kind to all creatures.

Discuss: How can you be kind to all of God's creatures?

 Learn more about Saint Francis at **aliveinchrist.osv.com**

Live Your Faith

Write a Story List four ways that people do God's work every day. Choose one way from the list and write about a person your age who does this.

1. _____
2. _____
3. _____
4. _____
_____
_____
_____
_____
_____
_____

The Church Gathered **69**

People of Faith

Tell the children about Saint Francis of Assisi.

- Francis had a special gift of sympathy—for people, animals, and all of nature.
- He was extremely honest, and wanted people to see him as God could see him.
- He believed in the circle of life and that we are all God's creatures.

Read aloud the paragraph on Saint Francis.

- Discuss the question with the children.

 Encourage the children to go to **aliveinchrist.osv.com** at home to learn more about Saint Francis of Assisi.

Activity

Read aloud the directions for the Live Your Faith activity.

- The children will be making a list and then writing about a young person. Allow time for them to think, plan, and write.
- Ask for volunteers to share their answers, if they are comfortable doing so.

Catholic Social Teaching

Catholic Social Teaching

To integrate Catholic Social Teaching into your lesson, choose one of the following features: Call to Community, pages 292–293; or Solidarity of the Human Family, pages 300–301.

- Start the Live step of the process by talking about Saint Francis on page 69. Then move directly to the Catholic Social Teaching feature.
- Or, to expand the lesson, complete both pages 68 and 69, then move to the Catholic Social Teaching feature.
- Return to Chapter 2 for the prayer on page 70.

Live

 Let Us Pray

Prayer of Thanksgiving

Explain that this prayer is a prayer of thanks for the Church.

Prepare

Select six readers and allow them to practice their parts. You will be the leader.

 Rehearse with the children "We Come Today," downloaded from **aliveinchrist.osv.com**.

Gather

Invite the children to gather in the prayer space with their books.

Pray

Follow the order of prayer on the student page.

Leader's concluding prayer: Lord, we thank you for the gift of community. Help us work together to praise your name forever.

 Conclude by singing with the children "We Come Today" as they exit the prayer space and make their way back to their seats.

 Let Us Pray

Prayer of Thanksgiving

Gather and begin with the Sign of the Cross.

Leader: Jesus, you call us in so many ways. We thank you now for being part of the Catholic Church.

Reader 1: The Church is the People of God

Reader 2: gathered in the name of Jesus.

All: Thank you for calling us to be a part of your Church.

Reader 3: The Church helps us to understand the Bible

Reader 4: and to share the message and love of Jesus.

All: Thank you for calling us to be a part of your Church.

Reader 5: The Church helps us to honor God the Father

Reader 6: and to grow closer to Jesus.

All: Thank you for calling us to be a part of your Church.

Leader: Let us pray.

Bow your heads as the leader continues to pray.

 Sing "We Come Today"

70 Chapter 2

 Liturgy Link

Gestures

Use these gestures with the *All* response to the readings:

- *Thank you* (hands folded in prayer)
- *for calling us* (cupped hands over mouth)
- *to be part* (hug self)
- *of your Church* (hands together with pointer fingers in steeple shape)

Go to **aliveinchrist.osv.com** for Sunday readings, Scripture background, questions of the week, and seasonal resources.

FAMILY+FAITH
LIVING AND LEARNING TOGETHER

YOUR CHILD LEARNED >>>

This chapter explains how the Church community works together to act in Jesus' name.

God's Word

Read **John 17:20–23** and talk about the ways each of you can be one with God.

Catholics Believe

- The Bible is the Word of God written in human words.
- The Church is the community of all baptized people who believe in God and follow Jesus.

To learn more, go to the *Catechism of the Catholic Church* #781, 782 at usccb.org.

People of Faith

This week, your child met Saint Francis of Assisi, who helped bring about a renewal of Church through his simple way of life.

CHILDREN AT THIS AGE >>>

How They Understand the Church Community Third grade is an age when the social group often becomes important to children. They want to know that they belong and have friends. This is the perfect age to talk with your child about the Church as our community of faith. It's especially important that they have time to spend with peers at church and are able to form friendships in their parish community.

CONSIDER THIS >>>

When someone looks at you do they see Christ in you?

Have you ever asked yourself this? It may seem like an odd question. Yet, as baptized people we believe that God has invited us into his Divine life. "Only Jesus can transform us into himself. Our inner receptivity [our openness] is critical. To receive love, we need to be open to it." Offering ourselves at Mass together with the gifts of bread and wine is the best way to continuously give Christ the opportunity to transform us. "Then in Christ we become bread for the world's bodily and spiritual hungers" (*USCCA, p. 227*).

LET'S TALK >>>

- As a family, talk about ways that you could live a more simple life.
- Talk about the different times you gather as a Church community.

LET'S PRAY >>>

Saint Francis, pray for us that we may work together to build the Church. Amen.

For a multimedia glossary of Catholic Faith Words, Sunday readings, seasonal and Saint resources, and chapter activities go to **aliveinchrist.osv.com**.

Family + Faith

Distribute the page to the children or parents/adult family members. Point out the chapter highlights, insights on how third graders understand concepts, the opportunity for the adults to reflect on their own experience and faith journey, and the family prayer.

Chapter 2 Review

A **Work with Words** Complete the following statements.

Word Bank
Church
Good News
community
People of God
Bible

1. One way to serve God and the Church is by living out the **Good News** of Jesus Christ.

2. A **community** is a group of people who come together for a shared purpose.

3. Through Baptism, God called you to be part of a special community called the **Church**.

4. The **Bible** is the Word of God written in human words.

5. A name for the Church community is **People of God**.

B **Check Understanding** Match each description in Column A with the correct term in Column B.

Column A	Column B
6. Was sent to guide the Church	Sacred Tradition
7. Means "belonging to the Lord"	the Holy Spirit
8. Showing respect for others is one way to do this	love one another
9. God's Word handed down verbally through the Apostles and bishops	Church
10. God wants people to do this	serve God

Go to **aliveinchrist.osv.com** for an interactive review.

Chapter Review

Use Catechist Quick Reviews to highlight lesson concepts.

A **Work with Words**
Review the Word Bank with the children. Have them use the correct words to complete the statements.

B **Check Understanding**
Explain to the children that they will be matching each description with the correct term.

Go to **aliveinchrist.osv.com** to prepare customized and downloadable assessments, send eAssessments, and assign interactive reviews.

The Church Gathered **71–72**

Family + Faith

KEY CONCEPT

Mary is a special member of God's family and the greatest Saint. The family home is called the "domestic Church."

DOCTRINAL CONTENT

- Families teach us how to care for, respect, and help one another. (CCC, 1657, 2207)

- We honor Mary as the Mother of God, the greatest of Saints, and our Mother, too. (CCC, 963)

- The Hail Mary begins with the words Elizabeth used to greet Mary. (CCC, 435, 2676)

- The Catholic family is the domestic Church where we experience love, and learn about God and how we pray and live as Catholics. (CCC, 2204)

TASKS OF CATECHESIS

Helping children grow in a faith that is "known, celebrated, lived, and expressed in prayer" (NDC, 20).

This chapter focuses on the following tasks of catechesis:

- Promoting Knowledge of the Faith

- Education for Community Life

Catechist Background

Then his mother and his brothers came to him but were unable to join him because of the crowd. He was told, "Your mother and your brothers are standing outside and they wish to see you." He said to them in reply, "My mother and my brothers are those who hear the word of God and act on it." **Luke 8:19–21**

➜ **Reflect** Do you act on the Word of God?

The first school of Christian life is the Christian family. (See *CCC,* 1657.) The family shapes a child's primary image of God when it mirrors his life and love in the communion among the three Divine Persons of the Holy Trinity. A child learns from parents who display a loving relationship that results in the physical, emotional, and spiritual well-being of the child. The family also transmits Christian values to the child, especially as family members, bonding together in love, build a community of faith, hope, and charity. The child learns Christian values in a family community that lives and acts as Jesus did by praying, worshipping God his Father, and reaching out to help others. Even when the earthly bonds of the family are damaged by divorce, alienation, or estrangement, the child can still learn God the Father's love and fidelity if parents respect each other and love their child.

When its members learn to love, to give and receive respect, and to forgive and be forgiven, a faithful family is like leaven in the bread of today's world. Such acts of charity and justice in daily life help others grow in faith. In this way the Christian family spreads the Kingdom of God in the world outside itself. Consequently, the family is called the "domestic Church."

➜ **Reflect** In what ways has your family acted as leaven in today's world?

Catechist's Prayer

God the Father, I thank you for the children in my care and for their families. Guide me that I may give them the support and guidance that will help them grow in your friendship. Amen.

Lesson Plan

Objectives	Process	Materials

⏱ Invite, 10 minutes

Families Teach Love Page 73

- ♥ **Psalm 133:1** Pray the opening prayer.
- 📖 **Luke 8:19–21** Reflect prayerfully on the Word.
- Discuss What Do You Wonder questions.

📶 **Optional Activity**
Chapter Poem:
"A Family"

⏱ Discover, 35 minutes

A Model for Our Families
Pages 74–75

- Appreciate that families teach us how to care for, respect, and help one another
- Recognize the importance of Mary as the Mother of God and our Mother, too
- Connect the words Elizabeth used to greet Mary with the Hail Mary

- **Catholic Faith Words** Visitation, Mary
- Discuss what Mary teaches us about being a part of a family.
- 📖 **Luke 1:39–56** Proclaim "Mary Visits Elizabeth."
- ☆ Fill in the blanks to complete the Hail Mary prayer.
- **Share Your Faith Activity** Write one way family members love and care for one another.

- ☐ pencils or pens
- ☐ board or chart paper
- ☐ index cards, two per child
- **Optional Activity** Prayer Puzzle
- ☐ Activity Master 3 (Page 73E)

The Church of the Home
Pages 76–77

- Identify the Catholic family as the domestic Church where we experience love, and learn about God and how we pray and live as Catholics

- **Catholic Faith Words** domestic Church
- Explain that families are part of the Church.
- ☆ Underline how family shows the love of the Holy Trinity.
- **Connect Your Faith Activity** Write words and actions that show love.

- ☐ pencils or pens
- ☐ board or chart paper
- ☐ index cards, one per child

⏱ Live, 15 minutes

Our Catholic Life Pages 78–79

- Remind the children that respect is honoring God and other people.
- ☆ Write ways to respect God and others.
- **People of Faith** Learn about Blessed Luigi and Maria.
- **Live Your Faith Activity** Draw a comic strip about a family that cares for one another.

- ☐ pencils or pens
- ☐ colored pencils or markers
- ☐ board or chart paper

Prayer of Petition Page 80

- Choose four volunteers for the reader parts.
- Follow the order of prayer.
- ▶ Conclude with "The Family of God."

📶 Download "The Family of God."

Family + Faith Page 81

Point out that the Catholic Families page provides chapter highlights, information on how third graders understand faith concepts, and family prayer.

Chapter Review Page 82

📶 aliveinchrist.osv.com

- Customize and Download Assessments
- Email Links to eAssessments
- Interactive Student Reviews

ONLINE RESOURCES

 Go to **aliveinchrist.osv.com**

You will find:

- Interactive lesson planning with web specific content and additional activities
- Step by step lesson instruction from printed Catechist Edition for integrated lesson planning
- Custom-built assessments to download and eAssessment links
- Interactive reviews that provide scores and the option to review answers
- Sunday readings with background and questions of the week

 Go to **osvparish.com**

You will find:

- Ask the Experts Q and A
- General Catechist Helps
- Community Connections and Blogs

Sharing the Message with Third Graders

The Family as Domestic Church A family's professed beliefs, and especially their example, are very important and powerful forces that shape the faith of children. It's important that the two match as much as reasonably possible, because third graders are now at the age when they can notice discrepancies between words and actions.

Teaching Tip: Use content from the family page during the lesson as a way to remind the children to bring the page home and share it with their families.

How Third Graders Understand

- Third graders are often proud of their families. Allow them to share their family's activities.
- Children this age want to feel important in a group. Call them by name.
- Young people tend to imitate the adults who care for them. Your positive attitude will help them to be positive as well.

"I'm proud of my family. Allow me to share some of the things that we enjoy doing together."

Chapter Connections

Chapter Poem

Invite

"A Family"

Use this poem to expand the chapter introduction.

- Some of the children will live in a complex family situation. A caretaker might be a parent, a grandparent, another relative, or someone designated by the court.
- Have the children decide an important quality of a strong family.

 Go to **aliveinchrist.osv.com** Lesson Planning section for this poem.

NCEA IFG: ACRE Edition

Discover

Knowledge of the Faith

- Objective: To know and understand basic Catholic teaching about the Incarnate Word Jesus Christ as the way, truth, and life

Communal Life

- Objectives: To know the origin, mission, structure, and communal nature of the Church; to know the rights and responsibilities of the Christian faithful

Catholic Social Teaching

Live

 Use one of these features to introduce a principle and engage the children with an activity.

- Life and Dignity, Pages 290–291
- Call to Community, Pages 292–293

Music Options

 Use one or more of the following songs to enhance catechetical learning or for prayer.

- "The Family of God," Live Prayer, Page 80
- "God Keeps His Promises," Discover, Page 75
- "All Over the World," Discover, Page 77
- "Hail Mary," Discover, Page 77
- "Loving Others," Live, Page 78

LECTIONARY CONNECTION

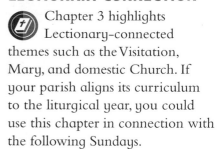 Chapter 3 highlights Lectionary-connected themes such as the Visitation, Mary, and domestic Church. If your parish aligns its curriculum to the liturgical year, you could use this chapter in connection with the following Sundays.

Year A

The Holy Family of Jesus, Mary, and Joseph—Duties for Parents

Fifth Sunday of Easter—Living Stones

Year B

Twenty-second Sunday in Ordinary Time—God's Laws

Twenty-seventh Sunday in Ordinary Time—Family

Year C

The Holy Family of Jesus, Mary, and Joseph—Love of Family

Fifth Sunday of Easter—Love of Family

Go to **aliveinchrist.osv.com** for a complete correlation ordered by the Sundays of the year and suggestions for how to integrate the Scripture readings into chapter lessons.

Name _____   Date _____

Prayer Puzzle

Use the words in the Word Bank to fill in the blanks of The Hail Mary. When you have finished, read the words in the darker outlined boxes going down. Those letters will spell a message.

Word Bank

among   Hail   death   now

womb   Lord   Mother   blessed

, Mary, full of grace,

the [____] is with thee.

Blessed art thou [____] women

and [____] is the fruit

of thy [____], Jesus.

Holy Mary, [__**I**__] of God,

[__**H**__]

pray for us sinners, [__**G**__]

and at the hour of our [____]. Amen.

Message: ⬭ ⬭ ⬭ ⬭   ⬭ ⬭ ⬭ ⬭   ⬭ ⬭ ⬭

CHAPTER 3

Families Teach Love

Let Us Pray

Leader: God, our Father, help us to live as your people.

"How good and how pleasant it is,
when brothers dwell together as one!" **Psalm 133:1**

All: God, you give us our families to teach us about you.
Help us to listen, learn, and follow your ways. Amen.

God's Word

Jesus' Mother and others from his family came to see him but could not get near him because of the crowd. Someone told him, "Your family is outside and they want to see you." Jesus said, "My mother and my brothers are those who hear the word of God and act on it." **Based on Luke 8:19–21**

? What Do You Wonder?

- How are you a part of Jesus' family?
- Does God really care if you obey your parents?

73

© Our Sunday Visitor

Optional Activity

Chapter Poem: "A Family" *Verbal/Linguistic*

Use this poem after the opening prayer, before you tell the children that families are from God.

- Read aloud the poem and ask the children to think of their own families. Give them time to respond with their thoughts.
- After having the children tell what they have learned about family, transition back to the lesson instruction.

 Go to **aliveinchrist.osv.com** for Chapter Poem.

Invite

Let Us Pray

Invite the children to gather in the prayer space and make the Sign of the Cross. Ask a volunteer to read aloud the leader's prayer and the Psalm verse. Prompt the group's response. Have the children return to their seats.

Explain that our families are one of God's first gifts to us. They help us to live as God's People. But we have another family as well.

Say: Let's listen to this story about Jesus.

God's Word

Guide the children through the process of Scripture reflection.

- Invite them to close their eyes, be still, and open their minds and hearts to what God is saying to them in this passage.
- Proclaim the Scripture.
- Maintain several moments of silence.
- *Ask:* What did you hear God say to you today?
- Invite volunteers to share.

What Do You Wonder?

Say: Jesus helps us to understand that our families belong to a bigger family we call the Church. Learning how to love each other in our family helps us to learn how to love other people in the world. God uses our families to teach us about love.

Invite the children to respond to the questions. Ask what else they might wonder about family.

Objectives

- Appreciate that families teach us how to care for, respect, and help one another
- Recognize the importance of Mary as the Mother of God and our Mother, too
- Connect the words Elizabeth used to greet Mary with the Hail Mary

A Model for Our Families

Read aloud the question.

- List the children's responses on the board or on chart paper.

Ask a volunteer to read the opening paragraph.

- Remind the children that it is important for family members to spend time together.

 God's Word

Proclaim the Scripture story.

- Ask the children what the Scripture tells about how Mary and Elizabeth felt. Possible responses: happy to be together, grateful for God's blessings, full of wonder about the changes happening in their lives
- *Ask:* How did Mary and Elizabeth show that they were caring family members?
- Encourage volunteers to share their responses.
- Direct the children's attention to the illustration on the page. Invite them to describe what they see.

A Model for Our Families

What does Mary teach us about being part of a family?

In our families, we learn to care about and respect each other. We learn how important it is to listen to each other and be there when someone needs help. We share our lives. This story from the Bible, called the **Visitation**, tells us about a visit between **Mary** and her cousin Elizabeth.

Catholic Faith Words

Visitation the name of Mary's visit to Elizabeth before Jesus was born

Mary the Mother of Jesus, the Mother of God. She is also called "Our Lady" because she is our Mother and the Mother of the Church.

God's Word

Mary Visits Elizabeth

Mary's cousin, Elizabeth, was happy and surprised when Mary visited. Filled with the Holy Spirit, Elizabeth said to Mary,

"Most blessed are you among women, and blessed is the fruit of your womb. And how does this happen to me, that the mother of my Lord should come to me?"

Elizabeth's greeting made Mary happy. She answered, "My soul proclaims the greatness of the Lord; my spirit rejoices in God my savior."

Based on Luke 1:39–56

74

Songs of Scripture

Mary, O Blessed One

In the Gospel according to Luke, the story of the Annunciation is immediately followed by Mary's visit to Elizabeth. The Hail Mary recalls Elizabeth's words of recognition.

- Point out that Mary's "yes" to the angel was part of a lifetime of saying "yes" to God.
- Teach the children the song "Mary, O Blessed One."

 Use *Songs of Scripture*, Grades 1–3 CD, Track 17

The Greatest Mother

Like the Angel Gabriel who said to Mary, "Hail, favored one! The Lord is with you," Elizabeth knew how special Mary was (Mathew 1-28). As Catholics, we have always recognized Mary as a special member of God's family and the greatest Saint. She perfectly lived God's plan for her. We honor Mary as the Mother of God and our Mother. One way we do this is when we pray the Hail Mary.

➜ How can we honor Mary?

 Complete the prayer and then pray it together as a group

The Hail Mary

Hail, Mary, full of _____ **grace** _____,
the Lord is with thee.

_____ **Blessed** _____ art thou among women

and blessed is the fruit of thy womb, _____ **Jesus** _____.

Holy Mary, _____ **Mother** _____ of God,
pray for us sinners, now and at the hour of our death. Amen.

Share Your Faith

Think Write one way your family members love and care for one another.

_____

_____

_____

Share Share with a partner.

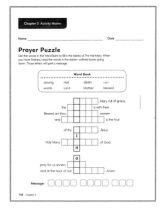

75

The Greatest Mother

Ask a volunteer to read aloud the paragraph and the question that follows.

- Discuss with the children how they can honor Mary.
- ⭐ Have the children work independently to complete the prayer.
- Pray the prayer as a group.

Activity

Read aloud the directions.

- Allow the children to choose a partner to share their work with.

 Music Option: Invite the children to sing, "God Keeps His Promises," downloaded from **aliveinchrist.osv.com**.

Work with Words

Ask two volunteers to read aloud the Catholic Faith Words and definitions from page 74.

- Give each child two index cards.
- Have the children make vocabulary cards for each term.
- Encourage them to use the cards to prepare for chapter and unit reviews.

Quick Review

We need to appreciate all the things that families teach us, and recognize the importance of Mary as the Mother of the Church.

Optional Activity

Activity Master 3: Prayer Puzzle

Distribute copies of the activity found on catechist page 63E.

- Tell the children that they will reveal a message when they have completed the puzzle.
- As an alternative, you may wish to send this activity home with the children.

Chapter 3 Activity Master

Name _____ Date _____

Prayer Puzzle
Use the words in the Word Bank to fill in the blanks of The Hail Mary. When you have finished, read the words in the darker outlined boxes going down. Those letters will spell a message.

Word Bank
among Hail death now
womb Lord Mother blessed

73E Chapter 3

Discover

Objectives

- Identify the Catholic family as the domestic Church where we experience love, and learn about God and how we pray and live as Catholics

The Church of the Home

Invite a volunteer to read aloud the question.

- List the children's answers on the board or on chart paper.

Have the children silently read the first three paragraphs.

- Ask them which family members taught them safety rules and how to do chores.

Read aloud the fourth paragraph.

- *Ask:* What is something you have learned about the Catholic Church from your family?
- Allow the children to share.

Work with Words

Point out the reference in the text to the *domestic Church*.

- Ask a volunteer to read aloud the definition from the Catholic Faith Words box.
- Give each child one index card. Have the children write the vocabulary word on one side of the card and its definition on the other side.
- Encourage the children to use this card, with the others they have created, to prepare for chapter and unit reviews.

The Church of the Home

How can our families help to show us God's love?

Catholic Faith Words

domestic Church a name for the Catholic family, because it is the community of Christians in the home. God made the family to be the first place we learn about loving others and following Christ.

In the story of the Visitation, Mary and Elizabeth helped us see how family members' actions show love. Your family members may show their love in actions, in words, or both.

You first learn about God's love for you from your family. Your family also teaches you how to love God and others.

You learn the basics of healthy living from your family. They teach you important safety rules. You may learn how to care for pets or do other chores.

Your family helps you learn prayers, such as the blessing before meals, the Lord's Prayer, and the Hail Mary. Your family introduces you to the Catholic Church. If you are baptized, you are already a member of this special family of God. The Church builds on what you have learned in your home. For this reason, the family is called the **"domestic Church,"** or the Church of the home.

76

© Our Sunday Visitor

🧍 Reaching All Learners

Examples

Some children find an abstract concept (like the family as a domestic Church) easier to understand when they are able to apply the concept to a particular situation.

- Encourage the children to share appropriate stories from their lives on lessons they have learned about the Church.
- Have the children write stories, plays, or skits to help them apply the concept.
- Share a story from your own experience.

Communities of Love

The Church of the home can be a special sign that shows others how the three Persons of the Holy Trinity love one another. Your family is a sign of this love when you live together in faith, hope, and love.

God shares his authority with parents. He invites them to love and care for you just as he does. God wants you to respect your parents and others who care for you. This includes teachers and community officials. Their authority comes from God, too.

God Loves Everyone

Sometimes members of families may be busy or tired. They may let you down. They are still loved by God, just as you are. It is important to treat the members of your family with love and respect and to pray for them.

Underline how your family is a sign of the love of the Holy Trinity.

Connect Your Faith

Make a Caring Chart What words and actions show love in each of these situations? Write your ideas in each column.

The Visitation	My Family Life
_____	_____
_____	_____
_____	_____
_____	_____

Families Teach Love **77**

(i) Catechist Background

Authority and Obligation

To most children, authority means being in charge and making decisions for other people. While that is true, it is a very simplistic explanation.

- True authority, as granted by God, comes with the obligation to care for those over whom one has authority.
- Jesus is a powerful example of this when he washes the feet of his disciples. (See John 13:1–20.)

Communities of Love

Invite two volunteers to read aloud the first two paragraphs.

 Have the children underline how their family is a sign of the love of the Holy Trinity.

- Ask the children what they think *authority* means. Allow time for their responses.
- Tell them that authority means the right or power to enforce rules or give orders. The power to make decisions is based on responsibility for the good of all.
- Explain that families are part of the Church. Emphasize that families can be a sign of love.

God Loves Everyone

Read aloud the text.

- Remind the children that our family members may sometimes let us down, but it is important to love, respect, and pray for them.

Activity

Read aloud the directions.

- Allow the children to look back at the Scripture story on page 74.

 Music Option: While the children work, play "All Over the World" or "Hail Mary," downloaded from **aliveinchrist.osv.com**.

Quick Review

The family is where we learn about love, God, and how to pray and live as Catholics.

Our Catholic Life

Ask: How do you show respect for God and others?

- Record the children's responses on the board or on chart paper.

- Remind the children that respect is honoring God and other people.

Respect

Review the chart content with the children.

 Instruct the children to write one more way they can show respect for God and one more way they can show respect for others.

- Allow the children to work in pairs to come up with ideas.

- In addition to discussing the children's responses, invite the children to act out ways of showing respect.

> ▶ Music Option: Have the children sing "The Family of God," downloaded from **aliveinchrist.osv.com**.

To read and pray the Hail Mary, have the children turn to page 321 of the Our Catholic Tradition section in the back of their books. Have them also practice the prayer in Latin.

Live

Our Catholic Life

How do you show respect for God and others?

God cares for you more than anyone else can. He showed that he cares about you by giving you life. God also gave you a family and the Church to guide you. He wants you to treat your family members with respect because they are a gift.

 Write one more way you can show respect for God and one more way you can show respect for others.

Respect

Respect for God	Respect for Others
You can show respect for God by • following the Ten Commandments. • teaching others about God. • taking part in Mass. • helping your Church community.	You show respect • for family members by treating them with love and care. • for your friends by taking turns and sharing your games. • for your teachers by doing your assignments and by being polite. • for your classmates by listening when they talk and by inviting them into your games.
_____ _____ _____ _____	_____ _____ _____ _____

78 Chapter 3

 Quick Tip

Respect Everywhere

Point out that simple gestures show respect in church.

- Genuflecting to the Tabernacle shows a person's respect for Jesus Christ's True Presence in the Eucharist.

- Praying quietly shows respect for God and for others who wish to pray.

- Walking quietly and speaking only when necessary (and then in a quiet voice) are ways of showing respect.

People of Faith

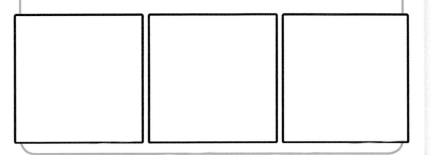

Blessed Luigi Beltrame Quattrocchi, 1880–1951 and Blessed Maria Corsini, 1884–1965   November 25

Blessed Luigi and Maria were a married couple. They lived in Rome, Italy. Luigi was a lawyer. Maria was a writer and a catechist. They had four children whom they loved very much. The family had a lot of fun together, but they always made time for prayer and helping other people. During World War II, they let people who had lost their homes stay with them. They showed the love of Jesus to everyone they met. Blessed Luigi and Maria help us see how our homes and families can be a "domestic Church."

Discuss: How does your family show the love of Jesus?

 Learn more about Blessed Luigi and Maria at **aliveinchrist.osv.com**

Live Your Faith

Draw a Comic Strip Draw a comic strip about a family whose members use words and actions to show that they care for one another.

People of Faith

Tell the children about Blessed Luigi Beltrame Quattrocchi and Blessed Maria Corsini.

- Care of the family was Maria's and Luigi's main concern and commitment.
- Maria had a little girl prematurely, but healthy nevertheless.
- Prayer was central to the lives of this family.
- Read aloud the paragraph.
- Ask the Discuss question and invite volunteers to respond.

 Encourage the children to go to **aliveinchrist.osv.com** at home to learn more about Blessed Luigi and Maria.

Activity

Read aloud the directions for the Live Your Faith activity.

- Provide the children with colored pencils or markers.
- Let them work in small groups to discuss ideas and plan a comic strip.
- With their permission, display their work.

🌐 Catholic Social Teaching

Chapter Connections

To integrate Catholic Social Teaching into your lesson, choose one of the following features: Life and Dignity, pages 290–291; or Call to Community, pages 292–293.

- Start the Live step of the process by talking about Blessed Luigi and Maria on page 79. Then move directly to the Catholic Social Teaching feature.
- Or, to expand the lesson, complete both pages 78 and 79, then move to the Catholic Social Teaching feature.
- Return to Chapter 3 for the prayer on page 80.

Let Us Pray
Prayer of Petition

Explain that this is a prayer of petition asking God to help us show love and care for our families.

Prepare

Choose volunteers for the four reader parts. Allow them to practice their parts. You will be the leader.

> ▶ Rehearse with the children "The Family of God," downloaded from **aliveinchrist.osv.com**.

Gather

Invite the children to come to the prayer space with their books.

- Lead the children into the prayer space while playing or singing "The Family of God."

Pray

Follow the order of prayer on the student page.

Leaders' concluding prayer: God our Father, please bless our families and help us grow in your love.

▶ Conclude by processing around the room with the children singing the refrain for "The Family of God."

Live

 Let Us Pray

Prayer of Petition

Gather and begin with the Sign of the Cross.

Leader: Dear God, you give us families to love and guide us. With your help, we will try to show them our love and care.

Reader 1: When we are together,

All: Help us show love and care.

Reader 2: When family members are sad,

All: Help us show love and care.

Reader 3: When we are full of energy and ideas,

All: Help us show love and care.

Reader 4: When we are tired and grouchy,

All: Help us show love and care.

Leader: Dear God, thank you for caring families.

All: Amen.

Leader: Let us pray.

Bow your heads as the leader prays.

All: Amen.

▶ Sing "The Family of God"
We gather together to celebrate family.
Our Church is the Family of God.
Sharing together the blessing of Jesus,
the Family of God.
© 2010, Chet A. Chambers. Published by Our Sunday Visitor, Inc.

80 Chapter 3

Liturgy Link

Read and Respond

Encourage the children to be active participants in prayer services.

- Explain that their participation shows their respect and love for God, as well as their belonging to a community of worship.
- Encourage all the children to respond and sing with all their hearts and voices.

> Go to **aliveinchrist.osv.com** for Sunday readings, Scripture background, questions of the week, and seasonal resources.

FAMILY+FAITH
LIVING AND LEARNING TOGETHER

YOUR CHILD LEARNED >>>
This chapter explores Mary as a model for family living and how families show love and respect and the role of the family as the "domestic Church."

God's Word
Read **Luke 8:19–21** and talk about how each of you hears God's Word and tries to live by it.

Catholics Believe
- Mary is a special member of God's family and the greatest Saint.
- The family home is called the "domestic Church."

To learn more, go to the *Catechism of the Catholic Church* #1657, 1666 at usccb.org.

People of Faith
This week, your child met Blessed Luigi Beltrame Quattrocchi and Blessed Maria Corsini, the first married couple to be beatified together.

CHILDREN AT THIS AGE >>>
How They Understand the Family as Domestic Church
A family's professed beliefs, and especially their example, are very important and powerful forces that shape the faith of children. It's important that the two match as much as reasonably possible, because your child is now at the age when he or she can notice discrepancies between words and actions.

CONSIDER THIS >>>
How do electronic devices keep your family from being present to each other?

When we are checking emails, texting, talking on the phone, and playing games on our tablet with no boundaries, sacred family time starts to disappear. Being in the same room is not enough. Being present to one another is the first obligation and privilege of family life. "When family members pray together, engage in lifelong learning, forgive one another, [and] serve each other…they help each other live the faith and grow in faith" (*USCCA, p. 376*).

LET'S TALK >>>
- Ask your child to name someone in his or her life, other than a parent, who helps him/her live a holy life?
- Talk about the different ways you can treat the members of your family with love and respect.

LET'S PRAY >>>
Heavenly Father, like Blessed Luigi and Blessed Maria, help us serve you and one another through a holy family life. Amen.

For a multimedia glossary of Catholic Faith Words, Sunday readings, seasonal and Saint resources, and chapter activities go to aliveinchrist.osv.com.

Family + Faith

Distribute the page to the children or parents/adult family members. Point out the chapter highlights, insights on how third graders understand concepts, the opportunity for adults to reflect on their own experience and faith journey, and the family prayer.

Chapter 3 Review

(A) Work with Words Complete each sentence with the correct word or words from the Word Bank.

Word Bank
- domestic Church
- authority
- respect
- love
- Hail Mary

1. You can show ___**respect**___ for God by following the Ten Commandments.

2. Elizabeth's words to Mary are found in the ___**Hail Mary**___.

3. ___**Domestic Church**___ is a name for the Catholic family and the first place we learn about God.

4. Families are a sign of God's ___**love**___.

5. The Church wants you to respect ___**authority**___.

(B) Check Understanding Write the letter T if the sentence is TRUE. Write the letter F if the sentence is FALSE.

6. Mary's visit to Elizabeth is called the Holy Greeting. **F**

7. Parents and teachers are given authority to love and care for you. **T**

8. Family members show one another care by giving gifts and money. **F**

Write responses on the lines below.

9. Why should you respect God and your family members?
Responses will vary.

10. How do you show respect for your family members?
Responses will vary.

Go to aliveinchrist.osv.com for an interactive review.

Chapter Review

Use Catechist Quick Reviews to highlight lesson concepts.

(A) Work with Words
Review the Word Bank. Have the children write the correct word from the Word Bank to complete each sentence.

(B) Check Understanding
Explain to the children that they will be writing a *T* if they think the statement is true and an *F* if they think it is false.

Go to **aliveinchrist.osv.com** to prepare customized and downloadable assessments, send eAssessments, and assign interactive reviews.

At Home with God 81–82

Unit Review

Use Catechist Quick Reviews in each chapter to highlight lesson concepts for this unit and prepare for the Unit Review.

Have the children complete the Review pages. Then discuss the answers as a group. Review any concepts with which the children are having difficulty.

A **Work with Words**

Have the children solve the crossword puzzle using words that were covered during the review of the chapters in this unit.

A Work with Words
Solve the crossword puzzle.

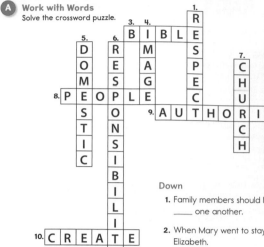

Across

3. The Word of God written in human words.

8. A name for the Church is the _____ of God.

9. God gives this to parents and those who care for you.

10. The Holy Trinity worked as one to _____ the world.

Down

1. Family members should love and _____ one another.

2. When Mary went to stay with Elizabeth.

4. Humans were created in God's _____.

5. The _____ Church is called the Church of the home.

6. A duty or job that you are trusted to do.

7. Community gathered in the name of Jesus Christ.

Revelation **83**

UNIT 1 — Unit Review

B **Check Understanding** Match each description in Column A with the correct term in Column B.

Column A

11. We call God the Father, God the Son, and God the Holy Spirit this.

12. The most blessed of all creatures.

13. A group of people who come together for a shared purpose.

14. All creation is this.

15. The Church is gathered in his name.

Column B

humans

Holy Trinity

good

Jesus Christ

community

(11 → Holy Trinity; 12 → humans; 13 → community; 14 → good; 15 → Jesus Christ)

84   Unit 1 Review

C **Make Connections** Name five ways you can show respect for God.

16. **Responses will vary.**

17. _____

18. _____

19. _____

20. _____

Name five ways you can show respect for others.

21. **Responses will vary.**

22. _____

23. _____

24. _____

25. _____

B **Check Understanding**
Direct the children to match each description in Column A with the correct term in Column B.

C **Make Connections**
Tell the children to name five ways they can show respect for God in problems 16–20. Then have them name five ways they can show respect for others in 21–25.

Go to **aliveinchrist.osv.com** to prepare customized and downloadable assessments, send eAssessments, and assign interactive reviews.

Unit 1 Review   **84–85**

Trinity

Our Catholic Tradition

- The mystery of the Holy Trinity is the most important mystery of our faith. (CCC, 261)

- The Trinity is the one God in three Divine Persons who are united in love. (CCC, 263)

- Each of the Divine Persons of the Trinity is distinct, and they work together in love. (CCC, 267)

- We worship the Trinity when we gather for Mass and in personal prayer. (CCC, 1325, 2565)

How do we grow in love with God the Father, God the Son, and God the Holy Spirit?

The assembly comes together at Mass to worship the Holy Trinity.

© Our Sunday Visitor

Unit 2 Overview

Chapter 4

The Holy Trinity 87

The children will:

- recognize that a mystery is a truth that is difficult to perceive or understand with our senses, but is known through faith and through signs
- examine Jesus' teachings about God the Father and God the Holy Spirit
- identify God the Father, God the Son, and God the Holy Spirit as a perfect communion of love
- describe the Creed as a statement of the Church's beliefs

 Songs of Scripture
"I Am the Way"

 Catholic Social Teaching:
Live Your Faith

- Call to Community, Pages 292–293
- Solidarity of the Human Family, Pages 300–301

Chapter 5

The Church Celebrates 97

The children will:

- describe worship as adoring and honoring God, especially at Mass and in prayer
- discover that at the Last Supper Jesus celebrated the Passover with his Apostles
- identify liturgy, including the Seven Sacraments and forms of daily prayer, as the public prayer of the Church
- understand that Catholics are required to attend Mass on Sundays and Holy Days of Obligation
- recognize the Blessed Sacrament as the Holy Eucharist, especially the Body of Christ, which is kept in the Tabernacle

 Catholic Social Teaching:
Live Your Faith

- Call to Community, Pages 292–293
- Rights and Responsibilities, Pages 294–295

Chapter 6

Pray Always 107

The children will:

- describe prayer as talking and listening to God
- name the Lord's Prayer as the prayer Jesus taught his followers to pray to God the Father
- discuss the importance of daily prayer
- recall the various ways to pray: using traditional prayers and our own words, out loud or silently, and at any time
- identify the five basic forms of prayer as blessing and adoration, praise, petition, intercession, and thanksgiving

 Catholic Social Teaching:
Live Your Faith

- Life and Dignity, Pages 290–291
- Solidarity of the Human Family, Pages 300–301

Preview Unit Theme

Ask: What is the unit theme?

Confirm that the unit focus is on the Trinity.

Invite volunteers to read aloud each of the bullet points under Our Catholic Tradition.

Ask: How do we grow in love with God the Father, God the Son, and God the Holy Spirit?

Have the children study the photos. Ask volunteers to describe what they see and how these images tie in to the bullet points and/or the unit theme.

After some discussion, explain that the group will be exploring all of this information in the next three chapters.

KEY CONCEPT

The Holy Trinity is one God in three Divine Persons. Jesus, God the Son, taught about God the Father and God the Holy Spirit.

DOCTRINAL CONTENT

- A mystery is a truth that is difficult to perceive or understand with our senses, but is known through faith and through signs. (CCC, 237)

- Jesus teaches us about God his Father and the Holy Spirit. (CCC, 240, 2780)

- God the Father, God the Son, and God the Holy Spirit are a perfect communion of love. (CCC, 850)

- The Creed is a statement of the Church's beliefs. (CCC, 187)

TASKS OF CATECHESIS

Helping children grow in a faith that is "known, celebrated, lived, and expressed in prayer" (NDC, 20).

This chapter focuses on the following tasks of catechesis:

- Promoting Knowledge of the Faith

- Education for Community Life

Catechist Background

This is how we know that we remain in him and he in us, that he has given us his Spirit. Moreover, we have seen and testify that the Father sent his Son as savior of the world… We have come to know and to believe in the love God has for us. **1 John 4:13–14, 16**

➤ **Reflect** How do you know the Spirit is with you?

The most fundamental teaching of faith is that of the Holy Trinity. The Church has repeatedly testified to this teaching in its earliest history, in its creeds, and in other statements of faith. The Hebrew people believed in the profound truth that there is only one God. Jesus' Resurrection and the coming of the Holy Spirit showed the faithful that there is one God in three Divine Persons—Father, Son, and Holy Spirit.

Although the doctrine of the Trinity is a religious mystery, it is the mystery that helps probe more deeply into the nature of God. The Church holds this image of the communion of three Divine Persons as a profound truth.

The images of Father, Son, and Holy Spirit provide some insight into the nature of God as a relational being. All three Divine Persons of the Trinity play a part in creation, redemption, and sanctification. The Trinity embodies the energy and power of love that draws all creation into his embrace. The love that exists among Father, Son, and Spirit cannot be contained; it can only overflow into a relationship with all people.

➤ **Reflect** How have your loving relationships reflected the love of the Trinity?

Catechist's Prayer

Triune God, I believe in your presence as Father, Son, and Spirit. May the example of your love help me be more loving toward others. Amen.

Lesson Plan

Objectives	Process	Materials

🕐 Invite, 10 minutes

The Holy Trinity Page 87

- 💗 **2 Corinthians 13:13** Pray the opening prayer.
- 📖 **1 John 4:13–14, 16** Reflect prayerfully on the Word.
- Discuss What Do You Wonder questions.

🌐 **Optional Activity**
Chapter Story: "Mysteries of Nature"

🕐 Discover, 35 minutes

One God, Three Divine Persons
Pages 88–89

- Recognize that a mystery is a truth that is difficult to perceive or understand with our senses, but is known through faith and through signs
- Examine Jesus' teachings about God the Father and God the Holy Spirit
- Identify God the Father, God the Son, and God the Holy Spirit as a perfect communion of love

- **Catholic Faith Words** mystery, Incarnation
- Share a story about Saint Patrick.
- 📖 **John 14:6–7, 16–17** Proclaim: "The Father and the Spirit."
- ☆ Underline what Jesus said about the Father.
- **Share Your Faith Activity** Discuss how symbols can help us understand the Trinity.

- ☐ pencils or pens
- **Optional Activity** Trinity Puzzle
- ☐ Activity Master 4 (Page 87E)

Communion of Love
Pages 90–91

- Describe the Creed as a statement of the Church's beliefs

- Discuss the work of the Trinity.
- **Catholic Faith Words** creed, Apostles' Creed
- ☆ Underline the most important thing about the Holy Trinity.
- **Connect Your Faith Activity** Write a prayer.

- ☐ pencils or pens
- ☐ board or chart paper

🕐 Live, 15 minutes

Our Catholic Life Pages 92–93

- Emphasize our responsibility to get correct information about Church issues.
- ☆ Place a check mark next to a resource for answers.
- **People of Faith** Learn about Saint John of Matha.
- **Live Your Faith Activity** Draft a letter.

- ☐ pencils or pens

Celebration of the Word Page 94

- Select a reader.
- Follow the order of prayer.
- ▶ Finish by singing "Yes, Lord, I Believe."

🌐 Download "Yes, Lord, I Believe."

Family + Faith Page 95

Point out that the Catholic Families page provides chapter highlights, information on how third graders understand faith concepts, and family prayer.

Chapter Review Page 96

🌐 **aliveinchrist.osv.com**
- Customize and Download Assessments
- Email Links to eAssessments
- Interactive Student Reviews

ONLINE RESOURCES

 Go to **aliveinchrist.osv.com**

You will find:

- Interactive lesson planning with web specific content and additional activities

- Step by step lesson instruction from printed Catechist Edition for integrated lesson planning

- Custom-built assessments to download and eAssessment links

- Interactive reviews that provide scores and the option to review answers

- Sunday readings with background and questions of the week

 Go to **osvparish.com**

You will find:

- Ask the Experts Q and A
- General Catechist Helps
- Community Connections and Blogs

Sharing the Message with Third Graders

The Trinity Because community is so important to many third–grade children, this is a perfect age to explore our understanding that God himself is a communion of Divine Persons. Third graders are learning that community (and communion) between persons means mutual giving of self, and this is certainly the case in God's revelation of himself to us.

Teaching Tip: When decorating your space, look for images that show a relationship between Divine Persons of the Trinity, such as Jesus praying to God the Father or the Holy Spirit descending upon Jesus.

How Third Graders Understand

- Third graders usually want to learn more about God. Help them explore the mysteries of faith.

- Children this age have a growing sense of competence and independence. Encourage them to do more things on their own.

- Young people tend to believe in themselves when you believe in them first.

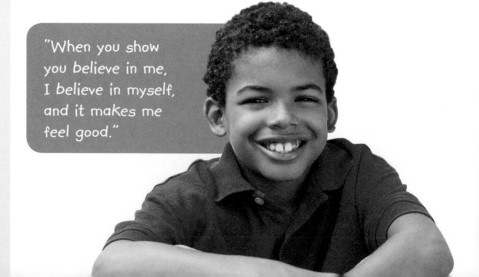

"When you show you believe in me, I believe in myself, and it makes me feel good."

Chapter Story

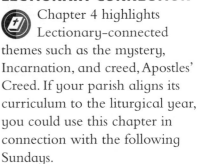

Invite

"Mysteries of Nature"

Use this story to expand the chapter introduction.

- Organize the children in several small groups.
- Have the groups share and discuss questions they have about nature.
- Ask each small group to choose one question to share with the larger group. Discuss all questions posed by the groups.

 Go to **aliveinchrist.osv.com** Lesson Planning section for this story.

NCEA IFG: ACRE Edition

Discover

Knowledge of the Faith

- Objective: To know and understand basic Catholic teaching about the Incarnate Word Jesus Christ as the way, truth, and life

Communal Life

- Objective: To know the origin, mission, structure, and communal nature of the Church

Catholic Social Teaching

Live

 Use one of these features to introduce the principle and engage the children with an activity.

- Call to Community, Pages 292–293
- Solidarity of the Human Family, Pages 300–301

Music Options

 Use one or more of the following songs to enhance catechetical learning or for prayer.

- "Yes, Lord, I Believe," Live Prayer, Page 94
- "The Trinity," Discover, Page 89
- "Jesus Is the Word," Page 92

LECTIONARY CONNECTION

Chapter 4 highlights Lectionary-connected themes such as the mystery, Incarnation, and creed, Apostles' Creed. If your parish aligns its curriculum to the liturgical year, you could use this chapter in connection with the following Sundays.

Year A

Sixth Sunday of Easter—The Paraclete

The Most Holy Trinity—The Son is sent by the Father.

Year B

Seventh Sunday in Ordinary Time—God's Promise Fulfilled by Jesus

The Most Holy Trinity— Holy Trinity

Year C

Fifteenth Sunday in Ordinary Time—Son of God

Twenty-first Sunday in Ordinary Time—God the Father

Go to **aliveinchrist.osv.com** for a complete correlation ordered by the Sundays of the year and suggestions for how to integrate the Scripture readings into chapter lessons.

Name _____   Date _____

Trinity Puzzle

Solve this puzzle by unscrambling the words. Write each message correctly on the lines below each puzzle. Then find the message below the stem.

GOD
The Father

E T A R S C E

_____

The Son

E V S A S and
S H E C A T E

_____

The Holy Spirit

U D I G E S

_____

The three Divine Persons of the

O H Y L   N T I I R Y T

_____

The Holy Trinity

 Let Us Pray

Leader: Lord God, send the Holy Spirit to set our hearts on fire!

"The grace of the Lord Jesus Christ and the love of God and the fellowship of the holy Spirit be with all of you." **2 Corinthians 13:13**

All: God, you are so much more than our minds can ever understand. Be with us as we explore the mystery of your great love. Amen.

God's Word

This is how we know that we remain in Jesus, and he is with us, that he has given us his Spirit. Moreover, we have seen and testify that the Father sent his Son as savior of the world. "We have come to know and to believe in the love God has for us."

Based on 1 John 4:13–14, 16

© Our Sunday Visitor

What Do You Wonder?

- Who is God?
- If you cannot see God right now, how do you know he is here?

Optional Activity

Chapter Story: "Mysteries of Nature" *Verbal/Linguistic*

Use this story after the opening prayer, before you tell the children that God created us with a gift.

- Ask the children to share different mysteries of creation.
- After the children have discussed questions about the mysteries of nature, transition back to the lesson instruction.

 Go to **aliveinchrist.osv.com** for Chapter Story.

Invite

Let Us Pray

Invite the children to gather in the prayer space and make the Sign of the Cross. Read aloud the leader's prayer and the Scripture verse. Prompt the children's response.

Have the children move from the prayer space back to their seats.

Explain that God created human beings with a great gift. Unlike all the rest of creation, we have the ability to know God. We can use our minds and our hearts to think about him.

Say: Let's listen to God tell us who he is, through his Word.

God's Word

Guide the children through the process of Scripture reflection.

- Invite them to close their eyes, be still, and open their minds and hearts to what God is saying to them in this passage.
- Proclaim the Scripture.
- Maintain several moments of silence.
- *Ask:* What did you hear God say to you today?
- Invite volunteers to share.

What Do You Wonder?

Say: We know that God is so great that even when we try, we can never fully understand his great mystery.

Invite the children to respond to the questions. Ask what else they might wonder about who God is.

Objectives

- Recognize that a mystery is a truth that is difficult to perceive or understand with with our senses, but is known through faith and through signs

- Examine Jesus' teachings about God the Father and God the Holy Spirit

- Identify God the Father, God the Son, and God the Holy Spirit as a perfect communion of love

One God, Three Divine Persons

Ask a volunteer to read aloud the question.

- Tell the children they may learn a few things as the group covers the next two pages.

Read aloud the introductory paragraph.

Saint Patrick

Have three volunteers each read aloud one of the paragraphs.

- Have the children place their finger on the highlighted word and ask a volunteer to read the definition for *mystery* from the Catholic Faith Words box.

- Ask the children to discuss what it means to accept an idea on faith. Possible response: to believe without fully understanding

- *Ask:* What helped the people Saint Patrick spoke to better understand the mystery of the Holy Trinity? the shamrock

---

Discover

One God, Three Divine Persons

What can we learn about the Holy Trinity?

Have you ever learned something that was hard to understand? The story of Saint Patrick tells how the people of Ireland learned about the Holy Trinity.

Saint Patrick

Long ago, the people of Ireland had questions about God. As a bishop, Patrick was teaching about the three Divine Persons in one God. Someone asked, "How can you say that there is only one God when you pray to the Father, the Son, and the Holy Spirit?"

Patrick explained the mystery of the Holy Trinity by plucking a shamrock from the ground. He held it up for the people to see.

"The shamrock is one plant, but it has three leaves. The Father, Son, and Holy Spirit are not three gods. They are one God in three Divine Persons. This is a **mystery** that we accept on faith."

Catholic Faith Words

mystery a spiritual truth that is difficult to perceive or understand with our senses, but is known through faith and through signs

Incarnation the mystery that the Son of God became man to save all people

© Our Sunday Visitor

88   Chapter 4

 Songs of Scripture

I Am the Way

Teach the children the chorus of the song. Ask them what we mean when we say Jesus is the way, the truth, and the life?

- Give each child a piece of art paper with one verse from the song written on it; ask them to illustrate the verse.

- Have the group sing "I Am the Way."

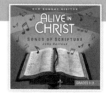

Use *Songs of Scripture*, Grades 1–3 CD, Track 18

Jesus Makes the Mystery Known

Patrick helped the people understand that there is only one God. You can also learn from Jesus, who told his followers about the Father and the Holy Spirit.

Along with the shamrock, a triangle or three interlocking rings are also used to explain the Holy Trinity.

God's Word

The Father and the Spirit

One day Jesus was talking with his followers about God. Jesus told them, "No one comes to the Father except through me. If you know me, then you will also know my Father."

Jesus promised to ask the Father to send the Holy Spirit to teach and guide the people. **Based on John 14:6–7, 16–17**

Underline what Jesus said about the Father.

There are three persons in one God:

- **God the Father** Jesus called God "Father," and he taught his followers to call God "Father," too.

- **God the Son** By his actions, Jesus showed that he is God the Son, who became man to save all people. This is known as the Incarnation.

- **God the Holy Spirit** Jesus asked his Father to send the Holy Spirit, who is God's love and grace, to be present with us.

Share Your Faith

Think How can symbols help you understand that the Trinity is one God in three Divine Persons?

Share Share your answer with a partner.

The Holy Trinity **89**

Jesus Makes the Mystery Known

Read aloud the introductory paragraph.

God's Word

Invite one child to practice and then proclaim Jesus' part in the Scripture story as another child narrates.

⭐ Direct the children to underline what Jesus said about the Father.

Read the beginning of the sentence following the Scripture, and ask three volunteers to read aloud the bullet points that follow.

- Ask the children to place their finger on the highlighted word *Incarnation*. Read aloud the definition in the Catholic Faith Words box on page 88.

Activity

Read aloud the Think portion of the Share Your Faith activity.

- Provide an opportunity for the children to share their answers with a partner.

 Have the children sing "The Trinity," downloaded from **aliveinchrist.osv.com**.

Quick Review

The Father, Son, and Holy Spirit are the Holy Trinity—one God in three Divine Persons. This mystery may be difficult to understand with our senses, but it can be known through faith and through signs.

Optional Activity

Activity Master 4: Trinity Puzzle

Distribute copies of the activity found on catechist page 87E.

- The puzzle will help the children learn more about the Holy Trinity.

- As an alternative, you may wish to send this activity home with the children.

Chapter 4 Activity Master

Name _____ **Date** _____

Trinity Puzzle
Solve this puzzle by unscrambling the words. Write each message correctly on the lines below each puzzle. Then find the message below the stem.

GOD
The Father
ETARSCE

The Son
EVSAS and
SHECATE

The Holy Spirit
UDIGES

The three Divine Persons of the
OHYL NTIIRYT

87E Chapter 4

Discover

Objectives
- Describe the Creed as a statement of the Church's beliefs

Communion of Love

Read aloud the question and all three paragraphs.

- Invite the children to compare the communion of love found in the Holy Trinity to the bond of special groups to which they belong. Ask them to name some of those groups. Possible responses: families, scouts, sports teams
- Point out the bonds of love and commitment that make such groups successful.
- ⭐ Have the children underline the most important thing about the Holy Trinity.
- Allow enough time for the children to find and underline the correct sentence.

For more information on each of the three Divine Persons of the Holy Trinity, refer the children to page 304 of the Our Catholic Tradition section in the back of the Student Book.

- Read aloud the opening paragraph.
- Ask volunteers to read the remaining paragraphs.

Communion of Love

What is the work of the Holy Trinity?

<u>The most important thing about the Holy Trinity is that he is a loving communion of Divine Persons joined as one in love.</u>

The Holy Trinity is a mystery, a truth of faith that Catholics believe even though we cannot understand it completely. A mystery is a truth that only God can fully understand. But, Jesus came to help us begin to see that God the Father, God the Son, and God the Holy Spirit are a perfect communion of love. The Holy Trinity is one God in three Divine Persons.

Through God's revelation and with his help, you can understand more about a mystery like the Trinity. You can see the Trinity at work when you see love in the world. You can see the reflection of the Trinity in the Church. You will better understand the Trinity when you see God in Heaven.

Catholic Faith Words

creed a statement of the Church's beliefs

Apostles' Creed one of the Church's oldest creeds. It is a summary of Christian beliefs taught since the time of the Apostles. This creed is used in the celebration of Baptism.

Underline the most important thing about the Holy Trinity.

© Our Sunday Visitor

90   Chapter 4

✓ Quick Tip

Pretzels

Long ago an Italian monk twisted extra bread dough into a loose knot shape.

- The three spaces came to symbolize the Trinity, and the dough strips resembled praying arms. These first pretzels were given to the children as a reward for knowing their prayers.
- After checking for food allergies, distribute traditionally shaped pretzels to the children.

Honoring the Trinity

The Church remembers and honors the one God in three Divine Persons in such prayers as the Sign of the Cross and the Glory Be and in the creeds. A **creed** is a summary of faith developed by the Church. One of the oldest creeds is the **Apostles' Creed**. It is a summary of faith in the Holy Trinity. Here is how the three parts begin.

"I believe in God, the Father …

I believe in Jesus Christ …

I believe in the Holy Spirit …"

Working Together

God the Father created you. God the Son, Jesus Christ, saved you and is your brother. God the Holy Spirit is with you now, making you holy and helping you bring God's love and peace to the world. All three Persons of the Trinity work together as one God.

→ When can the Holy Spirit help and guide you?

Connect Your Faith

Write a Prayer Finish each prayer in your own words.

God our Father, _____

_____

Jesus, Son of God, _____

_____

Holy Spirit, help us _____

_____

The Holy Trinity **91**

© Our Sunday Visitor

Honoring the Trinity

Ask the children to silently read the text to learn about creeds.

- Have the children read together the phrases that begin the three main parts of the Apostles' Creed.

Working Together

Ask a proficient reader to read the text aloud.

- Invite the children to describe the actions of the Persons of the Trinity. Possible responses: creating, saving, guiding/helping

Work with Words

Invite two volunteers to read the definitions of the highlighted words: *creed* and *Apostles' Creed*.

Activity

Read aloud the directions for the Connect Your Faith activity.

- Allow time for the children to write their prayers.
- Ask volunteers to share their prayers.

ⓘ Catechist Background

Creeds

Creed comes from the Latin *credo*, meaning "I believe." Two well-known creeds are the Apostles' Creed and the Nicene Creed.

- The Nicene Creed was adopted at an ecumenical council in the city of Nicaea in the fourth century.
- In November 2011, the translation of both Creeds were revised when the English translation of the Third Edition of the *Roman Missal* was implemented.

Quick Review

The Trinity is the central mystery of our faith. The Apostles' Creed, which is a statement of the Church's beliefs, honors the Blessed Trinity.

Our Catholic Life

Ask: Who answers your questions about the Church?

- List the children's responses on the board or on chart paper.

Ask the children to silently read the paragraph, then have a volunteer read it aloud.

Finding Answers

Read aloud the text.

- Tell the children that the chart on this page provides even more places to look for answers.

Resources

 Tell the children that they are going to place a check mark next to one resource they will use this week to help them find answers.

- Ask a volunteer to read aloud the list of resources.

- While the children make their marks, point out that they can grow in wisdom and grace when they learn about the Catholic faith.

- Remind the children to make an effort to find an answer to at least one question they have this week.

> ▶ Have the children sing "Jesus Is the Word," downloaded from **aliveinchrist.osv.com**.

Live

Our Catholic Life

Who answers your questions about the Church?

You are growing in your understanding of the Catholic faith. You probably have some questions about what you have been learning this year. It is all right to ask questions when you want to understand something better. There are people in the Church who will be glad to help you find the answers.

Finding Answers

There are many places to go to find answers to your questions about the Catholic faith. Ask your parents or guardians, your parish priest, or a religious education teacher to help you find the answers. They can probably lead you to the correct information source. Here are some places to look:

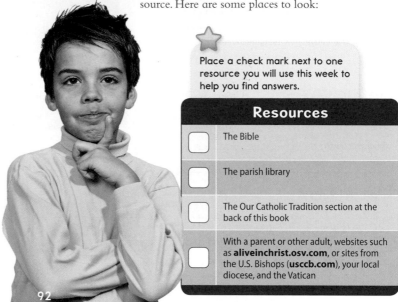

 Place a check mark next to one resource you will use this week to help you find answers.

Resources	
☐	The Bible
☐	The parish library
☐	The Our Catholic Tradition section at the back of this book
☐	With a parent or other adult, websites such as **aliveinchrist.osv.com**, or sites from the U.S. Bishops (**usccb.com**), your local diocese, and the Vatican

92

✔ Quick Tip

Be Accountable

Point out to the children that they are accountable for what they learn about the Church.

- Emphasize the duty to get correct information about Church issues. Indicate that after people acquire knowledge, they must apply it to their lives.

- Most questions begin with one of six words. When the children appear to have run out of questions, encourage them to think about the following list of question words: *Who, What, When, Where, Why,* and *How.*

People of Faith

Saint John of Matha, 1160–1213

December 17

Saint John of Matha was born in France. From the time he was a very little boy he tried to show his love for the Trinity. He obeyed his parents and studied hard. For a while, he lived alone as a hermit. But he decided that God wanted him to become a priest, so he went to Paris. After he was ordained, he started a group of priests called the Order of the Most Holy Trinity or Trinitarians. They worked to free Christians who were slaves. There are still Trinitarian priests today. They honor the Trinity by working in schools and churches.

Discuss: How can you show that you love the Father, the Son, and the Holy Spirit?

 Learn more about Saint John at **aliveinchrist.osv.com**

Live Your Faith

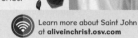

Write a Letter Who do you think can help you learn more about the Catholic faith? Draft a letter to that person and ask a question about your Catholic faith.

Dear _____,

_____

_____

_____

_____

_____

⊕ Catholic Social Teaching

Chapter Connections

To integrate Catholic Social Teaching into your lesson, choose one of the following features: Call to Community, pages 292–293; or Solidarity of the Human Family, pages 300–301.

- Start the Live step of the process by talking about Saint John of Matha on page 93. Then move directly to the Catholic Social Teaching feature.
- Or, to expand the lesson, complete both pages 92 and 93, then move to the Catholic Social Teaching feature.
- Return to Chapter 4 for the prayer on page 94.

People of Faith

Tell the children about Saint John of Matha.

- When Saint John was young, he loved to serve the poor.
- He was a student of such distinction that he decided to become a priest in order to share his talents with the Church.
- Once, Saint John was attacked by his enemies at sea while rescuing slaves. They took his sails and rudders. So, he tied his cloak to the mast, said a prayer, and safely sailed into port with God's help.
- Read aloud the paragraph on Saint John of Matha.
- Have a volunteer read aloud the Discuss question.
- Invite the other group members to respond.

 Encourage the children to go to **aliveinchrist.osv.com** at home to learn more about Saint John of Matha.

Activity

Read aloud the directions.

- As a group, brainstorm a list of possible recipients for the letters. Encourage the children to choose someone important to them.
- Allow time for the children to draft their letters.
- Walk among them to offer suggestions and assistance.
- Invite the children to share their questions and letters with the group.

Let Us Pray

Profess Our Faith

Explain that with this prayer, we will pray with the reading of God's Word.

Prepare

Select a reader for the celebration.

- Help him or her find the Scripture passage and practice reading it.
- You will be the leader.

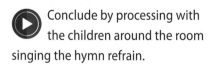 Rehearse with the children "Yes, Lord, I Believe," downloaded from **aliveinchrist.osv.com**.

Gather

Invite the children to come to the prayer space with their books.

- With "Yes, Lord, I Believe" playing in the background, lead the children into the prayer space.

Pray

Follow the order of prayer on the student page.

- Have the children stand for the Scripture reading.

 Conclude by processing with the children around the room singing the hymn refrain.

- Afterwards, invite the children to share a sign of peace.

Live

 Let Us Pray

Profess Our Faith

Gather and begin with the Sign of the Cross.

Leader: Joined together as one community, we are called to one faith.

Reader: A reading from the Letter to the Ephesians.

Read Ephesians 4:1–6.

The Word of the Lord.

All: Thanks be to God.

Leader: Let us share our belief in the Trinity. Do you believe in God the Father?

All: I do.

Leader: Do you believe in Jesus Christ, his only Son?

All: I do.

Leader: Do you believe in the Holy Spirit, the Lord and giver of life?

All: I do.

Leader: This is our faith. This is the faith of the Church.

All: Amen.

Sing "Yes, Lord, I Believe"

 Liturgy Link

We Do Believe

Invite the children to stand during this prayer.

- Tell them that people usually stand when making a very important statement, such as a speech or a serious promise (a wedding vow, for instance).
- The statement "I do" speaks to the very heart of the faith.

Go to **aliveinchrist.osv.com** for Sunday readings, Scripture background, questions of the week, and seasonal resources.

FAMILY+FAITH
LIVING AND LEARNING TOGETHER

YOUR CHILD LEARNED >>>

This chapter examines the mystery of the Holy Trinity and the relationship between God the Father, God the Son, and God the Holy Spirit.

God's Word
 Read **1 John 4:13–14, 16** and talk about how each of you know and believe in the Trinity.

Catholics Believe
• The Holy Trinity is one God in three Divine Persons.
• Jesus, God the Son, taught about God the Father and God the Holy Spirit.

To learn more, go to the *Catechism of the Catholic Church* #253, 237 at **usccb.org.**

People of Faith
This week, your child met Saint John of Matha, the founder of the Trinitarians. Saint John is known for his work in freeing Christian slaves in Tunis.

CHILDREN AT THIS AGE >>>

How They Understand The Trinity Because community is so important to many third-grade children, this is a perfect age to explore our understanding that God himself is a communion of Divine Persons. Your child is learning that community (and communion) between persons means mutual giving of self (especially important in parent-child and spousal relationships). This self-giving love is also evident in God's revelation of himself to us. The Trinity is a communion of three Divine Persons.

CONSIDER THIS >>>

How important is it to live what you believe?

Most people want to be seen as a person of integrity—a person who lives what he or she believes. So, we must be clear about what we believe. "The Church hears the perennial questions that each person asks at some point: 'How shall I live?' 'What values or principles shall I accept?' 'What norms shall I make my own?' 'What gives meaning to my life?' To answer questions such as these, we turn to a wise teacher. Christ is the ultimate teacher, and he continues to be heard in and through the Church today" (*USCCA, p. 330*).

LET'S TALK >>>
• Ask your child to explain how the shamrock helps us understand the Holy Trinity.
• Give examples of how the Holy Spirit has helped guide you in your life.

LET'S PRAY >>>
Saint John, pray for us that we may honor the Trinity by serving others at work, at school, and at home. Amen.

For a multimedia glossary of Catholic Faith Words, Sunday readings, seasonal and Saint resources, and chapter activities go to **aliveinchrist.osv.com.**

Alive in Christ. Grade 3 Chapter 4 **95**

Chapter 4 Review

A **Work with Words** Complete the following statements.

1. Summaries of faith are called ____**creeds**____.

2. The name given to the one God in three Divine Persons is the ____**Holy Trinity**____.

3. A truth that only God can fully understand is called a ____**mystery**____.

4. All three Persons of the Trinity work together as one ____**God**____.

5. Saint Patrick taught about the Trinity by using a ____**shamrock**____.

B **Check Understanding** Fill in the circle beside the correct answer.

6. ____ describes that the Son of God became man.
- ● Incarnation
- ○ Mystery
- ○ Annunciation

7. Jesus called God ____.
- ○ Trinity
- ● Father
- ○ Sir

8. One of the Church's oldest creeds is the ____.
- ○ prayers
- ○ Scriptures
- ● Apostles' Creed

9. The Holy Spirit helps bring ____ to the world.
- ● peace
- ○ sin
- ○ riches

10. You ____ learn more about your Catholic faith from people in the Church.
- ● can
- ○ cannot
- ○ should not

 Go to **aliveinchrist.osv.com** for an interactive review.

96 Chapter 4

Family + Faith

Distribute the page to the children or parents/adult family members. Point out the chapter highlights, insights on how third graders understand concepts, the opportunity for the adults to reflect on their own experience and faith journey, and the family prayer.

Chapter Review

Use Catechist Quick Reviews to highlight lesson concepts.

A **Work with Words**
Have the children complete the statements.

B **Check Understanding**
Explain to the children that they will be filling in the circle beside the correct answer.

 Go to **aliveinchrist.osv.com** to prepare customized and downloadable assessments, send eAssessments, and assign interactive reviews.

The Holy Trinity **95–96**

KEY CONCEPT

The celebration of the Eucharist is the Church's most important form of worship. In the Eucharist, the Church remembers what Jesus said and did at the Last Supper and receives the Body and Blood of Christ.

DOCTRINAL CONTENT

- Worship is adoring and honoring God, especially at Mass and in prayer. (CCC, 2097)

- At the Last Supper Jesus celebrated the Passover with his Apostles. (CCC, 1339–1440)

- Liturgy is the public prayer of the Church. It includes the Seven Sacraments and forms of daily prayer. (CCC, 1069–1070)

- Catholics are required to attend Mass on Sundays and Holy Days of Obligation. (CCC, 1389)

- The Blessed Sacrament is the Holy Eucharist, especially the Body of Christ, which is kept in the Tabernacle. (CCC, 1379)

TASKS OF CATECHESIS

Helping children grow in a faith that is "known, celebrated, lived, and expressed in prayer" (NDC, 20).

This chapter focuses on the following tasks of catechesis:

- Promoting Knowledge of the Faith
- Liturgical Education

Catechist Background

Then, taking the five loaves and two fish and looking up to heaven he said the blessing, broke the loaves, and gave them to [his] disciples to set before the people; he also divided the two fish among them all. They all ate and were satisfied. **Mark 6:41–42**

➔ **Reflect** How does Jesus nourish you?

Although there are many ways to worship God in private, when Catholics gather at Sunday Mass or at any sacramental liturgy, they gather as a people and publicly proclaim their gratitude with one voice. Anything from sitting in stillness to joyful singing can give rise to praising God for his infinite goodness. However, liturgy is always public worship, a gathering of the Body of Christ, with Christ, in the Spirit, to worship God and give thanks. It is always a celebration of Jesus' suffering, Death, Resurrection, and Ascension; for through this Paschal Mystery, the hope of salvation is made real. The sufferings and delights of the entire community are joined and offered to God in the Paschal Mystery. Every liturgy is an encounter with the loving God.

The liturgy is an encounter with God par excellence. Here Catholics experience Christ's presence most fully in the Eucharist, but also in the Word, the priest, and the assembly. As we come together week after week to be nourished, we find help to face daily joys and struggles with hope and faith. With strength renewed in Christ, we leave Mass each week to carry the presence of Christ to all those we meet. Then we return to the table to celebrate God's goodness and be nourished once again. The Eucharist is the source and summit of Christian life.

➔ **Reflect** How does worshipping God help you serve him?

Catechist's Prayer

God our Father, thank you for all of your wondrous gifts, especially the gift of your Son. Accept my love and worship. I join with the whole Christian community to praise you. Amen.

Lesson Plan

Objectives	Process	Materials

Invite, 10 minutes

The Church Celebrates Page 97

- ♥ **Psalm 150:4** Pray the opening prayer.
- 📖 **Mark 6:34–42** Reflect prayerfully on the Word.
- • Discuss What Do You Wonder questions.

🌐 **Optional Activity**
Chapter Story
"Giving Thanks"

Discover, 35 minutes

Special Celebrations Pages 98–99
- • Describe worship as adoring and honoring God, especially at Mass and in prayer
- • Discover that at the Last Supper Jesus celebrated the Passover with his Apostles

- • **Catholic Faith Words** Seven Sacraments, Last Supper
- • Discuss why and what Catholics celebrate.
- 📖 **Luke 22:14–20** Proclaim: "The Last Supper."
  - ⭐ Underline what Jesus did with the bread.
- • **Share Your Faith Activity** Write about and share a favorite celebration.

☐ pencils or pens
  - • **Optional Activity**
    Invitation to Worship
☐ Activity Master 5 (Page 97E)

The Heart of Our Worship
Pages 100–101
- • Identify liturgy, including the Seven Sacraments and forms of daily prayer, as the public prayer of the Church
- • Understand that Catholics are required to attend Mass on Sundays and Holy Days of Obligation
- • Recognize the Blessed Sacrament as the Holy Eucharist, especially the Body of Christ, which is kept in the Tabernacle

- • **Catholic Faith Word** liturgy, Nicene Creed, Tabernacle, Blessed Sacrament
- • Review ways to worship God.
- • Review what happens at Mass.
- • Share that Jesus Christ remains truly present in the Blessed Sacrament.
- • **Connect Your Faith Activity** Write a verse of joy.

☐ pencils or pens
☐ board or chart paper

Live, 15 minutes

Our Catholic Life Pages 102–103

- • Talk about showing respect at Mass.
- • **People of Faith** Learn about Saint Mary MacKillop.
- • **Live Your Faith Activity** The children will draw themselves at Mass.

☐ pencils or pens
☐ crayons and markers
☐ board or chart paper

Glory to God Page 104

- • Follow the order of prayer.
- ▶ End by singing "Praise the Lord."

🌐 Download "Praise the Lord."

Family + Faith Page 105

Point out that the Catholic Families page provides chapter highlights, information on how third graders understand faith concepts, and family prayer.

Chapter Review Page 106

🌐 **aliveinchrist.osv.com**
- • Customize and Download Assessments
- • Email Links to eAssessments
- • Interactive Student Reviews

ONLINE RESOURCES

 Go to **aliveinchrist.osv.com**

You will find:

- Interactive lesson planning with web specific content and additional activities
- Step by step lesson instruction from printed Catechist Edition for integrated lesson planning
- Custom-built assessments to download and eAssessment links
- Interactive reviews that provide scores and the option to review answers
- Sunday readings with background and questions of the week

 Go to **osvparish.com**

You will find:

- Ask the Experts Q and A
- General Catechist Helps
- Community Connections and Blogs

Sharing the Message with Third Graders

The Mass The Mass is the gathering of the parish community to remember and be present with Jesus Christ. At Mass, we gather to praise God and give him thanks for the many gifts he has given us, most especially the gift of Jesus' Body and Blood. This understanding of the Mass as a community celebration and the vehicle Jesus has chosen to be continually present with us is an important one to third graders, who are developing in their understanding of community.

Teaching Tip: Plan a time when the group can meet to attend Mass together. Meet at the church a few minutes early and encourage the families from your group to sit together in the same section.

How Third Graders Understand

- Third graders don't always remember to say "thank you." Help them express gratitude for all of God's gifts.
- Children this age like to observe how people show respect in church. Show them the ritual actions.
- Young people can be taught to show respect for people and places. Teach them words and actions that will help them.

"I like to observe how people show respect in church. Show me the ritual actions."

Chapter Connections

Chapter Story

Invite

"Giving Thanks"

Use this story to expand the chapter introduction.

- Tell the children that the Psalms were written to worship and thank God. At that time, dance was an accepted part of worship.
- Point out that dance and song were both part of celebrating historic events.
- Explain that dance was not a performance; it was a way of glorifying God.

 Go to **aliveinchrist.osv.com** Lesson Planning section for this story.

NCEA IFG: ACRE Edition

Discover

Knowledge of the Faith

- Objective: To know and understand basic Catholic teaching about the Incarnate Word Jesus Christ as the way, truth, and life

Liturgical Life

- Objective: To know the Paschal Mystery of Jesus: in the Church's liturgical life—feasts, seasons, symbols, and practices and in the Sacraments as signs and instruments of grace

Catholic Social Teaching

Live

 Use one of these features to introduce a principle and engage the children with an activity.

- Call to Community, Pages 292–293
- Rights and Responsibilities, Pages 294–295

Music Options

 Use one or more of the following songs to enhance catechetical learning or for prayer.

- "Praise the Lord," Live Prayer, Page 104
- "Five Loaves," Discover, Page 99

LECTIONARY CONNECTION

 Chapter 5 highlights Lectionary-connected themes such as worship, Seven Sacraments, Last Supper, liturgy, and Nicene Creed. If your parish aligns its curriculum to the liturgical year, you could use this chapter in connection with the following Sundays.

Year A

Thursday of Holy Week (Holy Thursday)—Passover/Lord's Supper

The Most Holy Body and Blood of Christ—The Living Bread

Year B

Sixth Sunday of Easter—Eucharist

The Most Holy Body and Blood of Christ—Eucharist

Year C

Fifth Sunday of Lent—Eucharist

Thursday of Holy Week (Holy Thursday)—Last Supper

Go to **aliveinchrist.osv.com** for a complete correlation ordered by the Sundays of the year and suggestions for how to integrate the Scripture readings into chapter lessons.

Name _____ Date _____

Invitation to Worship

In the space below, write an invitation to worship with your parish community. Include the name, address, and Mass times for your parish church. Illustrate the invitation with a picture of your church. Ask family members to help you choose someone to whom you can send the invitation, or post the invitation where it will remind your family to attend.

Welcome to Our Church	**You Are Invited!**
	To _____ *Name of Church* Address _____ _____ _____ Date _____ Mass Times _____ _____ _____ _____ My Personal Message _____ _____ _____ _____ _____

The Church Celebrates

 Let Us Pray

Leader: Holy Father, we celebrate your love for us. Let us look at all that you have made and say, "This is awesome!"

"Give praise with tambourines and dance, praise him with strings and pipes." **Psalm 150:4**

All: With all that you have given us God, our hearts are full of praise and we thank you. Amen.

 God's Word

A very large crowd gathered to listen to Jesus. They were hungry. Jesus told the people to sit down. "Then, taking the five loaves and two fish and looking up to heaven he said the blessing, broke the loaves, and gave them to [his] disciples to set before the people; he also divided the two fish among them all." Everyone ate until they were full. **Based on Mark 6:34–42**

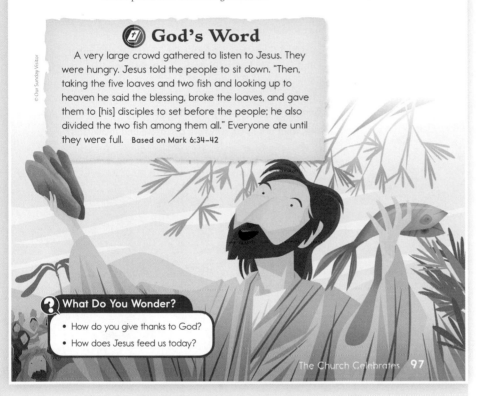

? What Do You Wonder?

• How do you give thanks to God?
• How does Jesus feed us today?

The Church Celebrates **97**

Optional Activity

Chapter Story: "Giving Thanks" *Verbal/Linguistic*

Use this story after the opening prayer, before talking about our gifts from God.

• Ask the children about times when they have been thankful to God.
• Invite them to share what emotions they felt.
• After inviting the children to write a verse of thanks and worship to God, transition back to the lesson instruction.

 Go to **aliveinchrist.osv.com** for Chapter Story.

 Invite

 Let Us Pray

Have the children move to the prayer space. Invite them to dance in procession around the room praying aloud the Psalm verse and playing simple musical instruments. Afterwards, have them return to their seats.

Say: Long ago, dance was an accepted part of worship. It was a way of glorifying God and showing him the joy and thankfulness we felt for all of his gifts. Let's hear about some gifts Jesus shared.

 God's Word

Guide the children through the process of Scripture reflection.

• Invite them to close their eyes, be still, and open their minds and hearts to what God is saying to them in this passage.
• Proclaim the Scripture.
• Maintain several moments of silence.
• *Ask:* What did you hear God say to you today?
• Invite volunteers to share.

What Do You Wonder?

Say: Jesus ate many meals with his family and friends. But, he knew that people were hungry for more than food. Jesus knew that they were hungry to learn about God and his love.

Invite the children to respond to the questions. Ask what else they might wonder about being fed and giving thanks.

Objectives

- Describe worship as adoring and honoring God, especially at Mass and in prayer
- Discover that at the Last Supper Jesus celebrated the Passover with his Apostles

Special Celebrations

Read aloud the question.

- List the children's responses on the board or on chart paper.
- Tell the children that one of the main things Catholics come together for is to celebrate the Mass.

Read aloud the first two paragraphs and invite the children to silently read along with you.

- Tell the children to listen for ways to honor God.

Invite a volunteer to read aloud the last paragraph.

- Ask the children when they have celebrated special occasions.
- Say that God's people have special celebrations, too.
- Invite a group discussion of the question.

Work with Words

Have the children place their finger on each highlighted word, one at a time, and ask a volunteer to read the definitions from the Catholic Faith Words box.

- Have the children copy the words and definitions on a separate sheet of paper to help them retain the meanings.

Special Celebrations

Why do Church members celebrate together?

Catholic Faith Words

Seven Sacraments special signs and celebrations that Jesus gave his Church. The Sacraments allow us to share in the life and work of God.

Last Supper the meal Jesus shared with his disciples on the night before he died. At the Last Supper, Jesus gave himself in the Eucharist.

Parties or meals with family and friends are great ways to celebrate important events, birthdays, and holidays. As Catholics, we celebrate special times in our faith and the life of the Church. We come together to worship God, honoring him with prayers and actions. We do this in a special way when we celebrate the **Seven Sacraments**.

Jesus taught his followers how to celebrate and thank God. He told stories and shared meals with them. His last meal with them was the most memorable one of all.

When Catholics celebrate the Mass, we remember what Jesus said and did at the **Last Supper**. We gather to give praise and thank God for the many gifts he has given us, most especially the gift of Jesus' Body and Blood, our greatest reason to celebrate.

➜ **What are some ways we celebrate and thank God?**

98

© Our Sunday Visitor

Optional Activity

Activity Master 5: Invitation to Worship

Distribute copies of the activity found on catechist page 97E.

- The activity will help the children share what they have learned with others.
- As an alternative, you may wish to send this activity home with the children.

God's Word

The Last Supper

Jesus and his disciples were together to celebrate the Jewish feast of Passover.

Jesus blessed the bread and broke it. He gave the bread to his friends, saying, "This is my body, which will be given for you; do this in memory of me."

Jesus then took the cup of wine and said, "This cup is the new covenant in my blood, which will be shed for you." **Based on Luke 22:14–20**

At Mass, the priest blesses the bread as Jesus did at the Last Supper and it becomes the Body of Christ.

 Underline what Jesus did with the bread.

Share Your Faith

Think Write about your favorite special celebration that you share with your family.

_____

_____

_____

_____

_____

Share Share with a partner.

The Church Celebrates **99**

 © Our Sunday Visitor

The Last Supper

Point out the photo at the top of the page and read aloud the caption.

 God's Word

Proclaim the Scripture.

- Ask the children why Jesus and his friends were celebrating. Possible response: It was the Jewish feast of Passover.
- Discuss how Jesus' words are used at every celebration of the Mass.
- ⭐ Ask the children to underline the sentences telling what Jesus did with the bread.
- Invite a volunteer to share which sentences he or she underlined.

Activity

Read aloud the directions for the Share Your Faith activity.

- Allow the children to select a partner to share their answers with.
- Invite volunteers to share with the group what their celebrations are like.

 Music Option: Have the children sing "Five Loaves," downloaded from **aliveinchrist.osv.com**.

 Scripture Background

Luke 22:14–20

In the Last Supper story, Jesus refers to the new covenant and recalls the covenant, or solemn agreement, between God and the leaders of his People.

- The Old Testament recounts that God made a covenant with Noah, Abraham, and Moses.
- The new covenant, established by Jesus' Death on the Cross, began a new relationship between God and humans.

Quick Review

When we adore and honor God in prayer and action, we are worshipping him. At the Last Supper Jesus celebrated the Passover with his friends.

Objectives

- Identify liturgy, including the Seven Sacraments and forms of daily prayer, as the public prayer of the Church

- Understand that Catholics are required to attend Mass on Sundays and Holy Days of Obligation

- Recognize the Blessed Sacrament as the Holy Eucharist, especially the Body of Christ, which is kept in the Tabernacle

The Heart of Our Worship

Tell the children that the group is going to talk about what happens in the Mass.

Have the children silently read the text.

- Ask them to state their favorite times to worship with the Church community.

Ask: Why is worshipping with others important?

- Encourage the children to explore the meaning of community worship.

At Mass

Read aloud the paragraph.

- Have the children tell what they remember about the story of the Last Supper.

Discover

© Our Sunday Visitor

The Heart of Our Worship

What happens in the Mass?

You can worship God alone or with your Church parish community. Worship is a way to return the love that God shows you. You can worship God with words, silence, music, and actions.

At the celebration of the Eucharist and in the other Sacraments, Catholics worship as a community. This kind of public, community worship is called **liturgy**.

Although Catholics have many ways to pray and worship, the Eucharist, or the Mass, is the most important. In the Eucharist, the community joins with Jesus to worship God the Father through the power of the Holy Spirit. The community joins in the love of the Holy Trinity.

At Mass

At Mass, Catholics gather to hear God's Word in Scripture. We profess our faith, or say what we believe about the Holy Trinity and the Church. We usually do this by saying the **Nicene Creed**. During the Mass, we remember and celebrate what Jesus said and did with his disciples at the Last Supper.

> ### Catholic Faith Words
>
> **liturgy** the public prayer of the Church. It includes the Sacraments and forms of daily prayer.
>
> **Nicene Creed** a summary of basic beliefs about God the Father, God the Son, and God the Holy Spirit and about other Church teachings. We usually say the Nicene Creed during Mass.

 ## Catechist Background

Worship

Early Christian worship grew out of Jewish worship, but it took on new meaning because of Jesus.

- The Eucharist is a sacrifice and a sacred meal.
- The sacrifice offered is Jesus' suffering and Death on the Cross.
- The meal that Christians share unites them with Jesus and with one another and nourishes them to do God's work.
- The Mass today celebrates this memorial.

Every time you go to Mass, you are encouraged to receive Jesus' Body and Blood in Holy Communion. The Church requires that you do this at least once during the Easter Season.

The Church teaches that Catholics must attend Mass on Sundays, or Saturday evenings, and Holy Days of Obligation. The celebration of the Eucharist is the center of the Church's life. When you do this, you follow the Third Commandment, "Remember to keep holy the Lord's Day."

Outside of Mass, Catholics also show love and respect for Jesus in the Eucharist by visiting the **Blessed Sacrament** in church. The Body of Christ, are kept in the **Tabernacle**. Jesus Christ remains truly present in the Blessed Sacrament.

→ **How does your family keep holy the Lord's Day?**

Catholic Faith Words

Tabernacle the special place in the church where the Blessed Sacrament is reserved after Mass for those who are ill or for Eucharistic Adoration

Blessed Sacrament a name for the Holy Eucharist, especially the Body of Christ kept in the Tabernacle

Connect Your Faith

Give Praise Write a verse of joy, praise, or thanks for the gift of the Eucharist in the space below.

_____

_____

_____

_____

_____

_____

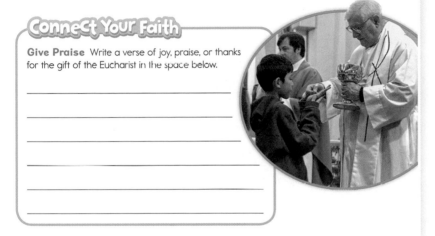

The Church Celebrates **101**

At Mass, continued

Ask volunteers to read aloud the remainder of this section.

- Describe how to visit the Blessed Sacrament and pray quietly there.
- Ask the children why the Church requires us to attend Mass on Sundays. to keep holy the Lord's Day, to participate in the Eucharist

Read aloud the final question.

- Write the children's responses on the board or on chart paper.

Work with Words

Point out the Catholic Faith Words on both pages 100 and 101, and have the children make vocabulary cards for each term.

Activity

Read aloud the directions.

- Allow time for the children to compose their verse.
- Ask volunteers to share what they wrote with the group.

🕴 Reaching All Learners

Linguistic Learners

These children will benefit from studying the prayers of the Mass. Provide printed versions of Mass prayers. Explain that in 2011, the translation of some prayers changed after the implementation of the English translation of the Third Edition of the *Roman Missal.*

- Challenge the children to memorize selected prayers and repeat them for you.
- Invite the children to explain what the prayer means and how it fits into the Mass.

Quick Review

Liturgy is the public prayer of the Church. Catholics are obligated to attend Mass on Sunday and Holy Days of Obligation. The Blessed Sacrament is the Holy Eucharist reserved in the Tabernacle.

Our Catholic Life

Ask: How do you show respect at Mass?

- List the children's responses on the board or on chart paper.
- You probably remember how difficult it was to pay attention during Mass when you were younger. Discuss with the children how your view of the Mass has changed since you were a child.

Read aloud the first sentence.

- Ask volunteers to read aloud each of the bullet points.
- ⭐ Instruct the children to underline one way they have shown respect for God at Mass.
- Ask several volunteers to share what they underlined.

Worship Together

Have a volunteer read aloud both paragraphs.

Ask: What are some of the actions you use to show respect for God during Mass? Sign of the Cross, sit, stand, or kneel, at certain times; pray

To share some of the prayers we honor God with at Mass, refer the children to page 320 of Our Catholic Tradition section in the back of the Student Book. Read aloud the opening paragraph.

- Invite the children to pray together the Sign of the Cross and the Lord's Prayer.

Our Catholic Life

How do you show respect at Mass?

One way to show honor and respect for God is to always act your best at Mass.

Underline one way that you have shown respect for God at Mass.

- Bow or genuflect before sitting down. When you bow, bend the upper part of your body from the waist. When you genuflect, you respectfully bend one knee and touch it to the floor.
- Sing the songs and pray the prayers.
- Listen to the priest.
- Stand in line with your hands folded when processing up to receive Holy Communion and bow slightly as the person before you is receiving.
- Stand up straight and tall, and be a part of the celebration!

Worship Together

Members of the Church use certain actions during Mass to show respect for God. You make the Sign of the Cross and sit, stand, and kneel at certain times.

The prayers of the Church are special ways of honoring God. At Mass, you pray the Lord's Prayer and other prayers. When you pray the prayers of the Church, you join Catholics all over the world.

102   Chapter 5

© Our Sunday Visitor

✓ **Quick Tip**

Celebrate

The children should know that Christians celebrate both inside and outside of the church building.

- Within a church, Church members gather for Mass and joyously celebrate the Sacraments.
- Point out that family gatherings are often held as extensions of Church celebrations such as Baptisms, First Communions, and weddings.

People of Faith

Saint Mary MacKillop, 1842–1909

August 8

Saint Mary MacKillop is the first person to become a Saint from Australia. She was a teacher. She rode horses a long way into the desert, called the Australian Outback, to teach children. She taught the children of farmers and miners. She also used to teach the native Australians, called Aborigines. When she was made a Saint, many Aborigines came to the ceremony in Italy. They wore face paint, danced traditional dances, and played special musical instruments called didgeridoos during the Mass. It was their way of showing how much they loved Saint Mary. Saint Mary loved them, too.

Discuss: What is your favorite part about going to Mass?

 Learn more about Saint Mary MacKillop at **aliveinchrist.osv.com**

Live Your Faith

Draw Yourself Under each picture, describe what is happening. Then, draw yourself at Mass in the empty box.

_____ _____   _____Me at Mass_____

103

(i) Catholic Social Teaching

Chapter Connections

To integrate Catholic Social Teaching into your lesson, choose one of the following features: Call to Community, pages 292–293; or Rights and Responsibilities, pages 294–295.

- Start the Live step of the process by talking about Saint Mary MacKillop on page 103. Then move directly to the Catholic Social Teaching feature.
- Or, to expand the lesson, complete both pages 102 and 103, then move to the Catholic Social Teaching feature.
- Return to Chapter 5 for the prayer on page 104.

People of Faith

Tell the children about Saint Mary MacKillop.

- Saint Mary started her first school with her brother and sisters in a renovated horse stable with 50 children.
- She began wearing black when she started teaching.
- She was known as Sister Mary of the Cross.
- She was also involved with an orphanage, neglected children, girls in danger, the aged poor, a reformatory, a home for the aged, and the incurably ill.
- Read aloud the paragraph on Saint Mary MacKillop.
- Allow several volunteers to answer the Discuss question.

> Encourage the children to go to **aliveinchrist.osv.com** at home to learn more about Saint Mary MacKillop.

Activity

Read aloud the directions for the Live Your Faith activity.

- Provide crayons and markers for drawing.
- Allow time for the children to identify the pictures and then draw themselves taking part in the Mass.

Live

 Let Us Pray
Glory to God

Prepare
Tell the children that everyone will read this prayer together.

 Rehearse with the children "Praise the Lord," downloaded from **aliveinchrist.osv.com**.

Gather
Invite the children to gather in the prayer space with their books.

Pray
Follow the order of prayer on the student page.

Optional readings include Psalm 138:1–3, Psalm 150, or Philippians 4:4–9.

 Conclude by joyfully singing with the children "Praise the Lord."

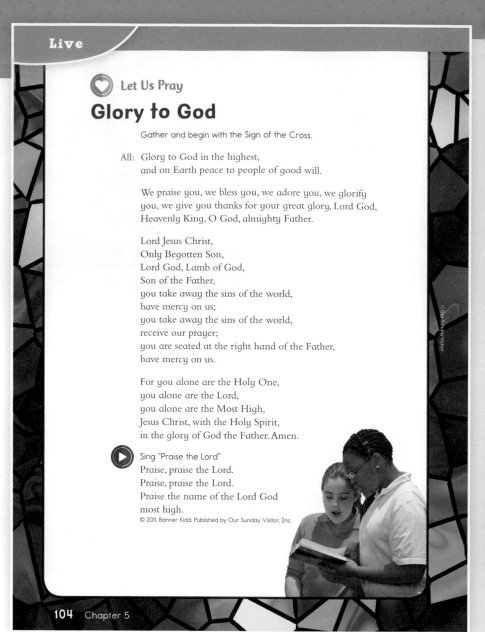

 Let Us Pray
Glory to God

Gather and begin with the Sign of the Cross.

All: Glory to God in the highest,
and on Earth peace to people of good will.

We praise you, we bless you, we adore you, we glorify you, we give you thanks for your great glory, Lord God, Heavenly King, O God, almighty Father.

Lord Jesus Christ,
Only Begotten Son,
Lord God, Lamb of God,
Son of the Father,
you take away the sins of the world,
have mercy on us;
you take away the sins of the world,
receive our prayer;
you are seated at the right hand of the Father,
have mercy on us.

For you alone are the Holy One,
you alone are the Lord,
you alone are the Most High,
Jesus Christ, with the Holy Spirit,
in the glory of God the Father. Amen.

Sing "Praise the Lord"
Praise, praise the Lord.
Praise, praise the Lord.
Praise the name of the Lord God most high.
© 2011, Banner Kidd. Published by Our Sunday Visitor, Inc.

104 Chapter 5

 Liturgy Link

Add Music

Some children may recognize that the prayer service is based on the Glory to God.

- You may wish to reintroduce the rhythm instruments or movement that was used for the Psalm verse on the Invite page, or you could have the children raise their arms and sway back and forth as they sing "Praise the Lord."

Go to **aliveinchrist.osv.com** for Sunday readings, Scripture background, questions of the week, and seasonal resources.

FAMILY + FAITH
LIVING AND LEARNING TOGETHER

YOUR CHILD LEARNED >>>

This chapter explains how we worship as Catholics and the special place of the Eucharist among the Seven Sacraments.

God's Word

Read **Mark 6:34–42** and talk about how God gives you what you need.

Catholics Believe

- The celebration of the Eucharist is the Church's most important form of worship.
- In the Eucharist, the Church remembers what Jesus said and did at the Last Supper and receive the Body and Blood of Christ.

To learn more, go to the *Catechism of the Catholic Church* #1333, 1407 at **usccb.org**.

People of Faith

This week, your child met Saint Mary MacKillop, the first Saint from Australia. Point out the continents on a map and talk about how there have been Saints from every part of the world.

CHILDREN AT THIS AGE >>>

How They Understand the Mass The Mass is the gathering of the parish community to remember and be present with Jesus Christ. At Mass, we gather to praise God and give him thanks for the many gifts he has given us, most especially the gift of Jesus' Body and Blood. This understanding of the Mass as a community celebration and the vehicle Jesus has chosen to be continually present with us is an important one to third-graders, who are developing in their understanding of community.

CONSIDER THIS >>>

Why do you teach your children to say thank-you?

Gratitude has its own rewards. It creates a loving connection to those we thank. It acknowledges that we understand the value of the gift. If we pay attention to our lives, we begin to recognize that everything is a gift from God. Our hearts fill to the point of bursting—with gratitude. We devotedly participate in Mass to say thank-you. "The Eucharistic sacrifice is offered to adore and thank God, to pray for all our needs, and to gain pardon for sins" (*USCCA, p. 221*). As a result of our participation, our relationship with God intensifies.

LET'S TALK >>>

- Explain that the Mass is the same no matter where you go.
- Share what you find most meaningful in the Mass and then have your child do so as well.

LET'S PRAY >>>

Dear God, Saint Mary MacKillop brought God's Word to different parts of the world. Help us to worship you with our minds, our hearts, and our bodies at Mass. Amen.

For a multimedia glossary of Catholic Faith Words, Sunday readings, seasonal and Saint resources, and chapter activities go to **aliveinchrist.osv.com**.

Family + Faith

Distribute the page to the children or parents/adult family members. Point out the chapter highlights, insights on how third graders understand concepts, the opportunity for the adults to reflect on their own experience and faith journey, and the family prayer.

Chapter 5 Review

A **Work with Words** Complete each sentence with the letter of the correct word or words from the Word Bank.

Word Bank

a. Tabernacle
b. Blessed Sacrament
c. holy
d. Passover
e. Scripture

1. At his last meal, Jesus and his friends celebrated the Jewish feast of **d**.

2. The Holy Eucharist, especially the Body of Christ kept in the Tabernacle is called the **b**.

3. At Mass, Catholics gather to hear God's Word in **e**.

4. The Third Commandment says to keep **c** the Lord's day.

5. After Mass, the Eucharist is kept in the **a**.

B **Check Understanding** Fill in the blanks with the correct answers.

6. What is worship? **To honor God in prayer and action.**

7. What is the most important way Catholics worship God?
By celebrating the Eucharist.

8. How often and when must Catholics receive Holy Communion?
Once a year, during the Easter season.

9. What is liturgy?
The Church worshipping together in public.

10. When must Catholics attend Mass?
On Sundays, or Saturday evenings, and holy days.

Go to **aliveinchrist.osv.com** for an interactive review.

Chapter Review

Use Catechist Quick Reviews to highlight lesson concepts.

A **Work with Words**
Have the children complete each sentence by writing in the letter that corresponds to the correct term in the Word Bank.

B **Check Understanding**
Explain to the children that they will fill in the blanks with the correct answers.

Go to **aliveinchrist.osv.com** to prepare customized and downloadable assessments, send eAssessments, and assign interactive reviews.

The Church Worships **105–106**

KEY CONCEPT

Prayer is the raising of one's mind and heart to God. Prayer is an important part of a Catholic's daily life.

DOCTRINAL CONTENT

- In the Lord's Prayer, Jesus taught his followers to pray to God the Father. (CCC, 2765)

- Daily prayer is important. We can pray using traditional prayers and our own words, out loud or silently, and at any time. (CCC, 2659)

- The five basic forms of prayer are blessing and adoration, praise, petition, intercession, and thanksgiving. (CCC, 2644)

TASKS OF CATECHESIS

Helping children grow in a faith that is "known, celebrated, lived, and expressed in prayer" (NDC, 20).

This chapter focuses on the following tasks of catechesis:

- Teaching to Pray
- Liturgical Education

Catechist Background

"When you pray, do not be like the hypocrites, who love to stand and pray in the synagogues and on street corners so that others may see them. Amen, I say to you, they have received their reward. But when you pray, go to your inner room, close the door, and pray to your Father in secret. And your Father who sees in secret will repay you." **Matthew 6:5–6**

➜ **Reflect** What is your manner of prayer?

Any time you consciously acknowledge God, turn toward him, or become aware of him, you are at prayer. You allow your heart, your mind, and your soul to be in communion with God. Saint Thérèse of Lisieux experienced prayer as a movement of the heart, a heavenward gaze. Her prayer did not necessarily need words.

Prayer has many forms. One of the most important is making and taking the time to be with God in silence. He is always present. You must make yourself present to him. Prayer can be this type of very uncomplicated awareness of God's power, goodness, generosity, and care. When you are constantly aware of God's presence in your life, you are praying constantly.

In addition to the very specific teachings on prayer that Jesus gave his followers, Jesus' relationship with God the Father offers an important insight. Jesus was God's own Son. He prayed to God with faith and confidence, saying "Abba," which in Hebrew is an affectionate term for "father." By virtue of their Baptism in Christ, Christians are also children of God and share in that union with God. You can come before God in prayer with the confidence that Jesus demonstrated.

➜ **Reflect** How can you rejoice and pray always?

Catechist's Prayer

Lord, I need your help to be the best catechist I can be. Help me use the talents you have given me to lead these children to know, love, and serve you. Amen.

Lesson Plan

Objectives	Process	Materials

⏱ Invite, 10 minutes

Pray Always Page 107

- ♥ **Psalm 5:3** Pray the opening prayer.
- 📖 **Matthew 6:5–6** Reflect prayerfully on the Word.
- Discuss What Do You Wonder questions.

🔊 **Optional Activity**
Chapter Story:
"Hear Me, God"

⏱ Discover, 35 minutes

Jesus Teaches Us How to Pray
Pages 108–109

- Describe prayer as talking and listening to God
- Name the Lord's prayer as the prayer Jesus taught his followers to pray to God the Father

- **Catholic Faith Words** prayer, Lord's Prayer
- Talk about prayer as talking and listening to God.
- 📖 **Matthew 6:9–13** "Proclaim "The Lord's Prayer."
- ☆ Underline what we ask for in the Lord's Prayer.
- 📖 **Matthew 6:6–8** Proclaim "Praying Well."
- **Share Your Faith Activity** Describe an ideal prayer place.

☐ pencils or pens

Ways We Pray Pages 110–111

- Discuss the importance of daily prayer
- Recall the various ways to pray: using traditional prayers and our own words, out loud or silently, and at any time
- Identify the five basic forms of prayer as blessing and adoration, praise, petition, intercession, and thanksgiving

- **Catholic Faith Words** blessing and adoration, praise, petition, intercession, thanksgiving
- Discuss different ways to pray.
- ☆ Circle some times when Jesus prayed.
- Review the definitions in the text.
- **Connect Your Faith Activity** Identify the forms of prayer used in Scripture verses.

☐ pencils or pens
☐ board or chart paper
☐ Bibles
☐ five index cards per child
• **Optional Activity**
Time for Prayer
☐ Activity Master 6 (Page 107E)

⏱ Live, 15 minutes

Our Catholic Life Pages 112–113

- Remind the children that all prayer is conversation with God.
- ☆ Write some more ways to pray.
- **People of Faith** Learn about Saint Gertrude the Great.
- **Live Your Faith Activity** Make a Prayer Wheel.
- Organize the group into to sides.

☐ pencils or pens
☐ colored pencils or markers

Prayer of Petition Page 114

- Follow the order of prayer.
- ▶ Conclude by singing "Open My Eyes."

🔊 Download "Open My Eyes."

Family + Faith Page 115

Point out that the Catholic Families page provides chapter highlights, information on how third graders understand faith concepts, and family prayer.

Chapter Review Page 116

🔊 **aliveinchrist.osv.com**

- Customize and Download Assessments
- Email Links to eAssessments
- Interactive Student Reviews

ONLINE RESOURCES

 Go to **aliveinchrist.osv.com**

You will find:

- Interactive lesson planning with web specific content and additional activities
- Step by step lesson instruction from printed Catechist Edition for integrated lesson planning
- Custom-built assessments to download and eAssessment links
- Interactive reviews that provide scores and the option to review answers
- Sunday readings with background and questions of the week

 Go to **osvparish.com**

You will find:

- Ask the Experts Q and A
- General Catechist Helps
- Community Connections and Blogs

Sharing the Message with Third Graders

Prayer Third graders are capable of talking with Jesus as a friend. This is a good time to encourage children to speak to God in their own words. Their social nature also makes them especially amenable to praying with the family of with groups if they are given the structure and guidance necessary.

Teaching Tip: Send home family prayer ideas, especially at significant times of the year such as during Lent and Advent.

How Third Graders Understand

- Third graders worry about the people they love. Help them learn to turn to God when they are afraid.
- Children this age are able to respond to God's presence. Help them learn to pray.
- Some children learn and interact better with others when they know what to expect. Keep a regular schedule so that they feel comfortable.

"I like to know what to expect. Keeping a regular schedule makes me feel comfortable."

Chapter Connections

Chapter Story

 Invite

"Hear Me, God"

Use this story to expand the chapter introduction.

- As a group, brainstorm what you want to say to or ask of God.
- Allow the children to vote on which ideas to include. Select the three most popular ideas.
- Arrange and write the prayer on the board or on chart paper.

 Go to **aliveinchrist.osv.com** Lesson Planning section for this story.

NCEA IFG: ACRE Edition

Discover

Prayer

- Objective: To recognize and learn how to engage in Catholic forms of personal prayer and ways of deepening ones spiritual life

Liturgical Life

- Objective: To know the Paschal Mystery of Jesus: in the Church's liturgical life—feasts, seasons, symbols, and practices and in the Sacraments as signs and instruments of grace

Catholic Social Teaching

Live

 Use one of these features to introduce a principle and engage the children with an activity.

- Life and Dignity, Pages 290–291
- Solidarity of the Human Family, Pages 300–301

Music Options

 Use one or more of the following songs to enhance catechetical learning or for prayer.

- "Open My Eyes," Live Prayer, Page 114
- "Our Father," Discover, Page 108
- "God Is Our Father," Discover, Page 110
- "Jesus, Please Hear Our Prayer," Discover, Page 111

LECTIONARY CONNECTION

Chapter 6 highlights Lectionary-connected themes such as prayer and the Lord's Prayer. If your parish aligns its curriculum to the liturgical year, you could use this chapter in connection with the following Sundays.

Year A

Second Sunday of Advent—Prayer of Encouragement

Third Sunday of Advent—Patience

Year B

Third Sunday of Advent—Pray Unceasingly

Fourth Sunday in Ordinary Time—Prayer for Healing

Year C

Fourth Sunday of Advent—Prayer

Third Sunday of Lent— Forgiveness

Go to **aliveinchrist.osv.com** for a complete correlation ordered by the Sundays of the year and suggestions for how to integrate the Scripture readings into chapter lessons.

Name _____ Date _____

Time for Prayer

Read the following stories. Below each story, write a prayer that
the character might say. Then, write your own story and prayer.

Wayne just had the best day ever at school. He got an A on
his math quiz. His teacher said that she liked his painting of a
giraffe, and he and his friends won their soccer game during
gym class. Wayne's prayer:

_____

_____

Gab is afraid. Her mother just told her that they will soon
be moving to another town in another state. Gab thinks
she will be lonely in a new town. Gab's prayer:

_____

_____

Todd is angry. He had a fight with his best friend, Theo.
Now Todd's mother tells him that he has to apologize and
make up with Theo, but Todd still thinks that the fight was
all Theo's fault. Todd's prayer:

_____

_____

Your story _____

_____

_____

Your character's prayer _____

_____

_____

Pray Always

Let Us Pray

Leader: O God, listen to our prayers. We offer you our hearts filled with love.

"Attend to the sound of my cry, my king and my God!" Psalm 5:3

All: Jesus, you ask us to be people who pray. Help us to trust that you listen to our prayers. Amen.

© Our Sunday Visitor

God's Word

Jesus told his disciples not to be like the people who pray loudly in public so that others can see and hear them. Jesus said to go to a private place, close the door, and pray quietly to the Father. God will hear you.

Based on Matthew 6:5–6

What Do You Wonder?

- How does God hear the prayers of all the people in the world?
- Can you pray to God about anything that is bothering you?

Pray Always **107**

Optional Activity

Chapter Story: "Hear Me, God" *Verbal/Linguistic*

Use this story after the opening prayer, before talking about the importance of prayer.

- Read aloud the part of Joel. Pause after each line, and have the children share what God could be saying to answer him.
- After having the children recall times when God answered their prayers, transition back to the lesson instruction.

 Go to **aliveinchrist.osv.com** for Chapter Story.

Let Us Pray

Invite the children to gather in the prayer space and make the Sign of the Cross. Read aloud the leader's prayer and the Psalm verse. Prompt the children's response. Have them return to their seats.

Explain that prayer is an important part of our life with God.

Say: We give thanks and we ask forgiveness. We tell God about what worries us and ask for help. Most of all we give God praise. It is also important to think about how we should pray.

God's Word

Guide the children through the process of Scripture reflection.

- Invite them to close their eyes, be still, and open their minds and hearts to what God is saying to them in this passage.
- Proclaim the Scripture.
- Maintain several moments of silence.
- *Ask:* What did you hear God say to you today?
- Invite volunteers to share.

What Do You Wonder?

Say: Talking with God is even better than talking to one of our friends. God knows us so well that he understands exactly what is in our hearts.

Invite the children to respond to the questions. Ask what else they might wonder about prayer.

 **Discover**

Objectives

- Describe prayer as talking and listening to God
- Name the Lord's Prayer as the prayer Jesus taught his followers to pray to God the Father

Jesus Teaches Us How to Pray

Read aloud the question.

- List the children's responses on the board or on chart paper.

Summarize the text.

- Remind the children that Jesus taught his followers that prayer is talking and listening to God.

 God's Word

Proclaim the Scripture story.

⭐ Have the children underline what we ask for in the Lord's Prayer.

- Tell them that although Jesus gave us this special prayer to pray, they can always just tell God what is in their hearts.

Work with Words

Ask the children to locate the words *prayer* and *Lord's Prayer* in the text.

- Invite a volunteer to read aloud both definitions from the Catholic Faith Words box.

▶ Music Option: Have the children sing "Our Father," downloaded from **aliveinchrist.osv.com**.

Jesus Teaches Us How to Pray

What do we learn from Jesus about prayer?

Jesus taught his followers that **prayer** is talking and listening to God. It is raising your mind and heart to God. When Jesus' followers asked him to teach them how to pray, he taught them the **Lord's Prayer**.

Catholic Faith Words

prayer talking and listening to God. It is raising your mind and heart to God.

Lord's Prayer the prayer that Jesus taught his disciples to pray to God the Father

⭐ Underline what we ask for in the Lord's Prayer.

 God's Word

The Lord's Prayer

This is how you are to pray:
Our Father in heaven,
hallowed be your name,
your kingdom come,
your will be done,
on earth as in heaven.
Give us today our daily bread;
and forgive us our debts,
as we forgive our debtors;
and do not subject us to the final test,
but deliver us from the evil one.

Matthew 6:9–13

© Our Sunday Visitor

108 Chapter 6

 Catechist Background

Answers to Prayers

The idea that prayer is a way of having all of one's wishes come true is common among children and can lead to frustration and turning away from God

- Explain to the children that God answers prayers, but not always in the time frame or in the way that they might wish.
- Tell them that God is always with them and that he always has their best interests in mind.

How to Pray

The Lord's Prayer is also called the Our Father. It is a summary of all that we need to live a Christian life. Jesus told his disciples to call upon God the Father, as he did. He also gave this advice.

 God's Word

Praying Well

Jesus told his disciples to pray quietly to the Father. God will hear you. Some people think that God will hear them better if they use lots of fancy words to pray. Do not be like that. The Father knows what is in your heart even before you say it. **Based on Matthew 6:6–8**

Jesus taught his disciples how to pray to God the Father.

→ Where and for what do you pray most often?

Share Your Faith

Think Do you have a quiet place in which to pray? Describe what you would want in your ideal prayer space.

_____

_____

_____

Share With a partner, share your ideas for quiet "prayer places."

Optional Activity

Praying with Music *Musical*

Enrich the children's music and prayer lives by praying with music.

- With the help of the parish's director of music ministries, find several different musical arrangements of the Lord's Prayer. Or, research online for other appropriate version to download.
- Have the children vote for their favorite arrangement. Teach them the version that receives the most votes, and include it in prayers and liturgies.

How to Pray

Read aloud the text

 God's Word

Ask the children to listen quietly to the directions Jesus gives for praying.

- Then proclaim the Scripture story.

Ask the children what God knows about their prayers. God knows what is in their hearts.

Read aloud the question.

- Allow time for the children to share their answers with the group.

Ask a volunteer to read the caption to the illustration.

Activity

Read aloud the directions for the Share Your Faith activity.

- Allow the children time to describe their prayer spaces.
- Have them share with a partner.
- Ask volunteers to share their work with the group.
- If time allows, have the children draw what their ideal prayer space would look like.

Quick Review

Prayer is talking and listening to God. We should pray often the prayer that Jesus taught us, the Lord's Prayer.

Discover

Objectives

- Discuss the importance of daily prayer
- Recall the various ways to pray: using traditional prayers and our own words, out loud or silently, and at any time
- Identify the five basic forms of prayer as blessing and adoration, praise, petition, intercession, and thanksgiving

Ways We Pray

Ask: What are some different ways to pray?

- List the children's responses on the board or on chart paper.

Have three volunteers read the three paragraphs.

- *Ask:* Does God *always* hear our prayers? yes
- Recall for the children that Jesus was praying on the night before he died.

⭐ Ask them to circle some times when Jesus prayed.

- Review the children's answers.

Read aloud the photo caption.

- Discuss with the children some possible places to pray.
- Write all responses on the board or on chart paper.

 Music Option: Have the children sing "God Is Our Father," downloaded from **aliveinchrist.osv.com**.

Discover

Ways We Pray

What are some different ways to pray?

⭐ Circle some times when Jesus prayed.

Prayer was an important part of Jesus' life. Sometimes he got up early to pray. At other times, he prayed all night. Jesus prayed for other people. He also prayed when he needed help.

Prayer should be an important part of your day, too. You can use your own words or prayers that you have memorized. You can even pray without words by just being quiet in the presence of God's love. But whenever you pray, you can be sure that many other Christians are praying at the very same time.

You don't ever have to worry that your prayers won't be heard. No matter where, when, or how you pray, God is always listening. Even if you are loud or very quiet, he can hear your prayers when no one else can.

We can pray anywhere and at anytime. God always hears us.

110 Chapter 6

✓ Quick Tip

Find Favorites

As a group, look over the prayers of the Church on pages 320–327.

- Expand prayer with your group by using new prayers occasionally.
- Encourage the children to memorize the basic prayers of the Church, such as the Lord's Prayer, the Hail Mary, and the Nicene Creed or Apostles' Creed.

Prayer Forms

We pray for different reasons. To help you understand prayer better, here are five types, or forms, of prayer.

Catholic **Faith Words**

blessing and adoration in this prayer form, we show that we understand God is the Creator of all and that we need him. We give him respect and honor his greatness.

praise in this prayer form, we give God honor and thanks because he is God

petition in this prayer form, we ask God for what we need

intercession in this prayer form, we ask God to help others

thanksgiving in this prayer form, we give thanks to God for all he has given us

Connect Your Faith

Identify Prayers Work with a partner to find these Scripture verses. Tell which form of prayer each verse shows.

Psalm 51:3–5: _____

Psalm 107:1: _____

Psalm 125:4: _____

Prayer Forms

Read aloud the introductory paragraph.

Invite five volunteers to each read aloud one of the five forms of prayer and its definition listed in the Catholic Faith Words box.

- Have the children make flash cards of the words, writing the word on one side of an index card and the definition on the other. Working in pairs, have them quiz each other until they feel comfortable with the definitions.

Activity

Invite a volunteer to read aloud the directions for the Connect Your Faith activity.

- Provide the children with Bibles.
- Have them work with a partner to look up the Scripture verses.

 Music Option: Have the children sing "Jesus, Please Hear Our Prayer," downloaded from **aliveinchrist.osv.com**.

Optional Activity

Activity Master 6: Time for Prayer

Distribute copies of the activity found on catechist page 107E.

- The children will use what they have learned about prayer to complete the activity.
- As an alternative, you may wish to send this activity home with the children.

Quick Review

We can pray at different times, for different reasons, and in several different ways. Whatever we do, it is important to pray every day.

Our Catholic Life

Read aloud the question at the top of the student page.

- Encourage the children to share their thoughts.

Invite the children to look at the photo at the top of the page and describe what is happening.

- Ask a volunteer to read aloud the caption.

Read aloud the first paragraph.

Ways to Pray

Invite several volunteers to read aloud the different suggestions for ways to pray.

- ⭐ Instruct the children to write in some more ways they can pray.

- Allow the children to work in pairs to complete the chart.

- Invite them to share their responses.

- Remind the children that all prayer is conversation with God.

To review personal and family prayers, invite the children to turn to page 324 in the Our Catholic Tradition section in the back of the Student Book. Have volunteers read some or all of the prayers.

Live

We pray with our families to give thanks and, to ask for God's blessings for ourselves and others.

Our Catholic Life

How can you communicate with God?

You have conversations with God when you pray. He is always with you and hears your prayers. There are many ways to communicate with him. There are different ways to pray.

 Write some more ways you can pray.

Ways to Pray

You can pray during the day by offering your good works to God.

You can use your own words to pray. God hears simple prayers, such as "Help, please," or "Thank you, Lord."

You can pray by using other people's words, such as the Lord's Prayer or prayers from Mass.

You can pray by sitting and listening to God.

You can pray with your family or with friends.

_____

_____

_____

112 Chapter 6

© Our Sunday Visitor

✓ Quick Tip

How to Pray

At the heart of Christians' relationship with God is their willingness to communicate with him. It is important for the children to recognize that their thoughts are among the most precious prayers.

- Teach the children to sit quietly and offer their thoughts to God.

- Initially, you may want to allow one or two minutes of silence. As children become more familiar with this type of prayer, they may be able to sit quietly for five minutes or more.

- Remind the children that if they are quiet, they are more likely to hear and understand how God is helping them.

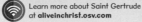

People of Faith

Saint Gertrude the Great, 1256–c.1302   November 16

Saint Gertrude was a German nun. Her parents died when she was very young, so she lived in a convent. Gertrude was very smart and loved to read. She was especially good at reading Latin, but she liked to read all different kinds of books. Another thing Gertrude loved to do was pray. She especially liked to pray for people who had died, asking God to take them to Heaven. She prayed for her family, her friends, and everyone she met. Many other Saints have used Saint Gertrude as an example of a very holy woman.

Discuss: Who do you like to pray for?

 Learn more about Saint Gertrude at **aliveinchrist.osv.com**

Live Your Faith

Make a Prayer Wheel
Write the name of a prayer you know in each section of the wheel. Use a pencil as a spinner and recite the prayer your eraser points to.

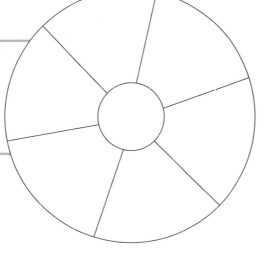

Catholic Social Teaching

Chapter Connections

To integrate Catholic Social Teaching into your lesson, choose one of the following features: Life and Dignity, pages 290–291; or Solidarity of the Human Family, pages 300–301.

- Start the Live step of the process by talking about Saint Gertrude the Great on page 113. Then move directly to the Catholic Social Teaching feature.

- Or, to expand the lesson, complete both pages 112 and 113, then move to the Catholic Social Teaching feature.

- Return to Chapter 6 for the prayer on page 114.

People of Faith

Tell the children about Saint Gertrude the Great.

- She had the gifts of miracles and prophecy.

- She was devoted to the Sacred Heart of Jesus.

- Saint Gertrude was very humble.

- The King of Spain declared her Patroness of the West Indies.

- Ask a proficient reader to read aloud the paragraph on Saint Gertrude.

- Discuss the question as a group.

> Encourage the children to go to **aliveinchrist.osv.com** at home to learn more about Saint Gertrude the Great.

Activity

Read aloud the directions for the Live Your Faith activity.

- As a guide, direct the children to Our Catholic Tradition pages 320–327.

- Provide the children with colored pencils or markers.

- Have the children write in the prayer titles and color the wheel.

- Allow time for the children to work in small groups and pray the prayers as part of a game.

Let Us Pray
Prayer of Petition

Point out that this prayer is an asking prayer.

Prepare

Arrange the children in two groups.

- Let them work in the groups to practice their parts.

 Rehearse with the children "Open My Eyes," downloaded from **aliveinchrist.osv.com**.

Gather

Invite the children to come to the prayer space with their books.

- Lead them into the prayer space while playing or singing together "Open My Eyes."

Pray

Follow the order of prayer on the student page.

Leaders concluding prayer: God our Father, help us follow your will for our lives. We ask this through Jesus Christ, our Lord.

Conclude by having the children process around the room while singing the song refrain.

Live

Let Us Pray
Prayer of Petition

Gather and begin with the Sign of the Cross.

Group 1: Help us remember to bless and adore you.

All: Our help comes from the Lord, who made Heaven and Earth (Psalm 121)

Group 2: Help us remember to praise you, for you are wonderful.

All: Our help comes from the Lord, who made Heaven and Earth (Psalm 121)

Group 1: Help us remember to turn to you whenever we need help.

All: Our help comes from the Lord, who made Heaven and Earth (Psalm 121)

Group 2: Help us remember to thank you, for you are so good to us.

All: Our help comes from the Lord, who made Heaven and Earth (Psalm 121)

Leader: Let us pray.
Bow your head as the leader prays.

All: Amen

Sing "Open My Eyes"

114 Chapter 6

 ## Liturgy Link

Gestures

Remind the children that prayer involves the whole human person—heart, mind, and body.

- Positions such as raising arms high, kneeling, standing, and sitting are integral to prayer.
- Prepare the children to add gestures to the terms *bless, praise, turn to God, ask,* and *thank.*

 Go to **aliveinchrist.osv.com** for Sunday readings, Scripture background, questions of the week, and seasonal resources.

FAMILY+FAITH
LIVING AND LEARNING TOGETHER

YOUR CHILD LEARNED >>>
This chapter describes prayer as talking and listening to God and the ways Jesus taught us to pray, including the Lord's Prayer. It identifies the various ways we pray.

God's Word
Read **Matthew 6:9–13**, the Lord's Prayer. Pray with your family and talk about what the prayer means to you.

Catholics Believe
- Prayer is the raising of one's mind and heart to God.
- Prayer is an important part of a Catholic's daily life.

To learn more, go to the *Catechism of the Catholic Church* #2559, 2659 at usccb.org.

People of Faith
This week, your child meet Saint Gertrude the Great, patron of Latin scholars. Gertrude is a model of intercessory prayer for those who have died.

CHILDREN AT THIS AGE >>>
How They Understand Prayer Third-graders are capable of talking with Jesus as a friend. This is a good time to encourage your child to speak to God in his or her own words. The social nature of third-graders also makes them especially amenable to praying with the family or in groups if they are given the structure and guidance necessary to do so. Take some time for family prayer, and encourage your child to take the lead.

CONSIDER THIS >>>
How necessary is it to be open to what someone has to say?

Real communication requires an openness of mind and heart. Opening our minds and hearts to hear what God has to say is the root of the sacred practice of prayer. "The Catechism reminds us that the Lord Jesus asks us to believe in order to pray and to pray in order to believe. There is a complementarity in which knowing and loving God support each other. Belief in the Father, Son, and Holy Spirit should be essentially and immediately connected to a prayerful and loving communion with the Trinity" (*USCCA, p. 491*).

LET'S TALK >>>
- Ask your child to talk about the things that he or she prays about most often.
- Talk about the different places you pray throughout the day.

LET'S PRAY >>>
Dear God, please bless everyone in my family, especially (mention family members here). Amen.

For a multimedia glossary of Catholic Faith Words, Sunday readings, seasonal and Saint resources, and chapter activities go to **aliveinchrist.osv.com**.

Alive in Christ, Grade 3 Chapter 6 **115**

Distribute the page to the children or parents/adult family members. Point out the chapter highlights, insights on how third graders understand concepts, the opportunity for the adults to reflect on their own experience and faith journey, and the family prayer.

Chapter 6 Review

A **Work with Words** Match the description in Column A with the correct word in Column B.

Column A   Column B

1. asking God to help other people   blessing

2. telling God that you are grateful   praise

3. responding to God's love   petition

4. asking God to help you   intercession

5. recognizing God's greatness   thanksgiving

B **Check Understanding** Fill in the circle beside the correct answer.

6. The prayer that Jesus taught his followers is called the _____.
   ● Lord's Prayer   ○ Hail Mary   ○ Apostles' Creed

7. Talking and listening to God is called _____.
   ○ liturgy   ○ Mass   ● prayer

8. You can use your own words or words that you have _____ to pray.
   ○ forgotten   ● memorized   ○ invented

9. Which person said that God knows what is in your heart even before you say it?
   ○ Peter   ● Jesus   ○ John

10. The Lord's Prayer is also called the _____.
    ● Our Father   ○ Hail Mary   ○ Glory Be to the Father

Go to **aliveinchrist.osv.com** for an interactive review.

116 Chapter 6 Review

Use Catechist Quick Reviews to highlight lesson concepts.

A **Work with Words**
Have the children draw a line to match the description in Column A with the correct word in Column B.

B **Check Understanding**
Explain to the children that they will be filling in the circle beside the correct answer.

Go to **aliveinchrist.osv.com** to prepare customized and downloadable assessments, send eAssessments, and assign interactive reviews.

Use Catechist Quick Reviews in each chapter to highlight lesson concepts for this unit and prepare for the Unit Review.

Have the children complete the Review pages. Then discuss the answers as a group. Review any concepts with which the children are having difficulty.

A **Work with Words**
Instruct the children to fill in the blanks with the correct word from the Word Bank.

B **Check Understanding**
Direct the children to complete each sentence by circling the correct word.

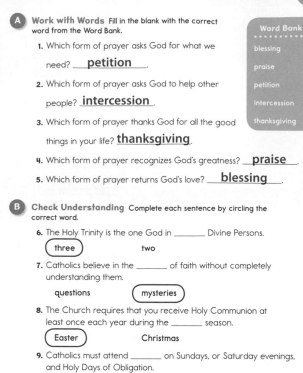

Unit Review

UNIT

2

A **Work with Words** Fill in the blank with the correct word from the Word Bank.

Word Bank

blessing

praise

petition

intercession

thanksgiving

1. Which form of prayer asks God for what we need? __**petition**__.

2. Which form of prayer asks God to help other people? __**intercession**__.

3. Which form of prayer thanks God for all the good things in your life? __**thanksgiving**__.

4. Which form of prayer recognizes God's greatness? __**praise**__.

5. Which form of prayer returns God's love? __**blessing**__.

B **Check Understanding** Complete each sentence by circling the correct word.

6. The Holy Trinity is the one God in _____ Divine Persons.

(three)   two

7. Catholics believe in the _____ of faith without completely understanding them.

questions   (mysteries)

8. The Church requires that you receive Holy Communion at least once each year during the _____ season.

(Easter)   Christmas

9. Catholics must attend _____ on Sundays, or Saturday evenings, and Holy Days of Obligation.

meetings   (Mass)

10. The _____ holds the Blessed Sacrament.

Rectory   (Tabernacle)

Trinity **117**

11. The _____ Creed is one of the Church's oldest creeds.
○ Jesus   ○ Gospel   ● Apostles'

12. A _____ is a truth that only God can fully understand.
● mystery   ○ prayer   ○ responsibility

13. _____ are statements of basic beliefs of the Church.
○ Sacraments   ○ Mysteries   ● Creeds

14. You _____ by honoring and praising God.
● worship   ○ listen   ○ have authority

15. The Holy Eucharist is also called the Blessed _____.
○ Creed   ○ Mystery   ● Sacrament

C Make Connections Write responses on the lines below.

16. What are two ways that you can pray?

<u>Possible responses: at Mass, with memorized</u>
<u>prayers, by listening for God's voice</u>

17. Why is it important for you to go to Mass?

<u>Possible response: to worship God as part of</u>
<u>the community of faith</u>

18. When might you say a prayer of intercession?

<u>Possible response: when a friend is in trouble</u>

19. How do you worship God?

<u>Possible responses: at Mass,</u>
<u>through prayer, by singing hymns</u>

20. When might you say a prayer of blessing?

<u>Possible response: when I think</u>
<u>about God's love</u>

Circle the words from the Word Bank in the word search.

21-25.

D	E	E	R	C	A	L	V
P	E	T	I	T	I	O	N
Y	T	I	N	I	R	T	G
C	M	D	L	Q	U	O	F
D	Z	E	E	E	K	R	R
A	F	I	M	O	V	X	V
N	L	I	T	U	R	G	Y
M	Y	S	T	E	R	Y	H

Word Bank
• • • • • • • • • •
Trinity
Petition
Creed
Liturgy
Mystery

B Check Understanding,
Direct the children to complete each sentence by filling in the circle next to the correct word.

C Make Connections
Tell the children to write their responses on the lines provided for the questions in problems 16–20. For 21–25, have them circle the words from the Word Bank in the word search.

Go to **aliveinchrist.osv.com** to prepare customized and downloadable assessments, send eAssessments, and assign interactive reviews.

Unit 2 Review   **118–119**

Jesus Christ

Our Catholic Tradition

- Jesus brought people the Good News of the Kingdom of God. (CCC, 542)

- Jesus sacrificed his own life to save everyone from sin. (CCC, 613)

- By his life, Death, Resurrection, and Ascension, Jesus Christ gives all people the gift of new life with God that will last forever. (CCC, 571)

- The Church continues to spread Christ's message of new life and hope. (CCC, 863)

What do we learn from the Gospels about Jesus' sacrifice of love?

© Our Sunday Visitor

Unit 3 Overview

Chapter 7

The children will:

- recall the Gospel message is the Good News of God's Kingdom and his saving love
- identify the Gospels as the four books in the New Testament that tell the stories of Jesus' life
- describe the Kingdom of God as the world of love, peace, and justice that is in Heaven and is still being built on Earth
- recall that in his miracles and parables, Jesus teaches that God's Kingdom is here and to come

 Catholic Social Teaching: Live Your Faith

- Life and Dignity, Pages 290–291
- Rights and Responsibilities, Pages 294–295

Chapter 8

The children will:

- recognize that Jesus offered the greatest sacrifice: he gave his life to save us from sin so we could have new life with God in Heaven
- recall that the Resurrection is the event of Jesus being raised from Death to new life
- define the Paschal Mystery as the mystery of Jesus' suffering, Death, Resurrection, and Ascension
- examine how the Church celebrates the Paschal Mystery in each of the Seven Sacraments

 Songs of Scripture
"Mary Magdalene"

 Catholic Social Teaching: Live Your Faith

- Life and Dignity, Pages 290–291
- Solidarity of the Human Family, Pages 300–301

Chapter 9

The children will:

- recognize that, with the help of the Holy Spirit, members of the Church continue Jesus' work here on Earth
- identify the Church as the Body of Christ of which Christ is the head
- recall that all the baptized use their gifts and talents to serve others
- name stewardship as the way we appreciate and use God's gifts, including our time, talent, and treasure and the gift of creation

 Catholic Social Teaching: Live Your Faith

- Call to Community, Pages 292–293
- Option for the Poor, Pages 296–297

Preview Unit Theme

Tell the children that the theme for this unit is Jesus Christ.

Direct the group's attention to the photo and the illustrations on the page. Ask volunteers to describe what they see and comment on how they believe these images relate to the unit theme.

Have four volunteers each read aloud one of the bullet points under Our Catholic Tradition.

Ask: What do we learn from the Gospels about Jesus' sacrifice of love?

Write the children's answers on the board or on chart paper.

Explain that the group will be exploring this question and the theme in general in the next three chapters.

KEY CONCEPT

Jesus taught about God's Kingdom of love, peace, and justice that is in Heaven and is still being built on Earth. Jesus established the Kingdom of God on Earth, and his teaching and miracles were signs of the Kingdom.

DOCTRINAL CONTENT

- The Gospel message is the Good News of God's Kingdom and his saving love. (CCC, 125)

- The four Gospel books in the New Testament tell about Christ's life, teaching, Death, and Resurrection. (CCC, 120, 127)

- The Kingdom of God is the world of love, peace, and justice that exists in its fullness in Heaven and is still being built on Earth. (CCC, 2818–2819)

- In his miracles and parables, Jesus shows us that God's Kingdom is here and yet to come fully. (CCC, 546)

TASKS OF CATECHESIS

Helping children grow in a faith that is "known, celebrated, lived, and expressed in prayer" (NDC, 20).

This chapter focuses on the following tasks of catechesis:

- Promoting Knowledge of the Faith
- Moral Formation

Catechist Background

"What woman having ten coins and losing one would not light a lamp and sweep the house, searching carefully until she finds it? And when she does find it, she … says … 'Rejoice with me because I have found the coin that I lost.' In just the same way, I tell you, there will be rejoicing among the angels of God over one sinner who repents." **Luke 15:8–10**

➜ **Reflect** Do you rejoice when you recover something lost?

Jesus came to proclaim that the reign of God is founded on love, justice, and peace. Every act of compassion, justice, forgiveness, and love performed in the name of Jesus is a realization and proclamation of the Good News. The Good News is that Jesus lived, died, and was raised from the dead for the salvation of all people. The Good News is Jesus Christ, who brought the Kingdom of God into the world. Jesus commissioned his followers to spread this message through the power of the Holy Spirit. As God's People, the Church also proclaims the Good News of the Kingdom of God.

Proclaiming the Good News through words and actions is called evangelizing. Broad and varied, at times outspoken and sometimes subtle, evangelization happens through preaching and teaching, celebrating the Sacraments, and bringing the gift of God's presence to others through acts of healing, freeing, forgiving, and reconciling.

Evangelization is the core of the mission of every member of the Church. Through evangelization, the Church constantly seeks to bring about the transformation of individuals, of cultures, and indeed of the whole world. For this reason, it is the responsibility of all Christians to use their gifts to proclaim the Good News in their everyday lives.

➜ **Reflect** When do your words and actions proclaim the Good News of the Gospel?

Catechist's Prayer

Gracious God, you are always ready to welcome each person with open arms. Teach me to love you more and more each day. Amen.

Lesson Plan

Objectives	Process	Materials

Invite, 10 minutes

The Good News Page 121	♥ **Psalm 16:11** Pray the opening prayer. 📖 **Luke 15:8–10** Reflect prayerfully on the Word. • Discuss What Do You Wonder questions.	📶 **Optional Activity** Chapter Story: "The Best News Ever"

Discover, 35 minutes

The Gospel Message Pages 122–123 • Recall the Gospel message is the Good News of God's Kingdom and his saving love • Identify the Gospels as the four books in the New Testament that tell the stories of Jesus' life	• **Catholic Faith Words** Gospel, Messiah • Discuss ways to share Jesus' Good News. ☆ Underline why Jesus came and what he was anointed to do. 📖 **Luke 4:16–21** Proclaim "The Rejection at Nazareth." • **Share Your Faith Activity** List words to describe the Good News.	☐ pencils or pens ☐ two index cards per child
The Kingdom of God Pages 124–125 • Describe the Kingdom of God as the world of love, peace, and justice that is in Heaven and is still being built on Earth • Recall that in his miracles and parables, Jesus teaches that God's Kingdom is here and to come	• **Catholic Faith Words** Kingdom of God, miracle, parable • Talk about the signs of the Kingdom. ☆ Circle what Jesus called people to do. 📖 **Mark 4:30–32** Proclaim "The Mustard Seed." • **Connect Your Faith Activity** Share things learned from others about God's love.	☐ pencils or pens ☐ board or chart paper ☐ three index cards per child

Live, 15 minutes

Our Catholic Life Pages 126–127	• Read descriptions of two of Jesus' parables. ☆ Draw the symbols from these parables. • **People of Faith** Learn about Saint Isaac Jogues. • **Live Your Faith Activity** List ways to work with God as he builds his Kingdom.	☐ pencils or pens ☐ crayons or colored pencils • **Optional Activity** Crossword Puzzle ☐ Activity Master 7 (Page 121E)
Prayer of Praise Page 128	• Divide the group into two sides. • Follow the order of prayer. ▶ Close by singing "When We Praise You."	📶 Download "When We Praise You."

Family + Faith Page 129

Point out that the Catholic Families page provides chapter highlights, information on how third graders understand faith concepts, and family prayer.

Chapter Review Page 130

📶 **aliveinchrist.osv.com**
• Customize and Download Assessments
• Email Links to eAssessments
• Interactive Student Reviews

ONLINE RESOURCES

 Go to **aliveinchrist.osv.com**

You will find:

- Interactive lesson planning with web specific content and additional activities
- Step by step lesson instruction from printed Catechist Edition for integrated lesson planning
- Custom-built assessments to download and eAssessment links
- Interactive reviews that provide scores and the option to review answers
- Sunday readings with background and questions of the week

 Go to **osvparish.com**

You will find:

- Ask the Experts Q and A
- General Catechist Helps
- Community Connections and Blogs

Sharing the Message with Third Graders

The Gospel Third graders don't often pause to wonder where the accounts of Jesus' life came from or why we have four Gospels in Scripture, told from different perspectives. As they get to know the Gospels better, they will become more aware of the different tones and character of the Gospel writers and the differences that arise from the stories having been told for different audiences.

Teaching Tip: Each year, the Lectionary focuses on one particular synoptic Gospel (Matthew, Mark, or Luke). Talk about this year's source for Gospel readings and what is unique about that Gospel.

How Third Graders Understand

- Third graders like stories that inspire them. Tell them stories of Jesus.
- Children this age don't always understand the underlying meaning of stories. Help them understand Jesus' parables.
- At this stage of their lives, most children are still discovering what it means to follow Jesus. Show them by your example.

"I don't always get what stories mean. Help me understand Jesus' parables."

Chapter Connections

Chapter Story

Invite

"The Best News Ever"

Use this story to expand the chapter introduction.

- The children will read aloud the questions and Taleshia's responses.
- Organize the children into pairs.
- Partners will work together to name three ways in which they shared their good news.

 Go to **aliveinchrist.osv.com** Lesson Planning section for this story.

NCEA IFG: ACRE Edition

Discover

Knowledge of the Faith

- Objective: To know and understand basic Catholic teaching about the Incarnate Word Jesus Christ as the way, truth, and life

Moral Formation

- Objective: To be knowledgeable about the teachings of Jesus and the Church as the basis of Christian morality and to understand Catholic Social Teaching

Catholic Social Teaching

Live

 Use one of these features to introduce a principle and engage the children with an activity.

- Life and Dignity, Pages 290–291
- Rights and Responsibilities, Pages 294–295

Music Options

 Use one or more of the following songs to enhance catechetical learning or for prayer.

- "When We Praise You," Live Prayer, Page 128
- "Act Justly," Discover, Page 123
- "Building God's Kingdom," Discover, Page 124
- "Jambo, Jesu," Live, Page 126

LECTIONARY CONNECTION

 Chapter 7 highlights Lectionary-connected themes such as the Gospel, the Messiah, Kingdom of God, parable, and miracle. If your parish aligns its curriculum to the liturgical year, you could use this chapter in connection with the following readings.

Year A

Fourteenth Sunday in Ordinary Time—Messiah

Eighteenth Sunday in Ordinary Time—Love of Christ

Year B

Twenty-third Sunday in Ordinary Time—Kingdom of God

Our Lord Jesus Christ, King of the Universe—Kingdom of God

Year C

The Immaculate Conception of the Blessed Virgin Mary—Birth of Jesus

The Most Holy Trinity—Jesus

 Go to **aliveinchrist.osv.com** for a complete correlation ordered by the Sundays of the year and suggestions for how to integrate the Scripture readings into chapter lessons.

Name _____ Date _____

Crossword Puzzle

This crossword puzzle contains many words that have to do with God's Good News. Use the Word Bank to complete the puzzle.

Across

2. one Gospel is named for him
4. the promised or anointed one
7. an Old Testament writer
9. _____ news makes people happy.
10. The word *Gospel* means "Good _____."
11. Twelve of Jesus' followers

Down

1. Church members _____ to worship.
3. God's Kingdom is full of this feeling.
5. God the Son
6. Humans are part of the _____ of God.
8. God _____ everyone.

Word Bank

Apostles
gather
good
happiness
Isaiah
Jesus
Kingdom
loves
Mark
Messiah
News

The Good News

 Let Us Pray

Leader: Dear God, help us to follow you always.

"You will show me the path to life,
abounding joy in your presence,
the delights at your right hand forever."
Psalm 16:11

All: Jesus, give us the courage to speak about your forgiving love. Amen.

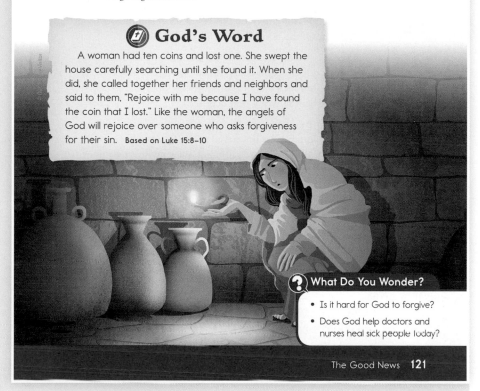

God's Word

A woman had ten coins and lost one. She swept the house carefully searching until she found it. When she did, she called together her friends and neighbors and said to them, "Rejoice with me because I have found the coin that I lost." Like the woman, the angels of God will rejoice over someone who asks forgiveness for their sin. **Based on Luke 15:8–10**

 What Do You Wonder?

- Is it hard for God to forgive?
- Does God help doctors and nurses heal sick people today?

The Good News **121**

Optional Activity

Chapter Story: "The Best News Ever" *Verbal/Linguistic*

Use this story after the opening prayer, before talking about God sending Jesus to teach us about his Kingdom.

- Ask volunteers to read aloud the questions and responses.
- Have the children work in pairs to list ways in which good news can be shared.
- After connecting sharing good news with sharing the Good News, transition back to the lesson instruction.

 Go to **aliveinchrist.osv.com** for Chapter Story.

Invite

 Let Us Pray

Invite the children to gather in the prayer space and make the Sign of the Cross. Read aloud the leader's prayer and the Psalm verse. Prompt the children's response.

Have the children move from the prayer space back to their seats.

Say: God sent Jesus, his Son, to teach us about his Kingdom where there will be peace and justice. Peace comes to many people when they know they are forgiven. Jesus offers us forgiveness for our sins.

God's Word

Guide the children through the process of Scripture reflection.

- Invite them to close their eyes, be still, and open their minds and hearts to what God is saying to them in this passage.
- Proclaim the Scripture.
- Maintain several moments of silence.
- *Ask:* What did you hear God say to you today?
- Invite volunteers to share.

What Do You Wonder?

Say: We see many times in the Gospels that people who are sick and suffering come to Jesus. He heals them. Healing is another sign of God's Kingdom.

Invite the children to respond to the questions. Ask what else they might wonder about forgiveness and healing.

Objectives

- Recall the Gospel message is the Good News of God's Kingdom and his saving love

- Identify the Gospels as the four books in the New Testament that tell the stories of Jesus' life

The Gospel Message

Read aloud the question.

- Tell the children that today's text will answer that question.

Read the text aloud.

- Have the children follow along in their books.

- After the reading, ask the children to state the Good News that Jesus shares. Possible response: God loves his People and saves them from the power of sin and everlasting death.

- *Ask:* How can you share Jesus' Good News with others?

- Brainstorm with the children specific responses to the question.

Work with Words

Read aloud the Catholic Faith Words and definitions from pages 122 and 123.

- Have the children make vocabulary cards for each term.

Discover

The Gospel Message

What Good News does Jesus share?

Catholic Faith Words

Gospel a word that means "Good News." The Gospel message is the Good News of God's Kingdom and his saving love.

Jesus came to share Good News with us. The news that God the Father loves his People and saves them from the power of sin and everlasting death.

Just as Jesus shares the Good News of God's love with you, you pass it on to others. The work of the Catholic Church is to share the Good News of Jesus Christ in words and actions.

Another word for Good News is **Gospel**. The Church gives this name to the four books of the New Testament that tell about Jesus' life, teachings, Death, and Resurrection. The Gospels are named for Matthew, Mark, Luke, and John. They are the most important books for the Church because they focus on Jesus.

Readings from the Bible, also called Scripture, are used every time the Church community gathers to worship. Scripture readings were used to worship in Jesus' day, too.

122

Reaching All Learners

Good News

Children who are experiencing problems at home may have difficulty appreciating Jesus' Good News.

- If possible, work with these children to help them find some positive aspects in their situations.

- It may be that your care and attention are the "good news" that will assist a child through a difficult time.

Jesus' Message

When Jesus' started his ministry in Nazareth, he used Hebrew Scriptures people knew to tell about his role in God's plan.

The people were surprised by Jesus' message. They were waiting for a **Messiah**, or savior. They did not expect him to be a man from Nazareth.

God's Word

The Rejection at Nazareth

One day, Jesus came back to his hometown of Nazareth. Everyone had gathered for worship. Jesus opened the Book of Isaiah and read words that described a person God promised to send.

"The Spirit of the Lord is upon me, because he has anointed me to bring glad tidings to the poor."

Jesus then said he had come to set people free and … announce a time of blessings from God.

Then Jesus surprised everyone. He said, "Today this scripture passage is fulfilled in your hearing."

Based on Luke 4:16–21

Catholic Faith Words

Messiah the promised one who would lead his People. The word Messiah means "God's anointed," or "God's chosen one." Jesus is the Messiah.

Underline why Jesus came and what he was anointed to do.

Share Your Faith

Think List words to describe the Good News.

1. _____   3. _____

2. _____   4. _____

Share In small groups, write a radio commercial using the words you each listed.

The Good News **123**

Jesus' Message

Read aloud both paragraphs.

- *Ask:* Where did Jesus begin his ministry? Nazareth
- *Ask:* Why were people surprised by Jesus' message? they didn't expect a savior to come from Nazareth
- Invite the children to respond to both questions.

God's Word

Tell the children that they will hear a story about how Jesus surprised people in his hometown. Point out that in Jesus' time, many people did not yet understand that Jesus was the Son of God.

Proclaim the Scripture story.

⭐ Instruct the children to underline why Jesus came and what he was anointed to do.

> ▶ Music Option: While the children work on the activity, play "Act Justly," downloaded from **aliveinchrist.osv.com**.

Activity

Read aloud the directions.

- Invite volunteers to share some of their words. Then arrange the children in groups to write a

Quick Review

The Gospels share the Good News of Jesus, and of Gods Kingdom and his saving love.

ⓘ Catechist Background

Gospel

The word *Gospel* comes from the Old English *godspel*—*god* meaning "good" and *spel* meaning "tale."

- The four Gospels were written thirty to sixty years after Jesus' Resurrection.
- The authors recognized the importance of writing the story of Jesus so that future generations could know him and believe in him.
- The Gospels share the Good News of Jesus.

Objectives

- Describe the Kingdom of God as the world of love, peace, and justice that is in Heaven and is still being built on Earth
- Recall that in his miracles and parables, Jesus teaches that God's Kingdom is here and to come

The Kingdom of God

Read aloud the question.

- Write the children's responses on the board or on chart paper.

Invite three volunteers to each read aloud one of the paragraphs.

- *Ask:* What were signs of the Kingdom during Jesus' time on Earth? his teaching and miracles

Have each child place a finger on the highlighted term, *Kingdom of God.*

- Ask a volunteer to read the definition for *Kingdom of God.*

Have each child place a finger on the highlighted word, *miracles.*

- Ask another volunteer to read the definition for *miracle.*
- Have the children make vocabulary cards for each term.

⭐ Direct the children to circle what Jesus called people to do.

 Music Option: Have the children sing "Building God's Kingdom," downloaded from **aliveinchrist.osv.com**.

The Kingdom of God

Where can we find God's Kingdom?

The reading from the Gospel of Luke tells of how Jesus began his work among the people. He called people to turn back to God and live as believers. He taught about God the Father's forgiveness and showed people to trust in and rely on the Father.

The words Jesus read from Scripture tell about the **Kingdom of God**, or God's reign of love, peace, and justice. In God's Kingdom, those who are poor hear joyful news. No one is a prisoner of sin and sadness. People who are sick are healed.

God's Kingdom is in Heaven and also on the Earth. In the Lord's Prayer, Jesus prayed that the Father's will would be done "on earth as it is in heaven." Jesus established the Kingdom of God on Earth, and his teaching and **miracles** were signs of the Kingdom that continues to grow. When we tell others about Jesus, show God's love and act with peace, we work with God to help his reign spread.

Catholic Faith Words

Kingdom of God the world of love, peace, and justice that is in Heaven and is still being built on Earth

miracle something that cannot be explained by science, but happened by the power of God

 Circle what Jesus called people to do.

© Our Sunday Visitor

124

✓ Quick Tip

The Kingdom

Point out to the children the literal meaning of *kingdom*: a place ruled over by a king.

- Explain that God's Kingdom includes the whole world.
- Remind the children that in the Lord's Prayer, we pray "thy kingdom come," which primarily refers to the final reign of God through Christ's return.
- Share with them that many artists depict God or Jesus dressed as a king.

Parables

Jesus often taught with **parables**. Parables are teaching stories that Jesus used to describe the Kingdom of God. One day, Jesus told this story.

God's Word

The Mustard Seed

Jesus said that the Kingdom of God was like a mustard seed. This seed grows from a tiny seed into a large, beautiful tree. **Based on Mark 4:30–32**

© Our Sunday Visitor

Jesus was planting the seed of the Kingdom. Jesus showed people how to live. He healed people and set them free from loneliness, sorrow, and sin. He helped people see and feel God's love. Jesus sends his Church to invite everyone into God's Kingdom.

Some other parables Jesus told were the Parable of the Lost Sheep, the Parable of the Good Samaritan, and the Parable of the Great Feast. He told these stories to teach people about God's love, how to treat one another with kindness and respect, and that everyone is welcome in God's Kingdom.

Catholic Faith Words

parable a short story Jesus told about everyday life to teach something about God

Connect Your Faith

Share Examples Who are some people who have taught you about God's love? Name one thing you learned from each of them.

125

(i) Catechist Background

Jesus' Parables

The children may need help recalling the parables that Jesus taught. Here are some you can share.

- The Unforgiving Servant, Matthew 18:23–35
- The Wedding Feast, Matthew 22:1–14
- The Sower, Mark 4:1–20
- The Good Samaritan, Luke 10:29–37
- The Lost Son, Luke 15:11–32

Parables

Summarize the first paragraph.

God's Word

Proclaim the Scripture story.

Have two volunteers read aloud the last two paragraphs.

- *Ask:* Why did Jesus use parables to teach? Possible response: Parables use comparisons and ideas that people can understand to explain difficult concepts.
- *Ask:* What was Jesus trying to teach with his stories? about God's love, how to treat one another, and that everyone is welcome in God's Kingdom

Activity

Read aloud the directions for the Connect Your Faith activity.

- Have the children work independently to make their lists.
- Ask them to share their lists with a partner.

Quick Review

Through his miracles and parables, Jesus shows us that the Kingdom of God (the world of love, peace, and justice) is here and yet to come.

Our Catholic Life

Ask: What do the parables really mean?

- Encourage group discussion.
- Point out that it is okay if different people get different meanings from the same story.

Invite two volunteers to read the two paragraphs.

Two Parables

Ask two more volunteers to each read aloud one of the bullet points in the chart.

 Tell the children that you want them to draw the symbols from the parables described in the chart.

- Provide crayons or colored pencils and allow time for the children to draw the symbols.

> ▶ Music Option: Sing with the children "Jambo, Jesu," downloaded from **aliveinchrist.osv.com**.

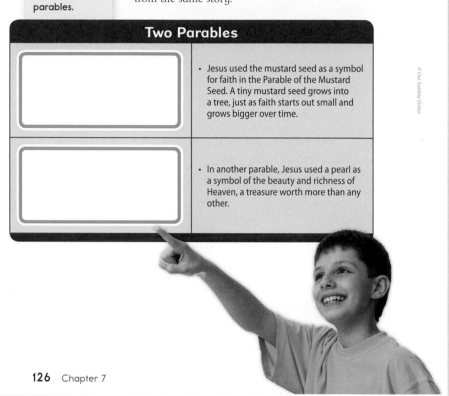

Live

Our Catholic Life

What do the parables really mean?

Jesus told many parables to help people learn about God. Sometimes you must think and study to understand what these stories mean.

One way to understand parables is to look for the symbols in them. The next time you read a parable, look for the symbols and think about what they stand for. Different people may get different meanings from the same story.

Draw symbols from Jesus' parables.

Two Parables

	• Jesus used the mustard seed as a symbol for faith in the Parable of the Mustard Seed. A tiny mustard seed grows into a tree, just as faith starts out small and grows bigger over time.
	• In another parable, Jesus used a pearl as a symbol of the beauty and richness of Heaven, a treasure worth more than any other.

© Our Sunday Visitor

126   Chapter 7

Optional Activity

Activity Master 7: Crossword Puzzle

Distribute copies of the activity found on catechist page 121E.

- Tell the children that this will be a fun way to review what they have learned about God's Good News.
- As an alternative, you may wish to send this activity home with the children.

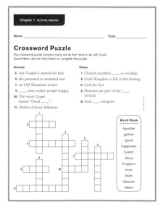

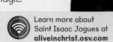

People of Faith

Saint Isaac Jogues, 1607–1646

October 19

Saint Isaac Jogues was a Jesuit priest in France. He was an explorer and wanted to bring the Gospel to North America. He sailed across the ocean to Canada. There, he was a missionary to the Native Americans where he spent six years preaching the Gospel. Saint Isaac was captured and tortured by some people who were afraid of him. They made him a slave. He was freed by Dutch settlers and went back to France. He still wanted to spread the Good News, so he returned to Canada. Sadly, Saint Isaac was killed by Native Americans who thought he was practicing bad magic.

Discuss: Talk about a time when you told someone about Jesus.

 Learn more about Saint Isaac Jogues at **aliveinchrist.osv.com**

Live Your Faith

List three ways you can work with God as he builds his Kingdom.

1. _____

2. _____

3. _____

Write one thing you can do this week to invite others to be part of God's Kingdom?

_____

_____

_____

The Good News **127**

 ## Catholic Social Teaching

Chapter Connections

To integrate Catholic Social Teaching into of the following features: Life and Dignity, pages 290–291; or Rights and Responsibilities, pages 294–295.

- Start the Live step of the process by talking about Saint Isaac on page 127. Then move to the Catholic Social Teaching feature.
- Or, to expand the lesson, complete both pages 126 and 127, then move to the Catholic Social Teaching feature.
- Return to Chapter 7 for the prayer on page 128.

People of Faith

Tell the children about Saint Isaac Jogues.

- Though he wanted to share the Good News with the Native Americans, they eventually killed him because they thought he was using bad magic.

- Saint Isaac gave the name *Blessed Sacrament* to the lake in Canada that is now called Lake George. He was the first Catholic priest to ever come to Manhattan Island, in New York.

- Read aloud the paragraph on Saint Isaac.

- Have a volunteer read aloud the Discuss statement.

- Allow the group to respond.

 Encourage the children to go to **aliveinchrist.osv.com** at home to learn more about Saint Isaac Jogues.

Activity

Read aloud the directions for the activity.

- Have the children work independently to write their answers.

While the children work, you might want to read to them about the coming of God's Kingdom from page 306 in the Our Catholic Tradition section of the Student Book. See "Life After Death" or "Last Judgment."

 Let Us Pray
Prayer of Praise

Prepare

Arrange the group into two sides.

Teach the gestures for the Psalm:

- *I will praise:* Make a full circle with your arms in front of you (praise circle).

- *Your name:* End your circle by crossing the pointer finger and middle finger on the right hand on top of the pointer finger and middle finger on the left hand (sign language for "name").

- *My King and my God:* Raise right arm toward the sky and bring it down by ear and cheek (God).

 Rehearse with the children "When We Praise You," downloaded from **aliveinchrist.osv.com**.

Gather

Invite the children to come to the prayer space with their books.

Pray

Follow the order of prayer on the student page.

- Encourage the children to use the gestures they practiced when they repeat the group response.

Leader's prayer: Lord, we praise your name and all your works. Thank you for your faithfulness.

 Conclude by singing with the children "When We Praise You."

Live

 Let Us Pray
Prayer of Praise

Gather and begin with the Sign of the Cross.

All: I will praise your name, my King and my God.

Side 1: I will give you glory, my God and King.

Side 2: Every day I will bless and praise your name forever.

All: I will praise your name, my King and my God.

Side 1: The Lord is full of grace and mercy.

Side 2: He is good in all his works and full of compassion.

All: I will praise your name, my King and my God.

Side 1: The Lord is faithful and always near. His name is holy.

Side 2: He lifts up those who fall.

All: I will praise your name, my King and my God.
Based on Psalm 145

Leader: Let us pray.

All: Amen.

Bow your head as the leader prays.

 Sing "When We Praise You"
We praise you,
we bless you,
we adore you,
and give glory to you
our God.

128 Chapter 7

 Liturgy Link

Procession

Have the children form a line in pairs and march to the prayer space as they sing the song.

- Have one child carry a Bible. Teach the child to hold the book high, walk slowly, and place the book reverently on the table, as is done with the Book of Gospels at the Sunday Liturgy.

Go to **aliveinchrist.osv.com** for Sunday readings, Scripture background, questions of the week, and seasonal resources.

FAMILY+FAITH
LIVING AND LEARNING TOGETHER

YOUR CHILD LEARNED >>>

This chapter explains the Good News that God the Father loves his People and saves them from the power of sin and everlasting death and that the Gospels in the New Testament tell the stories of Jesus' life and teachings, parables, and miracles.

God's Word

 Read **Luke 15:8–10** and talk about what these verses mean to you.

Catholics Believe

- Jesus taught about God's Kingdom of love, peace, and justice that is in Heaven and is still being built on Earth.
- Jesus established the Kingdom of God on Earth, and his teaching and miracles were signs of the Kingdom.

To learn more, go to the *Catechism of the Catholic Church* #546, 1154 at usccb.org.

People of Faith

This week, your child met Saint Isaac Jogues, one of the first martyrs in North America.

CHILDREN AT THIS AGE >>>

How They Understand The Gospel Third-graders don't often pause to wonder where the accounts of Jesus' life came from or why we have four Gospels in Scripture, told from different perspectives. As they get to know the Gospels better, they will become more aware of the different tones and character of the Gospel writers and the differences that arise from the stories having been told for different audiences.

CONSIDER THIS >>>

When you pray "thy kingdom come," how do you think that's going to happen?

Reflecting on the Kingdom of God requires us to keep one foot in the present and another in the future. We manifest, or participate as members of the Kingdom, when we live as disciples of Christ. The Kingdom is "the Good News that results in love, justice, and mercy for the whole world. The Kingdom is realized partially on earth and permanently in heaven. We enter this Kingdom through faith in Christ, baptismal initiation into the Church, and life in communion with all her members" (*USCCA, 79–80*).

LET'S TALK >>>

- Ask your child to name some ways he or she can share the Good News.
- Talk about some of your favorite parables and what they mean to you.

LET'S PRAY >>>

Saint Isaac, pray for us that we may have the courage to bring God's love to others. Amen.

For a multimedia glossary of Catholic Faith Words, Sunday readings, seasonal and Saint resources, and chapter activities go to **aliveinchrist.osv.com**.

Alive in Christ. Grade 3 Chapter 7 **129**

Distribute the page to the children or parents/adult family members. Point out the chapter highlights, insights on how third graders understand concepts, the opportunity for the adults to reflect on their own experience and faith journey, and the family prayer.

Chapter 7 Review

(A) Work with Words Complete each sentence with the correct answer.

1. God's __Kingdom__ is in Heaven and also on Earth.

2. Christians believe that Jesus is the __Messiah__.

3. Jesus used __parables__ to teach.

4. The word Gospel means __Good News__.

5. Jesus' __miracles__ were signs of God's Kingdom.

(B) Check Understanding To complete each statement use the same answer at the end of the first sentence and beginning of the second sentence.

6. Parables are stories told by __Jesus__.
__Jesus__ set people free from injustice and sin.

7. Jesus taught about the __Kingdom of God__. The __Kingdom of God__ is God's world of love, peace, and justice that is in Heaven and is still being built on Earth.

8. The books in the New Testament that tell stories of Jesus are the __Gospels__. __Gospels__ are named for Matthew, Mark, Luke, and John.

9. Readings from the Bible are also called __Scripture__. __Scripture__ was an important part of worship in Jesus' day.

10. Jesus is the __Messiah__. __Messiah__ is a Hebrew word that means "anointed."

Go to **aliveinchrist.osv.com** for an interactive review.

Chapter Review

Use Catechist Quick Reviews to highlight lesson concepts.

(A) Work with Words
Have the children complete each sentence with the correct answer.

(B) Check Understanding
Explain to the children that the same answer will be used to complete both statements.

Go to **aliveinchrist.osv.com** to prepare customized and downloadable assessments, send eAssessments, and assign interactive reviews.

KEY CONCEPT

Jesus died and rose to new life to save all people from the power of sin. The Church celebrates the Paschal Mystery in all of the Seven Sacraments.

DOCTRINAL CONTENT

- Jesus offered the greatest sacrifice: he gave his life to save us from sin so that we could have new life with God in Heaven. (CCC, 619, 623)

- The Resurrection is the event of Jesus being raised from Death to new life by God the Father through the power of the Holy Spirit. (CCC, 648)

- The Paschal Mystery is the mystery of Jesus Christ's suffering, Death, Resurrection, and Ascension. (CCC, 571)

- The Church celebrates the Paschal Mystery in each of the Seven Sacraments. (CCC, 1113)

TASKS OF CATECHESIS

Helping children grow in a faith that is "known, celebrated, lived, and expressed in prayer" (NDC, 20).

This chapter focuses on the following tasks of catechesis:

- Promoting Knowledge of the Faith

- Liturgical Education

Catechist Background

 "This is my commandment: love one another as I love you. No one has greater love than this, to lay down one's life for one's friend." **John 15:12–13**

➜ **Reflect** Are you dedicated to your friends and others?

In obedience to Christ's command to "do this in memory of me," the Church celebrates the Eucharist and gives thanks for Jesus' sacrifice. In doing so, the Church makes present Christ's sacrifice on Calvary. As the Body of Christ, the Church is one with that sacrifice, and thus her praise, sufferings, joys, and works are also offered to God.

With every celebration of the Eucharist, there is made present Jesus once again in his saving humanity by giving up his body and pouring out his blood. Salvation is an ongoing act by Christ that is made present and imbues the offerings of his Church.

The Paschal Mystery is the suffering, Death, Resurrection, and Ascension of Christ. These four events together comprise the mystery of our faith and give us hope that we, too, will rise from death to life. In the Death and Resurrection of Jesus, God has transformed defeat and death into victory and life. As a seed that has been buried grows roots, a stem, a flower, and, ultimately, fruit, so the miracle of life is born of death and burial in the Paschal Mystery.

This central mystery of Christianity celebrates God's power to bring light from darkness, order from chaos, hope from despair, beauty from squalor, life from death, and salvation from sin.

➜ **Reflect** How are you living the Paschal Mystery right now?

Catechist's Prayer

 Lord Jesus, you gave your life for me. Send me your Spirit so that I can live in your promise of the Resurrection. Amen.

Lesson Plan

Objectives	Process	Materials

⏱ Invite, 10 minutes

The Paschal Mystery Page 131

- ♥ **Psalm 50:14** Pray the opening prayer.
- **John 15:12–13** Reflect Prayerfully on the Word.
- Discuss What Do You Wonder questions.

🔊 **Optional Activity**
Chapter Poem:
"Changes"

⏱ Discover, 35 minutes

Being True to Our Promises
Pages 132–133

- Recognize that Jesus offered the greatest sacrifice: he gave his life to save us from sin so we could have new life with God in Heaven
- Recall that the Resurrection is the event of Jesus being raised from Death to new life

- **Catholic Faith Words** sacrifice
- Talk about making promises.
- ☆ Circle what was promised in the story.
- Discuss Jesus' sacrifice and what it means to us.
- **Share Your Faith Activity** Describe a sacrifice that was made.

☐ pencils or pens
☐ one index card per child

Jesus' Resurrection Pages 134–135

- Define the Paschal Mystery as the mystery of Jesus' suffering, Death, Resurrection, and Ascension
- Examine how the Church celebrates the Paschal Mystery in each of the Seven Sacraments

- **Catholic Faith Words** Resurrection, Ascension, Paschal Mystery
- **John 20:11–18** Proclaim "The Appearance to Mary Magdalene."
- ☆ Underline what Mary Magdalene saw.
- Review the Paschal Mystery with a graphic organizer.
- **Connect Your Faith Activity** Draw a crucifix.

☐ pencils or pens
☐ board or chart paper
☐ crayons or markers
☐ cross or crucifix
☐ three index cards per child

⏱ Live, 15 minutes

Our Catholic Life Pages 136–137

- Read about Gifts of Sacrifice.
- ☆ Write ways to share time, talent, and treasure with others.
- **People of Faith** Learn about Saint Mary Magdalene.
- **Live Your Faith Activity** Write sacrifices that could be made for someone else.

☐ pencils or pens
- 🔊 **Optional Activity**
  Word Search
☐ Activity Master 8 (Page 131E)
☐ board or chart paper

Act of Faith Page 138

- Explain the prayer.
- ▶ Rehearse the song.
- Conclude by processing around the prayer space with the children.

🔊 Download "We Proclaim Your Death, O Lord."

Family + Faith Page 139

Point out that the Catholic Families page provides chapter highlights, information on how third graders understand faith concepts, and family prayer.

Chapter Review Page 140

🔊 aliveinchrist.osv.com

- Customize and Download Assessments
- Email Links to eAssessments
- Interactive Student Reviews

ONLINE RESOURCES

 Go to **aliveinchrist.osv.com**

You will find:

- Interactive lesson planning with web specific content and additional activities
- Step by step lesson instruction from printed Catechist Edition for integrated lesson planning
- Custom-built assessments to download and eAssessment links
- Interactive reviews that provide scores and the option to review answers
- Sunday readings with background and questions of the week

 Go to **osvparish.com**

You will find:

- Ask the Experts Q and A
- General Catechist Helps
- Community Connections and Blogs

Sharing the Message with Third Graders

Jesus' Sacrifice It's difficult for third graders to understand why it was necessary for Jesus to die. The suffering, Death, Resurrection, and Ascension of Jesus Christ was in atonement for the sins of all mankind. The concept of atonement is still foreign to children this age, and can be difficult for many adults as well. For now, it is helpful for them to understand that Jesus loved us so much that he was willing to die to show his love.

Teaching Tip: Find or make a mini-poster of John 3:16 to display in the room. Pair this verse with an image of Jesus on the Cross.

How Third Graders Understand

- Third graders may act out when they don't understand. Encourage them to ask questions, and meet with them separately if you feel they are struggling.
- Children this age may be afraid of death. Be gentle when talking with them about it.
- Young people tend to want their needs met first. Show them ways to be generous to others.

"I may act out when I don't understand. Let me ask questions."

Chapter Poem

Invite

"Change"

Use this poem to expand the chapter introduction.

- Have the children write a *diamante* poem about selfishness. See the Chapter Poem for an example.
- Line 1 is the subject; line 2 is two words that describe it. Line 3 is three verbs; line 4 has two words about the subject and two about its opposite.
- Line 5 has three verbs about the opposite; line 6 has two words describing it. Line 7 contains the opposite.

 Go to **aliveinchrist.osv.com** Lesson Planning section for this story.

NCEA IFG: ACRE Edition

Discover

Knowledge of the Faith

- Objective: To know and understand basic Catholic teaching about the Incarnate Word Jesus Christ as the way, truth, and life

Liturgical Life

- Objective: To know the Paschal Mystery of Jesus: in the Church's liturgical life—feasts, seasons, symbols, and practices and in the Sacraments as signs and instruments of grace

Catholic Social Teaching

Live

 Use one of these features to introduce a principle and engage the children with an activity.

- Life and Dignity, Pages 290–291
- Solidarity of the Human Family, Pages 300–301

Music Options

 Use one or more of the following songs to enhance catechetical learning or for prayer.

- "We Proclaim Your Death, O Lord," Live Prayer, Page 138
- "Savior of the World," Discover, Page 133
- "Come to Us, Holy Spirit," Discover, Page 135

LECTIONARY CONNECTION

 Chapter 8 highlights Lectionary-connected themes such as sacrifice, Resurrection, Ascension, and Paschal Mystery. If your parish aligns its curriculum to the liturgical year, you could use this chapter in connection with the following readings.

Year A

Easter Sunday of the Resurrection of the Lord—Resurrection

Eleventh Sunday in Ordinary Time—Sinners Saved by Christ

Year B

Seventeenth Sunday in Ordinary Time—Sacraments

Thirty-second Sunday in Ordinary Time—Resurrection

Year C

Friday of the Passion of the Lord (Good Friday)—Jesus' Sacrifice

Holy Saturday: The Easter Vigil—Resurrection

Go to **aliveinchrist.osv.com** for a complete correlation ordered by the Sundays of the year and suggestions for how to integrate the Scripture readings into chapter lessons.

Chapter 8 Activity Master

Name ______________________________ Date ______________

Word Search

In the puzzle below, find and circle the words from the Word Bank. The words may appear vertically or horizontally. All of the words are related to Jesus' sacrifice.

Word Bank

Ascension	Courage	Cross	Giving	Heaven
Loving	Mystery	Paschal	Passover	Praise
Promise	Risen	Suffering	Unselfish	

F	J	G	H	E	S	I	A	R	P
N	O	I	S	N	E	C	S	A	A
E	Y	U	I	N	Y	G	H	E	S
S	U	F	F	E	R	I	N	G	S
I	N	S	L	V	E	V	L	A	O
M	E	S	E	A	T	I	O	R	V
O	S	O	S	E	S	N	V	U	E
R	I	R	N	H	Y	G	I	O	R
P	R	C	U	R	M	N	N	C	S
L	A	H	C	S	A	P	G	V	R

CHAPTER **8**

The Paschal Mystery

 © Our Sunday Visitor

Let Us Pray

Leader: Loving God, help us to give of ourselves.

"Offer praise as your sacrifice to God;
fulfill your vows to the Most High."
Psalm 50:14

All: As we think about your great sacrifice on the Cross, Jesus, we cannot imagine how great your love is for us. Fill us with your love today. Amen.

 God's Word

Jesus was talking to the disciples at the Last Supper. He said, "This is my commandment: love one another as I love you. No one has greater love than this, to lay down one's life for one's friends." **Based on John 15:12–13**

What Do You Wonder?

- Each time you go to Communion, is Jesus really offering his love to you?
- How can you love others as Jesus loves you?

131

Optional Activity

Chapter Poem: "Changes" *Verbal/Linguistic*

Use this poem after the opening prayer, before discussing the night before Jesus died.

- Read aloud the poem. Ask the children to listen for where the poem's tone shifts from selfish to self-giving.
- After connecting self-giving with Jesus' sacrifice, transition back to the lesson instruction.

Go to **aliveinchrist.osv.com** for Chapter Poem.

Let Us Pray

Invite the children to gather in the prayer space and make the Sign of the Cross. Have a volunteer read aloud the leader's prayer and the whole group pray the Psalm verse. Have the children return to their seats.

Explain that on the night before he died, Jesus ate the Last Supper with his disciples.

Say: Jesus wanted the Twelve to understand that, when you love someone, you are willing to make sacrifices for them.

God's Word

Guide the children through the process of Scripture reflection.

- Invite them to close their eyes, be still, and open their minds and hearts to what God is saying to them in this passage.
- Proclaim the Scripture.
- Maintain several moments of silence.
- *Ask:* What did you hear God say to you today?
- Invite volunteers to share.

What Do You Wonder?

Say: On Good Friday Jesus died on the Cross. He gave up his life because he loved his Father, and he loved us. He wanted to give us back what we had lost because of sin.

Invite the children to respond to the questions. Ask what else they might wonder about Jesus' love and life.

Objectives

- Recognize that Jesus offered the greatest sacrifice: he gave his life to save us from sin so we could have new life with God in Heaven
- Recall that the Resurrection is the event of Jesus being raised from Death to new life

Being True to Our Promises

Talk about making promises.

- Ask the children to give examples of promises they have made.

Read aloud the question at the top of the student page.

- Invite a volunteer to read the definition of the word *sacrifice*.

Read aloud the first paragraph.

Lindsey's Promise

Read the first paragraph.

Invite three volunteers to read the various parts.

Read aloud the question at the end of the text.

- Have the children discuss their answers with a partner.
- ⭐ Direct the children to circle what Lindsey promised.

Work with Words

Provide one index card per child. Have the children write the word on one side of the card and the definition on the other.

- Encourage the children to use this card, with the others they have created, to prepare for chapter and unit reviews.

132 Chapter 8

Being True to Our Promises

What does it mean to make a sacrifice?

Jesus made a promise to his Father. A promise can be easy or difficult to keep. You may need to give something up to keep a promise. Read this story about keeping promises.

Catholic Faith Words

sacrifice giving up something out of love for someone else or for the common good (the good of everyone). Jesus sacrificed his life for all people.

⭐ Circle what Lindsey promised.

Lindsey's Promise

One day, Lindsey was faced with a difficult choice. She was having fun with her friend when suddenly she stopped and looked at her watch.

"It's late. I have to go," Lindsey said.

"Call and say you're playing," Sarah said.

"I made a promise. I have to go," Lindsey said.

At the care center, Aunt Diane smiled brightly. "Hello, Lindsey. I am so glad to see you!"

"I promised to go for a walk with you."

Aunt Diane smiled and said, "Great! Let's go!"

→ Would you give up playing with your friends to help a family member?

© Our Sunday Visitor

132 Chapter 8

Optional Activity

Promise Art *Visual/Spatial, Verbal/Linguistic*

Have each child draw a picture of a time when he or she made a promise.

- Beneath the picture, ask each child to write how he or she kept that promise.
- On the back of the picture, have the children write about the importance of keeping promises.

Sacrifices Show Love

Lindsey gave up an afternoon with a friend because she made a promise. When you give up something or do something difficult out of love, it is called a **sacrifice**. It is not easy to make a sacrifice. It takes a lot of love and courage. You have to be unselfish when you make a sacrifice.

Jesus chose to make the greatest sacrifice of all. He did something that no one else could do. Jesus gave up his life so that people could be saved from the power of sin and everlasting death. He freely gave up his life so that all people could have new life with God forever.

The disciples mourn and pray at the foot of the Cross.

Share Your Faith

Think When have you made a sacrifice for someone? How do sacrifices show love? How did this sacrifice make you feel?

_____

_____

_____

_____

Share Share your answer with a partner.

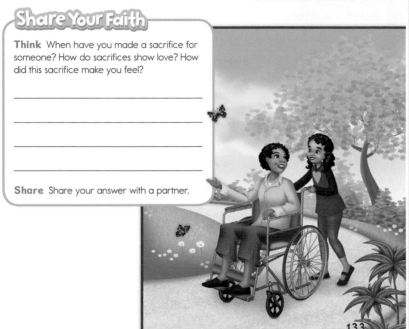

133

Sacrifices Show Love

Invite two volunteers to each read aloud one of the paragraphs.

- *Ask:* What did Jesus' sacrifice mean for the world? Possible response: Because of Jesus' sacrifice, all people can have new life with God in Heaven.
- Point out the illustration at the top of the page and have a volunteer read aloud the caption.
- *Ask:* When have you made a sacrifice for someone? How do sacrifices show love?
- Invite volunteers to respond to the questions.

Activity

Read aloud the directions for the Share Your Faith activity.

- Arrange the children in pairs.
- Have them work independently to answer the questions.
- Allow time for partners to share with each other what they wrote.

> Music Option: While the children work, play "Savior of the World," downloaded from **aliveinchrist.osv.com**.

✓ Quick Tip

Notice Sacrifices

Although the children may already make sacrifices, they might be unfamiliar with the term.

- Build the word *sacrifice* into their vocabulary by using it in everyday situations.
- Mention the sacrifices of members of the group as they help others, perhaps carrying something for another or running errands when they would rather do something else.

Quick Review

Jesus sacrificed his life to save us from sin. Jesus was raised from Death to new life at the Resurrection.

Discover

Objectives

- Examine how the Church celebrates the Paschal Mystery in each of the Seven Sacraments
- Define the Paschal Mystery as the mystery of Jesus' suffering, Death, Resurrection, and Ascension

Jesus' Resurrection

Ask: What does the Paschal Mystery mean?

- Tell the children that they will learn the meaning in this lesson.

Ask a volunteer to read the first paragraph.

God's Word

Proclaim the Scripture story.

 Have the children underline what Mary saw at Jesus' tomb.

- Allow time for the children to scan the text and underline the answer.

Work with Words

Read aloud the Catholic Faith Words and the definitions on pages 134 and 135.

- Provide three index cards per child. Have the children write the words on one side of the card and the definitions on the other.
- Encourage the children to use these cards, with the others they have created, to prepare for chapter and unit reviews.

Jesus' Resurrection

What does the Paschal Mystery mean?

Jesus' loving choice fulfilled God's plan to save his People. Through the work of the Holy Spirit, the Father raised Jesus from Death to new life. This is called the **Resurrection**. The Resurrection showed that God's power is stronger than death.

Catholic Faith Words

Resurrection the event of Jesus being raised from Death to new life by God the Father through the power of the Holy Spirit

Underline what Mary Magdalene saw when she went to Jesus' tomb.

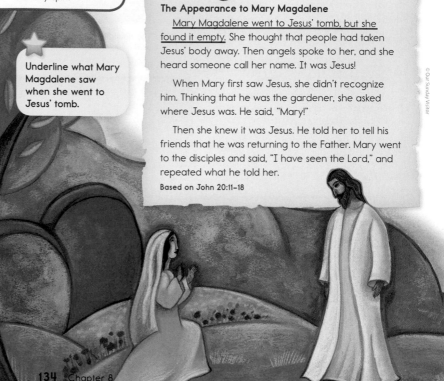

God's Word

The Appearance to Mary Magdalene

Mary Magdalene went to Jesus' tomb, but she found it empty. She thought that people had taken Jesus' body away. Then angels spoke to her, and she heard someone call her name. It was Jesus!

When Mary first saw Jesus, she didn't recognize him. Thinking that he was the gardener, she asked where Jesus was. He said, "Mary!"

Then she knew it was Jesus. He told her to tell his friends that he was returning to the Father. Mary went to the disciples and said, "I have seen the Lord," and repeated what he told her.

Based on John 20:11–18

134 Chapter 8

Songs of Scripture

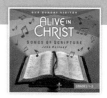

Mary Magdalene

Many children might think that Magdalene was Mary's last name. Explain that Magdala (Migdal) was a city on the Sea of Galilee.

- Mary left Magdala to follow Jesus. Ask the children what they think is the hardest thing to do to be a disciple of Jesus.
- Teach the children the song "Mary Magdalene."

Use *Songs of Scripture*, Grades 1–3 CD, Track 19

Christ's Saving Work

Jesus' suffering, Death, Resurrection, and Ascension are called the **Paschal Mystery**. The word Paschal comes from a word that means "passover." Jesus died to save people from their sins at the time of year when members of the Jewish faith celebrate Passover. Jesus was raised from the dead and at the **Ascension** returned to Heaven. He "passed over" from death to life so that all people can have new life with God in Heaven.

The Mass and the other Sacraments are ways that the Church lives out this great mystery. When you take part in the celebration of the Eucharist, you share in the saving power of Christ's Paschal Mystery.

➔ How is the news of Jesus' Resurrection and Ascension shared today?

Connect Your Faith

Draw a Crucifix Draw a picture of a crucifix and decorate it using words and images. Look at it during difficult times, and remember Jesus' saving actions.

Catholic Faith Words

Ascension when the Risen Jesus was taken up to Heaven to be with God the Father forever

Paschal Mystery the mystery of Jesus' suffering, Death, Resurrection, and Ascension

135

Christ's Saving Work

Ask two volunteers to read aloud the paragraphs.

Copy the graphic organizer in the Quick Tip box on the board or on chart paper. Begin by drawing the cross beneath the words *Paschal Mystery*.

- Ask the children to name the four events in Jesus' life that make up the Paschal Mystery. the suffering, Death, Resurrection, and Ascension of Jesus
- Write these words around the cross as they are named.
- Ask the children when the Church celebrates the Paschal Mystery. at Mass and in the Sacraments

Read aloud the question at the end of the text.

- Discuss with the group.

Activity

Read aloud the directions.

- Provide a cross or crucifix for the children to view as they work.

 Music Option: I have the children sing "Come to Us, Holy Spirit," downloaded from **aliveinchrist.osv.com**.

Quick Review

The Church celebrates the Paschal Mystery in all of the Sacraments. The Paschal Mystery is the mystery of Jesus' suffering, Death, Resurrection, and Ascension.

✓ Quick Tip

Graphic Organizer

Paschal Mystery

Suffering   Death

JESUS

Resurrection   Ascension

Live

Our Catholic Life

Read aloud the question.

- Write the children's responses on the board or chart paper.

Summarize the paragraph.

Gifts of Sacrifice

Assign the blue text in the chart to one child and the bullet points under each to three other children. Have the children read aloud the box content.

⭐ Direct the children to work in pairs to write another way for each gift to be given.

- Ask volunteers to share some of their ideas.

Ask: Why do you think gifts of sacrifice can help you become a better person?

- Encourage group discussion.

Remind the children that giving of their time, talent, and treasure is one of the Precepts of the Church. To review the rest of the Precepts, have the children turn to page 319 in the Our Catholic Tradition section of the Student Book.

Live

Our Catholic Life

How can your sacrifices help others?

When you make a sacrifice, you are offering a special gift. Most gifts involve time, talent, or treasure. In addition to helping others, gifts of sacrifice can help you feel good about yourself.

⭐ Write down some other ways you can share your time, talent, and treasure with others.

Gifts of Sacrifice

Gifts of time include paying attention to others.

- You give time when you play with a younger sister, brother, or neighbor.
- You can also visit elderly people in retirement centers.
- _____

A gift of treasure involves giving money to a worthy cause.

- You can give money to the Church or to other organizations that help people.
- You could donate some of your birthday money to the poor.
- _____

Gifts of talent include using your special abilities.

- You can give up some Saturday morning TV shows for choir practice.
- You could make cards for the elderly at a local senior center.
- _____

➔ Why do you think gifts of sacrifice can help you become a better person?

Optional Activity

Activity Master 8: Word Search

Distribute copies of the activity found on catechist page 131E.

- Tell the children that all of the words in this activity are related to Jesus' sacrifice.
- As an alternative, you may wish to send this activity home with the children.

People of Faith

Saint Mary Magdalene, first century A.D.   July 22

Saint Mary Magdalene was sick. We don't know what was wrong, but Jesus made her well. She then became one of his followers. Mary was with Jesus as he preached about God's love. She stood at the foot of his Cross as he suffered and died. She went to Jesus' tomb on the first Easter morning and was surprised that the tomb was empty. Jesus appeared to her and told her to tell others that he had risen from the dead. Mary did as she was told. Many people believed in Jesus' Resurrection because of her.

Discuss: Who was the first one to tell you about Jesus' Resurrection?

 Learn more about Saint Mary Magdalene at **aliveinchrist.osv.com**

Live Your Faith

Find Your Treasure On the coins labeled time, talent, and treasure, write a sacrifice that you plan to make for someone.

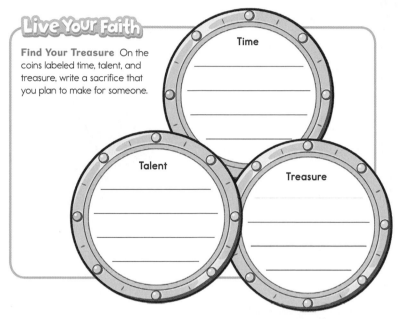

Time

_____

_____

_____

Talent

_____

_____

_____

Treasure

_____

_____

_____

The Paschal Mystery   **137**

 Catholic Social Teaching

Chapter Connections

To integrate Catholic Social Teaching into your lesson, choose one of the following features: Life and Dignity, pages 290–291, or Solidarity of the Human Family, pages 300–301.

- Start the Live step of the process by talking about Saint Mary Magdalene on page 137. Then move directly to the Catholic Social Teaching feature.

- Or, to expand the lesson, complete both pages 136 and 137, then move to the Catholic Social Teaching feature.

- Return to Chapter 8 for the prayer on page 138.

People of Faith

Tell the children about Saint Mary Magdalene.

- Explain that she had been sick, but Jesus made her well and she became one of his followers.

- She was with Jesus when he preached and stood at the foot of the Cross, unafraid for herself, when Jesus suffered and died.

- After Jesus' body had been placed in the tomb, Mary went to anoint it with spices early Easter Sunday morning. But Jesus was gone, and that made her sad.

- Risen from the dead, Jesus showed himself first to Mary Magdalene, who went and told others as Jesus instructed her.

Have a volunteer read aloud the Discuss question.

 Encourage the children to go to **aliveinchrist.osv.com** at home to learn more about Saint Mary Magdalene.

Activity

Read aloud the directions for the Live Your Faith activity.

- Allow time for the children to write their ideas for sacrifices.

- Invite volunteers to share what they wrote with the group.

Let Us Pray

Act of Faith

Explain to the children that this prayer is a statement of our faith as Catholics. With faith, God gives us grace to trust in him and his Word. The Act of Faith prayer reminds us that God's Word is truth.

Prepare

 Have the children rehearse "We Proclaim Your Death, O Lord," downloaded from **aliveinchrist.osv.com**.

Gather

With soft music playing in the background, invite the children to process to the prayer space. Have each child bring his or her book.

Have the children remain standing to pray the Act of Faith.

Pray

Follow the order of prayer on the student page.

- If there is time, share with the children some of the information on this prayer from the Liturgy Link box below.

 Have the children slowly process around the prayer space, singing the refrain for "We Proclaim Your Death, O Lord."

Live

 Let Us Pray

Act of Faith

Gather and begin with the Sign of the Cross.

All: O my God,
I firmly believe that you are one God in three Divine Persons,
Father, Son and Holy Spirit.
I believe that your Divine Son became man,
and died for our sins,
and that he will come to judge the living and the dead.
I believe these and all the truths which the holy Catholic Church teaches,
because you have revealed them,
who can neither deceive nor be deceived. Amen.

 Sing "We Proclaim Your Death, O Lord"
We proclaim your death, O Lord.
Jesus died for us.
We profess your Resurrection.
Jesus lives with us.
Until you come again,
we wait in joyful hope!

 Liturgy Link

Faith

The Act of Faith prayer acknowledges our trust and confidence in God and in his Word. Praying prayers like this, participating in the Sacraments, studying Scripture, and letting God's love and light shine through us are all ways we can keep our faith strong.

- The *Catechism of the Catholic Church* calls the gift of faith essential for our salvation. (CCC, 234)

Go to **aliveinchrist.osv.com** for Sunday readings, Scripture background, questions of the week, and seasonal resources.

FAMILY + FAITH
LIVING AND LEARNING TOGETHER

YOUR CHILD LEARNED >>>
The chapter explains that Jesus sacrificed his life to save us and examines how the Church celebrates the Paschal Mystery in each of the Seven Sacraments.

God's Word
 Read **John 15:12–13** to learn more about loving one another as Jesus loves us.

Catholics Believe
- Jesus died and rose to new life to save all people from the power of sin.
- The Church celebrates the Paschal Mystery in all of the Seven Sacraments.

To learn more, go to the *Catechism of the Catholic Church* #613, 1085 at **usccb.org**.

People of Faith
This week, your child met Saint Mary Magdalene, who was one of the first people to tell others about Jesus' Resurrection.

CHILDREN AT THIS AGE >>>
How They Understand Jesus' Sacrifice It's difficult for third-graders to understand why it was necessary for Jesus to die. The suffering, Death, Resurrection, and Ascension of Jesus Christ was in atonement for the sins of all mankind. The concept of atonement is still foreign to children this age, and can be difficult for many adults as well. For now, it is helpful for your child to understand that Jesus loved us so much that he was willing to die to show his love.

CONSIDER THIS >>>
What does it mean that we daily die and rise with Christ?

Life requires many "dyings." We die to being an adolescent, we die to being responsible only for ourselves, and we die to relationships that fail. Jesus' Death and Resurrection help us to understand that in every death, God can bring new life. "Faith in the resurrection of our bodies is inseparable from our faith in the Resurrection of Christ's body from the dead. He rose as our head, as the pattern of our rising, and as the life-giving source of our new life" (*USCCA, 155*).

LET'S TALK >>>
- Ask your child how making a sacrifice for someone else can help he or she feel good about themselves.
- Talk about a time you have made a sacrifice for someone else. How did that sacrifice show love?

LET'S PRAY >>>
Saint Mary, help us remember to ask Jesus for help when we are sick. Amen.

For a multimedia glossary of Catholic Faith Words, Sunday readings, seasonal and Saint resources, and chapter activities go to **aliveinchrist.osv.com**.

Chapter 8 Review

A **Work with Words** Complete the following paragraph with the correct words from the Word Bank.

1-5.

Jesus made a ___**promise**___ to his Father. He gave up his life so that people could be ___**saved**___ from sin and everlasting ___**death**___. Jesus' ___**Resurrection**___ showed people that God's power is ___**stronger**___ than death.

> **Word Bank**
> Resurrection
> death
> stronger
> saved
> promise

B **Check Understanding** Fill in the blank with the correct answer.

6. What is a special gift that you give by giving up something for a greater good? ___**sacrifice**___.

7. What is the word that means the Father raised Jesus to new life by the work of the Holy Spirit? ___**Resurrection**___.

8. Who told the disciples the news that Jesus was returning to the Father? __**Mary Magdalene**__.

9. The suffering, Death, Resurrection, and Ascension of Jesus are called the __**Paschal Mystery**__.

10. You share in the Paschal Mystery when you participate in the ___**Eucharist**___.

 Go to **aliveinchrist.osv.com** for an interactive review.

Family + Faith

Distribute the page to the children or parents/adult family members. Point out the chapter highlights, insights on how third graders understand concepts, the opportunity for the adults to reflect on their own experience and faith journey, and the family prayer.

Chapter Review

Use Catechist Quick Reviews to highlight lesson concepts.

A **Work with Words**
Review the Word Bank with the children. Have them write the correct word to complete each sentence.

B **Check Understanding**
Instruct the children to fill in the blanks with the correct answer.

Go to **aliveinchrist.osv.com** to prepare customized and downloadable assessments, send eAssessments, and assign interactive reviews.

The Paschal Mystery **139–140**

KEY CONCEPT

The Church is the Body of Christ, to which all her members belong. Stewardship is the way we appreciate and use God's gifts—including our time, talent, and treasure and the gift of creation—to serve God and others.

DOCTRINAL CONTENT

- With the help of the Holy Spirit, members of the Church continue Jesus' work here on Earth. (CCC, 1287–1288)
- The Church is the Body of Christ, of which Christ is the head. (CCC, 792)
- All the baptized must use their gifts and talents to serve others. (CCC, 791, 1937)
- Stewardship is the way we appreciate and use God's gifts, including our time, talent, and treasure and the gift of creation. (CCC, 2402)

TASKS OF CATECHESIS

Helping children grow in a faith that is "known, celebrated, lived, and expressed in prayer" (NDC, 20).

This chapter focuses on the following tasks of catechesis:

- Liturgical Education
- Education for Community Life

Catechist Background

There are different kinds of spiritual gifts but the same Spirit; there are different forms of service but the same Lord; there are different workings but the same God who produces all of them in everyone. **1 Corinthians 12:4–6**

➔ **Reflect** How do you purposefully use your gifts?

The doctrine of the Mystical Body of Christ means that rather than leaving his disciples behind, Jesus made his followers one with him. He told Peter and the rest of the disciples that he had to return to the Father but that his Spirit would come. Those disciples and their descendants, bound together in the Holy Spirit, are Christ's hands and feet, his eyes and ears, his heart and voice. The Holy Spirit has remained with and in the Body, guiding and empowering us through the centuries to continue the work of Jesus.

Saint Paul uses both the image of the human body and the image of the Body of Christ to convey the oneness of Christ and the Church (1 Corinthians: 12:12–27). Although the body has many diverse parts, each with its own function, the body acts as one.

A charism is a grace given by the Holy Spirit to a person or a group for the good of the community. It is more than a personal gift or talent. A charism is a call to live in a particular way that will serve the Church's mission, the continuation of the work of Jesus Christ. The Holy Spirit generously bestows charisms on all members of the Church. Each individual must discern his or her charism and then respond wholeheartedly.

➔ **Reflect** What gifts do you bring to the Church?

Catechist's Prayer

Lord, you love me as an individual and as part of your Body, the Church. Lead me to depend on your promise that you will never leave your faithful people. Amen.

Lesson Plan

Objectives	Process	Materials

Invite, 10 minutes

The Body of Christ Page 141

- ♥ **Psalm 82:3** Pray the opening prayer.
- **1 Corinthians 12:4–7** Reflect prayerfully on the Word.
- Discuss What Do You Wonder questions.

- 📶 **Optional Activity** Chapter Story: "A Big Success"

Discover, 35 minutes

We Each Have a Role Pages 142–143
- Recognize that, with the help of the Holy Spirit, members of the Church continue Jesus' work here on Earth
- Identify the Church as the Body of Christ of which Christ is the head

- **Catholic Faith Words** parish, Body of Christ
- Discuss how the people of the Church work together to get things done.
- ☆ Identify another name for the Church.
- Create a chart showing ways to do the work of Jesus.
- **Share Your Faith Activity** Write a poem to describe love of God.

- ☐ pencils or pens
- ☐ board or chart paper
- ☐ one index card per child
- • **Optional Activity** Important Messages
- ☐ Activity Master 9 (Page 141E)

Sharing in Jesus' Work of Helping Others Pages 144–145
- Recall that all the baptized use their gifts and talents to serve others
- Name stewardship as the way we appreciate and use God's gifts, including our time, talent, and treasure and the gift of creation

- **Catholic Faith Words** stewardship
- Talk about ways to respond to Jesus' call.
- **Matthew 26:31–40** Proclaim "Those Who Helped."
- ☆ Underline what Jesus will say at the end of time.
- **Connect Your Faith Activity** Draw ways to help people worship God.

- ☐ pencils or pens
- ☐ board or chart paper
- ☐ crayons, colored pencils, or markers
- ☐ one index card per child

Live, 15 minutes

Our Catholic Life Pages 146–147

- Share things the parish does for the community.
- ☆ Indicate ways to get involved in the parish.
- **People of Faith** Learn about Blessed Joseph Vaz.
- **Live Your Faith Activity** Make a banner encouraging others to use their talents.

- ☐ pencils or pens
- ☐ chart paper
- ☐ crayons, colored pencils, or markers

Prayer of Petition Page 148

- Select two readers.
- Follow the order of prayer.
- ▶ Close by singing the refrain for the song.

- 📶 Download "Somos el Cuerpo de Cristo/We Are the Body of Christ."

Family + Faith Page 149

Point out that the Catholic Families page provides chapter highlights, information on how third graders understand faith concepts, and family prayer.

Chapter Review Page 150

📶 aliveinchrist.osv.com
- Customize and Download Assessments
- Email Links to eAssessments
- Interactive Student Reviews

ONLINE RESOURCES

 Go to **aliveinchrist.osv.com**

You will find:

- Interactive lesson planning with web specific content and additional activities

- Step by step lesson instruction from printed Catechist Edition for integrated lesson planning

- Custom-built assessments to download and eAssessment links

- Interactive reviews that provide scores and the option to review answers

- Sunday readings with background and questions of the week

 Go to **osvparish.com**

You will find:

- Ask the Experts Q and A
- General Catechist Helps
- Community Connections and Blogs

Sharing the Message with Third Graders

Participation in Jesus' Work Third graders are sometimes initially surprised when they realize they can participate in God's work and that, in fact, everyone in the Church, young and old, has particular work to do. This is a good time in their lives to be presented with this concept, as they are now also becoming more aware of ways in which they can be helpful at home and at school.

Teaching Tip: Generate a "helpful hands" list that includes ways children can be helpful at home, at school, and in faith formation. Solicit ideas from the group.

How Third Graders Understand

- Third graders have gifts and talents they don't realize yet. Help them discover each one.

- Children this age want to be valued. Through your example, teach them to value themselves.

- Some young people like to help. Show them you appreciate the extra things they do.

"I like to help out, but it's nice when you thank me for what I do."

Chapter Connections

Chapter Story

Invite

"A Big Success"

Use this story to expand the chapter introduction.

- As a group, brainstorm the qualities necessary for working well together. Write the list on the board or on chart paper.
- For each quality listed, ask the children to describe an occasion in their lives when that quality proved helpful.

 Go to **aliveinchrist.osv.com** Lesson Planning section for this story.

NCEA IFG: ACRE Edition

Discover

Liturgical Life

- Objective: To know the Paschal Mystery of Jesus: in the Church's liturgical life—feasts, seasons, symbols, and practices and in the Sacraments as signs and instruments of grace

Communal Life

- Objectives: To know the origin, mission, structure, and communal nature of the Church; to know the rights and responsibilities of the Christian faithful

Catholic Social Teaching

Live

 Use one of these features to introduce a principle and engage the children with an activity.

- Call to Community, Pages 292–293
- Option for the Poor, Pages 296–297

Music Options

 Use one or more of the following songs to enhance catechetical learning or for prayer.

- "Somos el Cuerpo de Cristo/We Are the Body of Christ," Live Prayer, Page 148
- "Share the Light," Discover, Page 143
- "Gifts," Discover, Page 144

LECTIONARY CONNECTION

 Chapter 9 highlights Lectionary-connected themes such as Body of Christ and stewardship. If your parish aligns its curriculum to the liturgical year, you could use this chapter in connection with the following Sundays.

Year A

Twenty-fifth Sunday in Ordinary Time—Laborers in the Vineyard

Twenty-eighth Sunday in Ordinary Time—Generosity

Year B

Easter Sunday of the Resurrection of the Lord—Baptismal Promises

Third Sunday of Easter—Baptism

Year C

Second Sunday of Advent—Baptism

The Epiphany of the Lord—Baptism

Go to **aliveinchrist.osv.com** for a complete correlation ordered by the Sundays of the year and suggestions for how to integrate the Scripture readings into chapter lessons.

Name _____ Date _____

Important Messages

Using the pictures and letters, solve the two puzzles.

1

Them – m = _____

 = _____

 – land = _____

Thy – y + e = _____

 = _____

often – 10 = _____

 = _____

The important message =

_____

_____

_____

_____

2

U = _____

R = _____

 + ' = _____

 = _____

 = _____

and

 = _____

in

This – is + e = _____

 = _____

The important message =

_____

_____

_____

_____

CHAPTER 9

The Body of Christ

♥ Let Us Pray

Leader: Loving God, bring hope and comfort to all people.

"Defend the lowly and fatherless;
render justice to the afflicted and needy."
Psalm 82:3

All: You are the source of all hope. So many people in the world need basic things, or they are lonely or sad. Give me the eyes to see and the heart to act as your Son did. Amen.

📖 God's Word

The Holy Spirit gives us different kinds of gifts and different ways of serving. But, there is only one Lord. There are different ways to use your gifts, but it is God who gives them to each of us. **Based on 1 Corinthians 12:4–7**

❓ What Do You Wonder?

- How did God decide what gifts to give you?
- What happens when you only use your gifts to make things better for yourself?

141

○ Our Sunday Visitor

Optional Activity

Chapter Story: "A Big Success" *Verbal/Linguistic*

Use this story after the opening prayer, before you talk about Jesus' plan for each of us.

- Read aloud "A Big Success."
- Arrange the children into small groups, and have them share their experiences.
- After connecting working together with the Body of Christ, transition back to the lesson instruction.

 Go to **aliveinchrist.osv.com** for Chapter Story.

♥ Let Us Pray

Invite the children to gather in the prayer space and make the Sign of the Cross. Have a volunteer pray the leader's prayer, then you pray the Psalm verse. Prompt the group response.

Have the children move from the prayer space back to their seats

Say: Jesus has a plan for you. When you live according to his plan, you will honor God for his gifts and bring peace to the world. Listen to these words from Saint Paul.

📖 God's Word

Guide the children through the process of Scripture reflection.

- Invite them to close their eyes, be still, and open their minds and hearts to what God is saying to them in this passage.
- Proclaim the Scripture.
- Maintain several moments of silence.
- *Ask:* What did you hear God say to you today?
- Invite volunteers to share.

What Do You Wonder?

Say: We have all been given different gifts from the Holy Spirit. We must use these gifts to love God and serve others. We continue Jesus' work on Earth by doing so.

Invite the children to respond to the questions. Ask what else they might wonder about God's gifts.

Discover

Objectives

- Recognize that, with the help of the Holy Spirit, members of the Church continue Jesus' work here on Earth
- Identify the Church as the Body of Christ of which Christ is the head

We Each Have a Role

Read aloud the question.

- Tell the children that the people of the Church work together to get things done.

Read aloud the first paragraph.

The Church

Have three volunteers each read aloud one of the paragraphs.

- *Ask*: When have you worked with others to help solve a problem?
- Have the children discuss this question in pairs.
- Direct the children to draw a box around another name for the Church.

Work with Words

Read aloud the Catholic Faith Word and definition.

- Provide one index card per child. Have the children write the word on one side of the card and the definition on the other.
- Encourage the children to use this card, with the others they have created, to prepare for chapter and unit reviews.

We Each Have a Role

How do we continue Jesus' work today?

When people work together, the job is easier for everyone. God's Word tells us that we all have different gifts and talents we use together for the good of the Church.

The Church

The people of the Church work together. When Jesus lived on Earth, he did his Father's work. The Holy Spirit was with Jesus. At his Ascension, Jesus returned to his Father in Heaven. Then Jesus sent the Spirit to be with his Church. The Holy Spirit makes it possible for the Church to continue Jesus' work today.

As a baptized member of the Church family, you are part of a **parish**. Together as a community and as an individual, you are Jesus to other people. You use your hands and feet, your mouth and ears, and your mind and heart to do Jesus' work.

One name for the Church is the **Body of Christ**. This name tells you that all Church members are one body. Even though each member of the Church is unique, we are all one, just like the parts of a body are different parts of one body. We each have a special part to play in God's plan. This name also says that you belong to Jesus. Jesus is the head, and we follow him.

Catholic Faith Words

parish the local community of Catholics that meets at a particular place

Body of Christ a name for the Church of which Christ is the head. All the baptized are members of the Body.

 Draw a box around another name for the Church.

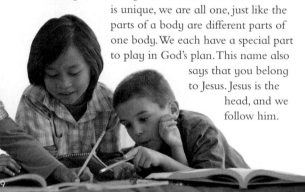

142 Chapter 9

(i) Catechist Background

Body of Christ

The Body of Christ is an image of the Church found in Saint Paul's Letters.

- This image helped early Christians understand their relationship to Jesus and to one another.
- Baptism connects the individual to Jesus and to others in the Church in much the same way that the parts of a body are connected.

Doing Jesus' Work

The Church continues to do Jesus' work on Earth. Jesus' mission was to help people know and give glory to God the Father. An important part of his work was caring for people who needed help.

As a Church, we continue Jesus' work by helping people know and worship God and also by caring for people who need help.

Saint Francis of Assisi taught that people can come to know God through our love for them. He said, "Preach the Gospel at all times. When necessary, use words." We can help fulfill Jesus' mission with our actions and our deeds.

We help others know God when we are good examples, make right choices, and put God first. Someday someone might ask you to explain why you live the way you do. When you talk about your love for God, you help others know him.

Members of parishes work together to help others in need and show love for God and others.

Share Your Faith

Think What would you say if someone asked why you love God? Write a poem using the words you used to describe your love for God.

_____

_____

_____

Share With a partner, share your reasons for living the way you do.

The Body of Christ **143**

Doing Jesus' Work

Have four children read aloud the four paragraphs on this page.

- Create a chart on the board or on chart paper. Use the headings hands, feet, mouth, ears, mind, and heart.

- Encourage the children to share ways of using each of these things to do the work of Jesus. Write their answers under the appropriate headings.

- *Ask:* What did Saint Francis of Assisi teach about people coming to know God's love "Preach the Gospel at all times. When necessary, use words."

- Explain that this means "actions speak louder than words."

Activity

Read aloud the directions.

- Have the children work independently on their poems.

Music Option: While the children work, play "Share the Light," downloaded from **aliveinchrist.osv.com**.

- Allow time for partners to share.

Quick Review

With the help of the Holy Spirit, members of the Church continue Jesus' work here on Earth. All baptized Catholics are members of the Body of Christ.

Optional Activity

Activity Master 9: Important Messages

Distribute copies of the activity found on catechist page 141E.

- Tell the children that when they solve the puzzle, they will find some important messages.

- As an alternative, you may wish to send this activity home with the children.

The Body of Christ **143**

Objectives

- Recall that all the baptized use their gifts and talents to serve others
- Name stewardship as the way we appreciate and use God's gifts, including our time, talent, and treasure and the gift of creation

Sharing in Jesus' Work of Helping Others

Ask: How can we respond to Jesus' call to help others?

- Write the children's responses on the board or on chart paper.

Read aloud the two sentences.

 God's Word

Have a proficient reader proclaim the Scripture story.

- *Ask:* How can you help Jesus by helping someone else?
- Have the group work together to come up with responses to the question.
- Write the children's responses on the board or on chart paper.

 Instruct the children to underline what Jesus will say to some people at the end of time.

> Music Option: Sing with the children "Gifts," downloaded from **aliveinchrist.osv.com**.

Discover

Sharing in Jesus' Work of Helping Others

How can we respond to Jesus' call to help others?

Jesus told his followers this story. In it, Jesus speaks of himself as a king, who praises those who have treated strangers and neighbors like they were Jesus himself.

Underline what Jesus will say to some people at the end of time.

 God's Word

Those Who Helped

At the end of time, the king will call all people before him. To some people, the king will say, "Enter into the kingdom and be joyful! When I was hungry, you fed me. You gave me water when I was thirsty and clothes when I needed them. When I was in prison, you visited me."

The people will say, "When did we do these things for you?"

The king will say, "Whenever you helped anyone in need, you helped me."

Based on Matthew 25:31–40

144

© Our Sunday Visitor

 Scripture Background

Matthew 25:31–40

In this Scripture passage, Jesus explains what will happen at the Last Judgment.

- He states clearly that his followers will be judged on how well they loved him by loving others.
- It is from this passage that the Church has identified specific Corporal Works of Mercy: feed the hungry, give drink to the thirsty, clothe the naked, shelter the homeless, visit the sick and imprisoned, and bury the dead.

Share Your Gifts

God gave each person special gifts, or talents. A talent is something you enjoy doing and can do well. You are called to use your talents to serve others. When you do this, you are being a good steward of the gifts that God has given you. **Stewardship** helps us have thankful hearts and a commitment to sharing our gifts with others.

When people put their talents together and work as the Body of Christ, they can do more than any one person can do alone.

At the end of Mass, you go forth to do Jesus' work in the world. The priest or deacon says, "Go in peace, glorifying the Lord by your life." You glorify the Lord by making good choices, by helping people know God, and by loving and serving all of God's people.

➔ **How many different talents can you count among the people around you?**

© Our Sunday Visitor

Catholic Faith Words

stewardship the way we appreciate and use God's gifts, including our time, talent, and treasure and the resources of creation

Connect Your Faith

Ways to Help Draw one way you help people worship God at your parish.

145

Share Your Gifts

Have three volunteers read aloud the three paragraphs in this section.

Ask another volunteer to read aloud the question at the end of the text.

- Write the children's responses on the board or chart paper.
- Connect a child's name to each talent listed. (All children within your group should be accounted for.)

Activity

Read aloud the activity directions.

- Provide crayons, markers, or colored pencils.
- Allow enough time for the children to finish their drawings.
- Encourage volunteers to explain their work.

Work with Words

Read aloud the Catholic Faith Word and its definition.

- Provide one index card per child. Have the children write the word on one side of the card and the definition on the other.
- Encourage the children to use this card, with the others they have created, to prepare for chapter and unit reviews.

Quick Review

People use their gifts and talents to serve God and others. We serve God when we serve our neighbor.

✓ Quick Tip

Encourage Children

Many children are already using their talents to help others.

- When you see a child using his or her gifts and talents to help others, praise and affirm that child.
- Call or send notes home to tell parents or guardians about a child's good work.
- Consider awarding stickers or other signs of recognition for good deeds.

Live

Our Catholic Life

Read aloud the question at the top of the page.

- Encourage the children to share what they know about their parish.

Read aloud the first paragraph.

Get Involved

Ask a volunteer to read aloud the paragraph.

⭐ Have the children place a check mark next to the ways they can or will get involved.

- Allow the children to discuss their answers with a partner.
- Invite volunteers to share what they marked.
- Encourage the children to share any other ideas they can think of for getting involved in the Church community.

Live

Our Catholic Life

How does your parish share in Jesus' work?

As a way to continue Jesus' work, parishes teach people about God the Father's great love and help those in need. This work can be done in the parish, in the community, or even in another country.

⭐ Place a check mark next to the ways you can or will get involved.

Get Involved

Your parish is already working to bring hope and understanding to your community and the world. Some ways that parishes get involved are listed below.

Get Involved	
☐ Collect money for the missions.	☐ Start a collection of baby items for a women's shelter.
☐ Serve food in a homeless shelter.	☐ Invite a friend to come to Mass or help someone get religious education class.
☐ Become an altar server.	☐ Clean a park.
	☐ Offer to help at computer classes for senior citizens.
	☐ Sing in the choir or play an instrument at Mass.
	☐ Become a greeter with your family.
	☐ Check your parish bulletin or website for announcements about your parish's involvement in the community.

© Our Sunday Visitor

146

Optional Activity

Liturgical Ministers *Interpersonal*

Ask the children to identify people who serve at the weekend liturgies.

- Explain that these parishioners are volunteers.
- Ask the children to take special notice of all liturgical ministers at Sunday Mass.
- Encourage them to thank the liturgical ministers for their gifts of service.

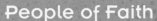

People of Faith

Blessed Joseph Vaz, 1651–1711　　　January 16

Blessed Joseph Vaz was born in India. Most people in India are Hindu. Joseph's family was Catholic. He wanted to share the Gospel with everyone. He used his gifts to help other people know God. He went to faraway places to teach about Jesus and build churches. Joseph decided to become a missionary and went to Ceylon (now Sri Lanka), even though the government there didn't allow priests in the country. Joseph helped bring others there to talk about Jesus and serve God's People.

Discuss: What are some things you can do to help others know God?

 Learn more about Blessed Joseph Vaz at **aliveinchrist.osv.com**

Share Your Talents Make a banner to encourage people to use their talents to help one another as members of the Body of Christ.

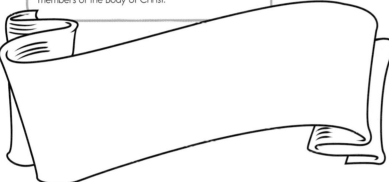

The Body of Christ **147**

🌐 Catholic Social Teaching

Chapter Connections

To integrate Catholic Social Teaching into your lesson, choose one of the following features: Call to Community, pages 292–293; or Option for the Poor, pages 296–297.

- Start the Live step of the process by talking about Blessed Joseph Vaz on page 147. Then move directly to the Catholic Social Teaching feature.
- Or, to expand the lesson, complete both pages 146 and 147, then move to the Catholic Social Teaching feature.
- Return to Chapter 9 for the prayer on page 148.

People of Faith

Tell the children about Blessed Joseph Vaz.

- Share that Joseph Vaz was born in India. Although most people in India are Hindu, Joseph's family was Catholic.
- Blessed Joseph wanted to share the Gospel with everyone. He used his gifts to help other people know God.
- As a missionary, he went to faraway places to teach about Jesus , to build churches, and to serve God's People.
- *Ask:* What are some things you can do to help others know God?

 Encourage the children to go to **aliveinchrist.osv.com** at home to learn more about Blessed Joseph Vaz.

Activity

Read aloud the directions for the Live Your Faith activity.

- Provide the children with crayons, markers, colored pencils, and chart paper.
- Allow time for the children to create their banners.
- While the children work on their Body of Christ banners, read aloud the paragraph on this topic on page 305 in the Our Catholic Tradition section from the Student Book.
- Display the banners around the room.

The Body of Christ **147**

 Let Us Pray

Prayer of Petition

Explain that this is an asking prayer.

Prepare

Select two readers for the prayer service. You will be the leader.

 Rehearse with the children "Somos el Cuerpo de Cristo/We Are the Body of Christ," downloaded from **aliveinchrist.osv.com**.

Gather

Invite the children to process to the prayer space with their books.

Pray

Follow the order of prayer on the student page.

An Optional reading to add if there is time is Matthew 25:31–40.

Leader's concluding prayer: Holy God, you give us all that we need to love and serve you. Thank you for helping us spread your message.

 Sing with the children the refrain for "Somos el Cuerpo de Cristo/We Are the Body of Christ" as together you process from the prayer space.

 Live

 Let Us Pray

Prayer of Petition

Gather and begin with the Sign of the Cross.

Leader: God our Father, we stand before you as the Body of Christ.

Reader 1: Help our eyes see work that needs to be done,

All: So that we can share in your work.

Reader 2: Help our ears hear your wisdom written in Scripture,

All: So that we can praise God and listen to his will.

Reader 1: Help our hands and feet be strong,

All: So that we can help one another.

Reader 2: Help our hearts be full of love,

All: So that we can share your love.

Leader: Let us pray.

Bow your heads as the leader prays.

All: Amen.

Sing "Somos el Cuerpo de Cristo/We Are the Body of Christ"
Somos el Cuerpo de Cristo.
We are the Body of Christ.
Hemos oído el llamado;
we've answered "Yes" to the call of the Lord.
Somos el Cuerpo de Cristo.
We are the Body of Christ.
Traemos su santo mensaje.
We come to bring the Good News to the world.

148 Chapter 9

 Liturgy Link

Gestures

Gestures are an effective way to help children remember a concept.

- Teach the children some gestures for indicating eyes, ears, hands, feet, and hearts.
- Instruct the group to use these gestures at the appropriate points in the prayer celebration when they hear the readers say the words aloud.

Go to **aliveinchrist.osv.com** for Sunday readings, Scripture background, questions of the week, and seasonal resources.

FAMILY+FAITH
LIVING AND LEARNING TOGETHER

YOUR CHILD LEARNED >>>

This chapter explains that all baptized Catholics are members of the Body of Christ and examines how people use their gifts and talents to serve God and others.

God's Word

 Read **1 Corinthians 12:4–7** and talk about how your family is part of the Body of Christ.

Catholics Believe

- The Church is the Body of Christ, to which all her members belong.
- Stewardship is the way we appreciate and use God's gifts— including our time, talent, and treasure and the gift of creation—to serve God and others.

To learn more, go to the *Catechism of the Catholic Church* #521, 1267 at usccb.org.

People of Faith

This week, your child met Blessed Joseph Vaz, a priest from India who traveled to other countries to help others know about God.

CHILDREN AT THIS AGE >>>

How They Understand Participation in Jesus' Work Third-graders are sometimes initially surprised when they realize they can participate in God's work and that, in fact, everyone in the Church, young and old, has particular work to do. This is a good time in your child's life to present this concept, as he or she is now also becoming more aware of ways to be helpful at home and at school.

CONSIDER THIS >>>

How do you foster your child's gifts and talents? Do you connect them to God's gifts and will for him/her?

As Catholic parents, we balance competition and the common good. It requires helping our children to become their personal best and helping them understand that this talent or gift has been given for the good of the community. "…it is fitting that parents always encourage their children to make life decisions with serious consideration about the best ways to live out the faith" (*USCCA, p. 379*).

LET'S TALK >>>

- Ask your child how he or she can help Jesus by helping someone else.
- Talk about a time when you've shared your talents to help others. What did you do and how did it help someone else?

LET'S PRAY >>>

Blessed Joseph Vaz, pray for us that we may help others know God. Amen.

For a multimedia glossary of Catholic Faith Words, Sunday readings, seasonal and Saint resources, and chapter activities go to aliveinchrist.osv.com.

Alive in Christ, Grade 3 Chapter 9 **149**

Distribute the page to the children or parents/adult family members. Point out the chapter highlights, insights on how third graders understand concepts, the opportunity for the adults to reflect on their own experience and faith journey, and the family prayer.

Chapter 9 Review

A **Work with Words** Complete each sentence with the correct word or words from the Word Bank.

Word Bank
- Church
- stewardship
- Body of Christ
- Holy Spirit
- glorify

1. The Church is sometimes called the __Body of Christ__.

2. You can __glorify__ the Lord by making good choices and helping people to know God.

3. Since Jesus returned to his Father, the __Church__ continues his work on Earth.

4. When Jesus returned to Heaven, he sent the __Holy Spirit__ to be with his followers.

5. __Stewardship__ means appreciating and using God's gifts for the good of God and others.

B **Check Understanding** Complete each sentence.

Column A	Column B
6. The Church continues Jesus' work with the help of	many members.
7. The Church is one, but it has	the Holy Spirit.
8. At his Ascension, Jesus returned to his	Baptism.
9. Your parish is a community that continues	Father in Heaven.
10. We become members of the Body of Christ at	Jesus' work.

Go to **aliveinchrist.osv.com** for an interactive review.

150 Chapter 9 Review

Use Catechist Quick Reviews to highlight lesson concepts.

A **Work with Words**
Have the children complete each sentence with the correct word or words from the Word Bank.

B **Check Understanding**
Direct the children to complete each sentence by matching Column A to Column B.

 Go to **aliveinchrist.osv.com** to prepare customized and downloadable assessments, send eAssessments, and assign interactive reviews.

Use Catechist Quick Reviews in each chapter to highlight lesson concepts for this unit and prepare for the Unit Review.

Have the children complete the Review pages. Then discuss the answers as a group. Review any concepts with which the children are having difficulty.

A Work with Words

Tell the children to match each description in Column A with the correct term in Column B for problems 1–5. Have them fill in the circle beside the correct answer for 6–10.

Unit Review

A Work with Words Match each description in Column A with the correct term in Column B.

Column A	Column B
1. Teaching stories that Jesus told	Messiah
2. Jesus made a great	Paschal Mystery
3. A name for the Church, of which Christ is the head	parables
4. A Hebrew word that means "anointed"	Body of Christ
5. Jesus' suffering, Death, Resurrection, and Ascension	sacrifice

Fill in the circle beside the correct answer.

6. The four books about Jesus in the New Testament are the _____.
○ parables ● Gospels ○ Bibles

7. The Kingdom of God is also called God's _____.
○ law ○ promise ● reign of love

8. What happened three days after Jesus' Death?
● Resurrection ○ Visitation ○ Ascension

9. The Gospels are named for Matthew, Mark, Luke, and _____.
○ James ○ Joseph ● John

10. Whom did Jesus send to us after he returned to Heaven?
● Holy Spirit ○ Apostles ○ Mary

B Check Understanding Complete each sentence with the correct word from the Word Bank.

Word Bank

Heaven

talents

Passover

Baptism

me

11. The word Paschal comes from a word that means

_____ **Passover** _____ .

12. Jesus passed over from Death to life so that all people can have life with God in

_____ **Heaven** _____ .

13. Catholics become members of the Body of Christ at

_____ **Baptism** _____ .

14. Jesus said, "Whenever you helped anyone in need, you helped

_____ **me** _____ ."

15. The Church has many members with special gifts, or

_____ **talents** _____ .

Write the letter T if the sentence is TRUE. Write the letter F is the sentence is FALSE.

16. [**T**] The Gospel message is the Good News of God's Kingdom.

17. [**F**] A miracle is something that can be explained by science.

18. [**T**] Jesus used a pearl as a symbol of the beauty of Heaven.

19. [**T**] After the Resurrection, Jesus told Mary Magdalene to tell others that he was returning to God the Father.

20. [**F**] Stewardship means keeping God's gifts to ourselves.

C Make Connections Write responses on the lines below.

21. In your own words, explain the Kingdom of God.

Possible response: The world of love, peace, and justice that is in Heaven and is still being built on Earth.

22. What does the word Ascension mean?

When the Risen Jesus was taken up to Heaven to be with God the Father forever.

23. What does it mean to you to be a part of the Body of Christ?

Possible response: I can help continue Jesus' work.

24. Why did Jesus say, "Whenever you helped anyone in need, you helped me"?

Possible response: To teach us how to love and serve.

25. How can you use your talents to help others?

Responses will vary.

B **Check Understanding**

Direct the children to complete each sentence with the correct word from the Word Bank for problems 11–15. For problems 16–20, have them write the letter *T* if the sentence is true or the letter *F* if the sentence is false.

C **Make Connections**

Have the children write their responses to the statements and questions on the lines provided.

Go to **aliveinchrist.osv.com** to prepare customized and downloadable assessments, send eAssessments, and assign interactive reviews.

The Church

Our Catholic Tradition

- The Holy Spirit is the soul of the Mystical Body of Christ, the Church and unites us. (CCC, 809)

- The Church is one and holy because she is united in the Trinity and to Christ. (CCC, 813–822)

- The Church is catholic, or universal, because she has all the truths and means of salvation. (CCC, 823–829)

- The Church is apostolic—founded by Jesus, on Peter and the Apostles. The Pope and bishops lead the Church. (CCC, 857–865)

How does the power of the Holy Spirit work in the Church through her bishops and all Catholics?

Saint Peter's Basilica Vatican City in Rome, Italy

© Our Sunday Visitor

Unit 4 Overview

Chapter 10
The children will:

- recognize that Peter was the leader of the Apostles and first Pope, head of the entire Church
- identify the Apostles as the first twelve leaders called by Jesus
- recognize the bishops as successors of the Apostles
- understand that the Pope, bishops, priests, and deacons, lead, guide, and make the Church holy

 Songs of Scripture
Come and Follow Me

 Catholic Social Teaching: Live Your Faith

- The Dignity of Work, Pages 298–299
- Care for Creation, Pages 302–303

Chapter 11
The children will:

- recognize the Marks of the Church as four characteristics that identify Christ's Church: one, holy, catholic, and apostolic
- describe Pentecost as the feast that celebrates the coming of the Holy Spirit
- discuss how the Holy Spirit continues to unify the Church and make her holy
- define the Communion of Saints as everyone who believes in and follows Jesus

 Catholic Social Teaching: Live Your Faith

- Call to Community, Pages 294–295
- Solidarity of the Human Family, Pages 300–301

Chapter 12
The children will:

- recognize that Saint Paul was one of the first to take the message of Jesus across many countries
- explore the Church's mission to announce the Good News of God's Kingdom
- identify the Church as catholic and apostolic
- recognize that the Church's mission is to share Jesus' Good News with the people of all nations
- discover that we are all part of the mission of the Church

 Catholic Social Teaching: Live Your Faith

- Option for the Poor, Pages 296–297
- The Dignity of Work, Pages 298–299

Preview Unit Theme

Tell the children the theme for this unit is the Church.

Ask: How does the power of the Holy Spirit work in the Church through her bishops and all Catholics?

Write the children's answers on the board or on chart paper.

Read aloud each of the bullet points.

Direct the children's attention to the photos and the illustration on the page. Ask volunteers to describe what they see and comment on how these images might relate to the unit theme and/or the bullet points.

After some discussion, explain that the group will be exploring this theme and the answers to the question in the next three chapters.

KEY CONCEPT

The bishops are the successors of the Apostles who teach, lead, and make the Church holy. The Pope is the successor of Peter, the bishop of Rome, and the leader of the entire Church.

DOCTRINAL CONTENT

- Peter was the leader of the Apostles and first Pope, head of the entire Church. (CCC, 552)

- The Apostles are the twelve disciples Jesus chose to be his closest followers. After the coming of the Holy Spirit, they shared in his work and mission in a special way. (CCC, 551)

- The bishops are successors of the Apostles. (CCC, 861–862)

- The Pope, bishops, priests, and deacons lead, guide, and make the Church holy. (CCC, 939)

TASKS OF CATECHESIS

Helping children grow in a faith that is "known, celebrated, lived, and expressed in prayer" (NDC, 20).

This chapter focuses on the following tasks of catechesis:

- Liturgical Education
- Education for Community Life

Catechist Background

Jesus sent out these twelve after instructing them thus,... "As you go, make this proclamation: 'The kingdom of heaven is at hand.' Cure the sick, raise the dead, cleanse lepers, drive out demons. Without cost you have received; without cost you are to give."
Matthew 10:5, 7, 8

→ **Reflect** Do you trust that God will provide all of your needs?

The Church needs good leadership to remain unified and to function effectively. All baptized members of the Body of Christ, with their diverse talents, share the responsibility of maintaining the spiritual and temporal life of the Church.

The primary teachers are bishops and priests, whom God calls to leadership by the power of the Holy Spirit. They are shepherds who guide and care for the spiritual health of the flock. Their first task is to preach the Good News of Jesus Christ.

A collegial group functions as a corporate whole, with each member having equal authority and power. The entire body of bishops throughout the world, sometimes called the episcopal college, is such a group. Together they function in union with the Pope to preserve the teaching and sacramental nature of the Church. The great number and diversity of the members of this group are signs of the Church's universality. The individual bishop exercises ministry in his diocese as well as within the collegial group.

The bishop of Rome, the Pope, has the primary place among all of the bishops and is head of the episcopal college. He is the visible sign of unity for the Church throughout the world.

→ **Reflect** How do you and your colleagues support one another in your ministry?

Catechist's Prayer

Holy Spirit, you are the first teacher. Guide all of the leaders of your Church, and guide me as I proclaim your Good News. Amen.

Lesson Plan

Objectives	Process	Materials

🕐 Invite, 10 minutes

Church Leaders Page 155	♥ **Psalm 73:24** Pray the opening prayer. 📖 **Matthew 10:5–10** Reflect prayerfully on the Word. • Discuss What Do You Wonder questions.	**Optional Activity** Chapter Story: "Everyone Needs Leaders"

🕐 Discover, 35 minutes

The First Leader Pages 156–157 • Recognize that Peter was the leader of the Apostles and first Pope, head of the entire Church	• **Catholic Faith Words** Pope 📖 **Matthew 16:15–19, 26:69–75, John 21:15–17** Proclaim "Peter's Belief," "Peter Denies Jesus," and "Jesus and Peter." • Discuss the Pope's responsibility. • **Share Your Faith Activity** Talk about leading a group.	☐ pencils or pens ☐ one index card per child
Chosen to Lead Pages 158–159 • Identify the Apostles as the first twelve leaders called by Jesus • Recognize the bishops as successors of the Apostles • Understand that the Pope, bishops, priests, and deacons, lead, guide, and make the Church holy	• **Catholic Faith Words** Apostolic Succession, bishop, Magisterium • Discuss the responsibilities of a bishop. ☆ Underline what a parish pastor does. • Talk about other ministries in the Church. • **Connect Your Faith Activity** Write one way the Church teaches us to serve.	☐ pencils or pens ☐ three index cards per child • **Optional Activity** Fill in the Blanks ☐ Activity Master 10 (Page 155E)

🕐 Live, 15 minutes

Our Catholic Life Pages 160–161	• Review the job of a Pope. ☆ Write one interesting thing the Pope does for the Church. • **People of Faith** Learn about Saint Gregory the Great. • **Live Your Faith Activity** Complete the statement on Church community.	☐ pencils or pens
Prayer of the Faithful Page 162	• Select three readers. ▶ Rehearse "Jesus Is with Us." • Follow the order of prayer.	🔊 Download "Jesus, Is with Us."

Family + Faith Page 163
Point out that the Catholic Families page provides chapter highlights, information on how third graders understand faith concepts, and family prayer.

Chapter Review Page 164
🌐 aliveinchrist.osv.com
• Customize and Download Assessments
• Email Links to eAssessments
• Interactive Student Reviews

ONLINE RESOURCES

 Go to **aliveinchrist.osv.com**

You will find:

- Interactive lesson planning with web specific content and additional activities
- Step by step lesson instruction from printed Catechist Edition for integrated lesson planning
- Custom-built assessments to download and eAssessment links
- Interactive reviews that provide scores and the option to review answers
- Sunday readings with background and questions of the week

 Go to **osvparish.com**

You will find:

- Ask the Experts Q and A
- General Catechist Helps
- Community Connections and Blogs

Sharing the Message with Third Graders

Leaders in the Church The adults in the parish that interact most with children, such as the catechists and sometimes the parish priests, are usually the Church leaders of whom children are most aware. They do not yet have much exposure to the Pope or even the local bishop. However, learning more about the larger Church and her leaders can help children feel more connected to the worldwide community of faith.

Teaching Tip: Have the group make cards for the Pope or the local bishop. Send them together in one package with a cover letter.

How Third Graders Understand

- Third graders need guidance. Lead them by your example.
- Children this age like to work with others. Provide group activities.
- Young people often find it easier to obey people who are interested in them. Be genuine in your interest.

"I like to work with others. Provide group activities when possible."

Chapter Story

Invite

"Everyone Needs Leaders"

Use this story to expand the chapter introduction.

- Ask each child to choose a partner; have one be the leader.
- Have the leader slowly move his or her hands while the partner mirrors the motions. Then have the children switch places.
- Ask the children to share what they learned about leaders.

 Go to **aliveinchrist.osv.com** Lesson Planning section for this story.

NCEA IFG: ACRE Edition

Discover

Liturgical Life

- Objective: To know the Paschal Mystery of Jesus: in the Church's liturgical life—feasts, seasons, symbols, and practices and in the Sacraments as signs and instruments of grace

Communal Life

- Objectives: To know the origin, mission, structure, and communal nature of the Church; to know the rights and responsibilities of the Christian faithful

Catholic Social Teaching

Live

 Use one of these features to introduce a principle and engage the children with an activity.

- The Dignity of Work, Pages 298–299
- Care for Creation, Pages 302–303

Music Options

 Use one or more of the following songs to enhance catechetical learning or for prayer.

- "Jesus Is with Us," Live Prayer, Page 162
- "The Family of God," Discover, Page 156
- "We Come Today," Discover, Page 159

LECTIONARY CONNECTION

 Chapter 10 highlights Lectionary-connected themes such as the Pope, bishop, Apostolic Succession, and Magisterium. If your parish aligns its curriculum to the liturgical year, you could use this chapter in connection with the following readings.

Year A

Fifth Sunday in Ordinary Time— The Disciples

Twenty-first Sunday in Ordinary Time—Peter the Rock

Year B

Seventh Sunday of Easter— The Apostles

The Ascension of the Lord— The Apostles

Year C

Palm Sunday of the Passion of the Lord—Imitate Christ

Third Sunday of Easter— Discipleship

Go to **aliveinchrist.osv.com** for a complete correlation ordered by the Sundays of the year and suggestions for how to integrate the Scripture readings into chapter lessons.

Name _____ Date _____

Fill in the Blanks

Fill in the blanks to complete the sentences.

1. A bishop heads a ☐ ___ ___ ___ ___ ___ ___.

2. ___ ___ ___ ___ ___ ___ ☐ take the place of the Apostles in today's world.

3. A diocese is made up of many ___ ☐ ___ ___ ___ ___ ___.

4. The Pope is the bishop of ___ ___ ___ ☐.

5. A ☐ ___ ___ ___ ___ ___ crowed, and Peter remembered Jesus' words.

6. Jesus asked Peter to feed his ☐ ___ ___ ___ ___ and sheep.

7. The word *bishop* means ___ ☐ ___ ___ ___ ___ ___.

Use the letters in the boxes above to complete the statement below. Use the numbers of the sentences below each blank to help you.

Pastors, bishops, and the Pope ___ ___ ___ ___ **and**

                                             6   4   3   1

___ ___ ___ ___ ___ **God's People.**

2   4   5   7   4

Church Leaders

 Let Us Pray

Leader: Caring God, help us follow your will for our lives.

"With your counsel you guide me,
and at the end receive me with honor."
Psalm 73:24

All: Jesus, you give us leaders to help us stay close to you. We give thanks for the priests and deacons who serve you by serving our Church. Amen.

 God's Word

Jesus sent out the Twelve after telling them, "As you go, make this proclamation: 'The kingdom of heaven is at hand.' Do not take any money, or a sack to carry things. Do not even take extra clothes or shoes. Depend on others for what you need." **Based on Matthew 10:5–10**

© Our Sunday Visitor

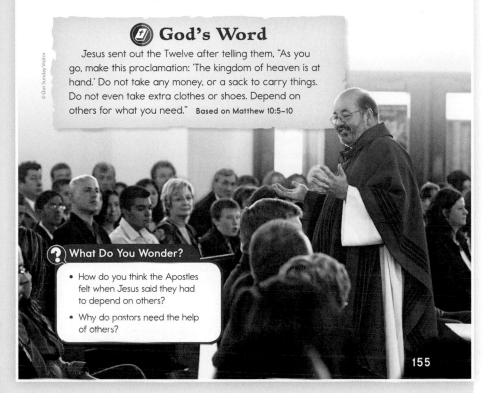

What Do You Wonder?

- How do you think the Apostles felt when Jesus said they had to depend on others?
- Why do pastors need the help of others?

155

Optional Activity

Chapter Story: "Everyone Needs Leaders"

Verbal/Linguistic

Use this story after the opening prayer, before you talk about the first leaders of the Church.

- Spend some time talking about the qualities of a good leader.
- After connecting leaders in general to leaders in the Church, transition back to the lesson instruction.

 Go to **aliveinchrist.osv.com** for Chapter Story.

 Let Us Pray

Invite the children to gather in the prayer space and make the Sign of the Cross. Have one volunteer read aloud the leader's prayer and another read the Psalm verse. Prompt the group's response. Have the children return to their seats.

Say: We rely on the Word of God to guide us in living a good Christian life. God gave us leaders to help us interpret his Word and show us how to live it.

 God's Word

Guide the children through the process of Scripture reflection.

- Invite them to close their eyes, be still, and open their minds and hearts to what God is saying to them in this passage.
- Proclaim the Scripture.
- Maintain several moments of silence.
- *Ask:* What did you hear God say to you today?
- Invite volunteers to share.

What Do You Wonder?

Say: The Church and all her members have Good News to share with everyone on Earth. Jesus entrusted us, the Church, with his mission.

Invite the children to respond to the questions. Ask what else they might wonder about being People of God with a mission to serve.

Objective

- Recognize that Peter was the leader of the Apostles and first Pope, head of the entire Church

The First Leader

Read aloud the question.

Explain to the children that they will learn about Saint Peter's special job as the group covers the next two pages.

- Choose readers for the parts of the narrator, Jesus, and Simon Peter.

God's Word

Tell the group to listen to the readers to find out what happens.

- After the readers have finished the first reading, ask the group why Jesus might call Peter a "rock." Possible response: Peter was firm in his faith.
- Continue with the second passage.

Work with Words

Once the Scripture reading is complete, invite a volunteer to read aloud the Catholic Faith Word and its definition.

- Pass out one index card per child.
- Have the children make a vocabulary card for use in chapter and unit reviews.

 Music Option: While the children work on their cards, play "The Family of God," downloaded from **aliveinchrist.osv.com**.

The First Leader

What special job did Jesus choose Peter for?

Here is a story about Saint Peter, the first leader of the Catholic Church.

> **Catholic Faith Words**
>
> **Pope** the successor of Peter, the bishop of Rome, and the head of the entire Catholic Church

God's Word

Peter's Belief

Jesus asked his disciples, "But who do you say that I am?" Simon answered him, "You are the Messiah, the Son of the living God." Then Jesus blessed Simon and told him that he could not know that from being human. Only his Father could make that known. "And so I say to you, you are Peter, and upon this rock I will build my church."

Peter Denies Jesus

A servant asked him if he had been with Jesus, but Peter denied that he had been with him. Two other people asked Peter if he was friends with Jesus, and Peter denied Jesus again both times.

Then a rooster crowed, and Peter remembered what Jesus had told him: "Before the cock crows you will deny me three times." Peter went out and began to weep bitterly.

© Our Sunday Visitor

156 Chapter 10

ⓘ Catechist Background

Simon Peter

The first part of the Scripture story takes place not long before the crucifixion.

- Jesus wanted his followers to know who he truly was. Simon's answer encouraged Jesus. Jesus entrusted the Church to Simon and changed his name to Peter.
- The second part of the Scripture reading reveals Peter's human weakness on the night before the crucifixion.
- The last part reinforces Peter's role as caretaker of the Church and her members.

Jesus and Peter

After his Resurrection, Jesus showed himself to his followers. Jesus asked Peter if he loved him. Peter responded yes, I love you. Jesus said to him, "Feed my lambs." Jesus asked Peter again, "Do you love me?" Peter answered, "Yes, Lord, you know that I love you." Jesus said, "Tend my sheep" and asked a third time, "Do you love me?" Peter said, "Lord, you know everything; you know that I love you." [Jesus] said to him, "Feed my sheep." Based on Matthew 16:15–19, 26:69–75, John 21:15–17

Jesus chose Peter to be the first leader of the Apostles and the head of the Church. The person in this position is now called the **Pope**. The Pope is in charge of caring for all of God's People.

Share Your Faith

Think Have you ever been asked to be a leader?

Share Talk about your experience in leading a group. Was leading easy or difficult?

 Songs of Scripture

Upon This Rock

Gather pictures of various Popes, including Peter and Pope Francis. Glue each one on paper and attach yarn to create a Pope breastplate for each child.

- Line the children up from Peter to Pope Franics. Explain that a symbol for the Pope is a key.
- Teach the song "Upon This Rock." During the chorus, have the children pass a key from one Pope to the next.

Use *Songs of Scripture,* Grades 1–3 CD, Track 20

Jesus and Peter

Before having the children continue with the third Scripture passage, ask the group why Peter said that he did not know Jesus. He was afraid.

Have the readers proclaim the last passage. When they have finished, ask the rest of the group what Jesus asked Peter to do. to feed his lambs and take care of his sheep

- *Ask:* Why do you think Jesus asked Peter the same question three times? Possible response: to make up for the three times Peter said he didn't know Jesus

Read aloud the concluding paragraph. Point out to the children that this is the answer to the question at the top of page 156.

Activity

Read aloud the directions.

- Have the children work in pairs to discuss and answer the questions.

Quick Review

Peter was the first Pope. The Pope is in charge of caring for all of God's People.

Discover

Objectives

- Identify the Apostles as the first twelve leaders called by Jesus
- Recognize the bishops as successors of the Apostles
- Understand that the Pope, bishops, priests, and deacons, lead, guide, and make the Church holy

Chosen to Lead

Tell the children that today someone else has the same job that Jesus gave to Peter.

- Ask a strong reader to read aloud the two paragraphs.
- *Ask:* Who takes the place of Jesus' Apostles today? The Pope and bishops
- *Ask:* What do you think the responsibilities of a bishop are?
- Invite the children to discuss the question with a partner.

Point out the photo at the top of the page.

- Have a volunteer read aloud the caption. Note that the caption answers both questions you asked the group.

For more information about the Apostles, turn to page 307 in the Our Catholic Tradition section of the Student Book.

Work with Words

Ask three volunteers to read the Catholic Faith Words and their definitions from pages 158–159.

- Have the children create vocabulary cards for each word.

Discover

The Pope and bishops carry on the work of the Apostles preaching the Good News. They lead, guide, and care for God's People.

Chosen to Lead

How do the Pope and bishops lead the Church?

The Apostles were the twleve men chosen by Jesus to be the first leaders of the Church, and Peter was their leader. The Apostles' teaching and authority have been handed down to the bishops, who are the leaders of the Church today. They are the people who now take the place of the Apostles on Earth. This is called **Apostolic Succession**.

The Pope is also the Bishop of Rome. The word **bishop** means "overseer." A bishop leads and serves a diocese. We use the word **Magisterium** to talk about the teaching office of the Church, which is all of the bishops in union with the Pope.

Catholic Faith Words

Apostolic Succession the term used to describe how the authority and power to lead and teach the Church is passed down from the Apostles to their successors, the bishops

bishop an ordained man who works together with other bishops and the Pope in teaching, leading, and making the Church holy. The bishops are the successors of the Apostles.

© Our Sunday Visitor

Optional Activity

Activity Master 10: Fill in the Blanks

Distribute copies of the activity found on catechist page 155E.

- Tell the children that this activity will be a fun way to review the chapter.
- As an alternative, you may wish to send this activity home with the children.

Leaders of the Parish

Dioceses are made up of many parishes. Each parish has leaders, too. The pastor is a priest who has been given the authority to lead a parish community. <u>He, along with other priests, celebrates the Sacraments and works with others to serve the people of a parish.</u> Deacons celebrate some of the Sacraments and do works of charity.

Church Members Serve

There are other people in a parish who are called to serve and lead. These men and women are not ordained, but they help with many parish ministries. Your catechist (religious education teacher) is one of these people. Other examples include liturgical ministers, parish committee members, and directors of religious education and youth ministry.

➜ What are some ways that the leaders of your parish help you?

Catholic Faith Words

Magisterium the teaching office of the Church, which is all of the bishops in union with the Pope

Underline what a parish pastor does.

Connect Your Faith

Serving Others On the lines below, write one way that each of the Church members can serve others.

1. Pastor: _____

2. Catechist: _____

3. You: _____

Leaders of the Parish

Read aloud the paragraph.

⭐ Ask the children to underline what a parish pastor does.

- Help the children learn the names of the priest(s) and deacon(s) of your parish.

Church Members Serve

Ask a volunteer to read aloud the paragraph.

- Tell the children to listen for the different kinds of ministries.
- Ask volunteers to name some of the ministries.

Read aloud the concluding question.

- Discuss responses as a group.

Activity

Read aloud the directions.

- Ask volunteers to share their answers.

 Music Option: Have the children sing "We Come Today," downloaded from **aliveinchrist.osv.com**.

Quick Review

The Apostles are the first Twelve leaders called by Jesus. The bishops are their successors. The Pope, bishops, and pastors lead and guide the Church.

(i) Catechist Background

Pastor

A pastor is a priest who has been assigned by the bishop of the diocese to lead one or more parishes in a diocese.

- The word *pastor* means "shepherd."
- Pastors are called to serve others. They are called to care for people as shepherds care for their flocks.
- The pastor of a parish community celebrates the Sacraments and works with others to serve the people of the parish.

Our Catholic Life

Ask: What is the Pope's job?

- Write the children's responses on the board or on chart paper.
- Tell them they will learn more about this as you cover the next two pages.

The Pope

Ask four volunteers to each read aloud a caption under one of the photographs.

- After each caption, stop and discuss what the children see in the photograph.
- ⭐ Instruct the children to write down one interesting thing that the Pope does for the Church.
- Allow volunteers to share their answers.
- Point out that the Pope leads all of the Church together with the bishops.
- *Ask:* What do you think would be the hardest thing about being the Pope?
- Write all responses on the board or on chart paper.
- Ask the children to remember to pray for the Pope and all Church leaders during Mass.

Live

Write down one interesting thing that the Pope does for the Church.

Our Catholic Life

What is the Pope's job?

The Pope has a special job in the Church. He is guided by the Holy Spirit to lead the Church. The more you learn about the Pope, the better you will understand the Church and your role in it.

The Pope

The Pope teaches.
The Pope is the highest teacher and guide in the Church. The Church learns about important matters of faith from what the Pope says and what he writes.

The Pope leads.
Together with the bishops, the Pope makes decisions about what Catholics should do to be better followers of Jesus.

The Pope travels.
The Pope goes all over the world to meet Catholics and people of other faiths. He helps bring peace and understanding.

The Pope cares for the whole world.
He celebrates Mass and meets with Catholics as well as with world leaders.

_____

_____

© Our Sunday Visitor

160 Chapter 10

Optional Activity

Vatican City *Verbal/Linguistic*

Tell the children that the Pope does not live in Rome or Italy—he lives in an independent state called Vatican City.

- Allow children who are interested to research Vatican City.
- Possible resources include the Vatican website and travel or history books.
- Schedule time during a future lesson for the children to share their findings.

People of Faith

Saint Gregory the Great, c. 540-604

September 3

Saint Gregory didn't want to be the Pope, but was elected Pope anyway. The Pope has a special job. He is guided by the Holy Spirit to lead the Church. Gregory was sad to give up his life as a monk, but he knew he had to do what God wanted. After he was Pope, he trained missionaries to preach the Gospel. Gregory thought beautiful music helped us pray better. Gregorian chant, a special kind of music, is named for him.

Discuss: How do you feel when you are asked to do something you don't want to do?

 Learn more about Saint Gregory the Great at **aliveinchrist.osv.com**

Live Your Faith

My Church Community Fill in the blanks to show how you belong to the community of the Church.

My name is _____.

I belong to a parish in the (Arch)diocese of _____.

Our pastor is _____. Our (arch)bishop Is

_____. Pope _____

and the bishops lead the Catholic Church.

Research Do some research with a family member to find out one thing that is unique about your parish or diocese.

People of Faith

Tell the children about Saint Gregory the Great.

- Being from a wealthy family, he gave up his estates in Italy to found six monasteries on the land.

- Saint Gregory was happiest as a monk in seclusion before being ordained one of seven deacons of Rome.

- He had missionary zeal. After he became Pope, he trained missionaries to preach the Gospel.

- Read aloud the paragraph on Saint Gregory.

- Have a volunteer read aloud the Discuss question.

- Allow volunteers to share their feelings.

 Encourage the children to go to **aliveinchrist.osv.com** at home to learn more about Saint Gregory the Great.

Activity

Read aloud the directions for the Live Your Faith activity.

- Provide the children with the name of your (arch)bishop and (arch)diocese.

- Encourage the children to complete the at-home research section.

Catholic Social Teaching

Chapter Connections

To integrate Catholic Social Teaching into your lesson, choose one of the following features: The Dignity of Work, pages 298–299; or Care for Creation, pages 302–303.

- Start the Live step of the process by talking about Saint Gregory the Great on page 161. Then move directly to the Catholic Social Teaching feature.

- Or, to expand the lesson, complete both pages 248 and 249, then move to the Catholic Social Teaching feature.

- Return to Chapter 10 for the prayer on page 162.

Let Us Pray

Prayer of the Faithful

Explain that this prayer is for leaders and members in the Church.

Prepare

Assign three readers. You will be the leader.

- Allow the readers to rehearse their lines.

 Rehearse with the children "Jesus Is with Us," downloaded from **aliveinchrist.osv.com**.

Gather

Invite the children to process to the prayer space. Have each child bring his or her book.

Pray

Follow the order of prayer on the student page.

An optional reading is Acts 6:1–7.

Leader's concluding prayer: Dear Lord, we thank you for the faithful people who lead us. May they help us continue to grow in faith.

 Conclude by singing together "Jesus Is with Us."

Have the children return to their seats.

Live

 Let Us Pray

Prayer of the Faithful

Gather and begin with the Sign of the Cross.

Leader: We gather today to pray for our leaders and for the needs of the Church.

Reader 1: For the Pope, the bishops, the priests, and other Church leaders, that they may act with wisdom and encourage hope, we pray to the Lord.

All: Lord, hear our prayer.

Reader 2: For our teachers and catechists, that they may help us understand your plan for us, we pray to the Lord.

All: Lord, hear our prayer.

Reader 3: For all members of the Church, that we may use our gifts to serve, we pray to the Lord.

All: Lord, hear our prayer.

Leader: Let us pray.

Bow your heads as the leader prays.

All: Amen.

 Sing "Jesus Is with Us"
Jesus is with us today,
beside us to guide us today.
Jesus teaches us, Jesus heals us,
for we are his Church; we are his chosen;
we are the children of God.

Based on Psalm 122. Text and music
© 1988, Christopher Walker.
Published by OCP.
All rights reserved.

162 Chapter 10

 Liturgy Link

Read Aloud

Because prayer services are a form of communal prayer, it is important that everyone understand the readings.

- Select readers who are highly motivated.
- Permit the readers to practice in a hallway or in another area apart from the rest of the group so that they may become familiar with their parts.

 Go to **aliveinchrist.osv.com** for Sunday readings, Scripture background, questions of the week, and seasonal resources.

FAMILY+FAITH
LIVING AND LEARNING TOGETHER

YOUR CHILD LEARNED >>>
This chapter explains how the Pope, bishops, and pastors lead and guide the Church and describes the Pope and bishops as successors of the Apostles.

God's Word
 Read **Matthew 10:5–10** and learn how Jesus sent the Apostles to announce the Good News.

Catholics Believe
- The bishops are the successors of the Apostles who teach, lead, and make the Church holy.
- The Pope is the successor of Peter, the bishop of Rome, and the head of the entire Church.

To learn more, go to the *Catechism of the Catholic Church* #816–939 at **usccb.org**.

People of Faith
This week, your child met Saint Gregory the Great, one of our past Popes. The Gregorian chant is named after him.

CHILDREN AT THIS AGE >>>
How They Understand Leaders in the Church The adults in the parish that interact most with children, such as the catechists and sometimes the parish priests, are usually the Church leaders of whom children are most aware. They do not yet have much exposure to the Pope or even the local bishop. However, learning more about the larger Church and her leaders can help your child feel more connected to the worldwide community of faith.

CONSIDER THIS >>>
How difficult is it to keep your whole family on the same page?

There are so many competing values and obligations in our lives. It may tend to pull the family in many directions. That is why it is important that each member of the family knows that faith is the priority in your family life. "When a family becomes a school of virtue and a community of love, it is an image of the loving communion of the Father, Son, and Holy Spirit. It is then an icon of the Trinity" *(USCCA, p. 377).*

LET'S TALK >>>
- Ask your child to name some of the responsibilities of a bishop.
- Take turns sharing what you think would be the most interesting thing about being the Pope.

LET'S PRAY >>>
 Saint Gregory, pray for us that we may use our talents to serve others. Amen.

 For a multimedia glossary of Catholic Faith Words, Sunday readings, seasonal and Saint resources, and chapter activities go to **aliveinchrist.osv.com**.

Distribute the page to the children or parents/adult family members. Point out the chapter highlights, insights on on how third graders understand concepts, the opportunity for the adults to reflect on their own experience and faith journey, and the family prayer.

Chapter 10 Review

A **Work with Words** Complete each sentence with the correct word or words from the Word Bank.

Word Bank
- Holy Spirit
- Apostolic
- diocese
- bishop
- Magisterium

1. Many parishes make up a ____diocese____.

2. The word ____bishop____ means "overseer."

3. The ____Holy Spirit____ guides the Pope to lead the Church.

4. The ____Magisterium____ is the teaching office of the Church—all of the bishops in union with the Pope.

5. ____Apostolic____ Succession describes how the authority given to the Apostles is passed down to the bishops.

B **Check Understanding** Match each description in Column A with the correct term in Column B.

Column A	Column B
6. leads the whole Church on Earth	Jesus
7. chose the Apostles to lead the Church	Pope
8. was the leader of the Apostles and first head of the Church	bishop
9. leads a diocese	Peter
10. leads a parish	pastor

 Go to **aliveinchrist.osv.com** for an interactive review.

Use Catechist Quick Reviews to highlight lesson concepts.

A **Work with Words**
Review the Word Bank. Have the children write the correct word from the Word Bank to complete each sentence.

B **Check Understanding**
Explain to the children that they will match each description in Column A to the correct term in Column B.

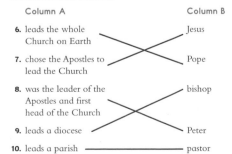 Go to **aliveinchrist.osv.com** to prepare customized and downloadable assessments, send eAssessments, and assign interactive reviews.

KEY CONCEPT

The Marks of the Church are the four characteristics that identify Christ's Church: one, holy, catholic, and apostolic. The Communion of Saints includes all members of the Church, both living and dead, and form one Body in Christ.

DOCTRINAL CONTENT

- The Marks of the Church are the four characteristics that identify Christ's Church: one, holy, catholic, and apostolic. (CCC, 811)

- Pentecost is the feast that celebrates the coming of the Holy Spirit fifty days after Easter. (CCC, 731)

- The Holy Spirit continues to unify the Church and make her holy. (CCC, 2623–2625)

- The Communion of Saints is everyone who believes in and follows Jesus—people on Earth and those who have died and are in Purgatory or Heaven. (CCC, 960–962)

TASKS OF CATECHESIS

Helping children grow in a faith that is "known, celebrated, lived, and expressed in prayer" (NDC, 20).

This chapter focuses on the following tasks of catechesis:

- Promoting Knowledge of the Faith
- Education for Community Life

Catechist Background

So then you are no longer strangers and sojourners, but you are fellow citizens with the holy ones and members of the household of God, built upon the foundation of the apostles and prophets, with Christ Jesus himself as the capstone. Through him the whole structure is held together and grows into a temple sacred in the Lord. **Ephesians 2:19–21**

➜ **Reflect** Do you feel held-together by the cornerstone, Jesus?

Jesus prayed to the Father for the unity of all who believed in and followed him. He also sent the Holy Spirit to help his disciples spread the Good News to the ends of the Earth. As Christianity spread, the Church encountered a wide variety of peoples, customs, and cultures; yet the unity of the one holy Church was preserved.

The Church recognizes and affirms the goodness and truth found in all cultures. The value of unity in diversity is that the Gospel can be lived fully within a specific culture and that the culture can help the Church express the faith in a variety of ways.

The Communion of Saints is a special relationship of the faithful, who are formed into the Body of Christ in Baptism and nourished by the Eucharist. This communion is bonded in faith, Seven Sacraments, goods, and fraternal love. Its members are holy people from all ages, living and dead, who share all of these holy things in common, not just for themselves, but also for the good of the whole Church.

➜ **Reflect** What are some ways in which you promote unity in the Church?

Catechist's Prayer

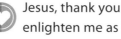 Jesus, thank you for being with me always. Strengthen and enlighten me as I share my faith and work to promote the unity of the Church. Amen.

Lesson Plan

Objectives	Process	Materials

Invite, 10 minutes

Objectives	Process	Materials
One and Holy Page 165	● **Psalm 127:1** Pray the opening prayer. ● **Ephesians 2:19–21** Reflect prayerfully on the Word. • Discuss What Do You Wonder questions.	● **Optional Activity** Chapter Poem: "One from Many"

Discover, 35 minutes

Objectives	Process	Materials
United as One Pages 166–167 • Recognize the Marks of the Church as four characteristics that identify Christ's Church: one, holy, catholic, and apostolic	• **Catholic Faith Words** Marks of the Church, one, holy, catholic, apostolic • Point out how we are all one in Christ • Discuss the Marks of the Church. • **Share Your Faith Activity** Research how people celebrate Mass around the world.	☐ pencils or pens ☐ index cards, five per child ☐ maps, globes • **Optional Activity** Create a Haiku ☐ Activity Master 11 (Page 165E)
Made Holy Pages 168–169 • Describe Pentecost as the feast that celebrates the coming of the Holy Spirit • Discuss how the Holy Spirit continues to unify the Church and make her holy • Define the Communion of Saints as everyone who believes in and follows Jesus	• **Catholic Faith Words** Pentecost, Saint, Communion of Saints ● **Acts 2:1–12** Proclaim "The Coming of the Spirit." ☆ Underline what the Apostles experienced at Pentecost. • Point out that the arrival of the Holy Spirit fulfilled Jesus' promise to the Apostles. • **Connect Your Faith Activity** Name someone who belongs to the Communion of Saints.	☐ pencils or pens ☐ index cards, three per child

Live, 15 minutes

Objectives	Process	Materials
Our Catholic Life Pages 170–171	• Discuss how Saints help us live better. ☆ Find the feast day for each Saint listed. • **People of Faith** Learn about Saints Perpetua and Felicity. • **Live Your Faith Activity** Illustrate a holy card.	☐ pencils or pens ☐ crayons, colored pencils, or markers ☐ art supplies ☐ resources for research of Saints
Praying Together to the Holy Spirit Page 172	• Explain the prayer form. ▶ Rehearse "Come to Us, Holy Spirit." • Follow the order of prayer.	☐ flowers, one per child ● Download "Come to Us, Holy Spirit"

Family + Faith Page 173
Point out that the Catholic Families page provides chapter highlights, information on how third graders understand faith concepts, and family prayer.

Chapter Review Page 174
● aliveinchrist.osv.com
• Customize and Download Assessments
• Email Links to eAssessments
• Interactive Student Reviews

ONLINE RESOURCES

 Go to **aliveinchrist.osv.com**

You will find:

- Interactive lesson planning with web specific content and additional activities
- Step by step lesson instruction from printed Catechist Edition for integrated lesson planning
- Custom-built assessments to download and eAssessment links
- Interactive reviews that provide scores and the option to review answers
- Sunday readings with background and questions of the week

 Go to **osvparish.com**

You will find:

- Ask the Experts Q and A
- General Catechist Helps
- Community Connections and Blogs

Sharing the Message with Third Graders

The Oneness of the Church To a third grader, it might not seem like the Church is one at all. Children this age have often had friends and family that are part of other faith communities (or other parishes, if they are Catholic). It's important for them to know that Christians generally, and Catholics specifically, are united by their faith in Jesus as God's Son and by other core beliefs and practices.

Teaching Tip: Pray the Apostles' Creed together. Talk about how all Catholics (and many other Christians) are united by the truths we profess in the Creed.

How Third Graders Understand

- Third graders want to be part of the group. Help them feel as though they belong to the parish community.
- Children this age like stories. Help them interpret the stories.
- Young people can keep their attention focused better when they are interested in the topic or activity. Connect the topics to their life experiences.

"I like to read stories. But sometimes I need help in interpreting them."

Chapter Connections

Chapter Poem

Invite

"One from Many"

Use this poem to expand the chapter introduction.

- Point out that many threads make a piece of cloth strong and that these threads also contribute to a beautiful pattern.
- Explain that in the same way that many single threads make up a larger, stronger piece of cloth, many different people make up the Church.

   Go to **aliveinchrist.osv.com** Lesson Planning section for this poem.

NCEA IFG: ACRE Edition

Discover

Knowledge of the Faith

- Objective: To know and understand basic Catholic teaching about the Incarnate Word Jesus Christ as the way, truth, and life

Communal Life

- Objectives: To know the origin, mission, structure, and communal nature of the Church; to know the rights and responsibilities of the Christian faithful

Catholic Social Teaching

Live

Use one of these features to introduce the principle and engage the children with an activity.

- Call to Community, Pages 292–293
- Solidarity of the Human Family, Pages 300–301

Music Options

 Use one or more of the following songs to enhance catechetical learning or for prayer.

- "Come to Us, Holy Spirit," Live Prayer, Page 172
- "Around Your Throne," Live, Page 170
- "Litany of Saints," Live, Page 171
- "Sing a Song to the Saints," Live, Page 171

LECTIONARY CONNECTION

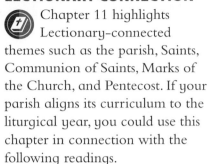 Chapter 11 highlights Lectionary-connected themes such as the parish, Saints, Communion of Saints, Marks of the Church, and Pentecost. If your parish aligns its curriculum to the liturgical year, you could use this chapter in connection with the following readings.

Year A

Pentecost Sunday—Descent of the Holy Spirit

All Saints Day—Children of God

Year B

Pentecost Sunday—Holy Spirit

Fourteenth Sunday in Ordinary Time—Saints

Year C

Sixth Sunday of Easter— Holy Spirit

Seventh Sunday of Easter— Holy Spirit

Go to **aliveinchrist.osv.com** for a complete correlation ordered by the Sundays of the year and suggestions for how to integrate the Scripture readings into chapter lessons.

Name _____ Date _____

Create a Haiku

A haiku is a special form of poem from the Japanese tradition. The first line of the poem must have five syllables. For example, syl - la - bles has three syllables. The second line must have seven syllables, and the third line must have five syllables.

Use the words from the Word Bank to fill in the blanks in the first haiku. Then see whether you can write your own haiku. Use the Idea Box to help.

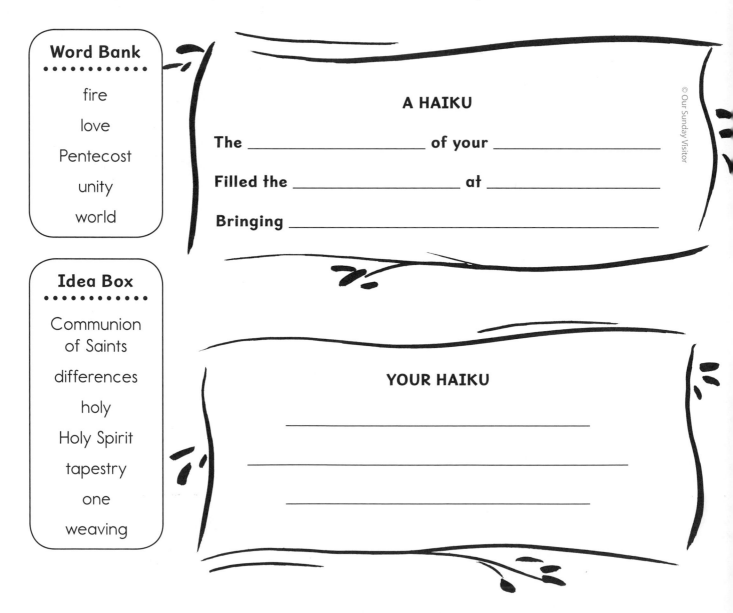

Word Bank

fire

love

Pentecost

unity

world

A HAIKU

The _____ of your _____

Filled the _____ at _____

Bringing _____

Idea Box

Communion of Saints

differences

holy

Holy Spirit

tapestry

one

weaving

YOUR HAIKU

_____

_____

_____

© Our Sunday Visitor

One and Holy

 Let Us Pray

Leader: Lord, God, you welcome all into your home. Help us to do your work.

"Unless the LORD build the house, they labor in vain who build." **Psalm 127:1**

All: Jesus, when we become one with you in Baptism, we become one with others in your Church. Let the Church be a sign of unity and welcome. Amen.

 God's Word

Jesus came and preached peace to everyone. So now, you are no longer strangers or wanderers. You are fellow citizens with the Saints and members of God's family. The Church is built upon the foundation of the Apostles and the prophets. Jesus is the center stone that holds everyone together. **Based on Ephesians 2:19–21**

? What Do You Wonder?

- Could you really have the same courage as the Apostles?
- How can the Holy Spirit make us one?

Optional Activity

Chapter Poem: "One from Many" *Verbal/Linguistic*

Use this poem after the opening prayer, before telling the children about the word *church*.

- Read aloud the poem.
- Point out that a loom joins many threads to make a single piece of cloth.
- After connecting many threads to diversity in people, transition back to the lesson instruction.

 Go to **aliveinchrist.osv.com** for Chapter Poem.

Invite

Let Us Pray

Invite the children to gather in the prayer space and make the Sign of the Cross. Read aloud the leader's prayer and Psalm verse. Prompt the group's response.

Explain that we sometimes use the word *church* to talk about a building, but it's important to remember the Church is most importantly the baptized people who are disciples of Jesus.

Say: Let's listen to hear what Saint Paul said about the Church.

God's Word

Guide the children through the process of Scripture reflection.

- Invite them to close their eyes, be still, and open their minds and hearts to what God is saying to them in this passage.
- Proclaim the Scripture.
- Maintain several moments of silence.
- *Ask:* What did you hear God say to you today?
- Invite volunteers to share.

What Do You Wonder?

Say: Jesus sent his Spirit to the Twelve on the Feast of Pentecost. The Holy Spirit made the Apostles one community and gave them the courage to tell the Good News about Jesus. The Holy Spirit does the same for you.

Invite the children to respond to the questions. Ask what else they might wonder about how the Holy Spirit makes us one.

Objective

- Recognize the Marks of the Church as four characteristics that identify Christ's Church: one, holy, catholic, and apostolic

United as One

Read aloud the question.

- Write the children's responses on the board or on chart paper.

Read aloud both paragraphs.

Ask a volunteer to read the three captions that go with the photos on pages 166 and 167. Pause between each caption to discuss the following:

- Ask what the children see in the photographs.
- Have them identify from which countries the photographs were taken.
- Invite the children to find their location on the map in relation to the ones shown here.

Point out that it is not unusual for our parish community to be made up of many cultures. But we are all one in Christ.

To prepare for the review of the Marks of the Church on page 167, turn to page 307 in the Our Catholic Tradition section of the Student Book.

Discover

United as One

How is the Catholic Church one?

Church communities are sometimes different, but all are one in Jesus. In other cultures, you would see some differences in the Mass celebration than what you would see in your own parish.

The same Mystery of Faith is being celebrated in all these places. The main parts of the Mass are the same everywhere because the Catholic Church is united as one.

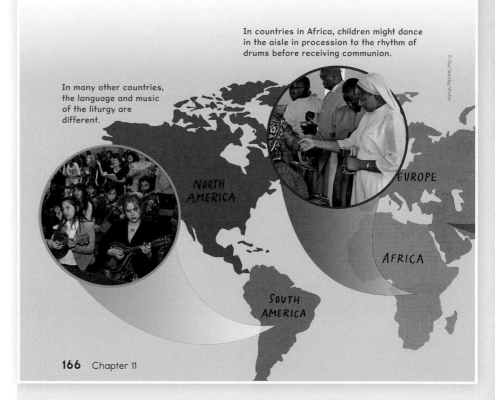

In countries in Africa, children might dance in the aisle in procession to the rhythm of drums before receiving communion.

In many other countries, the language and music of the liturgy are different.

© Our Sunday Visitor

NORTH AMERICA

EUROPE

AFRICA

SOUTH AMERICA

166 Chapter 11

Optional Activity

Activity Master 11: Create a Haiku

Distribute copies of the activity found on catechist page 165E.

- The children will write a poem focusing on chapter concepts.
- As an alternative, you may wish to send the activity home with the children.

Identifying Characteristics

There are four **Marks of the Church: one, holy, catholic, and apostolic.** These Marks are linked together and show the essential features of the Church and her mission. The Church is one because the Holy Spirit unites members of the Church all over the world through one faith and one Baptism.

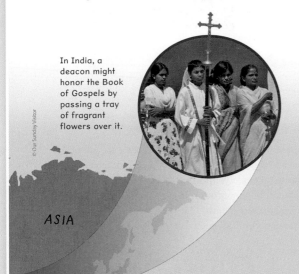

In India, a deacon might honor the Book of Gospels by passing a tray of fragrant flowers over it.

ASIA

AUSTRALIA

Catholic Faith Words

Marks of the Church the four characteristics that identify Christ's Church

one the Church is one because the power of the Holy Spirit unites all the members through one faith and one Baptism

holy the Church is holy because she is set apart for God and his purposes

catholic the Church is meant for all people in all times and all places

apostolic the teaching authority of the Church comes directly from Jesus and his chosen Apostles because the bishops of the Church are direct successors of the Apostles

Share Your Faith

Think How do you think Mass is celebrated in different parts of the world? Using a map or a globe, choose a country; then research how people celebrate Mass in that country.

Share Discuss with your group how Mass in that country might be different from Mass in the United States.

One and Holy **167**

Identifying Characteristics

Have a volunteer read aloud the paragraph.

- Write the title *Marks of the Church* on the board or on chart paper. Beneath the title, list the four Marks.

Work with Words

To review the Marks of the Church, invite five volunteers to each read aloud one of the Catholic Faith Words and its definition.

- Pass out five index cards per child. Have them write the word on one side of the card and the definition on the other, creating one card for each word.

- Encourage the children to use these cards, with the others they have created, to prepare for chapter and unit reviews.

Activity

Read aloud the directions for the Share Your Faith activity.

- Have the children work in small groups, and using a globe or map, select a country to research.

- Allow volunteers to share their findings.

Reaching All Learners

Tactile Learners

Hands-on experience with cloth may help the children grasp the concept of strength in numbers.

- Obtain some loosely woven cloth or ribbon.
- Direct the children to find and pull a loose thread.
- Have the children compare the strength of the single thread to that of the whole piece of cloth.

Quick Review

There are four Marks of the Church: one, holy, catholic, and apostolic. These essential characteristics identify Christ's Church and her mission.

Objectives

- Describe Pentecost as the feast that celebrates the coming of the Holy Spirit
- Discuss how the Holy Spirit continues to unify the Church and make her holy
- Define the Communion of Saints as everyone who believes in and follows Jesus

Made Holy

Ask: What makes the Catholic Church holy?

- Discuss with the children.

Ask a volunteer to read aloud the paragraph.

Work with Words

Ask three volunteers to read aloud the Catholic Faith Words and their definitions on this page and on page 169.

- Pass out three index cards per child.
- Have the children write the words on one side of the card and the definitions on the other side.
- Encourage the children to use these cards, with the others they have created, to prepare for chapter and unit reviews.

God's Word

Proclaim the Scripture. Include the part that appears on page 169.

 Instruct the children to underline the sentence that explains what happened to the Apostles when they were filled with the Holy Spirit.

Fifty days after Jesus' Resurrection the Apostles were filled with the Holy Spirit at Pentecost.

Made Holy

What makes the Catholic Church holy?

People from many different countries were united when the Holy Spirit came to followers of Jesus on **Pentecost**. Pentecost marks the day the work of the Church began. From that day on, the people understood more clearly that they were one body of believers who had been made holy.

Catholic Faith Words

Pentecost the feast that celebrates the coming of the Holy Spirit fifty days after Easter

 Underline what happened to the Apostles when they were filled with the Holy Spirit at Pentecost.

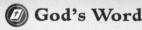 God's Word

The Coming of the Spirit

Fifty days after Jesus was raised from the dead, his followers were together in a house in Jerusalem. Suddenly, the house was filled with a noise like wind. Tongues of fire came to rest on each person in the room. All were filled with the Holy Spirit. They began speaking languages that they did not know.

(i) Catechist Background

Tongues of Fire

Third graders tend to interpret things literally. Take a moment to explain that the "tongues of fire" symbolize the presence of the Holy Spirit.

- Point out the illustration and caption on the student page.
- Find other examples of artwork depicting the Pentecost scene, and share them with the group.
- See if the children can name or identify other things that symbolize the Holy Spirit.

> Jerusalem was filled with Jews from all over the world that day. They heard the Apostles preaching. They were amazed that they could understand people from Galilee in their own languages. **Based on Acts 2:1–12**

Communion of Saints

The Holy Spirit continues to unify the Church today. The Spirit guides the leaders of the Church. The Spirit guides you to follow Jesus more closely and makes the Church holy.

Catholics all over the world are united by their faith in Christ. The Church is even united with the **Saints**, holy people of faith who are with God in Heaven. The Church honors the Saints, especially Mary, the Mother of Jesus, for their holiness. Christians can learn from the examples of the Saints.

The Church is also called the **Communion of Saints**. This means that the members of the Church, both living and dead, form one Body in Christ. Even the Saints join you in worshipping the Father, the Son, and the Holy Spirit!

© Our Sunday Visitor

Catholic Faith Words

Saint a hero of the Church who loved God very much, led a holy life, and is now with God in Heaven

Communion of Saints everyone who believes in and follows Jesus—people on Earth and people who have died and are in Purgatory or in Heaven

Connect Your Faith

Name a Saint Write down the name of someone you know who belongs to the Communion of Saints.

_____

_____

belongs to the Communion of Saints.

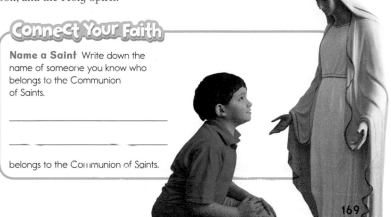

169

✓ Quick Tip

Today's Feast

Help the children become more aware of the Saints throughout the year.

- Show the children how to use a Church calendar to find the Saint whose feast is celebrated on a particular day. Encourage the children to research the life of that Saint.
- Celebrate name days by finding the feast day of each child's patron Saint or of a favorite Saint.

Communion of Saints

Invite the children to discuss what they think happened after Pentecost.

Ask a volunteer to read aloud the first paragraph. Have the children listen to find out what the Holy Spirit does.

- Point out that the arrival of the Holy Spirit fulfilled Jesus' promise to the Apostles.

Read aloud the second paragraph. Tell the children to listen to find out how Catholics are united.

- Explain that unity and holiness are not limited to the earthly Church.

Have a volunteer read aloud the last paragraph.

Ask: Whom do you know who belongs to the Communion of Saints?

- Ask the children to reflect in silence.

Activity

Read aloud the directions.

- Allow time for the children to reflect and write a name.

Quick Review

Pentecost celebrates the coming of the Holy Spirit, who continues to unify the Church and make her holy. The Communion of Saints is made up of all people, living and dead, who believe in and follow Jesus.

Live

Our Catholic Life

Read aloud the question. Allow the children to share their thoughts. Then tell them that we will review this page and find the answer.

Read aloud the introductory paragraph.

Saints

Ask five volunteers to each read aloud one example of how the Saints help us.

Point out the photos in the chart. Ask the children to share how these tie in to what they have read.

⭐ Have the children look up the feast day for each Saint listed at the end of the chart and write this information below their names.

• Provide the children with research material on Saints.

• Allow them to work in pairs to research and fill in the answers.

• Invite volunteers to share their answers.

• Remind the children that the Saints are special people, that they offer a beautiful example of how we can lead holy lives in service to God and others.

 Sing with the children "Around Your Throne," downloaded from **aliveinchrist.osv.com**.

Live

Our Catholic Life

How do Saints help us live better?

The holy people of the past can teach you many things. From them, you can learn how to love God, lead a holy life, and make good choices. Saints are good examples and role models.

⭐ Look up the feast day for each Saint and write it under their names.

Saints

Saints are models or examples.
Someone who teaches you how to live is called a role model. Saints can show you how to love God and serve others.

We can turn to the Saints in prayer.
Because the Saints share God's life and love in Heaven, we can ask the Saints to pray for us and to help us know God's will.

Saints are patrons for jobs, people, and parishes.
Sometimes Saints are called patron Saints. This means that these Saints may have had particular jobs or talents that we share. People who have certain jobs or talents can look up to the Saints who had those same jobs and talents.

People named for Saints look to their name Saints for help.
If your parish church is named for a Saint, you can honor that Saint and ask him or her to pray for you to be a faithful follower of Jesus.

We remember the Saints' lives on their feast days.
At liturgies and celebrations, we learn more about the Saints and their holy actions.

• Saints Anne and Joachim

Feast Day: _____

• Saint Bede

Feast Day: _____

• Saint Katharine Drexel

Feast Day: _____

• Saint Martin de Porres

Feast Day: _____

✓ **Quick Tip**

Discern What Is Right

The Saints are a resource for helping Catholic make difficult decisions.

• Occasionally tell stories that emphasize how God guided the choices of Saints.

• Remind the children that they may look to the life of a Saint for guidance or pray to a Saint for assistance.

People of Faith

Saints Perpetua and Felicity, died c. AD 202–203

March 7

Saints Perpetua and Felicity lived in Northern Africa. They died together for their faith. Perpetua was a rich woman who became a Christian. Felicity was a slave. She was a Christian, too. Both women had young children. Perpetua wrote about being in prison. She and Felicity helped each other be brave until they died. The Communion of Saints goes back to the start of the Church. In one of the prayers of the Mass, we remember many early Saints, like Perpetua and Felicity.

Discuss: Who are some of your favorite Saints?

 Learn more about Saints Perpetua and Felicity at **aliveinchrist.osv.com**

Live Your Faith

Illustrate a Holy Card Choose a Saint, and then illustrate a holy card. Draw a picture on the front of the card and write the Saint's name below your drawing. Then write a prayer on the back of the card.

Amen

🌐 Catholic Social Teaching

Chapter Connections

To integrate Catholic Social Teaching into your lesson, choose one of the following features: Call to Community, pages 292–293; or Solidarity of the Human Family, pages 300–301.

- Start the Live step of the process by talking about Saints Perpetua and Felicity on page 171. Then move directly to the Catholic Social Teaching feature.

- Or, to expand the lesson, complete both pages 170 and 171, then move to the Catholic Social Teaching feature.

- Return to Chapter 11 for the prayer on page 172.

People of Faith

Tell the children about Saints Perpetua and Felicity.

- Perpetua was only twenty-two when she was imprisoned. No matter how long they kept her, she would not forsake her faith.

- Perpetua had an infant son, and Felicity was eight months pregnant. Felicity suffered from the heat during her pregnancy while imprisoned.

- Ask a strong reader to read aloud the paragraph on these two Saints.

- Allow the children to share some of their favorite Saints and what makes them favorites.

 Encourage the children to go to **aliveinchrist.osv.com** at home to learn more about Saints Perpetua and Felicity.

Activity

Read aloud the directions for the Live Your Faith activity.

- Provide crayons, colored pencils, or markers and various art supplies.

- Allow the children time to be creative and finish decorating their cards.

- Ask volunteers to share their work with the group.

 Music Options: While the children work, play "Litany of Saints" or "Sing a Song to the Saints," downloaded from **aliveinchrist.osv.com**.

Live

 Let Us Pray

Praying Together to the Holy Spirit

Explain that this prayer is a reminder of the Communion of Saints.

Prepare

You will be the leader.

Provide each child with a flower.

Invite the children to think of people they would like to remember during this service.

- Provide examples for the children such as patron Saints or Saints associated with family members.

 Rehearse with the children "Come to Us, Holy Spirit" downloaded from **aliveinchrist.osv.com**.

Gather

- Invite the children to gather in the prayer space with their books.

Pray

Follow the order of prayer on the student page.

- When the children read the Saints names, they will lay their flowers around the Bible.

Leader's concluding prayer: Jesus, you said, "I am the resurrection and the life; whoever believes in me, even if he dies, will live, and everyone who lives and believes in me will never die" (John 11:25–26). May our hope in the Resurrection strengthen our faith in you. Amen.

 Conclude the celebration by singing with the children "Come to Us, Holy Spirit."

Live

 Let Us Pray

Praying Together to the Holy Spirit

Gather and begin with the Sign of the Cross.
Children read their names and present their flowers.

Leader: So many people belong to the Communion of Saints. Let us prayerfully name some. After every two names we will pray:

All: Be with us in praising God the Father, God the Son, and God the Holy Spirit.

Leader: Let us pray.

Bow your heads as the leader continues to pray.

All: Amen.

Offer one another a Sign of Peace.

 Sing "Come to Us, Holy Spirit"
Come to us Holy Spirit
So we can know God's love
Come to us Holy Spirit
So we can know God's love
© 2010, Chet A. Chambers. Published by Our Sunday Visitor.

172   Chapter 11

 Liturgy Link

The Communion of Saints

Remind the children that all people living and dead who believe in Jesus and follow his way are part of the Communion of Saints.

- This includes people now alive on Earth and people who have died and are now in Purgatory or Heaven.
- We join in the Communion of Saints when we celebrate the Eucharist.

Go to **aliveinchrist.osv.com** for Sunday readings, Scripture background, questions of the week, and seasonal resources.

FAMILY+FAITH
LIVING AND LEARNING TOGETHER

YOUR CHILD LEARNED >>>
This chapter explains how the Holy Spirit continues to unify the Church and make her holy. One and holy are two Marks of the Church.

God's Word
 Read **Ephesians 2:19–21** and discuss how we are all members of God's family.

Catholics Believe
- The Marks of the Church are the four characteristics that identify Christ's Church: one, holy, catholic, and apostolic.
- The Communion of Saints includes all members of the Church, both living and dead, and form one Body in Christ.

To learn more, go to the *Catechism of the Catholic Church* #813, 814 at usccb.org.

People of Faith
This week, your child met Saints Perpetua and Felicity, early martyrs who are remembered in Eucharistic Prayer I.

CHILDREN AT THIS AGE >>>
How They Understand the Oneness of the Church To a third-grader, it might not seem like the Church is one at all. Children this age have often had friends and family that are part of other faith communities (or other parishes, if they are Catholic). It's important for them to know that Catholics are united through the Communion of Saints, by their faith in Jesus as God's Son, and by other core beliefs and practices.

CONSIDER THIS >>>
Have you ever wondered if you are speaking the same language as everyone else in the room?

People often hear what they want and not what is said. It might lead someone to wonder how the Church can speak clearly about God's revelation. "…the Holy Spirit, dwelling in the Church, draws the whole body of the faithful to believe what truly belongs to the faith. 'By this appreciation of the faith, aroused and sustained by the Spirit of truth, the People of God, guided by the sacred teaching authority (*magisterium*), and obeying it, receives not the mere word of men, but truly the word of God… (*LG, no. 12*)" (*USCCA, p. 25*).

LET'S TALK >>>
- Ask your child to name some differences between Mass at your parish and Mass in other parts of the world.
- Talk about all of the people in your family who are part of the Communion of Saints.

LET'S PRAY >>>
Saints Perpetua and Felicity, we remember and honor you and ask you to pray for us now and at the hour of our death. Amen.

For a multimedia glossary of Catholic Faith Words, Sunday readings, seasonal and Saint resources, and chapter activities go to **aliveinchrist.osv.com**.

Distribute the page to the children or parents/adult family members. Point out the chapter highlights, insights on how third graders understand concepts, the opportunity for the adults to reflect on their own experience and faith journey, and the family prayer.

Chapter 11 Review

A **Work with Words** Match each description in Column A with the correct term in Column B.

Column A	Column B
1. unifies the Church today	Jerusalem
2. heroes of the Church who are with God in Heaven	Saints
3. another name for the Church	Pentecost
4. city where the Apostles received the Holy Spirit	Holy Spirit
5. celebrated fifty days after Easter	Communion of Saints

B **Check Understanding** Fill in the circle beside the correct answer.

6. Pentecost celebrates the coming of the ____.
   - ○ New World
   - ● Holy Spirit

7. The Church honors the Saints, especially ____.
   - ● Mary
   - ○ the Pope

8. The main parts of the Mass are ____ around the world.
   - ● the same
   - ○ different

9. ____ unites Catholics all over the world.
   - ○ The music at Mass
   - ● Faith in Jesus

10. You can learn how to ____ from studying the Saints.
   - ● lead a holy life
   - ○ pray

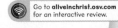 Go to **aliveinchrist.osv.com** for an interactive review.

Use Catechist Quick Reviews to highlight lesson concepts.

A **Work with Words**
Have the children match each description in Column A with the correct term in Column B.

B **Check Understanding**
Explain to the children that they will be filling in the circle beside the correct answer.

 Go to **aliveinchrist.osv.com** to prepare customized and downloadable assessments, send eAssessments, and assign interactive reviews.

KEY CONCEPT

The Church's mission is to share Jesus' Good News with the people of all nations. The Church is catholic because she is everywhere and she welcomes everyone.

DOCTRINAL CONTENT

- Saint Paul was one of the first to take the message of Jesus across many countries, establishing Church communities and writing them letters that became part of the New Testament. (CCC, 849, 856)

- All Church members participate in her mission to announce the Good News of God's Kingdom to people of all nations. (CCC, 863)

- The Church is catholic because she is everywhere and welcomes everyone. (CCC, 830–831)

- The Church is apostolic because Jesus gave his Apostles the mission of sharing his Good News with people all over the world. (CCC, 869)

TASKS OF CATECHESIS

Helping children grow in a faith that is "known, celebrated, lived, and expressed in prayer" (NDC, 20).

This chapter focuses on the following tasks of catechesis:

- Education for Community Life
- Missionary Initiation

Catechist Background

Let the word of Christ dwell in you richly, as in all wisdom you teach and admonish one another, singing psalms, hymns, and spiritual songs with gratitude in your hearts to God. And whatever you do, in word or in deed, do everything in the name of the Lord Jesus, giving thanks to God the Father through him.
Colossians 3:16–17

→ **Reflect** Do you do all that you do in Jesus' name?

The mission of the Church is to proclaim God's Reign of love, justice, and peace. This mission may sound simple, but it is not always easy to accomplish. Jesus commanded his disciples to proclaim the Good News of salvation in words and in actions. At the Last Supper, he also gave them a model of service to follow. Jesus, the teacher, washed the feet of his disciples, a work done by slaves in his time.

In reaching out to and serving people, Jesus showed his disciples how to be present to one another. He demonstrated how to cooperate with God's reign on Earth by bringing people into communion with him. Today Jesus' followers bring the Church's mission to life in acts of compassion and forgiveness, in works of justice and peace. All baptized Christians share in the mission of the Church. Their words and deeds proclaim the Good News—They show people the face of God.

The apostolate, the work of spreading the Good News of Jesus throughout the whole world as Jesus did, is the vocation of every Christian. Ordained persons, lay people, and those in religious life all bring their particular gifts and ministries to the mission of the Church in a variety of ways. The heart of the apostolate is the practice of the virtue of charity, which is nourished by the Eucharist. Therefore, one's relationship with Christ is important for the quality of apostolic work.

→ **Reflect** What gifts do you bring to the apostolate?

Catechist's Prayer

 Holy Spirit, be with me as I work to spread the seeds of faith and help move the world toward the harvest that is your Kingdom. Amen.

Lesson Plan

Objectives	Process	Materials

🕐 Invite, 10 minutes

Catholic and Apostolic Page 175

- 💙 **Psalm 19:5** Pray the opening prayer.
- 📖 **Colossians 3:16–17** Reflect prayerfully on the Word.
- Discuss What Do You Wonder questions.

🌐 **Optional Activity**
Chapter Story: "On a Mission"

🕐 Discover, 35 minutes

A Man with a Mission Pages 176–177
- Recognize that Saint Paul was one of the first to take the message of Jesus across many countries
- Explore the Church's mission to announce the Good News of God's Kingdom

- Tell the children you will be learning about Saint Paul's mission.
- ☆ Circle the ways Saint Paul helped the early Church.
- 📖 **1 Corinthians 3:5–9** Proclaim "Doing God's Work."
- **Share Your Faith Activity** Write about one good work to spread the Good News.

☐ pencils or pens

Universal and Missionary
Pages 178–179
- Identify the Church as catholic and apostolic
- Recognize that the Church's mission is to share Jesus' Good News with the people of all nations
- Discover that we are all part of the mission of the Church

- **Catholic Faith Words** evangelization, mission, missionaries
- Discuss the work of missionaries.
- ☆ Underline the things that missionaries do.
- Review the definitions in the text.
- **Connect Your Faith Activity** Write about someone in the parish serving as a missionary.

☐ pencils or pens
☐ index cards, three per child
- 🌐 **Optional Activity**
The Good News
☐ Activity Master 12 (Page 178E)

🕐 Live, 15 minutes

Our Catholic Life Pages 180–181

- Talk about sister parishes.
- ☆ Provide a suggestion that partner parishes can do together.
- **People of Faith** Learn about Saint Elizabeth Ann Seton.
- **Live Your Faith Activity** Create an image to show how special your parish is.

☐ pencils or pens
☐ magazines, art supplies, parish bulletins

Prayer of Naming and Blessing
Page 182

- Prepare the planters with soil.
- ▶ Rehearse the song.
- Follow the order of prayer.

☐ Seeds, soil, planters, one set per child
🌐 Download "Gathered as One."

Family + Faith page 183
Point out that the Catholic Families page provides chapter highlights, information on how third graders understand faith concepts, and family prayer.

Chapter Review Page 184
🌐 aliveinchrist.osv.com
- Customize and Download Assessments
- Email Links to eAssessments
- Interactive Student Reviews

ONLINE RESOURCES

 Go to **aliveinchrist.osv.com**

You will find:

- Interactive lesson planning with web specific content and additional activities
- Step by step lesson instruction from printed Catechist Edition for integrated lesson planning
- Custom-built assessments to download and eAssessment links
- Interactive reviews that provide scores and the option to review answers
- Sunday readings with background and questions of the week

 Go to **osvparish.com**

You will find:

- Ask the Experts Q and A
- General Catechist Helps
- Community Connections and Blogs

Sharing the Message with Third Graders

Mission People often ask children what they want to be when they grow up, but the idea of a mission, either a personal or collective one, may not be familiar to children in third grade unless people in their lives have encouraged them to consider what God is calling them to be. It's never too early for children to begin reflecting on this concept of God-given mission, especially as they begin to learn more about their talents and explore their interests.

Teaching Tip: Occasionally ask the children, "What do you think might be God's plan for you when you get older?" or point out things you notice they do well and say, "I wonder if, by giving you that talent, God might be telling you something about his plan for you."

How Third Graders Understand

- Third graders see and hear about different places in the world. Help them find them on a map or a globe.
- Children this age know that many children around the world live difficult lives. Discuss ways they can help them.
- Often, young people have ideas about ways to help others. Let them share their ideas.

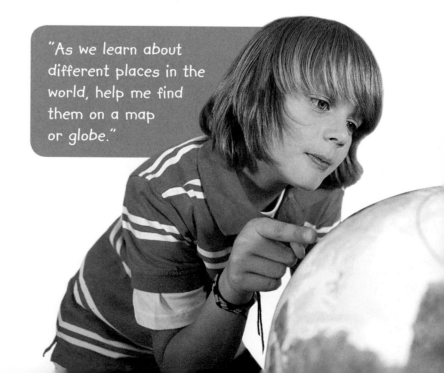

"As we learn about different places in the world, help me find them on a map or globe."

Chapter Story

Invite

"On a Mission"

Use this story to expand the chapter introduction.

- Ask the children who are involved in a group, scouting, or sports team to share their group's mission or goal.
- Have them discuss other kinds of missions.
- Have the children tell what they have learned about missions.

 Go to **aliveinchrist.osv.com** Lesson Planning section for this story.

NCEA IFG: ACRE Edition

Discover

Communal Life

- Objectives: To know the origin, mission, structure, and communal nature of the Church; to know the rights and responsibilities of the Christian faithful

Missionary Spirit

- Objectives: To recognize the centrality of evangelization as the Church's mission and identity embodied in vocation and service; to be aware of how cultures are transformed by the Gospel

Catholic Social Teaching

Live

 Use one of these features to introduce a principle and engage the children with an activity.

- Option for the Poor, Pages 296–297
- The Dignity of Work, Pages 298–299

Music Options

 Use one or more of the following songs to enhance catechetical learning or for prayer.

- "Gathered As One," Live Prayer, Page 182
- "Share the Light," Discover, Page 176
- "Walk in the Light," Discover, Page 176
- "Allelu! Let the Children Come," Discover, Page 179

LECTIONARY CONNECTION

 Chapter 12 highlights Lectionary-connected themes such as mission, evangelization, and missionaries. If your parish aligns its curriculum to the liturgical year, you could use this chapter in connection with the following readings.

Year A

The Epiphany of the Lord—Preach God's Plan

Twentieth Sunday in Ordinary Time—The Lord's House

Year B

Fifteenth Sunday in Ordinary Time—Share the Good News

Twenty-first Sunday in Ordinary Time—Mission

Year C

The Ascension of the Lord—Church

Twenty-ninth Sunday in Ordinary Time—Helping Others

 Go to **aliveinchrist.osv.com** for a complete correlation ordered by the Sundays of the year and suggestions for how to integrate the Scripture readings into chapter lessons.

Name _____ Date _____

The Good News

The following boxes show Jesus sharing God's Good News with others.

In the boxes below, draw three scenes of yourself. Show the different ways in which you share God's Good News with others.

Catholic and Apostolic

 Let Us Pray

Leader: Jesus, help us share your message.

"A report goes forth through all the earth, their messages, to the ends of the world." **Psalm 19:5**

All: We want to spread the Good News of your love with joy to all the world. Give us courage and fill us with desire. Amen.

 God's Word

Let the word of Jesus live deeply in you. While you teach, remind one another of his ways. "And whatever you do, in word or in deed, do everything in the name of the Lord Jesus, giving thanks to God the Father through him." **Based on Colossians 3:16–17**

What Do You Wonder?

- How can you bring the Good News of Jesus to others?
- Where are you supposed to bring the Good News of Jesus?

175

Optional Activity

Chapter Story: "On a Mission" *Verbal/Linguistic*

Use this story after the opening prayer, before telling the children that the Church has a mission.

- Read aloud "On a Mission." Discuss the definition of *mission*.
- Have the children share other kinds of missions they know about.
- After connecting secular missions with the mission of the Church, transition back to the lesson instruction.

 Go to **aliveinchrist.osv.com** for Chapter Story.

 Let Us Pray

Invite the children to gather in the prayer space and make the Sign of the Cross. Read aloud the leader's prayer and the Psalm verse. Prompt the children's response.

Have the children move from the prayer space back to their seats.

Explain that the Church has a mission to share Jesus' Good News with the people of all nations. The Church is for everyone.

Say: Let's listen to the words of Saint Paul.

 God's Word

Guide the children through the process of Scripture reflection.

- Invite them to close their eyes, be still, and open their minds and hearts to what God is saying to them in this passage.
- Proclaim the Scripture.
- Maintain several moments of silence.
- *Ask:* What did you hear God say to you today?
- Invite volunteers to share.

What Do You Wonder?

Say: You have a mission to bring the Good News of Jesus to everyone through your words and actions. That is part of what it means to be Catholic.

Invite the children to respond to the questions. Ask what else they might wonder about sharing the Good News of Jesus.

Objectives

- Recognize that Saint Paul was one of the first to take the message of Jesus across many countries
- Explore the Church's mission to announce the Good News of God's Kingdom

A Man with a Mission

Ask a volunteer to read aloud the question.

- Invite the children to share ideas.

Read aloud the first paragraph.

Paul's Mission

Ask three volunteers to read aloud the three paragraphs.

⭐ Instruct the children to circle the ways Saint Paul helped the early Church.

- Allow the children to work in pairs to reread the text and circle the sentences.

Invite volunteers to describe and interpret what they see in the illustration.

- Read aloud the caption.

 Music Options: Have the children sing "Share the Light" or "Walk in the Light," downloaded from **aliveinchrist.osv.com**.

While on journeys and even from prison, Saint Paul wrote letters to new Christian communities.

A Man with a Mission

How did Saint Paul spread the Good News?

An important part of believing in Jesus is sharing his story. Saint Paul was one of the first people to share Jesus' story. This was his mission.

Paul's Mission

 Circle the ways Saint Paul helped the early Church.

Saint Paul was one of the great Saints of the early Church. He traveled far from the Holy Land to preach about Jesus.

Wherever he traveled, Saint Paul tried to gather a group of people. He told them about Jesus. He helped them grow into a community. After staying with them for a while, Saint Paul would leave to tell others the Good News. The communities he left behind missed his guidance and would ask for his help even though he was far away.

Saint Paul wrote many letters to the groups he had started. He used the letters to answer questions, encourage them, and teach even more about Jesus and his teachings. We still read the letters today. They are part of the Bible. We listen to them at Mass.

176 Chapter 12

Optional Activity

Share the Good News *Verbal/Linguistic*

Tell the children to use what they have learned to become missionaries of the Good News.

- Explain that they will be writing a letter to share the Good News, just as Saint Paul did.
- Distribute stationery or extra paper and envelopes.
- Tell the children to address the letter to a friend.

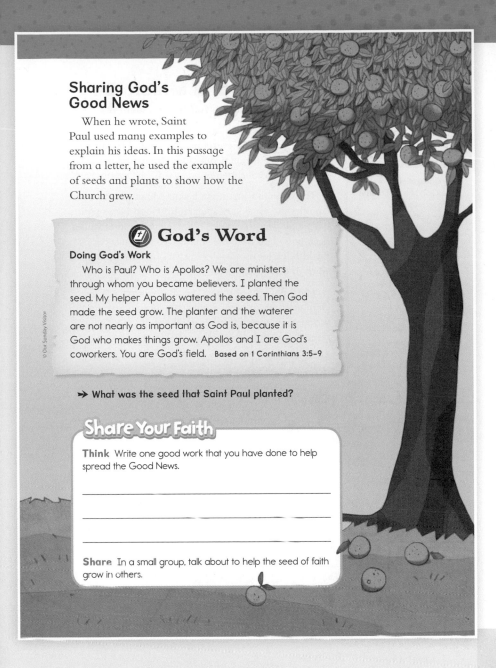

Sharing God's Good News

When he wrote, Saint Paul used many examples to explain his ideas. In this passage from a letter, he used the example of seeds and plants to show how the Church grew.

 God's Word

Doing God's Work

Who is Paul? Who is Apollos? We are ministers through whom you became believers. I planted the seed. My helper Apollos watered the seed. Then God made the seed grow. The planter and the waterer are not nearly as important as God is, because it is God who makes things grow. Apollos and I are God's coworkers. You are God's field.   **Based on 1 Corinthians 3:5–9**

➜ What was the seed that Saint Paul planted?

Share Your Faith

Think Write one good work that you have done to help spread the Good News.

_____

_____

_____

Share In a small group, talk about to help the seed of faith grow in others.

Scripture Background

1 Corinthians

In this Letter, Saint Paul refers to another missionary, Apollos. Both Saint Paul and Apollos worked to establish a Christian community at Corinth.

- Sometimes the Corinthians placed more importance on the leader and his gifts than on God.

- Saint Paul emphasizes that God is the one who is really responsible for a person's growth in faith. Those who are sent by God cooperate with him.

Sharing God's Good News

Invite a volunteer to read aloud the paragraph.

- Point out that in Saint Paul's world, writing letters was the primary form of long-distance communication.

God's Word

Proclaim the Scripture.

- Read aloud the question below the Scripture.

- Invite the children to respond.

Activity

Read aloud the directions for the Share Your Faith activity.

- Allow the children to work independently.

- Then have them work together in groups of two or three expand the topic.

- Allow volunteers to share what they wrote.

Quick Review

Saint Paul was one of the first to take the message of Jesus across many countries, establishing Church communities and writing Letters that became part of the New Testament. The Church's mission is to announce the Good News of God's Kingdom.

Discover

Objectives

- Identify the Church as catholic and apostolic
- Recognize that the Church's mission is to share Jesus' Good News with the people of all nations
- Discover that we are all part of the mission of the Church

Universal and Missionary

Read aloud the question.

- Tell the children we will find the answer as we work on the following pages.

Have four volunteers each read aloud one of the paragraphs.

⭐ Have the children underline the things that missionaries do.

Work with Words

Ask three volunteers to read aloud the Catholic Faith Words and their definitions.

- Pass out three index cards per child.
- Have the children write the words on one side of the card and the definitions on the other.
- Encourage the children to use these cards, with the others they have created, to prepare for chapter and unit reviews.

Direct the children's attention to the photograph. Read aloud the caption and use the content in the Quick Tip box to discuss missionaries.

Discover

Universal and Missionary

How does the Church fulfill her mission?

Saint Paul helped the early Christians know that the Church was for everyone. The Church is catholic because she is for all people in all times and places. The word catholic means "universal" or "everywhere."

The Church is apostolic because Jesus gave his Apostles the mission of sharing his Good News with people all over the world. This teaching authority has been passed on from the Apostles to their successors, the bishops. Jesus calls all of us, in our ways, to the work of **evangelization**.

The word **mission** also means a Church community in another country or in a remote place where people need to hear the Word of God. The term is sometimes used to describe a church with very few members.

Missionaries are people who travel to share Jesus' Good News, just as Paul did. You can help the Church's missionaries by praying for them and the people with whom they work. You can write letters to them and help raise money for things that the missionaries need.

Catholic Faith Words

evangelization sharing the Good News of Jesus through words and actions in a way that invites people to accept the Gospel

mission a job or purpose. The Church's mission is to announce the Good News of God's Kingdom.

missionaries people who answer God's call to bring the message of Jesus and announce the Good News of his Kingdom to people in other places

⭐ Underline the things that missionaries do.

Missionaries travel the world and share the Good News with people in far away places.

178 Chapter 12

✓ Quick Tip

Missionaries

Missionaries may be ordained ministers, members of religious communities, or lay persons.

- Some missionaries also help by building schools and clinics. They might teach farming and other skills.
- If possible, invite someone with ties to a mission to speak to your group, or bring in articles from missionary magazines to share with them.

Missionaries teach about Jesus and help people with their basic needs, such as a safe place to live.

Sharing with Others

Along with spreading the Good News of Jesus, missionaries also share food, shelter, medical supplies, and other things with the people who need their help. These things are important because they provide for people's basic needs. Christians have always shared with others and been concerned for their needs.

God wants you to share not only physical things, such as food, but also spiritual, or holy, things. That is why Christian missionaries teach people about Jesus and build churches, hospitals, and schools. They want people everywhere to hear God's Good News.

➜ How can you share the Good News with other people?

Connect Your Faith

Doing God's Work Find out who in your parish is serving God as a missionary. Write their name, where they are, and a brief sentence about what they are doing to spread the Good News.

179

Optional Activity

Activity Master 12: The Good News

Distribute copies of the activity found on catechist page 175E.

- The children will draw ways to spread the Good News.
- As an alternative, you may wish to send the activity home with the children.

Sharing with Others

Ask: What do people need in order to be physically healthy? Possible responses: food, adequate clothing, housing, medical care

Ask: What do people need in order to be spiritually healthy? Possible responses: help in learning about God, prayer, the Sacraments

Point out that missionaries share with others all of these things.

Read aloud the text.

Ask a volunteer to read aloud the question.

- Write the children's responses on the board or on chart paper.

Activity

Read aloud the directions for the Connect Your Faith activity.

- Provide the children with names of missionaries from your parish.
- Have the children work independently to write about the missionary.

 Music Option: Have the children sing, "Allelu! Let the Children Come," downloaded from **aliveinchrist.osv.com**

Quick Review

The Church is catholic because she is everywhere and apostolic because Jesus gave the Apostles the mission of sharing his Good News. We are all part of the mission of the Church.

Our Catholic Life

Ask: How can partner parishes work together?

- Write the children's responses on the board or on chart paper

Ask the children to listen carefully as you read aloud the paragraph.

- Share with the children if your parish has a sister parish.

To review the Marks of the Church turn to page 307 in the Our Catholic Tradition section of the Student Book.

Partner Parishes

Read aloud the content in the chart.

⭐ Have the children write one more suggestion that partner parishes can do together.

- Encourage the children to share their ideas with the rest of the group.

Live

One way we can help is to write letters to children our own age in our partner parish.

Our Catholic Life

How can partner parishes work together?

Sometimes a parish will have a special relationship with another parish. The two parishes may call each other "partner parishes" or "sister parishes." Here are some things that partner parishes do with and for each other.

© Our Sunday Visitor

Write one more suggestion that partner parishes can do to work together.

Partner Parishes
If the parishes are near each other, members of one parish sometimes attend Mass at the other parish; they also do activities together.
If the parishes are far apart, the members send letters, pray for one another, and sometimes exchange gifts.
If one of the parishes is a mission parish, the partner parish may send money, medicines, clothing, or send parishioners with useful skills to help the mission parish.
_____
_____
_____

180 Chapter 12

Optional Activity

Global Community *Verbal/Linguistic*

If your parish has a sister parish, find out where it is and answer the following questions. If you do not have a sister parish, choose a country on another continent for this lesson, designate it as your group's sister parish. As a group, explore the following.

- What kind of climate does the parish have?
- What do the people need?
- What can you do to help?

People of Faith

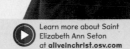

Saint Elizabeth Ann Seton, 1774–1821

May 26

Saint Elizabeth Ann Seton is the first Saint who was born in the United States. She was married and had five children. After her husband died, Elizabeth became a Catholic. She wanted to do Jesus' work on Earth by serving others. She knew that people all over the world needed simple things. They need food, clothing, and to be able to go to school. She said that we must "live simply so that others may simply live." One of the things Saint Elizabeth did was open schools for poor children. She helped start the system of Catholic schools in the United States.

Discuss: How can you help do Jesus' work on Earth?

 Learn more about Saint Elizabeth Ann Seton at **aliveinchrist.osv.com**

© Our Sunday Visitor

Live Your Faith

Promote Your Parish What's special about your parish? Write, draw, or attach pictures of things that make your parish special.

glue

Catholic and Apostolic **181**

People of Faith

Tell the children about Saint Elizabeth Ann Seton.

- She was born two years before the American Revolution.
- She lost her mother at a young age, and thought of the Blessed Mother as her mother.
- God's will, or "The Will," as she called it, would be a keynote in her spiritual life.
- Read aloud the paragraph on Saint Elizabeth Ann Seton.
- Encourage the children to respond to the Discuss question.

Encourage the children to go to **aliveinchrist.osv.com** at home to learn more about Saint Elizabeth Ann Seton.

Activity

Ask a volunteer to read aloud the directions for the Live Your Faith activity.

- Provide art supplies, old magazines, bulletins, or anything that can be used to portray a parish.
- Allow the children plenty of time to be creative.
- Display their work.

🌐 Catholic Social Teaching

Chapter Connections

To integrate Catholic Social Teaching into your lesson, choose one of the following features: Option for the Poor, pages 296–297; or The Dignity of Work, pages 298–299.

- Start the Live step of the process by talking about Saint Elizabeth Ann Seton on page 181. Then move directly to the Catholic Social Teaching feature.
- Or, to expand the lesson, complete both pages 180 and 181, then move to the Catholic Social Teaching feature.
- Return to Chapter 12 for the prayer on page 182.

Let Us Pray

Prayer of Naming and Blessing

Explain that this prayer gives us a chance to name good works and to bless the Church's mission.

Prepare

You will be the leader.

 Have the children rehearse "Gathered as One," downloaded from **aliveinchrist.osv.com**.

Gather

Invite the children to come to the prayer space with their books. Lead the children into the prayer space while playing or singing "Gathered as One."

Pray

Follow the order of prayer on the student page.

Leader's concluding prayer: Though we are many, we are one Body in Christ. May we always remain faithful to the mission of the Church. Amen.

 Conclude by processing around the room with the children singing the refrain from "Gathered as One."

Live

 Let Us Pray

Prayer of Naming and Blessing

Gather and begin with the Sign of the Cross.

Leader: God, you have called us, your Church, to spread your goodness in the world. We take the time today to recall the times when we have seen others share your goodness.

As we plant seeds in our "planters," we will name a good work that we have seen or know is happening somewhere in the world. The seeds will remind us that there is someone sharing the Good News, somewhere the seeds of love and goodness are being planted.

Take turns planting seeds and mentioning good works.

Leader: As our seeds grow, they will remind us of our mission to plant the seeds of faith by praying and doing good works.

Bow your heads as the leader continues to pray.

All: Amen.

 Sing "Gathered as One"
Gathered as one, united we stand.
Your chosen people here in this land. Gathered to hear the Word of our God.
One Body alive in our faith.
© 2007, John Burland. All rights reserved.

 Liturgy Link

Invite Others

You may wish to dramatize the fact that this prayer service is about sharing God's word by inviting special people to share your prayer time.

- Parents and other family members may enjoy visiting the group and sharing the service.

- If possible, invite the catechist and children from another room to join in the prayer.

Go to **aliveinchrist.osv.com** for Sunday readings, Scripture background, questions of the week, and seasonal resources.

FAMILY+FAITH
LIVING AND LEARNING TOGETHER

YOUR CHILD LEARNED >>>
This chapter covers the Marks of the Church: Catholic and Apostolic. The Church's mission is to share Jesus' Good News with the people of all nations.

God's Word

Read **Colossians 3:16–17** to learn how the Word of Jesus can live in you.

Catholics Believe
- The Church's mission is to share Jesus' Good News with the people of all nations.
- The Church is catholic because she is everywhere and she welcomes everyone.

To learn more, go to the *Catechism of the Catholic Church #830, 831* at usccb.org.

People of Faith
This week, your child met Saint Elizabeth Ann Seton, the first Saint born in the United States and the founder of the parochial school system. She said that we must "live simply so that others may simply live."

CHILDREN AT THIS AGE >>>
How They Understand the Mission of the Church People often ask children what they want to be when they grow up. The idea of a mission, either a personal or collective one, may not be familiar to children in third grade. Encourage them to consider what God is calling them to be. It's never too early for children to begin reflecting on this concept of God-given mission, especially as they begin to learn more about their talents and explore their interests.

CONSIDER THIS >>>
Have you ever been to Mass in another country or another state?

No matter where you are in the world, if you go to Mass you can be sure that every person that day is hearing the same Scripture proclaimed and receiving the real presence of Christ in the Eucharist. It is what we mean when we say we are one, catholic church. Although we are one, we express that diversity in many cultures. "The Catholic Church...continues to live in a diversity of cultures and languages because she is led by the Spirit of Christ to bring the Gospel to all peoples. She has known how to accept what is true and good in all cultures and...to infuse the truth and goodness of her tradition and life into them" (*USCCA, p. 129*).

LET'S TALK >>>
- Ask your child to name some ways he or she has shared Jesus' Good News with others.
- Talk about missionaries you have met and the countries they serve.

LET'S PRAY >>>
God, bless and protect all missionaries throughout the world. Amen.

For a multimedia glossary of Catholic Faith Words, Sunday readings, seasonal and Saint resources, and chapter activities go to aliveinchrist.osv.com.

Alive in Christ, Grade 3 Chapter 12 **183**

Family + Faith

Distribute the page to the children or parents/adult family members. Point out the chapter highlights, insights on on how third graders understand concepts, the opportunity for the adults to reflect on their own experience and faith journey, and the family prayer.

Chapter 12 Review

A **Work with Words** Complete each sentence with the correct word from the Word Bank.

Word Bank
- faith
- churches
- mission
- sharing
- apostolic
- missionaries

1. Paul traveled on a ___**mission**___ to tell others about Jesus.

2. Jesus gave his Apostles the mission of ___**sharing**___ the Good News.

3. The Apostle Paul planted the seed of ___**faith**___.

4. ___**Missionaries**___ bring the Good News of the Kingdom to people in other places.

5. Some missionaries help build ___**churches**___, hospitals, and schools.

6. ___**Apostolic**___ means the teaching authority of the Church that comes directly from Jesus and his Apostles.

B **Check Understanding** Fill in the circle beside the correct answer.

7. Saint Paul shared the Good News by writing ____.
   - ● letters to new Christians
   - ○ a newspaper

8. The job of a missionary is to ____.
   - ○ give money
   - ● share God's message

9. You can share in the mission of the Church by ____.
   - ○ mailing letters
   - ● sharing the Good News

10. The Church is called catholic because ____.
   - ● she is universal
   - ○ she is only for some

Go to aliveinchrist.osv.com for an interactive review.

184 Chapter 12

Chapter Review

Use Catechist Quick Reviews to highlight lesson concepts.

A **Work with Words**
Review the Word Bank. Have the children write the correct word from the Word Bank to complete each sentence.

B **Check Understanding**
Explain to the children that they will be filling in the circle beside the correct answer.

Go to **aliveinchrist.osv.com** to prepare customized and downloadable assessments, send eAssessments, and assign interactive reviews.

Catholic and Apostolic **183–184**

Use Catechist Quick Reviews in each chapter to highlight lesson concepts for this unit and prepare for the Unit Review.

Have the children complete the Review pages. Then discuss the answers as a group. Review any concepts with which the children are having difficulty.

A **Work with Words**
Tell the children to answer each question by writing in the letter of the correct word from the Word Bank.

B **Check Understanding**
Have the children circle the correct word to complete each sentence.

Unit Review

A **Work with Words** Answer each question by writing the letter of the with the correct word from the Word Bank.

1. **a** We travel to share Jesus' Good News. Who are we?

2. **d** This feast celebrates the coming of the Holy Spirit. What is it?

3. **b** We are the twelve men chosen by Jesus to be leaders. Who are we?

4. **e** We work with the Pope in teaching, guiding, and making the Church holy. Who are we?

5. **c** This is a job or duty for which someone is responsible. What is it?

Word Bank
a. missionaries
b. Apostles
c. mission
d. Pentecost
e. bishops

B **Check Understanding** Circle the correct word to complete each sentence.

6. The name Peter means _____.
(rock)   Church

7. The word bishop means _____.
leader   (overseer)

8. The Pope is the bishop of _____.
Italy   (Rome)

9. Saint _____ traveled on a mission to start new Christian communities.
(Paul)   Peter

10. A bishop leads a _____.
parish   (diocese)

The Church **185**

Match each description in Column A with the correct term in Column B.

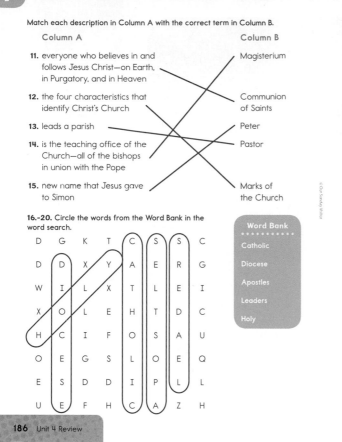

Column A | Column B

11. everyone who believes in and follows Jesus Christ—on Earth, in Purgatory, and in Heaven

12. the four characteristics that identify Christ's Church

13. leads a parish

14. is the teaching office of the Church—all of the bishops in union with the Pope

15. new name that Jesus gave to Simon

Magisterium

Communion of Saints

Peter

Pastor

Marks of the Church

© Our Sunday Visitor

16.-20. Circle the words from the Word Bank in the word search.

D	G	K	T	C	S	S	C
D	D	X	Y	A	E	R	G
W	I	L	X	T	L	E	I
X	O	L	E	H	T	D	C
H	C	I	F	O	S	A	U
O	E	G	S	L	O	E	Q
E	S	D	D	I	P	L	L
U	E	F	H	C	A	Z	H

Word Bank

Catholic

Diocese

Apostles

Leaders

Holy

C **Make Connections** Write a response to each question or statement on the lines below.

21. What is apostolic succession?

   <u>How the authority and power to lead and</u>
   <u>teach the Church is passed down from the</u>
   <u>Apostles to their successors, the bishops</u>

22. How do the Saints help you grow in friendship with God?

   <u>Responses will vary.</u>
   _____

23. Why is it important that the Church is united?

   <u>Responses will vary.</u>
   _____

24. How could you use one of your talents to support the Church?

   <u>Responses will vary.</u>
   _____

25. When have you noticed the Holy Spirit guiding you to follow Jesus?

   <u>Responses will vary.</u>
   _____

B **Check Understanding,**
continued

Direct the children to match each description in Column A with the correct term in Column B for 11–15. For 16–20, have them circle the words from the Word Bank in the word search.

C **Make Connections**

Have the children write their responses to the statements and questions on the lines provided.

Go to **aliveinchrist.osv.com** to prepare customized and downloadable assessments, send eAssessments, and assign interactive reviews.

Unit 4 Review **186–187**

Morality

Our Catholic Tradition

- The Beatitudes are teachings of Jesus that show the way to true happiness and tell how to live in God's Kingdom. (CCC, 1725)

- Jesus' New Commandment calls us to love and forgive one another as Jesus does. (CCC, 1985)

- We are lights to the world when we practice the virtues of faith, hope and charity. (CCC, 1813)

- The Holy Spirit and Church teachings help us make good choices and avoid evil. (CCC, 2041)

How does God help you to make a good decision?

Unit 5 Overview

 Songs of Scripture
"LOVE God"

 Catholic Social Teaching: Live Your Faith

- Life and Dignity, Pages 290–291
- Option for the Poor, Pages 296–297

 Catholic Social Teaching: Live Your Faith

- Rights and Responsibilities, Pages 294–295
- Care for Creation, Pages 302–303

 Catholic Social Teaching: Live Your Faith

- Rights and Responsibilities, Pages 294–295
- The Dignity of Work, Pages 298–299

Preview Unit Theme

Ask the children to name the theme for the unit. Confirm that it is Morality.

Have volunteers read aloud the four bullet points.

Ask: How does God help you to make a good decision?

Have a volunteer write the other children's answers on the board or on chart paper. Tell the group they will be able to check their answers and find out more during the review of this unit.

Direct the children's attention to the photo and the illustrations on the page. Ask them to describe what they see and comment on how these images relate to the unit theme.

After some discussion, explain that the group will be exploring all these things in the next three chapters.

KEY CONCEPT

Jesus' New Commandment is to love one another as he loves each of us. The Beatitudes are teachings of Jesus that show the way to true happiness and tell how to live in God's Kingdom.

DOCTRINAL CONTENT

- The Story of Joseph in the Old Testament shows us to forgive and love. (CCC, 312)
- Jesus teaches us to love our enemies. (CCC, 1825)
- The Beatitudes are teachings of Jesus that show the way to true happiness and tell how to live in God's Kingdom. (CCC, 1716)
- Jesus' New Commandment is for his disciples to love one another as he has loved us. (CCC, 1970–1971)

TASKS OF CATECHESIS

Helping children grow in a faith that is "known, celebrated, lived, and expressed in prayer" (NDC, 20).

This chapter focuses on the following tasks of catechesis:

- Promoting Knowledge of the Faith
- Moral Formation

Catechist Background

"But to you who hear I say, love your enemies, do good to those who hate you, bless those who curse you, pray for those who mistreat you... Do to others as you would have them do to you." Luke 6:27–31

➜ **Reflect** Do you pray for those who hate, curse, and mistreat you?

Just as the Old Law is given to Moses on Mount Sinai, Jesus proclaims the new law of love on a mountain in his Sermon on the Mount. Jesus' sermon begins with the Beatitudes and includes many examples of how to live them. The Jewish people who heard this message were probably challenged to hear that leading a good life went beyond keeping the Mosaic Law.

Jesus asks his followers to move beyond anger, retaliation, and hatred. He calls them to give without expecting a return, to pray from the heart, and to live humbly. Blessed are those who choose to follow this way of life, for their reward is eternal happiness.

The Law of Moses is more than a set of rules to be followed. It is a part of the covenant of salvation that God established with Moses. It was also meant to prepare people for the coming of Christ. God's covenant is fulfilled in Jesus, who brings a new covenant—one that is written on the hearts of people and flows from the grace and freedom of the Holy Spirit. Jesus' teachings in the Beatitudes are more than a set of rules. The Beatitudes require a transformation of the heart to love as Jesus did.

➜ **Reflect** How are the Beatitudes important in your life?

Catechist's Prayer

Loving God, you turn cares and troubles into opportunities to approach and appreciate you. Hold me in your love as I love others. Amen.

Lesson Plan

Objectives	Process	Materials

Invite, 10 minutes

Choose Love Page 189

- **Psalm 19:8** Pray the opening prayer.
- **Luke 6:27, 28, 31** Reflect prayerfully on the Word.
- Discuss What Do You Wonder questions.

- **Optional Activity** Chapter Poem: "Which One?"

Discover, 35 minutes

Learning to Forgive Pages 190–191
- Examine how the story of Joseph in the Old Testament shows us the importance of forgiving and loving

- Talk about free will and forgiveness.
- **Genesis 37–45** Proclaim "The Story of Joseph."
- ☆ Underline what Joseph's brothers did to him.
- **Share Your Faith Activity** Recall forgiving someone without judgment.

- ☐ pencils or pens

The Way of Love Pages 192–193
- Discuss Jesus' command to love our enemies
- Describe the Beatitudes as teachings of Jesus that show the way to true happiness and tell how to live in God's Kingdom
- Identify that Jesus' New Commandment is to love one another as he loves us

- **Catholic Faith Words** Beatitudes, mercy, New Commandment
- Review why we should be loving.
- **Matthew 5:43–47** Proclaim "Love of Enemies."
- ☆ Underline what Jesus wants us to do.
- Review definitions in the text.
- Talk about living the New Commandment.
- **Connect Your Faith Activity** Solve the code.

- ☐ pencils or pens
- ☐ board or chart paper
- ☐ three index cards per child
- **Optional Activity** Crossword Puzzle
- ☐ Activity Master 13 (Page 189E)

Live, 15 minutes

Our Catholic Life Pages 194–195

- Discuss why Catholics offer the sign of peace.
- ☆ Underline one way to obey Jesus' command.
- **People of Faith** Learn about Saint Peter Canisius.
- **Live Your Faith Activity** Draw a picture of making peace with a friend.

- ☐ pencils or pens
- ☐ crayons, colored pencils, or markers

Act of Love Page 196

- Select a reader.
- Follow the order of prayer.
- ▶ Sing "Greatest Gift."

- Download "Greatest Gift."

Family + Faith Page 197
Point out that the Catholic Families page provides chapter highlights, information on how third graders understand faith concepts, and family prayer.

Chapter Review Page 198
aliveinchrist.osv.com
- Customize and Download Assessments
- Email Links to eAssessments
- Interactive Student Reviews

Teaching This Grade

ONLINE RESOURCES

 Go to **aliveinchrist.osv.com**

You will find:

- Interactive lesson planning with web specific content and additional activities
- Step by step lesson instruction from printed Catechist Edition for integrated lesson planning
- Custom-built assessments to download and eAssessment links
- Interactive reviews that provide scores and the option to review answers
- Sunday readings with background and questions of the week

 Go to **osvparish.com**

You will find:

- Ask the Experts Q and A
- General Catechist Helps
- Community Connections and Blogs

Sharing the Message with Third Graders

The New Commandment Loving God above all things and loving our neighbors as God loves us may sound simple to a third grader—until it comes to practical applications. We are often tested in these commands by the things we get most excited about or the people we are with every day. Third graders will need many reminders of how they can apply these principles in daily life.

Teaching Tip: The *Catechism* teaches that the family is the first place we learn to love others. Let the children know that our families are like "schools" where we learn to love others. Times when it is challenging to love may be opportunities that God has given us to learn an important lesson.

How Third Graders Understand

- Third graders like having a choice about what they can do. Teach them ways to make good choices.
- Children this age can sometimes say mean things to others when they feel threatened. Try to see what is really happening.
- At this point in their lives, young people are beginning to be more aware of right and wrong. Help them form a good conscience.

"Sometimes I say mean things when I feel threatened. Talk to me about what is really going on."

Chapter Connections

Chapter Poem

Invite

"Which One?"

Use this poem to expand the chapter introduction.

- Ask each child to take a moment to think of a gift he or she has received that has shown love.
- If time allows, invite children to share their stories with the rest of the class.

 Go to **aliveinchrist.osv.com** Lesson Planning section for this poem.

NCEA IFG: ACRE Edition

Discover

Knowledge of the Faith

- Objective: To know and understand basic Catholic teaching about the Incarnate Word Jesus Christ as the way, truth, and life

Moral Formation

- Objective: To be knowledgeable about the teachings of Jesus and the Church as the basis of Christian morality and to understand Catholic Social Teaching

Catholic Social Teaching

Live

 Use one of these features to introduce the principle and engage the children with an activity.

- Life and Dignity, Pages 290–291
- Option for the Poor, Pages 296–297

Music Options

 Use one or more of the following songs to enhance catechetical learning or for prayer.

- "Greatest Gift," Live Prayer, Page 196
- "Shalom," Discover, Page 190
- "This Is My Commandment," Discover, Page 192

LECTIONARY CONNECTION

 Chapter 13 highlights Lectionary-connected themes such as the Beatitudes, mercy, and New Commandment. If your parish aligns its curriculum to the liturgical year, you could use this chapter in connection with the following Sundays.

Year A

Fourth Sunday in Ordinary Time—Beatitudes

Twenty-third Sunday in Ordinary Time—Love Fulfills the Law

Year B

Third Sunday of Lent—Forgiveness

Eleventh Sunday in Ordinary Time —Love of Others

Year C

Sixth Sunday in Ordinary Time—Love Others

Seventh Sunday in Ordinary Time—Forgiveness

 Go to **aliveinchrist.osv.com** for a complete correlation ordered by the Sundays of the year and suggestions for how to integrate the Scripture readings into chapter lessons.

Name _____ Date _____

Crossword Puzzle

Complete the crossword puzzle using words in the Word Bank.

Word Bank
• • • • • • • • • • • • • • • • • • • •

Beatitudes   Joseph

decisions   law of love

Egypt   perfect

enemies   shepherd

forgave

Across

2. The brother who was sold as a slave was _____.

4. The summary of the Beatitudes and the Ten Commandments is known as the _____.

6. Joseph's job when he lived with his father was that of a _____.

8. Jesus said to love both friends and _____.

Down

1. Joseph _____ his brothers for selling him.

3. Jesus' law of love can help you make good _____.

5. You must try to be perfect as God is _____.

7. Teachings of Jesus that show the way to happiness are called _____.

9. After Joseph was sold, he lived in _____.

© Our Sunday Visitor

Choose Love

 Let Us Pray

Leader: Loving God, teach us to love as you love.

"The law of the LORD is perfect,
refreshing the soul." **Psalm 19:8**

All: Teach me to love as you love. Amen.

God's Word

"But to you who hear I say, love your enemies, do good to those who hate you, bless those who curse you, pray for those who mistreat you. ... Do to others as you would have them do to you." **Luke 6:27-28, 31**

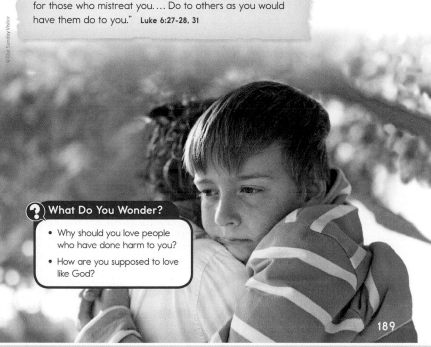

What Do You Wonder?

- Why should you love people who have done harm to you?
- How are you supposed to love like God?

189

Optional Activity

Chapter Poem: "Which One?" *Verbal/Linguistic*

Use this poem after the opening prayer, before talking about love.

- Ask the children to listen for the choices as you read the poem aloud. Encourage them to think of a gift they have received.
- Discuss the meaning of the poem.
- Connect the topic of gifts with God's gift of love, then return to the lesson instruction.

 Go to **aliveinchrist.osv.com** for Chapter Poem.

Let Us Pray

Invite the children to gather in the prayer space and make the Sign of the Cross. Read aloud the leader's prayer and the Psalm verse. Prompt the children's response. Have the children return to their seats.

Explain that when we do something loving, we are usually glad we did it. But acting in loving ways can sometimes be difficult.

Say: How many times a day do you hear the word *love*? It is a wonderful feeling when someone tells us they love us. Listen to these words of Jesus about love.

 God's Word

Guide the children through the process of Scripture reflection.

- Invite them to close their eyes, be still, and open their minds and hearts to what God is saying to them in this passage.
- Proclaim the Scripture.
- Maintain several moments of silence.
- *Ask:* What did you hear God say to you today?
- Invite volunteers to share.

What Do You Wonder?

Say: Jesus challenges us to love our enemy. When we do the difficult things that love asks, we love as God loves.

Invite the children to respond to the questions. Ask what else they might wonder about sacrifice and love.

Objectives

- Examine how the story of Joseph in the Old Testament shows us the importance of forgiving and loving

Learning to Forgive

Read aloud the question. Tell the children that we will learn the answer from the Scripture story.

Ask a volunteer to read aloud both paragraphs to introduce the lesson.

- Explain to the children that today's story is from the Old Testament, the part of the Bible that tells about the lives of God's People before Jesus was born.

 God's Word

Proclaim the Scripture story.

⭐ Have the children underline what Joseph's brothers did to hiim.

- Review the answer as a group.
- *Ask:* Have you ever done something you knew was wrong because you were jealous of your brother, sister, or friend?
- Remind the children that they do not need to share this information. Just have them take a moment to think about it.

Discover

Learning to Forgive

How did Joseph show forgiveness?

The Book of Genesis is the first book in the part of the Bible called the Old Testament. In it, we learn that God created human beings in his image and likeness. He gave us love and free will, which is the ability to choose.

During your life, you will have to make some hard choices. The following Scripture tells the story of a man who made a difficult choice after he was separated from his family. Joseph's story is found in the Old Testament.

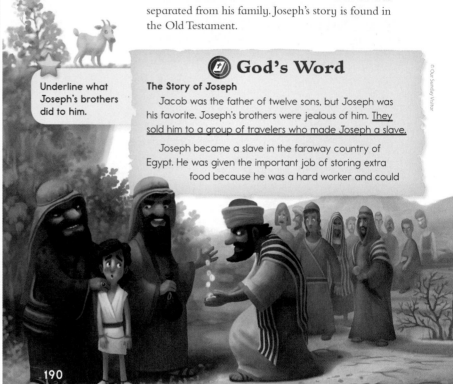

Underline what Joseph's brothers did to him.

God's Word

The Story of Joseph

Jacob was the father of twelve sons, but Joseph was his favorite. Joseph's brothers were jealous of him. They sold him to a group of travelers who made Joseph a slave.

Joseph became a slave in the faraway country of Egypt. He was given the important job of storing extra food because he was a hard worker and could

190

 Scripture Background

Genesis 37–45

The story of Joseph is one of the most well-known stories in the Old Testament.

- One of twelve sons of the patriarch Jacob, Joseph was known as his father's favorite and received from him the "coat of many colors."
- Joseph's story explains how the Hebrew people got to Egypt and provides a model of forgiveness.

explain dreams. During this time, Joseph's family needed food because they were starving, so they traveled all the way to Egypt. Joseph's brothers did not recognize him because so many years had passed.

At first, Joseph did not tell them who he was. He was still angry with them. **Based on Genesis 37–45**

Joseph chose to forgive his brothers because he loved them. Long before the time of Jesus, Joseph showed how to love those who hurt you.

➜ How do you think Joseph's brothers felt when Joseph told them who he was?

➜ What other choices could Joseph have made?

Think Have you ever had to forgive someone else without making a judgment?

Share Take turns sharing your thoughts with a partner.

The Story of Joseph

Continue with the Scripture.

- Pause at the end of the second paragraph and ask the children what they think Joseph should do now that he knows that his brothers do not recognize him.

- Read the end of the Scripture story.

- *Say:* Joseph was angry because of what his brothers had done to him. Let's find out how he responded.

- Read aloud the concluding paragraph.

- Invite volunteers to read the questions. Have them pause after each to allow the group to respond.

Read aloud the directions for the Share Your Faith activity.

- Let the children work with a partner to answer the question and share their thoughts.

Quick Review

The story of Joseph shows us how to forgive and to love.

✓ Quick Tip

Clarify Concepts

Point out that at some time in his or her life, everyone needs help with making choices. This could be help from God, help from other people, or help from the Church.

- Remind the children not to be afraid to ask for help when difficult problems or confusing situation arise.

- Point out that parents, guardians, teachers, catechists, and other trusted adults are happy to help.

- Tell the children that prayer also helps.

Objectives

- Discuss Jesus' command to love our enemies
- Describe the Beatitudes as teachings of Jesus that show the way to true happiness and tell how to live in God's Kingdom
- Identify that Jesus' New Commandment is to love one another as he loves us

The Way of Love

Ask: What does Jesus teach about love?

- List the children's answers on the board or on chart paper.

Ask a volunteer to read aloud the opening paragraph.

God's Word

Proclaim the Scripture.

⭐ Have the children underline what Jesus wants us to do.

- Ask a volunteer to read aloud the closing paragraph.

Work with Words

Invite three volunteers to read aloud the Catholic Faith Words and their definitions on page 193.

- Distribute three index cards.
- Have the children create vocabulary cards.
- Encourage the children to use the cards to prepare for chapter and unit reviews.

The Way of Love

What does Jesus teach about love?

One day, Jesus was talking with his followers about how to treat people. This is what he told them.

Underline what Jesus wants us to do.

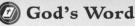 God's Word

Love of Enemies

You have been told to love your friends and hate your enemies. But now I am telling you: <u>Love your enemies, and pray for people who hurt you.</u> This will make you children of God. God doesn't want you to do only what is easy. If you are friendly only to people who are friendly to you, why is that special? **Based on Matthew 5:43–47**

Jesus said that it is easier to love those who love you. He also said that you must love your enemies! That can be as difficult for people as it was for Joseph to forgive his brothers.

192

© Our Sunday Visitor

Optional Activity

Activity Master 13: Crossword Puzzle

Distribute copies of the activity found on catechist page 189E.

- The children will review concepts from the chapter in this activity.
- As an alternative, you may wish to send this activity home with the children.

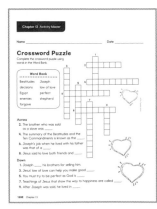

The New Commandment

Jesus' main teachings are about the love and care you are called to show God and others. In a teaching called the **Beatitudes**, Jesus said that those who make peace and show **mercy** are blessed by God. Jesus' **New Commandment** sums up the Ten Commandments and the Beatitudes in one statement

"…Love one another. As I have loved you, so you also should love one another." (John 13:34)

Living the New Commandment

People in your parish try to live by Jesus' New Commandment, too. There are probably volunteers who build houses, teach people to read, or give food to people who are hungry. They show their love by praying for and helping others. They show love by putting others' needs before their own.

© Our Sunday Visitor

Catholic Faith Words

Beatitudes teachings of Jesus that show the way to true happiness and tell how to live in God's Kingdom now and always

mercy kindness and concern for those who are suffering. God has mercy on us even though we are sinners.

New Commandment Jesus' command for his disciples to love one another as he has loved us

Connect Your Faith

Find the Message Solve the code by placing the correct letter in each blank to answer the question.

G	O	D		N	E	I	G	H	B	O	R		E	N	E	M	Y
1	2	3		4	5	6	7	8	9	10	11		12	13	14	15	16

What do these three words have in common?

W (E) A (R) (E) C A L L (E) (D)
   5   11 14   12 3

T (O) L (O) V (E) T (H) (E) (M)
 2   10   12   8 14 15

Choose Love **193**

Songs of Scripture

LOVE God

This song emphasizes that we must love God first and then our neighbor.

- When the children sing the first two lines of the chorus, have them face the center of the room, as a sign of God at the center of our lives. With the next two lines, have them turn and face the outside, as a sign of sharing God's love with the world.

Use *Songs of Scripture*, Grades 1–3 CD, Track 4

The New Commandment

Read aloud the opening paragraph, including the verse from Scripture.

- *Ask:* How can Jesus' New Commandment help us make good decisions?
- Write all responses on the board or on chart paper.

Living the New Commandment

Invite a volunteer to read aloud the paragraph.

- Ask the children to share examples of people they know who live the New Commandment.
- Explain how receiving love with an open and grateful heart is part of Jesus' command to love one another.
- To further discuss God's Laws, have the children turn to pages 316–317 in the Our Catholic Tradition section in the back of the Student Book.

Activity

Read aloud the directions.

- Have the children work together in pairs to solve the puzzle.
- Invite a volunteer to share the solution.

Quick Review

Jesus wants us to love everyone, even our enemies. He gave us the Beatitudes to show us how to live in God's Kingdom.

Our Catholic Life

Tell the children that they will be learning why we make the sign of peace.

Discuss the meaning of the word *peace* with the group. Explain that peace is more than the absence of conflict; it is related to contentment and love.

Ask several volunteers to read aloud the paragraphs.

⭐ Direct the children to underline one way to obey Jesus' command to make peace with one another.

- *Ask:* During which part of the Mass do we give the sign of peace? Allow time for the children to think before calling on a volunteer to respond. If the children do not recall the exact name of the part of the Mass, share it with them. We give the sign of peace during the Liturgy of the Eucharist.

Live

© Our Sunday Visitor

Our Catholic Life

Why do we make the sign of peace?

There are many reasons that Catholics make the sign of peace during the Mass. Jesus told his followers to make peace with one another before they brought their gifts to the altar. <u>The sign of peace is a way to obey Jesus' command</u>.

Giving the sign of peace shows that the people gathered in the church are united as one community of believers.

God wants the whole world to live in peace. Remember to share a sign of peace with your family and neighbors. You get to know more people in your church family when you greet one another during the sign of peace.

Underline one way to obey Jesus' command.

194 Chapter 13

ℹ️ **Catechist Background**

Sign of Peace

The children's text refers to Matthew 5:23–24, in which Jesus tells his followers to make peace with one another before offering sacrifices in the temple.

- This highlights the connection between humans' worship of God and their relationships with one another: We must have peace among ourselves in order to be free to worship God.

- We must make an effort to establish external peace before receiving Communion; however, God gives us the grace to achieve internal peace as well.

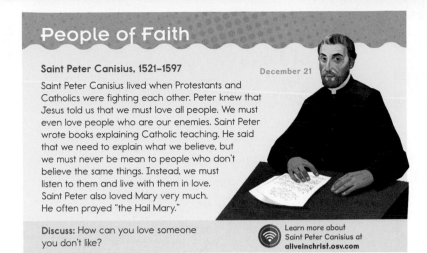

People of Faith

Saint Peter Canisius, 1521–1597

December 21

Saint Peter Canisius lived when Protestants and Catholics were fighting each other. Peter knew that Jesus told us that we must love all people. We must even love people who are our enemies. Saint Peter wrote books explaining Catholic teaching. He said that we need to explain what we believe, but we must never be mean to people who don't believe the same things. Instead, we must listen to them and live with them in love. Saint Peter also loved Mary very much. He often prayed "the Hail Mary."

Discuss: How can you love someone you don't like?

Learn more about Saint Peter Canisius at **aliveinchrist.osv.com**

Live Your Faith

Making Peace Draw a picture about a time when you made up with a friend or family member after an argument.

Choose Love **195**

People of Faith

Tell the children about Saint Peter Canisius.

- Peter's mother died shortly after his birth.
- He taught at the university and was confessor at the hospital and prison in Vienna.
- Saint Peter defended Catholic truths by writing about them.
- He was obedient to those he worked for and caring to those who worked for him.
- Read aloud the paragraph.
- Invite the children to answer the Discuss question.

 Encourage the children to go to **aliveinchrist.osv.com** at home to learn more about Saint Peter Canisius.

Activity

Read aloud the directions for the Live Your Faith activity.

- Allow time for them to draw their pictures.
- Encourage them to share their drawings with a partner.

Catholic Social Teaching

Chapter Connections

To integrate Catholic Social Teaching into your lesson, choose one of the following features: Life and Dignity, pages 290–291; or Option for the Poor, pages 296–297.

- Start the Live step of the process by talking about Saint Peter Canisius on page 195. Then move directly to the Catholic Social Teaching feature.
- Or, to expand the lesson, complete both pages 194 and 195, then move to the Catholic Social Teaching feature.
- Return to Chapter 13 for the prayer on page 196.

Let Us Pray

Act of Love

Explain to the children that they will be praying an Act of Love, asking for help from God to forgive.

Prepare

Choose a volunteer for the reader part. You will be the leader.

- Invite the children to practice reading the Act of Love.

 Have the children rehearse "Greatest Gift," downloaded from **aliveinchrist.osv.com**.

Gather

Invite the children to come to the prayer space with their books. Lead them into the prayer space while playing or singing "Greatest Gift."

Pray

Follow the order of prayer on the student page.

Leader's concluding prayer: God who loves so generously, thank you. We promise to always spread your love throughout our world.

 Conclude by singing with the children the refrain for "Greatest Gift."

Live

Let Us Pray

Act of Love

Gather and begin with the Sign of the Cross.

Leader: God our Father, help us love as Jesus did.

Reader: When someone is mean to us, as Joseph's brothers were to him,

All: Help us forgive as Joseph did.

Reader: When we find it difficult to love,

All: Help us love as Jesus did.

Leader: We pray together an Act of Love.

All: O God, we love you above all things, with our whole heart and soul, because you are all-good and worthy of all love. We love our neighbor as ourselves for love of you. We forgive all who have injured us and ask pardon of all whom we have injured.

Leader: Let us pray.

Bow your heads as the leader prays.

All: Amen.

 Sing "Greatest Gift"
Love, love, Jesus is love.
God's greatest gift is the gift of love.
All creation sings together,
praising God for love.

Liturgy Link

Pray Together

It may be difficult for children to read the prayer in unison, especially if they are unfamiliar with it.

- Have the children practice reading the prayer.
- Go over unfamiliar words and pronunciations when necessary.
- Encourage the children to speak at a comfortable pace that is neither too fast nor too slow.

 Go to **aliveinchrist.osv.com** for Sunday readings, Scripture background, questions of the week, and seasonal resources.

FAMILY+FAITH
LIVING AND LEARNING TOGETHER

YOUR CHILD LEARNED >>>
This chapter describes the need to seek God's mercy and to ask for and offer forgiveness. It also focuses on Jesus' teachings to love others, especially our enemies.

God's Word
Read **Luke 6:27-31** and think about ways you can show your love for each family member.

Catholics Believe
- Jesus' New Commandment is to love one another as he loves each of us.
- The Beatitudes are teachings of Jesus that show the way to true happiness and tell how to live in God's Kingdom.

To learn more, go to the *Catechism of the Catholic Church* #1933, 1716 at **usccb.org**.

People of Faith
This week, your child met Saint Peter Canisius who urged us to always speak kindly to those with whom we disagree. He is credited with adding the sentence beginning, "Holy Mary, Mother of God" to the Hail Mary.

CHILDREN AT THIS AGE >>>
How They Understand the New Commandment Loving God above all things and loving others as God loves us may sound simple to a third-grader—until it comes to practical applications. We are often tested in these commands by the things we get most excited about or the people we are with every day. Your child will need many reminders of how he or she can apply these principles in daily life choices. For example, he or she might choose to go to church rather than staying home to play a video game or make a choice to not fight with a friend or sibling.

CONSIDER THIS >>>
How difficult is it to show kindness to someone who has harmed you?

Forgiveness may be the greatest challenge in our spiritual journey. It is sometimes difficult to imagine how people can let go of the resentment and bitterness they feel when they are wronged. Yet, "the best way to obtain mercy is to be merciful. As Jesus taught us, 'Blessed are the merciful, for they will be shown mercy' (Mt 5:7). Failure to forgive others is a major human problem. Holding grudges is common. Failure to forgive routinely tears apart families, neighborhoods, and even nations. Jesus stressed mercy and forgiveness in numerous ways" *(USCCA, p. 488)*.

LET'S TALK >>>
- Talk about a time when you've found it difficult to forgive. What did that experience teach you?
- Ask your child to name some times when he or she has asked forgiveness from someone else. How did it feel to receive that forgiveness?

LET'S PRAY >>>
Holy Mary, Mother of God, pray for us sinners now and at the hour of our death. Amen.

For a multimedia glossary of Catholic Faith Words, Sunday readings, seasonal and Saint resources, and chapter activities go to **aliveinchrist.osv.com**.

Alive in Christ, Grade 3 Chapter 13 **197**

Family + Faith

Distribute the page to the children or parents/adult family members. Point out the chapter highlights, insights on how third graders understand concepts, the opportunity for the adults to reflect on their own experience and faith journey, and the family prayer.

Chapter 13 Review

A **Work with Words** Match each description in Column A with the correct term in Column B.

Column A	Column B
1. Teachings of Jesus that show the way to true happiness	our enemies
2. Sums up the Ten Commandments and the Beatitudes	love and forgiveness
3. A way to show that the people gathered in the church are one community of believers	Beatitudes
4. Jesus wants us to love	sign of peace
5. The story of Joseph is about this	New Commandment

B **Check Understanding** Put these events from the story of Joseph in order by numbering the sentences correctly.

6. [4] Joseph recognizes his brothers, but they do not recognize him. Then Joseph tells his brothers who he is.

7. [1] Joseph's father loves him very much. Joseph's brothers grow jealous.

8. [5] Joseph forgives his brothers.

9. [3] Joseph's brothers come to Egypt to ask for food.

10. [2] Joseph's brothers sell him as a slave.

Go to **aliveinchrist.osv.com** for an interactive review.

198 Chapter 13

Chapter Review

Use Catechist Quick Reviews to highlight lesson concepts.

A **Work with Words**
Have the children match the description in Column A with the correct term in Column B.

B **Check Understanding**
Explain to the children that they will be numbering the sentences about Joseph's life in the correct order.

 Go to **aliveinchrist.osv.com** to prepare customized and downloadable assessments, send eAssessments, and assign interactive reviews.

Choose Love **197–198**

KEY CONCEPT

Each of us has a purpose and vocation that helps us follow God's plan and be a light to the world. God's gifts of faith, hope, and charity (love) help you live a good and moral life.

DOCTRINAL CONTENT

- Vocation is God's plan for our lives, the purpose for which he made us. (CCC, 1877)

- Virtues are good spiritual habits that make you stronger and help you do what is right and good. (CCC, 1803)

- The Theological Virtues of faith, hope, and charity are gifts from God that help us live in relationship with the Holy Trinity. (CCC, 1813)

- Virtues grow over time with our practice and openness to God's grace. (CCC, 1830)

TASKS OF CATECHESIS

Helping children grow in a faith that is "known, celebrated, lived, and expressed in prayer" (NDC, 20).

This chapter focuses on the following tasks of catechesis:

- Promoting Knowledge of the Faith

- Moral Formation

Catechist Background

 Jesus spoke to them again, saying, "I am the light of the world. Whoever follows me will not walk in darkness, but will have the light of life." John 8:12

➔ **Reflect** How do you show that you walk in the light of life?

Throughout life, people develop both good and bad habits. Indeed, many people have spent a good number of New Year's Eves dreaming up new habits or resolutions for the coming year. Good habits and bad habits do not just happen. Repeated practice reinforces them until, finally, they become almost automatic.

Virtues are good habits. The Theological Virtues of faith, hope, and love are gifts from God. Christians accept these gifts and practice them until they become second nature, a blending of the human and the Divine. Jesus gave his followers an example of how to live these virtues. The Holy Spirit inspires and enables Christians to practice the virtues and, in the end, to be with God eternally.

In the presence of hardship, illness, evil, or death, hope can be difficult to sustain. Those who have practiced lifelong hope will not succumb to feelings of despair or abandonment, even when they are severely tempted or tested. Instead, they will cling to the promise of resurrection in Christ, who overcame the power of evil and everlasting death once and for all. Even in the face of the most horrendous evil, God's grace will triumph.

➔ **Reflect** Which of the three Theological Virtues is most prominent in your life? How do you practice it?

Catechist's Prayer

 Holy Spirit, enkindle my desire to share the light of Christ. Burn within me, so that I may overcome darkness. Amen.

Lesson Plan

Objectives	Process	Materials

🕐 Invite, 10 minutes

Live in the Light Page 199

- 💗 **Psalm 43:3** Pray the opening prayer.
- 📖 **John 8:12** Reflect prayerfully on the Word.
- Discuss What Do You Wonder questions.

📶 **Optional Activity**
Chapter Poem: "Candle"

🕐 Discover, 35 minutes

The Light of the World
Pages 200–201

- Discover that Christians are called by Jesus to be the light of the world
- Be aware that our vocation is God's plan for our lives
- Describe virtues as good spiritual habits that make us stronger and help us do what is right and good

- **Catholic Faith Words** vocation
- Talk about the light of Christ.
- 📖 **Matthew 5:14–16** Proclaim "Your Light Must Shine."
  - ☆ Underline consequences of sharing the light.
- Discuss bringing light and peace to others through vocation.
- **Share Your Faith Activity** Write one way to be a light to others.

☐ pencils or pens
☐ board or chart paper
☐ one index card per child

The Virtues Pages 202–203

- Explore the Theological Virtues of faith, hope, and charity and how they help us live in relationship with the Holy Trinity
- Illustrate the need to practice the virtues so they will grow over time

- **Catholic Faith Words** virtues, Theological Virtues, faith, hope, charity
- Discuss the Theological Virtues and how they guide us.
- Review the definitions in the text.
- **Connect Your Faith Activity** Design and decorate a bookmark.

☐ pencils or pens
☐ crayons, colored pencils, or markers
☐ five index cards, per child
• **Optional Activity** Virtues
☐ Activity Master 14 (Page 199E)

🕐 Live, 15 minutes

Our Catholic Life Pages 204–205

- Talk about making prayer a part of every day.
- ☆ Place a check mark next to prayer times.
- **People of Faith** Learn about Saint Genevieve.
- **Live Your Faith Activity** List times of day to pray and ideas for reminders.

☐ pencils or pens
☐ board or chart paper

Prayer of Petition Page 206

- Choose volunteers for the three reader parts.
- Follow the order of prayer.
- ▶ Sing "Share the Light."

📶 Download "Share the Light."

Family + Faith Page 207

Point out that the Catholic Families page provides chapter highlights, information on how third graders understand faith concepts, and family prayer.

Chapter Review Page 208

📶 **aliveinchrist.osv.com**
- Customize and Download Assessments
- Email Links to eAssessments
- Interactive Student Reviews

ONLINE RESOURCES

 Go to **aliveinchrist.osv.com**

You will find:

- Interactive lesson planning with web specific content and additional activities
- Step by step lesson instruction from printed Catechist Edition for integrated lesson planning
- Custom-built assessments to download and eAssessment links
- Interactive reviews that provide scores and the option to review answers
- Sunday readings with background and questions of the week

 Go to **osvparish.com**

You will find:

- Ask the Experts Q and A
- General Catechist Helps
- Community Connections and Blogs

Sharing the Message with Third Graders

Sharing the Light of Christ It's a powerful feeling for children when they realize they can have an impact on others. And they can do this in both positive and negative ways. Particularly if they have younger siblings at home, but also with peers and even people who are older, children can spread the light of Christ through kind actions and virtuous example. This will usually mean something different for each child, but third graders often need to be reminded that they serve as examples for others.

Teaching Tip: Periodically invite the children to share a way they had a positive impact on someone else this past week.

How Third Graders Understand

- Children this age tend to stay with the same small group of friends for security. Encourage them to work with different groups and get to know others.
- Most young people like praise and affirmations. It helps them know they are on the right track.
- Some third graders like to observe things in the world around them. They may need your help in finding the right words to describe their observations.

"I like to observe things in the world around me. Help me put words to my observations."

Chapter Connections

Chapter Poem

Invite

"Candle"

Use this poem to expand the chapter introduction.

- Take a moment to discuss how light comforts us and how people can comfort one another.
- Encourage the children to share their thoughts with the group.

 Go to **aliveinchrist.osv.com** Lesson Planning section for this poem.

NCEA IFG: ACRE Edition

Discover

Knowledge of the Faith

- Objective: To know and understand basic Catholic teaching about the Incarnate Word Jesus Christ as the way, truth, and life

Moral Formation

- Objective: To be knowledgeable about the teachings of Jesus and the Church as the basis of Christian morality and to understand Catholic Social Teaching

Catholic Social Teaching

Live

 Use one of these features to introduce the principle and engage the children with an activity.

- Rights and Responsibilities, Pages 294–295
- Care for Creation, Pages 302–303

Music Options

 Use one or more of the following songs to enhance catechetical learning or for prayer.

- "Share the Light," Live Prayer, Page 206
- "Christ Is Light," Discover, Page 200
- "Walk in the Light," Discover, Page 200

LECTIONARY CONNECTION

 Chapter 14 highlights Lectionary-connected themes such as vocation and the Theological Virtues. If your parish aligns its curriculum to the liturgical year, you could use this chapter in connection with the following readings.

Year A

Fourth Sunday of Lent—Duty to Live in the Light

Thirtieth Sunday in Ordinary Time—The Greatest Commandment

Year B

The Holy Family of Jesus, Mary, and Joseph—Virtues

Nineteenth Sunday in Ordinary Time—Imitate God

Year C

The Nativity of the Lord (Christmas)—Light of God

First Sunday of Lent—Choices

 Go to **aliveinchrist.osv.com** for a complete correlation ordered by the Sundays of the year and suggestions for how to integrate the Scripture readings into chapter lessons.

Name _____ Date _____

Virtues

Virtues are gifts from God. We grow close to God when we practice habits of faith, hope, and charity (love).

Next to each box, write one way that you can practice that virtue.

| **Faith** | _____
 _____
 _____ |

| **Hope** | _____
 _____
 _____ |

| **Charity** | _____
 _____
 _____ |

Live in the Light

Let Us Pray

Leader: God our Father, help us to be a light in the darkness.

"Send your light and your fidelity,
    that they may be my guide." **Psalm 43:3**

All: God, with you as our guide, we will learn how to love our neighbor. Amen.

God's Word

Jesus spoke to them again, saying, "I am the light of the world. Whoever follows me will not walk in darkness, but will have the light of life."

John 8:12

? What Do You Wonder?

- Does your choice to shine the light of Jesus in the world really matter?
- How do you "practice" faith and hope?

199

Optional Activity

Chapter Poem: "Candle" *Verbal/Linguistic*

Use this poem after the opening prayer, before talking about how hard it is to see in the dark.

- Read aloud the poem. Ask the children what other words they would use to describe a candle. Possible responses: hot, bright, burning, light
- After connecting the light of a candle with Jesus as the Light of the World, transition back to the lesson instruction.

  Go to **aliveinchrist.osv.com** for Chapter Poem.

Invite

Let Us Pray

Invite the children to gather in the prayer space and make the Sign of the Cross. Invite a volunteer to read aloud the leader's prayer and the Psalm verse. Prompt the children's response.

Have the children move from the prayer space back to their seats.

Explain that we all know how hard it is to see in the dark. Even the littlest bit of light can help us to see.

Say: Let's listen to the words of Jesus as he talks about light.

God's Word

Guide the children through the process of Scripture reflection.

- Invite them to close their eyes, be still, and open their minds and hearts to what God is saying to them in this passage.
- Proclaim the Scripture.
- Maintain several moments of silence.
- *Ask:* What did you hear God say to you today?
- Invite volunteers to share.

What Do You Wonder?

Say: Jesus helps us to see what we must do to be his light in the world. But just like when we are learning to ride a bike or dance, we must practice how to be faith-filled, hope-filled, loving people.

Invite the children to respond to the questions. Ask what else they might wonder about how we can shine the light of Jesus.

Objectives

- Discover that Christians are called by Jesus to be the light of the world
- Be aware that our vocation is God's plan for our lives
- Describe virtues as good spiritual habits that make us stronger and help us do what is right and good

The Light of the World

Read aloud the question.

- Invite the children to respond.
- Write their responses on the board or on chart paper.

Invite a volunteer to read aloud the opening paragraph.

- Ask the children to listen for the sharing and caring nature of Jesus' words.

God's Word

Proclaim the Scripture story.

- Emphasize that Jesus' words apply to modern times, too.
- Read the questions that follow and allow the children to respond.
- Write their responses to each question on the board or on chart paper.
- ⭐ Instruct the children to underline what Jesus said others may see when you share your light.

▶ Music Option: Have the children sing "Christ Is Light" or "Walk in the Light," downloaded from **aliveinchrist.osv.com**.

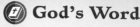
The Light of the World

Who has shared the light of Christ with you?

Jesus talked about how people should help others find their way. One day, Jesus told his followers what the world needed from them.

 Underline what Jesus said others may see when you share your light.

God's Word

Your Light Must Shine

"You are the light of the world," Jesus said. "A city set on a mountain cannot be hidden."

He went on, "Nor do they light a lamp and then put it under a bushel basket; it is set on a lampstand, where it gives light to all in the house."

Finally he said, "Just so, your light must shine before others, that they may see your good deeds and glorify your heavenly Father."   Based on Matthew 5:14–16

➤ What are some things you say or do that can bring light?

➤ Why do you think it's important to share your light with others?

We share Jesus' light during the Service of Light at Easter Vigil

200

Scripture Background

Matthew 5:14–16

In this passage, Jesus addresses a group of his followers.

- The purpose of the Church is to be a sign of God's Kingdom. The members of the Church are to further her purpose by sharing the Good News and doing good deeds.
- Good works should be done for the glory of God, not for personal glory.
- By our good works, we are to influence the world for good.

Be a Light

Jesus taught about the many ways that we are called to show love and care for others. The good things you do for others show that you believe in God's Kingdom.

God's plan for your life is called your **vocation**. Each person has a purpose and our vocation helps us live that calling. When you choose loving actions, you are following God's plan. You are letting your light shine.

You are a light for the world when you help bring peace to others. Sometimes you work for peace in your own family and neighborhood. Sometimes you need to help people who live far away. Wherever help is needed, Jesus calls his followers to bring his peace.

© Our Sunday Visitor

Catholic Faith Words

vocation God's plan for our lives; the purpose for which he made us

Share Your Faith

Think Write one way you've been a light to others.

_____

_____

_____

Share With a group, discuss ways you have shared the light of Christ with someone.

201

ⓘ Catechist Background

Candles

The Church uses candles to symbolize the light of faith and Jesus as the Light of the World.

- At the Easter Vigil, the Paschal Candle is lit. It is used in Baptisms, at funerals, and throughout the Easter season.
- Other candles in the church include the sanctuary candle, which tells us that the Blessed Sacrament is in the Tabernacle, and altar candles, which are lit for Mass.

Be a Light

Invite three volunteers to each read aloud one of the paragraphs.

- Ask the children to explain how we can be a light for the world.

Work with Words

Invite a volunteer to read aloud the Catholic Faith Word.

- Distribute one index card per child.
- Ask the children to write the word on one side of the card and the definition on the other side.
- Encourage them to use this card, with others they have created, to prepare for chapter and unit reviews.

Activity

Read aloud the directions.

- Allow time for the children to think about their answers and write them down.
- Organize the children into groups of three or four.
- Encourage them to share their answers with their group.

Quick Review

We are called to be the light of the world. We can do this through our vocation. By practicing good spiritual habits, or virtues, these gifts from God will help us know and do what is right.

Discover

Objectives

- Explore the Theological Virtues of faith, hope, and charity and how they help us live in relationship with the Holy Trinity
- Illustrate the need to practice the virtues so they will grow over time

The Virtues

Ask: How do the Theological Virtues help us?

- Encourage group discussion.

Ask a volunteer to read aloud the first paragraph.

- *Ask:* When do we first receive these virtues? at Baptism

The Theological Virtues

Have a volunteer read aloud the first paragraph.

- Invite the group to repeat together the names of the three Theological Virtues.

Work with Words

Before continuing with the content on the page, review the Catholic Faith Words on both pages 202 and 203 with the children.

- As you read aloud the definition, have the children locate the highlighted word and place their finger on it.
- Repeat this pattern for all words.
- Distribute five index cards per child.
- Have the children create vocabulary cards for chapter and unit reviews.

Ask a volunteer to read aloud the paragraph on faith.

202 Chapter 14

Discover

The Virtues

How do the Theological Virtues help us?

Making good and loving choices helps you develop habits of goodness, called **virtues**. The word virtue means "strength." Practicing these good habits helps you make even more loving choices. The Theological Virtues come from God and help us to relate to him. We are first given these virtues in our Baptism.

The Theological Virtues

The **Theological Virtues** are faith, hope, and charity (love). They help us to live in a relationship with the Holy Trinity.

Faith leads us to obey God. True faith is believing in God and all that he helps us understand about himself. As a follower of Jesus, you believe in him. Faith is both a gift from God and something we choose. Scripture tells us that real faith also produces good works.

Catholic Faith Words

virtues good spiritual habits that make you stronger and help you do what is right and good. They grow over time with our practice and openness to God's grace.

Theological Virtues the virtues of faith, hope, and charity (love), which are gifts from God that guide our relationship with him

faith the theological virtue that makes it possible for us to believe in God and all that he helps us understand about himself. Faith leads us to obey God.

202

ⓘ Catechist Background

Virtue

The word *virtue* comes from the Latin word *virtus*, meaning "strength."

- Faith, hope, and charity (or love) are strengths given by God to help people act in believing, trusting, and generous ways.
- Explain to the children that when Christians practice these virtues, they grow in knowledge of God, anticipate the coming of God's Kingdom, and share the love of the Holy Trinity.

Hope is the virtue that helps you trust in all that God the Father has made known, in Jesus' promises of eternal life, and in the help of the Holy Spirit. Sometimes at Mass we pray, "Our hope is in the name of the Lord who made Heaven and Earth." As the Church, we hope for a world that is more like God's Kingdom.

Charity directs people to love God above all things and their neighbor as themselves. You show your love for God by helping people, loving others, and listening to friends who have problems. The Church helps you show love for God by teaching you how to treat everyone with kindness and respect.

In order to get better at something, you need to practice. You have to practice virtues. When you do, these gifts from God—faith, hope, and charity—grow strong in you.

Catholic Faith Words

hope the theological virtue that helps us trust in the true happiness God wants us to have and in Jesus' promises of eternal life, and to rely on the help of the Holy Spirit

charity the theological virtue of love. It directs us to love God above all things and our neighbor as ourselves, for the love of God.

Connect Your Faith

Create a Reminder Design and decorate a bookmark about practicing one of the virtues as you share the light of Christ with others.

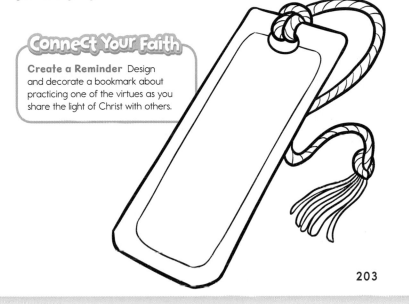

203

The Theological Virtues, *continued*

Invite two more volunteers to read aloud the paragraphs on hope and charity.

- Ask the children to share anything new they learned about the Theological Virtues.
- Remind them that, like anything else, they will get better at the virtues with practice.

Activity

Have a volunteer read aloud the directions for the Connect Your Faith activity.

- Provide the children with crayons, colored pencils, or markers.
- Encourage them to think about ways to practice the virtues while they work.
- You might also suggest that they include symbols of the virtues on their bookmarks.
- Allow time for the children to complete their bookmarks.

Optional Activity

Activity Master 14: Virtues

Distribute copies of the activity found on catechist page 199E.

- Tell the children that they will write one way to practice each virtue.
- As an alternative, you may wish to send this activity home with the children.

Chapter 14 Activity Master

Name _____ Date _____

Virtues

Virtues are gifts from God. We grow close to God when we practice habits of faith, hope, and charity (love).

Next to each box, write one way that you can practice that virtue.

Faith _____
Hope _____
Charity _____

199E Chapter 14

Quick Review

Practicing the Theological Virtues of faith, hope, and charity (love) will help us live in relationship with the Holy Trinity. Over time, they will grow in us and help us lead holy lives.

Our Catholic Life

Read aloud the question at the top of the page.

- Write the children's responses on the board or on chart paper.

- Tell them that the group is going to cover some ways to add prayer to our days.

- Ask a volunteer to be prepeared to add anything new that comes up to the list you already started.

Read aloud the first paragraph and the three bullets.

- Answer any questions the children might have.

Ask a volunteer to read aloud the concluding paragraph.

Pray Every Day

Have the children review the chart.

 Direct them to place a check mark next to the times they already pray during the day.

- Allow time for the children to read and mark their prayer time.

- Ask volunteers if there are other times that they would add to the chart.

Live

Our Catholic Life

How can you make prayer a part of your day?

The virtues of faith, hope, and charity help you develop your prayer life.

- **Prayers of faith** show God that you believe in him.

- **Prayers of hope** tell God that you trust in him, even when times are tough.

- **Prayers of charity** (love) show God that you love him and will show your love to others by being kind.

There are many ways to add prayer to your day. If you aren't already saying morning prayers, mealtime prayers, and bedtime prayers, you can easily develop the habit of praying at these times. Some families say prayers at special times, such as before leaving on a trip. Talk to your family about adding more prayer to your lives.

⭐ Place a check mark next to the times you pray during the day.

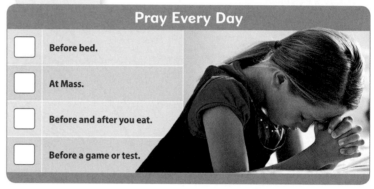

Pray Every Day

☐ Before bed.

☐ At Mass.

☐ Before and after you eat.

☐ Before a game or test.

© Our Sunday Visitor

204 Chapter 14

Optional Activity

Categorize Prayers *Verbal/Linguistic*

The children will benefit from using the acts of faith, hope, and love to further establish the connection between these virtues and prayer.

- Instruct the children to turn to pages 320–327 in the Our Catholic Tradition section of the Student Book.

- Have them look through the prayers and identify those that mention any of the virtues.

People of Faith

Saint Genevieve, c. 422–500

January 3

Saint Genevieve lived in France. When she was young, she decided that she wanted to share the light of Christ with everyone she met. She lived the virtues her whole life and showed her faith by praying. Attila the Hun and his army didn't attack Paris because Saint Genevieve led the people in prayer. She showed her hope by building a church that people still use. She gave food to hungry people and asked the King to have mercy on prisoners. Saint Genevieve often wore a crucifix to remind her to think about Jesus.

Discuss: When have you helped others in need?

 Learn more about Saint Genevieve at **aliveinchrist.osv.com**

Live Your Faith

Remember to Pray With a group, list several times of day when you can pray. Make a list of ways to remind yourself to pray.

When to Pray:	Reminders to Pray:
_____	_____
_____	_____
_____	_____
_____	_____
_____	_____
_____	_____

Live in the Light **205**

People of Faith

Tell the children about Saint Genevieve.

- When she was a young girl, Genevieve was noticed in a crowd and encouraged by someone to persevere with her virtues.
- Read aloud the paragraph about Saint Genevieve.
- *Ask:* When have you helped others in need?
- Allow the children to share their answers with a partner.

> Encourage the children to go to **aliveinchrist.osv.com** at home to learn more about Saint Genevieve.

Activity

Read aloud the directions for the Live Your Faith activity.

- Allow the children to work in groups of three or four to complete the chart.
- Ask volunteers to share their group's findings.

Catholic Social Teaching

Chapter Connections

To integrate Catholic Social Teaching into your lesson, choose one of the following features: Rights and Responsibilities pages 294–295; or Care for Creation, pages 302–303.

- Start the Live step of the process by talking about Saint Genevieve on page 205. Then move directly to the Catholic Social Teaching feature.
- Or, to expand the lesson, complete both pages 204 and 205, then move to the Catholic Social Teaching feature.
- Return to Chapter 14 for the prayer on page 206.

Let Us Pray
Prayer of Petition

Explain that this prayer is an asking prayer. In it, we spend time thinking and praying about others who have been lights of the world. We also pray for ourselves, asking God's help so we can continue to be doers of good deeds.

Prepare

Choose volunteers for the three reader parts.

 Rehearse with the children "Share the Light," downloaded from **aliveinchrist.osv.com**.

Gather

Invite the children to gather in the prayer space with their books.

Pray

Follow the order of prayer on the student page.

Leader's concluding prayer: Generous Father, we thank you for the gifts of faith, hope, and charity and for the people in our lives who have been a light to the world, showing your gifts in action. Help us to be like them and to use your gifts well. We pray in Jesus' name.

 Conclude by processing around the room with the children singing "Share the Light."

 ### Let Us Pray
Prayer of Petition

Gather and begin with the Sign of the Cross.

Leader: We pray together, asking Jesus to help us grow in faith, hope, and charity.

All: We know you, and so we have faith in you, O Jesus.

Reader 1: Help us act with love toward one another.

Reader 2: Help us share the light of your love.

Reader 3: Give us the hope of living with you in Heaven.

All: Amen.

Leader: Let us pray.

Bow your heads as the leader prays.

All: Amen.

 Sing "Share the Light"
Share the light of Jesus.
Share the light that shows the way.
Share the light of Jesus.
Share God's spirit today. Share God's spirit today.
Repeat Verse

Share the word…
Share the love…
Share the smile…
Share the light…

 ## Liturgy Link

Add Light

Because light has been the theme of this chapter, you may wish to add light to the prayer celebration.

- Have the children make construction-paper flames and decorate the prayer space with them.
- Include battery-powered candles in the prayer space or use them as you process to and from the prayer space.

Go to **aliveinchrist.osv.com** for Sunday readings, Scripture background, questions of the week, and seasonal resources.

FAMILY+FAITH
LIVING AND LEARNING TOGETHER

YOUR CHILD LEARNED >>>

This chapter explores the importance of sharing Christ's light with others and the Theological Virtues of faith, hope, and charity (love).

God's Word

 Read **John 8:12** to learn how you can help others to see Jesus' light.

Catholics Believe

- Each of us has a purpose and vocation that helps us follow God's plan and be a light to the world.
- God's gifts of faith, hope, and charity (love) help you live a good and moral life.

To learn more, go to the *Catechism of the Catholic Church* #1813, 1877 at **usccb.org**.

People of Faith

This week, your child met Saint Genevieve, the patron Saint of Paris. She is said to have thwarted the attack of Attila the Hun through prayer.

CHILDREN AT THIS AGE >>>

How They Understand Sharing the Light of Christ It's a powerful feeling for children when they realize they can have an impact on others. Your child can do this in both positive and negative ways. Particularly if he or she has younger siblings at home, but also with peers and even people who are older, your child can spread the light of Christ through kind actions and virtuous example. This will usually mean something different for each child, but third graders often need to be reminded that they serve as examples for others

CONSIDER THIS >>>

How quick are you to recognize the bad habits of yourself or others?

It is easy to see other's bad habits. We are familiar with our own as well—so much so that it may be easier to name our bad habits than recognize our good ones. "[Virtues] are acquired by frequent repetition of virtuous acts that establish a pattern of virtuous behavior.... Yet it is through doing good acts in the concrete that the virtue within us is strengthened and grows" (*USCCA, p. 317*).

LET'S TALK >>>

- Talk about a time when your trust in God has given you hope.
- Ask your child to name some good habits that he or she has.

LET'S PRAY >>>

Saint Genevieve, help us to be the light of Christ and share God's love with all we meet. Amen.

For a multimedia glossary of Catholic Faith Words, Sunday readings, seasonal and Saint resources, and chapter activities go to **aliveinchrist.osv.com**.

Alive in Christ, Grade 3 Chapter 14 **207**

Distribute the page to the children or parents/adult family members. Point out the chapter highlights, insights on how third graders understand concepts, the opportunity for the adults to reflect on their own experience and faith journey, and the family prayer.

Chapter 14 Review

A **Work with Words** Complete Jesus' message with the correct words from the Word Bank.

1-5. Jesus said, "You are the _____**light**_____.

A city on a mountaintop cannot be

_____**hidden**_____.""Your light must

_____**shine**_____ before others, that they may

see your good _____**deeds**_____ and glorify

your Heavenly _____**Father**_____."

Word Bank
- deeds
- Father
- hidden
- shine
- light

B **Check Understanding** Match each description in Column A with the correct term in Column B.

Column A

Column B

6. This virtue helps you trust in God's promise of happiness and eternal life.

faith

7. This virtue helps you believe in God and all that he has made known to us.

charity

8. You can do this at any time of day, not just at meals or bedtime.

virtue

9. This virtue helps you love and show kindness.

pray

10. This is a good quality or good habit that you can develop.

hope

 Go to **aliveinchrist.osv.com** for an interactive review.

208 Chapter 14

Chapter Review

Use Catechist Quick Reviews to highlight lesson concepts.

A **Work with Words**
Have the children use the words from the Word Bank to complete Jesus' message.

B **Check Understanding**
Instruct the children to match each description in Column A with the correct term in Column B.

Go to **aliveinchrist.osv.com** to prepare customized and downloadable assessments, send eAssessments, and assign interactive reviews.

KEY CONCEPT

Conscience is the ability given to us by God that helps us make choices about right and wrong. God's grace in the Sacraments, and the Holy Spirit, help us make changes and good choices.

DOCTRINAL CONTENT

- Conscience is an ability given to us by God that helps us make choices about right and wrong. (CCC, 1777)
- The Precepts of the Church are some of the minimum requirements given by Church leaders for deepening our relationship with God and the Church. (CCC, 2041)
- The Holy Spirit and the teachings of the Church help us to make good choices. (CCC, 1783–1785)
- In the Sacrament of Penance and Reconciliation, we receive God's forgiveness and the grace to help us change. (CCC, 1422–1423)

TASKS OF CATECHESIS

Helping children grow in a faith that is "known, celebrated, lived and expressed in prayer" (NDC, 20).

This chapter focuses on the following tasks of catechesis:

- Promoting Knowledge of the Faith
- Moral Formation

Catechist Background

> Probe me, God, know my heart; try me, know my thoughts. See if there is a wicked path in me; lead me along an ancient path. **Psalm 139:23–24**
>
> ➜ **Reflect** Are you willing to be judged or examined by God?

The Israelites looked on the Torah, their Law, with the utmost reverence. They regarded it as sacred because it confirmed the covenant between God and the people of Israel. Traditionally, laws have helped groups of people live together rightly and justly. Rules guide life at home and at work; in clubs, teams, and organizations; and in parishes. Behavioral codes and guidelines direct and preserve communities everywhere.

The Ten Commandments and the Sermon on the Mount, which includes the Beatitudes, serve to guide the moral life of Church members. The Precepts of the Church assist Catholics in determining those minimal actions expected of members of the Catholic faith. These precepts specify some of the behaviors that will enhance Christian growth in love of God and neighbor. This guidance helps Christians choose moral living and faithfulness.

Although the Church provides guidance, Christians still choose sin. Yet God is always ready to forgive, and the Church is always ready to celebrate God's forgiveness in the Sacrament of Penance and Reconciliation. Sin weakens our relationship with God and others. This Sacrament celebrates the restoration of these relationships.

➜ **Reflect** Describe an event of reconciliation in your life.

Catechist's Prayer

 Forgiving Father, you show me a love beyond what I deserve or understand. Teach me to love more and to forgive myself and others. I ask in Jesus' name. Amen.

Lesson Plan

Objectives	Process	Materials

Invite, 10 minutes

Help with Choices Page 209

- 💜 **Psalm 25:5** Pray the opening prayer.
- 📖 **Psalm 139:23–24** Reflect prayerfully on the Word.
- Discuss What Do You Wonder questions.

🔊 **Optional Activity**
Chapter Story: "Making Choices"

Discover, 35 minutes

Many Choices Pages 210–211

- Recognize conscience as an ability given to us by God that helps us make choices about right and wrong
- Define the Precepts of the Church as some of the minimum requirements given by Church leaders for deepening our relationship with God and the Church

- **Catholic Faith Word** grace, conscience, Precepts of the Church
- Discuss making good choices.
- Review how each Precept provides guidance.
- **Share Your Faith Activity** Choose a Precept and discuss how it helps Catholics become holy.

- ☐ pencils or pens
- ☐ three index cards, per child
- **Optional Activity** Moral Choice Maze
- ☐ Activity Master 15 (Page 209E)

Changing Directions Pages 212–213

- Recall that the Holy Spirit and the teachings of the Church help us to make good choices
- Appreciate receiving God's forgiveness and the grace to help us change in the Sacrament of Penance and Reconciliation

- **Catholic Faith Words** sin
- Talk about overcoming bad choices.
- 📖 **Acts 9:1–30** Proclaim "Saul and Jesus."
- ☆ Underline what the voice said to Saul.
- Discuss ways to make things right.
- **Connect Your Faith Activity** Talk with a partner about making good choices.

- ☐ pencils or pens
- ☐ one index card, per child

Live, 15 minutes

Our Catholic Life Pages 214–215

- Review steps to form a good conscience.
- ☆ Write the first word of each step in order.
- **People of Faith** Learn about Saint Padre Pio.
- **Live Your Faith Activity** Play a conscience game.

- ☐ pencils or pens
- ☐ a coin and markers for game

Prayer for Forgiveness Page 216

- Select one child to read the first four leader parts.
- ▶ Rehearse "God of Mercy."
- Follow the order of prayer.

🔊 Download "God of Mercy."

Family + Faith Page 217

Point out that the Catholic Families page provides chapter highlights, information on how third graders understand faith concepts, and family prayer.

Chapter Review Page 218

🌐 **aliveinchrist.osv.com**
- Customize and Download Assessments
- Email Links to eAssessments
- Interactive Student Reviews

ONLINE RESOURCES

 Go to **aliveinchrist.osv.com**

You will find:

- Interactive lesson planning with web specific content and additional activities
- Step by step lesson instruction from printed Catechist Edition for integrated lesson planning
- Custom-built assessments to download and eAssessments links
- Interactive reviews that provide scores and the option to review answers
- Sunday readings with background and questions of the week

 Go to **osvparish.com**

You will find:

- Ask the Experts Q and A
- General Catechist Helps
- Community Connections and Blogs

Sharing the Message with Third Graders

Making Good Choices Third graders often define good choices in terms of the parameters they have been given by people they trust. These parameters are often specific to place or situation. Because children this age depend a great deal on social expectations, it's important that this early conscience formation occur in environments that are trustworthy and supportive of Catholic moral values.

Teaching Tip: Review your expectations with the children and discuss how they relate to God's commandment to love God and others.

How Third Graders Understand

- Third graders expect laws to have certain consequences. Be consistent with your rules and in your behavior.
- Children this age need to know that they can have a second chance. Help them learn from their mistakes.
- All children desire forgiveness. If they messed up, show them how they can make things right again.

"When I need forgiveness for something I've done, show me how to make things right."

Chapter Connections

Chapter Story

Invite

"Making Choices"

Use this story to expand the chapter introduction.

- Ask the children to think about difficult choices they have made.
- Discuss why some choices are not good moral choices.

 Go to **aliveinchrist.osv.com** Lesson Planning section for this story.

NCEA IFG: ACRE Edition

Discover

Knowledge of the Faith

- Objective: To know and understand basic Catholic teaching about the Incarnate Word Jesus Christ as the way, truth, and life

Moral Formation

- Objective: To be knowledgeable about the teachings of Jesus and the Church as the basis of Christian morality and to understand Catholic Social Teaching

Catholic Social Teaching

Live

 Use one of these features to introduce the principle and engage the children with an activity.

- Rights and Responsibilities, Pages 294–295
- The Dignity of Work, Pages 298–299

Music Options

 Use one or more of the following songs to enhance catechetical learning or for prayer.

- "God of Mercy," Live Prayer, Page 216
- "Christ Is Light," Discover, Page 210
- "I'm Sorry," Discover, Page 213
- "Kyrie," Discover, Page 213

LECTIONARY CONNECTION

 Chapter 15 highlights Lectionary-connected themes such as grace, sin, conscience, and Precepts of the Church. If your parish aligns its curriculum to the liturgical year, you could use this chapter in connection with the following readings.

Year A

Ash Wednesday—Reconciliation

Twenty-fourth Sunday in Ordinary Time—Call to Forgiveness and Mercy

Year B

Second Sunday of Advent— Reconciliation

Third Sunday in Ordinary Time— Reconciliation

Year C

Twenty-sixth Sunday in Ordinary Time—Forgiveness

Our Lord Jesus Christ, King of the Universe—Reconciliation

 Go to **aliveinchrist.osv.com** for a complete correlation ordered by the Sundays of the year and suggestions for how to integrate the Scripture readings into chapter lessons.

Name _____   Date _____

Moral Choice Maze

Use the words in the maze to fill in the blanks. Then draw a line through
the maze in the same order as your answers.

1. A deliberate choice to
disobey God is a

   _____.

2. The inner voice that helps
you decide right and wrong

   is your _____.

3. A great Christian
preacher and writer:

   _____.

4. Church teachings and

   _____ are guides to
help you make good moral choices.

5. The book that contains God's Word

   is called the _____.

6. You sometimes need help to make

   good _____.

7. The _____ are some
of the basic duties of members of
the Catholic Church.

8. A _____ is a group
of people who come together to
share their belief in Jesus.

9. The Holy _____ helps
you choose to do what is right.

10. God's loving gift to humans is called

    _____.

11. After _____ appeared
to Saul, Saul was baptized.

12. He forgives our sins:

    _____.

13. The celebration of God's forgiveness
through the Church is the

    _____.

Maze words: ← start → / sin / conscience / community / faith / Spirit / obey / Saint Paul / decisions / precepts / grace / wrong choice / laws / Bible / Jesus / saints / right choice / Sacrament of Reconciliation / God / finish

© Our Sunday Visitor

Help with Choices

♡ Let Us Pray

Leader: God, help me to follow you.

"Guide me by your fidelity and teach me,
for you are God my savior." **Psalm 25:5**

All: Jesus, help me to listen for the voice of the Holy
Spirit in your Word and in the Church so that I
may choose what is right. Amen.

God's Word

Look deep into my heart, O God. You know
my deepest thoughts. See if I am going in the
wrong direction, then lead me back to you.
Based on Psalm 139:23–24

? What Do You Wonder?

- Is God mad when you do
  something wrong?
- Who do you trust to help you
  learn what is right and wrong?

Help with Choices **209**

Optional Activity

Chapter Story: "Making Choices" *Verbal/Linguistic*

Use this story after the opening prayer, before talking about listening
for the voice of the Holy Spirit.

- Point out that making good choices is not always easy.
- Emphasize that we can find help in choosing to do the right
  thing. Review sources of help, then transition back to the lesson
  instruction.

 Go to **aliveinchrist.osv.com** for Chapter Story.

♡ Let Us Pray

Invite the children to gather in the
prayer space and make the Sign of
the Cross. Pray the leader's prayer,
including the Psalm verse. Prompt
the children's response. Have the
children return to their seats.

Say: Jesus taught his disciples how
to live by loving God and loving
others. He asks us to listen for the
voice of the Holy Spirit so that we
can know what is right.

God's Word

Guide the children through the
process of Scripture reflection.

- Invite them to close their eyes,
  be still, and open their minds and
  hearts to what God is saying to
  them in this passage.
- Proclaim the Scripture.
- Maintain several moments
  of silence.
- *Ask:* What did you hear God say
  to you today?
- Invite volunteers to share.

What Do You Wonder?

Say: It can sometimes seem difficult
to know what is right. God helps us
to know his will through the
Church's teaching. He can give us
the strength to do what is right,
even when it is hard for us. If we fail,
God is waiting to forgive us.

Invite the children to respond to
the questions. Ask what else they
might wonder about learning and
doing what is right.

Objectives

- Recognize conscience as an ability given to us by God that helps us make choices about right and wrong

- Define the Precepts of the Church as some of the minimum requirements given by Church leaders for deepening our relationship with God and the Church

Many Choices

Read aloud the question.

- Write the children's responses on the board or on chart paper.

Invite two volunteers to read aloud the first two paragraphs.

- Encourage the children to share examples of easy decisions and hard decisions.

Summarize the last paragraph.

- Read aloud the questions and invite the children to respond.

Work with Words

Ask three volunteers to read aloud the words and definitions from the Catholic Faith Words box.

- Distribute three index cards per child.

- Have them write the words on one side of the card and the definitions on the other side.

- Encourage them to use these cards, with others they have created, to prepare for chapter and unit reviews.

Discover

Many Choices

How do you make good choices?

Your life is full of choices. Some don't make much of a difference, such as which color of shirt you wear on a Saturday.

Some choices do make a big difference, though. Sometimes you must choose between a bad thing and a good thing. If you are lucky, the choice is easy. Sometimes, the choice can be difficult.

Everyone needs help to make good choices. The Holy Spirit helps you. God's **grace** in the Sacraments can help you. Parents, priests, and teachers can help you prepare for choices by helping you form your **conscience**.

> ➜ Why are some choices harder to make than others?
>
> ➜ What do you do when you have a choice to make?

Catholic Faith Words

grace God's free and loving gift to humans of his own life and help

conscience an abiltiy given to us by God that helps us make choices about right and wrong

Precepts of the Church some of the minimum requirements given by Church leaders for deepening our relationship with God and the Church

210 Chapter 15

Optional Activity

Activity Master 15: Moral Choice Maze

Distribute copies of the activity found on catechist page 209E.

- Tell the children this will be a fun way to review the chapter material.

- As an alternative, you may wish to send this activity home with the children.

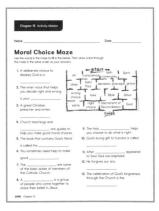

The Church Guides Choices

The Church helps us make good choices, too. We use the teachings of the Church to guide our choices. The Church teaches us to follow the Ten Commandments and the Beatitudes. The Church tells us we must also follow its basic laws. These basic laws are called the **Precepts of the Church**.

Precepts of the Church

Precept	How Each Precept Guides You
1. Take part in Mass on Sundays and Holy Days of Obligation. Keep these days holy and avoid unnecessary work.	Makes sure that you take time to be with Jesus and your parish community, strengthens your faith, rests your body, and encourages you to enjoy the world God has given you
2. Celebrate the Sacrament of Penance and Reconciliation at least once a year if there is serious sin.	Helps you look at your life to see how you need God's forgiveness and which actions you need to improve
3. Receive Holy Communion at least once a year during Easter time.	Strengthens your faith and makes you one with Jesus
4. Fast and abstain on days of penance.	Helps you share in the sacrifice of Jesus, train yourself spiritually, and experience the hunger of people who are poor
5. Give your time, gifts, and money to support the Church.	Encourages you to support the Church and participate in her works

© Our Sunday Visitor

Share Your Faith

Think Pick out one of the Precepts. How does it help Catholics become holy?

Share Share your answer with a partner and talk about why the precepts are important.

211

✓ Quick Tip

Graphic Organizer

Precept · Precept · Precept · Precept · Precept

Christian Life → God

The Church Guides Choices

Read aloud the paragraph.

- Draw the graphic organizer from the Quick Tip box on the board or on chart paper. Explain that the Precepts are like road signs that show the way to eternal life with God.

Precepts of the Church

Have two strong readers take turns reading from the chart. The first child will read the Precept; then the other child will read the copy under "How Each Precept Guides You."

- Go back to your drawing. Have volunteers write some key words from one of the Precepts next to each of the signs.

Activity

Read aloud the directions

- Encourage the children to share their answer with a partner.

Quick Review

Our conscience helps us make choices about right and wrong. The Precepts of the Church also guide us and help deepen our relationship with God and the Church.

Discover

Objectives

- Recall that the Holy Spirit and the teachings of the Church help us to make good choices
- Appreciate receiving God's forgiveness and the grace to help us change in the Sacrament of Penance and Reconciliation

Changing Directions

Ask: How do you overcome making a bad choice?

- Allow the children to share what they would do.

Read aloud the opening paragraph.

God's Word

Select proficient readers to proclaim the parts of Saul, the narrator, and Jesus.

⭐ Have the children underline what the voice said to Saul.

- Ask the children how Saul changed. Possible response: He changed from hurting Jesus' followers to becoming one of them.
- Remind the children that people who make selfish choices can change and make better choices. Jesus appeared to Saul, who changed from an enemy of Jesus' followers to a faithful Christian.

Changing Directions

How do you overcome making a bad choice?

What happens when someone makes bad choices? This Scripture story shows how someone who made bad choices can change.

Underline what the voice said to Saul.

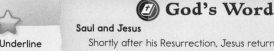 God's Word

Saul and Jesus

Shortly after his Resurrection, Jesus returned to his Father in Heaven. A man named Saul began turning in followers of Jesus to the authorities.

One day, Saul was traveling between towns. A bright light flashed around him. He heard a voice say, "Saul, Saul, why are you persecuting me?"

Saul asked, "Who are you?"

The voice answered, "I am Jesus. Go into the city and do what you are told to do."

Saul did as Jesus said. He was baptized and became a great Christian preacher and writer. He is now known as Saint Paul, his new name in Christ.

Based on Acts 9:1–30

212 Chapter 15

Scripture Background

Acts 9:1–30

The conversion of Saul is one of the pivotal events in the history of the early Church.

- The full text of Saul's story can be found in the Acts of the Apostles.
- After his conversion, Saul became known by his other name, Paul. Saint Paul is recognized as one the Church's major missionaries and writers.

The Sacrament of Penance and Reconciliation

Like Saul, everyone makes wrong choices at times. The deliberate choice to disobey God is called **sin**. When you sin, you hurt your relationship with God and other people. But there are things you can do to help make things right again.

You can experience God's forgiveness in the Sacrament of Penance and Reconciliation, also called confession. Through this Sacrament, God gives you a chance to take these actions through his Church:

- Look at what you have done.
- Say you are sorry, seek forgiveness, and receive absolution.
- Repair or make up for the wrong you have done, and change your behavior.

> ### Catholic Faith Words
>
> **sin** a person's choice to disobey God on purpose and do what he or she knows is wrong. Sins hurts our relationship with God and other people.

© Our Sunday Visitor

Connect Your Faith

Talk It Over With a partner, talk about making good choices in the following situation, and list your choices in the space below.

You can see your best friend's test paper from where you are sitting, and you know that she always gets the highest grade.

_____

_____

_____

213

The Sacrament of Penance and Reconciliation

Read aloud the first paragraph.

- Distinguish between a sin and an accident or a mistake. Remind the children that the choice to sin is intentional, but that an accident or a mistake is not intentional.

Read aloud the second paragraph and the bullet points.

- Point out that Jesus and the Church have provided the Sacrament of Penance and Reconciliation as a way of repairing the harm that sin does.
- *Ask:* Why is the Sacrament of Reconciliation important? Possible responses: It repairs a wrong or helps you change your behavior.

Work with Words

Have the children create a vocabulary card for the word *sin*.

Activity

Read aloud the directions.

- Allow the children to choose a partner to work with.

Quick Review

The Holy Spirit and the teachings of the Church help us make good choices. When we mess up, we can still receive the grace of God through the Sacrament of Penance and Reconciliation.

Optional Activity

Mimes and Role-Plays *Bodily/Kinesthetic*

The situation in the Connect Your Faith Activity can easily be adapted as a role-play or mime.

- After the partners discuss the situation and the right moral choice, ask volunteers to act out or mime the scene, including their solutions.
- Invite the rest of the group to guess the solution being acted out.
- Encourage some of the pairs to team up if the children would like to include making a bad choice in their role-play.

Live

Our Catholic Life

Tell the children that they are going to learn about telling right from wrong in this lesson.

Read aloud the first paragraph.

Form Your Conscience

Ask five volunteers to each read aloud one of the bullet points in the chart.

⭐ Instruct the children to write the first word of each step in order on the blanks provided.

• Have the children work independently to complete the chart.

• *Ask:* Why is forming your conscience important?

• List the children's responses on the board or on chart paper.

• Point out that the Ten Commandments (p. 316), the Beatitudes (p. 317), and the Precepts of the Church (p. 319) can be found in the Our Catholic Tradition section of the Student Book.

Remind the children that while it is okay for us to think about whether or not we are making good choices, we should not try to point out the poor moral choices others have made. Emphasize that only God can judge people.

Our Catholic Life

How do you tell right from wrong?

You know that your conscience guides you in making right decisions. It is up to you to learn what is right and wrong so that you can use that knowledge when you need to make a choice. Information about what is right and wrong can be found in many different places.

Write the first words of each step in order below.

Form Your Conscience

• **Pray** to the Holy Spirit, asking for help to make a right choice.	1. <u>Pray</u>
• **Learn** the Ten Commandments, the Beatitudes, and the Precepts of the Church.	2. <u>Learn</u>
• **Listen** to the homily at Mass, and pay attention during religion lessons to learn God's laws.	3. <u>Listen</u>
• **Ask** a parent or another trusted adult.	4. <u>Ask</u>
• **Receive** the Sacraments, and be strengthened to follow God's will.	5. <u>Receive</u>

214

© Our Sunday Visitor

✓ Quick Tip

Free Choice

Keep in mind that many important decisions are made for children by adults.

• Emphasize that parents, guardians, and teachers have God's authority to make decisions for children.

• Tell the children that although they may not get to make all their own decisions, they are responsible for the decisions and choices that they do make.

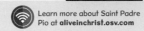

People of Faith

Saint Pio (Padre Pio), 1887–1968

September 23

Saint Padre Pio was born in Italy. His parents were farmers. At age 15, he began studying to become a Capuchin priest. He took the name Pio in honor of Pope Saint Pius V. Padre Pio knew that confession was very important. He said that going to confession was like dusting the soul. He heard the confessions of people who traveled from all over. He helped them feel God's mercy and forgiveness. Padre Pio was known for having the stigmata, the visible wounds of Christ. He would tell people "Pray, hope, and don't worry."

Discuss: When have you felt God's mercy?

Learn more about Saint Padre Pio at **aliveinchrist.osv.com**

Live Your Faith

The Path of Conscience With a partner, flip a coin to move along the path. Heads moves one space; tails moves two spaces. The first player to finish is the winner.

215

Catholic Social Teaching

Chapter Connections

To integrate Catholic Social Teaching into your lesson, choose one of the following features: Rights and Responsibilities, pages 294–295; or The Dignity of Work, pages 298–299.

- Start the Live step of the process by talking about Saint Pio on page 215. Then move to the Catholic Social Teaching feature.
- Or, to expand the lesson, complete both pages 214 and 215, then move to the Catholic Social Teaching feature.
- Return to Chapter 15 for the prayer on page 216.

People of Faith

Tell the children about Saint Pio.

- He was born Francesco, named in honor of Saint Francis of Assisi.
- Padre Pio had the ability to read people's hearts when he heard their confessions.
- He heard confessions ten to twelve hours a day. He used this opportunity to help people become closer to God.
- Read aloud the paragraph on Saint Padre Pio.
- Discuss the question with the children.

Encourage the children to go to **aliveinchrist.osv.com** at home to learn more about Saint Pio.

Activity

Read aloud the directions for the Live Your Faith activity.

- Tell the children that they will play a game based on forming a good conscience. Point out that by thinking about situations in advance, they will know how to react to similar situations in the future.
- Organize the children in pairs to play the game.
- Supply coins and small objects for players to use as markers.
- Have the children play the game.
- Walk among the group to determine how the children are reacting to the situations in the game.

Let Us Pray
Prayer for Forgiveness

Prepare
Choose one child to read the first four leader parts. You will read the concluding prayer.

 Have the children rehearse "God of Mercy," downloaded from **aliveinchrist.osv.com**.

Gather
Invite the children to come to the prayer space with their books. Lead the children into the prayer space while playing or singing "God of Mercy."

Pray
Follow the order of prayer on the student page.

Leader's concluding prayer:
Dear Lord, we are so thankful that you always give us another chance to do better. Thank you for your guidance and your mercy.

 Conclude by singing with the children "God of Mercy" as they process from the prayer space back to their seats.

Live

Let Us Pray
Prayer for Forgiveness

Gather and begin with the Sign of the Cross.

Leader: God our Loving Father, we come to you to ask forgiveness. Sometimes we have not behaved as we should.

Leader: If we have quarreled and called each other names,

All: Lord, let your mercy be on us, as we place our trust in you.

Leader: If we are lazy at home and in school,

All: Lord, let your mercy be on us, as we place our trust in you.

Leader: If we have not done good for others when we had the chance,

All: Lord, let your mercy be on us, as we place our trust in you.

Leader: Let us pray.

Bow your heads as the leader prays.

All: Amen.
Based on the Rite of Penance.

 Sing "God of Mercy"

Liturgy Link

Children as Leaders
The children will be more involved in the prayer celebrations if you give them leadership roles. In this prayer service, you have selected someone to act as a prayer leader.

• You may also wish to select a song leader. Ask whether any children sing in a choir or determine if they demonstrate musical ability.

Go to **aliveinchrist.osv.com** for Sunday readings, Scripture background, questions of the week, and seasonal resources.

FAMILY + FAITH
LIVING AND LEARNING TOGETHER

YOUR CHILD LEARNED >>>
This chapter explains how grace, conscience, and the Precepts of the Church help us follow God and make good choices.

God's Word
 Read **Psalm 139:23–24** and discuss how God leads you in the right direction.

Catholics Believe
- Conscience is the ability given to us by God that helps us make choices about right and wrong.
- God's grace in the Sacraments, and the Holy Spirit, help us make changes and good choices.

To learn more, go to the *Catechism of the Catholic Church* #1777, 1785 at **usccb.org**.

People of Faith
This week, your child met Saint Padre Pio. He said that regular confession was one of the keys to a holy life.

CHILDREN AT THIS AGE >>>
How They Understand Making Good Choices Third graders often define good choices in terms of the parameters they have been given by people they trust. These parameters are often specific to place or situation. Because children this age depend a great deal on social expectations, it's important that this early conscience formation occur in family environments that are trustworthy and supportive of Catholic moral values.

CONSIDER THIS >>>
Who in your life do you trust to give you good advice?

We are careful about who we trust to give us advice. We realize that even those we trust can be wrong because of our limitedness as human beings. "Wisdom enables us to see the world from God's viewpoint, which can help us come to grasp the purpose and plan of God. It grants us the long-range view of history, examining the present in the light of the past and the mystery of the future. It saves us from the illusion that the spirit of the times is our only guide" (USCCA, p. 208).

LET'S TALK >>>
- Ask your child to name one of the actions he or she can do to experience God's forgiveness.
- Talk about how you've experienced God's forgiveness in the Sacrament of Penance and Reconciliation.

LET'S PRAY >>>
Saint Pio, pray for us that we may learn to turn to God often for forgiveness and mercy. Amen.

For a multimedia glossary of Catholic Faith Words, Sunday readings, seasonal and Saint resources, and chapter activities go to **aliveinchrist.osv.com**.

Distribute the page to the children or parents/adult family members. Point out the chapter highlights, insights on how third graders understand concepts, the opportunity for the adults to reflect on their own experience and faith journey, and the family prayer.

Chapter 15 Review

A **Work with Words** Fill in the circle beside the correct answer.

1. Your conscience is a ____ in making good decisions.
   ○ prayer   ● guide   ○ sin

2. A sin is a(n) ____ to disobey God.
   ● deliberate choice   ○ accident   ○ mistake

3. God's ____ in the Sacraments can help you make the right choices.
   ○ spirit   ● grace   ○ words

4. Some basic duties of Catholics are the ____ of the Church.
   ○ laws   ○ guidance   ● Precepts

5. The Church offers God's ____ in the Sacrament of Penance and Reconciliation.
   ○ anger   ● forgiveness   ○ conscience

B **Check Understanding** Write responses on the lines below.

6. Whose voice did Saul hear? **Jesus' voice**

7. What did Saul do after he heard the voice?
   stopped persecuting Christians

8. What was another name for Saul? **Paul**

9. Why do you need to form your conscience?
   Possible response: to make better choices

10. What can help you form your conscience?
    Possible responses: the Holy Spirit, the Ten Commandments

Go to **aliveinchrist.osv.com** for an interactive review.

Use Catechist Quick Reviews to highlight lesson concepts.

A **Work with Words**
Have the children fill in the circle beside the correct answer.

B **Check Understanding**
Explain to the children that they will write their responses to the questions on the lines provided.

Go to **aliveinchrist.osv.com** to prepare customized and downloadable assessments, send eAssessments, and assign interactive reviews.

Help with Choices **217–218**

Use Catechist Quick Reviews in each chapter to highlight lesson concepts for this unit and prepare for the Unit Review.

Have the children complete the Review pages. Then discuss the answers as a group. Review any concepts with which the children are having difficulty.

A **Work with Words**

Have the children match each description in Column A with the correct term in Column B for problems 1–5. They will determine whether sentences are true or false for 6–10..

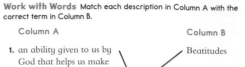

Unit Review

UNIT
5

A **Work with Words** Match each description in Column A with the correct term in Column B.

Column A

Column B

1. an ability given to us by God that helps us make choices about right and wrong

Beatitudes

2. teachings of Jesus that show the way to true happiness

virtues

3. basic duties of Catholics

Precepts of the Church

4. good qualities, or habits of goodness

New Commandment

5. sums up the Ten Commandments and the Beatitudes

conscience

Write the letter T if the sentence is TRUE. Write the letter F if the sentence is False.

6. **T** Catholics should receive Holy Communion at least once a year.

7. **F** Charity (love) means believing in God.

8. **T** Theological virtues are a gift from God.

9. **T** The Church tells us we must follow the Precepts of the Church.

10. **F** Jesus wants us to hold grudges against others.

Morality **219**

B Check Understanding
Complete each sentence by circling the correct word.

11. You can experience God's forgiveness in the Sacrament of ____.

(Penance and Reconciliation)   Baptism

12. Jesus said, "You are the ____ of the world."

leader   (light)

13. When you sin, you hurt your relationship with ____.

yourself   (God)

14. ____ was sold by his brothers into slavery.

(Joseph)   Paul

15. After his Baptism, Saul became known as ____.

(Paul)   Simon

Write responses on the lines below. What are the five Precepts of the Church?

16–20. Take part in Mass on Sundays.

Receive the Sacrament of Penance and Reconciliation.

Receive Holy Communion.

Fast and abstain on days of Penance.

Give your time, gifts, and money to support the Church.

C Make Connections
Write responses on the lines below.

21. How do you show your faith?

Possible response: I pray to and trust God.

22. What did the story of Joseph and his brothers teach you about forgiveness?

Responses will vary.

23. List two of the Beatitudes and what you have done to follow them.

Possible response: I can choose to forgive instead of staying angry.

24. Give an example of the difference between sinning and making a mistake.

Possible response: Lying is a sin. Getting a wrong answer on a test is a mistake.

25. How do you follow Jesus' New Commandment?

Possible response: I show love to neighbors by helping them with chores.

B Check Understanding
Direct the children to complete each sentence by circling the correct word for 11–15. On lines 16–20, have them write their responses to the question.

C Make Connections
On the lines provided, tell the children to write their responses to the statements.

Go to **aliveinchrist.osv.com** to prepare customized and downloadable assessments, send eAssessments, and assign interactive reviews.

Sacraments

Our Catholic Tradition

- The three Sacraments of Initiation celebrate membership into the Church: Baptism, Confirmation, and Eucharist. (CCC, 1212)

- The Sacraments of Healing help people in need of forgiveness and healing during times of physical and spiritual sickness. (CCC, 1421)

- The Sacraments at the Service of Communion celebrate people's commitment to serve God and the community. (CCC, 1534)

Why are the symbols, words, and actions of the Seven Sacraments important in our worship?

Bishops receive the authority to lead, teach, and make holy the Church.

© Our Sunday Visitor

Unit 6 Overview

Chapter 16

The children will:

- understand that people of all ages can be baptized into the Church

- identify that the Sacraments of Initiation include Baptism, Confirmation, and Eucharist

- recall that Baptism removes Original Sin, forgives personal sin, and gives us new life in Christ; Confirmation seals and completes Baptism

- recognize that Jesus shares himself with us in the Eucharist

 Catholic Social Teaching: Live Your Faith

- Life and Dignity, Pages 290–291
- Call to Community, Pages 292–293

Chapter 17

The children will:

- reflect on the connection between faith and healing

- recognize that God's forgiveness and healing are given through the Sacraments of Healing

- understand that during Reconciliation, you confess your sins to a priest and are forgiven in the name of Christ, while in the Anointing of the Sick, the priest prays that God will send you his healing love

 Songs of Scripture
"Healing Grace"

 Catholic Social Teaching: Live Your Faith

- Rights and Responsibilities, Pages 294–295
- The Dignity of Work, Pages 298–299

Chapter 18

The children will:

- understand that vows are sacred promises made to or before God

- explore serving God and community through the Sacraments at the Service of Communion

- describe Holy Orders as the Sacrament in which baptized men are ordained as deacons, priests, or bishops

- identify Matrimony as the Sacrament that joins a baptized man and a baptized woman in Christian marriage to serve God

 Catholic Social Teaching: Live Your Faith

- Call to Community, Pages 292–293
- Solidarity of the Human Family, Pages 300–301

Preview Unit Theme

Have the children name the theme for this unit—Sacraments.

Point out the main photo on the page and, without reading the caption, see if the children can identify which Sacrament it represents. Holy Orders

Ask a volunteer to read aloud the caption.

Read aloud the three bullet points under the Our Catholic Tradition head.

Ask: Why are the symbols, words, and actions of the Seven Sacraments important in our worship?

Write the children's answers on the board or on chart paper. Tell the group they will be able to check their answers and find out more about the Sacraments as the group reviews the next three chapters.

KEY CONCEPT

Baptism removes Original Sin, forgives personal sin, and gives new life in Christ. Confirmation seals and completes Baptism. In the Eucharist, Jesus shares himself with us, giving us the gift of his Body and Blood.

DOCTRINAL CONTENT

- People of all ages can be baptized into the Church. (CCC, 1247, 1250)

- The Sacraments of Initiation celebrate membership into the Catholic Church: Baptism, Confirmation, and Eucharist. (CCC, 1212)

- Baptism removes Original Sin, forgives personal sin, and gives new life in Christ. Confirmation seals and completes Baptism. (CCC, 1217)

- In the Eucharist, Jesus shares himself with us, giving us the gift of his Body and Blood. (CCC, 1323)

TASKS OF CATECHESIS

Helping children grow in a faith that is "known, celebrated, lived, and expressed in prayer" (NDC, 20).

This chapter focuses on the following tasks of catechesis:

- Promoting Knowledge of the Faith

- Liturgical Education

Catechist Background

But you are "a chosen race, a royal priesthood, a holy nation, a people of his own, so that you many announce the praises" of him who called you out of darkness into his wonderful light. Once you were "no people" but now you are God's people; you "had not received mercy" but now you have received mercy. **1 Peter 2:9–10**

➔ **Reflect** Do you announce the praises of the One who called you out of darkness?

Whether you were a babe in arms, an adolescent, or an adult, your Baptism united you to Christ Jesus. Whether the baptismal water was poured over your forehead or you were immersed, the sacred waters united you to the mystery of Christ's Death and Resurrection. You were welcomed into the life of the Church and invited to journey toward life with God forever.

Whether you were confirmed when you were baptized or you celebrated Confirmation at a later age, the Sacred Chrism sealed your Baptism. The Holy Spirit gave you strength. And, you came to the table of the Lord and received the Body and Blood of Christ. Through these three Sacraments, you were fully initiated into the life of Christ and the Christian community.

In the early Church, many catechumens were initiated at the Easter Vigil, celebrating Baptism, Confirmation, and Eucharist at a single ritual. The present-day Eastern Rite continues this practice for all new members. However, many Western (Latin) Rite Catholic dioceses baptize infants and celebrate First Eucharist several years later. Confirmation is celebrated still later, when the bishop or his delegate is present. Whether the Sacraments are celebrated together or separately, the Eucharist is the culmination of Initiation. It is the source and summit of the Christian life.

➔ **Reflect** How does the Eucharist nourish your spiritual life?

Catechist's Prayer

 Jesus, Light of the World, be with me in the dark times, and let me burn with love for you. Amen.

Lesson Plan

Objectives	Process	Materials

🕐 Invite, 10 minutes

Sacraments of Initiation Page 223	💗 **Psalm 149:1** Pray the opening prayer. 📖 **1 Peter 2:9–10** Reflect prayerfully on the Word. • Discuss What Do You Wonder questions.	📶 **Optional Activity** Chapter Poem: "Butterfly"

🕐 Discover, 35 minutes

New Life in God Pages 224–225 • Understand that people of all ages can be baptized into the Church	• **Catholic Faith Words** Sacred Chrism • Read a story on finding new life in Christ. ⭐ Underline three things that took place in a celebration of three Sacraments. • Summarize similarities and differences in celebrations. • **Share Your Faith Activity** Illustrate a First Communion.	☐ pencils or pens ☐ crayons, colored pencils, or markers ☐ one index card per child
Church Membership Pages 226–227 • Identify that the Sacraments of Initiation include Baptism, Confirmation, and Eucharist • Recall that Baptism removes Original Sin, forgives personal sin, and gives us new life in Christ; Confirmation seals and completes Baptism • Recognize that Jesus shares himself with us in the Eucharist	• **Catholic Faith Words** Sacraments of Initiation, Eucharist, Real Presence • Review the Sacraments of Initiation. 📖 **Acts 2:38–41** Proclaim "Many Are Baptized." ⭐ The children will underline important words from the Sacraments. • **Connect Your Faith Activity** Write one way the Church family welcomes new members.	☐ pencils or pens ☐ 3 index cards per child

🕐 Live, 15 minutes

Our Catholic Life Pages 228–229	• Discuss ways to welcome Church members. • **People of Faith** Learn about Saint John the Baptist. • **Live Your Faith Activity** Write names of those who have been welcoming.	☐ pencils or pens ☐ board or chart paper **Optional Activity** Sacraments of Initiation ☐ Activity Master 16 (Page 223E)
Pray with God's Word Page 230	• Choose volunteers for the three reader parts. ▶ Rehearse "The Seven Sacraments." • Follow the order of prayer.	☐ Bible 📶 Download "The Seven Sacraments."

Family + Faith Page 231

Point out that the Catholic Families page provides chapter highlights, information on how third graders understand faith concepts, and family prayer.

Chapter Review Page 232

📶 **aliveinchrist.osv.com**
• Customize and Download Assessments
• Email Links to eAssessments
• Interactive Student Reviews

ONLINE RESOURCES

 Go to **aliveinchrist.osv.com**

You will find:

- Interactive lesson planning with web specific content and additional activities
- Step by step lesson instruction from printed Catechist Edition for integrated lesson planning
- Custom-built assessments to download and eAssessment links
- Interactive reviews that provide scores and the option to review answers
- Sunday readings with background and questions of the week

 Go to **osvparish.com**

You will find:

- Ask the Experts Q and A
- General Catechist Helps
- Community Connections and Blogs

Sharing the Message with Third Graders

The Sacraments of Initiation Because third graders are just beginning to form social groups and understand what it means to belong to a community, this is an ideal time for them to understand the Sacraments of Initiation as the way in which one enters the Church community. While many third graders will not remember their Baptism, many of them celebrated another Sacrament of Initiation, Eucharist, for the first time just last year. Their continued celebration of Eucharist reinforces their participation at the family table.

Teaching Tip: Take a trip to the sacristy and discuss how the vessels used at Mass are similar to items we use for special meals on our family tables.

How Third Graders Understand

- Third graders learn best when the see, touch, and experience things for themselves. Provide activities that allow them to use their senses.
- Sometimes children this age need reassurance. Listen attentively to their questions and answers.
- Most children like to feel special but still be a part of the group. Do not single them out in unnecessary ways.

"I learn *best* when I *see*, touch, and experience. Provide activities that allow me to use my *senses*."

Chapter Poem

Invite

"Butterfly"

Use this poem to expand the chapter introduction.

- Provide props, or take the children outside, and show them flowers, eggs, butterflies, and other natural symbols of renewal.
- Encourage the children to share their stories about renewal or transformation. butterfly from cocoon, baby chick from egg, new baby in family, sibling moving away to college

 Go to **aliveinchrist.osv.com** Lesson Planning section for this poem.

NCEA IFG: ACRE Edition

Discover

Knowledge of the Faith

- Objectives: To know and understand basic Catholic teaching about the Incarnate Word Jesus Christ as the way, truth, and life; to know and understand God's activity in human history

Liturgical Life

- Objective: To know the Paschal Mystery of Jesus: in the Church's liturgical life—feasts, seasons, symbols, and practices and in the Sacraments as signs and instruments of grace

Catholic Social Teaching

Live

 Use one of these features to introduce a principle and engage the children with an activity.

- Life and Dignity, Pages 290–291
- Call to Community, Pages 292–293

Music Options

 Use one or more of the following songs to enhance catechetical learning or for prayer.

- "The Seven Sacraments," Live Prayer, Page 230
- "If You Believe and I Believe," Discover, Page 225

LECTIONARY CONNECTION

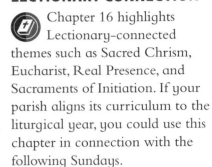 Chapter 16 highlights Lectionary-connected themes such as Sacred Chrism, Eucharist, Real Presence, and Sacraments of Initiation. If your parish aligns its curriculum to the liturgical year, you could use this chapter in connection with the following Sundays.

Year A

Second Sunday in Ordinary Time—John's Testimony to Jesus

Sixteenth Sunday in Ordinary Time—Intercession of the Spirit

Year B

Baptism of the Lord—Baptism of Jesus

Second Sunday of Easter—Sacraments of Initiation

Year C

Fourth Sunday of Lent Sacraments of Initiation

Nineteenth Sunday in Ordinary Time—Sacraments of Initiation

Go to **aliveinchrist.osv.com** for a complete correlation ordered by the Sundays of the year and suggestions for how to integrate the Scripture readings into chapter lessons.

Name _____ Date _____

Sacraments of Initiation

1. Find everything relating to Baptism and color those circles in your favorite color.

2. Find everything relating to Confirmation and color those circles in a second color.

3. Find everything relating to Eucharist and color those circles in a third color.

4. Watch for one word, action, or effect that is used in more than one Sacrament.

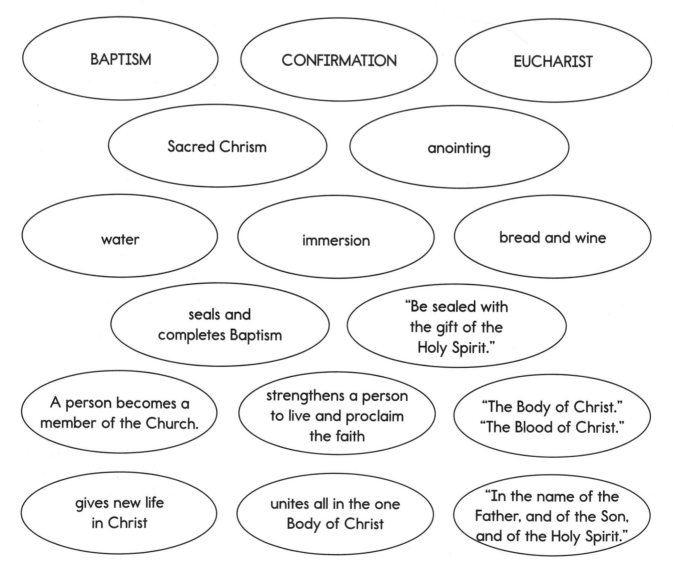

Sacraments of Initiation

Let Us Pray

Leader: Loving God, help us answer your call.

"Sing to the LORD a new song,
his praise in the assembly of the
faithful." **Psalm 149:1**

All: In Baptism, we receive your call to grow in
holiness. We ask you, Jesus, to give us the eyes to
see the many ways we can grow deeper in love
with you. Amen.

God's Word

Peter wrote a letter to the
Christians in the early Church.
He told them, "You are a people
chosen by God, a people who
serve and worship God. You give
praise to Jesus for he called
you out of darkness into his
wonderful light. Once you
were not a family, but now
you are God's family. You
had not received mercy,
but now you have received
mercy." **Based on 1 Peter 2:9–10**

❓ What Do You Wonder?

- How are you chosen by God?
- Why did your parents want you to be baptized?

Sacraments of Initiation **223**

Optional Activity

Chapter Poem: "Butterfly" *Verbal/Linguistic*

Use this poem after the opening prayer, before you tell the children
that Baptism is the first Sacrament we receive.

- Read aloud the poem.
- Ask the children what happens in this poem. A caterpillar becomes
  a butterfly.
- Discuss some changes that a human undergoes during a life cycle.
  Then transition back to the lesson instruction.

 Go to **aliveinchrist.osv.com** for Chapter Poem.

 Invite

♥ Let Us Pray

Invite the children to gather in the
prayer space and make the Sign of
the Cross. Read aloud the leader's
prayer and the Psalm verse. Prompt
the children's response. Have the
children return to their seats.

Explain that Baptism is the first
Sacrament we receive.

Say: Remember that In Baptism,
God shares his life with us through
Jesus. We become part of the Body
of Christ here on Earth. Listen to
what Saint Peter said.

🔲 God's Word

Guide the children through the
process of Scripture reflection.

- Invite them to close their eyes, be
  still, and open their minds and
  hearts to what God is saying to
  them in this passage.
- Proclaim the Scripture.
- Maintain several moments of
  silence.
- *Ask:* What did you hear God say
  to you today?
- Invite volunteers to share.

What Do You Wonder?

Say: Through the Sacraments of
Initiation, we are welcomed into
God's family and we celebrate
membership in the Catholic Church.

Invite the children to respond to the
questions. Ask what else they might
wonder about being chosen by God.

© Our Sunday Visitor

Objectives

- Understand that people of all ages can be baptized into the Church

New Life in God

Ask a volunteer to read aloud the question at the top of the student page.

- Tell the children that we will learn more about this as we cover the next two pages.

Read aloud the first paragraph.

New Life Begins

Invite two volunteers to each read aloud one of the paragraphs.

⭐ Instruct the children to underline the three things that took place when Aunt Kim received three Sacraments in one celebration.

- Review the answers with the group.

Work with Words

Pass out one index card per child.

- Have the children write the term *Sacred Chrism* on one side of the card and the definition on the other side.

- Encourage the children to use this card, with the others they have created, to prepare for chapter and unit reviews.

Invite the children to share their impressions of the photograph on the bottom of the page.

Discover

New Life In God

How does someone become a member of the Catholic Church?

Most people receive new life in God and become members of the Catholic Church when they are baptized as babies. This story is about an adult who found new life in Christ.

New Life Begins

Steve's family was watching a video of the Easter Vigil celebration. Aunt Kim and the other adults had celebrated three Sacraments in one evening. First, they were baptized. Then, they were confirmed with the anointing of **Sacred Chrism**. Finally, they received Holy Communion.

After Mass, everyone was laughing and hugging Aunt Kim and the others. Steve enjoyed all the excitement. He looked very happy on the video!

Catholic Faith Words

Sacred Chrism perfumed oil used for anointing in the Sacraments of Baptism, Confirmation, and Holy Orders

⭐ Underline the three things that took place when Aunt Kim received three Sacraments in one celebration.

224

© Our Sunday Visitor

Optional Activity

Field Trip *Bodily/Kinesthetic*

Take the group to see your parish's baptismal font.

- If necessary, get permission in advance to bring the children to the church.

- If possible, arrange for the parish priest or deacon to meet the group in church and talk briefly about the celebration of Baptism.

Life in the Church

After they saw the video, the family looked at photos. "Look, Steve," his sister Laura said. "Here are pictures of your Baptism. And here you are on your First Communion day."

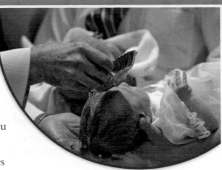

In Baptism, holy water is poured over the person's head or the person is immersed in water three times, in the name of the Holy Trinity.

The family noticed some differences between the celebrations. Baby Steve wore a white baptismal gown, but Aunt Kim wore a brown robe before her Baptism and changed into a white one after. Steve received First Communion in second grade. Kim was an adult, and she received the Eucharist on the same day she was baptized.

Still, some things were the same. Steve's godfather was Aunt Kim's sponsor, too. Father John had baptized both Steve and Aunt Kim.

Aunt Kim celebrated three Sacraments at the Easter Vigil. Sacraments are signs that come from Jesus. Through the power of the Holy Spirit, Jesus works in and through the Sacraments to give grace, a share in God's life and work.

➜ What do you remember most from your First Communion, or from that of a friend or family member?

Share Your Faith

Think Draw a picture to illustrate how your parish celebrates First Communions.

Share Share your drawing with a small group.

225

Life in the Church

Point out the photograph at the top of page 225. Ask the children to explain how it is the same and how it is different from the photograph on page 224.

- Read aloud the caption.

Invite four volunteers to each read aloud one of the four paragraphs.

- Ask volunteers to summarize the story, and point out the similarities and the differences they found between Aunt Kim's and Steve's celebrations.

- Invite the children to answer the question following the text.

 Music Option: Have the children sing "If You Believe and I Believe" downloaded from **aliveinchrist.osv.com.**

Activity

Read aloud the directions for the Share Your Faith activity.

- Provide the children with crayons, colored pencils, or markers.

- Allow time for them to draw their pictures.

Quick Review

People of all ages can be baptized and become members of the Catholic Church.

 ## Catechist Background

Baptism

Tell the children that immersing a person in flowing water was a common way of baptizing in the early Church.

- Baptism by immersion has been brought back in many parishes today. A baptismal pool is used for this purpose.

- Some parishes use temporary pools for the Easter Vigil; others have permanent pools.

- Still others continue to use the baptismal font where they pour the holy water over a person's head.

Objectives

- Identify that the Sacraments of Initiation include Baptism, Confirmation, and Eucharist
- Recall that Baptism removes Original Sin, forgives personal sin, and gives us new life in Christ; Confirmation seals and completes Baptism
- Recognize that Jesus shares himself with us in the Eucharist

Church Membership

Ask: What are the Sacraments of Initiation?

- Based on the text covered in the previous pages, see if the children can name all three Sacraments.

Invite a volunteer to read aloud the first paragraph.

God's Word

Proclaim the Scripture story.

- *Ask:* Who did Peter say Jesus' promise of the Holy Spirit was for? everyone

Encourage the children to share their impressions of the illustration on the bottom of page 226.

Work with Words

Pass out three index cards per child.

- Have the children create vocabulary cards for each term listed in the Catholic Faith Words box.

Church Membership

What are the Sacraments of Initiation?

Sacraments of Initiation the three Sacraments that celebrate membership into the Catholic Church: Baptism, Confirmation, and Eucharist

Eucharist the Sacrament in which Jesus shares himself, and the bread and wine become his Body and Blood

Real Presence the teaching that Jesus is really and truly with us in the Eucharist. We receive Jesus in his fullness.

From the beginning of the Church, the **Sacraments of Initiation** have been an important and necessary part of our faith. Baptism is the first Sacrament we receive. It leads to the other Sacraments of Initiation: Confirmation and **Eucharist**. Listen to Peter speak about Baptism to a crowd of people who did not know about Jesus.

God's Word

Many Are Baptized

On Pentecost, Peter said to the crowd, "Repent and be baptized, every one of you, in the name of Jesus Christ for the forgiveness of your sins; and you will receive the gift of the Holy Spirit."

Peter told the people that Jesus' promise was meant for everyone. Many of them accepted his message. About 3,000 people were baptized that day. **Based on Acts 2:38–41**

226

© Our Sunday Visitor

Scripture Background

Acts of the Apostles

Peter's sermon was delivered immediately after the Holy Spirit's presence filled the Apostles on Pentecost.

- In telling the crowd to repent, Peter asked the people to change their ways and accept Jesus' message.
- Those who were baptized on that day accepted the Gospel and the gift of the Holy Spirit.

Receiving and Sharing God's Love

In each of the Sacraments of Initiation, you see the actions and hear the words of the minister, who acts in the name of the Holy Trinity. Jesus, the Son, by the power of the Holy Spirit, shares with you the love of the Father. In the Sacrament of the Eucharist we honor Christ's **Real Presence** and receive him in Holy Communion.

Underline important words we hear in each Sacrament.

Sacraments of Initiation

	Words and Actions	Effects
Baptism	The priest or deacon pours water on or immerses the person, saying, "I baptize you in the name of the Father, and of the Son, and of the Holy Spirit."	Removes Original Sin, forgives personal sin, and gives new life in Christ; marks the person as a member of Christ's Body, the Church; unites all Christians
Confirmation	The bishop or priest lays hands on the person's head and then anoints him or her with Sacred Chrism, saying, "Be sealed with the Gift of the Holy Spirit."	Seals and completes Baptism; strengthens the person's bond with the Church; unites the person more fully with Christ; strengthens him or her in living the faith
Eucharist	The priest prays the Eucharistic Prayer, consecrating bread and wine, saying, "This is my Body, which will be given up for you....This is the chalice of my blood... shed for you and for many." Then he shares Christ's Body and Blood with the Church community.	Brings forgiveness of venial sins and an increase of grace; unites all who share the Eucharist into the one Body of Christ

© Our Sunday Visitor

Connect Your Faith

Show Welcome Write one way your Church family welcomes a new member.

_____

_____

✓ Quick Tip

Common Elements

While reviewing the Sacraments of Initiation, point out the elements that are common to all Sacraments.

- All have their foundation in Jesus' words or actions.
- All reflect Jesus' presence in a special way.
- All are special signs of God's grace.
- All are acts of worship.
- In all, the Holy Spirit unites members and helps them be like Jesus.

Receiving and Sharing God's Love

Read aloud the paragraph.

Sacraments of Initiation

Choose six volunteers to help you review the chart with the group.

- Begin by having one child read aloud the *Words and Actions* that go with Baptism. Have another child read aloud the accompanying *Effects*.
- Continue in this manner until all of the chart content has been read.
- ☆ Direct the children to underline important words we hear in each Sacrament.

Read aloud the directions for the Connect Your Faith activity.

- Allow the children to pair up, discuss their answers, and write down one way their Church family welcomes new members.

Quick Review

The Sacraments of Initiation include Baptism, Confirmation, and Eucharist. Baptism gives us new life in Christ; Confirmation seals and completes Baptism; and Jesus gives us the gift of his Body and Blood in the Eucharist.

Live

Our Catholic Life

Ask a volunteer to read aloud the question at the top of the student page.

- Invite the children to respond.
- Write their responses on the board or on chart paper.

Read aloud the first two paragraphs.

Have three volunteers each read aloud one of the bullet points on ways to welcome new members of the Church.

- Afterwards, point out that it is okay to let others know you have prayed for them. In fact, it will probably make them feel more welcome.
- *Ask:* What makes you feel welcome in your parish?
- Encourage the children to share their thoughts with the rest of the group.

Point out that another name for the members of the Church is "The Body of Christ." Read aloud the paragraph on this topic on page 305 in the Our Catholic Tradition section of the Student Book.

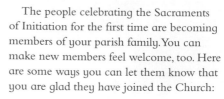

Our Catholic Life

How can you help welcome new members into the Catholic Church?

When a good friend or relative visits your family, or when a baby brother or sister joins your family, you welcome that person. You might have a party. You might make a sign that says "Welcome!" You might show a visitor where to sit at the dinner table.

The people celebrating the Sacraments of Initiation for the first time are becoming members of your parish family. You can make new members feel welcome, too. Here are some ways you can let them know that you are glad they have joined the Church:

- In some parishes, babies are baptized at a Sunday Mass. If you are present during one of these celebrations, pay close attention and pray for those being baptized.
- Every year at the Easter Vigil, people join the Catholic Church. They receive the Sacraments of Christian Initiation. Pray for those joining the Church. As a class project, create "Welcome to the Church" cards for them.
- First Communions and Confirmations take place as part of parish life, too. Ask a parish leader for a list of those preparing to receive these Sacraments. Select one name and pray for that person.

➜ **What makes you feel welcome in your parish?**

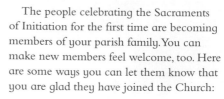

Optional Activity

Activity Master 16: Sacraments of Initiation

Distribute copies of the activity found on catechist page 223E.

- This activity is a good way for the children to review what they learned in this chapter.
- As an alternative, you may wish to send this activity home with the children.

People of Faith

June 24

Saint John the Baptist, first century

Saint John the Baptist was Jesus' cousin. An angel came to Saint John's father, Zechariah, to say that he and his wife Elizabeth would have a baby. Mary, the Mother of Jesus, visited Elizabeth when she was pregnant. John grew up to be a preacher. He prepared the way for Jesus by telling people the Good News that God would come to save his People. When Jesus was ready to start his ministry, Saint John baptized him in the River Jordan. He was killed by King Herod for telling Herod that he was doing bad things.

Discuss: Talk about a Baptism that you have seen. Who was baptized? What happened?

 Learn more about Saint John the Baptist at **aliveinchrist.osv.com**

Live Your Faith

Helped You Feel Welcome Write your name and the names of three people in your parish who have helped you feel welcome.

_____ _____ _____ _____

Sacraments of Initiation **229**

People of Faith

Tell the children about Saint John the Baptist.

- Saint John the Baptist was probably born about six months before his cousin, Jesus.
- He dressed in camel's hair and a leather belt.
- His food was honey and locusts.
- Saint John the Baptist got his name from being "the baptizer."
- Have a proficient reader read aloud the paragraph on Saint John the Baptist.
- Review the Discuss statement and questions with the children.

 Encourage the children to go to **aliveinchrist.osv.com** at home to learn more about Saint John the Baptist.

Activity

Read aloud the directions for the Live Your Faith activity.

- Give the children time to think about those who welcomed them.

⊕ Catholic Social Teaching

Chapter Connections

To integrate Catholic Social Teaching into your lesson, choose one of the following features: Life and Dignity, pages 290–291; or Call to Community pages, 292–293.

- Start the Live process by talking about Saint John the Baptist on page 229. Then move to the Catholic Social Teaching feature.
- Or, to expand the lesson, complete both pages 228 and 229, then move to the Catholic Social Teaching feature.
- Return to Chapter 16 for the prayer on page 230.

Let Us Pray

Pray with God's Word

Explain that this prayer is prayed along with a reading from the Word of God.

Prepare

Choose volunteers for the three reader parts.

You will be the leader.

Help Reader 1 find the Scripture and rehearse it.

> ▶ Rehearse with the children "The Seven Sacraments" downloaded from **aliveinchrist.osv.com**.

Gather

Invite the children to come to the prayer space with their books.

- Lead them into the prayer space while playing or singing "The Seven Sacraments."
- Then lead them to the prayer table that holds the Bible.

Pray

Follow the order of prayer on the student page.

Leader's concluding prayer: Father in Heaven, we thank you for the new life we have gained through your Son. We pray in Jesus' name.

> ▶ Conclude by processing around the room with the children singing the refrain for "The Seven Sacraments."

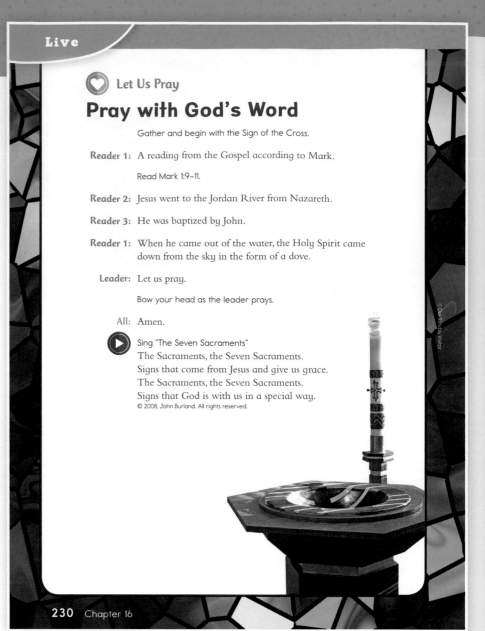

Live

Let Us Pray

Pray with God's Word

Gather and begin with the Sign of the Cross.

Reader 1: A reading from the Gospel according to Mark.

Read Mark 1:9–11.

Reader 2: Jesus went to the Jordan River from Nazareth.

Reader 3: He was baptized by John.

Reader 1: When he came out of the water, the Holy Spirit came down from the sky in the form of a dove.

Leader: Let us pray.

Bow your head as the leader prays.

All: Amen.

▶ Sing "The Seven Sacraments"
The Sacraments, the Seven Sacraments.
Signs that come from Jesus and give us grace.
The Sacraments, the Seven Sacraments.
Signs that God is with us in a special way.
© 2008, John Burland. All rights reserved.

230 Chapter 16

Liturgy Link

Include Symbols

Enhance the atmosphere in your prayer space by displaying symbols of the Sacraments.

- A baptismal candle, grapes and broken bread, perfumed oil, and a shell placed next to holy water are possible additions.
- You might even consider celebrating this prayer service while gathered around the parish baptismal font or pool.

> 🛜 Go to **aliveinchrist.osv.com** for Sunday readings, Scripture background, questions of the week, and seasonal resources.

FAMILY+FAITH
LIVING AND LEARNING TOGETHER

YOUR CHILD LEARNED >>>
This chapter discusses the words and actions of the Sacraments of Initiation which celebrate membership into the Catholic Church: Baptism, Confirmation, and Eucharist.

God's Word
Read **1 Peter 2:9–10** to read how we are all part of God's family.

Catholics Believe
- Baptism removes Original Sin, forgives personal sin, and gives new life in Christ. Confirmation seals and completes Baptism.
- In the Eucharist, Jesus shares himself with us, giving us the gift of his Body and Blood.

To learn more, go to the *Catechism of the Catholic Church* #1212, 1271, 1323 at **usccb.org**.

People of Faith
This week, your child met Saint John the Baptist who baptized Jesus. Share pictures from your own family Baptisms.

CHILDREN AT THIS AGE >>>
How They Understand the Sacraments of Initiation
Because third-graders are just beginning to form social groups and understand what it means to belong to a community, this is an ideal time for your child to understand the Sacraments of Initiation as the way in which one enters the Church community. While many third-graders will not remember their Baptism, many of them celebrated another Sacrament of Christian Initiation, Eucharist, for the first time just last year. Their continued celebration of Eucharist reinforces their participation at the family table.

CONSIDER THIS >>>
Do you think of your Baptism as an event, or the beginning of a relationship?

While many of us think of Baptism as a happy event that happened in our lives or the lives of our children, we often do not see it as a moment that began a life of relationship, much like a wedding. Baptism sets us on a lifetime journey of growing ever more deeply in knowledge and love of Jesus Christ. "In Baptism, the Holy Spirit moves us to answer Christ's call to holiness. In Baptism, we are asked to walk by the light of Christ and to trust in his wisdom. We are invited to submit our hearts to Christ with ever deeper love" (USCCA p. 196).

LET'S TALK >>>
- Talk about the ways that your family celebrates new beginnings.
- Ask your child to name some ways he or she can welcome new members of the Church.

LET'S PRAY >>>
John the Baptist, pray for us, that we may continue to live the faith we received at Baptism and share that faith with others. Amen.

For a multimedia glossary of Catholic Faith Words, Sunday readings, seasonal and Saint resources, and chapter activities go to **aliveinchrist.osv.com**.

Alive in Christ. Grade 3 Chapter 16 **231**

Family + Faith

Distribute the page to the children or parents/adult family members. Point out the chapter highlights, insights on how third graders understand concepts, the opportunity for the adults to reflect on their own experience and faith journey, and the family prayer.

Chapter 16 Review

A **Work with Words** Fill in the circle beside the correct answer.

1. _____ is the perfumed oil used in some Sacraments.
   ○ Eucharist   ○ Baptism   ● Sacred Chrism

2. Baptism, Holy Eucharist, and Confirmation are all Sacraments of _____.
   ● Initiation   ○ Childhood   ○ Holiness

3. Initiation is a word that means _____.
   ○ faith   ● beginning   ○ Church

4. Holy Eucharist brings _____.
   ○ resolution   ○ Sainthood   ● unity with Christ

5. Confirmation strengthens your bond with _____.
   ○ your parents   ● the Church   ○ yourself

B **Check Understanding** Match each description in Column A with the correct term in Column B.

Column A	Column B
6. Removes Original Sin	Sacraments
7. Signs that come from Jesus and give grace	Sacraments of Initiation
8. Catholics receive the Body and Blood of Christ	Baptism
9. Grants membership in the Catholic Church	Confirmation
10. Seals and completes Baptism	Eucharist

Go to **aliveinchrist.osv.com** for an interactive review.

232 Chapter 16

Chapter Review

Use Catechist Quick Reviews to highlight lesson concepts.

A **Work with Words**
Have the children fill in the circle beside the correct answer.

B **Check Understanding**
Explain to the children that they will be matching each description in Column A with the correct term in Column B.

Go to **aliveinchrist.osv.com** to prepare customized and downloadable assessments, send eAssessments, and assign interactive reviews.

Sacraments of Initiation **231–232**

KEY CONCEPT

In the Sacraments of Healing, God's forgiveness and healing are given to those suffering physical and spiritual sickness. In Penance, a priest absolves sin. In the Anointing of the Sick, the priest anoints and prays for God to send his healing love.

DOCTRINAL CONTENT

- In the Sacraments of Healing, God's forgiveness and healing are given to those suffering physical and spiritual sickness. (CCC, 1421)

- In Penance and Reconciliation, we confess our sins to a priest who forgives in the name of Christ and his Church. (CCC, 1424)

- In the Anointing of the Sick, the priest prays that God will send his healing love to the person who is being anointed. (CCC, 1517)

TASKS OF CATECHESIS

Helping children grow in a faith that is "known, celebrated, lived, and expressed in prayer" (NDC, 20).

This chapter focuses on the following tasks of catechesis:

- Promoting Knowledge of the Faith
- Liturgical Education

Catechist Background

People brought to him all those who were sick and begged him that they might touch only the tassel on his cloak, and as many as touched it were healed. **Matthew 14:35, 36**

→ **Reflect** Do you have the kind of faith that believes Jesus' power of healing is absolute?

Illness and sin are a very real part of life. Every person knows the feelings of helplessness, powerlessness, and desperation that are part of the human condition. During these times of physical and spiritual need, the Church reaches out to reveal the goodness and power of God's grace.

The Sacraments of Healing are Penance and Reconciliation and the Anointing of the Sick. In these Sacraments, the Church mediates God's forgiveness and healing. The Sacraments of Healing restore broken bonds and reunite the individual with the Church. Within the Body of Christ, Christians find strength, rest, and freedom. In the Sacrament of Reconciliation, a person receives the forgiveness of sin. In the Anointing of the Sick, a person is strengthened with the presence of the Holy Spirit. The Church does what Christ would do. The Church brings healing in the name of the Lord.

The anointing of a person's forehead and hands during the Anointing of the Sick and the extension of the priest's hands during the Sacrament of Penance are sacred actions. These human gestures signify the healing, forgiving power of God. The Holy Spirit frees the human spirit from the grip of pain, fear, guilt, and sin. God uses human hands to radiate the power of his loving touch.

→ **Reflect** How have you recently experienced reconciliation or healing?

Catechist's Prayer

Loving God, you touch me with your healing embrace; help me be a healing presence for others. Amen.

Lesson Plan

Objectives	Process	Materials

⏱ Invite, 10 minutes

Sacraments of Healing Page 233	♥ **Psalm 30:3** Pray the opening prayer. 📖 **Matthew 14:34–36** Reflect prayerfully on the Word. • Discuss What Do You Wonder questions.	🌐 **Optional Activity** Chapter Story: "Making Things Right"

⏱ Discover, 35 minutes

Jesus Heals Pages 234–235 • Reflect on the connection between faith and healing	• Discuss how faith can lead to healing. 📖 **Luke 8:40–42; 49–56** Proclaim "Jesus Gives New Life." • **Share Your Faith Activity** Make a plan and act out the story of the healing of Jarius's daughter.	☐ pencils or pens
Signs of Healing Pages 236–237 • Recognize that God's forgiveness and healing are given through the Sacraments of Healing • Understand that during Reconciliation, you confess your sins to a priest and are forgiven in the name of Christ, while in the Anointing of the Sick, the priest prays that God will send you his healing love	• **Catholic Faith Words** Sacraments of Healing • Review a chart on the Sacraments of Healing. ☆ Underline the effects of sin and sickness. • **Connect Your Faith Activity** Create words or phrases that tell how the Church helps us.	☐ pencils or pens ☐ board or chart paper • **Optional Activity** Links to Healing ☐ Activity Master 17 (Page 233E)

⏱ Live, 15 minutes

Our Catholic Life Pages 238–239	• Review ways to participate in the Sacraments of Healing. • **People of Faith** Learn about Saint Marianne. • **Live Your Faith Activity** Write a story about a child who receives healing.	☐ pencils or pens
Prayer for Healing Page 240	• Choose two readers. • Follow the order of prayer. ▶ Close with the song "Heal Us, Lord."	☐ bowl of holy water 🌐 Download "Heal Us, Lord."

Family + Faith Page 241

Point out that the Catholic Families page provides chapter highlights, information on how third graders understand faith concepts, and family prayer.

Chapter Review Page 242

🌐 **aliveinchrist.osv.com**
• Customize and Download Assessments
• Email Links to eAssessments
• Interactive Student Reviews

ONLINE RESOURCES

 Go to **aliveinchrist.osv.com**

You will find:

- Interactive lesson planning with web specific content and additional activities
- Step by step lesson instruction from printed Catechist Edition for integrated lesson planning
- Custom-built assessments to download and eAssessment links
- Interactive reviews that provide scores and the option to review answers
- Sunday readings with background and questions of the week

 Go to **osvparish.com**

You will find:

- Ask the Experts Q and A
- General Catechist Helps
- Community Connections and Blogs

Sharing the Message with Third Graders

The Sacraments of Healing The beginning awareness of community that is characteristic of third graders can help children this age to see the Sacraments of Healing as a way in which the Catholic community shows its care of those who are in need of physical and spiritual healing. It is also a good time to raise awareness of ways in which the children can personally show care to someone who is suffering through direct actions or prayer.

Teaching Tip: Include the names of ill parishioners in your session prayer times. You may find these names in your parish bulletin or through your parish office.

How Third Graders Understand

- Sometimes third graders act out in anger. Teach them not to strike out against others when they are frustrated.
- Adults can influence children this age greatly. You might calm them down with a gentle hand on their shoulder.
- Third grade children are growing in confidence. When you believe in them, they continue to grow.

"Adults can influence me greatly. A gentle hand on my shoulder is a good way to calm or reassure me."

Chapter Connections

Chapter Story

"Making Things Right"

Use this story to expand the chapter introduction.

- Remind the children that becoming a better person improves all of society.
- Have them discuss how Russell's problem started and what he could have done to avoid it.
- Plan a practice session on what the children can do and say when they are tempted to carry tales from one child to another.

 Go to **aliveinchrist.osv.com** Lesson Planning section for this story.

NCEA IFG: ACRE Edition

Knowledge of the Faith

- Objectives: To know and understand basic Catholic teaching about the Incarnate Word Jesus Christ as the way, truth, and life; to know and understand God's activity in human history

Liturgical Life

- Objective: To know the Paschal Mystery of Jesus: in the Church's liturgical life—feasts, seasons, symbols, and practices and in the Sacraments as signs and instruments of grace

Catholic Social Teaching

 Use one of these features to introduce a principle and engage the children with an activity.

- Rights and Responsibilities, Pages 294–295
- The Dignity of Work, Pages 298–299

Music Options

 Use one or more of the following songs to enhance catechetical learning or for prayer.

- "Heal Us, Lord," Live Prayer, Page 240
- "Coming Back Together," Discover, Page 237

LECTIONARY CONNECTION

Chapter 17 highlights Lectionary-connected themes such as the Sacraments of Healing. If your parish aligns its curriculum to the liturgical year, you could use this chapter in connection with the following Sundays.

Year A

Fifth Sunday of Lent—Restoration

Eleventh Sunday in Ordinary Time—Sinners Saved by Christ

Year B

Fifth Sunday in Ordinary Time—Sacraments of Healing

Sixth Sunday in Ordinary Time—Anointing of the Sick

Year C

Tenth Sunday in Ordinary Time—Jesus as Healer

Twenty-eighth Sunday in Ordinary Time—Jesus Heals

Go to **aliveinchrist.osv.com** for a complete correlation ordered by the Sundays of the year and suggestions for how to integrate the Scripture readings into chapter lessons.

Name _____ Date _____

Links to Healing

Unscramble the letters before each sentence to find the sentence's missing word.

VERSOFNIGES   You receive God's

⬚⬚⬚⬚⬚⬚⬚⬚⬚⬚ in the

Sacrament of Penance and Reconciliation.

DEARAPEST   Sin is choosing to be

⬚⬚⬚⬚⬚⬚⬚⬚ from God.

SNECOFS   Catholics hear God's forgiveness through the words of the

priest when they ⬚⬚⬚⬚⬚⬚ their sins.

ISPRET   A ⬚⬚⬚⬚⬚ presides at the two Sacraments

of Healing.

NUMHA   ⬚⬚⬚⬚⬚ life is sacred.

LOSABEV   The priest will ⬚⬚⬚⬚⬚⬚⬚ you from

your sins.

NONAIST   The priest ⬚⬚⬚⬚⬚⬚⬚ the sick person's

head and hands.

HRITG   The Sacraments of Healing help you make relationships

⬚⬚⬚⬚⬚ again.

Sacraments of Healing

 Let Us Pray

Leader: O God, give me strength.

"O LORD, my God,
I cried out to you for help and you
healed me." **Psalm 30:3**

All: Son of God, you comforted those you met as you
taught and traveled. So many people are sick
today. Bless them, Jesus, and help them to know
that you are there with them. Amen.

God's Word

After crossing the sea, Jesus and his disciples came
to a small town. When the men of that town recognized
him, they sent word to the surrounding villages. People
brought all those who were sick and begged Jesus to let
them touch the hem of his robe. All who touched it were
healed. **Based on Matthew 14:34–36**

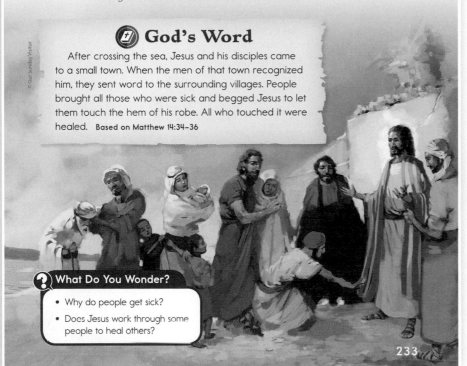

What Do You Wonder?

- Why do people get sick?
- Does Jesus work through some
  people to heal others?

233

Optional Activity

Chapter Story: "Making Things Right" *Verbal/Linguistic*

Use this story after the opening prayer, before talking about how
seeing sick people made Jesus sad.

- Explain that damaged relationships, like hurt or sick bodies, need
  to be healed. Invite the children to share stories of repaired
  friendships.

- Connect this to the Sacraments of Healing and transition back to
  the lesson instruction.

 Go to **aliveinchrist.osv.com** for Chapter Story.

 Invite

 Let Us Pray

Invite the children to gather in the
prayer space and make the Sign of
the Cross. Ask a volunteer to read
aloud the leader's prayer and the
Psalm verse. Prompt the group's
response.

Have the children move from the
prayer space back to their seats.

Say: Jesus was sad when he saw
people who were hungry, or hurt, or
sick. He wanted everyone to be well
and have what they need.

God's Word

Guide the children through the
process of Scripture reflection.

- Invite them to close their eyes, be
  still, and open their minds and
  hearts to what God is saying to
  them in this passage.

- Proclaim the Scripture.

- Maintain several moments of
  silence.

- *Ask:* What did you hear God say
  to you today?

- Invite volunteers to share.

What Do You Wonder?

Say: The people believed that Jesus
would make them better, that he
would heal them. Today Jesus gives
us the healing we need through the
Sacrament of the Anointing of the
Sick and the Sacrament of Penance
and Reconciliation.

Invite the children to respond to the
questions. Ask what else they might
wonder about the Sacraments of
Healing.

Objectives

- Reflect on the connection between faith and healing

Jesus Heals

Ask a volunteer to read aloud the question at the top of the student page.

- Tell the children that we will learn more about this as we review the next two pages.

Read aloud the first paragraph as an introduction to the Scripture story. Tell children that they will present the story as a play.

God's Word

Select individuals to play the speaking parts (Jairus, the Woman, Jairus's servant, Jesus, and Jarius's wife). The rest of the group can play the part of the crowd.

- Allow time for the children to review their parts.
- Have the children read through the section of the Scripture story on page 234.
- Point out the illustration at the bottom of the page, showing the servant bringing Jarius the sad news.

Ask: Do you think Jesus is too late?

Discover

Jesus Heals

How can faith lead to healing?

During his life, Jesus cared for people who were sick or in need of forgiveness. He healed people who had faith in him. Read this story about Jesus healing a man's daughter.

God's Word

Jesus Gives New Life

Jairus: Please let me through. I must talk to Jesus.

Woman: You look worried. Stand aside. Let this man through to see Jesus.

Jairus: Jesus, please. I beg you to come to my home. My only daughter is dying.

Jairus's servant: Jairus, I have sad news. Your daughter is dead.

234

Songs of Scripture

Healing Grace

While this song recounts the Gospel story of a woman with a hemorrhage, the chorus emphasizes that God listens with great love when we ask for healing for ourselves and others.

- Tell the children that healing comes in many ways.
- Teach the children the song "Healing Grace."

 Use *Songs of Scripture,* Grades 1–3 CD, Track 21

Jesus: Jairus, don't be afraid. Have faith, and your daughter will be all right. (Jesus walks to Jairus's house.)

Jairus's wife: Jesus, thank you for coming to our home. Our daughter has died and we are very sad.

Jesus: She isn't dead. She is sleeping. Now everyone except her parents and my three friends must leave.

Crowd: He doesn't know what he's talking about. She really is dead!

Jesus: [touching the girl] Child, wake up! [The girl wakes up; her parents hug her.]

Jesus: Please don't tell anyone about what I did here today.

Jairus's wife: Thank you so much, Jesus! You have given us back our daughter. **Based on Luke 8:40-42, 49-56**

Share Your Faith

Think Reflect on the story of the healing of Jairus's daughter. Make a list of the characters in the story and the props you would need to act it out.

1. Scene: _____

2. Characters: _____

3. Props: _____

Share Act out the story with a small group.

Sacraments of Healing **235**

Jesus Gives New Life

Have the children continue reading the play.

- Challenge them to read with feeling and to use appropriate gestures.
- *Ask:* Why did Jesus want to help Jairus? Possible response: Jairus had great faith.
- *Ask:* How is Jairus a role model for us? Possible response: When we are troubled, we can remember that Jairus had great faith and that Jesus helped him and his daughter.

Activity

Read aloud the directions for the Share Your Faith activity.

- Arrange the children in groups of four or more.
- Have them work together to make a list and a plan and then act out the story.

Quick Review

Jesus has power over illness and death. There is a strong connection between faith and healing.

Optional Activity

Healing *Interpersonal*

Point out that people usually experience healing for the first time in their families.

- Invite the children to recount stories of when they have been sick and who has cared for them.
- Sometimes Jesus uses the hands of others to help us get better.
- Emphasize that these healing experiences can be similar to the healing experiences in the Church family.

Objectives

- Recognize that God's forgiveness and healing are given through the Sacraments of Healing

- Understand that during Reconciliation, you confess your sins to a priest and are forgiven in the name of Christ, while in the Anointing of the Sick, the priest prays that God will send you his healing love

Signs of Healing

Ask: How do these Sacraments help us?

- Write the children's answers on the board or on chart paper.

Invite three children to each read aloud one of the paragraphs.

Work with Words

Read aloud the highlighted term and its definition.

- Pass out one index card per child.
- Have the children create vocabulary cards.
- Encourage them to use this card to prepare for chapter and unit reviews.

Sacraments of Healing

Review the contents of the chart.

- Ask two volunteers to assist by acting out the actions described while you read them aloud. You may need to review with them the correct way to perform the actions first.

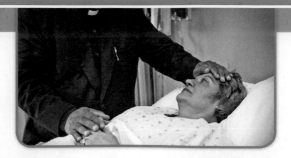

Signs of Healing

How do these Sacraments help us?

The **Sacraments of Healing** are Penance and Reconciliation, and the Anointing of the Sick. These Sacraments help people in times of sin or sickness.

During Penance, you confess your sins to a priest and are absolved, which means forgiven. In the Anointing of the Sick, the priest prays that God will send his healing love to the sick person. This Sacrament shows that every person is special and that life is sacred.

Only a priest can preside at the Sacraments of Healing. Like all Sacraments, these Sacraments use words and actions to show God's love.

> ### Catholic Faith Words
>
> **Sacraments of Healing** Penance and Reconciliation and the Anointing of the Sick. In these Sacraments, God's forgiveness and healing are given to those suffering physical and spiritual sickness.

© Our Sunday Visitor

Sacraments of Healing

	Reconciliation	Anointing of the Sick
Actions	The priest extends his hand in blessing.	The priest uses the oil of the sick to anoint the head and hands of the person who is very sick or aged.
Words	"I absolve you from your sins in the name of the Father, and of the Son, and of the Holy Spirit."	"Through this holy anointing may the Lord in his love and mercy help you with the grace of the Holy Spirit. May the Lord who frees you from sin save you and raise you up."

 Quick Tip

The Need for Reconciliation

The children may wonder why they must confess their sins when God's forgiveness is always available.

- Explain that the Sacrament of Reconciliation was given by Jesus to his followers to experience God's forgiveness and mercy through the priest.

- The Sacrament of Reconciliation allows us to be reconciled with God and with the Christian community.

Sin and Sickness

Sin and sickness are different in a very important way. Sickness may separate you from others, but you do not choose to be sick. When you sin, you make a choice to turn away from God and others; and you are responsible for that decision.

The effects of sin and sickness can be similar. Both can make you feel separated from God and from people you love. The Sacraments of Healing allow the community a chance to share your sorrows and joys. These Sacraments show God's mercy and our trust in his loving care. The Church prays for spiritual and physical healing from God.

Underline the effects of sin and sickness.

Connect Your Faith

Use Healing Words Sin and sickness often separate you in some way from those you love. Using the letters below, create words or phrases that tell how the Church helps you.

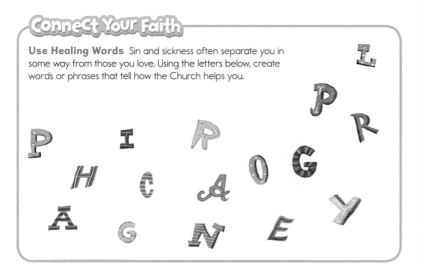

Sacraments of Healing **237**

Sin and Sickness

Invite two volunteers to read aloud the paragraphs.

⭐ Have the children underline the effects of sin and sickness.

- Allow the children time to reread or scan the text and underline the appropriate words.
- Stress that sin hurts the entire community because sin almost always injures someone else as well as the one who commits the sin.

Activity

Read aloud the directions for the Connect Your Faith activity.

- Have the children work in pairs to create words or phrases that tell how the Church helps them.

 Music Option: While the children work, play "Coming Back Together," downloaded from **aliveinchrist.osv.com**.

Quick Review

The Sacraments of Healing are Reconciliation, or Penance, and the Anointing of the Sick. These Sacraments help us when we are suffering from physical or spiritual sickness.

Optional Activity

Activity Master 17: Links to Healing

Distribute copies of the activity found on catechist page 233E.

- The puzzle activity will help review the concepts presented in this chapter.
- As an alternative, you may wish to send this activity home with the children.

Chapter 17 Activity Master

Name _____ Date _____

Links to Healing
Unscramble the letters before each sentence to find the sentence's missing word.

VERSOFNSGES You receive God's ☐☐☐☐☐☐☐☐☐☐ in the Sacrament of Penance and Reconciliation.

DEARAPEST Sin is choosing to be ☐☐☐☐☐☐☐☐☐ from God.

SHECOFS Catholics hear God's forgiveness through the words of the priest when they ☐☐☐☐☐☐☐ their sin.

23PRET A ☐☐☐☐☐☐☐ presides at the two Sacraments of Healing.

NUMHA ☐☐☐☐☐ life is sacred.

LOSABEV The priest will ☐☐☐☐☐☐☐☐ you from your sin.

NONA2ST The priest ☐☐☐☐☐☐☐ the sick person's head and hands.

HR2TG The Sacraments of Healing help you make relationships ☐☐☐☐☐ again.

233E Chapter 17

Sacraments of Healing **237**

Our Catholic Life

Direct the children's attention to the question at the top of the page. Tell them that we can all participate in the Sacraments of Healing.

- *Say:* Let's learn how.

Have volunteers read aloud the first paragraph and the bulleted list.

- *Ask:* When can you participate in the Sacrament of Penance and Reconciliation? whenever you want to and whenever a priest is available

Draw the children's attention to the photo at the bottom of the page.

- *Ask:* Which Sacrament of Healing is the priest performing here? the Anointing of the Sick

- Read aloud the caption.

Tell the children that they can pray a blessing prayer over a family member who is ill.

- Have them turn to page 315 in the Our Catholic Tradition section of the Student Book to read about blessings.

Our Catholic Life

How can you participate in the Sacraments of Healing?

Everyone has been hurt at one time or another. Healing from an injury can be fast or slow. The Sacraments of Healing are the Church's way to help those who need healing. Your parish celebrates the Sacraments of Healing often.

- Your parish might celebrate Reconciliation every week on Saturdays or before Mass.

- A priest may anoint someone who has been or may be sick for a long time.

- You can participate in Penance and Reconciliation whenever you need to. You may or may not need to receive the Sacrament of Anointing of the Sick in your lifetime. Both Sacraments give God's grace and strengthen you to live as a follower of Jesus.

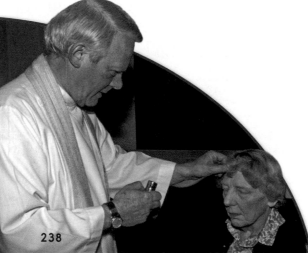

© Our Sunday Visitor

Priests anoint those who are aged or seriously ill with the Oil of the Sick.

238

Quick Tip

Reconcile

One of the greatest tests of humanity is to make peace with another after you have wronged or been wronged by that person.

- Remind the children to recognize their faults and practice humility by asking forgiveness.
- Point out that in forgiving others we become more like God.
- Encourage the children to leave the past behind and begin anew after reconciling with another.

People of Faith

Saint Marianne Cope, 1838–1918

January 23

Saint Marianne Cope was born in Germany, but came to the United States as a baby. After her father died, she helped raise her brothers and sisters. When she was 24, she became a Franciscan sister. She worked in hospitals in New York. One day she learned that King Kalakaua of Hawaii was asking for sisters to come to the islands to work with lepers. Saint Marianne and six other sisters traveled to Honolulu. She worked at the leper colony on the island of Molokai helping Saint Father Damien, who was dying of leprosy himself. Saint Marianne's feast day is January 23.

Discuss: What do you do when you are sick? How can Jesus make you feel better?

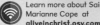 Learn more about Saint Marianne Cope at **aliveinchrist.osv.com**

Live Your Faith

Write a Story of Healing Write a short story about a child who receives one of the Sacraments of Healing.

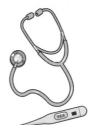

_____

_____

_____

_____

_____

_____

_____

_____

Sacraments of Healing **239**

Catholic Social Teaching

Chapter Connection

To integrate Catholic Social Teaching into your lesson, choose one of the following features: Rights and Responsibilities, pages 294–295; or The Dignity of Work, pages 298–299.

- Start the Live process by talking about Saint Marianne Cope on page 239. Then move to the Catholic Social Teaching feature.
- Or, to expand the lesson, complete both pages 238 and 239, then move to the Catholic Social Teaching feature.
- Return to Chapter 17 for the prayer on page 240.

People of Faith

Tell the children about Saint Marianne Cope.

- Sister Marianne Cope helped direct the opening of the first two Catholic hospitals in central New York.
- When she moved to Hawaii, she managed a hospital on the island of O'ahu, where victims of leprosy were cared for.
- She was responsible for orphans of women who had contracted the disease as well as clergy who had contracted the disease while working with lepers.
- She was canonized by Pope Benedict XVI in 2012.
- Read aloud the paragraph.
- Have the children discuss the questions with a partner.

> Encourage the children to go to **aliveinchrist.osv.com** at home to learn more about Saint Marianne Cope.

Activity

Read aloud the directions for the activity.

- Allow time for the children to write their stories.
- Walk around the room to offer assistance as needed.
- Invite volunteers to share their story with the group.

Let Us Pray

Prayer for Healing

Explain that this prayer is based on a prayer from the Rite of the Anointing of the Sick.

Prepare

Select two readers and allow them to rehearse their parts.

You will be the leader.

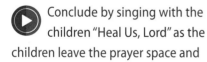 Rehearse with the children "Heal Us, Lord," downloaded from **aliveinchrist.osv.com**.

Gather

Invite the children to come to the prayer space with their books. Begin with Sign of the Cross, using the holy water.

- Lead the children into the prayer space while playing or singing "Heal Us, Lord."

Pray

Follow the order of prayer on the student page.

- An optional Scripture reading to include is James 5:14–16.

 Conclude by singing with the children "Heal Us, Lord" as the children leave the prayer space and return to their seats.

Live

 Let Us Pray

Prayer for Healing

Gather and begin with the Sign of the Cross.

Leader: God wants us to ask for what we need in prayer. We pray now for those people we know who need God's healing.

Reader 1: Loving God, you take every family under your care.

Reader 2: You know our physical and spiritual needs.

All: Strengthen us with your grace so that we may grow in faith and love.

Reader 1: Loving God, you provide comfort for those who are sick.

Reader 2: You give them courage and peace.

All: Strengthen them with your grace so that they may know your love and care.

Reader 1: We ask this through our Lord Jesus Christ, your Son,

Reader 2: Who lives and reigns with you and the Holy Spirit.

All: One God, forever and ever. Amen.

Based on a prayer from the
Rite of the Anointing of the Sick.

 Sing "Heal Us, Lord"
Heal us, Lord.
We feel the power of your love.
Let your Spirit come unto us.

 Liturgy Link

Pray for Others

After the leader's opening prayer, you may want to invite the children to speak aloud the names of people they know who are sick.

- Find out from a parish staff member or parish bulletin some of the people in the parish who need prayers, and add them to the list.

- Keep this list short and specific.

Go to **aliveinchrist.osv.com** for Sunday readings, Scripture background, questions of the week, and seasonal resources.

FAMILY + FAITH
LIVING AND LEARNING TOGETHER

YOUR CHILD LEARNED >>>

This chapter describes the words and actions of the Sacraments of Healing: Penance and Reconciliation and the Anointing of the Sick.

God's Word
 Read **Matthew 14:34–36** and discuss any healing you may need.

Catholics Believe
- In the Sacraments of Healing, God's forgiveness and healing are given to those suffering physical and spiritual sickness.
- In Penance, a priest absolves sin. In the Anointing of the Sick, the priest anoints and prays for God to send his healing love.

To learn more, go to the *Catechism of the Catholic Church* #1420, 1421, 1424 at **usccb.org.**

People of Faith
This week, your child met Saint Marianne Cope, who worked to help sick people in New York and, later, lepers in Hawaii.

CHILDREN AT THIS AGE >>>

How They Understand the Sacraments of Healing   As mentioned in earlier chapters, the beginning awareness of community is characteristic of third-graders. Because of this, children this age can see the Sacraments of Healing as a way in which the Catholic community shows its care for those who are in need of physical and spiritual healing. This is also a good time to raise awareness of ways in which your child can personally show care to someone who is suffering through direct actions and through prayer.

CONSIDER THIS >>>
Have you ever prayed for someone to be healed?

We suffer when we see others in pain. The sense of helplessness and sorrow moves us to turn to God for help. "When the Sacrament of Anointing of the Sick is given the hoped-for effect is that, if it be God's will, the person be physically healed of illness. But even if there is no physical healing, the primary effect of the Sacrament is a spiritual healing by which the sick person receives the Holy Spirit's gift of peace and courage to deal with the difficulties that accompany serious illness or the frailty of old age" *(USCCA, p. 254).*

LET'S TALK >>>
- Talk about a time when someone you know has been anointed while they were sick.
- Ask your child to name some ways that the Sacraments of Healing can help people.

LET'S PRAY >>>
Saint Marianne Cope, help us to be kind and loving to all who are sick. Amen.

For a multimedia glossary of Catholic Faith Words, Sunday readings, seasonal and Saint resources, and chapter activities go to **aliveinchrist.osv.com.**

Alive in Christ, Grade 3 Chapter 17   **241**

Distribute the page to the children or parents/adult family members. Point out the chapter highlights, insights on how third graders understand concepts, the opportunity for the adults to reflect on their own experience and faith journey, and the family prayer.

Chapter 17 Review

A **Work with Words** Complete each sentence with the correct word from the Word Bank.

Word Bank
- priest
- forgiven
- Sin
- physical
- spiritual

1. During Penance Reconciliation you confess your sins and are _____**forgiven**_____.

2. Illness, such as a cold or flu, is called _____**physical**_____ sickness.

3. Only a _____**priest**_____ can perform a Sacrament of Healing.

4. _____**Sin**_____ is choosing to turn away from God.

5. Living with sin and not participating in Reconciliation can be called _____**spiritual**_____ sickness.

B **Check Understanding** Write the letter T if the sentence is TRUE. Write the letter F if the sentence is FALSE.

6. Faith in Jesus' healing power was important in the story of Jairus's daughter. **T**

7. Penance is a Sacrament of Intiation. **F**

8. The Sacraments of Healing help people physically and spiritually. **T**

9. Oil is used for Penance and Reconciliation. **F**

10. The Sacraments show God's mercy and loving care. **T**

Go to **aliveinchrist.osv.com** for an interactive review.

242 Chapter 17

Use Catechist Quick Reviews to highlight lesson concepts.

A **Work with Words** Review the Word Bank with the children. Have them complete each sentence with the correct word from the Word Bank.

B **Check Understanding** Have the children determine if the sentences are true or false.

 Go to **aliveinchrist.osv.com** to prepare customized and downloadable assessments, send eAssessments, and assign interactive reviews.

Sacraments of Healing   **241–242**

KEY CONCEPT

Holy Orders is the Sacrament in which baptized men are ordained as deacons, priests, or bishops to lead and serve the Church. Matrimony joins a baptized man and a baptized woman in Christian marriage to serve God by loving and serving each other and any children God gives them.

DOCTRINAL CONTENT

- Sacraments at the Service of Communion celebrate people's commitment to serve God and the community and help build up the People of God. (CCC, 1534)

- Holy Orders is the Sacrament in which baptized men are ordained as deacons, priests, or bishops to lead and serve the Church. (CCC, 1536)

- Matrimony joins a baptized man and a baptized woman in Christian marriage to serve God by loving and serving each other and any children God gives them. (CCC, 1601)

TASKS OF CATECHESIS

Helping children grow in a faith that is "known, celebrated, lived, and expressed in prayer" (NDC, 20).

This chapter focuses on the following tasks of catechesis:

- Liturgical Education
- Moral Formation

Catechist Background

For you were called for freedom, brothers. But do not use this freedom as an opportunity for the flesh; rather, serve one another through love. For the whole law is fulfilled in one statement, namely, "You shall love your neighbor as yourself." But if you go on biting and devouring one another, beware that you are not consumed by one another. **Galatians 5:13–14**

➜ **Reflect** Do you love all your neighbors as yourself?

What an honor and a privilege it is that God considers Christians to be so precious that they share in the priesthood of Christ. In Baptism, God calls all Christians to holiness and to mission. Whether single, married, or religious, lay or ordained, all share in this common priesthood. They experience this priesthood by participating in the life of the Church through prayer, witness, and service.

Those who are married live out their common priesthood in the domestic Church, creating a partnership of equals that will blossom into a loving home and family. Those who are ordained live out their common ministerial priesthood in service to the entire Church, proclaiming the Good News in Word and Sacrament. Those who choose the single life live out their common priesthood as Jesus did, completely open to the extended family of humanity. Like Peter's "living stones," each unique way of life builds up the Kingdom of God.

No Sacrament is an end in itself. Baptism, Confirmation, and Eucharist initiate new members into the community of priestly people. Matrimony and Holy Orders call those members to a particular lifestyle of service.

➜ **Reflect** How do you serve others in the life to which you have been called?

Catechist's Prayer

Jesus, may your example of compassion and service be my inspiration and guide me as I continue the mission you have entrusted to me. Amen.

Lesson Plan

Objectives	Process	Materials
Invite, 10 minutes		
Sacraments at the Service of Communion Page 243	♥ **Psalm 34:23** Pray the opening prayer. 📖 **Galatians 5:13–14** Reflect prayerfully on the Word. • Discuss What Do You Wonder questions.	🌐 **Optional Activity** Chapter Story: "A Special Day"
Discover, 35 minutes		
Learning about Service Pages 244–245 • Understand that vows are sacred promises made to or before God	• **Catholic Faith Words** vows, priest, deacon • Read a story about a special day of love. • **Share Your Faith Activity** Share different meanings and expressions of love.	☐ pencils or pens ☐ 3 index cards per child
Serving God's People Pages 246–247 • Explore serving God and community through the Sacraments at the Service of Communion • Describe Holy Orders as the Sacrament in which baptized men are ordained as deacons, priests, or bishops • Identify Matrimony as the Sacrament that joins a baptized man and a baptized woman in Christian marriage to serve God	• **Catholic Faith Words** Sacraments at the Service of Communion • Discuss how we can continue Jesus' work. 📖 **1 Corninthians 3:21–4:12** Proclaim the Scripture. ☆ Circle the two Sacraments at the Service of Communion. • Review a chart on Holy Orders and Matrimony. • **Connect Your Faith Activity** Write two questions to ask a priest or married person about how they serve others.	☐ pencils or pens
Live, 15 minutes		
Our Catholic Life Pages 248–249	• Talk about ways to serve in the Church Family. • **People of Faith** Learn about Saint Jean-Baptiste de la Salle. • **Live Your Faith Activity** Write a thank you letter to a leader.	☐ pencils or pens ☐ board or chart paper ☐ stationery • **Optional Activity** Service to Others ☐ Activity Master 18 (Page 243E)
Prayer of Thanks Page 250	• Select a leader and five readers. • Follow the order of prayer. ▶ Sing "All That God Wants You to Be."	☐ bowl of holy water 🌐 Download "All That God Wants You to Be."

Family + Faith Page 251

Point out that the Catholic Families page provides chapter highlights, information on how third graders understand faith concepts, and family prayer.

Chapter Review Page 252

🌐 aliveinchrist.osv.com

- Customize and Download Assessments
- Email Links to eAssessments
- Interactive Student Reviews

ONLINE RESOURCES

 Go to **aliveinchrist.osv.com**

You will find:

- Interactive lesson planning with web specific content and additional activities
- Step by step lesson instruction from printed Catechist Edition for integrated lesson planning
- Custom-built assessments to download and eAssessment links
- Interactive reviews that provide scores and the option to review answers
- Sunday readings with background and questions of the week

 Go to **osvparish.com**

You will find:

- Ask the Experts Q and A
- General Catechist Helps
- Community Connections and Blogs

Sharing the Message with Third Graders

The Sacraments at the Service of Communion The third grader's emerging awareness of others makes this an ideal time to consider how God might call him or her to serve others in the Church and in society. Particular considerations should be given to Matrimony, Holy Orders, or religious life. While they will ultimately have many years to discern this, an early awareness of a life of service can help keep them oriented in a direction that is compatible with God's plan for their lives.

Teaching Tip: Invite a priest and married couple to give a brief (5–10-minute) talk about how they serve others in their vocations.

How Third Graders Understand

- Family is important to third graders. Help them see how God loves their family.
- Children this age are beginning to see and learn about the world outside their home. Help them see how they can help the Church family.
- Often, young people like to do things for others. Help them understand that in serving others they serve God.

"As I begin to learn more about the world around me, help me see how I can help the Church."

Chapter Connections

Chapter Story

Invite

"A Special Day"

Use this story to expand the chapter introduction.

- Be sensitive to the children who do not live in traditional family situations.
- Explain that when families have problems that keep them from living God's plan fully, he still loves and cares for them. God loves all families.

 Go to **aliveinchrist.osv.com** Lesson Planning section for this story.

NCEA IFG: ACRE Edition

Discover

Liturgical Life

- Objective: To know the Paschal Mystery of Jesus: in the Church's liturgical life—feasts, seasons, symbols, and practices and in the Sacraments as signs and instruments of grace

Moral Formation

- Objective: To be knowledgeable about the teachings of Jesus and the Church as the basis of Christian morality and to understand Catholic Social Teaching

Catholic Social Teaching

Live

 Use one of these features to introduce a principle and engage the children with an activity.

- Call to Community, Pages 292–293
- Solidarity of the Human Family, Pages 300–301

Music Options

 Use one or more of the following songs to enhance catechetical learning or for prayer.

- "All That God Wants You to Be," Live Prayer, Page 250
- "Jesu, Jesu," Discover, Page 246
- "For the Fruits of this Creation," Live, Page 250

LECTIONARY CONNECTION

 Chapter 18 highlights Lectionary-connected themes such as vows, Matrimony, and Holy Orders. If your parish aligns its curriculum to the liturgical year, you could use this chapter in connection with the following Sundays.

Year A

Tenth Sunday in Ordinary Time—Inheritance through Faith

Thirteenth Sunday in Ordinary Time—Representatives of Christ

Year B

The Epiphany of the Lord—Share Good News

Second Sunday in Ordinary Time—Holy Orders

Year C

Third Sunday of Advent—Love of God

Eighth Sunday in Ordinary Time—Love for Others

Go to **aliveinchrist.osv.com** for a complete correlation ordered by the Sundays of the year and suggestions for how to integrate the Scripture readings into chapter lessons.

Name _____ Date _____

Service to Others

Write each word from the Word Bank under the correct Sacrament of Service. Some words may be used for both Sacraments.

Word Bank

witnesses   bishop

priest   marriage

anniversary   ordain

deacon   vows

Matrimony

_____

_____

_____

_____

Holy Orders

_____

_____

_____

_____

All Christians are called to use their gifts in service to God's People.

Draw a picture that shows you helping others.

Sacraments at the Service of Communion

 Let Us Pray

Leader: Dear God, we are your servants forever.

"The LORD is the redeemer of the souls of
    his servants;
    and none are condemned who take
      refuge in him." **Psalm 34:23**

All: You want us to serve each other, Jesus. Let my heart
be like yours so that I serve out of love and not
because "I have to." Amen.

 God's Word

For you were called to be free. Do not use
this freedom so you can sin. Instead, serve
each other in love. For all the commandments
can be put together in one statement,
"You shall love your neighbor as
yourself." **Based on Galatians 5:13–14**

? What Do You Wonder?

- How can third-graders serve
others in love?
- How will you know whether God
is calling you to be married or to
the priesthood or religious life?

243

© Our Sunday Visitor

Optional Activity

Chapter Story: "A Special Day" *Verbal/Linguistic*

Use this story after the opening prayer, before talking about the
importance of serving others.

- Ask volunteers to share memories of special family celebrations
and what they contributed or how they helped.
- After reading the story, connect family service with serving God,
and transition back to the lesson instruction.

 Go to **aliveinchrist.osv.com** for Chapter Story.

 Invite

 Let Us Pray

Invite the children to gather in the
prayer space and make the Sign of
the Cross. Read aloud the leader's
prayer and the Psalm verse. Prompt
the children's response.

Have the children move from the
prayer space back to their seats.

Say: We should always be looking
for ways that we can be of service to
others. Listen to what Saint Paul
told the people who lived in Galatia.

 God's Word

Guide the children through the
process of Scripture reflection.

- Invite them to close their eyes, be
still, and open their minds and
hearts to what God is saying to
them in this passage.
- Proclaim the Scripture.
- Maintain several moments
of silence.
- *Ask:* What did you hear God say
to you today?
- Invite volunteers to share.

What Do You Wonder?

Say: Serving God and each other is
such a necessary part of the life of a
baptized Catholic that Jesus gave us
two Sacraments to give us the help
we need. In the Sacraments of
Matrimony and Holy Orders, God
calls us to honor him by serving
others.

Invite the children to respond to the
questions. Ask what else they might
wonder about serving others.

Objective

- Understand that vows are sacred promises made to or before God

Learning about Service

Ask a volunteer to read aloud the question at the top of the student page.

- Tell the children that we will learn the answer in today's story.

Read aloud the opening paragraph.

The Wedding Story

Assign strong readers to the roles of Samantha, her mother, Dad, and Jeremy. Have the rest of the children follow along in their books as the readers begin.

- Point out that all families suffer through difficult times. But family members can help one another through the hard times, and we can always turn to God.
- *Ask:* What good memories of weddings and married life have family members shared with you?
- Allow volunteers to share a few stories.

Draw the children's attention to the illustration at the bottom of the page.

- *Ask:* Would you consider this to be a good family time? Why?

Learning about Service

How do married people and ordained men serve others?

Catholic Faith Words

vows solemn promises that are made to or before God

An anniversary is a time to remember a special day of love and commitment. Jeremy and Samantha learn about their parents' wedding day.

The Wedding Story

"Mom, you looked pretty," Samantha said.

"It's because I was so happy," said her mother.

"We said our **vows** and promised to love each other and to be faithful before God through good and bad times," Dad said.

"I know it's fun to share good times," said Samantha. "But bad times?"

"Well, Samantha," said Mom, "everyone has bad times, but mine would be worse if I didn't have your dad. We often ask God to help us through the bad times. And the good times are even better because I get to share them with someone I love."

© Our Sunday Visitor

ⓘ Catechist Background

The Sacrament of Matrimony

The marriage of a baptized man and a baptized woman is sacramental.

- The couple's vows are a covenant blessed by God. Jesus is present through the Holy Spirit, providing the couple with the grace to serve each other, their children, and the larger community.
- The couple's new life together is sacred.

Sharing Wedding Memories

"Look, there's a picture of Father Hernandez, witnessing our wedding vows," said Mom. "He also met with us before we were married. He shared with us how important it is to understand that marriage is a Sacrament. That means that God gives us the grace to love each other and help each other grow in his image. Our **priest** and **deacon** do a lot of work that we don't always see."

"What kind of work?" asked Jeremy.

"They teach people about the faith and guide them in making good decisions. They visit people who are sick and serve the parish in many other ways. Priests celebrate Mass and other Sacraments. Deacons baptize and witness marriages. Priests and deacons do important work," said Dad.

"Just like married people," said Samantha.

"Yes, just like married people. God helps all of us do his work," said Mom.

> ### Catholic Faith Words
>
> **priest** an ordained man who helps his bishop by leading a parish, preaching the Gospel, and celebrating the Eucharist and other Sacraments
>
> **deacon** an ordained man who serves the Church by assisting in the Eucharist, baptizing, witnessing marriages, and doing works of charity

Share Your Faith

Think What is love? Think about the different types of ways that people show love to one another.

Share Share with a partner about the different meanings of love and how you can show love for others.

Sacraments of Service **245**

Optional Activity

Interview *Interpersonal*

Suggest that the children talk with at least one married couple in their families—perhaps parents, grandparents, or an aunt and uncle.

- The children should ask why the couple married.
- Encourage the children to ask how marriage has helped the couple serve God, each other, and other people.
- Invite the children to bring the results of their interviews back at a later session to share with the group.

Sharing Wedding Memories

Have the children continue reading their parts.

- Have them pause after the first paragraph so you can emphasize the roles of deacons and priests in ministering to parishes.
- At the conclusion of the story, thank the readers for providing a service to the group.

Ask: How are the lives of married people, deacons, and priests similar. Possible response: All involve the promise of a lifetime commitment and the use of talents to serve God and others.

Work with Words

Point out the Catholic Faith Words from pages 244 and 245 and have the children make vocabulary cards for each term.

Activity

Read aloud the directions.

- Have the children work in pairs to define *love* and discuss its expressions.

Quick Review

Vows are sacred promises made to God. In Matrimony, a man and woman profess their vows to love and serve God and one another. When a man celebrates Holy Orders, he vows to live a life of service to the Church community.

Objectives

- Explore serving God and community through the Sacraments at the Service of Communion

- Describe Holy Orders as the Sacrament in which baptized men are ordained as deacons, priests, or bishops

- Identify Matrimony as the Sacrament that joins a baptized man and a baptized woman in Christian marriage to serve God

Serving God's People

Read aloud the question at the top of the student page.

- Tell the children to think about this question as the group reviews the next two pages.

Invite two volunteers to read aloud the two paragraphs.

⭐ Instruct the children to circle the names of the two Sacraments at the Service of Communion.

God's Word

Ask a volunteer to proclaim the Scripture.

- Read aloud the question at the bottom of the page.

- Encourage the children to share what they have learned about bishops, priests, and deacons in earlier chapters.

> ▶ Music Option: Have the children sing "Jesu, Jesu," downloaded from **aliveinchrist.osv.com**.

Discover

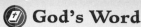

Serving God's People

How do the Sacraments at the Service of Communion continue Jesus' work?

The priest and the parents in the story had something in common. They had each celebrated one of the **Sacraments at the Service of Communion**. The two Sacraments are Holy Orders and Matrimony.

Holy Orders is the Sacrament in which baptized men become deacons, priests, or bishops. When a man receives Holy Orders, he is ordained. He shares Jesus' ministry in a special way. Saint Paul wrote about the work of the Church's early ministers.

> *© Our Sunday Visitor*

Catholic Faith Words

Sacraments at the Service of Communion the two sacraments that celebrate people's commitment to serve God and the community: Holy Orders and Matrimony

 Circle the two Sacraments at the Service of Communion.

God's Word

The place of the preachers is not to establish themselves as leaders among men; instead, think of us as servants of Christ and stewards of the mysteries of God. Stewards must be trustworthy. **Based on 1 Corinthians 3:21–4:2**

> ▶ What are some ways deacons, priests, and bishops serve the Church?

🔹 Scripture Background

1 Corinthians 3:21–4:2

This passage comes near the end of Saint Paul's description of how the Apostles serve the Church and, in so doing, serve God.

- The purpose of Saint Paul's Letter was to heal divisions in the Corinthian community.

- Saint Paul describes his life as one of building up the Church through service; he asks that the Corinthians (and therefore we) do the same.

Sacraments of Service

	Holy Orders	Matrimony
Action	A bishop lays his hands on the man to be ordained and prays to the Holy Spirit.	In front of a priest or deacon and other witnesses, a baptized woman and man promise to love each other and to be faithful.
Effects	The authority to minister as a priest, with the authority to lead the Church community, to teach, and to govern or as a deacon to serve the Church through sacramental ministries and works of charity.	The grace to love each other as Christ loves his Church and to remain faithful; the grace to welcome and raise children

Serving One Another

Married people share Jesus' ministry, too. The Sacrament of Matrimony joins a baptized man and a baptized woman in Christian marriage. They serve God by loving and serving each other and any children God gives them.

Sometimes husbands and wives must both work at jobs so that their families will have food and shelter. Other times, one of them may stay home with the children while the other goes to work.

Sometimes a couple has to live apart from each other. However, they must still do their best to serve their families. The Church cares for and supports all families.

Through Baptism and Confirmation, all Church members are called to use their gifts to serve God's People. Any way you answer that call, you serve God and your community.

Connect Your Faith

Learn About Sacraments at the Service of Communion In this space, write two questions that you would like to ask your pastor and a married person about how they serve others.

_____

_____

Sacraments of Service **247**

✓ Quick Tip

Pray for Leaders

Remind the children to listen carefully at Mass to hear the prayers for Church leaders during the petitions.

- As a group, write a petition for Church leaders. Ask your parish priest to include it in the petitions.
- Discuss with the children why Church leaders need our prayers.

Sacraments of Service

Lead the group in a review of the contents of the chart. You might want to have a volunteer read aloud the *Actions* of each Sacrament, followed by you reading aloud the *Effects*.

Serving One Another

Invite four volunteers to each read aloud one of the paragraphs.

- Answer any questions the children might have on the content.
- *Ask:* How do married people serve God? by loving and serving each other and their children
- *Ask:* How do priests and deacons serve the Church. They act as servants of God and stewards of the faith, leading and serving the Church.

For more information about the Church and her mission, invite the children to turn to page 305 in the Our Catholic Tradition section of the back of the Student Book.

Read aloud the directions for the Connect Your Faith activity.

- When the children finish, invite volunteers to share their questions with the group.

Quick Review

People can serve God and the community through the Sacraments at the Service of Communion, which include Holy Orders and Matrimony.

Our Catholic Life

Ask a volunteer to read aloud the question at the top of the student page.

- Invite the children to respond.
- Write the children's responses on the board or on chart paper.

Invite three volunteers to each read aloud one of the paragraphs.

- Point out that not every adult must be ordained or married. Many people lead lives of service as single adults or as men and women religious.
- *Ask:* When you serve others, should you be thinking of how this will help you or how it will help the one(s) you are serving? how it will help the ones you are serving

Point out the photos at the bottom of the page as examples of ways to serve God and others.

- After you read each caption, invite the children to give their impressions of the subjects in the photographs.

Live

Our Catholic Life

How can you serve the family of God?

Being part of a family brings many responsibilities. Being part of God's family, the Church, brings responsibilities, too. Many people serve through their vocation to marriage or through Holy Orders.

When you serve others, you do not think about how the service will help you. You serve others because God calls you to share your time and talents with others.

You can serve others through small acts of kindness. You can assist a neighbor by carrying groceries. You can help your parents care for your brothers or sisters or a pet. There are many ways to serve God and others.

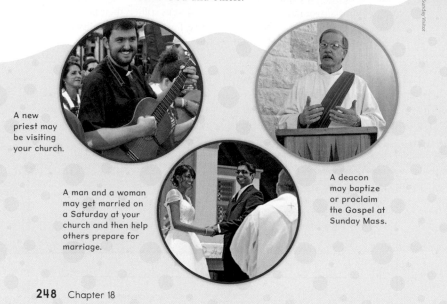

A new priest may be visiting your church.

A man and a woman may get married on a Saturday at your church and then help others prepare for marriage.

A deacon may baptize or proclaim the Gospel at Sunday Mass.

248 Chapter 18

Optional Activity

Activity Master 18: Service to Others

Distribute copies of the activity found on catechist page 243E.

- Tell the children that they will identify words that apply to Holy Orders and Matrimony.
- As an alternative, you may wish to send this activity home with the children.

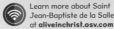

People of Faith

Saint Jean-Baptiste de la Salle, 1651–1719

April 7

Saint Jean-Baptiste de la Salle knew he wanted to be a priest when he was eleven years old. He came from a wealthy French family. He used his money to build schools for poor children. He founded a group of men called the Christian Brothers, who were teachers. He also founded a college to train teachers. He said that when he became a priest, he didn't know he would be a teacher, too. He knew he had a vocation to be a priest, but God also gave him a vocation to teach. Even today, Christian Brothers teach in schools all around the world.

Discuss: How have you served the poor?

 Learn more about Saint Jean-Baptiste de la Salle at **aliveinchrist.osv.com**

Live Your Faith

Write a Thank You Letter Bishops, priests, and deacons do many things for Church members. Draft a thank-you letter to one of these leaders. Then write your final letter on nice paper and send it to the person.

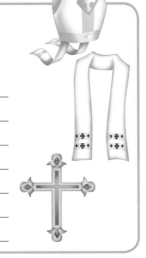

_____

_____

_____

_____

_____

_____

_____

249

People of Faith

Tell the children about Saint Jean-Baptiste de la Salle.

- Saint Jean-Baptiste de la Salle housed and fed the teachers he trained so they would not be discouraged.

- He was modest and didn't mind if others got the honors or credit for his work.

- He never allowed himself to be discouraged, even in the face of persecution.

- His last words were "In all things, I adore the will of God in my regard."

- Ask a proficient reader to read aloud the paragraph on Saint Jean-Baptiste de la Salle.

- Prompt the children to answer the Discuss question.

 Encourage the children to go to **aliveinchrist.osv.com** at home to learn more about Saint Jean-Baptiste de la Salle.

Activity

Read aloud the directions for the Live Your Faith activity.

- Provide the children with stationery and pens.

- Allow time for them to write a draft in their books and then a final version on nice paper to be mailed or delivered.

Catholic Social Teaching

Chapter Connections

To integrate Catholic Social Teaching into your lesson, choose one of the following features: Call to Community, pages 292–293; or Solidarity of the Human Family, pages 300–301.

- Start the Live step of the process by talking about Saint Jean-Baptiste de la Salle on page 249. Then move directly to the Catholic Social Teaching feature.

- Or, to expand the lesson, complete both pages 248 and 249, then move to the Catholic Social Teaching feature.

- Return to Chapter 18 for the prayer on page 250.

Let Us Pray

Prayer of Thanks

Prepare

Select a leader and five readers. Give them time to review their parts.

 Rehearse with the children "All That God Wants You to Be," downloaded from **aliveinchrist.osv.com**.

Gather

Invite the children to bring their books and assemble quietly in the prayer space.

Pray

Follow the order of prayer on the student page.

A good optional Scripture reading to add would be 1 John 4:7.

 Conclude by processing around the room with the children singing "All That God Wants You to Be."

Alternate Music Option: "For the Fruits of This Creation"

 Let Us Pray

Prayer of Thanks

Gather and begin with the Sign of the Cross.

Leader: Generous God, we thank you for the gifts of service of bishops, priests, deacons, and married people.

Reader 1: For priests who lead us to you,

All: We thank you, God.

Reader 2: For deacons who help us find you,

All: We thank you, God.

Reader 3: For bishops who guide your people,

All: We thank you, God.

Reader 4: For married people who lead each other to God,

All: We thank you, God.

Reader 5: For parents who show us how to love you,

All: We thank you, God.

 Sing "All That God Wants You to Be"
You can become all that
God wants you to be!

Here am I, O Lord! I come
to do your will.
Help me become all that
you want me to be!

 Liturgy Link

Sing Responses

You may want to have the children sing their responses to the prayers.

- Teach them, "We thank you, God," as a simple chant. Ask a child to suggest a melody.
- As an alternative, you may wish to teach the children the American Sign Language gestures for this response. Go to **aliveinchrist.osv.com** to find the gestures.

 Go to **aliveinchrist.osv.com** for Sunday readings, Scripture background, questions of the week, and seasonal resources.

FAMILY+FAITH
LIVING AND LEARNING TOGETHER

YOUR CHILD LEARNED >>>
This chapter explores serving God and community through the Sacraments at the Service of Communion: Holy Orders and Matrimony.

God's Word
 Read **Galatians 5:13–14** to read about how we should serve one another.

Catholics Believe
- Holy Orders is the Sacrament in which baptized men are ordained as deacons, priests, or bishops to lead and serve the Church.
- Matrimony joins a baptized man and a baptized woman in Christian marriage to serve God by loving and serving each other and any children they may have.

To learn more, go to the *Catechism of the Catholic Church* #1534, 1535 at **usccb.org**.

People of Faith
This week, your child met Saint Jean-Baptiste de la Salle, a priest, teacher, and the founder of the Christian Brothers, whose mission is to educate youth.

CHILDREN AT THIS AGE >>>
How They Understand the Sacraments at the Service of Communion Your child's emerging awareness of others makes this an ideal time to consider how God might call him or her to serve others in the Church and in society. Particular consideration should be given to Matrimony, Holy Orders, or religious life. While your child will ultimately have many years to discern a vocation, an early awareness of a life of service can help keep your child oriented in a direction that is compatible with God's plan for his or her life.

CONSIDER THIS >>>
In how many ways do you see yourself as a servant?

If you are a parent you may see your whole life through the eyes of service! The choice is in being begrudging angry servants, or eager servants, knowing that our service is an act of love. "God's people share in Christ's kingly mission, which is to lead others through loving service to them. Jesus came not 'to be served but to serve and to give his life as a ransom for many' (Mt 20:28). We are called in imitation of the Lord Jesus, to be people who offer ourselves willingly in service to others" (*USCCA, p. 118*).

LET'S TALK >>>
- Ask your child to name some ways that the people in your family serve God and others.
- Share some good memories of weddings and family life that you have seen or experienced.

LET'S PRAY >>>
Saint Jean-Baptiste, help us know what God is calling us to do. May we listen to that call and willingly follow it. Amen.

For a multimedia glossary of Catholic Faith Words, Sunday readings, seasonal and Saint resources, and chapter activities go to **aliveinchrist.osv.com**.

Chapter 18 Review

A **Work with Words** Complete each sentence with the letter of the correct word or words from the Word Bank.

Word Bank

a. vows
b. Holy Orders
c. service
d. ordained
e. deacon

1. A baptized man is **d** in the Sacrament of Holy Orders.

2. The **a** made during the Sacrament of Matrimony last a lifetime.

3. Only baptized men are called to receive **b** .

4. Holy Orders celebrates a man's commitment to Jesus' ministry as a **e** , priest, or bishop.

5. Husbands and wives can serve the family of God by doing acts of **c** for others.

B **Check Understanding** Match each description in Column A with the correct term in Column B.

Column A	Column B
6. What a man is called after the Sacrament of Matrimony.	Holy Orders
7. The Sacrament in which a bishop ordains a baptized man.	priest
8. The Sacrament that unites a man and woman in love and faithfulness.	husband
9. An ordained man.	Matrimony
10. Sacred promises.	vows

Go to **aliveinchrist.osv.com** for an interactive review.

Family + Faith

Distribute the page to the children or parents/adult family members. Point out the chapter highlights, insights on how third graders understand concepts, the opportunity for the adults to reflect on their own experience and faith journey, and the family prayer.

Chapter Review

Use Catechist Quick Reviews to highlight lesson concepts.

A **Work with Words**
Have the children complete each sentence with the letter of the correct term from the Word Bank.

B **Check Understanding**
Have the children match each description in Column A with the correct term in Column B.

Go to **aliveinchrist.osv.com** to prepare customized and downloadable assessments, send eAssessments, and assign interactive reviews.

UNIT 6

Unit Review

Use Catechist Quick Reviews in each chapter to highlight lesson concepts for this unit and prepare for the Unit Review.

Have the children complete the Review pages. Then discuss the answers as a group. Review any concepts with which the children are having difficulty.

A Work with Words

Direct the children to write the correct answer to complete each sentence for problems 1–5. For 6–10, have them complete the chart with the names of the Sacraments.

Unit Review

UNIT 6

A Work with Words Write the correct answer to complete each sentence.

1. ___Vows___ are sacred promises that are made to or before God.
2. Sacraments at the ___Service___ of Communion celebrate people's commitment to serve God and the community.
3. ___Sacraments___ are signs that come from Jesus and give grace.
4. Sacraments of ___Initiation___ celebrate membership into the Catholic Church.
5. Sacred ___Chrism___ is perfumed oil used in some Sacraments.

Complete the chart below with the names of the Sacraments.

Sacraments	
Initiation	Healing
6. Baptism	9. Penance and Reconciliation
7. Confirmation	
8. Eucharist	10. Anointing of the Sick

UNIT 6 Unit Review

B Check Understanding Match each description in Column A with the correct Sacrament in Column B.

Column A

Column B

11. received by people who are very sick

Penance and Reconciliation

12. removes Original Sin, forgives personal sin, and gives new life in Christ

Baptism

13. unites a person more fully with Christ

Eucharist

14. celebrates the gift of the Body and Blood of Christ in Holy Communion

Confirmation

15. absolves you of your sins

Anointing of the Sick

Write the letter T if the sentence is TRUE. Write the letter F if the sentence is FALSE.

16. **T** In the Sacrament of the Eucharist we honor Christ's Real Presence in Holy Communion.

17. **T** Confirmation strengthens our bond with the Church.

18. **F** Jesus did not want to help those who were sick or in need.

19. **F** Only a deacon can preside at the Sacraments of Healing.

20. **T** When a man receives Holy Orders, he is ordained.

254 Unit 6 Review

C Make Connections Write responses to each question or statement on the lines below.

21. Name a person who has received the Sacrament of Holy Orders, and tell one way in which he serves others.

Responses will vary.

22. What did you learn from the story of Jairus and his daughter?

Possible response: Faith in Jesus brings hope and sometimes healing.

23. Why is celebrating the Eucharist important?

Possible response: It helps me grow in God's love.

24. How do married couples serve God and others?

Possible response: By being faithful, by starting loving families

25. How can an unmarried person serve God?

Possible response: By serving as a reader or catechist

B Check Understanding
Direct the children to match each description in Column A with the correct Sacrament in Column B for 11–15. Then have them review the statements in 16–20 and write the letter *T* if the sentence is true or the letter *F* if the sentence is false.

C Make Connections
Tell the children to write their responses to the questions or statements on the lines provided.

Go to **aliveinchrist.osv.com** to prepare customized and downloadable assessments, send eAssessments, and assign interactive reviews.

Kingdom of God

Our Catholic Tradition

- The Church is a sign of God's covenant. (CCC, 762)

- We share in the Church's mission to spread the Good News. (CCC, 852)

- We are all signs of God's Kingdom. (CCC, 567)

- If we die in God's friendship, we will live with him forever. (CCC, 1023)

- At the end of the world, Christ will judge all people by how they lived their lives. (CCC, 681)

How does the covenant that God made with Abraham continue in Jesus and throughout the Church?

© Our Sunday

Unit 7 Overview

Chapter 19
The Church Through Time

The children will:

- define a covenant as a sacred promise between God and humans
- examine the covenant between Abraham and God, which led to the beginning of God's People
- recall that through Jesus the Church continues to be a sign of God's covenant, which extends to all people
- recognize the faithfulness and commitment of early Christians to the covenant and to God

 Catholic Social Teaching: Live Your Faith

- Rights and Responsibilities, Pages 294–295
- Solidarity of the Human Family, Pages 300–301

Chapter 20
The Work of the Church

The children will:

- examine how the Church continues Jesus' work on Earth through her worship, teaching, care for others, and work for peace and justice
- recognize that the Church is a sign of God's Kingdom and helps people share in the love of the Holy Trinity
- recall that by our Baptism, all members of the Church share in her mission to share the Good News and serve God and others

 Catholic Social Teaching: Live Your Faith

- Rights and Responsibilities, Pages 294–295
- The Dignity of Work, Pages 298–299

Chapter 21
Everlasting Life

The children will:

- reflect on Jesus' Resurrection as proof of his promise of eternal life
- recognize that the last book of the Bible, Revelation, ends with John's vision of God's everlasting Kingdom
- understand that Particular Judgment is the individual judgment by God at the time of a person's death
- identify the Last Judgment as God's final triumph over evil, when Christ will come again and bring the Kingdom of God to its fullness

 Songs of Scripture
"God Is So Big"

Catholic Social Teaching: Live Your Faith

- Life and Dignity, Pages 290–291
- Rights and Responsibilities, Pages 294–295

Preview Unit Theme

Ask the children to name the theme for this unit— Kingdom of God.

Ask: How does the covenant that God made with Abraham continue in Jesus and throughout the Church?

Invite the children to respond, but point out that they will get a better understanding of this as the group reviews the next three chapters.

Read aloud the bullet points under the Our Catholic Tradition head.

Point out the photos on the page and ask the children how they might connect with the theme.

Tell the group they will find out more about the Kingdom of God in the next three chapters.

KEY CONCEPT

God kept his promise to be forever faithful when he sent his Son, Jesus. Throughout her history the Church strives to be faithful to God's covenant and proclaim the Good News.

DOCTRINAL CONTENT

- A covenant is a sacred promise or agreement between God and humans. (CCC, 56–58)
- God established a covenant with Abraham, and from that came the beginning of God's People. (CCC, 72)
- As the Son of God, Jesus fulfills God's promise and his covenant extends to all people. (CCC, 73, 706)
- The first Christians faced difficult times, but they tried to be faithful to him and to the covenant, and the Church grew. (CCC, 2471–2472)

TASKS OF CATECHESIS

Helping children grow in a faith that is "known, celebrated, lived, and expressed in prayer" (NDC, 20).

This chapter focuses on the following tasks of catechesis:

- Promoting Knowledge of the Faith
- Liturgical Education

Catechist Background

 They devoted themselves to the teaching of the apostles and to the communal life, to the breaking of the bread and to the prayers. **Acts 2:42**

➔ **Reflect** How often do you pray? Is it enough?

The Church is the People of God. From the time of our first parents, humans gathered in community and made efforts to relate to God. After many generations, God called Abraham and Sarah to form a people who would be particularly his own. He made an explicit, everlasting covenant, or promise, between himself and the Israelites, the chosen descendants of Abraham.

Even though the Israelites were unfaithful to the covenant at times, God was always faithful to them. Through the prophets, he prepared the people for salvation. Then God sent his Son to establish a new and eternal covenant through his own Death and Resurrection. Throughout her history, the Church has been protected and guided by our faithful God. He remains faithful to the eternal covenant and continues to be present in the Church through the power of the Holy Spirit.

In the earliest days of the Church, Christians were anointed for mission. Even to the present day, they are anointed with Sacred Chrism after they are baptized. Baptism initiates them into the Christian life. Strengthened by the Holy Spirit, they are enabled to carry on the ministry of Jesus. Today's Christians stand in a long line with the anointed ones who have gone before them, doing the work of the Church. Together they are the Saints, the holy people who are signs of the Kingdom of God.

➔ **Reflect** What meaning does being anointed have for you?

Catechist's Prayer

 Faithful Father, be with me as I strive to keep your promise alive within my heart and in my actions. In Jesus' name I pray. Amen.

Lesson Plan

Objectives	Process	Materials

Invite, 10 minutes

The Church Through Time Page 257

- ♥ **Psalm 25:10** Pray the opening prayer.
- 📖 **Acts 2:42** Reflect prayerfully on the Word.
- Discuss What Do You Wonder questions.

Optional Activity Chapter Story: "Those Who Came Before"

Discover, 35 minutes

God's Covenant Pages 258–259

- Define a covenant as a sacred promise between God and humans
- Examine the covenant between Abraham and God, which led to the beginning of God's People

- **Catholic Faith Words** covenant, proclaim
- Learn how God first called his People.
- 📖 **Genesis 17:1–19** Proclaim "I Will Be Your God."
- ☆ Underline God's promises to Abraham.
- **Share Your Faith Activity** Write a promise that can be made to God.

- ☐ pencils or pens
- ☐ two index cards per child

The Early Church Pages 260–261

- Recall that through Jesus the Church continues to be a sign of God's covenant, which extends to all people
- Recognize the faithfulness and commitment of early Christians to the covenant and to God

- **Catholic Faith Words** faithful
- Learn about the early Christians.
- Discuss the growth of the Church.
- **Connect Your Faith Activity** Describe ways to identify someone as Catholic.

- ☐ pencils or pens
- ☐ board or chart paper
- ☐ one index card per child
- **Optional Activity** My Story of Faith
- ☐ Activity Master 19 (Page 257E)

Live, 15 minutes

Our Catholic Life Pages 262–263

- Talk about the Church's past.
- ☆ Choose a topic on Church history to research.
- **People of Faith** Learn about Saint Clement of Rome.
- **Live Your Faith Activity** Record information on a topic of research from Church history.

- ☐ pencils or pens
- ☐ research materials

Prayer of Faith Page 264

- Choose volunteers for the three reader parts.
- Follow the order of prayer.
- ▶ Close by singing "Get on the Boat."

Download "Get on the Boat."

Family + Faith Page 265

Point out that the Catholic Families page provides chapter highlights, information on how third graders understand faith concepts, and family prayer.

Chapter Review Page 266

aliveinchrist.osv.com

- Customize and Download Assessments
- Email Links to eAssessments
- Interactive Student Reviews

ONLINE RESOURCES

 Go to **aliveinchrist.osv.com**

You will find:

- Interactive lesson planning with web specific content and additional activities
- Step by step lesson instruction from printed Catechist Edition for integrated lesson planning
- Custom-built assessments to download and eAssessment links
- Interactive reviews that provide scores and the option to review answers
- Sunday readings with background and questions of the week

 Go to **osvparish.com**

You will find:

- Ask the Experts Q and A
- General Catechist Helps
- Community Connections and Blogs

Sharing the Message with Third Graders

The Historical Church Learning about their faith ancestors and the great things they have done can be exciting for third graders, who enjoy feeling a part of something larger than themselves. It's especially helpful if children this age can place themselves within the context of the story, for example in the way that they are emulating a particular Saint in their own talents, actions, or goals for the future.

Teaching Tip: When you see obvious connections between particular children and a Saint (e.g., birthdays near the Saint's feast day, interests that are similar), be sure to point them out to the child. In doing so, you can help foster devotion to a particular Saint that is relevant to the child.

How Third Graders Understand

- Third graders are starting to form friendships. Help them realize that people who are different from them can be their friends.
- Children this age like group activities. Encourage them to work with someone who is working alone.
- Young people sometimes like to choose with whom they interact. Allow times when they can choose their own partners or groups.

"I am starting to form friendships. Help me realize that people who are different from me can be my friends."

Chapter Connections

Chapter Story

Invite

"Those Who Came Before"

Use this story to expand the chapter introduction.

- Ask the children to explain how archaeologists learn about the past. Possible response: They dig up things that ancient people once used.
- Tell the children that they are going to make discoveries in this chapter about the lives of Christians who came before them.

 Go to **aliveinchrist.osv.com** Lesson Planning section for this story.

NCEA IFG: ACRE Edition

Discover

Knowledge of the Faith

- Objective: To know and understand basic Catholic teaching about the Incarnate Word Jesus Christ as the way, truth, and life

Liturgical Life

- Objective: To know the Paschal Mystery of Jesus: in the Church's liturgical life—feasts, seasons, symbols, and practices and in the Sacraments as signs and instruments of grace

Catholic Social Teaching

Live

 Use one of these features to introduce the principle and engage the children with an activity.

- Rights and Responsibilities, Pages 294–295
- Solidarity of the Human Family, Pages 300–301

Music Options

 Use one or more of the following songs to enhance catechetical learning or for prayer.

- "Get on the Boat," Live Prayer, Page 264
- "Share the Light," Discover, Page 261
- "Building God's Kingdom," Live, Page 262

LECTIONARY CONNECTION

 Chapter 19 highlights Lectionary-connected themes such as covenant, Christians, and faithfulness. If your parish aligns its curriculum to the liturgical year, you could use this chapter in connection with the following Sundays.

Year A

Fourth Sunday of Easter—The Good Shepherd

Twenty-ninth Sunday in Ordinary Time—Model for Believers

Year B

Fourth Sunday of Easter—Church/People of God

Sixteenth Sunday in Ordinary Time—Followers of Jesus

Year C

Third Sunday in Ordinary Time—Love for Others

Pentecost Sunday—Church

 Go to **aliveinchrist.osv.com** for a complete correlation ordered by the Sundays of the year and suggestions for how to integrate the Scripture readings into chapter lessons.

Name _____ Date _____

My Story of Faith

You and others who follow Jesus are an important part of the story of faith. Follow the directions below to tell about your own story of faith.

Directions

- Cut on the solid lines.

- Fold on the dashed lines.

- On page 1, paste your picture or make a drawing or a symbol for yourself.

- On pages 2, 3, and 4, write your story. You can write about your whole life or a time when you came to know God better and grew in your faith.

Page 1	Page 4
My Story of Faith by	End your story of faith.
Begin your story of faith.	**Continue your story of faith.**
Page 2	**Page 3**

The Church Through Time

 Let Us Pray

Leader: Faithful God, help us to follow your path of love.

"All the paths of the LORD are mercy and truth toward those who honor his covenant and decrees." **Psalm 25:10**

All: O God, you promised to always be with us. Give us the strength to live our promise to put you first in our lives. Amen.

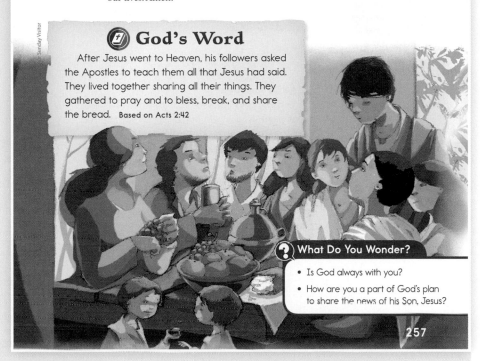

God's Word

After Jesus went to Heaven, his followers asked the Apostles to teach them all that Jesus had said. They lived together sharing all their things. They gathered to pray and to bless, break, and share the bread. **Based on Acts 2:42**

? What Do You Wonder?

• Is God always with you?

• How are you a part of God's plan to share the news of his Son, Jesus?

257

Our Sunday Visitor

Optional Activity

Chapter Story: "Those Who Came Before"

Verbal/Linguistic

Use this story after the opening prayer, before telling the children that Jesus wasn't always well known.

• Invite volunteers to read aloud this story of discovery.

• Connect learning about the past with making discoveries about early Christians, then transition back to the lesson instruction.

 Go to **aliveinchrist.osv.com** for Chapter Story.

Invite

Let Us Pray

Invite the children to gather in the prayer space and make the Sign of the Cross. Read aloud the leader's prayer and the Psalm verse. Prompt the children's response.

Have the children move from the prayer space back to their seats.

Explain that after Jesus was raised from the dead and ascended into Heaven, not many people outside of his own country knew about him.

Say: The first disciples, strengthened by the Holy Spirit, learned how to live together and went out to spread the Good News.

God's Word

Guide the children through the process of Scripture reflection.

• Invite them to close their eyes, be still, and open their minds and hearts to what God is saying to them in this passage.

• Proclaim the Scripture.

• Maintain several moments of silence.

• *Ask:* What did you hear God say to you today?

• Invite volunteers to share.

What Do You Wonder?

Say: A very long time ago, God promised to always be with us. The Son of God's coming shows us that God keeps his promises.

Invite the children to respond to the questions. Ask what else they might wonder about God's plan.

Objectives

- Define a covenant as a sacred promise between God and humans

- Examine the covenant between Abraham and God, which led to the beginning of God's People

God's Covenant

Tell the children that this section will focus on how God cares for his People.

Read aloud the first paragraph.

 God's Word

Proclaim the Scripture story.

- Emphasize the point in the story where God changed Abram's name to Abraham.

Say: This is when God made a covenant with Abraham and his family.

⭐ Have the children underline God's promises to Abraham.

- Finish the Scripture at the top of page 259 before reviewing the Catholic Faith Words.

Work with Words

Ask two volunteers to read aloud the Catholic Faith Words and their definitions.

- Have the children make vocabulary cards for each term and use the cards to prepare for chapter and unit reviews.

God's Covenant

How does God care for his People?

The beginnings of the Church's history go back to ancient times. Here is the story of the time when God first called his People.

© Our Sunday Visitor

 God's Word

I Will Be Your God

Sarai and Abram were sad. They had no children. One night Abram went outside and he heard God call to him. God said, "Abram, I want to make a promise to you, a covenant. I will be your God and you will become the father of many people."

Abram said to God, "You know that Sarai and I trust you, but we are old and we have no children."

God said, "I want to begin a covenant with you. You will now be called Abraham. You will become the father of many nations. Your wife's name will now be Sarah. I will bless her and give you a son."

Catholic Faith Words

covenant a sacred promise or agreement between God and humans

proclaim to tell about Jesus in words and actions

 Underline God's promises to Abraham.

258 Chapter 19

 Scripture Background

Genesis 17:1–8

In this Scripture passage, God enters into a covenant with Abram.

- God changes Abram's name to Abraham, which is Hebrew for "father of a multitude." God also changes Abram's wife's name from Sarai to Sarah.

- Through these faithful ones, the Jewish people came to have faith in God's promises—promises that are fulfilled through Jesus.

> God told Abraham to look up at the stars. He then said, "Your family will outnumber the stars. They will be my People, and I will be their God. All nations will be blessed through you. This is my covenant, my promise to you." **Based on Genesis 17:1–19**

Fulfilled in Jesus

God kept his promise. Abraham and Sarah had a son. Their family grew and they were God's Chosen People, the people of Israel. God was faithful to the **covenant** he had made with Abraham.

When Jesus, God's own Son, was born, God the Father extended the covenant to all people. Through Jesus' Death, Resurrection, and Ascension, God's promise was fulfilled. All people were saved from the power of sin and everlasting death through Jesus.

Followers of Jesus and members of the Church continue to be a sign of God's covenant. They do this as they **proclaim** the Good News of God's Kingdom.

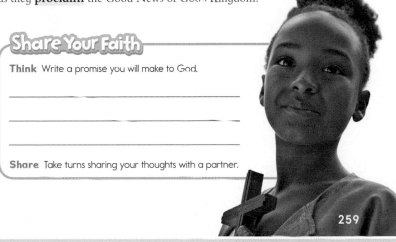

Share Your Faith

Think Write a promise you will make to God.

_____

_____

_____

Share Take turns sharing your thoughts with a partner.

259

I Will Be Your God

Continue proclaiming the story.

- *Ask:* What family stories do you enjoy hearing again and again?
- Invite the children to share family stories that have been told to them.

Fulfilled in Jesus

Ask the children to silently read the text.

- Point out that this lesson may seem to be on "fast forward" as it moves from Abraham to Jesus.
- Explain that the Bible contains so many stories about people's faith in God that one lesson cannot tell all of them.

Activity

Read aloud the directions for the Share Your Faith activity.

- Allow time for the children to write their promise and share with a partner.

Quick Review

A covenant is a sacred promise or agreement between God and humans. God established a covenant with Abraham, and from that came the beginning of God's People.

 Catechist Background

The Past Is Present

The Eucharistic Prayer tells the story of all that God has done throughout salvation history. It remembers those who have been part of salvation history and those who live it now.

- Use copies of parish missals to review Eucharistic Prayer I.
- List the people who are mentioned in salvation history.
- You can walk the children through the parts of the Eucharistic Prayer using page 313 in the Our Catholic Tradition section of the Student Book.

Objectives

- Recall that through Jesus the Church continues to be a sign of God's covenant, which extends to all people
- Recognize the faithfulness and commitment of early Christians to the covenant and to God

The Early Church

Ask a volunteer to read aloud the question.

- Tell the children that we will learn the answer as we cover the next two pages.

Invite three volunteers to read aloud the three paragraphs.

- Explain that some people did not want to hear the Good News about Jesus and made laws against the Christian faith. Help the children understand the term *persecution*—harassment of or harm done to a group because of some difference.
- *Ask:* Why is it important to learn about the early Christians?
- Write the responses on the board or on chart paper.

Ask the children what they think the photo on the page represents.

- Have a volunteer read the caption.

Work with Words

Read aloud the Catholic Faith Word and its definition.

- Have the children make a vocabulary cards to be used for memory games or for review.

The Early Church

How did the Church grow?

> ### Catholic Faith Words
>
> **faithful** to be constant and loyal to your promises and commitments to God and others, just as he is faithful to you

The ruins at Dura Europos in Syria, one of the earliest known house churches where Christians gathered.

Jesus and his first followers were Jewish. After Jesus returned to the Father, some of his followers continued to attend Jewish services on the Sabbath. They also gathered to celebrate the Eucharist in secret places like their homes or hidden catacombs.

The followers of Christ became known as Christians. They saw themselves as a new people, as the Church. Christians spread the Good News to other lands.

The early years of the Church were times of persecution, when many Christians were imprisoned or put to death. Even in difficult times, Jesus' followers remembered God's promises and tried to be **faithful** to him and to the covenant.

➜ **Why is it important to learn about the early Christians?**

260

© Our Sunday Visitor

Optional Activity

Activity Master 19: My Story of Faith

Distribute copies of the activity found on catechist page 257E.

- Tell the children that they are an important part of the story of faith.
- As an alternative, you may wish to send the activity home with the children.

The Church Grows

Christians kept the Church alive and growing. When invaders from the North attacked Rome, Christians in Ireland and Scotland kept the Gospel alive in monasteries. Saints including Patrick, Brigid, Kevin, and Columba carried on the Church's mission.

Into the Present

Many Saints you have read about this year in People of Faith have bravely carried the Word of God to distant lands. The Catholic faith has spread throughout Africa, Asia, Europe, and the Americas.

The Church's history is still being written today. You and all people who follow Jesus are an important part of the story of faith as well.

Mass of the Chrism at Saint Mary's Church in Secunderabad, India.

Connect Your Faith

Describe Christians How do people know that you are a Catholic?

People know that I am a follower of Jesus because:

_____

My parish family shows that it follows Jesus by:

_____

When I think of Catholics I think of:

_____

Quick Tip

Locations

Help the children use a map or globe to locate the places mentioned on page 261.

- List the places on the board or on chart paper so you can check them off as you find them.
- Ask volunteers to point out the places on the map or globe.
- Help the children find any remaining locations.
- This is an excellent time to reinforce the idea that the Church is catholic, or universal.

The Church Grows

Have a volunteer read aloud the paragraph.

- Explain that many years passed between the beginnings of the Church and the time of the Irish and Scottish Saints. Even more time passed before the Church spread to the Americas.

Into the Present

Ask a volunteer to read aloud the text.

- Ask the children how they are part of the Church's history. Possible response: They follow Jesus and share their faith with others.

Activity

Read aloud the directions for the Connect Your Faith activity.

- Have the children work independently to answer the questions.

 Music Option: Have the children sing "Share the Light," downloaded from **aliveinchrist.osv.com**.

Quick Review

As the Son of God, Jesus fulfills God's promise and his covenant extends to all people. The first Christians faced difficult times, but they were faithful to God and to the covenant, and the Church grew.

Our Catholic Life

Ask a volunteer to read aloud the question at the top of the student page.

• Invite the children to respond.

Ask a volunteer to read aloud the first paragraph.

Dig into the Past

Read aloud the paragraph.

Church History Research Topics

Have a volunteer read aloud the entries in the chart.

 Ask the children to place a check mark next to the topic they would like to research and write one reason they chose it.

• Allow time for the children to make their selections.

• Encourage volunteers to share their responses.

• Allow the children to comment on or ask questions about the suggested topics.

• Help them understand the connection between the topics and Church history.

• Make parish-approved research materials available to the group.

• Allow class time for the children to do their research.

> Music Option: While the children work, play "Building God's Kingdom," downloaded from **aliveinchrist.osv.com**.

Live

Our Catholic Life

What can you learn from the Church's past?

It can be fun to find out how people lived long ago. Studying the past can help you understand people's ideas and actions. You can learn how people solved problems. Their ideas can help you see how to solve problems today.

Dig into the Past

Think of a time in Church history that you would like to learn more about, or think of a Saint or another person who did special work for the Church.

Research a topic about Church history. Place a check mark next to it and write one reason you chose it.

Church History Research Topics

☐ **One of the Apostles**

☐ **Missions to Africa and Asia**

☐ **Saint Patrick, Saint Brigid, Saint Kevin, or Saint Columba**

☐ **Blessed Junipero Serra**

☐ **Padre Eusebio Kino**

_____

_____

_____

_____

262 Chapter 19

 ### Catechist Background

Make Changes

Like all history, Church history reflects changes in people and in organizations.

• Point out to the children some of the changes to the Mass that were made when we began to implement the English translation of the Third Edition of the *Roman Missal*, such as the *Gloria* or the Creed.

• Explain that these changes made the language in the Mass closer to the original Latin, so they more closely resemble the words from Scripture.

People of Faith

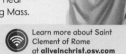

Saint Clement of Rome, died c. A.D. 100

November 23

Saint Clement was the bishop of Rome. He was one of the first Popes after Saint Peter. In fact, he learned about Jesus from Saint Peter himself. One of the things we know about Saint Clement is that he wrote a special letter. It was sent to Christians in a place called Corinth. It is one of the oldest letters we have from a Pope. In it, he talks about the Eucharist. Sometimes you will hear Saint Clement's name read in a list of Saints during Mass.

Discuss: How does the Pope communicate to people today?

 Learn more about Saint Clement of Rome at **aliveinchrist.osv.com**

Live Your Faith

Record Your Findings Record information you've learned about the topic you chose to research.

My topic:

_____

Why this topic interests me:

_____

What I learned:

_____

_____

Why this topic is important to Church history:

_____

_____

Catholic Social Teaching

Chapter Connections

To integrate Catholic Social Teaching into your lesson, choose one of the following features: Rights and Responsibilities, pages 294–295; or Solidarity of the Human Family, pages 300–301.

- Start the Live step of the process by talking about Saint Clement on page 263. The move directly to the Catholic Social Teaching feature.
- Or, to expand the lesson, complete both pages 262 and 263, then move to the Catholic Social Teaching feature.
- Return to Chapter 19 for the prayer on page 264.

People of Faith

Tell the children about Saint Clement of Rome

- Saint Clement was the fourth Pope. He learned about Jesus from Saint Peter himself.
- He wrote a Letter to the Church of Corinth; it is one of the oldest letters we have from a Pope. Other Letters have also been attributed to him.
- *Ask:* How does the Pope communicate to people today?
- Allow volunteers to share what they know.

 Encourage the children to go to **aliveinchrist.osv.com** at home to learn more about Saint Clement of Rome.

Activity

Read aloud the directions for the Live Your Faith activity.

- Give the children time to write in their information.
- As a take-home assignment, encourage the children to make posters or gather other visual materials to enhance their presentations.
- Assign days on which the children may share their information with the group.

Live

 Let Us Pray

Prayer of Faith

Explain that this prayer is a reminder of God's faithfulness through time and place.

Prepare

Choose volunteers for the three reader parts. Allow them to practice their lines.

- You will be the leader.

 Rehearse with the children "Get on the Boat," downloaded from **aliveinchrist.osv.com**.

Gather

Invite the children to come to the prayer space with their books.

- Lead the children into the prayer space while playing or singing "Get on the Boat."

Pray

Follow the order of prayer on the student page.

- Optional readings include 2 Thessalonians 2:13–17 and John 14:27.

 Conclude by processing around the room with the children singing "Get on the Boat."

Live

 Let Us Pray

Prayer of Faith

Gather and begin with the Sign of the Cross.

Leader: God our Father, we remember today our ancestors who have walked in faith with you.

Reader 1: Faith is getting what we have hoped for. It is our hope of what we have not seen.

Reader 2: By faith, we believe that God created the world.

Reader 3: By faith, Noah built an ark when he could see no water.

Reader 1: By faith, Abraham obeyed when God sent him to a faraway place.

Reader 2: By faith, Moses led God's People across the Red Sea as if it were dry land.

Reader 3: Yet God had something even better for his People.
Based on Hebrews 11

All: Thanks be to God.

 Sing "Get on the Boat"
Get on the boat! Get on the boat!
Get on! Noah, tell your friends.
Get on the boat! Get on the boat
before the rain begins.
© 1999, Mark Friedman and Janet Vogt.
Published by OCP. All rights reserved.

 Liturgy Link

Get Comfortable

Have the children sit for the reading part of the prayer service so that they will be more comfortable and will be less likely to fidget.

- If you use the optional reading from 2 Thessalonians, the children may sit as they do for the first two readings of the Mass.

- If you use the Gospel verse, have the children stand for it as they do at Mass.

 Go to **aliveinchrist.osv.com** for Sunday readings, Scripture background, questions of the week, and seasonal resources.

YOUR CHILD LEARNED >>>

This chapter examines the covenant between Abraham and God and recalls that through Jesus the Church continues to be a sign of God's everlasting covenant.

God's Word
 Read **Acts 2:42** and learn how the early Christians lived and worshiped together.

Catholics Believe
- God kept his promise to be forever faithful when he sent his Son, Jesus.
- Throughout her history the Church strives to be faithful to God's covenant and proclaim the Good News.

To learn more, go to the *Catechism of the Catholic Church* #781, 1612 at **usccb.org.**

People of Faith
This week, your child met Saint Clement, one of the first Popes after Saint Peter.

CHILDREN AT THIS AGE >>>

How They Understand the Historical Church Learning about their faith ancestors and the great things they have done can be exciting for third-graders, who enjoy feeling a part of something larger than themselves. It's helpful if children this age can place themselves within the context of the story, for example in the way that they are emulating a particular Saint in their own talents, actions, or goals for the future.

CONSIDER THIS >>>

How important is it to keep your promises to others?

Being able to trust someone to keep their promise of faithfulness or dependability is the foundation of a relationship. A sacred promise is called a covenant. "The covenant between God and humanity was first established with Noah after the great Flood,... God entered into a covenant later with Abraham and then with the people of Israel at the time of their exodus from slavery in Egypt under the leadership of Moses. He affirmed that they will always be his people" *(USCCA, p. 14).*

LET'S TALK >>>

- Ask your child to describe the covenant between God and the people of Israel.
- Talk about a Saint or someone you've learned about who did special work for the Church.

LET'S PRAY >>>

Saint Clement, pray for us that we may stand up for our faith. Help us remember all the Christians who lived before us and taught us about the faith. Amen.

For a multimedia glossary of Catholic Faith Words, Sunday readings, seasonal and Saint resources, and chapter activities go to **aliveinchrist.osv.com.**

Family + Faith

Distribute the page to the children or parents/adult family members. Point out the chapter highlights, insights on how third graders understand concepts, the opportunity for the adults to reflect on their own experience and faith journey, and the family prayer.

Chapter 19 Review

A **Work with Words** Fill in the circle beside the correct answer.

1. God made a covenant with _____.
   - ○ Isaac
   - ● Abraham

2. A covenant is a sacred _____ between God and humans.
   - ● agreement
   - ○ sacrifice

3. Jesus and his first followers were _____.
   - ● Jewish
   - ○ Christian

4. Followers of Christ became known as _____.
   - ○ Jews
   - ● Christians

5. Jesus _____ the covenant between God and his People.
   - ○ destroyed
   - ● fulfilled

B **Check Understanding** Write the letter T if the sentence is TRUE. Write the letter F if the sentence is False.

6. **F** There is no way to learn more about Church history or people from the past who have done special work for the Church.

7. **T** Early Jewish Christians met to pray at Jewish services and in homes.

8. **T** Early Christians shared their faith and were sometimes persecuted for doing so.

9. **T** The Church's history is still being written today.

10. **F** The Church never spread out of Israel.

Go to **aliveinchrist.osv.com** for an interactive review.

Chapter Review

Use Catechist Quick Reviews to highlight lesson concepts.

A **Work with Words**
Have the children fill in the circle beside the correct answer.

B **Check Understanding**
Explain to the children that they will write the letter *T* if the sentence is True and write the letter *F* if the sentence is False.

Go to **aliveinchrist.osv.com** to prepare customized and downloadable assessments, send eAssessments, and assign interactive reviews.

KEY CONCEPT

We can use our time, talent, and treasure to worship God, help others know about him, and respect and help others. The Church is a sign of the Kingdom of God.

DOCTRINAL CONTENT

- The Church continues Jesus' work on Earth through her worship, teaching, care for others, and work for peace and justice. (CCC, 759)

- The Church is a sign of God's Kingdom and helps people share in the love of the Holy Trinity. (CCC, 763)

- By our Baptism, we are called to participate in the Church's mission to share the Good News and serve God and others. (CCC, 2044–2046)

TASKS OF CATECHESIS

Helping children grow in a faith that is "known, celebrated, lived, and expressed in prayer" (NDC, 20).

This chapter focuses on the following tasks of catechesis:

- Moral Formation
- Missionary Initiation

Catechist Background

Finally, brothers, rejoice. Mend your ways, encourage one another, agree with one another, live in peace, and the God of love and peace will be with you. **2 Corinthians 13:11**

➜ **Reflect** How do you encourage the catechists and children you work with?

The Church today is called to participate in the Kingdom of God. Those who live as Jesus did spread his Kingdom through their everyday actions and attitudes when they act uprightly, practice patience, and love genuinely. Relying on God's power and grace, Christians are called to promote justice and speak the truth to help bring about the fullness of his Kingdom in the world.

According to the *Pastoral Constitution on the Church in the Modern World* (1), "The joy and hope, the grief and anguish of the men of our time, especially of those who are poor or afflicted in any way, are the joy and hope, the grief and anguish of the followers of Christ as well." This statement is a reminder that when Christians work to cooperate with God's Kingdom, they must look not only into their own homes, but also outward to those who are most in need of the Good News. Aiding those who are poor or in need shows solidarity with all humanity. When the Church works for the care and liberation of those who are poor, it is fulfilling a most important task in its mission. In serving these people, the Church follows the example of Jesus. The virtue of solidarity goes beyond giving material resources. It also involves sharing the gifts of faith.

➜ **Reflect** In what ways have you shown solidarity by aiding those who are poor?

Catechist's Prayer

Loving God, help me be an instrument of your peace. May my words and actions prepare me for the coming of your Kingdom and help me show the way to others. Amen.

Lesson Plan

Objectives	Process	Materials

🕐 Invite, 10 minutes

The Work of the Church Page 267	♥ **Psalm 118:22** Pray the opening prayer. 📖 **2 Corinthians 13:11** Reflect prayerfully on the Word. • Discuss What Do You Wonder questions.	📶 **Optional Activity** Chapter Story: "What Would You Do?"

🕐 Discover, 35 minutes

Doing Jesus' Work Pages 268–269 • Examine how the Church continues Jesus' work on Earth through her worship, teaching, care for others, and work for peace and justice	• Discuss the Church's mission. ☆ Find ways to share time, talent, and treasure. 📖 **Matthew 10:5–14** Proclaim "The Commissioning of the Twelve." • **Share Your Faith Activity** Provide instructions for being disciples and members of the Church.	☐ pencils or pens ☐ board or chart paper
The Church in the World Pages 270–271 • Recognize that the Church is a sign of God's Kingdom and helps people share in the love of the Holy Trinity • Recall that by our Baptism, all members of the Church share in her mission to share the Good News and serve God and others	• **Catholic Faith Words** peace, justice • Review how we work for God's Kingdom today. ☆ Check things to do right now as work for the Church. • Think about why we follow the example of Jesus. • **Connect Your Faith Activity** Create a T-shirt message about the Church's mission.	☐ pencils or pens ☐ art supplies ☐ two index cards per child • **Optional Activity** A Certificate of Honor ☐ Activity Master 20 (Page 267E)

🕐 Live, 15 minutes

Our Catholic Life Pages 272–273	• Talk about giving witness. ☆ Write ways to give witness in our community. • **People of Faith** Learn about Saint Peter Claver. • **Live Your Faith Activity** Draw a picture of what justice and peace looks like in action.	☐ pencils or pens ☐ board or chart paper ☐ art supplies
Prayer for Peace Page 274	• Follow the order of prayer. ▶ Sing "Peace Is Flowing Like a River."	📶 Download "Peace Is Flowing Like a River."

Family + Faith Page 275

Point out that the Catholic Families page provides chapter highlights, information on how third graders understand faith concepts, and family prayer.

Chapter Review Page 276

📶 aliveinchrist.osv.com

• Customize and Download Assessments
• Email Links to eAssessments
• Interactive Student Reviews

ONLINE RESOURCES

 Go to **aliveinchrist.osv.com**

You will find:

- Interactive lesson planning with web specific content and additional activities
- Step by step lesson instruction from printed Catechist Edition for integrated lesson planning
- Custom-built assessments to download and eAssessment links
- Interactive reviews that provide scores and the option to review answers
- Sunday readings with background and questions of the week

 Go to **osvparish.com**

You will find:

- Ask the Experts Q and A
- General Catechist Helps
- Community Connections and Blogs

Sharing the Message with Third Graders

The Work of the Church Today In our increasingly secular society, children may view the Church as quite separate from everyday life. It is important that we talk about our identity as members of the Catholic community and how this identity is one we carry with us into all places and situations. This calls us to responsibility. We are Jesus' voice, hands, and feet in the world.

Teaching Tip: In conversation during an open-ended activity, invite the children to talk about a way in which they have told others about Jesus either through their words or through their actions.

How Third Graders Understand

- Sometimes the world news is frightening. Help third graders find ways to pray and work for peace in the world.
- Children this age are reading about people who make a difference. Help them see that they, too, can make a difference.
- Sometimes children use the phrase "It's not fair!" Help them see that there are often two sides to a disagreement.

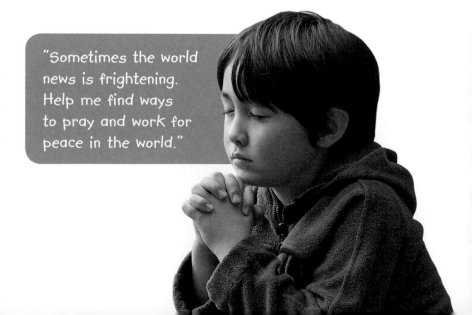

"Sometimes the world news is frightening. Help me find ways to pray and work for peace in the world."

Chapter Connections

Chapter Story
Invite

"What Would You Do?"

Use this story to expand the chapter introduction.

- Supply the children with newspapers. Help them find articles that describe problems in the world.

- Read the articles and brainstorm ways to solve the problem.

 Go to **aliveinchrist.osv.com** Lesson Planning section for this story.

NCEA IFG: ACRE Edition
Discover

Moral Formation

- Objectives: To be aware of the importance of a well-formed conscience for decision making; to be knowledgeable about the teachings of Jesus and the Church as the basis of Christian morality and to understand Catholic Social Teaching

Missionary Spirit

- Objectives: To recognize the centrality of evangelization as the Church's mission and identity embodied in vocation and service; to be aware of how cultures are transformed by the Gospel

Catholic Social Teaching
Live

 Use one of these features to introduce the principle and engage the children with an activity.

- Rights and Responsibilities, Pages 294–295
- The Dignity of Work, Pages 298–299

Music Options

 Use one or more of the following songs to enhance catechetical learning or for prayer.

- "Peace Is Flowing Like a River," Live Prayer, Page 274
- "Act Justly," Discover, Page 269
- "Raise Your Voice for Justice," Discover, Page 270
- "Take the Word of God with You," Live, Page 272

LECTIONARY CONNECTION

 Chapter 20 highlights Lectionary-connected themes such as peace, mission, and Church work. If your parish aligns its curriculum to the liturgical year, you could use this chapter in connection with the following Sundays.

Year A

Ninth Sunday in Ordinary Time—Justice

Twenty-seventh Sunday in Ordinary Time—Joy and Peace in Christ

Year B

Second Sunday of Lent—Justice

Twelfth Sunday in Ordinary Time—Peace

Year C

Fifth Sunday in Ordinary Time—Followers of Jesus

Twenty-fifth Sunday in Ordinary Time—Justice

Go to **aliveinchrist.osv.com** for a complete correlation ordered by the Sundays of the year and suggestions for how to integrate the Scripture readings into chapter lessons.

Name _____ Date _____

A Certificate of Honor

Complete this certificate for a person whose abilities and actions help make the world a better place and spread the news of the Kingdom of God. After filling in the blanks, decorate the certificate appropriately.

Then cut along the lines below, and present the certificate to the person you named.

Cut here
- -

Certificate of Honor

_____

is hereby recognized for

_____

This action helps God build his Kingdom because

_____

_____

_____   _____
Date   Presenter
- -
Cut here

The Work of the Church

 Let Us Pray

Leader: God our Father, help us build your Church.

"The stone the builders rejected
has become the cornerstone." **Psalm 118:22**

All: Jesus, through Baptism we have become members of your Body, the Church. Help us to always remember that you are the center of our lives. Amen.

 God's Word

Be happy! Change your bad habits, encourage each other, be agreeable with each other, live in peace. The God of love and peace is always with you.
Based on 2 Corinthians 13:11

What Do You Wonder?

- What does Saint Paul mean by live in peace?
- What would make people stop fighting so that we could have peace in the world?

267

Optional Activity

Chapter Story: "What Would You Do?" *Verbal/Linguistic*

Use this story after the opening prayer, before explaining that we have a mission.

- Ask the children to name some problems in the world.
- Brainstorm with them ideas to solve the problems.
- Invite the children to listen as you read "What Would You Do?"

 Go to **aliveinchrist.osv.com** for Chapter Story.

 Let Us Pray

Invite the children to gather in the prayer space and make the Sign of the Cross. Ask a volunteer to read aloud the leader's prayer and the Psalm verse. Prompt the children's response.

Have the children move from the prayer space back to their seats.

Say: The Church's mission is to share the Good News and to serve God and each other. Saint Paul told the people who lived in Corinth how they should act.

God's Word

Guide the children through the process of Scripture reflection.

- Invite them to close their eyes, be still, and open their minds and hearts to what God is saying to them in this passage.
- Proclaim the Scripture.
- Maintain several moments of silence.
- *Ask:* What did you hear God say to you today?
- Invite volunteers to share.

What Do You Wonder?

Say: When we respect others, we help bring God's peace to the world. When you work to make the world a place where people have what they need to live, you work for justice. As a member of the Church you share in God's work.

Invite the children to respond to the questions. Ask what else they might wonder about living in peace.

Objective

- Examine how the Church continues Jesus' work on Earth through her worship, teaching, care for others, and work for peace and justice

Doing Jesus' Work

Ask a volunteer to read the question.

- Tell the children that we will learn the answer to the question over the next two pages.

Summarize the paragraph.

- Emphasize the idea that as baptized members of the Church, the children are called on to perform positive actions and work for the Kingdom of God.

Point out the illustration at the top of the page, which ties in with the Scripture reading.

God's Word

Proclaim the Scripture story.

- Remind the children that Jesus sent the Holy Spirit to help the disciples on their mission.
- Have a volunteer read aloud the question.
- Write the children's responses on the board or chart paper.

Discover

Doing Jesus' Work

What is the Church called to do?

The Church continues Jesus' work on Earth. We work together with Jesus to do his work. The work of the Church is to worship God, to help others know and worship God the Father, Son, and Holy Spirit and live holy lives, to help and protect all life, especially people who are most vulnerable and those who are poor and needy, and to work for peace and justice. Jesus sent his disciples on a mission to spread the Good News and gave them special instructions.

© Our Sunday Visitor

God's Word

The Commissioning of the Twelve

Jesus sent his disciples on a mission to spread the Good News. These are the instructions he gave them.

Travel to visit the people of Israel. Tell them that the Kingdom of God is at hand. Cure people who are sick. Don't take supplies or extra clothes or sandals. Whenever you come to a town, find a good person's home, and stay there as long as you are in the town. When you go into a house, bless it. If people do not accept you or listen to you, leave the house or town and have nothing to do with it. **Based on Matthew 10:5–14**

➜ Why do you think Jesus asked his disciples to do these things?

Scripture Background

Matthew 10:5–14

The Gospel according to Matthew reports that Jesus sent the Apostles to share the Good News with the Jewish people, just as he had done.

- The disciples received from God the free gift of salvation, and they should be similarly generous.
- The instructions indicate that the Apostles were to depend upon the generosity of those whom they evangelized.

Called to Work

Each of us has talents, gifts, and interests that God has given us. They can be a call from God to do a particular kind of work for his Church.

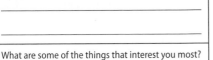
Fill in the blanks with ways you can share your time, talent, and treasure.

Give Your Time, Talent, and Treasure

What are some of the talents and gifts God has given you?

_____

_____

What are some of the things that interest you most?

_____

_____

How can you use your talents and interests to help in the work of the Church?

_____

_____

DONATIONS

Share Your Faith

Think What instructions would you give fellow disciples on how to follow Christ and be members of the Catholic Church?

Share Share your ideas with the other groups.

The Work of the Church **269**

Called to Work

Ask a volunteer to read aloud the paragraph.

- *Ask:* What can you do right now to make the world better?
- Encourage the children to explain how a simple action could help make a better future.

Give Your Time, Talent, and Treasure

Ask the children to look over the chart.

 Direct them to fill in the blanks with ways they can share their time, talent, and treasure.

Activity

Read aloud the directions.

- Ask the children to work in pairs to answer the question.
- Invite volunteers to share their ideas with the group.

 Music Option: Have the children sing "Act Justly," downloaded from **aliveinchrist.osv.com**.

Quick Review

The Church continues Jesus' work on Earth through her worship, teaching, care for others, and work for peace and justice.

✓ Quick Tip

Help Others

Avoid giving the impression that specific ethnic groups are more likely to be the recipients of help than others.

- The children will benefit from hearing about organizations that emphasize people helping others within their own ethnic community. Check the Internet and learn about these organizations and share the information with the children.
- Be sure to include stories of African and Asian Saints and missionaries; these can be found on the USCCB website.

© Our Sunday Visitor

Objectives

- Recognize that the Church is a sign of God's Kingdom and helps people share in the love of the Holy Trinity
- Recall that by our Baptism, all members of the Church share in her mission to share the Good News and serve God and others

The Church in the World

Tell the children that this section will focus on how the Church does Jesus' work in the world today.

Start out by having the children silently read the three paragraphs.

- Emphasize the idea that all members of the Church are called on to work for the Kingdom of God.

Working for God's Kingdom

Ask a volunteer to read aloud the suggestions in the chart.

⭐ Have the children place a check mark next to things they can do right now to be a part of the work of the Church.

- Ask volunteers to share their decisions and have them explain how and why.

 Music Option: Have the children sing "Raise Your Voice for Justice," downloaded from **aliveinchrist.osv.com**.

Discover

The Church in the World

How does the Church do Jesus' work in the world today?

You know that there are many problems in the world. Some of the problems are so big that you may think someone your age can't help solve them or make a difference. Think about the Twelve who set out with Jesus' Good News.

Every time you work as the disciples did to help others know God you are working for God's Kingdom. Every time you encourage someone to turn to God in prayer, feed a person who is hungry, stop a fight, or give someone hope, you are sharing the Good News of Jesus.

The Catholic faith is about the past, future, and present. Right here, right now, the Holy Spirit is with us, and we are the Church.

© Our Sunday Visitor

⭐ Place a check mark next to the things you can do right now to be part of the work of the Church.

Working for God's Kingdom

☐	helping people worship God
☐	teaching people about God
☐	sending missionaries to other places to share the Gospel
☐	standing up for people's rights for life, water, work, and freedom
☐	helping those who are poor or in need

We can build the Kingdom of God by helping others.

270

ⓘ Catechist Background

The Kingdom of God

The Kingdom of God exists in two dimensions—the beginning of the Kingdom, which Jesus proclaimed is present now on Earth, and the fulfillment of the Kingdom, which God will bring about at the end of time. Explain to the children the following.

- The Kingdom is both present and still to come.
- All followers of Jesus are called through Baptism to be signs of God's Kingdom through their words and actions.

Sharing a Mission

The mission of the Church is to share the Good News, make the world holy, and serve God and one another. The Church is a sign of God's Kingdom and helps people share in the love of the Holy Trinity. Your words and actions show God's **justice**, love, and **peace**. You are asked to do this at your Baptism.

As a member of the Church, you join in her work. The Spirit strengthens you to tell others about Jesus. You can help the Church worship God in the Mass. You can work for everyone's basic rights, such as food, clothing, shelter, and dignity. You can care for people who are poor, ill, or lonely.

Why Help with the Church's Work?

When you help with the Church's mission, you follow the example of Jesus. You do this because you love God and put him first. You also do this because all people are your sisters and brothers. God calls all people to be united in his family and to share what they have.

Catholic Faith Words

peace a state of calm when things are in their proper order and people settle problems with kindness and justice

justice giving God what is due to him, and giving each person what he or she is due because that person is a child of God

Connect Your Faith

Send a Message Design a T-shirt that helps spread the message about the Church's mission.

© Our Sunday Visitor

Sharing a Mission

Tell the children that they will find out how they can share in the Church's mission.

Ask two children to each read aloud one of the paragraphs.

Work with Words

Have a volunteer read aloud the Catholic Faith Words and their definitions.

- Pass out two index cards per child.
- Have the children write the word on one side of the card and the definition on the other.
- Encourage them to use the cards for a chapter or unit review.

Why Help with the Church's Work?

Read aloud the paragraph.

- Remind the children that all people are called to share their gifts and serve one another.

Activity

Read aloud the directions.

- Provide art supplies for the children to create a message on the T-shirt image.
- Ask volunteers to share their message and their art.

Quick Review

The Church is a sign of God's Kingdom and helps us share in the love of the Holy Trinity. By our Baptism, all members of the Church share in her mission to work for peace and justice.

Optional Activity

Activity Master 20: A Certificate of Honor

Distribute copies of the activity found on catechist page 267E.

- Tell the children they will be creating a certificate for a person who helps build God's kingdom.
- As an alternative, you may wish to send this activity home with the children.

> Chapter 20 Activity Master
>
> Name _____ Date _____
>
> **A Certificate of Honor**
> Complete this certificate for a person whose abilities and actions help make the world a better place and spread the news of the Kingdom of God. After filling in the blanks, decorate the certificate appropriately.
> Then cut along the lines below, and present the certificate to the person you named.
>
> Cut here
>
> **Certificate of Honor**
>
> _____
> is hereby recognized for
> _____
>
> This action helps God build his Kingdom because
> _____
> _____
>
> Date _____ Presenter _____
> Cut here
>
> 267E Chapter 20

Our Catholic Life

Ask a volunteer to read aloud the question.

- Define the term *witness* as a verb that means to testify or tell the truth about something.
- Invite the children to respond to the question.
- Write their responses on the board or on chart paper.

Ask two children to read aloud the two paragraphs.

Get Involved

Read aloud the three bullet points.

- Discuss how participating in the listed activities shows the children's faith to others.
- Have the children write some ways they can give witness in their community.
- Allow time for them to think and write.
- Encourage creative responses.
- Ask volunteers to share their ideas.

> ▶ Music Option: Have the children sing "Take the Word of God with You," downloaded from **aliveinchrist.osv.com**.

Remind the children that starting the day off with a prayer like the "Morning Offering" on page 324 in the Our Catholic Tradition section of their books will help them focus on being good witnesses.

Our Catholic Life

How do you give witness?

Through Baptism, all Catholics are called to live their faith every day. This is known as giving witness. Sometimes giving witness can be done without saying anything.

Living your faith means acting according to your beliefs, with the Holy Spirit's help, to bring the Good News of God's Kingdom to the world. You can give witness to your faith throughout your community.

 Write some ways that you can give witness in your community.

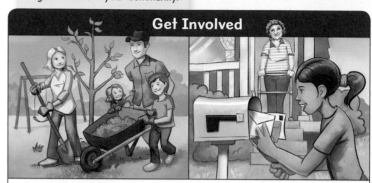

Get Involved

- Volunteer with other members of your church to clean up a local park.
- Do small jobs or chores for a neighbor who is sick or elderly.
- Show respect for others by using good manners.

_____

_____

_____

_____

_____

✓ Quick Tip

Constant Witness

Point out to the children that organizations within their community and parish will give them opportunities to give witness to their faith.

- Ask a member of the Society of Saint Vincent de Paul or a member from another volunteer organization in the parish to talk to the class about how the society gives witness.
- Ask the children how belonging to such groups as Boy Scouts and Girl Scouts can be witnessing.

People of Faith

Saint Peter Claver, 1581–1654

September 9

Saint Peter Claver was from Spain. He moved to Columbia and became a Jesuit priest. When slave ships came from Africa, Saint Peter would meet them at the docks to give the slaves food and medicine. He would tell the slaves how much God loved them and talk to them about Jesus. He wanted to stop all slavery but until that happened, he made sure slaves were given food and clothes and treated kindly. He also helped sick people in the hospital, prisoners in jail, and sailors.

Discuss: To whom can you bring God's message of love?

Learn more about Saint Peter Claver at **aliveinchrist.osv.com**

Live Your Faith

Draw a Picture of yourself working for justice and peace.

© Our Sunday Visitor

People of Faith

Tell the children about Saint Peter Claver.

- Though he was timid and lacking in self-confidence, he became a daring and ingenious organizer.

- He assembled a group of interpreters of various nationalities, of whom he made catechists to interpret for the slaves.

- While the slaves were penned up waiting to be purchased and dispersed, Saint Peter Claver instructed and baptized them in the faith.

- Have a proficient reader read aloud the paragraph on Saint Peter Claver.

- Encourage the children to answer the Discuss question.

 Encourage the children to go to **aliveinchrist.osv.com** at home to learn more about Saint Peter Claver.

Activity

Read aloud the directions for the Live Your Faith activity.

- Provide art supplies to the children.

- Allow time for them to create their pictures.

- Ask volunteers to share.

Catholic Social Teaching

Chapter Connections

To integrate Catholic Social Teaching into your lesson, choose one of the following features: Rights and Responsibilities, pages 294–295; or The Dignity of Work, pages 298–299.

- Start the Live step of the process by talking about Saint Peter Claver on page 273. The move directly to the Catholic Social Teaching feature.

- Or, to expand the lesson, complete both pages 272 and 273, then move to the Catholic Social Teaching feature.

- Return to Chapter 20 for the prayer on page 274.

Let Us Pray

Prayer for Peace

Explain that this prayer is the prayer of Saint Francis of Assisi calling for peace in the world to begin within him.

Prepare

Ask the children to pray for themselves to become instruments of peace that flows to others so that others can also share in the peace.

 Rehearse with the children "Peace Is Flowing Like a River," downloaded from **aliveinchrist.osv.com**.

Gather

Invite the children to come to the prayer space with their books.

• Lead the children into the prayer space while playing or singing "Peace Is Flowing Like a River."

Pray

Follow the order of prayer on the student page.

• An optional reading is John 20:19–22.

Leader's concluding prayer: Heavenly Father, help us share your peace and kindness with everyone we meet.

 Conclude by processing around the room with the children singing the hymn refrain.

Live

Let Us Pray

Prayer for Peace

Gather and begin with the Sign of the Cross.

All: Pray together.
Lord, make me an instrument of your peace.
Where there is hatred, let me sow love;
where there is injury, pardon;
where there is doubt, faith;
where there is despair, hope;
where there is darkness, light;
and where there is sadness, joy.

O Divine Master, grant that I may not so much seek
to be consoled as to console;
to be understood as to understand;
to be loved as to love.
For it is in giving that we receive;
it is in pardoning that we are pardoned;
and it is in dying that we are born to eternal life. Amen.
Prayer of Saint Francis

Sing "Peace Is Flowing Like a River"
Peace is flowing like a river,
flowing out of you and me.
Flowing out into the desert,
setting all the captives free.

His love is flowing…
Alleluia, Alleluia…
Traditional, adapted by Carey Landry.
Text and music adaptation
© 1975, 1979, OCP.
All rights reserved.

Liturgy Link

Gestures

During the prayer, you may wish to have the children make appropriate gestures whenever specific words are said.

• Help the children come up with and agree on gestures for the words *peace, love, faith, light, joy, pardon,* and *life.*

Go to **aliveinchrist.osv.com** for Sunday readings, Scripture background, questions of the week, and seasonal resources.

YOUR CHILD LEARNED >>>

This chapter recalls that all members of the Church share in her mission to work for peace and justice and Jesus' instruction to his disciples to tell the Good News.

God's Word
 Read **2 Corinthians 13:11** and see ways that we can help and encourage one another.

Catholics Believe
- We can use our time, talent, and treasure to worship God, help others know about him, and respect and help others.
- The Church is a sign of the Kingdom of God.

To learn more, go to the *Catechism of the Catholic Church* #2044–2046 at **usccb.org**.

People of Faith
This week, your child met Saint Peter Claver who helped African slaves when they arrived in the Americas.

CHILDREN AT THIS AGE >>>

How They Understand the Work of the Church Today In our increasingly secular society, children may view the Church as quite separate from everyday life. It is important that we talk about our identity as members of the Catholic community and how this identity is one we carry with us into all places and situations. This calls us to responsibility. We are Jesus' voice, hands, and feet in the world.

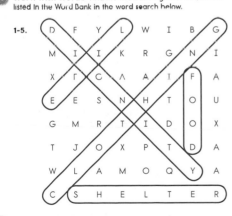

CONSIDER THIS >>>

When have you experienced the peace that Jesus alone can give?

People describe peace in many ways including a lack of conflict or everyone just doing what they want. Jesus reminds us that the peace he alone can give comes from the hard work of dying to our ego. "Jesus' life, teaching, death, and Resurrection show us the meaning of love and justice in a broken world. Sacred Scripture and traditional ethical principles define what it means to make peace" (*Living with Faith and Hope after September 11, 2001*, quoted in USCCA, p. 332).

LET'S TALK >>>
- Ask your child what he or she can do right now to follow Jesus' example.
- Discuss some ways your family can share their time, talent, and treasure.

LET'S PRAY >>>
Dear God, lead us to be like Saint Peter Claver and help those who are hungry or sick. Amen.

For a multimedia glossary of Catholic Faith Words, Sunday readings, seasonal and Saint resources, and chapter activities go to **aliveinchrist.osv.com**.

© Our Sunday Visitor

Distribute the page to the children or parents/adult family members. Point out the chapter highlights, insights on how third graders understand concepts, the opportunity for the adults to reflect on their own experience and faith journey, and the family prayer.

Chapter 20 Review

A **Work with Words** Find the five basic rights of all humans listed in the Word Bank in the word search below.

1-5.

D	F	Y	L	W	I	B	G
M	I	I	K	R	G	N	I
X	T	C	A	A	I	F	A
E	E	S	N	H	T	O	U
G	M	R	T	I	D	O	X
T	J	O	X	P	T	D	A
W	L	A	M	O	Q	Y	A
C	S	H	E	L	T	E	R

Word Bank
food
shelter
clothing
dignity
life

B **Check Understanding** Match each description in Column A with the correct term in Column B.

Column A

6. Giving God and others what's due to them

7. Settling problems with kindness

8. Share the Good News

9. Sign of God's Kingdom

10. Living your faith

Column B

the Church

giving witness

justice

peace

our mission

Go to **aliveinchrist.osv.com** for an interactive review.

Use Catechist Quick Reviews to highlight lesson concepts.

A **Work with Words**
Have the children find the five basic rights of humans in the word search.

B **Check Understanding**
Instruct the children to match each description in Column A with the correct term in Column B.

Go to **aliveinchrist.osv.com** to prepare customized and downloadable assessments, send eAssessments, and assign interactive reviews.

The Work of the Church **275–276**

KEY CONCEPT

People who die in God's friendship will live forever in his presence. At the end of the world, Christ will judge all people on the way they lived their lives.

DOCTRINAL CONTENT

- Jesus' Resurrection is proof of his promise of eternal life. (CCC, 655)

- The last book of the Bible, Revelation, ends with John's vision of a new creation, God's everlasting Kingdom. (CCC, 1044–1045)

- The Particular Judgment is the individual judgment by God at the time of a person's death when God decides where that person will spend eternity according to his or her faith and works. (CCC, 1022)

- The Last Judgment is God's final triumph over evil, when Christ will come again and bring the Kingdom of God to its fullness. (CCC, 1038–1040)

TASKS OF CATECHESIS

Helping children grow in a faith that is "known, celebrated, lived, and expressed in prayer" (NDC, 20).

This chapter focuses on the following tasks of catechesis:

- Promoting Knowledge of the Faith

- Moral Formation

Catechist Background

And this is the testimony: God gave us eternal life, and this life is in his Son. Whoever possesses the Son has life; whoever does not possess the Son of God does not have life. **1 John 5:11–12**

➜ **Reflect** Do you live your testimony?

Although no one knows what the future holds, Jesus did promise that the Kingdom of God will come in its fullness at the end of time. Someday there will be a new Heaven and a new Earth where injustice, war, and hatred will be no more. Justice, peace, and love will reign.

Eschatology, the study of these last things, speaks of Heaven as a state of supreme happiness and fulfillment in the presence of God. Hell, then, is a state marked by the permanent absence of God. To prepare for participation in the new Heaven and the new Earth, the Lord calls people to develop relationships based on justice and love. Eternal life belongs to those who choose to cooperate with God's grace.

Thoughts of the last judgment can make people uncomfortable. Jesus teaches that God is merciful and compassionate, just and loving. He gave humans free will; they are responsible for their actions. Upon death, it is time to face the ultimate truth. By their actions in this life, especially their accetance or rejection of the grace and friendship God offers, all people choose everlasting life in Heaven or Hell.

➜ **Reflect** Which of your actions will God judge as merciful?

Catechist's Prayer

 Living God, you are the source of my hope and salvation. Hold me and never let me go. Amen.

Lesson Plan

Objectives	Process	Materials

Invite, 10 minutes

Everlasting Life Page 277

- ♥ **Psalm 145:13** Pray the opening prayer.
- **1 John 5:11–12** Reflect prayerfully on the Word.
- Discuss What Do You Wonder questions.

- 🌐 **Optional Activity**
Chapter Story:
"The Gift of Life"

Discover, 35 minutes

Cycles of Life Pages 278–279
- Reflect on Jesus' Resurrection as proof of his promise of eternal life
- Recognize that the last book of the Bible, Revelation, ends with John's vision of God's everlasting Kingdom

- Read a story about the cycle of life.
- ☆ Underline what the sunflower said to the daisy.
- **Revelation 21:1–4** Proclaim "The New Heaven and the New Earth."
- **Share Your Faith Activity** Unscramble the words to find John's vision.

- ☐ pencils or pens
- ☐ board or chart paper

Our Future Pages 280–281
- Understand that Particular Judgment is the individual judgment by God at the time of a person's death
- Identify the Last Judgment as God's final triumph over evil, when Christ will come again and bring the Kingdom of God to its fullness

- **Catholic Faith Words** Heaven, Hell, Purgatory, Last Judgment
- Review the definitions in the text.
- Discuss God as the Alpha and Omega.
- Talk about new life in God's everlasting Kingdom.
- **Connect Your Faith Activity** Write a message to share God's love with those who don't know it.

- ☐ pencils or pens
- ☐ four index cards per child
- 🌐 **Optional Activity**
Code Breaker
- ☐ Activity Master 21 (Page 277E)

Live, 15 minutes

Our Catholic Life Pages 282–283

- Discuss ways to comfort people who are sad due to a death.
- ☆ Write one way to comfort someone.
- **People of Faith** Learn about Saint Joseph.
- **Live Your Faith Activity** Design a sympathy card.

- ☐ pencils or pens
- ☐ board or chart paper
- ☐ colored pencils or markers

Prayer for the Kingdom Page 284

- Select three readers.
- ▶ Rehearse "Seek Ye First."
- Follow the order of prayer.

- 🌐 Download "Seek Ye First."

Family + Faith Page 285
Point out that the Catholic Families page provides chapter highlights, information on how third graders understand faith concepts, and family prayer.

Chapter Review Page 286
🌐 aliveinchrist.osv.com
- Customize and Download Assessments
- Email Links to eAssessments
- Interactive Student Reviews

ONLINE RESOURCES

 Go to **aliveinchrist.osv.com**

You will find:

- Interactive lesson planning with web specific content and additional activities
- Step by step lesson instruction from printed Catechist Edition for integrated lesson planning
- Custom-built assessments to download and eAssessment links
- Interactive reviews that provide scores and the option to review answers
- Sunday readings with background and questions of the week

 Go to **osvparish.com**

You will find:

- Ask the Experts Q and A
- General Catechist Helps
- Community Connections and Blogs

Sharing the Message with Third Graders

Life after Death One of the most common and intense fears of children in third grade (although it is usually unspoken) is that someone close to them (especially a parent) will die. Having an opportunity to talk about death and to learn about what we as Catholics believe about our hope for the future can be comforting for children this age, and might also allow them to express their individual thoughts, questions, and fears.

Teaching Tip: Sometimes we are at a loss for words when children are talking about a sensitive subject like death. It's okay not to know what to say. Sometimes listening and reflecting what you are hearing is the most helpful response we can give.

How Third Graders Understand

- Third graders are beginning to read stories about death. Help them understand more about Christian hope in life after death.
- The group has covered a lot in faith formation this year. Encourage the children to go out and live what they have learned.
- While the children are probably looking forward to summer vacation, help them realize that God is always with them.

"I have learned much in my religion class this year. Encourage me to live what I have learned."

Chapter Connections

Chapter Story

Invite

"The Gift of Life"

Use this story to expand the chapter introduction.

- Invite volunteers to share their thoughts about welcoming a new life.
- Accept responses that include welcoming a new pet or having a relative move into the house. These are new beginnings as well.
- Ask the children to recall what a person does that makes him or her a new member of God's family. celebrates the Sacraments of Initiation

 Go to **aliveinchrist.osv.com** Lesson Planning section for this story.

NCEA IFG: ACRE Edition

Discover

Knowledge of the Faith

- Objectives: To know and understand basic Catholic teaching about the Incarnate Word Jesus Christ as the way, truth, and life; to know and understand God's activity in human history

Moral Formation

- Objectives: To be aware of the importance of a well-formed conscience for decision making; to be knowledgeable about the teachings of Jesus and the Church as the basis of Christian morality and to understand Catholic Social Teaching

Catholic Social Teaching

Live

 Use one of these features to introduce the principle and engage the children with an activity.

- Life and Dignity, Pages 290–291
- Rights and Responsibilities, Pages 294–295

Music Options

 Use one or more of the following songs to enhance catechetical learning or for prayer.

- "Seek Ye First," Live Prayer, Page 284
- "Now Thank We All Our God," Live, Page 284

LECTIONARY CONNECTION

 Chapter 21 highlights Lectionary-connected themes such as Heaven, Hell, Purgatory, and Last Judgment. If your parish aligns its curriculum to the liturgical year, you could use this chapter in connection with the following Sundays.

Year A

First Sunday of Advent—Need for Watchfulness

The Epiphany of the Lord— Preach God's Plan

Year B

First Sunday of Advent—Waiting for Jesus

Tenth Sunday in Ordinary Time— Heaven

Year C

First Sunday of Advent—Coming of Jesus

Fourth Sunday of Easter— Resurrection

Go to **aliveinchrist.osv.com** for a complete correlation ordered by the Sundays of the year and suggestions for how to integrate the Scripture readings into chapter lessons.

Name _____   Date _____

Code Breaker

Use the clues beneath the blank spaces and the letters in the grid to spell the missing words. Here is an example:

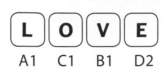

L   O   V   E
A1   C1   B1   D2

D	P	E	R	A
C	O	S	T	W
B	V	I	M	D
A	L	G	C	N
	1	**2**	**3**	**4**

1. The Church is a sign of God's ⬜⬜⬜⬜⬜⬜⬜⬜.
       A3 C1 B1 D2 A4 D4 A4 C3

2. Christians are ⬜⬜⬜⬜⬜⬜⬜⬜⬜ of Christ.
       B4 B2 C2 A3 B2 D1 A1 D2 C2

3. As a Christian, you are a ⬜⬜⬜⬜⬜⬜⬜ to God's
       C4 B2 C3 A4 D2 C2 C2
love, justice, and peace.

4. You are empowered by the ⬜⬜⬜⬜⬜⬜ to help with
       C2 D1 B2 D3 B2 C3
the Church's mission.

5. You look forward to Christ's ⬜⬜⬜⬜⬜⬜
       C2 D2 A3 C1 A4 B4

⬜⬜⬜⬜⬜⬜ at the end of time.
A3 C1 B3 B2 A4 A2

6. Those who live in love will be in God's ⬜K⬜⬜⬜⬜⬜⬜
       B2 A4 A2 B4 C1 B3
forever.

Everlasting Life

 Let Us Pray

Leader: Loving Father, we praise your name forever.

"Your reign is a reign for all ages,
    your dominion for all generations." **Psalm 145:13**

All: By his Death and Resurrection, Jesus gave us
eternal life. Loving Father, help us to live in this
world in a way that reflects your goodness. Amen.

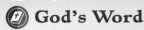 **God's Word**

And this is our belief. "God gave us eternal life, and
this life is in his Son. Whoever knows Jesus has life."
Based on 1 John 5:11–12

© Our Sunday Visitor

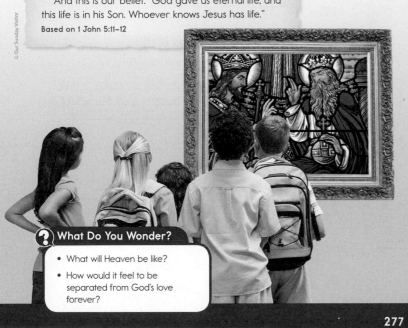

? What Do You Wonder?

- What will Heaven be like?
- How would it feel to be
  separated from God's love
  forever?

277

Optional Activity

Chapter Story: "The Gift of Life" *Verbal/Linguistic*

Use this story after the opening prayer, before talking about proof of
eternal life.

- Ask volunteers to read the parts of the family members in "The Gift
  of Life." Give the children time to practice.
- Connect welcoming a new family member with being a member
  of God's family, then transition back to the lesson instruction.

 Go to **aliveinchrist.osv.com** for Chapter Story.

Let Us Pray

Invite the children to gather in the
prayer space and make the Sign of
the Cross. Ask one volunteer to read
aloud the leader's prayer and
another to read the Psalm verse.
Prompt the group's response.

Have the children move from the
prayer space back to their seats.

Explain that when Jesus rose from
the dead, we had proof of his
promise of eternal life.

Say: Eternal life means that when
we die, we too can live forever with
God, if we believe and accept his
grace in our lives. Listen to Saint
John describe the gift of eternal life.

God's Word

Guide the children through the
process of Scripture reflection.

- Invite them to close their eyes, be
  still, and open their minds and
  hearts to what God is saying to
  them in this passage.
- Proclaim the Scripture.
- Maintain several moments of
  silence.
- *Ask:* What did you hear God say
  to you today?
- Invite volunteers to share.

What Do You Wonder?

Say: If we are faithful to God, we
will live forever with him in
happiness.

Invite the children to respond to the
questions. Ask what else they might
wonder about everlasting life.

Discover

Objectives

- Reflect on Jesus' Resurrection as proof of his promise of eternal life
- Recognize that the last book of the Bible, Revelation, ends with John's vision of God's everlasting Kingdom

Cycles of Life

Ask a volunteer to read aloud the question at the top of the student page.

- Tell the children that we will learn the answer as we cover the text in this chapter.

Read aloud the first paragraph.

- Point out that the story on this page tells about both the beginning and the ending of life.

The Little Daisy

Read aloud the story, using your voice to express the character's feelings.

Ask: Why did Daisy feel better after learning that flowers would bloom from her seeds?

- Write the children's responses on the board or on chart paper.
- Ask the children when they have heard another story about a death that led to new life. Affirm those who mention Jesus' Resurrection.
- ⭐ Have the children underline what the sunflower said to the daisy.
- Allow the children time to reread and underline the appropriate text.

Cycles of Life

What happens after death?

⭐ Underline what the Sunflower said to the Daisy.

The cycle of life begins with birth and ends in death. Read this story about the cycle of life and dealing with loss.

The Little Daisy

Early one spring, a little bud named Daisy grew from a seed. She became friends with another bud named Sunflower.

Daisy grew into a small white flower with a little yellow head. Sunflower grew very tall with yellow petals and a large brown head. They both loved the fresh morning dew and the warm summer sun.

One day the wind got very cold. Daisy noticed that ice had formed on her leaves.

"What is happening?" she asked.

Sunflower said, "At the end of summer, it is time for us to die. When you die, your seeds will fall back into the ground and then new flowers will bloom from your seeds!"

"I feel much better now," said Daisy.

She laid her head down and said, "I've had a beautiful life."

© Our Sunday Visitor

278

Optional Activity

Funerals *Interpersonal*

Consider extending the text question by inviting the children to think about things that made Daisy's life beautiful. Tell them we can do the same thing for the people we have lost in our lives.

- Invite the parish priest or deacon to meet with your group to explain aspects of a funeral liturgy that celebrate the life of the deceased and the hope of eternal life.
- Direct the children to prepare questions for the speaker in advance.

New Life

When Jesus came to Earth, he told people that if they believed in him, they would have everlasting life. His own Resurrection is the proof that his promise is true. His followers saw him alive after he had died. Later, John, who was one of Jesus' followers, had a vision from God of what would come at the end of time. This is what John said about his vision.

God's Word

The New Heaven and the New Earth

I saw a new heaven and a new earth. The old creation had passed away. I saw a holy city coming out of the sky. It was like a new Jerusalem. I heard God's voice saying that there would be no more tears or sadness, no more suffering or death.

Based on Revelation 21:1–4

© Our Sunday Visitor

Share Your Faith

Think Unscramble the words to find John's vision of what the new Heaven and Earth will look like.

A LHYO YICT MGOINC UTO FO HTE YKS

A H O L Y   C I T Y   C O M I N G
O U T   O F   T H E   S K Y

Share Share your answer with a partner.

Songs of Scripture

God Is So Big

This song teaches the children many of the attributes of God in a developmentally appropriate way. These include: omnipotence, all powerful; omniscience, all knowing; transcendent, so big; immanent, close to you; eternal, always was and forever will be.

- Teach the children the song "God Is So Big."

 Use *Songs of Scripture*, Grades 1–3 CD, Track 22

New Life

Read aloud the text to introduce the Scripture story.

God's Word

Ask a volunteer to proclaim the Scripture.

- Invite the children to close their eyes and imagine John's vision.
- Ask how John described the city in his vision. Possible response: a holy city of justice, love, and peace; a life with no more tears, sadness, suffering, or death
- Explain that the holy city is John's way of describing his vision of the new life Christians will have when Jesus returns.
- Tell the children that although death is an ending, it is also a beginning. Remind them that Jesus promised his followers everlasting life.

Activity

Read aloud the directions for the Share Your Faith activity.

- Ask the children to work with a partner to solve the puzzle
- Invite volunteers to share their work.

Quick Review

Jesus' Resurrection is proof of his promise of eternal life. The last book of the Bible, Revelation, ends with John's vision of a new creation, God's everlasting Kingdom.

Discover

Objectives

- Understand that Particular Judgment is the individual judgment by God at the time of a person's death

- Identify the Last Judgment as God's final triumph over evil, when Christ will come again and bring the Kingdom of God to its fullness

Our Future

Point out that this section will cover what the Church believes about life after death.

Invite three volunteers to each read aloud one of the paragraphs.

Work with Words

Invite four children to read the Catholic Faith Words and their definitions.

- Pass out four index cards per child.

- Have the children create vocabulary cards.

- Encourage them to use these cards, with others they have created, to prepare for chapter and unit reviews.

Have the children turn to page 308 in the Our Catholic Tradition section of the Student Book. Read aloud the last part of the creed, emphasizing our belief in "the resurrection of the body and life everlasting."

Our Future

What does the Church teach about life after death?

We look forward to a reunion with God. The Church looks beyond death to the coming of God's Kingdom in its fullness.

When we die we will be judged on our faith and works. This is called the Particular Judgment. God decides where each person will spend eternity: **Heaven**, **Hell**, or **Purgatory**. At the end of time, all people will be judged, as Jesus said. Those who have loved God and die in his friendship will live with him forever in Heaven.

As you look forward to good times on Earth, you can also look forward to Christ's Second Coming and the **Last Judgment** at the end of time. Catholics live in hope that God's grace and our loving actions will lead to everlasting life with God. Our trust in God gives us hope that we will be reunited with our loved ones.

Catholic Faith Words

Heaven the full joy of living with God forever

Hell being separated from God forever because of a choice to turn away from him and not seek forgiveness

Purgatory a state of final cleansing after death and before entering into Heaven

Last Judgment God's final triumph over evil that will occur at the end of time, when Christ returns and judges all the living and the dead

© Our Sunday Visitor

280

ⓘ Catechist Background

Second Coming

Parousia is a Greek word meaning "presence" or "arrival." In the New Testament, this word is used to describe the expectation that Christians have for the return of Christ in glory. Explain to the children the following:

- Christ's return will complete salvation history and will definitively establish God's Kingdom on Earth.

- In Matthew 24:36, Jesus says that no one but the Father knows exactly when the Second Coming will occur.

The Beginning and the End

The Bible begins and ends with stories of creation. In the Book of Genesis, the first book of the Bible, you read how God created all things out of love. The last book, the Book of Revelation, ends with John's vision of a new creation. This is God's everlasting Kingdom. The world and the Church will then be perfect. All faithful people will be raised to new life.

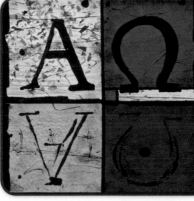

The Son of God, the Word of God, was present at the creation, and he will be present at the end of time. In John's vision, Jesus Christ says,

"I am the Alpha and the Omega, the first and the last, the beginning and the end." **Revelation 22:13**

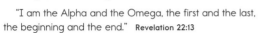

Write a Message Write a message to share with those who do not know God's love.

_____

_____

_____

_____

Optional Activity

Activity Master 21: Code Breaker

Distribute copies of the activity found on catechist page 277E.

- This activity will help the children review chapter content.
- As an alternative, you may wish to send this activity home with the children.

The Beginning and the End

Read aloud these paragraphs.

- Remind the children that as followers of Jesus, they can look forward to a reunion with God. The Catholic Church looks forward to the time when the Reign of God will come in fullness.
- Invite the children to explain in their own words what the Scripture passage on the Alpha and the Omega means.

Activity

Read aloud the directions for the Connect Your Faith activity.

- Have the children work in groups of three or four to create the message.
- They will then return to their seats to write out the message in a decorative way or in their very best handwriting.
- Invite volunteers to share their message and their designs.

Quick Review

In Particular Judgment, God will judge us individually and determine where we will spend eternity. The Last Judgment is God's final triumph over evil, when Christ will come again and bring the Kingdom of God to its fullness.

Our Catholic Life

Ask a volunteer to read aloud the question.

- Invite the children to respond.
- Write the children's responses on the board or on chart paper.
- Explain that comforting a person shows that you share his or her feelings of grief usually because someone the person cared about has died.

Read aloud the two paragraphs.

Ways to Comfort

Read and briefly explain the different ways of comforting others.

 Have the children write one more way to comfort someone.

- Invite volunteers to share their responses.

 Music Option: Sing with the children "The King of Love, My Shepherd Is," downloaded from **aliveinchrist.osv.com**.

Our Catholic Life

How do you give comfort to others?

Even though there is life after death, people are usually sad when someone dies. The friends and family members of the person who has died are sad because they cannot see and talk with the person anymore. They know that it could be a long time before they meet their loved one in Heaven.

The Church asks you to find ways to comfort people who are sad because of a death.

 Write one more way you can comfort someone.

Ways to Comfort

- Find ways to make their lives easier. Take them food, or help with chores around their homes.
- Visit the funeral home with your family, or go to the funeral.
- Talk about the person who died, telling why that person was special.
- Say that you are sorry about the death.
- _____

_____

282 Chapter 21

✓ Quick Tip

Be Mindful of Losses

Before presenting this lesson, recall or determine whether any children in the group have experienced the death of a loved one. Adjust the lesson accordingly.

- Avoid asking such a child pointed questions, but do affirm appropriate comments.
- If someone you love has died, use the insights you gained through that experience to respond to the children's questions.

People of Faith

Saint Joseph, first century

March 19

Saint Joseph was Mary's husband and the foster father of Jesus on Earth. When Jesus was a baby, Joseph took Jesus and Mary to Egypt to protect them from King Herod who wanted to kill Jesus. When Jesus was lost in the Temple at age 12, Joseph helped Mary look for Jesus. He was a carpenter and taught Jesus how to build things. We don't know how he died, but we believe that Mary and Jesus were with him. Today, we pray to Saint Joseph for a happy and peaceful death.

Discuss: Who do you know in your family who has died?

 Learn more about Saint Joseph at **aliveinchrist.osv.com**

Live Your Faith

Make a Card Use this space to design a sympathy card for someone who has recently lost a loved one. Decorate it with flowers or trees to represent new life. Include drawings, verses of Scripture, or a prayer.

Catholic Social Teaching

Chapter Connections

To integrate Catholic Social Teaching into your lesson, choose one of the following features: Life and Dignity, pages 290–291; or Rights and Responsibilities, pages 294–295.

- Start the Live step of the process by talking about Saint Joseph on page 283. The move directly to the Catholic Social Teaching feature.
- Or, to expand the lesson, complete both pages 282 and 283, then move to the Catholic Social Teaching feature.
- Return to Chapter 21 for the prayer on page 284.

People of Faith

Tell the children about Saint Joseph.

- It is probably at Nazareth that Joseph betrothed and married Mary who was to become the Mother of God.
- The angel of the Lord appeared to Joseph in his sleep, guiding Joseph to make decisions.
- Joseph was a humble Jew, supporting himself and his family by his work, and faithful to the religious practices commanded by the Law or observed by pious Israelites.
- Read aloud the paragraph on Saint Joseph.
- Approach the question carefully, being especially aware of any recent losses.

> Encourage the children to go to **aliveinchrist.osv.com** at home to learn more about Saint Joseph.

Activity

Ask a volunteer to read aloud the directions for the Live Your Faith activity.

- Provide the children with colored pencils or markers.
- Allow time for the children to draw and come up with a message.
- Invite volunteers to share their work.

Live

Live

 Let Us Pray

Prayer for the Kingdom

Explain that this prayer is for the coming of the Kingdom of God here on Earth as it is in Heaven.

Prepare

Choose three readers and allow them to practice their parts.

- You will be the leader.

 Rehearse with the children "Seek Ye First," downloaded from **aliveinchrist.osv.com**.

Gather

Invite the children to bring their books and gather in the prayer space.

Pray

Follow the order of prayer on the student page.

- Recall some favorite moments from the year, and invite members of the group to do the same.

 Conclude by processing around the room with the children singing "Seek Ye First."

Alternate Music Option: "Now Thank We All Our God"

 Let Us Pray

Prayer for the Kingdom

Gather and begin with the Sign of the Cross.

Leader: We gather and share a prayer for the coming of the Kingdom.

Reader 1: God, we have learned so much about you this year.

Reader 2: We have taught one another about your love.

Reader 3: Help us learn even more about you in school, at home, and at play.

Reader 1: Help us grow to be more caring people, who will show your love to all who know us.

Reader 2: When our earthly lives end, judge us by our loving deeds.

Reader 3: We hope to join your Saints and rejoice in your presence forever.

All: Come, Lord Jesus! Amen.

Sing "Seek Ye First"

284 Chapter 21

 Liturgy Link

Closing Prayer

Because this may be the last prayer service for meetings with this group, make it especially memorable.

- If you have saved any group projects, place them in the prayer center. You could also print out a list of the activities on chart paper.

- Prepare your highlights of the year and hopes for the group so that you will be ready to share them.

Go to **aliveinchrist.osv.com** for Sunday readings, Scripture background, questions of the week, and seasonal resources.

YOUR CHILD LEARNED >>>

This chapter identifies the Last Judgment as God's final triumph over evil, when Christ will come again and bring the Kingdom of God to its fullness.

God's Word

 Read **1 John 5:11–12** to learn about the promise of eternal life that God shared with John.

Catholics Believe

- People who die in God's friendship will live forever in his presence.
- At the end of the world, Christ will judge all people on the way they lived their lives.

To learn more, go to the *Catechism of the Catholic Church* #1023–1029, 1039 at **usccb.org**.

People of Faith

This week, your child met Saint Joseph, the husband of Mary, and patron of happy and peaceful death.

CHILDREN AT THIS AGE >>>

How They Understand Life after Death One of the most common and intense fears of children in third grade (although it is usually unspoken) is that someone close to them, especially a parent, will die. Having an opportunity to talk about death and to learn about what we as Catholics believe about our hope for the future can be comforting for children this age. It also allows them to express their individual thoughts, questions, and fears.

CONSIDER THIS >>>

Do you think your child is a work in progress?

As human beings we grow emotionally, physically, and intellectually. We are also called to grow spiritually. We are moving ever toward the fullness of life God offers us in Heaven. "The Christian family forms an environment within which faith is professed and witnessed. When family members pray together, engage in lifelong learning, forgive one another, serve each other, welcome others, affirm and celebrate life, and bring justice and mercy to the community, they help each other live the faith and grow in faith" (*USCCA, p. 376*).

LET'S TALK >>>

- Talk about a time when you have needed comfort and the things others did to comfort you.
- Ask your child to name some reasons why Catholics look forward to the Second Coming of Christ.

LET'S PRAY >>>

Saint Joseph, protect us as we live and watch over us at the end of our lives. Amen.

For a multimedia glossary of Catholic Faith Words, Sunday readings, seasonal and Saint resources, and chapter activities go to **aliveinchrist.osv.com**.

Alive in Christ, Grade 3 Chapter 21 **285**

Distribute the page to the children or parents/adult family members. Point out the chapter highlights, insights on how third graders understand concepts, the opportunity for the adults to reflect on their own experience and faith journey, and the family prayer.

Chapter 21 Review

Chapter Review

A **Work with Words** Complete each sentence with the correct word or words from the Word Bank.

Word Bank
- Heaven
- Hell
- death
- Last Judgment
- Purgatory

1. Our earthly life will end in _____**death**_____.

2. _____**Heaven**_____ is being with God forever.

3. A state of final cleansing is called _____**Purgatory**_____.

4. Separation from God forever is called _____**Hell**_____.

5. God's final triumph over evil, when Christ will come again and bring the Kingdom of God to its fullness is called _____**Last Judgment**_____.

B **Check Understanding** Fill in the circle beside the correct answer.

6. You can comfort someone who has lost someone by ____.
   ○ ignoring them   ○ telling jokes   ● going to the funeral

7. The ____ is the Catholic belief that Jesus will come again.
   ○ Holy Trinity   ● Second Coming   ○ Lord's Prayer

8. Catholics look forward to ____ in God's Kingdom.
   ● new life   ○ big parties   ○ eternal separation

9. God's grace and people's ____ will lead to everlasting life with God.
   ○ families   ● loving actions   ○ good grades

10. John's vision of the end of time is called the Book of ____.
    ○ Mystery   ○ Praise   ● Revelation

Go to **aliveinchrist.osv.com** for an interactive review.

286 Chapter 21 Review

Use Catechist Quick Reviews to highlight lesson concepts.

A **Work with Words**
Have the children complete each sentence with the correct word or words from the Word Bank.

B **Check Understanding**
Explain to the children that they will be filling in the circle of the correct answer.

Go to **aliveinchrist.osv.com** to prepare customized and downloadable assessments, send eAssessments, and assign interactive reviews.

Everlasting Life **285–286**

Unit Review

Use Catechist Quick Reviews in each chapter to highlight lesson concepts for this unit and prepare for the Unit Review.

Have the children complete the Review pages. Then discuss the answers as a group. Review any concepts with which the children are having difficulty.

A Work with Words

Direct the children to fill in the circle beside the correct answer for problems 1–5. For 6–10, have them determine whether each sentence is true or false.

A Work with Words Fill in the circle beside the correct answer.

1. A _____ is a sacred promise between God and humans.
   ○ vow   ● covenant   ○ commitment

2. _____ is the state of cleansing before Heaven.
   ○ Purification   ○ Hell   ● Purgatory

3. _____ is being separated from God forever.
   ○ Purgatory   ● Hell   ○ Darkness

4. _____ is the virtue that moves people to give God and their neighbors what is their due.
   ○ Peace   ○ Charity   ● Justice

5. _____ is the full joy of living with God forever.
   ○ Peace   ○ Justice   ● Heaven

Write the letter T if the sentence is TRUE. Write the letter F if the statement is FALSE.

6. [F] Isaac made a covenant with God.

7. [T] The work of the Church is to worship God, help others know about the Holy Trinity, and work for peace and justice.

8. [F] Giving witness means that we sit by and watch what others do to build the Kingdom and do nothing ourselves.

9. [T] John had a vision of a new Heaven and Earth.

10. [T] All faithful people will be raised to new life with God in Heaven.

Kingdom of God **287**

B Check Understanding Circle the correct word to complete each sentence.

11. Early Christians remained _____ to God even when they were being persecuted.

   (faithful)   fearful

12. Jesus and his early followers were _____.

   Catholic   (Jewish)

13. God remained loyal to his covenant with the people of _____.

   Egypt   (Israel)

14. Purgatory is a state of final _____ before entering Heaven.

   judgment   (cleansing)

15. Basic human rights are food, clothing, shelter, and _____.

   money   (dignity)

C Make Connections Complete each sentence with the correct word or words from the Word Bank.

> **Word Bank**
> • • • • • • • • • • •
> Last Judgment
> Israel
> witness
> death
> peace

16. Abraham's family grew to become the people

   of _____**Israel**_____.

17. To show by words or actions is to

   _____**witness**_____.

18. _____**Peace**_____ makes people want to respect one another.

19. Our earthly lives will end in _____**death**_____.

20. At the **Last Judgment**, Christ will come again and bring the Kingdom of God to its fullness.

Write a response to each question or statement on the lines below.

21. How have you been a peacemaker?

   Responses will vary.

22. Give an example of a way that you could show solidarity.

   Responses will vary.

23. What does everlasting life mean?

   Responses will vary.

24. What are you doing to prepare for the coming of God's Kingdom?

   Responses will vary.

25. How can you help keep the Church alive and growing?

   Responses will vary.

B Check Understanding
Direct the children to circle the correct word to complete each sentence.

C Make Connections
Tell the children to complete each sentence with the correct word or words from the Word Bank from problems 16–20. Then have them write a response to each question or statement for 21–25.

Go to **aliveinchrist.osv.com** to prepare customized and downloadable assessments, send eAssessments, and assign interactive reviews.

Live Your Faith
&
Our Catholic Tradition
Reference Section

Live Your Faith

" Let us keep a place for Christ in our lives, let us care for one another and let us be loving custodians of creation. "

—Pope Francis via Twitter, March 19, 2013

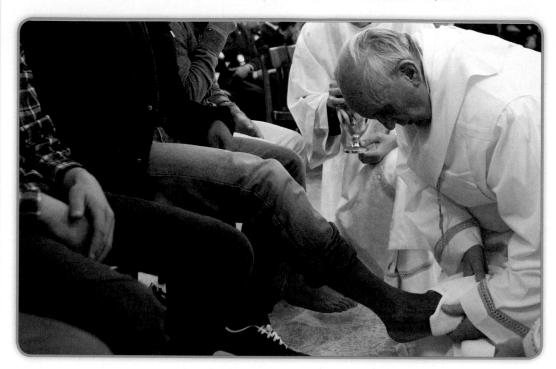

The Seven Themes of Catholic Social Teaching

The Catholic Church's Social Teaching helps build a just society and shows how to live lives of holiness amidst the challenges of modern society. The wisdom of this tradition can be understood best through a direct reading of Church documents, but here is a synopsis of each of the seven key themes that are part of our Catholic Social Tradition.

Life and Dignity of the Human Person

Each person is created in God's image and all people have rights that flow from their human dignity. The equal dignity of all people means we must work to eliminate social and economic inequalities. We strive to value all people over our personal wealth or possessions.

Call to Family, Community, and Participation

In order for our society to be healthy, we must all make positive contributions to it, bringing to it the light of the Gospels. We can do this by finding practical ways to participate more fully in our own families, in our parishes, and in our communities.

Rights and Responsibilities

Every person has a right to life and the rights needed to live in dignity. The fundamental rights of all people are freedom, justice, and the basic necessities of everyday life. As individuals and as a society, we must work to protect these rights for all people.

Option for the Poor and Vulnerable

God loves all people, and he calls us to love one another as he loves us. In a world where many people live in great poverty while others enjoy great wealth, we must pay special attention to the needs of the poor and reach out to them in Christian charity.

The Dignity of Work and the Rights of Workers

Through labor all people participate in the work of creation and all workers have the following rights that must be protected: the right to productive work, to fair wages, and to pursue economic opportunity. Catholics believe that our work can be a valuable way to serve God and others.

Solidarity

All people—rich and poor, young and old, weak and strong—have equal dignity and rights that flow from that dignity. As part of one human family, we are all dependent on one another and responsible for one another, and must work to reduce social inequalities and provide for one another's needs.

Care for God's Creation

God is the Creator of all people and all that exists in nature. He has given us the bounty of the Earth and its resources and has entrusted us with its care. We are called to respond by protecting and caring for all God's creation for generations to come.

 Go to **aliveinchrist.osv.com** for a complete listing of chapters and Church year lessons correlated to the themes of Catholic Social Teaching.

About This Principle This section presents an overview of the theological foundation of the theme so that catechists have background information at point of use.

Wrap Instruction An easy to follow side column provides catechists with directions and activities for presenting the Catholic Social Teaching in developmentally appropriate ways.

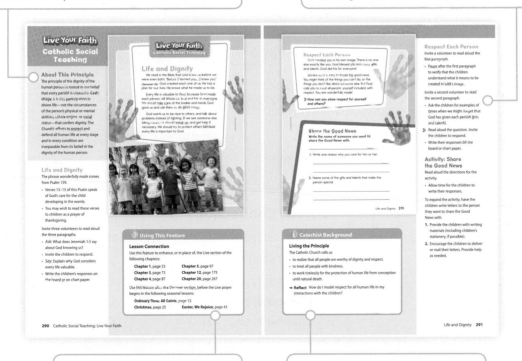

Using This Feature This box identifies core chapters and seasonal lessons to which the Live Your Faith feature is connected.

Living This Principle This box identifies ways the Church calls us to practice the principle and includes a question for catechist reflection.

About This Principle

This principle focuses on the equality of every person before God. Today some value systems prejudice people against anyone with physical or mental disabilities or anyone who is financially disadvantaged. Many people think that to have more is to be more. God has created every human being with dignity and equality, and yet millions of the world's citizens live in hopeless poverty. As Catholics, we must work to bring about societal changes to ensure that everyone is treated with dignity and respect because all are children of God.

Life and Dignity

Introduce the topic. See pages CE52–CE53 for more information on all seven Catholic Social Teaching principles.

Have a volunteer read the first paragraph, and another find Jeremiah 1:5 in the Bible and read it.

- *Ask:* What does the Jeremiah 1:5 Scripture passage say about God's plans for us? God knows the plans he has for us before we are born.
- Invite the children to respond.

Read aloud the next two paragraphs.

- *Ask:* What does God want us to do when we disagree with others?
- Invite the children to discuss.

Live Your Faith
Catholic Social Teaching

Life and Dignity

We read in the Bible that God knew us before we were even born: "Before I formed you...I knew you" **(Jeremiah 1:5)**. God created each one of us. He has a plan for our lives. He knows what he made us to be.

Every life is valuable to God. Because God made each person, we should be kind and fair to everyone. We should take care of the bodies and minds God gave us and use them to do good things.

God wants us to be nice to others, and talk about problems instead of fighting. If we see someone else being mean, we should speak up, and get help if necessary. We should help to protect others because every life is important to God.

God wants you to treat each other with respect, even when you are upset.

© Our Sunday Visitor

 Using This Feature

Lesson Connection

Use this feature to enhance, or in place of, the Live section of the following chapters:

Chapter 1, page 53   **Chapter 13,** page 189

Chapter 3, page 73   **Chapter 16,** page 223

Chapter 6, page 107   **Chapter 21,** page 277

Use this feature after the Discover section, before the Live Prayer begins in the following seasonal lessons:

All Saints, page 9   **Easter,** page 39

Christmas, page 23

Respect All People

At times, you might be tempted to think that people's value comes from how much money they have or the nice clothes they wear. When you think that, you are seeing as the world sees. God calls you to see as he sees!

When you see as God sees, you know that every human is a beloved child of God. Even when a person's actions make it hard to see God's goodness in him or her, that person is still created in God's image and is loved by God. Every Catholic is called by faith to respect all persons and to see the value in their lives.

≫ **How can you treat everyone you meet with dignity and respect?**

Share Life and Respect

God wants you to treat everyone fairly and with respect. He also wants all people to live happy, healthy lives. Place a heart next to the things that are needed for life. Place a star next to things you can do to show respect for other people.

Life	Respect
☐ lots of candy and treats	☐ ignore people you don't like
☐ warm clothing	☐ be friendly and polite
☐ good health	☐ share what you have
☐ a swimming pool	☐ laugh at people who are different

Life and Dignity **291**

Catechist Background

Living the Principle

The Catholic Church calls us

- to respect the dignity of each individual as a person created in God's image.
- to work to ensure that everyone has the basic necessities of life.
- to find ways to eliminate systems that oppress people.

➜ **Reflect** What is my personal value system?

Respect All People

Invite a volunteer to read aloud the first paragraph.

- Pause to be sure the children understand what it means to see as God sees.

Invite a volunteer to read the second paragraph.

- Ask the children for examples of times when we forget that God has given each person value.
- Explain that we are not seeing as God sees when we disrespect a child of God.

≫ Read aloud the question.

- Invite the children to respond.

Activity: Share Life and Respect

Read aloud the directions for the activity.

- Allow time for the children to mark the items.

To expand the activity, work together as a group to prepare bags of healthful snacks and personal hygiene articles to donate to a local shelter.

1. Assign tasks to individuals or teams.
2. Set up a time and place for the bags to be assembled.
3. Arrange for bags to be distributed.

Live Your Faith
Catholic Social Teaching

About This Principle

This principle calls us to honor family as the first and most important community to which we belong. God created families so that humans could support and sustain one another. Family members work together to help one another. Today, however, many families are in crisis. Families are scattered; other pursuits intrude on family time. Commitment to family first is rare. Catholics are called to witness to the substance and nature that God intended families to have.

Call to Community

Introduce the topic. See pages CE52–CE53 for more information on all seven Catholic Social Teaching principles.

Ask the children to describe what they see in the photo and how they think it relates to the theme.

Invite two volunteers to read aloud the paragraphs.

- *Ask:* Why does God give us families? Because God knows it would not be good for us to be alone; to help us learn who he is and how to love one another
- Invite the children to respond.
- *Ask:* How does our parish community help us learn about God?
- Discuss responses with the children.

Live Your Faith
Catholic Social Teaching

Call to Community

God gives us families and communities because he knows it would not be good for us to live our lives alone. In fact, the Bible says that this is why God created Eve to be a companion and friend to Adam, the first human being. (See Genesis 2:18.)

The Church teaches that God gives us families to help us learn who God is and how to love one another. Our parish community also helps us to learn about God. In families and in parish communities, we work together to take care of one another and to become the people God made us to be.

 ### Using This Feature

Lesson Connection

Use this feature to enhance, or in place of, the Live section of the following chapters:

Chapter 2, page 63   **Chapter 5**, page 97

Chapter 3, page 73   **Chapter 9**, page 141

Chapter 4, page 87   **Chapter 11**, page 165

Use this feature after the Discover section, before the Live Prayer begins in the following seasonal lessons:

Advent, page 15   **Pentecost**, page 45

Holy Week, page 35

Live in Community

The one God in three Divine Persons (God the Father, God the Son, and God the Holy Spirit) is a communion of Divine love. God made humans to live in community. To teach people how to live in their first community—the family—God sent his own Son to live in a family with Mary and Joseph.

Catholics are called by their faith to participate in family life. Each time a family member acts with love, the family grows stronger. Each time a person shares in community life, the community grows stronger.

≫ **How can you help your family and your community grow stronger?**

Improve Your Community

What would make a stronger, better community? Does your playground need cleaning? Does anyone need help with homework? Or maybe your school needs a new computer. As a group decide on one item or service that would help, and plan to make it a reality.

_____

_____

_____

_____

Call to Community **293**

ⓘ Catechist Background

Living the Principle

The Catholic Church calls us

- to recognize that the family God created is an image of the communion of persons found in the Holy Trinity.
- to respect the family as the most basic Christian community: the domestic Church.
- to act with a consciousness of Christ's presence in our family lives.

→ **Reflect** How present am I to my family?

Live in Community

Invite volunteers to read the paragraphs.

- Ask the children why the Holy Trinity is called a communion of love.
- Recall stories of the Holy Family.
- *Ask:* How is the Holy Family an example of family and community?

≫ Read aloud the question.

- Write the children's responses on the board or on chart paper.

Activity: Improve Your Community

Invite a volunteer to read aloud the directions for the activity.

- Allow the children to work in pairs to brainstorm ideas.
- Encourage the pairs to share their list with the group.
- Have the children vote on one item or service.

To expand the activity, encourage the children to enlist the help and involvement of others outside the group to implement a service the group decided on.

1. Send an announcement to to families and other community members.
2. Schedule a community work day.

Live Your Faith
Catholic Social Teaching

About This Principle

This principle of human rights is at the heart of Catholics' identity as children of God. Human rights are not given by governments, nor are they conditions of birth. Rather, these rights are God-given and are shared by all people of all times and places. The Catholic tradition teaches that human dignity can be protected and a healthy community can be achieved only if human rights are protected and responsibilities are met.

Rights and Responsibilities

Introduce the topic. See pages CE52–CE53 for more information on all seven Catholic Social Teaching principles.

Invite a strong reader to read aloud both paragraphs.

- *Ask:* What is the difference between a right and a responsibility? Rights are the freedoms or things every person needs and should have. Responsibilities are our duties, or the things we must do.

- Invite the children to share their thoughts.

Direct the children's attention to the photo. Ask them to explain how the people in the photo are protecting human rights.

Live Your Faith
Catholic Social Teaching

Rights and Responsibilities

Because God made every person, everyone has rights and responsibilities. Rights are the freedoms or things every person needs and should have. Responsibilities are our duties, or the things we must do.

Jesus said, "You shall love your neighbor as yourself" **(Mark 12:31)**. Following this command means making sure everyone's rights are protected. We also have a responsibility to treat others well and work together for the good of everyone.

294   Faith in Action

🌐 Using This Feature

Lesson Connection

Use this feature to enhance, or in place of, the Live section of the following chapters:

Chapter 5, page 97   **Chapter 17**, page 233

Chapter 7, page 121   **Chapter 19**, page 257

Chapter 14, page 199   **Chapter 20**, page 267

Chapter 15, page 209   **Chapter 21**, page 277

Use this feature after the Discover section, before the Live Prayer begins in the following seasonal lesson:

Lent, page 29

Basic Rights

Every person has human rights. These are the basic things that people need to live happy, healthy lives according to God's plan. All people should have a safe place to live, clean water, and enough food. All people should be treated fairly.

As followers of Jesus, Christians have a special responsibility. One of the most important jobs is helping when someone's human rights have been taken away. When Catholics help protect the rights of others, they are doing the work of Jesus.

> **Why are Christians responsible for the human rights of others?**

Show That You Are Jesus' Friend

Jesus showed you how to care for others. When you live as Jesus lived, you are acting with justice, forgiveness, and love. Draw one way you can act with love so that people know you are a friend of Jesus.

Basic Rights

Be sensitive to the range of economic and social circumstances represented in your class.

- Make sure not to ask the children to disclose personal information about their family circumstances.
- Read aloud the paragraphs.

> Ask a volunteer to read aloud the question.

- Invite the children to respond.

Activity: Show That You Are Jesus' Friend

Read aloud the introduction.

- Give the children enough time to draw their responses.
- Invite volunteers to share their drawings with the group.

To expand the activity, arrange the children in three groups and encourage them to put on a skit.

1. Assign each group to portray justice, forgiveness, or love.
2. Ask each group to act out a scene portraying their topic.
3. Give the children time to practice and then perform their skits.

(i) Catechist Background

Living the Principle

The Catholic Church calls us

- to know that every person has a fundamental right to life and to all that is required to live in human decency.
- to recognize that human dignity demands that human rights be protected.
- to understand that Catholics have a responsibility to protect the rights of everyone.

→ **Reflect** What have you done to help those whose human rights are being denied?

Live Your Faith
Catholic Social Teaching

About This Principle

This principle reminds us of our obligation as Christians to reach out to those living in poverty and those who cannot defend themselves. These are the people who are ignored or taken advantage of by society. Yet, those who are poor and vulnerable are the very people to whom Christ asks us to reach out in love.

Option for the Poor

Introduce the topic. See pages CE52–CE53 for more information on all seven Catholic Social Teaching principles.

Read aloud both paragraphs.

Ask: What does Jesus say about how we should treat those who are poor? We should treat people the way we would treat him.

- Invite the children to respond.
- Point out that Jesus is in everyone's heart, so when you treat others with kindness, you are treating Jesus with kindness as well.

Direct the children's attention to the photo and ask a volunteer to read the caption.

- See if the children can name some potential places their families could volunteer.

Live Your Faith
Catholic Social Teaching

Option for the Poor

In Scripture, Jesus says that whatever we have done for people who are poor or needy, we have also done for him. (See Matthew 25:40.) We should treat people the same way we would treat Jesus himself. When people need food, drink, clothing, housing, or medical care, or when they are lonely, we should try extra hard to help.

Saint Rose of Lima said, "When we serve the poor and the sick, we serve Jesus." Our Church teaches that we should have special love and care for those who are poor and put their needs first. When we do this, God will bless us.

One way we can give our time to help others is to volunteer for an organization that helps those in need.

© Our Sunday Visitor

296 Faith in Action

🌐 Using This Feature

Lesson Connection

Use this feature to enhance, or in place of, the Live section of the following chapters:

Chapter 9, page 141   **Chapter 13**, page 189
Chapter 12, page 175

Use this feature after the Discover section, before the Live Prayer begins in the following seasonal lessons:

Our Lady of Guadalupe, page 19   **Pentecost**, page 45

The Needs of Others

Jesus' actions showed that he loved and cared for people who were poor, sick, or lonely. Your mission is to help others by imitating his loving actions. But who needs your help most? Like Jesus, you are called to help those who are poor and in need.

The Catholic Church teaches its members to be responsible for everyone in need, especially those who are poor. Organized groups, such as the St. Vincent de Paul Society, care for the needs of those who are poor. Individual Catholics give money, volunteer their time, and pray for those in need.

≫ **What Church groups do you know about that serve those who are poor in your area?**

Saint Vincent de Paul

Start Helping

Make a list of those who need your help the most. Write one thing you can do to help.

1. _____

2. _____

3. _____

I can help by _____

_____

ⓘ Catechist Background

Living the Principle

The Catholic Church calls us

- to realize that love of neighbor is inseparable from love of God.
- to understand that justice in each society is dependent upon our respecting the God-given dignity of all people.
- to work for change in societal structures that oppress those who are poor and vulnerable.

→ **Reflect** Do I show compassion and caring for the poor, or do I turn away?

The Needs of Others

Invite a volunteer to read aloud the first paragraph.

- Discuss what it means to help those who are in need. Ask the children whether many people do this.

Invite another volunteer to read aloud the second paragraph.

- Discuss why and how Christians are responsible for everyone in need, especially the poor.

≫ Read aloud the question.

- List all responses on the board or on chart paper.

Activity: Start Helping

Read aloud the directions for the activity.

- Allow time for the children to discuss with a partner and write down a plan.
- Encourage the pairs to share their plans with the group.

To expand the activity, encourage the children to write letters encouraging others to reach out to help those in need in your community.

1. Let them select from writing to the editor of the local newspaper or an elected official.
2. Provide stationery and envelopes.
3. Help the children, as needed, with the wording of their letters.
4. Encourage them to mail the letters.

Live Your Faith
Catholic Social Teaching

About This Principle
The Church believes that work should be meaningful and it should affirm the dignity of the worker. Through work we are able to provide the necessities of life for ourselves and for our families. It is a way to contribute our gifts and talents and cooperate with all of God's creation. All workers have the right to a just wage, to work in safe conditions, and to be treated with respect.

The Dignity of Work
Introduce the topic. See pages CE52–CE53 for more information on all seven Catholic Social Teaching principles.

Have the children name people who help in school, in the city, in stores, and in neighborhoods.

- Talk about the things these people do and how they make life better for others.

Invite two volunteers to read aloud the paragraphs.

- Explain to the children that work is one of the ways we can cooperate with God's plan.
- Point out that when we love and serve others, we are doing the most important work of the Church.

Live Your Faith
Catholic Social Teaching

The Dignity of Work
The different jobs people have help them earn money to buy food and other things they need to live. Jobs also allow people to work together with God and his creation. Work is part of God's plan for people, and everyone should work, either in the home or in a job outside the home.

All adults should be able to have a job if they want one. Scripture teaches that workers should be treated fairly by their bosses. (See Deuteronomy 24:14.) They should be given fair pay for their work. (See Leviticus 19:13; and Deuteronomy 24:15.) If workers are unhappy, they should be able to talk about this and work things out together with their bosses.

298 Live Your Faith

 ### Using This Feature

Lesson Connection
Use this feature to enhance, or in place of, the Live section of the following chapters:

Chapter 10, page 155   **Chapter 17**, page 233
Chapter 12, page 175   **Chapter 20**, page 267
Chapter 15, page 209

Use this feature after the Discover section, before the Live Prayer begins in the following seasonal lessons:

Our Lady of Guadalupe, page 19
Holy Week, page 35

Rights of Workers

Work is not just a way to make money. Through work each day, humans join in God's work of creation. All work and all workers have dignity and value.

Workers are not always treated with the dignity and respect they deserve. Some workers earn too little pay and work too many hours. Others work in places that have unsafe conditions.

The Catholic Church wants all workers to be treated with respect and dignity. All workers must earn enough money to take care of their families. All workers should be able to work in safe places.

≫ How can you appreciate the work your family does?

Value Your Own Work

Use the chart below to track how you value yourself as a worker and the work you do. In each space, write at least one way you brought dignity to the work you do in your daily life.

The Dignity of Work		
At Home	At School	With Others

The Dignity of Work **299**

(i) Catechist Background

Living the Principle

The Catholic Church calls us

- to appreciate work as a right of all people.
- to honor work as a cooperation with God's creation.
- to protect the basic rights of workers.

→ **Reflect** Do I purchase products made or harvested by people whose rights are being exploited?

Rights of Workers

Ask three volunteers to each read aloud one of the paragraphs.

- Have the children pause after each paragraph to invite questions and comments.

≫ Read aloud the question.

- Invite the children to respond.

Point out the safety sign on the page.

- *Ask:* Why is safety important to our dignity and why is it one of our rights to work in a safe environment? Possible response: If we don't work in a safe environment, we could get hurt or accidentally hurt others. This could create a lot of medical bills and cause us to be unable to work.

Activity: Value Your Own Work

Read aloud the directions.

- Have the children work individually to complete the chart.
- Invite volunteers to share their responses.

To expand the activity, encourage the children to pray about ways they can improve in bringing dignity to the work they do.

1. Lead the group in prayer.
2. Pause after mentioning each of the three areas from the activity above for the children to silently add their personal prayers.

About This Principle

This principle reminds us that we are all joined in one human family. As both Catholics and as citizens of the world, we have a responsibility to work with God to bring about peace and justice in the world. We cannot live in isolation from others, for we are interdependent on one another. Communication in the twenty-first century has made us more of a global community than ever before. This makes it possible for us to work with others throughout the world in new ways, to ensure that people everywhere can live in peace with justice.

Solidarity of the Human Family

Introduce the topic. See pages CE52–CE53 for more information on all seven Catholic Social Teaching principles.

Ask the children to describe what they see in the photo and how it relates to this theme.

Read aloud the text.

- *Ask:* What does the Scripture quote from Matthew 5:9 mean? Peacemakers are blessed because treating others fairly helps us all live in peace.

- Remind the children that people around the world are different, but we are all made by God.

Live Your Faith
Catholic Social Teaching

Human Solidarity

People around the world are different in many ways. Our hair, eyes, and skin are many different colors. There are people who are rich, people who are poor, and people who are in-between. People believe many different things about how we should live.

But one way we are all alike is that God made us. We are one human family. (See Galatians 3:28.) God calls everyone to be his children. Because God made everyone, we should treat everyone with love, kindness, and fairness. In the Beatitudes, Jesus says, "Blessed are the peacemakers" (Matthew 5:9). Treating others fairly will help us to live in peace with one another.

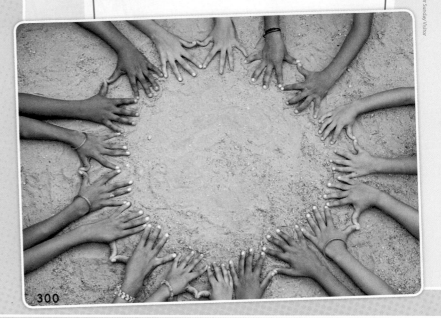

300

© Our Sunday Visitor

🌐 Using This Feature

Lesson Connection

Use this feature to enhance, or in place of, the Live section of the following chapters:

Chapter 2, page 63   **Chapter 8**, page 131
Chapter 4, page 87   **Chapter 18,** page 243
Chapter 6, page 107   **Chapter 19,** page 257

Use this feature after the Discover section, before the Live Prayer begins in the following seasonal lessons:

All Saints, page 9   **Easter,** page 39
Lent, page 29

The Human Family

About seven billion people live on Earth today. All of those people are brothers and sisters in the family of God. When your brothers and sisters on Earth have troubles, you should find ways to help them. Taking care of others in the world shows solidarity, which means friendship and unity with everyone God created.

You show solidarity when you help bring peace to others. Sometimes you work for peace in your own family and neighborhood. Sometimes you need to help people who live far away. Wherever help is needed, Jesus calls his followers to bring his peace.

≫ **How can you be a person of peace every day?**

Discover the World

You can learn about people around the world by reading books that share information on people and life in other places. Discover the names and authors of three such books and write them here.

_____

_____

_____

Combine your list with those of your classmates to make a Friends Around the World reading list. Read at least a few of these books during the school year or over the summer.

Solidarity **301**

ⓘ Catechist Background

Living the Principle

The Catholic Church calls us

- to recognize that as members of the universal Church, we are one with the world.
- to understand that peacemaking is an essential dimension of our faith.
- to foster communities in which the virtue of peace can take root and be nourished.

→ **Reflect** How do I bring about peace in my family and in my community?

The Human Family

Invite two volunteers to read aloud the paragraphs.

- *Ask*: How can you show solidarity? by doing what you can to bring peace to your home and neighborhood

≫ Read aloud the question.

- Invite the children to respond.
- Write the children's answers on the board or on chart paper.

Activity: Discover the World

Have the children form small groups.

- Read aloud the directions for the activity.
- Provide the groups with catalogs of books or access to an online bookstore.
- Allow time for groups to complete their research and make their lists. If the children will be working on this at home, have each child in a group bring in one book title and author.

To expand the activity, invite a children's librarian in your community to come in and talk to the group.

1. Contact the librarian and ask him/her to share some stories of children who live in other lands.

2. See if the librarian can bring in photos, books, or videos on other countries that the children can look through.

Live Your Faith
Catholic Social Teaching

About This Principle

God created the world for humans to use and enjoy. But in the twenty-first century, many of Earth's resources are used and, at times, exploited by wealthier countries. As Catholics, we have a responsibility to ensure that the resources of the Earth benefit all people and that these resources are preserved for future generations.

Care for Creation

Introduce the topic. See pages CE52–CE53 for more information on all seven Catholic Social Teaching principles.

Invite two volunteers to read aloud the paragraphs.

- *Ask:* What does Genesis 1:28 say about people and our responsibility to creation? God put people in charge of taking care of all living things.

- Invite the children to discuss.

- Ask the children why we need to protect the gifts of creation that God has given us. Possible response: so these things can still be enjoyed in the future

Point out the photograph on the page. Ask the children how the boy is caring for creation.

- Invite the children to respond.

Live Your Faith
Catholic Social Teaching

Care for Creation

God created the whole world—the Earth and sky, the mountains and deserts, and all of the plants, animals, and people. When God made these things, he called them "very good" (Genesis 1:31). God put people in charge of the "fish of the sea, the birds of the air, and all the living things that crawl on the earth" (Genesis 1:28). God wants us to enjoy and take care of everything he has made.

Our Church teaches us that God gave the plants and animals for the good of all people. We should work to take care of the plants and animals and the places where they live, so everyone can enjoy them now and in the future. We should also be kind to animals, because they are God's creatures.

302 Live Your Faith

Using This Feature

Lesson Connection

Use this feature to enhance, or in place of, the Live section of the following chapters:

Chapter 1, page 53   **Chapter 14**, page 199
Chapter 10, page 155

Use this feature after the Discover section, before the Live Prayer begins in the following seasonal lessons:

Advent, page 15   **Christmas**, page 23

A Good Steward

When you show God that you are grateful for creation, you are being a good steward, or caregiver, of creation. Here are some ways to show you care.

Be grateful for foods that come from the Earth. Apples, berries, corn, and other fruits and vegetables are gifts from the Earth that help keep people healthy. Care for other people. People are the most important part of creation. Use natural resources with care. The water you drink, the air you breathe, and the land used to grow food are needed for all life on Earth. Taking care of them and using them well shows that you are a good steward.

≫ **How do you already care for creation?**

Show Thanks and Care

Draw a thank you card to show God that you are thankful for the wonderful world he created. Include some ways that you will care for God's creation.

 © Our Sunday Visitor

Care for Creation **303**

ⓘ Catechist Background

Living the Principle

The Catholic Church calls us

- to use the resources of the Earth responsibly.
- to ensure that our resources are used for the good of all.
- to make certain that our resources are preserved.

→ **Reflect** How responsibly do I use God's gift of creation?

A Good Steward

Invite a strong reader to read aloud both paragraphs.

- *Ask:* What does it mean to be a steward of creation? to care for the Earth; to take responsibility for it

≫ Read aloud the question.

- Invite the children to respond.
- Write their responses on the board or on chart paper.

Activity: Show Thanks and Care

Ask a volunteer to read aloud the directions for the activity.

- Help the children brainstorm ways they can care for creation.

To expand the activity, invite the children to grow a small plant.

1. Distribute seeds, disposable cups, and potting soil.
2. Have each child write his or her name on the cup, fill it with soil, and plant the seeds.
3. If possible, place all of the containers on a windowsill or near another light source. Water when the soil feels dry.
4. Let the children care for the growing plants when they come for lessons.
5. When the plants are established, allow the children to offer their plants to relatives or neighbors.

The Holy Trinity

There are three Persons in one God—God the Father, God the Son, and God the Holy Spirit. The word for three Persons in one God is Holy Trinity.

God the Father, First Divine Person of the Trinity
We honor God the Father as the creator of all that exists. The Church prays to God the Father. Jesus taught his followers that God was his Father and their Father, too. Jesus said to pray using the words, "Our Father, who art in Heaven."

God the Son, Second Divine Person of the Trinity
We honor Jesus, God the Son, as the Savior of all people. Jesus is God, and he also became human. Jesus is the Messiah, God's chosen one. Messiah is a Hebrew word that means "the anointed one" or "the one chosen by God." Jesus has been given many names and titles that tell something special about him or honor him. These include Christ, Savior, Lord, Lamb of God (Agnus Dei), Son of God, Son of Man, the Word, and the Suffering Servant.

God the Holy Spirit, Third Divine Person of the Trinity
We honor God the Holy Spirit as our Guide and Helper. The Holy Spirit supports and comforts us and helps us live holier lives. He unites the Church and makes her mission possible. The Church uses symbols to describe the Holy Spirit. A dove, a flame, and the wind are all symbols of the Holy Spirit.

The Church

The Church is the community of all baptized people who believe in God and follow Jesus. The word is often used for the Catholic Church because she traces our origins back to the Apostles. The word *church* comes from two different words. One means "a community called together." The other means "belonging to the Lord." The Church is also sometimes called the "People of God."

The Pope, cardinals, bishops and archbishops, pastors, and other priests lead and guide the followers of Christ.

Body of Christ

Another name for the Church is "The Body of Christ." This name shows that you are closely joined with others and with Jesus. Church members work together just as parts of the body work together. The Church's mission is to share with others the Good News of God's Kingdom.

305

Optional Activity

The Holy Spirit

Show the children some liturgical art that depicts the Holy Spirit as a dove, wind, or fire.

- Discuss what those symbols show about the Holy Spirit.
- Then have each child draw and cut out a symbol of the Holy Spirit.
- Take all of their symbols and create a border around a bulletin board or chalk board in your meeting space.

Optional Activity

Body of Christ Mural

Read the description of the Body of Christ on the student page.

- Encourage the children to visualize what the Body of Christ means to them.
- Roll out a large piece of paper and pass out crayons, colored pencils, and markers to the group.
- Have the children choose different spots on the paper to draw the images they see when they think of the Body of Christ.
- If possible, display the mural where others in the parish can enjoy it.

The Communion of Saints

All people living and dead who believe in Jesus and follow his way are part of the Communion of Saints. This includes people now alive on Earth and people who have died and are now in Purgatory or Heaven. People on Earth join in the Communion of Saints when they celebrate the Eucharist.

Life After Death

The Church looks forward to the coming of God's Kingdom. When a Christian dies, he or she looks forward to the promise of life forever with God. After people die, they will be in Heaven, Hell, or Purgatory.

- Heaven is the full joy of living with God forever.

- Hell is being separated from God forever because of a choice to turn away from him and not seek forgiveness.

- Purgatory is a preparation and final cleansing after death and before entering into Heaven. The word Purgatory means "making pure." Purgatory makes a person ready to be with God in Heaven.

Last Judgment

At the end of time, all Christians look forward to a time of happiness and peace. At that time Jesus will come again to judge the living and the dead. Then the Kingdom of God will come in fullness. The Church calls these events the Second coming and the Last Judgment. These are times of hope and joy for Christians. Jesus' followers believe in the promise of God's everlasting Kingdom.

Marks of the Church

There are four Marks of the Church: one, holy, catholic, and apostolic. These essential characteristics identify Christ's Church and her mission.

1. The Church is one because the power of the Holy Spirit unites all of her members through one faith and one Baptism.

2. The Church is holy because she is set apart for God and his purposes. The Church shows God's holiness.

3. The Church is catholic because Jesus sent his followers out to tell the Good News to the whole world. The Church is universal, meant for all people in all times and places.

4. The Church is apostolic because she is built on the faith and leadership of the Apostles. Today the Church teaches directly from what the Apostles taught, and the bishops lead as the successors of the Apostles.

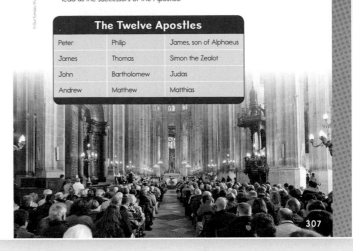

The Twelve Apostles

Peter	Philip	James, son of Alphaeus
James	Thomas	Simon the Zealot
John	Bartholomew	Judas
Andrew	Matthew	Matthias

Optional Activity

Communion of Saints

At each session, talk with the children about the Saints whose feast days are celebrated on the Church's calendar for that day or week.

- Assign each child to a different week. Ask him or her to find a story about a Saint whose feast day is during that week.

- Have the children share their stories with the rest of the group at the designated times.

Optional Activity

Marks of the Church

Distribute Catholic newspapers and parish bulletins, and ask the children to find examples of people who are living out each of the Marks of the Church.

- Make sure that the children have a basic understanding of the meaning of each of the Marks.

- Ask volunteers to share their examples with the rest of the group.

Creeds

The Creed tells the faith of the Church. It brings together the Church's most important beliefs.

Apostles' Creed

This creed gives a summary of the Apostles' beliefs. It is often used at Mass during the season of Easter and in Masses with children. This creed is part of the Rosary.

I believe in God,
the Father almighty,
Creator of heaven and earth,
and in Jesus Christ, his only Son, our Lord.

At the words that follow, up to and including the Virgin Mary, all bow.

who was conceived by the Holy Spirit,
born of the Virgin Mary,
suffered under Pontius Pilate,
was crucified, died and was buried;
he descended into hell;
on the third day he rose again from the dead;
he ascended into heaven,
and is seated at the right hand
of God the Father almighty;
from there he will come to judge
the living and the dead.

I believe in the Holy Spirit,
the holy catholic Church,
the communion of saints,
the forgiveness of sins,
the resurrection of the body,
and life everlasting. Amen.

Nicene Creed

This creed was written over a thousand years ago by leaders of the Church who met at a city named Nicaea. Christians over the centuries have prayed. Today we pray this creed during most Masses.

I believe in one God,
the Father almighty,
maker of heaven and earth,
of all things visible and invisible.

I believe in one Lord Jesus Christ,
the Only Begotten Son of God,
born of the Father before all ages.
God from God, Light from Light,
true God from true God,
begotten, not made, consubstantial
with the Father;
through him all things were made.
For us men and for our salvation
he came down from heaven,

At the words that follow up to and including and became man, all bow.

and by the Holy Spirit was incarnate
of the Virgin Mary, and became man.

For our sake he was crucified under
Pontius Pilate,
he suffered death and was buried,
and rose again on the third day
in accordance with the Scriptures.

He ascended into heaven
and is seated at the right hand of
the Father.
He will come again in glory
to judge the living and the dead
and his kingdom will have no end.

I believe in the Holy Spirit, the Lord,
the giver of life,
who proceeds from the Father and
the Son,
who with the Father and the Son is
adored and glorified,
who has spoken through the prophets.

I believe in one, holy, catholic and
apostolic Church.
I confess one Baptism for the
forgiveness of sins
and I look forward to the resurrection
of the dead
and the life of the world to come.
Amen.

Optional Activity

Life after Death

Point out the very last section of the Apostle's Creed where it mentions our belief in "the resurrection of the body, and life everlasting."

- Tell the children that humans can only imagine what eternal life will be like.
- The Church relies on images interpreted through the teachings of Jesus, and the guidance of the Holy Spirit, to help Christians understand what it means to live with God forever.
- Ask each child to write a paragraph describing his or her thoughts about what eternal life may be like.

Optional Activity

I Believe

Discuss how both Creeds profess the divine and human nature of Jesus. The translation in both the Nicene and the Apostles' Creeds was revised when we began to implement the Third Edition of the *Roman Missal* in November 2011.

- Create with the children a prayer service during which they will renew their baptismal promises.
- Use the question form of the Creed from the *Rite of Baptism for Children.*

The Church Teaches

The Catholic Church uses several terms and titles when she speaks about her teaching. These ways of talking about the Church help all her members to be clear on what we believe and why. They will also be helpful to you in learning about the Church.

- A **doctrine** or **dogma** is an important teaching revealed by Christ and taught by the Church's Magisterium. As a Catholic, you are required to believe these revealed truths.

- An important ministry of the **Pope** and **bishops** is to teach with the guidance of the Holy Spirit. It is their duty to interpret the Catholic faith and explain it to all people.

- **Priests** and **deacons** assist the bishops in carrying out the teaching ministry. They do so by preaching, celebrating the Sacraments, and guiding the people.

- A **catechist** or **teacher** is someone who teaches the faith and helps people learn how to live according to the faith. Most catechists are laypeople. Religious sisters and brothers are often involved in this work of catechesis and education.

The Sanctuary of Our Lady of Fátima in Portugal.

The Shrine to Our Lady of Lourdes in France.

Mary

Mary is Jesus' Mother. For this reason she is called the Mother of God. The Church honors Mary because she was willing to do what God asked. Mary is a model for Christians of all times and places.

Titles of Mary

The Church honors Mary with many titles. Each tells something about her and why she is so loved. Mary is called the Immaculate Conception, the Blessed Virgin, the Madonna, Our Lady of Perpetual Help, Queen of Heaven, Help of Christians, the Morning Star, and Queen of Angels.

Many Christians honor Mary by naming their children after her. Mary, Marie, and Maria are forms of the name you may know. Marilyn, Maureen, Moira, Marianne, and Marita are names that mean "Mary" in other languages.

The name Madonna means "my lady" in Italian. Regina means "queen" in Latin. And Virginia is a name that refers to Mary's virginity. In Spanish-speaking countries children are also named Lupe (for Our Lady of Guadalupe), Concepción (for the Immaculate Conception), Dolores (for Our Lady of Sorrows), or Gracia (for Our Lady of Grace).

310

Optional Activity

The Church Teaches

Invite the priest or a deacon to come and speak to the group about the role he plays in teaching members of the Church.

- Help the children prepare appropriate questions ahead of time.

- Ask your speaker to also explain more about the roles of the Pope and bishops in guiding the Church.

Optional Activity

Titles of Mary

Pray a Marian prayer with the children, pausing at the end of each line so that they can reflect on its meaning.

- Help the children by sharing your own reflections on the prayer.

- Have the children work together to compose a brief prayer in which they incorporate one of the titles of Mary.

- Then ask each child to create a prayer card by writing the prayer on card stock and decorating it.

The Seven Sacraments

Catholics share in the worship of the Church by participating in the Seven Sacraments. The Sacraments are special signs and celebrations that Jesus gave his Church. They allow us to share in God's life and work. The Sacraments are divided into three groups.

The Mass

The Mass is the celebration of the Sacrament of the Eucharist. The Mass includes two main parts: the Liturgy of the Word and the Liturgy of the Eucharist.

At the Liturgy of the Word you listen to readings from Scripture. The priest gives a homily. He explains the readings and how they apply to our lives. We all profess our faith by saying one of the creeds.

The Liturgy of the Eucharist includes prayers and songs thanking and praising God, and offering the gifts of bread and wine. Then the priest blesses the bread and wine, which become the Body and Blood of Christ. Those gathered pray the Lord's Prayer and give one another a sign of peace. This shows they are ready to come to the Lord's table. The people share in Jesus' sacrifice when they receive Holy Communion.

When the Mass ends, those gathered are sent to "Go and announce the Gospel of the Lord" in their own community.

The Seven Sacraments

Sacraments of Initiation	
The three Sacraments that celebrate membership into the Catholic Church.	• Baptism • Confirmation • Eucharist

Sacraments of Healing	
In these Sacraments, God's forgiveness and healing are given to those suffering physical and spiritual sickness.	• Penance and Reconciliation • Anointing of the Sick

Sacraments at the Service of Communion	
These Sacraments celebrate people's commitment to serve God and the community and help build up the People of God.	• Holy Orders • Matrimony (Marriage)

312   Our Catholic Tradition

Order of Mass

The Mass follows a pattern, with some differences according to the feast or season of the liturgical year. The main parts of the Mass are the Liturgy of the Word and the Liturgy of the Eucharist.

The Order of Mass

Introductory Rites

1. Entrance Chant
2. Greeting
3. Rite for the Blessing and Sprinkling of Water
4. Penitential Act
5. Kyrie
6. Gloria
7. Collect

Liturgy of the Word

1. First Reading (usually from the Old Testament)
2. Responsorial Psalm
3. Second Reading (from the New Testament letters)
4. Gospel Acclamation (Alleluia)
5. Gospel Dialogue
6. Gospel Reading
7. Homily
8. Profession of Faith (Creed)
9. Prayer of the Faithful

Liturgy of the Eucharist

1. Preparation of the Gifts
2. Invitation to Prayer
3. Prayer over the Offerings
4. Eucharistic Prayer
   • Preface Dialogue
   • Preface
   • Preface Acclamation
   • Consecration
   • Mystery of Faith
   • Concluding Doxology
5. Communion Rite
   • The Lord's Prayer
   • Sign of Peace
   • Lamb of God (Agnus Dei)
   • Invitation to Communion
   • Communion
   • Prayer after Communion

Concluding Rites

1. Greeting
2. Blessing
3. Dismissal

Faith Basics   313

Optional Activity

The Sacraments

Review "The Seven Sacraments" chart on the student page.

• Discuss any celebrations of the Sacraments planned for the parish community during the course of the year.

• Ask the children to share what they have seen, heard, smelled, tasted, or touched when participating in or attending a celebration of one of the Sacraments.

• Point out that the Sacraments are special signs and celebrations that Jesus gave the Church so that we could share in God's life and work.

Optional Activity

Order of Mass

Consider inviting the parish priest or a liturgical minister to attend a session and explain to the children the parts of the Mass. You may wish to have your speaker explain some of the changes made to the English translation of the Mass when we began to implement the Third Edition of the *Roman Missal*.

• Have the children prepare for the speaker by writing any questions they have about the Mass.

• If possible, consider holding this session in the parish church or day chapel.

Special Church Objects

 Altar the central table at the front of the church where the Eucharist is celebrated.

 Ambo (lectern) the place where Scripture is proclaimed and homilies preached. The lector (reader), deacon, and priest stand behind the lectern to announce God's Word.

 Baptismal Font/Pool the container that holds blessed holy water for celebrating Baptisms.

 Tabernacle the special place in the church where the Blessed Sacrament is reserved after Mass for those who are ill or for Eucharistic Adoration.

 Book of Gospels the special book that contains the Gospel readings used at Mass.

 Chalice the cup for the Blood of Christ.

 Ciborium the special container placed in the Tabernacle that holds the Eucharistic Hosts, the Body of Christ.

 Lectionary the special book used at Mass that contains readings from the Old and New Testament.

 Paschal Candle a large, decorated candle that is lit from the new fire at the Easter Vigil. This candle is lit at all masses during the Easter season. It is also lit at Baptisms and funerals.

 Roman Missal the special book that contains the prayers of the Mass.

Liturgical Colors

Certain colors are used during certain seasons of the Church year. These colors are used for parts of the priest's vestments.

Colors	
Green	Sundays in Ordinary Time
Red	Palm Sunday, Good Friday, Pentecost
Rose	Third Sunday of Advent and Fourth Sunday of Lent
Purple or Violet	Advent and Lent
White	Christmas, Easter, Feasts of the Lord, Mary, and the Saints not martyred, or funerals

Sacramentals

As a reminder of Jesus' presence, the Church uses special signs and symbols. They are called sacramentals. A sacramental can be an object, words, gesture, or action. They are made sacred through the prayers of the Church.

Sacramentals often include an action like the Sign of the Cross. Crucifixes, holy cards, and medals remind you of Jesus, the Blessed Mother, or the Saints. Palm branches remind you of Jesus' entry into Jerusalem. After the Palm Sunday service, you can keep and display the palm branches in your home. These are all popular sacramentals.

Blessings

A blessing is a special sign and prayer. Blessings praise God. They ask for God's care for a person, a place, a thing, or an action. In many churches on the feast day of Saint Francis of Assisi (October 4), the priest blesses pets or farm animals.

Devotions

Devotions are special prayers that honor God, Mary, or the Saints. Visits to the Blessed Sacrament are a popular devotion to honor Jesus. The Rosary is a devotion to honor Mary. Devotions help people remember to pray outside of the Mass.

Optional Activity

Special Church Objects

Strengthen the children's knowledge of their parish church and the special things within it by taking them on a tour of the church.

- Make arrangements ahead of time to bring the children to the church for a tour.
- Serve as the tour guide yourself or invite a parish staff member to guide your group.
- Point out all of the items listed on page 314 in the Student Book.

Optional Activity

Liturgical Colors

Review with the children the different colors used during the various seasons of the Church year.

- Point out that these colors are used for parts of the priest's vestments.
- If possible, show some of the liturgical vestments, or garments, to the children, while you refer to the different seasons and colors in the text on the student page.

God's Laws

God desires you to be in relationship with him. To help you do this and to know what is right, he has given you laws.

The Ten Commandments

	The Ten Commandments	Their Meaning
1	I am the Lord your God: you shall not have strange gods before me.	Keep God first in your life.
2	You shall not take the name of the Lord your God in vain.	Always use God's name in a reverent way.
3	Remember to keep holy the Lord's Day.	Attend Mass and rest on Sunday.
4	Honor your father and your mother.	Obey your parents and guardians.
5	You shall not kill.	Be kind to the people and animals God made; care for yourself and others.
6	You shall not commit adultery.	Be respectful in the things you do with your body.
7	You shall not steal.	Take care of other people's things; don't take what belongs to someone else. Respect other people and their property.
8	You shall not bear false witness against your neighbor.	Respect others by always telling the truth.
9	You shall not covet your neighbor's wife.	Keep your thoughts and words clean; don't be jealous of other people's friendships.
10	You shall not covet your neighbor's goods.	Be happy with the things you have; don't be jealous of what other people have.

The Great Commandment

[Jesus] said in reply, "You shall love the Lord, your God, with all your heart, with all your being, with all your strength, and with all your mind, and your neighbor as yourself." Luke 10:27

The Beatitudes

Blessed are the poor in spirit,
for theirs is the kingdom of heaven.
Blessed are they who mourn,
for they will be comforted.
Blessed are the meek,
for they will inherit the land.
Blessed are they who hunger and thirst
  for righteousness,
for they will be satisfied.
Blessed are the merciful,
for they will be shown mercy.
Blessed are the clean of heart,
for they will see God.
Blessed are the peacemakers,
for they will be called children of God.
Blessed are they who are persecuted for
  the sake of righteousness,
for theirs is the kingdom of heaven.
Matthew 5:3–10

Jesus' New Commandment

Jesus also gave his followers a New Commandment: "love one another. As I have loved you, so you also should love one another."
John 13:34

Corporal and Spiritual Works of Mercy

The Corporal Works of Mercy draw Catholics to the care of the physical needs of others. The Spiritual Works of Mercy guide us to care for the spiritual needs of people.

Corporal
- Feed the hungry
- Give drink to the thirsty
- Clothe the naked
- Shelter the homeless
- Visit the sick
- Visit the imprisoned

Spiritual
- Warn the sinner
- Teach the ignorant
- Counsel the doubtful
- Comfort the sorrowful
- Bear wrongs patiently
- Forgive injuries
- Pray for the living and the dead

Optional Activity

The Ten Commandments

Review with the group the Ten Commandments.

- Have the children close their books.
- Red aloud individual entries from the column "Their Meaning" on page 316 in the Student Book.
- Call on volunteers to provide the correct Commandment that matches what you read.
- Tell the children it's okay if they don't use the exact wording; it's more important that they understand what God's laws mean.

Optional Activity

The Great Commandment

Have the children memorize the Great Commandment.

- Assign partners, and have the partners quiz each other.
- Discuss what the world would be like if no one followed the Great Commandment.
- Then discuss what the world would be like if everyone followed the Great Commandment.

Virtue

The word virtue means "strength." Virtues are good spiritual habits that make you stronger and help you do what is right and good. Practicing these habits of goodness helps you to make even more loving choices.

The Theological Virtues

These three virtues are gifts from God.

Faith—Faith makes it possible to believe in God and all that he has shown us. Faith leads you to obey God and all he has taught.

Hope—Hope is the virtue that helps you trust in what God has shown you. It is the gift of looking forward to the happiness of life forever with God and the coming of God's Kingdom.

Charity (Love)—You show your love for God by praising him and making him number one in your life. You also show love for God by loving other people, treating everyone with kindness and respect. You help people. You listen to friends who have problems. You do kind things.

Cardinal Virtues

The four principle moral virtues that help us live as children of God and from which the other moral virtues flow. We strengthen these good habits through God's grace and our own efforts.

Prudence—being practical and making correct decisions on what is right and good, with the help of the Holy Spirit and a formed conscience.

Justice—giving God what is due him. It also means to give each person what he or she is due because that person is a child of God.

Fortitude—showing courage, having strength to get through difficult times, not giving up when doing good.

Temperance—using moderation, being disciplined, and having self-control.

Precepts of the Church

The following precepts are important duties of all Catholics.

1. Take part in Mass on Sundays and holy days. Keep these days holy and avoid unnecessary work.

2. Celebrate the Sacrament of Reconciliation at least once a year.

3. Receive Holy Communion at least once a year during the Easter season.

4. Fast and abstain on days of penance.

5. Give your time, gifts, and money to support the Church.

Gifts of the Holy Spirit

You receive the Gifts of the Holy Spirit through the Sacraments of Baptism and Confirmation. These gifts help you grow in relationship with God and others.

- Wisdom
- Understanding
- Right Judgment (Counsel)
- Courage (Fortitude)
- Knowledge
- Reverence (Piety)
- Wonder and Awe (Fear of the Lord)

Examination of Conscience

1. Pray to the Holy Spirit to help you examine your conscience.

2. Read the Beatitudes, the Ten Commandments, the Great Commandment, and the Precepts of the Church.

3. Ask yourself these questions:

- When have I not done what God wants me to do?
- Whom have I hurt?
- What have I done that I knew was wrong?
- What have I not done that I should have done?
- Have I done penance and tried to change?
- With what am I still having trouble?
- Am I sorry for all my sins?

Optional Activity

Virtue

Pray a simple act of faith, hope, or love with children. Then read aloud the Theological Virtues copy on the student page.

- Encourage the children to think about specific ways in which they can practice these virtues in their daily lives.

- Invite them to write petitions that ask God to help them practice these virtues.

Optional Activity

Examination of Conscience

Encourage the children to examine their consciences privately, perhaps each evening.

- Arrange the children in four small groups. Assign each group one of the following to read together: the Ten Commandments, the Beatitudes, the Great Commandment, and the Precepts of the Church.

- Instruct each group to write questions based on these readings; explain that these questions will be used to compose an examination of conscience.

- Have each group share their questions with the larger group.

- Based on all the questions, work together to compose an examination of conscience.

Basic Prayers

These are essential prayers that every Catholic should know. Latin is the official, universal language of the Church. As members of the Catholic Church, we usually pray in the language that we speak, but we sometimes pray in Latin, the common language of the Church.

Sign of the Cross

In the name of the Father,
and of the Son,
and of the Holy Spirit.
Amen.

Signum Crucis

In nómine Patris
et Fílii
et Spíritus Sancti.
Amen.

The Lord's Prayer

Our Father, who art in heaven,
hallowed be thy name;
thy kingdom come,
thy will be done
on earth as it is in heaven.
Give us this day our daily bread,
and forgive us our trespasses,
as we forgive those who trespass
   against us;
and lead us not into temptation,
but deliver us from evil. Amen.

Pater Noster

Pater noster qui es in cælis:
santificétur Nomen Tuum;
advéniat Regnum Tuum;
fiat volúntas Tua,
sicut in cælo, et in terra.
Panem nostrum
cotidiánum da nobis hódie;
et dimítte nobis débita nostra,
sicut et nos
dimíttus debitóribus nostris;
et ne nos indúcas in tentatiónem;
sed líbera nos a Malo.

Glory Be

Glory be to the Father
and to the Son
and to the Holy Spirit,
as it was in the beginning
is now, and ever shall be
world without end. Amen.

The Hail Mary

Hail, Mary, full of grace.,
the Lord is with thee.
Blessed art thou among women
and blessed is the fruit of thy womb,
   Jesus.
Holy Mary, Mother of God,
pray for us sinners,
now and at the hour of our death.
Amen.

Gloria Patri

Gloria Patri
et Fílio
et Spíritui Sancto.
Sicut erat in princípio,
et nunc et semper
et in sæcula sæculorem.
Amen.

Ave Maria

Ave, María, grátia plena,
Dóminus tecum.
Benedícta tu in muliéribus,
et benedíctus fructus ventris
   tui, Iesus.
Sancta María, Mater Dei,
ora pro nobis peccatóribus,
nunc et in hora mortis nostræ.
Amen.

Optional Activity

The Lord's Prayer

Pray the Lord's Prayer with the group.

- Have the children suggest simple, reverent gestures to accompany the phrases of this prayer.

- After the children have practiced the gestures while saying the prayer, share the gestures with parents and guardians or another group of children.

- Use the gestures as part of the Lord's Prayer during future prayer celebrations with the children.

Optional Activity

Hail Mary

Encourage the children to pray this prayer whenever the intercession of Mary would be especially welcome.

- Help the children think of specific situations in which someone might ask Mary to intercede on their behalf.

- Then have them create liturgical art that reflects the imagery of this prayer.

Prayers from the Sacraments

I Confess/Confiteor

I confess to almighty God
and to you, my brothers and sisters,
that I have greatly sinned,
in my thoughts and in my words,
in what I have done and in what I have
failed to do,

Gently strike your chest with a closed fist.

through my fault, through my fault,
through my most grievous fault;

Continue:

therefore I ask blessed Mary ever-Virgin,
all the Angels and Saints,
and you, my brothers and sisters,
to pray for me to the Lord our God.

The Apostles' Creed

See page 308 for this prayer.

The Nicene Creed

See page 309 for this prayer.

Gloria

Glory to God in the highest,
and on earth peace to people of
good will.

We praise you, we bless you, we adore
you, we glorify you, we give you
thanks for your great glory,
Lord God, heavenly King, O God,
almighty Father.

Lord Jesus Christ,
Only Begotten Son,
Lord God, Lamb of God,
Son of the Father,
you take away the sins of the world,
have mercy on us;
you take away the sins of the world,
receive our prayer;
you are seated at the right hand of
the Father, have mercy on us.

For you alone are the Holy One,
you alone are the Lord,
you alone are the Most High,
Jesus Christ, with the Holy Spirit,
in the glory of God the Father.
Amen.

Holy, Holy, Holy Lord

Holy, Holy, Holy Lord God of hosts.
Heaven and earth are full of your glory.
Hosanna in the highest.
Blessed is he who comes in the name of
the Lord.
Hosanna in the highest.

Lamb of God

Lamb of God, you take away the
sins of the world,
have mercy on us.
Lamb of God, you take away the
sins of the world,
have mercy on us.
Lamb of God, you take away the
sins of the world,
grant us peace.

Prayer to the Holy Spirit

Come, Holy Spirit, fill the hearts of your
faithful.
And kindle in them the fire of your love.
Send forth your Spirit and they shall be
created.
And you will renew the face of the
earth.

Act of Contrition

(From Rite of Penance)
*Often used at night after a brief
examination of conscience.*
My God, I am sorry for my sins
with all my heart.
In choosing to do wrong
and failing to do good,
I have sinned against you
whom I should love above all things.
I firmly intend, with your help,
to do penance, to sin no more,
and to avoid whatever leads me to sin.
Our Savior Jesus Christ
suffered and died for us.
In his name, my God, have mercy.

Optional Activity

I Confess/Confiteor

Have the children use the text of this prayer or the Act of Contrition on page 323 to make prayer cards.

- Point out that they can use these cards as reminders when they are celebrating the Sacrament of Reconciliation.

- As an alternative, ask each child to write a prayer of sorrow in his or her own words.

Optional Activity

Holy, Holy, Holy Lord

Celebrate with the children how Heaven and Earth are full of God's glory. Note that some of the words of the prayer changed when we began to implement the English translation of the Third Edition of the *Roman Missal* in November 2011.

- Have the children draw or find images of God's glory to post on a bulletin board.

- In the middle of the board, include a decorative version of the prayer.

- You may wish to play "Holy Lord God of Hosts," Track 9 of *And with Your Spirit* by John Burland, for the children as they work (available from Our Sunday Visitor Curriculum Division).

Personal and Family Prayers

Daily Prayer

We begin each day and end each day with prayer. That is because we want him to guide all that we say and do. We ask him to be with us as we go about our day. We then thank him for everything he does and gives, asking him to be with us as we sleep.

Grace Before Meals

Bless us, O Lord, and these thy gifts which we are about to receive from thy bounty, through Christ our Lord. Amen.

Grace After Meals

We give you thanks, Almighty God, for all these gifts which we have received from thy bounty, through Christ our Lord. Amen.

Morning Prayer

Blessed are you, Lord, God of all creation:
you take the sleep from my eyes
and the slumber from my eyelids.
Amen.

Morning Offering

Almighty God, we thank you
for the life and light of a new day.
Keep us safe today
and protect us from every evil.
We offer ourselves this day to you
through Jesus Christ your Son.
May your Holy Spirit
make our thoughts, words, and actions
pleasing in your sight.
Amen.

Evening Prayer

Protect us, Lord, as we stay awake;
watch over us as we sleep,
that awake, we may keep watch with
Christ,
and asleep, rest in his peace.
Amen.

Angel Guardian

An angel is a spiritual being that is a messenger of God. Angels are mentioned nearly 300 times in the Bible.

Three important angels are Gabriel, Michael, and Raphael.

Traditional

Angel of God,
my Guardian dear,
to whom his love commits
me here,
ever this day (night)
be at my side,
to light and guard,
to rule and guide.

Contemporary

Angel sent by God to guide me,
be my light and walk beside me;
be my guardian and protect me;
on the paths of life direct me.

Act of Faith, Hope, and Love

Often prayed in the morning to remind us that all gifts come from God, and that he can help us believe, trust, and love.

My God, I believe in you,
I trust in you,
I love you above all things,
with all my heart and mind and strength.
I love you because you are supremely
good and
worth loving;
and because I love you,
I am sorry with all my heart for
offending you.
Lord, have mercy on me, a sinner.
Amen.

Act of Contrition

Often used at night after a brief examination of conscience. See page 323 for this prayer.

Optional Activity

Morning Offering

Involve the children in a discussion about the different ways they wake up in the morning and the things they do to get ready for the day. Talk about ways they can make God a part of their first morning thoughts.

• Provide the children with construction paper and crayons.

• Encourage them to draw a picture of themselves saying "Good morning" to God to hang near their beds or where they brush their teeth as a reminder to focus on God each day.

Optional Activity

Angel Guardian

Remind the children that it is important to end each day in prayer, whether using an evening prayer, the Angel Guardian prayer, or one of their own creation.

• Provide construction paper, crayons or markers, some yarn, and a single hole punch.

• Have the children write either the traditional or the contemporary Angel Guardian prayer on construction paper and add a drawing of a guardian angel.

• Punch two holes at the top of the paper, run a piece of yarn through the holes, and tie it together to form a loop.

• Encourage the children to hang their prayer cards over their bedposts, on a nightstand, or on a wall near their beds.

Praying with the Saints

When we pray with the Saints, we ask them to pray to God for us and to pray with us. The Saints are with Christ. They speak for us when we need help.

As the Mother of Jesus, the Son of God, Mary is called the Mother of God, the Queen of all Saints, and the Mother of the Church. There are many prayers and practices of devotion to Mary.

Angelus

The Angelus is a prayer honoring the Incarnation. It is given its name by the first word of the Latin version of the prayer: Angelus Domini nuntiavit Maria, "The angel of the Lord declared unto Mary." To honor the Incarnation, it is recited three times each day—morning, noon, and evening, at the sound of the Angelus bell. Each response, where shown, is followed by reciting the Hail Mary.

V. The angel spoke God's message to Mary,
R. and she conceived of the Holy Spirit.
Hail, Mary,…

V. "I am the lowly servant of the Lord:
R. let it be done to me according to your word."

Hail, Mary,…
V. And the Word became flesh,
R. and lived among us.
Hail, Mary,…
V. Pray for us, holy Mother of God,
R. that we may become worthy of the promises of Christ.
Let us pray.

Lord,
fill our hearts with your grace:
once, through the message of an angel you revealed to us the Incarnation of your Son;
now, through his suffering and death lead us to the glory of his resurrection.

We ask this through Christ our Lord. Amen.

The Rosary

One of the most popular prayers is the Rosary. It focuses on the twenty mysteries that describe the events in the lives of Jesus and Mary.

How to Pray the Rosary

1. Pray the Sign of the Cross and say the Apostles' Creed.
2. Pray the Lord's Prayer.
3. Pray three Hail Marys.
4. Pray the Glory Be to the Father.
5. Say the first mystery; then pray the Lord's Prayer.
6. Pray ten Hail Marys while meditating on the mystery.
7. Pray the Glory Be to the Father.
8. Say the second mystery; then pray the Lord's Prayer. Repeat 6 and 7 and continue with the third, fourth, and fifth mysteries in the same manner.
9. Pray the Hail, Holy Queen.

The Mysteries of the Rosary

The Joyful Mysteries
The Annunciation
The Visitation
The Nativity
The Presentation in the Temple
The Finding in the Temple

The Luminous Mysteries
The Baptism of Jesus
The Wedding at Cana
The Proclamation of the Kingdom
The Transfiguration
The Institution of the Eucharist

Hail, Holy Queen

Hail, holy Queen, Mother of mercy, hail, our life, our sweetness, and our hope.
To you we cry, the children of Eve; to you we send up our sighs, mourning and weeping in this land of exile.
Turn, then, most gracious advocate, your eyes of mercy toward us; lead us home at last and show us the blessed fruit of your womb, Jesus;
O clement, O loving, O sweet Virgin Mary.

The Sorrowful Mysteries
The Agony in the Garden
The Scourging at the Pillar
The Crowning with Thorns
The Carrying of the Cross
The Crucifixion and Death

The Glorious Mysteries
The Resurrection
The Ascension
The Descent of the Holy Spirit
The Assumption of Mary
The Coronation of Mary in Heaven

Optional Activity

Praying with the Saints

Point out that Catholics often pray to the Saints asking them to intercede, or pray to God, for us. Since the Saints are with Christ, they can speak for us when we need help.

- Have the children pick one of the Saints that you have read about in your lessons.
- Ask them to compose a prayer to that Saint for guidance or assistance with some aspect in their lives.
- Encourage the children to take their prayers home and pray them when they feel the need for a little extra help.

Optional Activity

How to Pray the Rosary

Review with the children the prayers used and the steps followed in praying the Rosary. Post the following information on a chart visible to all: The Apostles' Creed is said on the crucifix; the Lord's Prayer is said on each of the large beads; the Hail Mary is said on each of the small beads; the Glory Be is said after the three Hail Marys at the beginning of the Rosary, and after each decade of small beads.

- Provide the children with a line art drawing or a picture of rosary beads.
- Using the information on the chart, ask them to write next to each bead which prayers apply to each bead.

Catholic Faith Words

A

Apostles' Creed one of the Church's oldest creeds. It is a summary of Christian beliefs taught since the time of the Apostles. This creed is used in the celebration of Baptism. **(90)**

Apostolic Succession the term used to describe how the authority and power to lead and teach the Church is passed down from the Apostles to their successors, the bishops **(158)**

apostolic the teaching authority of the Church comes directly from Jesus and his chosen Apostles because the bishops of the Church are direct successors of the Apostles; a Mark of the Church **(167)**

Ascension when the Risen Jesus was taken up to Heaven to be with God the Father forever **(135)**

B

Beatitudes teachings of Jesus that show the way to true happiness and tell how to live in God's Kingdom now and always **(193)**

Bible the Word of God written in human words. The Bible is the holy book of the Church. **(65)**

bishop an ordained man who works together with other bishops and the Pope in teaching, leading, and making the Church holy. The bishops are the successors of the Apostles. **(158)**

Blessed Sacrament a name for the Holy Eucharist, especially the Body of Christ, kept in the Tabernacle **(101)**

Blessing and Adoration in this prayer form, we show that we understand God is the Creator of all and that we need him. We give him respect and honor his greatness. **(111)**

Body of Christ a name for the Church of which Christ is the head. All the baptized are members of the body. **(142)**

C

catholic the Church is meant for all people in all times and all places; a Mark of the Church **(167)**

charity the theological virtue of love. It directs us to love God above all things and our neighbor as ourselves, for the love of God. **(203)**

Church the community of all baptized people who believe in God and follow Jesus. The word is often used for the Catholic Church because we trace our origins back to the Apostles. **(67)**

Communion of Saints everyone who believes in and follows Jesus—people on Earth and people who have died and are in Purgatory or Heaven (169)

conscience an ability given to us by God that helps us make choices about right and wrong (210)

covenant a sacred promise or agreement between God and humans (258)

creation everything made by God (55)

creed a statement of the Church's beliefs (90)

deacon an ordained man who serves the Church by assisting in the Eucharist, baptizing, witnessing marriages, and doing works of charity (245)

domestic Church a name for the Catholic family, because it is the community of Christians in the home. God made the family to be the first place we learn about loving others and following Christ. (76)

E–G

Eucharist the Sacrament in which Jesus shares himself, and the bread and wine become his Body and Blood (226)

evangelization sharing the Good News of Jesus through words and actions in a way that invites people to accept the Gospel (178)

faith the theological virtue that makes it possible for us to believe in God and all that he helps us understand about himself. Faith leads us to obey God. (202)

faithful to be constant and loyal to your promises and commitments to God and others, just as he is faithful to you (260)

Gospel a word that means "Good News." The Gospel message is the Good News of God's Kingdom and his saving love. (122)

grace God's free and loving gift to humans of his own life and help (210)

Heaven the full joy of living with God forever (280)

Hell being separated from God forever because of a choice to turn away from him and not seek forgiveness (280)

holy the Church is holy because she is set apart for God and his purposes; a Mark of the Church (167)

Holy Trinity the one God in three Divine Persons—God the Father, God the Son, and God the Holy Spirit (57)

hope the theological virtue that helps us trust in the true happiness God wants us to have and in Jesus' promises of eternal life, and to rely on the help of the Holy Spirit (203)

image of God the likeness of God that is in all human beings because we are created by him (57)

Incarnation the mystery that the Son of God became man to save all people (88)

Intercession in this prayer form, we ask God to help others (111)

justice giving God what is due him, and giving each person what he or she is due because that person is a child of God (271)

Kingdom of God the world of love, peace, and justice that is in Heaven and is still being built on Earth (124)

Last Judgment God's final triumph over evil that will occur at the end of time, when Christ returns and judges all the living and the dead (280)

Last Supper the meal Jesus shared with his disciples on the night before he died. At the Last Supper, Jesus gave himself in the Eucharist. (98)

liturgy the public prayer of the Church. It includes the Sacraments and forms of daily prayer. (100)

Lord's Prayer the prayer that Jesus taught his disciples to pray to God the Father (108)

Magisterium the teaching office of the Church, which is all of the bishops in union with the Pope. (158)

Marks of the Church the four characteristics that identify Christ's Church: one, holy, catholic, and apostolic (167)

Mary the Mother of Jesus, the Mother of God. She is also called "Our Lady" because she is our Mother and the Mother of the Church. (74)

mercy kindness and concern for those who are suffering. God has mercy on us even though we are sinners. (193)

Messiah the promised one who would lead his People. The word Messiah means "God's anointed," or "God's chosen one." Jesus is the Messiah. (123)

miracle something that cannot be explained by science, but happened by the power of God (124)

mission a job or purpose. The Church's mission is to announce the Good News of God's Kingdom. (178)

missionaries people who answer God's call to bring the message of Jesus and announce the Good News of his Kingdom to people in other places (178)

mystery a spiritual truth that is difficult to perceive or understand with our senses, but is known through faith and through signs (88)

New Commandment Jesus' command for his disciples to love one another as he has loved us **(193)**

Nicene Creed a summary of basic beliefs about God the Father, God the Son, and God the Holy Spirit and about other Church teachings. We usually say the Nicene Creed during Mass. **(100)**

one the Church is one because the power of the Holy Spirit unites all the members through one faith and one Baptism; a mark of the Church **(167)**

parable a short story Jesus told about everyday life to teach something about God **(125)**

parish the local community of Catholics that meets at a particular place **(142)**

Paschal Mystery the mystery of Jesus' suffering, Death, Resurrection, and Ascension **(135)**

peace a state of calm when things are in their proper order and people settle problems with kindness and justice **(271)**

Pentecost the feast that celebrates the coming of the Holy Spirit fifty days after Easter **(168)**

petition in this prayer form, we ask God for what we need **(111)**

Pope the successor of Peter, the bishop of Rome, and the head of the entire Church **(157)**

praise in this prayer form, we give God honor and thanks because he is God **(111)**

prayer talking and listening to God. It is raising your mind and heart to God. **(108)**

Precepts of the Church some of the minimum requirements given by Church leaders for deepening our relationship with God and the Church **(210)**

priest an ordained man who helps his bishop by leading a parish, preaching the Gospel, and celebrating the Eucharist and other Sacraments **(245)**

proclaim to tell about Jesus in words and actions **(258)**

Purgatory a state of final cleansing after death and before entering into Heaven **(280)**

Real Presence the teaching that Jesus is really and truly with us in the Eucharist. We receive Jesus in his fullness. **(226)**

Resurrection the event of Jesus being raised from Death to new life by God the Father through the power of the Holy Spirit **(134)**

Sacraments of Healing Penance and Reconciliation and the Anointing of the Sick. In these Sacraments, God's forgiveness and healing are given to those suffering physical and spiritual sickness. **(236)**

Sacraments of Initiation the three Sacraments that celebrate membership into the Catholic Church: Baptism, Confirmation, and Eucharist (226)

Sacred Chrism perfumed oil used for the Sacraments of Baptism, Confirmation, and Holy Orders (224)

Sacred Tradition God's Word handed down verbally through the Apostles and bishops (67)

sacrifice giving up something out of love for someone else or for the common good (the good of everyone). Jesus sacrificed his life for all people. (132)

Saint a hero of the Church who loved God very much, led a holy life, and is now with God in Heaven (169)

Seven Sacraments special signs and celebrations that Jesus gave his Church. The Sacraments allow us to share in the life and work of God. (98)

sin a person's choice to disobey God on purpose and do what he or she knows is wrong. Sins hurt our relationship with God and other people. (213)

stewardship the way we appreciate and use God's gifts, including our time, talent, and treasure and the resources of creation (145)

Tabernacle the special place in the church where the Blessed Sacrament is reserved after Mass for those who are ill or for Eucharistic Adoration (101)

thanksgiving in this prayer form, we give thanks to God for all he has given us (111)

Theological Virtues the virtues of faith, hope, and charity (love), which are gifts from God that guide our relationship with him (202)

virtues good spiritual habits that make you stronger and help you do what is right and good. They grow over time with our practice and openness to God's grace. (202)

Visitation the name of Mary's visit to Elizabeth before Jesus was born (74)

vocation God's plan for our lives; the purpose for which he made us (201)

vows solemn promises that are made to or before God (244)

Index

© Our Sunday Visitor

Index

The Subcommittee on the Catechism, United States Conference of Catholic Bishops, has found this catechetical series, copyright 2014, to be in conformity with the *Catechism of the Catholic Church*.

Nihil Obstat
Rev. Fr. Jeremiah L. Payne, S.Th.L.
Censor Librorum, Diocese of Orlando

Imprimatur
✠ Most Rev. John Noonan
Bishop of Orlando
March 26, 2013

Alive in Christ is a registered trademark of Our Sunday Visitor Curriculum Division, Our Sunday Visitor, 200 Noll Plaza, Huntington, Indiana 46750.

For permission to reprint copyrighted materials, grateful acknowledgment is made to the following sources:

English translation of the *Catechism of the Catholic Church for the United States of America* copyright © 1994, United States Catholic Conference, Inc.—Libreria Editrice Vaticana. English translation of the *Catechism of the Catholic Church: Modifications from the Editio Typica* copyright © 1997, United States Catholic Conference, Inc.—Libreria Editrice Vaticana. Used by permission. All rights reserved.

English translation of Glory Be (the Gloria Patri), Gloria in Excelsis, the Hail Mary, Lord, have mercy, the Apostles' Creed, Nicene Creed, the Lord's Prayer, and Lamb of God (Agnus Dei) by the International Consultation on English Texts (ICET). All rights reserved.

The English translation of a Psalm Response from *Lectionary for Mass* © 1969, 1981, 1997, International Commission on English in the Liturgy Corporation (ICEL); excerpts from the English translation of *Rite of Penance* © 1974, ICEL; excerpts from the English translation of *Pastoral Care of the Sick: Rites of Anointing and Viaticum* © 1982, ICEL; excerpts from the English translation of *Rite of Christian Initiation of Adults* © 1985, ICEL; excerpts from the English translation of *The Roman Missal* © 2010, ICEL. All rights reserved. Published with the approval of the Committee on Divine Worship, United States Conference of Catholic Bishops.

Excerpts from the *United States Catholic Catechism for Adults,* copyright © 2006, United States Catholic Conference, Inc.—Libreria Editrice Vaticana.

Music selections copyrighted or administered by OCP Publications are used with permission of OCP Publications, 5536 NE Hassalo, Portland, OR 97213. Please refer to songs for specific copyright dates and information.

Scripture selections taken from the *New American Bible, revised edition* © 2010, 1991, 1986, 1970 by the Confraternity of Christian Doctrine, Washington, D.C., and are used by license of the copyright owner. All rights reserved. No part of the *New American Bible* may be reproduced in any form without permission in writing from the copyright owner.

Additional Acknowledgments appear on page 336.

Alive in Christ Parish Grade 3 Student Book
ISBN: 978-1-61278-010-8
Item Number: CU5100

1 2 3 4 5 6 7 8 015016 17 16 15 14 13
Webcrafters, Inc.; Madison, WI; USA; August 2013, Job# 105390

Activity Master
Answer Keys

Activity Master Answer Keys

Chapter 1 Activity Master, p. 53E

Answers will vary.

Chapter 2 Activity Master, p. 63E

Answers will vary.

Chapter 3 Activity Master, p. 73E

| H | A | I | L |, Mary, full of grace,

the | L | O | R | D | is with thee.

Blessed art thou | A | M | O | N | G | women

and | B | L | E | S | S | E | D | is the fruit

of thy | W | O | M | B |, Jesus.

| I |

Holy Mary, | M | O | T | H | E | R | of God,

| H |

| G |

pray for us sinners, | N | O | W |

and at the hour of our | D | E | A | T | H |. Amen.

Message: H O M E   W I T H   G O D

Chapter 4 Activity Master, p. 87E

GOD
The Father
CREATES

The Son
SAVES and TEACHES

The Holy Spirit
GUIDES

The three Divine Persons of the
HOLY TRINITY

Chapter 5 Activity Master, p. 97E

Invitations will vary.

Chapter 6 Activity Master, p. 107E

Answers will vary.

Chapter 7 Activity Master, p. 121E

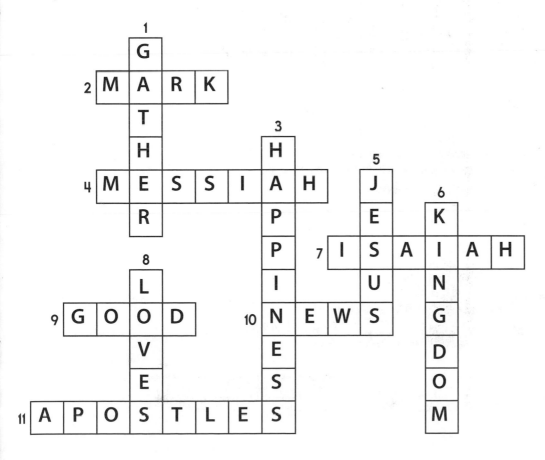

```
F    J    G    H    E    S    I    A    R    P
N    O    I    S    N    E    C    S    A    A
E    Y    U    I    N    Y    G    H    E    S
S    U    F    F    E    R    I    N    G    S
I    N    S    L    V    E    V    L    A    O
M    E    S    E    A    T    I    O    R    V
O    S    O    S    E    S    N    V    U    E
R    I    R    N    H    Y    G    I    R    R
P    R    C    U    R    M    N    N    C    S
L    A    H    C    S    A    P    G    V    R
```

Chapter 9 Activity Master, p. 141E

1. Them – m = THE

 = CHURCH

🏝 – land = IS

Thy – y + e = THE

🧍 = BODY

often – 10 = OF

 = CHRIST

The important message =
THE CHURCH
IS THE BODY OF CHRIST

2. U = YOU

R = ARE

👤 + ' = CHRIST'S

🤲 = HANDS,

👣 = FEET,

and

💛 = HEART

in

This – is + e = THE

🌍 = WORLD

The important message =
YOU ARE CHRIST'S HANDS, FEET
AND HEART IN THE WORLD

Chapter 10 Activity Master, p. 151E

1. ⬚D⬚IOCESE
2. BISHOP⬚S⬚
3. P⬚A⬚RISHES
4. ROM⬚E⬚
5. ⬚R⬚OOSTER
6. ⬚L⬚AMBS
7. O⬚V⬚ERSEER

Final statement: Pastors, bishops, and the Pope LEAD and SERVE God's People.

Chapter 11 Activity Master, p. 165E

A HAIKU
The FIRE of your LOVE
Filled the WORLD at PENTECOST
Bringing UNITY

YOUR HAIKU
Responses will vary.

Chapter 12 Activity Master, p. 175E

Drawings will vary.

Chapter 13 Activity Master, p. 189E

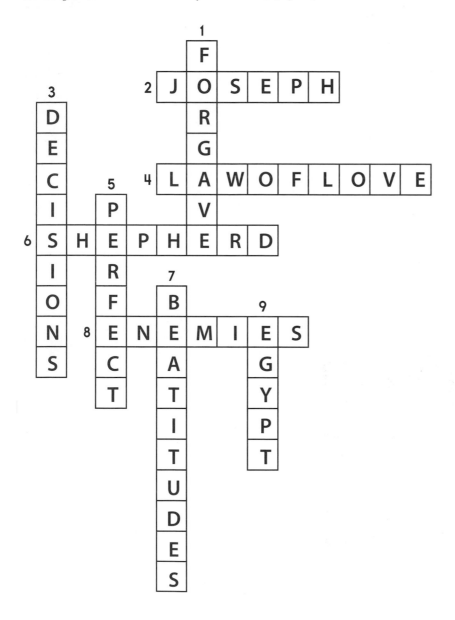

Chapter 14 Activity Master, p. 199E

Answers will vary.

Chapter 15 Activity Master, p. 209E

1. SIN
2. CONSCIENCE
3. SAINT PAUL
4. LAWS
5. BIBLE
6. DECISIONS
7. PRECEPTS
8. FAITH COMMUNITY
9. SPIRIT
10. GRACE
11. JESUS
12. GOD
13. SACRAMENT OF RECONCILIATION

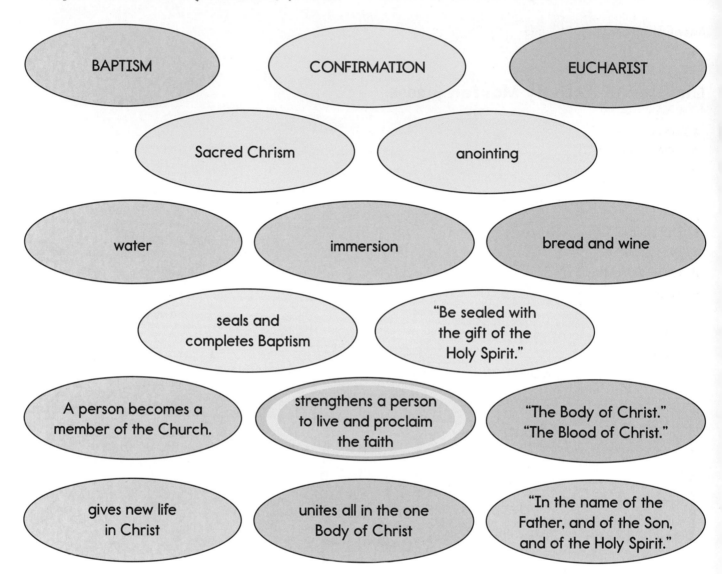

BAPTISM

CONFIRMATION

EUCHARIST

Sacred Chrism

anointing

water

immersion

bread and wine

seals and completes Baptism

"Be sealed with the gift of the Holy Spirit."

A person becomes a member of the Church.

strengthens a person to live and proclaim the faith

"The Body of Christ." "The Blood of Christ."

gives new life in Christ

unites all in the one Body of Christ

"In the name of the Father, and of the Son, and of the Holy Spirit."

Chapter 17 Activity Master, p. 233E

VERSOFNIGES = FORGIVENESS
DEARAPEST = SEPARATED
SNECOFS = CONFESS
ISPRET = PRIEST
NUMHA = HUMAN
LOSABEV = ABSOLVE
NONAIST = ANOINTS
HRITG = RIGHT

Chapter 18 Activity Master, p. 243E

Matrimony	Holy Orders
witnesses	bishop
priest	priest
marriage	ordain
anniversary	deacon
vows	vows

Chapter 19 Activity Master, p. 257E

Stories will vary.

Chapter 20 Activity Master, p. 267E

Certificates will vary.

Chapter 21 Activity Master, p. 277E

1. COVENANT
2. DISCIPLES
3. WITNESS
4. SPIRIT
5. SECOND COMING
6. KINGDOM

Photo Credits

CE4 Our Sunday Visitor; **CE5** Our Sunday Visitor; **CE6** Our Sunday Visitor; **CE7** (t) SuperStock; **CE9** (cl) iStockphoto.com/huronphoto; **CE9** (cr) iStockphoto.com/laflor; **CE9** (bl) Our Sunday Visitor; **CE9** (bcl) iStockphoto.com/redhumv; **CE9** (bcr) iStockphoto.com/Erdosain; **CE9** (br) Our Sunday Visitor; **CE11** iStockphoto.com/loops7; **CE12** Goodshoot/Thinkstock; **CE13** Sebastien Desarmaux/Corbis; **CE14** (t) United States Conference of Catholic Bishops; **CE14** (b) Our Sunday Visitor; **CE15** iStockphoto.com/asiseeit; **CE16** The Crosiers/Gene Plaisted, OSC; **CE17** Our Sunday Visitor; **CE22** Our Sunday Visitor; **CE23** United States Conference of Catholic Bishops; **CE26** (cl) Image Copyright Richard Paul Kane, 2012 Used under license from Shutterstock.com; **CE26** (cr) The Sacred Heart of Jesus, end of nineteenth century (mixed media), European School, (19th century)/Private Collection/Archives Charmet/The Bridgeman Art Library; **CE29** Amos Morgan/Photodisc/Thinkstock; **CE30** Our Sunday Visitor; **CE52** Osservatore Romano/Reuters; **53C** Tetra Images/Alamy; **63C** Image Copyright Edward Lara, 2013 Used under license from Shutterstock.com; **73C** John Henley/Blend Images/Corbis; **87C** MBI/Alamy; **97C** Myrleen Pearson/PhotoEdit; **107C** Image Copyright Ermolaev Alexander, 2013 Used under license from Shutterstock.com; **121C** iStockphoto/Thinkstock; 131C Tetra Images/Corbis; **141C** José Manuel Gelpi Díaz/Alamy; **155C** Image Copyright Apollofoto, 2013 Used under license from Shutterstock.com; **165C** Beau Lark/Corbis; **175C** Image Source/Alamy; **189C** Nathan Blaney/Photodisc/Getty Images; **199C** Konrad Wothe/LOOK/Getty Images; **209C** iStockphoto/Thinkstock; **223C** Myrleen Pearson/PhotoEdit; **233C** Image Source/Alamy; **243C** Glow Images/Getty Images; **257C** Mike Kemp/Getty Images; **267C** iStockphoto.com/CraigRJD; **277C** Amos Morgan/Photodisc/Thinkstock

Additional Acknowledgments:

English translation of the *Catechism of the Catholic Church for the United States of America* copyright © 1994, United States Catholic Conference, Inc.—Libreria Editrice Vaticana. English translation of the Catechism of the Catholic Church: *Modifications from the Editio Typica* copyright © 1997, United States Catholic Conference, Inc.—Libreria Editrice Vaticana. Used by permission. All rights reserved.

Excerpts from the English translation of Roman Missal © 2010, International Commission on English in the Liturgy Corporation (ICEL). All rights reserved.

Gadium et Spes ("Pastoral Constitution on the Church in the Modern World") © Libreria Editrice Vaticana.

Music selections copyright John Burland, used with permission, and produced in partnership with Ovation Music Services, P.O. Box 402 Earlwood NSW 2206, Australia. Please refer to songs for specific copyright dates and information.

Scripture selections taken from the *New American Bible, revised edition* © 2010, 1991, 1986, 1970 by the Confraternity of Christian Doctrine, Washington, D.C., and are used by license of the copyright owner. All rights reserved. No part of the *New American Bible* may be reproduced in any form without permission in writing from the copyright owner.